Latino/a Thought

Latino/a Thought

Culture, Politics, and Society

Francisco H. Vázquez and Rodolfo D. Torres

ROWMAN & LITTLEFIELD PUBLISHERS, INC.
Lanham • Boulder • New York • Oxford

ROWMAN & LITTLEFIELD PUBLISHERS, INC.

Published in the United States of America
by Rowman & Littlefield Publishers, Inc.
An Imprint of the Rowman & Littlefield Publishing Group
4720 Boston Way, Lanham, Maryland 20706
www.rowmanlittlefield.com

12 Hid's Copse Road, Cumnor Hill, Oxford OX2 9JJ, England

British Library Cataloguing in Publication Information Available

Library of Congress Cataloging-in-Publication Data

Latino/a thought : culture, politics, and society / Francisco H. Vázquez and Rodolfo D. Torres.
    p. cm.
    ISBN 0-8476-9940-4 (cloth : alk. paper)—ISBN 0-8476-9941-2 (pbk. : alk. paper)
    1. Hispanic Americans—Intellectual life. 2. Hispanic Americans—Politics and government. 3. Hispanic Americans—Social conditions. 4. United States—Ethnic relations. 5. United States—Ethnic relations—Political aspects. 6. Ethnicity—Political aspects—United States. I. Vázquez, Francisco H. (Francisco Hernández), 1949– II. Torres, Rodolfo D., 1949–
    E184.S75 L35545   2003
    973'.04968073—dc21   2002004905

Printed in the United States of America

But REALITY es una Gran Serpiente
a great serpent that moves and changes
and keeps crawling
out of its
dead skin

despojando su pellejo viejo
to emerge
clean and fresh
la nueva realidad nace de la realidad vieja.
—Luis Valdéz, *Pensamientos Serpentinos*

We welcome the new citizen, not as a stranger but as one entering his father's house.
—President Woodrow Wilson, April 1, 1917

O todos hijos, o todos entenados. [Either treat us all as if we are your children or treat us all as if we are your stepchildren, but treat us all the same.]
—Mexican saying

We are people! At least they didn't send an animal's lawyer!
—Luis Valdéz, *Zoot Suit*

I seek new images of identity, new beliefs about ourselves, our humanity and worth no longer in question.
—Gloria Anzaldúa, *Borderlands/La Frontera*

CONTENTS

ACKNOWLEDGMENTS

This work represents the voices of past generations that have converged into the subjectivity we are today. More immediately, this work is shaped by traces of countless knowledges from blood and other relatives, teachers and strangers. It is both a privilege and a responsibility to attempt to produce a discourse that will do justice to their desires. It is impossible to acknowledge them all by name and regrettable that, try as one may to recognize those who have made this work possible, some individuals are inadvertently left out. Our thanks to Dean Birkenkamp, editor at Rowman & Littlefield, and Janice Braunstein, assistant managing editor. Their support and intelligent judgment on all aspects of this project added considerably to the final product. Mil gracias to Dean and Janice!

A major influence on this work comes from our own experience(s) in the political and intellectual debates in Chicana/o and Latina/o studies. After many years of sharing stories of hope and resistance with youth at the university, with our own children, we have become aware of the need to put these stories in a context and in a format they can understand. This is no easy task given the increasing specialization of academic languages. In this regard, we received crucial assistance from the students of the Hutchins School of Liberal Studies, who worked with earlier drafts of this anthology in Liberal Studies 420 Analytics of Culture in the fall of 1998 and Liberal Studies 320 Quest for Citizenship in the spring of 2000. The critical questions they raised about the selections and the specific needs for context have served as an inner voice guiding the writing of the framing pieces for this book. We also want to thank Cheryl Craft, Anna Manring, Jane Kim, and Matt Ormond in the Department of Education at the University of California, Irvine, for their technical and editorial assistance. We especially want to thank Dave Compton for his detailed and careful editing of the manuscript.

No enterprise would be possible without family support. Without the time and space our compañeras Rosa and Patricia have so selflessly allowed us, this work would not be possible. Furthermore, Francisco has been inspired by Rosa's dedication to her own writing and by her first novel, *Silencio,* which addresses the insidious ways in which domination can take place even among those who love each other. Francisco extends special gracias to his daughter Vanessa Xochitl for her insights on the politics of everyday life in the Latino metropolis of Los Angeles. His son Joaquín Tizoc keeps sending him relevant information and challenging and questioning some of Francisco's assumptions about Latino political thought. His daughter Sofía Eréndira keeps forcing him to filter his intellectual somersaults through the fresh and concrete perspective of a young teenage Chicana.

Rudy wishes to thank his valued colleagues at the University of California, Irvine: Gilbert G. Gonzalez, Joan Bissell, Richard Brown, Leo Chávez, and Luis F. Mirón. In particular, Rudy has benefited from the ideas of a host of colleagues and friends. They include Mario Barrera, Antonia Darder, Zaragosa Vargas, Darrell Y. Hamamoto, Peter McLaren, and Victor Valle. Francisco expresses his deep appreciation to his colleagues at the Hutchins School of Liberal Studies for their support and for making the necessary schedule adjustments to accommodate his sabbatical. Special thanks from Francisco to Ardath Lee, Anthony Mountain, and Jeannine Thompson, from whom he has learned so much about student-centered teaching, and to Sue Foley for helping with the technical and clerical aspects of developing the manuscript. Francisco also wants to express his appreciation to Dean William Babula and President Rubén Armiñana for their continued support and to the faculty and staff at Sonoma State University for granting him a sabbatical. Special thanks to colleagues Teresa Córdova, Elizabeth Coonrod Martínez, Noel Samaroo, Anthony White, Peter Phillips, Raymund Castro, José Hernández, Elizabeth Gálvez, and Morena Noyes. We want to thank them for being our coconspirators in the quest for public citizenship.

We are indebted to many other intellectual guides, some of whom are represented in the anthology and others of whom are not, such as Rudy Acuña, Frank Bonilla, Carlos Cortés, Carlos Muñoz Jr., and Juan Gómez-Quiñonez. Finally, this book has its intellectual and political roots in a friendship of nearly thirty years. The two of us have wanted to collaborate on a project since our days in graduate school in Claremont and our first years teaching at Loyola Marymount University. This project gave us the opportunity to continue our intellectual conversation and strengthen our friendship in a truly democratic and exciting collaboration. We initially conceived of this volume as a coedited reader. It gradually grew into a hybrid book-length study with original material and reprints. Francisco Vázquez and Rudy Torres had coequal material in the volume with the exception of appendix 7B, which was authored solely by Francisco.

Francisco H. Vázquez
Rodolfo D. Torres
January 2002

GENERAL INTRODUCTION

The national elections in the United States in the year 2000 were so controversial they masked the fact that a political revolution of another sort was taking place. If the twentieth century was the American century, the new century points to the prominence of U.S. Latino/as. This group is projected to grow to 25 percent of the U.S. population by 2050 and those who are immigrants are becoming U.S. citizens at an unprecedented rate. There is an emergent, socially oriented middle class with economic clout that has spawned a cohesive national Latino/a lobby and they are considered to be a political Third Force.[1] With 7 percent of the one million voters in the 2000 elections, Latino/as were the deciding factor in many critical political races, including the contested presidential election. It is said that Mexicans gave the presidency to Gore in California and that Cubans took it away from him in Florida. Indeed, we can now say that Latino/as are no longer *becoming,* they *are* a major political, economic, and cultural force in the United States. It seems, nevertheless, that Latino/as in the United States do not feel included, accepted, and most importantly, treated with respect no matter how hard they work and try to participate in the American way of life.[2]

The need to understand this paradoxical situation is one of many reasons a reader on Latino/a political thought is necessary. This reader is also an important device to counteract the mantle of invisibility that seems to envelope this population. Informed people of the United States and abroad will find the reader useful for learning about the history of Latino/a political involvement and the possible directions that Latino/a political thought may take in the future. Foremost, though, this reader was assembled with young people in mind, for not only will they help shape the future, but they also express a genuine interest to learn about their fellow U.S. Americans. Latino/a youth, in particular, need to have a historical and political context in which to place themselves, make sense of and become active in their social- and political-economic realities. Most are not taught their own history and, if they are, this history is often biased, or one dimensional, or restricted to one particular

1

group. For each and every reader, the objective is to raise the level of discourse of, by, and for Latino/as in the United States.

To achieve this goal, we have gone beyond the usual reader or anthology that collects a number of related articles in between two covers and frames them with an introduction and conclusion. This contextualized reader on Latino/a political thought provides, in addition to the articles for scholars interested in further exploring a number of topics, conceptual and critical tools for students and lay readers to dissect, approach, evaluate, and interact with the articles. Also, it includes exercises, guidelines, suggestions, and models to put into practice the ideas discussed and elicited by the collection of articles and the extensive framing pieces.

While the editors' original intent was to address Latino/a political thought manifested by all Latino/a groups, our ultimate decision in limiting the scope of the reader was dictated by a combination of factors relating to space and pedagogy. Since most anthologies do not provide an adequate context for students or the lay reader to obtain an adequate understanding of the issues, we wanted to include a chronological as well as thematic compilation. There was barely enough room to give U.S. Mexicans, Cubans, and Puerto Ricans adequate treatment. Equally important, as we analyzed Latino/a political thought and uncovered a quest for public citizenship, we realized that such a quest applied to everyone inside and outside the United States, native, resident, immigrant, undocumented, or citizen. But we also became aware that there was something that made this quest more conspicuous among some groups of Latino/as. Mexicans, Puerto Ricans, and Cubans were first subjected to the U.S. government via treaties and acts that not only signaled the end of military conquest or invasion, but also served as symbolic "birth certificates" for these new territorial, involuntary, and cultural U.S. citizens. Starting with such status, focus on the permutations of the relations of each of these groups with the U.S. government and the dominant society yields special insights about the mechanisms and processes involved in the quest for economic, political, and cultural equity.

The need remains for chronological-thematic texts that adequately and specifically address the political thought of many other Latino/as who are also in the United States as a result of geopolitical-economic forces that have affected their countries and who are also in a quest for public citizenship: Dominicans, Ecuadorians, Salvadorians, Colombians, Nicaraguans, Panamanians, Chileans, and many others from the Americas. Diversity among Latino/as is not limited to national origin; as Octavio Romano has pointed out, Latino/as are the only group that proclaims its **mestizaje** (its mixture of races, its hibridity). Indeed, a Latino/a can be from any race or ethnic group. Latin America and the Caribbean have in some ways realized the U.S. American dream of a melting pot. There is, nevertheless, the lingering question of **pigmentocracy** (a hierarchy based on the color of skin), a form of unspoken, latent racism.

A demographic picture of the three groups featured in this reader would show that (20.5 million) Mexicans make up two thirds (32 million) of Latino/as in the United States and their population is increasing faster than that of any other group in the United States, including other Latino/a groups. There are 6.6 million Puerto Ricans (11 percent of all Latino/as); 2.8 million are in the mainland United States and 3.8 million are on the island. There are approximately 1.5 million Cubans living in the United States (5 percent of all Latino/as and nearly 10 percent of Cuba's entire population). South Americans make up 13 percent of all Latino/as and there are 7 percent who fall in the "Other" category in the U.S. Census. A close-up of this image would reveal almost one third of all Latinos living in the following six counties or metropolitan areas: Los Angeles County, California (4.1 million); Miami-Dade, Florida (1.2 million); Cook County, Illinois (930,887); Harris County, Texas (908,053); Orange County, California (801,797); and New York City (two million).[3] The political revolution is taking place because these human bodies are becoming active participants in the political process. Because of the age distribution of this population, there will be an increase in their portion of the electorate no matter what happens to immigration. More to the point, voter registration among Latino/as increased by 164 percent in 1976–96 (compared to 31 percent for non-Latino/as). Voter turnout increased by 135 percent (compared to 21 percent for non-Latinos).[4]

What is in a name? Could the invisibility of Latino/as be attributed to their sheer diversity of nationalities, races, ethnic groups, and religions? Perhaps the difficulty in representing them is that they do not lend themselves to an easy portrayal. A curious manifestation of subjugation is the constant search for adequate struggles and, along with these, suitable identities and names. Thus we have a Negro College Fund, the National Association for the Advancement of Colored People, Black Panthers, and African American studies. Similarly, we have the League of United Latin American Citizens, Movimiento Estudiantil Chicano de Aztlán, the Hispanic Chamber of Commerce, the National Council for La Raza, and the Mexican American Legal and Educational Fund. We also have Hispanics, Latino/as, Raza, Cuban Americans, Puerto Ricans and Nuyoricans, Mexicans, Mexican Americans, Spanish Americans, Chicano/as, Indio/as, Tex Mex, Manito/as, Cholo/as, Pocho/as and names within each group that refer to how dark the skin may be (*güero/a, trigueño/a, moreno/a, prieto/a, negro/a*) or to hair texture (*pelo liso* or *pelo quebrado*—straight or wavy hair).

Many of these terms are used in the readings, and the definitions not covered below are provided by the context of the anthologized texts or the framing pieces provided by the editors. Each term symbolizes the effort to assert or deny respect within the exercise of power relations, and each term has as a referent, a particular class, region, political consciousness, and level of acculturation. For example, "Hispanic" refers to Spain and the Spanish language and is preferred by the U.S. government and the light-skinned upper and upper-middle classes; however, using this term would be like calling all English speakers "Brittanics" and considering them a homogeneous group. "Latino/a" has its own historical problems (dating back to the French intervention in Mexico), but at least it is a term in the Spanish language and preferred by most people who consider themselves to be descendants of Latin Americans, and at least it cuts across class levels. "Raza" also encompasses all Latino/as, as in Raza Studies at San Francisco State University in California. The term has two sources: it was used colloquially to designate "lower" classes, "the rabble," but it was also derived from the philosophical concept of a cosmic (hybrid) race: La Raza Cósmica of José Vasconcelos.

"Mexican American" and "Spanish American" are names used by people who have been well established in the United States for several generations and want to differentiate themselves from the recently arrived poor Mexicans. The latter used to be called "Chicanos," but this pejorative term became a badge of courage for the militant student movement of the late sixties and seventies. In American popular culture, as well as among scholars like Juan Gómez Quiñonez and Rodolfo Acuña, the term "Mexican" is applied to Mexicans in the United States. The editors use "U.S. Mexican" when it becomes necessary to distinguish the latter from Mexicans from Mexico who are not subject to any type of U.S. **juridical** influence. "Cholo/a" is the modern term for "Pachuco" or gang member, while "Pocho/a" is a pejorative for a Mexican American who has supposedly "lost" her or his culture. To address a question that is frequently raised in "race awareness" workshops, it is here noted that these terms are situational, relational, subject to political games of truth. The individuals who are caught in the construction of these identities go "around the day in eighty worlds," as Julio Cortázar once titled a book. The terms are not essences tattooed into their flesh and therefore it is impossible to know in advance what to call a particular Latino/a (although to be precise, you might find a gang member who has tattooed his gang or barrio name on his body). Incidentally, Latino "ethnicity" is an idea that is subject to similar political maneuvers. That is to say, it is not a solid substance, a materiality, an "essence" that stays unchanged throughout history. And yet, when necessary, like the concept of "culture," it does serve as a tool for protection from and even struggle against racism.

Depending on the time period, the term "americano/a" has been applied to Latin Americans and to Anglo-Americans. Because of this inconsistency, and also because the term technically applies to anyone who is from this continent, in this reader we refer to the population of the United States in general by the term "U.S. American." When it is necessary to be more specific, we use the term "Anglo-American" or "white"; similarly, we use the term "U.S. Mexican" to refer to the Mexicans who come under the jurisdiction of the U.S. government and live under the dominant U.S. culture. When the context requires more specificity, we use the terms "Mexican American" and "Chicano/as."

To many people, the idea of a reader on Latino/a "political thought" raises questions such as: Do Latino/as have their own political philosophy? Their own politics? Is there a particular history of Latino/a political thought? Is there such a thing as Latino/a political thought? While there are no formal graduate programs on Latin American philosophy, there are many studies, mostly in Spanish, of the social and political thought of Latin American intellectuals. Three major political thinkers, for example, who have influenced Cubans, Puerto Ricans, and U.S. Mexicans are José Martí, Eugenio Maria de Hostos, and Ricardo Flores Magón, respectively. As to be expected, Latin American philosophy and, more concretely, Latino political thought cover a wide historical and **political spectrum:** from scholasticism to **Enlightenment** and from liberal ideals (which led to Mexican *independencia* in 1821 and the Mexican Constitutions of 1854 and 1917 as well as the constitutions of Cuba in 1900 and Puerto Rico in 1950) to the conservative and even fascist and racist thought of the positivists, known as *los científicos,* in the nineteenth century and that associated with U.S.-backed militarist, reactionary, and elitist politics of the twentieth century.[5] A complete history of Latino political philosophy, however, remains to be written, for most texts do not give expression to the wide diversity of voices that make up the Latin American political discourse.

This reader takes a different approach to political thought. What we are attempting to do here is an archaeological dig, a reconstruction of a discourse of Latino/a political thought. There is no attempt at completeness. While we try to provide a chronological context, we present statements and discourses as we find them and leave it up to the reader to glue them together in the way that makes the most sense to her or him. We are painfully aware that we are missing crucial pieces of information, necessary authorities, explanations, and theories.

More specifically, we attempt to detect political thought in the everyday life of the people, in their tactics and strategies for survival, for dignity, and for social justice. *Cada cabeza es un mundo* (every head is a world of its own) goes an often-quoted Mexican saying. Indeed, anyone attempting to present or describe these particular strands of American thought would come up with their own selection of readings. We have been inspired by many thinkers who have detected the less-visible workings of power; among them are, most immediately, women and men in our families and communities real and imagined who carry on a lifelong struggle for public citizenship. Academically, there are people like Gramsci, who has supplied his notion of hegemony; there is Rousseau's claim that the real law is not in the legal codes but resides in the hearts of the people; and there is Artaud's belief that "it is the action that shapes the thought." Mostly, though, we follow Foucault's suggestion that to study power, we should look not at the institutions but at their manifestations in the form of resistance and their focus on bio-power, the human body as a nexus of desire as well as production. This reader attempts to go beyond philosophy and to focus on the many ways that power ultimately leaves its mark on these human bodies.

Latino political thought is here defined as a discourse produced by diverse and multilevel actions: by Latino/as and the U.S. government and dominant culture, based on their corresponding material and cultural conditions, to (de)construct a space where the struggle for justice takes place. Examples of these manifold actions would be political voting behavior, proposed and opposed laws, protest demonstrations, economic decisions, representations, images, writings (philosophy, poetry, plans, strategies), and again, actions that ultimately impact the human body. Most recently this space has been defined by the California anti-immigrant Proposition 187, the Puerto Rican demand for the U.S. Navy to get out of Vieques, and the Cuban American internal and external conflict regarding U.S. and Cuban state policies affecting human bodies in both countries. This quest for public citizenship is a question of justice: justice in terms of the respect for the established law, justice in terms of the abuses based on light-skin supremacy, justice based on an equitable distribution of the social wealth, justice in terms of respect for the individual as moral and physical entity with cultural and gender differences.

In this scenario, there is a distinction between the ideals of truth, honor, love, equality, and democracy and the appropriation of these ideals for political purposes, for self-interest or what we call games of truth. In this scenario, moreover, there are no pure identities for victims or victimizers, there are no ethnic or racial, class, or gender essences. Though the historical record clearly shows a strong dose of anti-Latino/a sentiment among U.S. Americans, in the final analysis there is no reason for anyone to take the moral high ground. The point of studying political thought is not to feel guilty about what happened in the past, but to feel responsible for what may happen in the future. We all conspire for justice as well as for our own subjection. In short, we examine the birth of U.S. Latinos (Mexican Americans, Puerto Ricans, Cuban Americans) as (in)voluntary, territorial, and cultural U.S. citizens (similar to African Americans and American Indians) and the permutations of their relations with the U.S. government and the dominant society. We focus our gaze not only on what has been said but also on the illegitimate knowledges that are hidden behind the horizon of a dominant U.S. political culture.

STRUCTURE OF THE READER

This anthology of Latino/a political thought provides a historical yet thematic compilation of readings, cross-referencing and framing each one of them within the context of a quest for public citizenship defined as a struggle for social justice. It spans the period of the wars of independence from Britain, France, and Spain in the eighteenth and nineteenth centuries to the present. We discuss not only where these Latino/as are politically, but also how they got there. It also provides theoretical discussions regarding methods of study and research of social and political issues as well as pedagogical tools for classroom use.

The articles and other texts are drawn from books representing a variety of academic disciplines combined with pieces from scholarly journals and monographs. An effort has been made to represent diverse voices and differences in political tone and orientation, or at least to point to the existence of opposing views. As might be expected, it was in the historical and nationalist themes that a gender balance was difficult to attain. The feminist voice is loud and clear, however, in the practical and theoretical understanding of the predicament of Latino/a political thought, in particular in the notion of "public" that informs the overall theme of the reader. While the emphasis is on contemporary issues, an effort is made to include important pieces that are now out of print. The framing pieces provide a coherent story of U.S. Mexican, Puerto Rican, and U.S. Cuban political thought that stands on its own, yet refers to the contents in a relationship of text/subtext. In a special "Introduction for Students" and through the framing pieces and questions after each piece, students are encouraged to read the texts with critical minds, suspend judgment, and not take statements as given truths, but as truths in a complex game of truths, to do what no one power, divine or mortal, can make them do: think for themselves.

The reader is constructed so that it can be approached in a variety of ways depending on the needs of the reader: student and/or instructor. The chronological table of contents consists of four parts covering the following topics: (1) class/labor struggle, (2) Cubans, (3) feminisms, (4) genders/queer theory, (5) historical materialism (marxism), (6) Latino/as, (7) literature, (8) Mexicans, (9) nationalism, (10) **postmodernism,** (11) Puerto Ricans, (12) theory, and (13) violence in theory and practice.

The chronological table of contents has a postmodern structure in that the first and last parts are both beginnings and ends. Both provide theoretical frameworks and scaffoldings to understand contemporary political thought (Latino/a or not). Part I also includes literary and historical discourses to introduce the readers to the stories, characters, issues, and past events that inform Latino/a political thought. The main section, titled "Seduction and Aggression: The Birth of Territorial, Involuntary, and Cultural U.S. Citizens," plots the historical points when the U.S. government brought under its political control the three largest groups of Latino/as in the United States (Mexicans, Puerto Ricans, and Cubans). In a sliding scale of domination, the United States moved from outright conquest and annexation of Mexican territory in 1848, with the Treaty of Guadalupe Hidalgo, to the gradual incorporation of Puerto Rico through the Treaty of Paris, the Foraker Act of 1900, and additional amendments in 1917 (like the Jones Act, which made Puerto Ricans U.S. citizens). Similarly, the Treaty of Paris and the Platt Amendment to the Cuban Constitution (enacted into law by Congress in February 1901 and repealed in 1934) established U.S. hegemony over Cubans.

In part II, the texts in the first section illustrate what life was like within the empire (roughly from 1900 to the 1960s) for these newborn U.S. Americans, how they (de)constructed political positions and identities in response to local, national, and global political-economic changes. The second section of part II briefly presents the emergence of manifold identities and struggles (roughly from the 1960s to the present). Part III presents theories, strategies, and tactics that pertain to the national question. In contrast to this focus, part IV contains texts that go beyond the national–colonial dichotomy by exploring the politics or, better yet, the microphysics of power (see appendix 5).

Among the questions addressed by the reader from various perspectives are:

- What political philosophies serve as a model for, or are considered the origins of, contemporary Mexican, Puerto Rican, and Cuban political thought?
- What, if anything, differentiates U.S. Mexican, Puerto Rican, and U.S. Cuban political thought from other political thought in the United States?
- Do Mexicans, Puerto Ricans, and U.S. Cubans see themselves as part of the United States political framework or do they support a separatist position?
- To what extent is there an agreement between the political thought of U.S.

Mexican, Puerto Rican, and U.S. Cuban people and that of the intellectual and political leaders who speak for them or represent them?

- What are the most important issues for Mexican, Puerto Rican, and U.S. Cuban political thought?
- What are the visions and strategies for U.S. Mexican, Puerto Rican, and U.S. Cuban political action in the twenty-first-century United States?
- How do U.S. Mexican, Puerto Rican, and U.S. Cuban political thought address current issues such as racism; the globalization of the economy; immigration; gender; class relations among U.S. Mexicans, Puerto Ricans, and U.S. Cubans; pigmentocracy (superiority of light over dark skin); and relations with other ethnic groups?

The reader's distinctive "user-friendly" design and pedagogical tools will assist students and nonspecialists to further study the topic or to engage not only in the study but also in the practice of politics. Faculty who are not experts in Latino political thought may find these features useful from the standpoint of pedagogy. Those whose disciplines are political science or philosophy may find the dialogical seminar suggestions a useful alternative to lecture classes. Words in boldface are explained in the glossary.

NOTES AND SUGGESTED READINGS

1. Juan Gonzalez, *Harvest of Empire* (New York: Viking, 2000), 168.
2. William V. Flores and Rina Benmayor, eds., *Latino Cultural Citizenship: Claiming Identity, Space and Rights* (Boston: Beacon, 1997). As Raymund Paredes has shown in "The Origins of Anti-Mexican Sentiment in the United States" (in *New Directions in Chicano Scholarship*, ed. R. Romo and R. Paredes, Chicano Studies Monograph Series [San Diego: University of California, San Diego, 1978]), Latino and Anglo-American relations are part of an epic discourse going back at least four centuries to the "Black Legend," or the defeat of the invisible Armada. In 1900, José Enrique Rodó, referring to Shakespeare's *The Tempest*, claimed that whereas Latino/as are imbued with the aesthetic sensibilities characteristic of the spirit of Ariel, U.S. Anglo-Saxons covet materialism because they are possessed by the spirit of Calibán (Rodó, *Ariel*, trans. Margaret Sayers Peden [Austin: University of Texas Press, 1988]). For a critical perspective, see Roberto Fernández Retamar, *Caliban and Other Essays*, trans. Edward Baker (Minneapolis: University of Minnesota Press, 1989). *Arielismo* became a literary and political movement that is said to have spawned revolutionaries such as Victor Raul Haya de la Torre and, through his American Revolutionary Popular Alliance, Fidel Castro (Martin Staab, *In Quest of Identity* [Chapel Hill: University of North Carolina Press, 1967]). Nobel Prize–winner Octavio Paz says these two peoples, Latinos and Anglos, are the product of two different civilizations and are so essentially different that even economic equality cannot bridge their dissimilarities (*The Labyrinth of Solitude and the Other Mexico, Return to the Labyrinth of Solitude, Mexico and the United States, The Philanthropic Ogre* [New York: Grove Press, 1985]). Within the United States, some complain that Latinos crossed the border illegally; others retort that the border crossed them. Social scientists observe that Latino/as will eventually become assimilated like all other ethnic groups have in the past, while politi-

cians argue that Latino/as threaten to become another Quebec, and complain about a "chromosomatic invasion."

3. U.S. Census.

4. Gonzalez, *Harvest*, 168; Tomas Rivera Policy Institute (www.trpi.org).

5. Staab, *In Quest of Identity;* Mario de la Cueva et al., *Major Trends in Mexican Philosophy*, trans. R. A. Caponigri (Notre Dame, Ind.: University of Notre Dame Press, 1966); Harold Eugene Davis, *Latin American Social Thought* (Washington, D.C.: University Press of Washington, D.C., 1966); Juan Gómez-Quiñonez, *Sembradores Ricardo Flores Magón y el Partido Liberal Mexicano: A Eulogy and Critique* (Los Angeles: Aztlan, University of California, Los Angeles, 1973).

INTRODUCTION FOR STUDENTS
Power/Knowledge, Language, and Everyday Life

Francisco Hernández Vázquez

There are several assumptions the editors of this volume have made about you the student or, better yet, the lifelong learner who reads this collection of texts on Latino/a political thought. One is that you are interested in the concept of "power" and curious enough to want to learn as much as you can about it. Another assumption is that you are willing to wrestle with language and force it to yield the hidden meanings, codes, and secrets of power. If these assumptions are correct, then you must also want seriously to learn about this thing called "politics."

STUDENT QUESTIONS

But in reality, when a student is confronted with a reader on Latino/a political thought, there is a set of FAQs (frequently asked questions) that the student may not raise in class but may think of to themselves: Why should I care? I hate politics! What will I learn? How true is this? Whose side of the story is this? Is this another book on how Latino/as have been victimized by the dominant group? These are legitimate questions that need to be addressed, first briefly and then more extensively.

"Why Should I Care? I Hate Politics!"

According to a famous phrase by Aristotle, humans are political animals. This means there is a political dimension to everything we do, collectively or individually, whether we mean it as political or not. Another way of putting it is that every action is subject to interpretation and every interpretation has political implications and consequences.

"What Will I Learn?"

In this reader there is a history of political engagement of Latino/as in the United States, their struggles for respect and for justice. Latino/a political thought is presented in a format that can be accessed chronologically or thematically (like a game of *Serpientes y Escaleras*—Chutes and Ladders). In this introduction, you also may discover ways to understand yourself in terms of the relationship between power and knowledge, to increase your understanding of the politics of education, and to increase your learning strategies. In short, we invite you to play games of truth and power that shape your own identity and to make a map to navigate your own political reality.

"How 'True' Is This Representation of Latino/a Political Thought?"

What "truth" is and how it is involved with politics is the main concern of this reader. While we present one way to look at truth, the analysis of discourse, it is left up to you to decide your own truth based on the evidence presented in the reader.

"Whose Side of the Story Is This? Is This Another Book on How Latino/as Have Been Victimized by the Dominant Group?"

The editors have tried to represent a variety of positions and voices. However, the quest for public citizenship, for justice, inevitably includes victims and victimizers as well as social systems that oppress and liberate. Who is the hero and who is the fool depends, again, on your own perspective and your own interpretation.

"¿Y Qué Es la Política? What Is Politics, Anyway?"

When I was in elementary school in Mexico, my mother would admonish me: "No te metas a la política. No andes juzgando, criticando ni alegando." (Don't get involved in politics. Don't go around judging, criticizing, or arguing.) I knew what she meant; she wanted to protect me from a particular kind of "politics." Student politics in Mexico, as in many countries, can be deadly. When I visited Guadalajara after many years in the United States, I was sad to find that some of my childhood friends had been killed in junior high school and high school during political confrontations. Through my living and schooling experiences in the United States, however, I soon realized that everyone is political in one way or another; to be alive and even to die is to be political. I learned, furthermore, that judgment, criticism, and argument are *the* necessary tools for successful political involvement.

Politics can be defined in many ways. Let us dig deep to find the kind of politics that affects us in a personal way. When you look up "politics" in a dictionary or encyclopedia, it is very likely that you will find the following definitions:

1. The art or science of government or governing, especially the governing of a political entity, such as a nation, and the administration and control of its internal and external affairs.

   Here "politics" means the knowledge that would help you govern the United States, Aztlán, Puerto Rico, or Cuba, if or when you found yourself in that situation. Or, if you want to study and teach politics, the academic discipline is called "political science."
2. Within a country, what a government (federal, state, local), a politician, or a political party does is also "politics."
3. An individual can also be "into politics" in the sense that she or he dedicates her or his life or makes a career out of politics.
4. Intrigue or maneuvering within a political unit or a group in order to gain control or power.

   This could be as passionate as office politics or student government, as fervent as Republican or Democratic or ethnic politics, or as zealous and dangerous as fighting to the death to defend your territory, your family, your dignity. Control of a street gang or high-school cliques like the "populars" also fits into this definition of "politics."

5 and 6. The last of the definitions refers to the hidden sort of politics that most of us take for granted: "political attitudes and positions" and "the often internally conflicting interrelationships among people in a society."[1] Indeed, the psychologist R. D. Laing has written books on the *Politics of the Family* and the *Politics of Experience*. In Spanish, there are terms like *"tio/a politico/a"* (literally a "political" aunt or uncle who is not related by blood but by marriage, corresponding to the English usage of "in-law"). The point is that even if you hate politics, you are involved in them. The obvious implication is that whether you are conscious of it or not, you have a political attitude and you take political positions. Even refusing to take a position is a political position! You may be conservative, or liberal, or anarchist and not even know it! In this context, it is pertinent to note that during the 1960s, to the extent that Chicano and Puerto Rican youth became "politicized" by joining the Brown Berets or the Young Lords, gang membership dropped.

We need to question why the personal dimension of "politics" is the very last one in the list of definitions. This dimension reflects the attitude that leads people to say they hate politics. This is a disempowering notion. It is part of the illusion that "politics" is just something that "politicians" do, not what we the people do. This gives a sort of invisibility to the politics in our everyday life and to our role as political animals. And yet at the same time we profess that we have "a government of the people, by the people, and for the people." It is critical, then, to envision politics as building up from the political relationship you have with yourself (identity), with your parents, with relatives, with friends, with lovers, and with institutions like school, business, the courts, and the police. Then there are economic, social, and cultural relations among individuals and groups and finally the relations between the people and the **state** (the most complex political machine humans have ever built, next to corporations and, in another time, the Church). In short, politics is the way we manage power/knowledge at the many levels of existence. Such awareness is important not only for you to understand Latino/a political thought, but also for you to make sense of the world around you and for your own personal development.[2]

There is one incident that brought politics to its most fundamental level for me. I was once in a hotel in Mexico where the manager told me they had a *política* on cashing checks. It struck me as odd: what does cashing checks have to do with politics? To my surprise, I found that in Spanish *política* means both "politics" and "policy." Indeed, "policy" is such a close relative of "politics" that is first defined by dictionaries as "a plan or course of action, as of a government, political party, or business, intended to influence and determine decisions, actions, and other matters," such as "American foreign policy in Mexico" or "the company's personnel policy." Only secondly is it defined at the personal level as "a course of action, guiding principle, or procedure considered expedient, prudent, or advantageous," such as comments we hear in everyday conversation: "my policy is not to borrow money from friends" or "to date my friend's girl/boy friend." So the dress policy in your school and the store policy for returns are also politics. When you don't like these policies and you want to change them, you are involved in political action. So, you go talk to the principal and tell him you want the dress code changed—but is that all it takes? How do we use language to change our realities?

EXERCISE #1

(a) List the ten key events of your political life.

(b) Write a short essay describing the political beliefs, principles, or positions you "inherited" from your parents and ancestors. Include if or how these differ from your own politics or personal policies.

(c) Write a dialogue with one of your parents or ancestors about a political issue.

THE APPROPRIATION OF DISCOURSE, OR *PALABRAS QUE NO SE LAS LLEVA EL VIENTO* (WORDS THAT ARE NOT CARRIED AWAY BY THE WIND)

In addition to your realizing how "political" you may be without even knowing it, you will learn here about "discourse" as the product of the collision between language and power. The value of using the term "discourse" is that it points to the intimate relationship between language and power, or between "what is said" and economic/political institutional processes. By using this term we want to create a habit of mind, a reminder that language hides things at the same time that it reveals them. We need, therefore, to remember to think vertically, in depth, to dig for what remains invisible under the horizontal surface of language. We begin again with the necessity to counteract another commonly accepted belief. This notion goes something like this: "if only people knew about it, something would be done." There is, for example, a dramatic story of Ricardo Chávez Ortiz, a Mexican national who hijacked a Frontier Airlines 737 jet from Albuquerque, New Mexico, with an unloaded gun. The plane landed in Los Angeles, where he asked not for money but for radio time to talk about the unjust treatment of Mexicans, hoping that spreading such knowledge would bring about social change. He got the airtime but, as you might imagine, no major change occurred in the life of Mexicans in the United States. He paid with federal prison time for the right to speak to power.[3]

This is a big price to pay for misunderstanding the nature of language. This misconception about the way language affects our everyday lives, our notions of reality, of history, of our own sense of identity is, unfortunately, rather widespread. Let us explore in more detail the relationship between power and language. Imagine the voices of the people in any given community, in any social group. Some of these voices are just that, voices that are carried away by the wind. Some voices, though, intersect with power relations. That means that they have an impact on desire, politics, or economics. How do we know they have an impact? Because of the reaction these voices provoke. At a personal level there are voices you hear, remember, and repeat "in your mind" over and over again. What is it about some things that are said that affect you so much while others you forget almost immediately? At a social level, depending on the status of "who speaks," the voice(s) may be categorized as scientific, artistic, funny, or worth repeating, or they may be considered stupid, unworthy, or "fighting words." By "status" we mean class, culture, gender, and color and an infinite number of other factors. Why are some voices heard and not others? Imagine that some of these voices become "solidified" into what we call Statements: they acquire a certain "materiality" and become part of a Discourse. Words that seem to be carved in stone, for example, are called "laws." This particular discourse and its (moral, political, economic, and military) enforcement represent one of the most concrete and powerful realities that impact our everyday lives. This is what it means to have the property of, to appropriate discourse. These words are not easily carried away by the wind. Here the ideal is, of course, that *no one is above the law*. The reality is that there are individuals whose voices reach the White House, or the Congress, or the Supreme Court, or all of them. This is what the very popular song "El Rey," by José Alfredo Jiménez, means by "mi palabra es la ley" (my word is the law). The reality is also that there are voices that are silenced. There are bodies and doings and events that are rendered invisible by discourse. Their human experience does not fit into any of the socially accepted categories or Discourses (politics, economics, and desire relations). Desires and needs, joys and suffering are part of everyday life and of the reality of the world, but these voices remain more or less invisible until they become an object of Discourse (see for example "The Decolonial Imaginary," by Emma Pérez, in part IV of this reader). So, the struggle for community, for justice, and for dignity is the quest for public citizenship: it is also the constant fight to open up spaces for voices to be heard and bodies to be seen, the efforts to implant our Statements into positions of authority, policies, and institutional procedures until the desired social changes take place. In short, discourse is to the body politic as a tattoo is to the human body: the indelible trace of a transformative experience.

It is not, then, just a matter of speaking up, it is a *question* of investing our words with power. As you can see, this is not just an issue for Latino/as, but for everyone who cares about a democracy that is based on "the will of the people." A key to the misunderstanding of the relationship between language and power seems to arise because we tend to think of language and words as transparent things, as objects that obey our commands, as entities that carry our intentions and our thoughts without distorting them. We become frustrated when they don't do the job we tell them to do. That is because words have their own baggage, their own meanings. They are material things, like mountains and oceans and deserts. Their materiality makes them **commodities** in our political economy. We would not claim to be able to move a mountain with our bare hands and yet we firmly believe that we can say anything we want. We believe words come from us when in fact we were born into them. We build conceptual castles and philosophical shacks and poetic skyscrapers only to see them collapse under a discursive storm. We take the inherent power of language for granted when we should be establishing a respectful relationship with it. *¡Ponte trucha!* (Watch out!) A discourse is like a mine field. If you don't watch where you're going, words explode into contradictory meanings and semantical disturbances.

At this point we are counting on our assumption that you are still willing to wrestle with language (just like we are) and force it to yield the hidden meanings, codes, and secrets of power. Let us proceed by briefly illustrating a particular analysis of the production and appropriation of discourse. Then you can explore the implications of this approach for your education and for increasing critical and analytical skills.

In the appendix to this reader, you will find a "Chart of Discursive Analysis" and a "Chart of Latino/a Political Discourse as Presented in the Reader," as well as the "Rules and Procedures for the Control and Production of Discourse." Here, we will limit ourselves to a brief analysis of Chicano discourse in the form of a story.

Once upon a time (in 1940) the word "Chicano" was first used by the writer Mario Suárez in his short stories. Undoubtedly, the word was widely used by then, but it was not an Object supported by Discourse so, as the Mexican saying goes, "it was carried away by the wind." The word "Chicano" was visible to the U.S. Mexican border Chicano communities but invisible to the dominant society. As power relations shifted twenty years later, the word "Chicano/a" was born as a Statement and it became powerful enough to spawn other terms, such as "Brown Power" and "La Nueva Raza." (Another, more recent shift led to a decline of the visibility of "Chicano/a." Now, for example, we have Chicano/Latino or Raza Studies.) We say that "Chicano/a discourse" was born in the 1960s, when it was constructed as a "real Object." At that time there was a particular combination of Subjectivities (leaders such as César Chávez, José Angel Gutierrez, Corky Gonzales, and Reies Tij-erina) and a critical mass of individuals (students mostly) who appropriated discourse and gave their voices the status of Truth. There were also Chicano/a Concepts (such as Chicano Power, Internal Colonialism, marxism, Cultural Nationalism, the nation of Aztlán, Brown Berets, Hijas de Cuauhtémoc, Chicana feminism, and School Walkouts) that fit into the conceptual scheme of the dominant society (Black Power, Black Panthers, civil rights, feminism, the Vietnam War, the counterculture, revolution). Finally, Chicano/a discourse depended on the support of (or opposition by) numerous political and economic institutions (Movimento Estudiantil Chicano de Aztlán and many other political organizations, high schools, barrios, foundations, and universities, as well as the military and the police). When the prophetic Mario Suárez first used the word "Chicano/a," it was just that, a word; later it was infused with power and became a social movement with its own labor unions, political party, academic departments in universities, national association, journals, scholarships, and doctoral programs.

Chicano/a Discourse became a Chicano renaissance in areas such as visual art, music, poetry, theater, film, prose, and academic journals. But that is not all. There were also politics by other means: mass demonstrations, violence, and deaths. For Chicano Discourse was in reality just another version of a struggle against the Rules for the Control of Latino/a Discourse illustrated in this reader. Whether it is against institutional racism, anti-Mexican sentiment, or Chicanology, the struggle for public citizenship continues. The moral of the story, up to this point, is that when language combines with diverse power relations to form Statements and Discourses and there is a confluence of material conditions and historical circumstances, social change is likely to occur. The trick is, of course, to be able to read historical events to know when power relations will assume a propitious form. This is such a complex task because there is a principle of uncertainty involved; it is no wonder social change is so difficult to achieve, whether by peaceful or violent means.

You may wonder just how many explanations, charts, theories, and **taxonomies** there are to chop up and re-present social and political reality and whether there is one correct or true way to do it. There is no "correct" way. There are only interpretations, or rather struggles to invest Statements and Discourses with the status of Truth, to legitimize them, give them authority. This is what in this reader we call "Games of Truth." We could call them political games, except that everyone claims to be after "the Truth" but not after "politics." These Games of Truth are found in the history of political thought of every human society, every culture. In this reader, several texts allude to the Puerto Rican movement for independence or the Cuban revolution or counterrevolution as Objects that are constructed out of a particular arrangement of Subjects, Concepts, and Institutions. Or we could take Objects such as the Rights of Man (as opposed to the Divine Right of Kings—but women were invisible), or the Declaration of Independence (but Native Americans and African Americans were invisible), or the process by which Italian and Irish Americans became whites (by differentiating themselves from "blacks"), or how women or gay rights more recently have been acquiring political and cultural visibility and civil/

human rights. Ultimately, however, a discourse is a scar on history. It is a painful event that might have healed, but will never cease to remind us of the transgression against the political or human body. It is a material memory that endures precisely because the transgression is continually repeated.

Is there an Objective, a Real Truth? The relativity of interpretations stops where bloodshed begins. The closest we can come to it is to say that the ultimate effect of the power deployed by these Games of Truth can be read on the human body itself. When all is said and done, are the human bodies well fed, healthy, educated, and respected or are they not? In this respect, an ethical dimension that is central to the Games of Truth is the struggle between the notions of humans as moral entities or commodities. Consequently, this analysis reverts into a question of social justice, one that includes the distribution of wealth as well as of human dignity (therefore the quest for public citizenship). Indeed, political thought in general can be understood as a Game of Truth in which, depending on your position as a "Subject," sometimes the wager may be your own body, your dignity, your life. This reader itself, with its particular choice of articles (and its necessary exclusion of many others), with its Charts of Discourse, is itself a Game of Truth.

So the methodology we use in the reader is: Language plus Power equals Statements. Statements that appear on a regular basis equal a Discourse. The political struggles to have Discourses accepted as Truth equal Games of Truth. Appropriation of discourse equals the power to invest our voices into social realities. With these conceptual tools you will be able to stand in a critical relationship with language and with education (see appendixes 3, 4, and 5).

POWER/KNOWLEDGE: EDUCATION, SUBJECTIFICATION, AND CRITICAL THINKING

How is the above useful to understanding your subjective position within power/knowledge relations and to increasing your learning strategies? How do games of truth shape your own identity (your subjectivity) and how might you navigate this political reality? Let us begin by noting that so far we have addressed two misunderstandings: that we hate politics and can do without it and that language is there for us to use anyway we want. A third misconception is about the relation between power and knowledge. It is common to hear people say young people should get an education because "knowledge is power." (If this were true, presumably, every high school and college graduate would be powerful.) Why is it that people rarely say the inverse: "power is knowledge?" Like the language/power relation, the relation between power and knowledge is not simple and straightforward.

There are several ways in which power interacts with knowledge, either restricting it or producing it; among them are academic disciplines, fellowships of discourse (like secret societies), doctrines, and education (see appendix 5). Here let us focus first on a process of subjectification by the institution of education, meaning the distribution of human bodies along established social categories like class, gender, and color. Or, from the opposite perspective, how educational institutions assign subjectivities by "subjecting" you to one or more particular identities. Secondly, we will consider the fight against this type of subjectification, which as you well know takes many forms: you may go along with it and make it work for you, you may go along pretending you are learning, or you may just drop out. Indeed, as Paulo Freire taught, education can be for domination, but it can also be for liberation. This can be achieved through a student-centered method of teaching, such as the seminar (see appendix 7B) or by your practice of critical thinking skills (see appendix 7A). In terms of appropriating discourse, thinking critically means investing your words with power, inserting your voice in institutional processes and policies and thus (re)constructing your social reality and identity. All this sounds fairly direct; the hard part is determining what your "voice" is, to know who you are separate from the way you have been subjectified, from the identities that have been given to or forced upon you.

The educational system is not, of course, solely responsible for the process of subjectification. As usual, there are cultural, economic, and political factors involved. For example, academic performance can be determined by the socioeconomic level of the school district. There is also a correlation between a lower average income and the fact that Latino/as have a high percentage of school dropouts. As we shift from an industrial to a postindustrial global economy, most U.S. Americans no longer work in big factories. Instead, they do two main things: process information and provide services for other people. Most of the factories move to parts of the world where workers do not charge so much for their labor. So your place in the class structure determines, to a large extent, what kind of education you get and what position you will occupy in society. It is also known that race and gender (and even height!) enter into this process of subjectification. So we can conclude that in the games of truth we all must play, knowledge is necessary but not sufficient for power. This does not mean that everyone's destiny is determined. There is a principle of uncertainty at play here, too, and there are methods to use in struggling against this form of domination we call subjectification.

According to Paulo Freire, education can be for domination or for liberation. Education as domination operates on the basis of the "banking concept" and it works this way: sit in the classroom and absorb everything the teacher "deposits" in you via the lecture format; faithfully repeat it in a test to get good grades. Clearly, this method does not necessarily mean you will learn anything; it only means that you will have the ability to regurgitate what you have been told. It is important to note that this does not mean that every teacher who "lectures" is not practicing a pedagogy of liberation. The key question is about the nature of your relationship with the process of learning. Are you just learning to pass the test or do you take yourself seriously as a learner? That is, are you just going through the motions? Or are you aware of the relationship between what you learn (knowledge) and the issues that affect your personal and socioeconomic realities (power)?

Education as liberation or critical pedagogy, by contrast, is based on the transformation that occurs when learning takes place as a dialogue between the teacher and the student, and it leads to a transformation in both of their social outlooks. Or better yet, learning becomes a dialogue between the teacher *and* the student *with* the social world. This kind of learning you carry with you as part of yourself. School learning becomes similar to the way you learn from conversations with friends, family, and relatives, from your own experiences, or from movies and television. The difference is that you care about it because it makes a difference in your life.

A good vehicle for education as liberation is the seminar discussion format. As described in appendix 7B, "Introduction to Seminaring," a seminar is based on the premise that a teacher is not necessary. Furthermore, as expressed by a Hutchins School alumnus, "it was born as a way of education which told us we were capable of learning from our peers and that we were not empty little vessels into which learning had to be poured."[4] An ideal seminar creates a safe environment where there is tolerance for ambiguity and diversity of ideas, where people interact in a respectful and caring manner for the purpose of discussing a given text, and where they build knowledge that is relevant to all the members of the seminar. An important aspect of the seminar is that it promotes tolerance for ambiguity and for diversity of ideas and political or philosophical positions.

In contrast to an education as liberation and transformation is an education based on the "banking concept." Since the latter teaches people to rely on instructors, on experts, on those "with authority" to define the truth or at least to tell people what is important, there is little if any room for students to articulate their ideas and opinions. This leads to three related natural consequences among many new members at the start of a seminar class. There is a lack of self-validation to encourage members to express their opinions, a lack of trust in the notion that they can learn from their peers, and an inability to listen carefully to what others have to say. After a few weeks of following the basic seminaring skills, however, most students learn to appreciate the joy of learning without the imposition of authority.

One has to wonder about a democracy that depends on the expression of "the will of the people," yet has an educational system that does not teach most of the people to feel validated, to express their own beliefs and opinions, and to practice critical thinking. A system that does teach these things would seem a necessary prerequisite for any active citizen, especially one on a quest for public citizenship.

EXERCISE #2

While mostly reserved for graduate studies and elite or honors programs, seminar discussions can be conducted, even with large classes or outside of class on your own in "study groups." Ask your teachers to hold seminar discussions following the instructions in appendix 7B, or form your own seminar with members of your class outside of school. Write a one- to two-page response paper on your observations of the processes.

Now, let's say that you are participating in a seminar to discuss this reader or other readings that have been selected by the group. How do you distinguish between what is important and what is not important? How do you decide to take a position? How do you play this particular game of truth? Many students are swayed by the arguments in favor and then change their minds when they hear the argument against. But how do you begin to think critically? Antonio Gramsci put it this way:

> The starting-point of critical elaboration is the consciousness of what one really is, and is "knowing thyself" as a product of the historical process to date, which has deposited in you an infinity of traces, without leaving an inventory; therefore it is imperative at the outset to compile such an inventory.[5]

This means that to separate what is important from what is not important (to you, not to someone else) you need to know who you are. In effect, from our experience, students who do not know themselves as "a product of the historical process to date" usually agree with everything and have a difficult time making up their minds about a particular issue. This difficulty also appears in their writing and in their speaking, in which they tend to contradict themselves. So it is crucial to "know thyself."[6] How do you begin to compile an inventory of the historical fragments that define who you are? Obviously for Latino/a students, especially of Cuban, Mexican, and Puerto Rican heritage, this reader is a beginning. But for all students, the journal exercises in appendix 7A will facilitate a more personal process. As noted there, a journal may be used for the constitution of a sort of permanent political relationship to oneself: one must manage oneself as a governor manages the governed, as a head of an enterprise manages his enterprise, as a head of a household manages his household.

EXERCISE #3

(a) Following the directions in appendix 7A, list the ten key events, or stepping-stones, of your "educational life."
(b) Write a dialogue with society (specifically with your school principal or teacher).
(c) Write a short essay on your educational experiences using Paulo Freire's concepts of education.

A WORD ON HOW TO READ THE ARTICLES

While reading the articles in this collection, keep in mind that some of them are easier to read than others. Remember that language is as material as water and rocks and air. So you may breeze through a poem like *I Am Joaquín,* but feel like you are stuck in mud when reading treaties or scholarly articles. Don't be discouraged. It is in the nature of power to hide behind language. The texts also differ in political tone and orientation. Read with a suspicious mind, suspend judgment, don't take statements as "given truths" but as "truths" in a complex game of truths. An effort has been made to include different political perspectives or at least to point to the existence of opposing views. There is only one thing that you and only you can do (not even God has that power), and that is to think for yourself. Consequently, you must make up your mind about what you want to believe.

BECOMING POLITICALLY INVOLVED

Just like when you buy a car and begin noticing other cars that look like yours, when you "buy" a particular idea or theory, you also recognize its reflection in various settings. As you engage this reader, you may want to make "politics" your car. The contents of the reader as well as your everyday political experience will be your map. Then as you cruise down Working Class Boulevard and Middle Class Avenue, turning Left or Right, you become aware of the power relations in your 'hood, how they are ordered, arranged, categorized. You might also realize early on that to categorize experience or reality is to exercise power over it.

Indeed, as a critical thinker, you are ready to play games of truth. As you go through the political forests of everyday life you detect the workings of power, the rules for the manipulation of discourse and bio-power. You can recognize, assess, compare, analyze, and synthesize power relations. In short, you want to become politically involved. In appendix 7, you will find models for service learning and community involvement in research and policy making that may be helpful in this regard.

EXERCISE #4

Think about the ideas of politics, language, knowledge/power, and education as they affect your everyday life. What does your political world look like and what role do you play in it? Referring to the images in this section draw or paint a poster-sized map that illustrates your political realities, the many forces that affect you, and the ways you can affect them in return.

NOTES AND SUGGESTED READINGS

1. *The American Heritage Dictionary of the English Language,* 3d ed., electronic version (Houghton Mifflin Company, 1992).

2. See for example Carol Hardy-Fanta, "Political Consciousness: Being Political, Becoming Political," in her *Latina Politics/Latino Politics: Gender, Culture and Political Participation in Boston* (Philadelphia: Temple University Press, 1993).

3. Francisco H. Vázquez, "Chicanology: A Postmodern Analysis of Meshicano Discourse," *Perspectives in Mexican American Studies* 3 (1992): 132.

4. Michael Kahn, "The Seminar" (unpublished).

5. Quoted in Edward Said, *Orientalism* (New York: Pantheon, 1978), 25. As Said notes, the English translation inexplicably leaves out the second part of the sentence. Quintin Hoare and Geoffrey Nowell Smith, *The Prison Notebooks: Selections* (New York: International, 1971), 324.

6. Among the Greeks, the story goes that the Oracle of Delphi, who was like the voice of

the gods, said that Socrates was the smartest man in Athens. Socrates didn't believe it, so he went around trying to prove that there were others who knew more than he did. After a while Socrates realized that while there were others who knew more than he did, he knew the limits of his own knowledge and this made him smarter than anyone else! Over the entrance to the Oracle of Delphi's abode were the words "Know thyself."

PART I

HISTORICAL ORIGINS/THEORETICAL AND FEMINIST(S) CONTEXTS (ca. 1750 to 1900)

THE QUESTION OF THE ORIGIN OF LATINO/A political thought is a tricky one. Is Latino/a thought the extension of a history of Latin American political philosophy? Or is it the product of political actions required by the circumstances of becoming part of a new country? When Latino/as have to take political action, do they consider their pre-Colombian, colonial, or other legacies or do they react pragmatically, according to a given situation? If we take the case of the Chicano movement of the 1960s, we see that it makes heavy use of pre-Columbian, particularly Aztec, symbolism. And yet it has been argued that Chicano political thought was shaped by circumstances and not by tradition. Limón's article in part II points out that some Chicanos in the 1960s showed no awareness that previous political movements shared their outlook: a radical, feminist, militant, quasiseparatist ideology. Furthermore, Vázquez's article in part I, "América's Patriots Then and Now," claims that the dominant Latino/a political discourse is based on the liberal concepts of freedom that inspired North and South American anti-imperialist movements in the eighteenth and nineteenth centuries.

In terms of origins, then, we are dealing with a continuum that includes at least the following elements. There are memories of past injustices that, like the Greek **Furies,** erupt with such force that they seemingly write their politics with blood. This is the case with ethnic movements, uprisings, and riots. Other memories are designed to avoid injustices and are articulated as commandments and laws and engraved in stone (as in Aztec pyramids, Mayan stelae, or Moses's tables) so that everyone can remember them. Another way to keep memories is to embed them in discourses and **institutions** in which they function as contexts, as precedents that structure our present actions. These memories involve social issues that can be traced to the beginning of humankind and that repeatedly challenge us at the personal and institutional/legal levels. These are the issues of economic and criminal justice, of equality, of respect for the dignity and diverse desires of human beings, issues that are ultimately carved in the bodies of human beings, in this case Latino/as. The question of the origins of Latino political thought, therefore, is not an either/or question. It is an interplay between the "re-membering" of historical struggles and urgent, necessary, immediate action that gives birth to Latino/a political thought. In this vein, part I provides (1) a set of tools to approach Latino/a political thought, (2) the historical-literary contexts for this thought, and (3) the memories and juridical (legal) events that frame the birth of Latinos as Territorial, Involuntary, Cultural U.S. citizens.

In the first section of part I, *"Serpientes y Escaleras,"* we present three theoretical approaches to understanding Latino/a political thought. All three see Latino/a political thought as a struggle that features different opponents: is it a dialectic of class struggle, a struggle of feminine versus patriarchal politics, or an ongoing struggle to carve a meaningful life out of the material force of language, a struggle that may appear as based on class, gender, or race, or on any other combination of such factors?

In the second section, "Carved Out of Language," we entertain the question: how far back do we go in our search for origins—to the Aztecs, Taínos and Arawaks, or Siboneys (the indigenous people of Mexico, Puerto Rico, and Cuba)? Indeed, we include a text that poetically and analytically connects the gaps and continuities between the past and the present. This literary and historical discourse re-members the hybridity of peoples and cultures that began with the conquest, proceeded during three hundred years of colonization, and continues in the increasingly borderless world of global capitalism. The memories also reach to the seventeenth century, when Anglos and Latinos shared a common identity as patriots, based on the democratic concept of "we the people," and fought against the monarchies of Britain and Spain, respectively. Contrary to this common discourse, there is also the textual and political construction of anti-Mexican (and by implication anti-Latino/a) sentiment that started in the sixteenth century and continues to portray Latino/as as the undesirable Others.[1]

In the third section, "Seduction and Aggression," we look at the complex process of cultural seduction and military aggression in U.S.-Latin American relations; the long and difficult gestation of Mexicans, Cubans, and Puerto Ricans; and their births as territorial, involuntary, or cultural U.S. citizens. Indeed, the most obvious, clear, and immediate origins of Latino/a political thought are the treaties, acts, and amendments. These are in a real, legal sense the "birth certificates" of Mexicans, Puerto Ricans, and Cubans, who thereby came directly under the authority of the U.S. government and indirectly under the influence of the U.S. American dominant culture.

NOTE

1. Raymund Paredes, "The Origins of Anti-Mexican Sentiment in the United States," in *New Directions in Chicano Scholarship,* ed. R. Romo and R. Paredes, Chicano Studies Monograph Series (San Diego: University of California, San Diego, 1978), 139–165. Paredes' article analyzes U.S. American texts going back to the original thirteen colonies. It is an excellent example of discursive analysis, that is, analysis of the regular appearance of certain statements within a particular discourse over a period of time; this is sometimes called "intertextuality" because the same statements are repeated in many different texts and historical epochs. Eventually, the intertextuality Paredes studies was infused with scientific theories, and it is now endemic in U.S. culture; one might say it is engraved in the hearts and minds of many people in the United States and supports the hidden or overt assumptions about the inferiority of the Mexican/Latino people. We can almost feel the material weight and power of discourse in this particular game of truth that unfolds throughout centuries. Anti-Catholic and anti-Spanish statements merge with anti-Mexican Indian statements to construct a discourse that denies Mexicans and all Latinos their value as moral entities and have "rendered unlikely the possibility that nineteenth-century Americans would regard the people of Mexico [and of Cuba and Puerto Rico] with compassion and understanding."

Serpientes y Escaleras: Frameworks and Scaffolds for Understanding Latino/a Political Thought

When the student is ready the teacher will appear.

—Zen saying

Some teachers believe frameworks and scaffolds help students approach, enter, climb, or dig into a subject in a critical manner. We agree and therefore provide three articles in this section to assist you in understanding Latino/a political thought. These are echoed by the last three pieces in part IV. One of the three articles in this section says understanding Latino/a political thought is a matter of rational and conscious political action, another that it is a matter of the inclusiveness of feminist personal politics, and a third that it is the political implications of the material nature of language. These three articles represent three dominant explanations commonly used in Latino/a politics known as historical materialism, feminist analysis, and analysis of discourse. The objective is for you to grasp key concepts that appear throughout the texts in this reader, such as **citizenship,** culture, and power/knowledge/desire relations.

These dominant explanations are at the beginning and at the end of the book because we believe that critical thinking is like the board game *Serpientes y Escaleras* (known in English as Chutes and Ladders). This is a game in which you try to move to the top of the board according to the numbers on the dice, but in the process of doing so you either climb up ladders or slide down the backs of serpents. Similarly, as you engage in political thinking, you may proceed deductively and slide down to a conclusion from a general theory or a key historical point. Or you can think inductively and climb up to reach your own conclusions from pieces of evidence you find along the way. But in playing the game of critical thinking it is more likely that you will find yourself climbing and sliding as you come to *your own understanding* of Latino/a political thought. The goal is that you become aware of your political self and the way that this particular self has been constructed through history, literature, and law. Ultimately, the hope is that you will become an agent of change for a just society.

* 1 *

THE CHICANA WOMAN: AN HISTORICAL MATERIALIST PERSPECTIVE

Maria Linda Apodaca

This seminal piece was written in the late 1970s, a time when most analyses of the condition of Latinos were made from "cultural" or "sentimental" perspectives. This early piece by Maria Linda is useful on many counts.

It provides a class analysis that has been widely used to explain the status of Latinas in the United States, an extensive historical background from the Aztecs to the present, and explanations of transformations from a feudal to a capitalist system. It also provides a vocabulary of terms and concepts that may seem unfamiliar at first but that will appear in many of the pieces of this reader (see appendix 6 for a brief explanation of historical materialism). As to be expected in the games of truth we are playing, here, Marxist analysis itself is subjected to critique by more recent analyses. For example, Francisco H. Vázquez, Ramón Grosfoguel, Victor Valle, Rodolfo D. Torres, and Emma Pérez, in their articles in this reader, implicitly or explicitly consider marxism a necessary but not sufficient analysis for the understanding of Latino/a political realities. Even though Apodaca's article refers to Chicanas, her discussion of the development of productive forces and corresponding relations of production will be echoed by other readings that include discussion of other Latinas (and indeed all workers everywhere). If we had to put her message on a bumper sticker it would read: "It's rational and conscious political action."

✳   ✳   ✳

CHICANA HISTORIOGRAPHY: THEORETICAL QUESTIONS

The turbulence of the sixties and early seventies once again brought into question the inequalities that exist in the United States. Workers, students, women and other groups began questioning these conditions and attempted to understand the causes of inequality. National minorities began to demand equal rights, better education, jobs, and wages. Among these was the Chicano or Mexican American.[1]

In the universities and colleges Chicano historians and social scientists wrote papers and books to show that Chicanos were not inferior but a people with culture and history. These Chicano scholars often became integral elements in the Chicano people's demand for better education, jobs, and wages.

The history of the Chicano experience, as told by Chicano historians and Chicano social scientists, many times was clouded with sentiment and emotion resulting only in affirmations of the contributions made to so-called Anglo culture (e.g. Campa, 1973; Acuña, 1972). Many of these historiographies lacked historical analysis; some became limited to analyses of racial or cultural conflict. While the contributions made by the Spanish and Mexicans to the development of the Southwest cannot be slighted, since in many ways they paved the way for the entrance of U.S. pioneers into the Southwest, nevertheless, several facts must be clarified about the history of the Southwest.

It must first be understood that the society of Spanish colonialism in Mexico (including the territory which is now the U.S. Southwest) was not the idyllic portrait of benevolence and cooperation. In Mexico and in the Southwest countless Native Americans were enslaved to work the Spanish mines, herd cattle and sheep, and work the agricultural fields. As a result many were consumed by overwork and disease.[2] Secondly, it must be made clear that the early productive developments made by the Spanish and later the Mexicans were feudal in nature (Chevalier, 1972:49). Finally, if we objectively study the productive forces in the Southwest, we will find that it was not until the United States took over the Southwest that large investments of capital released these areas of production from their feudal bonds and allowed for their fuller development (Taylor, 1971:68; McWilliams, 1971). The majority of Chicano historiographers do not deal with these historical facts.

The development of history must be based on something more tangible than ideas, dates, and individuals. The production and reproduction of immediate life is, in the last analysis, the basis for historical development. *Production has a twofold character: on the one hand, the production of the means of existence, of food, clothing and shelter, and the tools necessary for that production; on the other hand, the propagation of human beings themselves, the reproduction of the species.* The social organization of a particular epoch and area are determined by both kinds of development: "by the stage of development of labor and of the family" (Engels, 1973:71). Analysis reveals that the historical development of Mexico after 1520 until approximately 1850 was based on feudal production and had a corresponding social organization. In the United States the case was different. Its historical development after 1800 until the present has been that of growing capitalist production and a corresponding bourgeois culture. Again Chicano historiographers rarely base their analysis on the productive and reproductive process in the Southwest.

Chicano historiographers have also tended to ignore the role and situation of Mexican and Chicana women in immigration, social production (i.e. agriculture, textile industry, etc.), and working-class struggle.[3] There are some studies (e.g., Green, 1971; Allen, 1931), but rarely are these incorporated into the general histories of the Chicano. In place of histories that show Chicanas as workers, we have been offered pictures of passivity, naiveness, weakness, in a word "femininity," the typical Mexican conception of what a woman's role should be. Yet the history of Mexico and the United States show us that the only women who could enjoy femininity, gentleness, and little or no work, were the women of the property-owning class. For the women of the laboring classes, including the majority of Chicanas and Mexicanas, their class situation has meant working in the fields, in factories, as well as at cooking, washing, and sewing. For working-class women and for Chicanas, work was not a choice but a necessity.

Any attempt to enter into an analysis of the historical and political situation of the Chicana has usually been frowned upon in the Chicano movement and by some Chicano historians. The reasons often given are that this type of discussion violates Chicano culture and divides the movement. The underlying reasons are much more fundamental. For a long time the Chicano movement was concerned only with the discrimination that had cut us off from our "historical," and more importantly, from our "cultural" past. The tendency developed to glorify all the cultural traits of the past. To bring up the question of Chicana oppression was to question the family, more specifically to question male dominance, in a word, to question machismo. In trying to understand the cause for the subjugation of women, and in particular the Chicana, the question many times led to an analysis of classes. Questions arose as to the difference between the women of the patron class and the peon class in Mexico, and to the difference between the women of the capitalist class and the wage-earning class. But these questions encountered resistance. Socially and historically two obstacles exist to hinder the development of an analysis of women's oppressed condition and although taken by some as *two* distinct phenomena, in practice they are mutually interdependent. The two basic factors discouraging analysis of the Chicana are (1) a class society based on private property with the need for inheritance and (2) male chauvinism. Interestingly enough, these two aspects not only discourage analysis, but in the real world are the material and ideological basis for the subjugation of women and other working-class people.

The development of private property in the means of production necessitated the development of certain forms of social relations. The socio-economic subjugation of women was one of those relations. Along with other rationales (i.e. magic, theology, human nature) used to explain the supremacy of one class over another, male superiority and its counterpart, female passivity, became an explanation and justification for the inferior position of women in society. Explanations of male superiority became embodied in the ideology of male chauvinism. Chicanos, including the historians, being products of two class cultures, feudal and bourgeois, have manifested the ideologies of these class societies. What we need to understand is that chauvinism, from either a Chicano worker or intellectual, or from a bourgeois intellectual, justifies private property, class oppression, and the subjugation of women.

Contrary to most Chicano historians, I believe that we must have histories that can be the basis for future social action, rather than mere academic interpretations. In this sense the need for a class analysis of the Chicana exists. Focusing on the development of the productive forces and the corresponding relations of production, it becomes possible to understand the purpose of forced sterilization, unequal pay, lack of education, etc. *Finally, it is only by understanding the relation between the development of private productive property in the Southwest, the subsequent requirement for labor power, and the nature of the subjugation of women under feudalism and capitalism, that the role of the Chicana in historical development becomes clear.* Furthermore, class analysis makes it possible to understand how politically and culturally the working class was forced to accept, at least temporarily, its conditions of exploitation. For women of various historical working classes as well as for the Chicana, class analysis allows one to understand:

1. the expropriation of their labor power and that of their families;
2. man's supremacy in the home and in society;
3. society's denial of their importance in social production.

Why has the role of the Chicana in society been hidden? Why has she been described as passive and fragile? How are these two questions related to social production and to domestic production? The answers can only be found in understanding how social production has changed in class society, specifically under monopoly capitalism. We can begin to answer these questions by simply saying that with the early development of private property and classes in ancient society, mother-right was replaced by father-right, and monogamy was imposed on women. Thereafter, it became necessary to veil the role of women in ideals of sacrifice and motherhood.

But the answers to the questions are much more fundamental, much more tied to the overall historical development of society. This development is the movement of production and classes. Because as production changes, so does the group or class which controls the society. The overthrow of mother-right was a partial answer. The development of private property and classes, the corresponding need to trace one's property (i.e., inheritance), and the final separation of domestic production from social production is the full answer.

History teaches us that the class or social group which plays the principal role in social production and performs the main functions in production must, in the course of time, inevitably take control of that production. There was a time, under the matriarchate, when women were regarded as the controllers of production. Why was this? Because under the kind of production then prevailing, primitive agriculture, women played the principal role in production, they performed the main functions, while the men roamed the forests in quest of game. Then came the time, under the patriarchate, when the predominant position in production passed to men. Why did this change take place? Because under the kind of production prevailing at that time, stockbreeding, in which the principal instruments of production were the spear, the lasso, and the bow and arrow, the principal role was played by men. (Marx et al., 1969, emphasis mine)

This is not to say that women were the first class to be subjugated, as some would like us to believe. No, the subjugation of women is integrally related to the subjugation of propertyless *women and men*. The particular subjugation of women must be understood in terms of class contradictions. By classes is meant the relation men and women have to the means of production: on the one hand are the property owners who reap the benefits of production, on the other are the laboring classes who are more or less propertyless and live on the meagre offerings of the propertied class.

The aspect of inheritance is something only propertied classes enjoyed. But in order to give inheritance validity, it had to become a universal cultural aspect; thus the institution of monogamy in all levels of society came into being. The aspect of women's historical position of inferiority results from the inability of any class society to give real economic and political equality. This inability necessitates the creation of explanations for positions of inferiority. For women this explanation became tied to her biological function and to the caring of newborn children.

The subjugation of women cannot be separated from the overall development of society. In studying this development we must focus on the movement of the productive forces in each mode of production and understand how this affected social relations.[4] In analyzing, we must not confuse social production with socialized production. Social production is the production for society's needs, including food, clothing, technology, and reproduction and maintenance of new members (i.e., labor power) (Marx and Engels, 1972:48). The definition of what a society is, thus what social production is, has changed with each new mode of production. For example, a society of hunters and gatherers rarely constituted more than a clan, a group of people of about ten to twenty related by blood. In this case there is no distinction between social and domestic production; social production is production for the clan only. With further developments in production (i.e., domestication of plants and animals), in division of labor (i.e., pastoral and agricultural, handicraft and agricultural, etc.), and especially the development of private property, there begins to be a differentiation between social production and domestic production. Domestic production became the area where labor power was reproduced and maintained.[5] Production of food, shelter, and technology was being taken more and more away from the domestic area. In a slave society, as in ancient Greece, Rome, and Aztec society, this division may not have been as developed. Under a feudal society, as in Spain and colonial Mexico, this division was to become more apparent. Capitalism, the mode of production that greatly accelerated production, made the division between social and domestic production complete. In a capitalist society production of food, clothing, tools, etc., was removed from the domestic area. Women were given the responsibility of the domestic area, although often participating in social production. Many times they were not allowed to express any authority; they were the property of the man in the house—be it father or husband.

In societies characterized by private property and classes, the condition of women is not the same. On the one hand, the women of the property-owning classes are generally excluded from having any real economic and political power. Many of these women only organize the household affairs, and even this is often taken care of by servants. On the other hand, while the women of the propertyless class are denied political and social power, economically they are important. Their economic importance is one of the aspects of Chicana history that will be presented in a later segment of this paper. For now let me clarify the preceding discussion with the following:

> The "savage" warrior and hunter had been content to take second place in the house, after the woman; the "gentler" shepherd, in the arrogance of his wealth, pushed himself forward into the first place and the woman down into the second. . . . The division of labor within the family had regulated the division of property between the man and the woman. *That division of labor had remained the same; and yet it now turned the previous domestic relation upside down simply because the division of labor outside the family had changed.* . . . The domestic labor of the woman no longer counted beside the acquisition of the necessities of life by the man; the latter was everything, the former an unimportant extra. (Engels, 1973:221, emphasis mine)

In each succeeding mode of production we found two requirements: (1) production for social needs (i.e., food, shelter, clothing, technology), and (2) reproduction and maintenance of labor power. In each new mode of production the relation between these two areas of production changed according to the level of development of the means of production and according to the manner by which property was distributed. As society developed, as more was being produced, as distinctions between property owner and worker developed, the division between social production and domestic work widened. In more developed modes of production (i.e., feudalism and capitalism), the separation of social production from domestic production continued until under capitalism this separation was made complete.

HISTORICAL ROOTS: ANCIENT AZTEC SOCIETY AND
SPANISH FEUDALISM

In 1520 the Spanish invaders to Mexico found a society that was highly developed. There were sophisticated systems of irrigation, extensive trade routes, developed sciences of astronomy and medicine, highly developed arts, complex systems of religious hierarchy, and a centralized government. This society called Tenotchtitlan granted to political and religious leaders the right to own various tracts of land and to exact tribute from the surrounding population. Private property existed amidst some communal control of land.

The development of what we now call Aztec civilization is predicated upon a long history of development (Soustelle, 1975). Anthropologists and archeologists have shown that the central valley area prior to Aztec domination underwent tremendous cultural changes. The earliest peoples are characterized as hunters and gatherers. They exhibited many of the cultural items that would place them in that stage of development Morgan and Engels termed "savagery" (Engels, 1973), and Marx termed primitive communalism (Marx, 1970:19). The situation of the women in these early societies was conditioned by the fact that the campsite (the domestic area) was the main area of production. Because there was no distinction between social and domestic production and because of the low level of technological development, the work of the women was equally important to that of men. In fact we can venture to say that because of the social need to care for the children, the subsequent division of labor made women the gatherers of seeds, plants, and small rodents, whereas men became the hunters, sometimes absent for long periods of time. The food provided by the women was much more important because it was more stable.

This overview of primitive communalism in Meso-America is brief. There remains a tremendous amount of work to be done by historians and anthropologists in this area. Research should be undertaken to examine the role of women in the transformation from primitive communalism to the Aztec stage of civilization. One further comment needs to be made before discussing feudalism and capitalism. Aztec society, contrary to the illusions some may have, was a class society. The whole religious and political organization exempted those at the top from work and gave them the right to extract tribute and mandatory work from those over whom they were given responsibility. Aztec society was based on the labor of masses of peasants who were required to produce corn, beans, and squash; to weave fine cloth; to mine precious stones for Aztec jewelry; and to build monuments for the Aztec ruling class. The condition of women at this time was greatly altered from the primitive communal stage. Further analysis of this time period I leave, hopefully, to other Chicana historians and anthropologists.

The Spanish conquest greatly altered the society that existed prior to 1520, but the essence of social relations remained based on private property. This is why some historians could state that for the peasant in the outlying Indian villages nothing had changed; the peasant still had to give involuntarily of his produce and labor, only now to the new Spanish landlord.

The society that Spain imposed on Meso-America was a particular organization of private property, namely feudalism. Feudalism as a mode of production has as its basis the relationship between a landlord and a peasant. The landlord owns the land and the peasant works the land. In return for use of the land, the peasant gives up a certain portion of his product. This rent many times took the form of personal service, such as working the land of the landlord, serving in the home of the landlord, and going to war for the landlord. Except for nominal protection, the peasant, therefore, received nothing from the landlord. In fact, in a feudal society the producer gives up a portion of his product to the landlord in return for the privilege of using the owner's land. The remainder of the product produced by the peasant is directly consumed by himself and his family.

The political organization of a feudal society is characterized by decentralization. With different landlords fighting to gain control of land and peasants, territory is broken up into warring fiefdoms. Each landlord conducts expeditions and wars at his own expense, taxing the peasantry with ever greater demands for rent and tribute.[6]

In Mexico, the Spanish imposed this social system on the Indian population by granting *encomienda*s and *repartimiento*s to the conquistadores.[7] Along with the various types of land grants conferred upon the conquistadores, the *repartimiento*s and *encomienda*s guaranteed the conquerers a source of labor. The Spanish, not satisfied with taking the land and enslaving the Indian, allocated to themselves the right to extract tribute from the various Indians living upon the land.

The Spanish, needing to reinforce their economic and political dominance, systematically destroyed the Native Americans' social, economic, political and cultural systems. They imposed a religion that pacified the Indians into accepting their condition of servitude. They reorganized the political system, giving all powers to the Spanish Crown, its viceroys, and its vassals (i.e., Cortez, Onate, and others). The former Indian rulers were converted into mere puppets. The economy of Meso-America, once a flourishing economy of trade and handicraft production based on a developed system of agriculture, came to a virtual standstill by the middle of the seventeenth century (Chevalier, 1972).

Spain, itself a nation dying under the feudal yoke, gave to Mexico its feudal structure and decaying feudal economy. Needing to maintain its armies and protect its hegemony in the world, the Spanish Crown invoked higher and higher taxes on its colonies. Silver production in New Spain was a source of wealth that the Crown and its conquistadores relished much more than the Mexican land. The mercury used for mining silver could only be bought from Spain, but higher taxes on mercury imposed by the Crown, made silver-mining very expensive. The Spanish in New Spain sent less and less silver to Spain, and those that did send silver and other commodities faced the possibility of British and Dutch raids. Spanish and Mexican trade became increasingly difficult (Cumberland, 1969:91).

The curtailing of silver production was only one of the changes that affected the Meso-American economy. In the early years of Spanish colonization, Catholic missionaries attempted to establish new industries, such as winemaking, silk and other textile production, which would encourage the development of the Mexican economy. The Spanish Crown, wanting to maintain a monopoly over trade and fearing the development of Mexican industries, passed laws against the development of any new small-commodity production (Cumberland, 1969:98).

Other factors which reinforced feudalism and slowed the development of the Mexican economy were the successful introduction of cattle breeding and the enormous decrease in the native population. The tremendous growth of cattle resulted in the destruction of many agricultural lands (Fernández, forthcoming:19). Farms, villages, and sometimes whole valleys were abandoned to cattle haciendas. The decline in the Indian population also added to the abandonment of agriculture and villages. As a result of forced labor, miserable working conditions, and the diseases brought by the Spanish, the native population decreased from approximately twenty million in 1520 to slightly more than a million in 1650 (Cumberland, 1969:49). With the Spanish Crown wanting more precious metals and the creoles and peninsulares in New Spain unwilling to work, further subjugation and exploitation of the remaining Indian population resulted (Chevalier, 1972:54).

Feudal relations of production were reinforced by the tendency of the Spanish Crown to encourage colonization under the domination of rich men. These conditions and the failing economy encouraged the development of a strong hacendado, or landlord, to control the area. Chevalier explains the process in this manner:

> Finally, each region and even each locality tended to become isolated and self-sufficient and to huddle under the authority of the large landowners or local leaders, who frequently took over the expenses required for maintaining a police force or waging war on the nomads. (Chevalier, 1972:49)

What was created, then, were feudal fiefdoms with the landlord having total authority over the people and the land under his control.

For the Mexican Indian woman, Spanish colonialism had particular effects. To analyze the condition of women in any mode of production, an understanding of the relationship between social production and domestic production is required. This relationship in a feudal society undergoes various changes as compared to the primitive communal society where social production is basically within the sphere of the domestic area. There was already in the Aztec empire a division between social production and domestic production which was predicated upon the development of large-scale agriculture and the existence of a privileged class that lived at the expense of the masses of peasants and artisans. This division was manifested in various ways. First, production had developed beyond the immediate needs of the clan. The product of the *calpulli*[8] was involuntarily given up either to tribute or taxes or to the empire's "privileged" priests and warriors. In addition, the product of the *calpulli* was traded for the wares of the *pochtecas.*[9] Corn, beans, and local handicrafts were exchanged for agricultural and handicraft items from different areas. Social production had expanded to maintain the "idle" ruling class and for purposes of trade and barter.

Social production had changed, but domestic work remained the same. This development must be understood in reference to the development of classes, for the condition of women in the property-owning class is entirely different from the condition of women in the working class. The women of the Aztec ruling class were virtually ostracized from producing their immediate subsistence. Their role in domestic work, the maintenance and reproduction of the species, was also minimal. Except for reproduction, the majority of the work in a ruling-class home was done by servants or slaves. Men and women slaves would be brought in to maintain the home (Soustelle, 1975:74).

The condition of the women in the peasant class during the Aztec empire was quite different. Because of their class position peasant women were denied any legal and political status. Economically, however, these women were very important. Based on the requirements for social production, the labor power of the woman of the *calpulli* was an important item. The product from her labor in weaving, spinning, basketry, and pottery-making would very likely be included in the items for tribute, taxes, and trade. In order to insure a good crop, women's and children's labor power was also needed in agricultural production. Although women shared in the productive process, they were still given the added responsibility of cooking, washing, and sewing for the whole family. The family organization was still that of the extended family, consisting of parents, aunts and uncles, grandparents, and cousins. Many times the lineage was based on patrilineal descent—father-right. The domestic work of the family, then, was not the sole responsibility of one woman.

The Spanish conquerers built upon this already stratified society. Except for the "legal" abolishment of slavery and a more developed division of labor, the relationship of social and domestic production in colonial Mexico remained the same. In feudal New Spain and later Mexico, women were denied any real political and social voice. Catholicism reinforced the feudal patriarchal society with its hierarchy of authority—God, Christ, Pope, King, landlord, father or husband—and its doctrine of obedience and salvation. The peasant man and woman was totally subjected to the authority of the priest and hacendado. For example, it was common for peasants to ask permission in order to marry, and then have to submit to the hacendado's first night rights. If peasants withheld crops, cheated, or in any way misbehaved, their only judge and jury was the hacendado. The woman, in Catholic doctrine, was to be a good mother, self-sacrificing, and especially obedient. The woman of the peasant class was completely subjected to the authority of men—the hacendado, the priest, the husband, and at times to the eldest son.

Again the relationship of social production to domestic production in colonial Mexico was essentially the same as in the Aztec empire. The essential difference was that the Aztec empire was a centralized, urban state, whereas, colonial Mexico was decentralized with much of the authority coming from the rural areas, from the haciendas.

The encomienda and repartimiento system of conscripting labor from the Indian population of New Spain usually required the labor of men (Cumberland, 1969:65). The resultant decrease in village populations combined with a decline due to disease, placed more of the agricultural and handicraft production in the hands of the women. Peasant women in agriculture and handicrafts were not something new; they had always been involved in social production. Because the means of production (i.e., plow, milpas, simple tools) belonged to the man and were located in the peasant's home (*solar*), the woman was able to participate in both social and domestic production (NACLA, 1975). Women from wealthier peasant families many times inherited property from their fathers, but once married this property came under the jurisdiction of the husband. Women of the peasant class were important in many areas of handicraft production. They wove cloth, spun yarn, made soap and candles; some were midwives and *curanderas,* they worked in carpentry and in shoemaking. As stated earlier, the labor of women was very important in agricultural production; they helped in planting, harvesting, and processing the crops; and they went to the various local markets to sell agricultural products and handicrafts. The gains from these activities were used to provide the rent for land and other taxes that were imposed. The remainder was used to maintain the peasant family. Women in a feudal society, therefore, were important in maintaining the society and the family. But because of the need to reinforce class distinctions and the subjugation of women, the work of peasant women was not recognized by the society, and later historians and social scientists sustained this omission.

This situation remained the same throughout New Spain until 1821; after this date changes began occurring in Mexico and the northern provinces of California and Texas. In 1821 Mexico gained its independence from Spain. In Texas growing trade with the United States developed, and American citizens received permission to colonize the state, finally culminating with Texas' independence in 1836. In California the church lands were taken over by private individuals, allowing for some improvement in productive output. However, for the Church Indians of California until 1848, and for the peasant man and woman in Chiapas and Morelia, the situation remained the same. It would not be until the regime of Porfirio Diaz and the introduction of foreign investment that there would begin to occur radical change in the mode of production of Mexico.

CONTEMPORARY ROOTS:
CAPITALISM AND IMPERIALISM

After 1848 the situation north of the Rio Grande developed in a completely different manner than in Mexico. Southwest United States was characterized by the development of extensive transportation lines, a development in cattle and shepherding, mining, fishing and world trade in California harbors. and the development of an industry that in the last half of the twentieth century would rival nations for power, namely agribusiness. The development of the major parts of the Southwest can be characterized as capitalist development, more contemporarily as monopoly capitalism.

Capitalism is a distinct mode of production. It changed the whole social development and the condition under which labor power was to be utilized and maintained. However, it is not the purpose of this paper to develop an exposé of the capitalist system and its development in the Southwest. For those who wish to know more about capital, I suggest they read Marx's *Capital.*

However, there are several characteristics of capitalism which are related to the question under discussion. The first is the general tendency of capitalism to concentrate private productive property in the hands of fewer and fewer people, leaving millions of expropriated petty producers in its wake. As the merchant, manufacturer, and the capitalist farmer accumulated wealth, peasants and artisans were left propertyless. On the one hand was created the new class that would dominate society, the bourgeoisie; on the other was created, from the expropriated peasants and artisans, the modern working class, the proletariat. The act of expropriating small property owners continues to this day with the collapse of small businesses and small farmers. Even more imporant, however, is the expropriation of the commodities produced by the proletariat, the appropriation of surplus value by the capitalist.

Dispossessed peasants and artisans, men, women, and children were forced to give up their labor power in exchange for a wage. Labor power became a commodity that could be purchased when needed, and the barest minimum paid for a subsistence existence. The wage given to the worker is never equal to the actual amount of value produced, and it is thus that surplus value is extracted. Thus another important characteristic of capital is developed, namely profit. Contrary to a feudal society where production is for use, production in a capitalist society is for profit. Profit is produced to reinvest in property to create more profit. These essential characteristics, production for profit, expropriation of small producers, and the expropriation of surplus value by the capitalist have manifested themselves in the various periods of capitalist development (i.e., pre-industrial capitalism, industrial capitalism, and finally monopoly capitalism). The main form of capitalism that has affected the lives of Mexicans and Chicanos has been monopoly capitalism (i.e., imperialism).

Imperialism is more than a preferred foreign policy, it is primarily characterized by the concentration of production and capital to such a high degree that monopolies are created which play a decisive role in economic life. *This is its fundamental attribute.* Other attributes are: (a) merging of industrial and bank capital to form a financial oligarchy; (b) the export of capital in the form of loans, and investment to get "cheaper wages and raw materials"; (c) division of the world among capitalist associations; (d) creation of colonies or sphere of influence; (3) state intervention in production (i.e., state capitalism); (f) migratory movements (i.e., immigration) (Lenin, 1965). There are other general characteristics, but these are the main ones that have affected the lives of Chicano men and women.

Capitalism separates the producer from the means of production and leaves the worker propertyless. Capitalism takes production entirely away from the peasant's farm, the artisan's cottage, and puts production into the factories. Whereas production under feudalism was individual, meaning each producer completed a particular commodity (i.e., shoes, wheat, etc.), under capitalism the production of commodities becomes socialized in that many persons are organized in one area producing one commodity. The worker under capitalism gives up to the capitalist all the commodities (value) produced. In return the laborer is paid a wage seemingly amounting to all the time spent at the workplace but in effect covering only part of the total value produced by the expansion of her/his labor power during that time. This separation of the producer from the means of production is the basis for the complete separation of social and domestic production.[10]

It is under capitalist production that the division between social production and domestic production is finally and completely made. Throughout class society women have been given the responsibility in the domestic area for the maintenance and reproduction of labor, but under capitalism this responsibility is separated from its relation to production. Under capitalism women are ideologically conditioned into believing that domestic work is the only area of work for which they are fitted, yet because of the requirements of the different modes of production, women have been and continue to be integral parts of production. Throughout the history of capitalism, women and children have been included as potential and actual sources of surplus value (Marx, 1973; Chicano Communication Center, 1976; Women's History Group, 1972; González, 1976). Under capitalist production, the maintenance and reproduction of labor is crucial; without it profit cannot be created, yet it remains individual and outside the sphere of social production. "The maintenance and reproduction of the working class is, and must *ever be,* a necessary condition to the reproduction of capital" (Marx, 1973:57).

If the reproduction and maintenance of the laboring class is such a necessary condition for capitalism, why then is this area of work not considered important? And furthermore, why has the role of women in social production been denied?

The answer to the first question is that private domestic consumption by the worker and his or her family is unproductive in that it does not create wages for the laborer, the family, nor wealth for the capitalist.[11] This is true for two reasons: first, because capitalists control society and because their mode of production thrives on profit, it follows that the only work which is important for the capitalist system is that which creates profit. The capitalists' only concern is that the worker appear for the time he or she is needed. The second reason has two aspects. Because the working class is deprived of the means of production, each person is responsible for his/ her survival. This objective condition is reinforced by the ideology of individualism which stresses "doing your own thing," and "you can make it if you try." Therefore how workers use the wage given them is not the concern of the capitalist as long as wages do not eat a large share of profit.

> All the capitalist cares for is to reduce the laborer's individual consumption as far as possible to what is strictly necessary . . . What the laborer consumes beyond his or her maintenance is unproductive consumption. (Marx, 1973:573)[12]

On the one hand because domestic production does not create wealth for the producers it is unimportant. On the other hand, while it is a prime requirement for the capitalist, its importance is covered up with the wage given to the laborer, and by the ideology of individualism.

The answer to the second question, the hiding of women's role in social production is part of the general tendency to deny to the working class its role in the building of society. Another aspect to this question is the need to explain why women are pulled out of work during periods of recession, after conclusion of wars (i.e., end of the Second World War, the Vietnam War, etc.), and why women tend to fill domestic related jobs, (i.e., waitress, nurse, elementary school teacher). Lastly, by perpetuating this ideology women will accept their responsibility in domestic work, and become members of that ready pool of cheap labor from which capitalism can draw in times of increased production.

THE BORDER BETWEEN FEUDALISM AND IMPERIALISM: A CONCRETE ILLUSTRATION

The preceding has been a theoretical explanation of how the various modes of production have affected the role of women in social development. However, the test of theory is in history. Many search and research history in the confines of libraries and museums, but historical data can become available to us by tracing the lives of those persons who have lived through history. The following is an essay written by José Lona. José Lona was a student in a course I taught at California State University Los Angeles called "Chicana Women in History and Society." As part of the required course work, students were asked to do an oral history of a woman in their lives. José's paper was chosen because the life of the woman clearly shows how women's role was conditioned by feudalism and imperialism.

The essay is included in this section of the paper because it concretely captures the condition of peasant women and also of women who were forced to immigrate with family and husband. Following it will be a brief analysis of the essay, and a brief historical analysis of imperialism in Mexico and the United States and how Chicanas are affected by this mode of production.

BIOGRAPHICAL SKETCH OF THE LIFE OF AN IMMIGRANT WOMAN

How many sunrises and sunsets has a person seen in seventy-eight years of life? How many times has one laughed? Cried? Hurt? How many miles has one traveled? How many meals has a woman prepared in a lifetime of being a housewife? How many tortillas can be made in seventy-eight years? How many? How many? How many?

No one knows I guess, because no one has ever really counted what to some are trivial things. But to a person that has lived such a life, these things/events are not trivial. Especially not when your worth is measured by how well you can "keep house," cook, and bear children.

Surely the female child born on July 1, 1898, on the hacienda of Peñuelas, state of

Aguascalientes, Mexico, never thought about her life from that perspective. All she knew was that she was God's gift to her parents and that as such, she was indebted to them and had to obey them and, of course, her elder brother also. She didn't have to obey her younger brothers or sister because of the simple fact that she herself from a very young age had had to fill the role of surrogate mother due to their mother's recurrent spells of illness. Little did it matter that her mother was a respected and known midwife, for her own illness often rendered her helpless. Picture thus, a child that since the age of seven or eight was already helping to cook, to sew, to spin, to help her mother in all the household chores and her father in the field. Indeed, one of the most cherished memories of this person is when, as a child, she and her father had to seek shelter from a brief shower by sitting under the belly of an ox until the storm blew over! This event is cherished because of the love felt for her father; of his warmth and closeness while seated under the ox. It didn't matter then, or now, that this family along with thousands of others, were being exploited. It didn't matter because the significance and impact were not understood!

It was simply accepted as part of one's life as a peon that your daily wages from the hacendado were to be twenty centavos and a dry liter of maize! The fact of the matter was that this particular family considered themselves lucky because the father was allowed to raise a little garden for the family's use. No, this family didn't consider themselves really bad off for they were existing . . . weren't they? The important thing was: that one preserve one's honor, and remain a cohesive family. And under the circumstances, this was best done by meeting head-on those challenges you could not avoid, and ignore those that you could—always humble, yet proud. To work was the best index of one's character if you were a man. If you were a woman, the abilities to run a home, to care for children, and to be docile and obedient were most cherished. Thus, for example, a girl learned not to cry in public; especially if such an action brought embarrassment to her father or to her husband! Thus when this child's father moved the family to another hacienda because of a promise that he could "share-crop," and then the ENTIRE crop was appropriated by the hacendado—leaving them hungry and even more destitute; even then she could not vent her hurt, her sorrow!

Perhaps tears and sorrow do erode one's will and resolve, and what begins as a trickle becomes a torrent that leads to collapse. I don't know. What I do know is that this particular child, woman, senior citizen, has shown strength when others were weak; resolve and determination in the worst of crises! Lest you misunderstand me, however, yes, she has, can, and does cry!

She didn't cry, however, when one fine day Zapata's revolutionaries suddenly appeared in the doorway of their hut asking for a bite to eat—*"una tortilla con frijoles."*

Nor did she cry when her father took her and the other young girls of the hacienda into the mountains to hide them and save them from possibly being raped and/or kidnapped. It is fitting to note, however, that to her recollection not a single girl or woman was raped or otherwise molested on her hacienda. The Revolution destroyed the hacienda and thus the peones lost their "jobs" and what little security they had. Employment was offered by the Mexican railroad to the peones and was taken—the beginning of an era of wandering from one estación or encampment to another; raising derailed trains and/or laying or repairing tracks in the process. This child, now a young woman, was still wandering between Aguascalientes and Zacatecas in 1914; however, she was now married. By the end of 1914, however, her husband and she, now swollen with child, had joined the rest of her family in Chihuahua, Chihuahua—still seeking roots, a better existence. In this case, however, existence coincided with bare survival! Chihuahua at this time was a city of refugees, of uprooted persons; all of them destitute, all of them hungry. Needless to say, the best memories are not the stuff of circumstances such as these. But nonetheless, memories there are . . . and plenty! Of father, husband, and older brother working all day at the railroad, coming home to a plate of beans, and leaving immediately again—each with an axe in hope of finding a pack-train with firewood that needed chopping. This dismal ritual was repeated day after incessant day, of waiting, pregnant, in long lines for *HOURS* in order to cash in a "ticket" for *TWO* French rolls and some flour . . . often reaching the door only to be told that the foodstuffs had run out, come back tomorrow!

What can one do to ease the crying, the ceaseless crying of children when they are hungry today . . . and hungrier tomorrow?

Under these circumstances, not a damn thing, except rock them and give them water; rock them when your own belly is swollen and bursting with a hungry life within! And when this life, a boy, enters this world demanding to be fed and you cannot feed it because your own body has been so decimated by hunger that you have no milk . . . what do you do? How do you explain to this mewling little creature that you, his mother, have had nothing to eat for three days since his birth, existing solely on tea made from orange-tree leaves! Yes, how much hurt can one person endure in a lifetime? How many tears can one shed? Especially when you realize that you entered the world crying and that sixteen years later, you are still in tears; in fact you are surrounded and engulfed by them!

Little wonder then that this woman-child eagerly followed her husband from Chihuahua to Texas and then to California. Again in hopes of a better life, again working for the railroad—this time however, in the United States. It must be rather disheartening, however, to suddenly find yourself with food and *nothing* to cook it in; with a home but with nothing to sleep on. Left in the middle of the desert in a country where you know neither the language nor the customs; where you know no one! Secundina adapted quickly however, and soon had food cooking . . . in clean empty coffee cans she had gathered along the tracks, along with firewood. Bedding was soon provided by another Mexican woman that was seemingly well-off, comparatively speaking. This woman soon made an offer that Secundina could not refuse—she offered her a job washing the railroad workers' clothes . . . by hand, naturally. This offer was accepted and Secundina worked daily at this chore until she developed an allergy to the strong, caustic detergent she had to use.

She declined the offer of her employer, however, to buy her son since in the opinion of her employer, she was too young and naive to care for him properly! And besides, they could use the money . . . couldn't they? Secundina and her husband soon moved to San Bernardino where another son was born and where they remained until 1918— another turning point in her life.

1918 brought with it both life and death. Life in that Secundina was again pregnant, and death in that the pandemic of flu claimed her husband.

Thus in the space of four years she became bride, mother, and widow! She returned to her family in Chihuahua where a third son was born; and vowed never to return to the United States. After the birth of her son she washed clothes in a boarding house for one Mexican peso a day—against the express wishes of her father who, however, was in no financial condition to help her nor stop her. Because of the terrible wages and the terrible hardships in Mexico, she was forced to return to the home of her compadres in

San Bernardino in 1919, paying two cents for the crossing of the border. The second phase of Secundina's life began in 1921, when she married for the second time to a man that was to remain her husband until his death in 1969.

With this man she was to have an additional eight children. All eleven children were destined to graduate from high school, one from college. I consider this a remarkable feat, given the fact that this woman never attended school formally but instead was taught to read and write by her mother while home as a child. Who taught her mother is open to question.

Her second husband, José, was born in Guanajuato, Mexico, and emigrated to the United States with his family at a young age. He attended school to the eighth grade, at which time he had to enter the labor market . . . working for the railroad full-time in order to support his now widowed mother and four younger brothers and sisters. When he married Secundina in 1921, he was thus forced to support nine persons, not counting himself. He eventually moved his family to Watts, California, where they lived in a tent on a plot of ground that he slowly purchased. He became a naturalized American citizen and was a steady and consistent voter until shortly before his death in 1969. This man was my father, José Romolo Lona.

Secundina Macias Lona is my mother. Her formal work-history is only that which is mentioned herein. Her reason for being in the United States is the same for her as for thousands of other Mexicans that have left their native land and can be summed up in one short word . . . necessity. This is her country; the country that has seen the blood of her sons flow in war. No, she would never leave, and we would *never* let her be taken against her will.

SUMMARY

It is open to conjecture as to whether male chauvinism or class oppression was most responsible for the subjugation of the person I interviewed, namely, my mother. This is because historically, the two have been linked much as Siamese twins and are thus inseparable. Yes, it is true that her family's original condition was caused by a class society, a semi-feudal system. And it is also true that this system was created by men to be perpetrated on other men . . . and women! As to her personal position vis-à-vis that of men it is also true that, to a point, she was also subjugated.

Given the circumstances of the family, "the times," and thus the constant struggle for survival, this subjugation was subtly shrouded in tradition and custom. And again it is open to conjecture as to whether this differentiation of the sexes did not serve a function—namely that of survival for the self, and for the family as we know it.

Perhaps now that the Chicana is more aware, more educated, more politically and socially attuned, and thus less dependent, she will assume her rightful place alongside her man—rather than below or behind him.

José Santos Lona

Secundina's life begins in the period of Porifirio Díaz. Although under Díaz many changes occurred in economic development, Mexico still manifested feudal relations of production. Her early life in Peñuelas is characteristic of many women who lived on haciendas as peasants, or lived in ejidos. At an early age the young women learn to do the household chores and work in the fields. At this time Secundina and her family were already becoming the kind of labor needed for capitalist production, namely propertyless wage labor. After 1910, Secundina and her family joined the countless immigrants coming into the United States. They were like the Chinese peasant of the 1850s and the European immigrant of the East—PEASANTS WITHOUT LAND AND PROLETARIANS WITHOUT JOBS!

José's analysis of the relation of male chauvinism and class oppression is accurately described by his statement, ". . . historically, the two have been linked much as Siamese twins and are thus, INSEPARABLE." As stated earlier, class society necessitates the explanation of the subjugation of women vis-à-vis male chauvinism. In understanding the basic relations of production, José has also exposed some of the myths surrounding domestic work and ties it to the question of survival:

> Given the circumstances of the family, "the times," and thus the constant struggle for survival, this subjugation was subtly shrouded in tradition and custom. And again it is open to conjecture as to whether this differentiation of the sexes did not serve a function—namely that of survival for the self, and for the family as we know it.

The condition that forced Secundina's family to migrate was not due to the natural economic development of Mexico. Porifirio Díaz was the consolidator of the Mexican nation as well as the instigator of economic programs which were to leave Mexico underdeveloped. Under the Díaz regime, mines were opened up, roads and railroads were built, and agricultural production began to grow. However, this seemingly progressive development occurred because of foreign investment. Foreign investment in many ways was the major reason why the migration of thousands of Mexican workers began to occur, and also the reason why Mexico today is characterized as "underdeveloped."

Foreign capital in the late 1800s greatly affected conditions in Mexico. On the one hand industrial development began to occur, but it was a development that favored the foreign investors. The profit produced from this development would go to the owners of foreign investment and loans. Foreign penetration into the Mexican economy left thousands of peasants landless, and hundreds of proletarians jobless. This situation was further aggravated in 1883 when the first land-survey laws were passed. When the last of these infamous laws were passed, approximately one-fifth of Mexico's land was in the hands of foreign interests. The interests that were favored were primarily the railroad and mining concessions. For example, in 1880 Mexico could boast of 700 miles of railroad tracks (in comparison, the United States in 1860 had over 30,000 miles of tracks), yet four short years later 3,600 miles of track existed in Mexico. This tremendous development was financed by foreign loans and investment. By 1910 there were over 12,000 miles of track in Mexico. The majority of railroads and roads were not built to develop the internal economy of Mexico, rather they were built by the United States, Britain, and other nations to facilitate their ventures in mining and their establishment of markets (Cumberland, 1969:216).

By 1910 the United States had become the main foreign investor in Mexico. United States capitalism claimed 82 percent of goods produced in Mexico, owned approximately three quarters of mineral holdings, and investments amounted to $2 billion (Cumberland, 1969:228). Foreign capital may have been beneficial to a certain sector in Mexico, but in the early 1900s, as in 1976, the majority of the people were left in a desperate situation. The people of Mexico had to face what some call "creeping" inflation. Between the years 1876 and 1910, the price of corn rose 108 percent; the price of beans rose 163 percent; the price of chili rose 147 percent; wages increased only 60 percent (in Acuña, 1972:126). These conditions culminated in the revolution of 1910. This disruption of the Mexican society gave the impetus to dislodging the Mexican peasant from the land. Thousands fled the tragedy of war and others were left landless. The Mexican people had two alternatives, either stay in Mexico and die, or leave and join the railroad lines in the United States and hope to live.

Thus began what some have called the greatest migration of a people. McWilliams (1968) gives us a hint as to its magnitude. Between 1900 and 1930 Arizona's Mexican immigrant population increased by approximately 100,000; California's by 360,000; New Mexico's by 53,000; and Texas' by 612,000. These figures are approximations and do not actually give us the total number of people who immigrated. The majority came not as property owners, but as workers. Workers who, because of their condition of being propertyless and also because of the conditions in their country, would go to work in any area that offered the hopes of a meal.

In the 1900s the conditions in Mexico were extremely aggravated by the presence of foreign investment. The Mexican state under Díaz and other Mexican presidents allowed not only for the penetration of foreign capital, but for the direct ownership of land and raw materials by the foreign nations. This economic development did not favor the Mexican nation, thus Mexico is characterized by a semi-capitalist, semi-feudal economy. This condition made Mexico a prime source of cheap labor, cheap raw materials, and a source of profit from loans and foreign aid. Mexico under these conditions also became the most reliable source of "cheap" labor for the growing "factories in the fields," and railroads in the U.S. Southwest. The U.S. government under pressure from agribusiness interests did not patrol the U.S.-Mexican border, thus allowing farmers associations, mining interests, and railroad companies to actively recruit and contract Mexican labor (Galarza, 1964:29).

Mexican labor was considered "reliable" not only because it was cheap, but because it was easily deportable in time of economic crisis. Time and time again the U.S. government has acted as an agent in recruiting and deporting Mexican workers. The U.S. government has also made the climate ripe for U.S. corporations by setting up such programs as the infamous "Bracero Program," and since 1965, the Border Industrial Program. These programs are just two examples of how the U.S. government not only serves the interest of the monopoly capitalist, but is their main tool to maintain economic dominance.

The state has invariably been used to stop striking men, women, and children in the mines of New Mexico, in the fields of the Imperial Valley in 1973, in the school blowouts of Los Angeles in 1968, and in August of 1970, during the Chicano moratorium. The list continues and will continue until the state no longer serves the interest of the property owners.

Unlike the immigration of the Chinese in the 1850s and later the Japanese, the early Mexican migrants in the 1900s came as families. The long miles of common boundaries made it easy for whole families to migrate from Mexico to the United States. Railroad work would provide the way for families to migrate. Other families came as the result of being contracted by agribusiness. Other Mexican families would join the railroad crews, finally making their way to the United States by living in boxcars (McWilliams, 1968:167).

The women and children, in this journey of work, would many times take on jobs in or near the railroad. Chicana women would many times be hired to wash the workers' clothes, or would be hired to cook for the crew. The children would help with whatever had to be done. At other times the women would go to the fields and work, or go to the homes of the wealthy and work as maids, cooks, and wet nurses.

In Texas and California, Chicanas went to work in the huge agricultural combines. They joined other migrant laborers who went from farm to farm to pick the fruit of the season. At other times, Chicanas would go to the packing houses and canneries to prepare the produce they had just picked. As the early immigrants began to settle in towns, barrios, and cities, many of the women went to the textile and garment factories to seek employment. As more time went on and as the Chicana became more stable, some changes began to occur. Instead of wandering endlessly, workers found homes in the old railroad campsite, for example, in Watts and Roseville, California, and El Paso, Texas. Some of the new generation began getting an education. For a small minority of Chicanas and Chicanos, education was a benefit. For the majority, education meant tracking into working-class jobs. For most Chicanas life meant continual work in the home, seasonal employment in factories and stores, or unemployment and welfare.

In coming to the United States, Mexican immigrants underwent culture change. The majority of Chicanos were forced to accept the values and behavior not of "Anglos" but of the bourgeoisie, and were molded by their work place and the educational system into proletarians. Those values of Mexican feudal culture stressing male dominance and obedience were reinforced to make Mexicans into the kind of proletarians needed by the U.S. bourgeoisie (González, 1976). However, because of their condition as proletarians, Chicanos and Chicanas began to develop those cultural values and behavior peculiar to proletarians (i.e., organization, planning, discipline). Under these conditions, and because Chicanas were in the labor force, they too changed their behavior. Chicanas, as *women and proletarians,* began to participate in struggles for equality and justice.

The Chicana as part of the U.S. working class has not always been at home praying, waiting for tomorrow to come. Politically the Chicana has been involved in many historical struggles which have been aimed at advancing the interests of the poor and propertyless. With the inception of the 1910 Mexican Revolution, the

Mexicana fought alongside the peasant man. While providing food and other necessities, she many times had to take a gun and fight to protect home and family.

In the fields of California and Texas, in the factories of Los Angeles and El Paso, and even in the mines of New Mexico, the Chicana has fought many a battle for better wages and better working conditions. In the communities, the Chicana has fought for decent housing and medical care, and for better education.

History is filled with the activities of the Chicana. Our task as Chicanas and as historians is to present the history of the Chicana and the Chicano in light of the capitalist development that permeated the United States and the world. To present a different history will mask the already hidden histories, and perpetuate the existence of exploitation and subjugation.

NOTES

I would like to express my appreciation to Rosalinda González and Gilbert González for their help in clarifying and organizing the main points in this paper. I also want to thank Getachew Alemu and Felicitas Apodaca for their consistent encouragement.

1. The international border created by the Treaty de Guadalupe Hidalgo is highly important and cannot be taken lightly. On the northern side the strongest capitalist nation would develop, rendering to its inhabitants a distinct social, cultural, and economic system. While on the southern side a nation would develop that would be plagued by imperialist penetration. In this sense I use the term Chicano and Mexican American to refer to those people born and living in the United States of Mexican parentage, and Mexicano to those born and living in Mexico. These categories are not finite, involved is the immigrant Mexican in the United States. For purposes of historical clarification these people are placed with Chicanos because of their objective condition as members of the working class in the United States. For more clarification on the differences between the United States and Mexico see Fernández and Ocampo (1974).

2. For further clarification on this point see Bailey (1966) and Forbes (1960).

3. For recent exceptions to this tendency see Arroyo (1974), Farah Strike Committee (1974), and González (1976).

4. Mode of production refers to a particular way in which society produces and reproduces itself. More concretely it refers to the forces of production, including raw materials, labor power, level of development of technology and silence. The second aspect of the mode of production is the relations of production, or the way society comes together to produce and exchange. Involved in this second aspect are class relations.

5. Reproduction and maintenance of labor power refers to the actual feeding, clothing, housing, and procreation of male and female labor.

6. For further information on feudal society see Bloch (1961), Dobb (1973), and Rowbotham (1974).

7. *Encomiendas* and *repartimientos* were the two main historical forms of land grants by which the Spanish landlord received tribute and labor services from the native population.

8. The *calpulli* was the town district occupied and used by a single clan possessing *use* but not property rights.

9. *Pochtecas* were the merchants during the time of the Aztec empire.

10. Social production begins to become distinguished from domestic production when

there begins to be produced a surplus in commodities. This development is reinforced by further divisions of labor, primarily by the division between property owners and the propertyless. Capitalism is the mode of production that thoroughly separates social production from domestic production; this is because capitalism leaves the working class with no private productive property, and because capitalism has the highest development of private property (i.e., monopoly capitalism).

11. Laborers engage in two types of consumption. One type is the consumption of the means of production. In other words, consuming the raw materials and machinery that go into the commodities which produce profit. The second type involves the consumption by which the individual provides for himself and the family. "The result of the first is, that the capitalist lives; of the other, that the laborer lives" (Marx, 1973:571).

12. In reading "Simple Reproduction" of *Capital*, it is interesting to note that while Marx reached his own conclusion on productive and unproductive consumption, Marx's footnotes indicate that the economist Ricardo and Malthus had advocated the necessity of limiting laborer's personal consumption (see Marx, 1973:573, footnote 3 and 4).

REFERENCES

Acuña, Rodolfo
   1972 *Occupied America: The Chicano's Struggle Toward Liberation.* San Francisco: Canfield
      Press.
Allen, Ruth
   1931 "Mexican Peon Women in Texas," *Sociology and Social Research,* 16 (November-
      December), 131–142.
Arroyo, Laura E.
   1974 "Industrial and Occupational Distribution of Chicana Workers," *Aztlán,* IV (2)
      243–382.
Bailey, L. R.
   1966 *Indian Slave Trade in the Southwest.* Los Angeles: Western Lore Press.
Bloch, Marc
   1961 *Feudal Society.* Chicago: University of Chicago Press.
Campa
   1973 "The Mexican-American in Historical Perspective," in Renato Rosaldo et al., *Chi-
      cano: The Evolution of a People.* Minneapolis: Winston Press.
Chevalier, François
   1972 *Land and Society in Colonial Mexico, The Great Hacienda.* Berkeley: University of
      California Press.
Chicano Communications Center
   1976 *450 Years of Chicano History.* Albuquerque: Chicano Communication Center.
Cumberland, Charles C.
   1968 *Mexico, the Struggle for Modernity.* New York: Oxford University Press.
Dobb, Maurice
   1973 *Studies in the Development of Capitalism.* New York: International Publishers.
Engels, Frederick
   1973 *The Origin of the Family, Private Property and the State.* New York: International
      Publishers.

Farah Strike Support Committee
  1974 *Chicanos Strike at Farah.* San Francisco: United Front Press.
Fernández, Raúl and José Ocampo
  1974 "The Latin American Revolution: A Theory of Imperialism, Not Dependence,"
    Latin American Perspectives, I (Spring), 30–61.
Forbes, J. D.
  1960 *Apache, Navajo and Spaniard.* Norman: University of Oklahoma Press.
Galarza, Ernesto
  1964 *Merchants of Labor.* Santa Barbara: McNally & Loftin Publishers.
González, Rosalinda M.
  1976 "A Review of the Literature on Mexican and Mexican American Women Workers in
    the United States Southwest, 1900–1975," Unpublished, University of California at
    Irvine, Program in Comparative Culture.
Green, George N.
  1971 "ILGWU in Texas, 1930–1970," *The Journal of Mexican American History,* (Spring),
    144–169.
Lenin, V. I.
  1965 *Imperialism, The Highest Stage of Capitalism.* Peking: Foreign Languages Press.
Marx, Karl
  1970 *A Contribution to the Critique of Political Economy.* New York: International Pub-
    lishers.
  1973 *Capital,* Vol. I, New York: International Publishers.
Marx, Karl and Frederick Engels
  1972 *The German Ideology.* New York: International Publishers.
Marx, Karl et al.
  1969 *The Woman Question.* New York: International Publishers.
McWilliams, Carey
  1968 *North from Mexico.* New York: Greenwood Press.
  1971 *Factories in the Field.* Santa Barbara and Salt Lake City: Peregrine Publishers.
NACLA
  1975 "Women's Labor," *Latin America and Empire Report,* IX (September).
Rowbotham, Sheila
  1974 *Hidden from History.* New York: Pantheon Books.
Soustelle, Jacques
  1975 *Daily Life of the Aztecs.* Stanford: Stanford University Press.
Taylor, Paul S.
  1971 *An American-Mexican Frontier.* New York: Russell and Russell.

QUESTIONS

1. Why "must" the development of history be based on something more tangible than ideas, dates, and individuals? What are the "tangible" foundations Apodaca suggests and why should we not accept other explanations as convincing?

2. Apodaca mentions magic, theology, human nature, and male superiority as explanations that have been

used to justify the supremacy of one class over another. What is your own explanation why there are social inequalities, why a few people are extremely rich and most are poor?

3. Why is the relation between domestic and social production so important for understanding the status of women, whether in Aztec society, colonial Mexico, or the Southwest of the United States in the nineteenth century? Does it have any importance in the twenty-first-century global economy? Generally speaking, in what sort of domestic production are women involved today?

4. To what extent is Secundina's life "conditioned" by feudalism and imperialism (material or objective conditions) as opposed to the choices she and her family made (subjective conditions)?

5. Apodaca implies that rather than an Anglo culture there is a bourgeoisie culture and that rather than a Mexican or Chicano culture there is a "proletariat" (working-class) culture. How does this definition of culture differ from other definitions in this reader or elsewhere?

✳ 2 ✳
LATINA POLITICS/LATINO POLITICS

Carol Hardy-Fanta

For Carol the question revolves around the inclusiveness of feminist personal politics. In the following excerpt, Carol raises many of the principal concerns of this reader. She raises critical questions regarding Latino/a political participation in the United States in view of the diversity and the noncitizen status of many Latino/as, and of the role of gender in developing a more participatory model of community and citizenship for all Americans. Her discussion of these different approaches to citizenship have substantial implications for political theory, the nature of politics, and the interaction of culture, class, and gender in political participation. If we had to put her message on a bumper sticker it would read: "It's the inclusiveness of feminist personal politics."

CONCLUSION

Despite the constraints that face them as women, and in the process of challenging the constraints that face Latinos in the United States as a group, Latina women in Boston envision a political life that is more participatory than that envisioned by Latino men. The vision of Latina women is based on connectedness rather than personal advancement; collective methods and collective organization rather than hierarchy; community and citizenship generated from personal ties rather than from formal structures; and consciousness raising rather than a response to opportunity. The story of Latina women in politics in Boston is one that deserves to be told, if only because it challenges myths about their supposed passivity and submissiveness and because it counters their invisibility in mainstream political science.

If this were only a story about Latina women who overcame the constraints of sexism and racism to become political mobilizers, however, the broader implications for our understanding of culture, gender, and political participation in America would be missed. In this conclusion, I explore some of the ways the experiences of Latina women and Latino men in Boston inform several key debates in political science today, debates about the meaning of gender differences for political theory, about the nature of politics, and about the interaction of culture and gender in political participation. The stories of Latina women and Latino men in Boston have much to teach us not only about engendering political participation in Latino communities but also about addressing the cynicism and disaffiliation in American politics today.

IMPLICATIONS FOR POLITICAL THEORY

Latinos in Boston provide substantial support for feminist theories that differences exist between women and men in how they view politics. The relational–positional debate posits that women stress relationships, whereas men are more focused on gaining and maintaining positions—positions as elected office, as government appointments, and as status. Feminist theories have suggested that relationships play an important role in women's psychological development; connection—connectedness—emerges as central to women's politics as well.

The relational aspects of political life dominate the stories of Latina women in Boston and are observable in their political work within the Latino community. For Latina women in Boston, politics is an interpersonal, interactive process—building bridges and making connections between people. In contrast, Latino men emphasize access to political positions and status, the development of formal political structures, hierarchical organizations, and politics as an opportunity—an opportunity for community advancement, yes, but for personal advancement as well.

A key issue within the debate about gender differences is whether there is an essential divide between the public and private dimensions of politics. For Latina women, much more than men, the boundary between these supposedly distinct spheres of life is blurred, indistinct. With their emphasis on grassroots politics, survival politics, the politics of everyday life and through their emphasis on the development of political consciousness, Latina women see connections between the problems they face personally and community issues stemming from government policies.

For Latina women, making connections between problems in their daily lives and institutional policies, "taking a stand" against oppression from any source, is the first step toward a political life; it creates a *chispa*—a spark—a passion for politics. The development of the personal self, as a woman, as a person with new capacities, as someone who can take action with others, is intimately linked with the development of the political self. Political mobilization occurs when the desire to *desenvol-*

verse—to develop oneself—is linked to working with other people on the government policies that affect one's ability to achieve personal and community goals.

A similar process occurs in relation to the debate about the nature of power. Latina women differ substantially from Latino men in how they perceive the meaning of power. Latino men talk more about power than do Latina women; they also reflect the mainstream, perhaps male, view of power as "power over," whereas Latina women see power as the "power to"—especially the power to achieve change. This finding lends support for feminist theories of gender differences in the meaning of power and suggests that these differences are valid cross-culturally. As Rosa López says, "It's promoting change. . . . That's political, that's what I mean by politics, that's what politics means to me."

Feminist contributions to political theory—contributions about gender differences, the public–private dimensions of politics, and power—are sometimes limited, unfortunately, by a lack of attention to diversity. Hurtado (1989), for example, contends that "most contemporary published feminist theory in the United States has been written by white, educated women" and that "the experiences of other women . . . are absent in much of white academic feminist theory" (838). Latina women in Boston lend considerable support for contemporary feminist theories that women—as women—are more focused on the relational aspects of politics than are men. Nevertheless, Latina women in Boston, like many black women and Latinas in other parts of the United States (Hurtado 1989, 842), are highly critical of Anglo feminism for not paying more attention to struggles faced by poor women of color. Economic subordination and racism have not been addressed within the feminist movement to the extent desirable for the mobilization of Latina women as women. Thus, while Latina women in Boston provide support for feminist theories about gender differences, they also help explain the dilemma of why some groups of women of color hesitate to embrace—or lend active support for—feminist causes.

An even more complex theoretical dilemma exists, however. In contending, as I do, that substantial differences exist between Latina women and Latino men around connectedness, collectivity, community, and consciousness, I am treading on dangerous ground. The contention that the politics of women differs in some essential way from the politics of men comes perilously close to the biological determinism and the "separate spheres" arguments of the nineteenth century, notions that contributed to the subordination of women. Dietz (1989), Flanagan and Jackson (1990), and Deutchman (1991) caution against any tendency toward what Dietz calls "binary opposition," in other words, against seeing women and men as promoting diametrically opposed visions of society and politics.

Many potential dangers exist when theory or empirical research concludes that there are intrinsic differences between women and men: (1) The truth may be distorted; even though Latina women are twice as likely as Latino men to focus on connectedness, and Latino men are five times as likely as women to emphasize politics as positions, some women and men share a common view of politics—a view that represents a meeting ground, a potential for common understanding and common action, a view that might be obscured when differences are highlighted.

(2) The role of patriarchal social structures consequently receives less attention. (3) Essentialist explanations of observed gender differences may contribute to antifeminist policies (Deutchman 1991) and the imposition of greater constraints on women.

In other words, when I couch observed gender differences as connectedness *versus* positions and status, collectivity *versus* hierarchy, community *versus* formal structures, and consciousness *versus* opportunity and formal affiliations, the occasions of common political understanding shared by Latino men and Latina women retreat from view. In addition, as I discussed in Chapter 2, the reasons Latina women do not stress positions more, for example, may originate in the sociopolitical structure: subordination, social conditioning, and blocked opportunities. Finally, by promoting a vision of Latina women's politics as more participatory, as superior, their potential activism in areas currently dominated by men may be further inhibited.

What purpose is served, then, by asserting and highlighting the gender differences? First, the differences exist; they cannot be ignored or rationalized away. Second, regardless of the source, the differences reveal a contribution by Latina women to a model of participatory politics, a model that may hold a key for political mobilization and political empowerment, especially in communities of color. By pointing to the differences, then, I do not wish to create the impression that these participatory qualities are the unique realm of women—there were indeed Latino men who exhibited some of them as well; in each analysis, some men responded like the women and some women resembled the men.

Nevertheless, by highlighting the different, more participatory, vision of politics voiced and acted upon by Latina women, participatory skills and values are likewise highlighted, brought to the forefront of political analysis. It is obviously possible that these skills and values are within the abilities of men—who may be constrained from their expression or may suppress their expression in action or words because of another kind of sexism that stifles men's relational abilities. Finally, by highlighting observed gender differences among Latinos, a vision of politics, of "What is political?" takes shape, a vision that holds promise for a revitalization of political participation. When Andrea del Valle, Barber (1984), and Dietz (1989) argue for participation, it is a participation of all, a revitalization of the truer image of citizenship.

WHAT IS POLITICAL?

What emerges from the stories of Latina women and Latino men is that the traditional focus on politics as positions, on politics as elections and interest groups, that frames much of our understanding of politics may be a gendered construct. It may be that the emphasis on the hierarchical organizations, elected offices, and formal structures that constitute the system of representative democracy prevalent in American politics reflects its origins in male concerns about positions, hierarchy, and formally organized structures. The dominance of these concerns in political *analysis* may also reflect the dominance of males in the profession of political science.

It is not my goal to dismiss the importance of elections, of voting, of promoting legal citizenship, and of traditional modes of political participation. As indicated previously, what Latino men do politically may contribute as much to the realignment of political power for Latinos in this country as what Latina women do. Redistricting challenges by Latino men, for example, were directly responsible for the election of the first Latino to statewide office in Massachusetts. In addition, this book begins by documenting the actions of Latina women in these traditional political roles. The fact that Latina women in Boston have run for office as often as Latino men, and in greater proportion than their non-Latina counterparts, shows that a more participatory vision of politics does not in any way preclude support for the electoral side of politics. Latina women are candidates; they also figure prominently in voter registration, in party politics, and in political education. Latina women even discuss voting slightly more than do Latino men. What Latina women contribute to our understanding of "What is political?" then, is not a dilution of support for electoral politics but a specification of the interactive process of political mobilization and a reexamination of the nature of politics.

Strategies built on an interpersonal, interactive, *process-oriented* type of politics involve mutuality, the *intercambio de ideas* (exchange of ideas), and the ability to truly listen. Organizational structures that encourage members to take on new roles, including political roles, and those that encourage participation in defining and implementing organizational goals enhance political participation. Building community through face-to-face, door-to-door conversations and discussion groups does more to create a sense of citizenship among neighbors—a sense of citizenship that transcends legal status—than campaign flyers and voting instructions. While elections and redistricting decisions in the courts determine representation and are important vehicles for Latino political success in *electoral* politics, political strategies built on interpersonal relationships may in fact contribute far more to mass *participation* within Latino communities.

Finally, a reexamination of the nature of politics via a study of Latina women and Latino men in Boston addresses the question whether gender affects the definition and study of politics in America. Too often, political analysis ignores the gender of the political actors involved in political mobilization; when women's political behavior is ignored, their politics and their ideas about "the political" are marginalized. When, for example, Uriarte-Gaston (1988) follows convention and does not identify the gender of many of the leaders and participants in the community development activism of Boston's Puerto Rican community during the 1960s and 1970s, many readers might assume the community organizers were men, or that the gender of the participators was unimportant. The contribution of the many women active in that period is thus lost. It is not sufficient, therefore, to discuss the roles of women only in research or theoretical works on women or, in a sense, to contain the politics of women within the bounds of feminist political theory and research; gender must be identified and included in general political analysis as well.

POLITICS AS AN INTERACTIVE PROCESS: "EVERYBODY WANTS PERSONAL POLITICS"

When I claim that connection, collectivity, community, and consciousness are the ingredients that create a passion for politics and translate political passion into political activity, am I somehow claiming that Latinos are unique, in other words, that they have a cultural need for a more personal politics? Or is there an implicit class dimension: Do poorer Latino groups, like Puerto Ricans and Dominicans, require personal politics because of a parochial, private-regarding, ethos? Finally, am I claiming that Latina women are unique in their ability to generate mobilization because they use connection, collectivity, community, and consciousness as mobilization methods? All these questions revolve around a central issue: What is the relationship between culture, class, and gender in the study of Latino politics?

On the surface, it seems clear that the Latino cultural value of *personalismo* could explain much of the need for a more personal style of political mobilization. A class perspective also seems suggested by my findings: traditional theories see lower-class people as having a parochial, private-regarding, view of politics; the consensus of Latinos in Boston is that they want something concrete for the community as a result of their political efforts. But then, where does the fact that Latina women focus on connectedness and personal politics to a much greater degree than Latino men fit into a culture class model of Latino political participation? Obviously, culture, class, and gender all interact in some way.

Latinos clearly do have cultural traditions that point to an expectation of personal politics, concrete benefits, and group-centered mobilization strategies. The discussion in Chapter 6 on home-country politics in Puerto Rico and the Dominican Republic, for example, demonstrates that men and women alike expect politicians and political organizers to "come and find out," to listen, to shake hands, and to promise benefits and respond to community needs.

Of course, this is not just a cultural tradition (in the sense of shared values transmitted through generations) but an expectation based on a different political structure. Latino countries such as Puerto Rico and the Dominican Republic have strong parties, dynamic campaigns, and a political style that integrates affiliative needs into political events. Latino politics in the United States, when compared to home-country politics, clearly demonstrates how culture alone does not determine political participation in a linear way—structure creates the conditions in which cultural values develop.

At the same time, the political-culture school implies that class determines political participation. There did seem to be a class gap between influential Latinos in Boston (*los profesionales*) and their mobilization targets (*la gente del pueblo*). Many Latinos, however, bridged that gap using a political style that blended culture and politics; many of these were Latina women. In addition, there may be a flaw in the argument that lower-status groups or different cultures require certain types of politics (i.e., private-regarding, personal politics). Perhaps the real reason higher socioeconomic groups seem to focus on more than concrete benefits is that, in comparison to poorer groups like Latinos, they already receive the benefits; their dominance of Congress, state legislatures, and other government decision-making bodies assures that their concrete needs are met, again, at least in comparison to poorer groups. Middle-class, white neighborhoods have better schools, cleaner streets, and more responsive police departments. The difference in political styles and political ethos between the upper and lower classes may be less the result of innate differences within the lower classes and more the consequence of who controls the economic resources. As the pained cry of Juana Oviedo, who is facing cuts in her disability allotment, shows, she knows who benefits from this control: "Who is it that is being hurt? It's us, the poor people. Because *those* people have money— the one who has money—this doesn't affect him at all. *He* has a good job, a nice house. . . . How is one supposed to survive? You tell me *that*!" Oviedo recognizes that having money, a good job, and a nice house protects people from the exigencies of life; I suggest that already having many of these concrete benefits also protects the higher socioeconomic groups from the need to engage in "parochial" politics.

Some would argue that middle- or upper-class people have received these benefits precisely because of their political activism and political talents. The socioeconomic model implies, however, that the middle- and upper-class groups are, in a sense, less concerned with these private benefits and more concerned with broader social or community needs. I suggest that concrete benefits are concrete benefits and that lower-status groups are not the only ones with "parochial needs." They are simply demanding what they do not have.

What about gender? Latina women in Boston clearly perceive politics differently from Latino men. But do they perceive politics differently from white women, or from black women? Mine was not a comparative study. Only future research can answer the question of culture-specific gender differences between Latina women and women of other ethnic or racial groups. However, the gender differences between Latino men and Latina women add another layer to the already complex task of sorting out culture and class. If Latino men value *personalismo* because of cultural expectations and because most people respond to a politics embedded in interpersonal relationships, why is it that Latina *women* are the ones in the community who are most successful at integrating personal politics into their political mobilization efforts? And if Latino men of *la gente del pueblo*—as men—prefer formal affiliations, hierarchical structures, and access to positions, why do they not respond in greater numbers to the appeals of like-minded Latino male leaders? Is it possible that Latino men are also looking for a more personal style of politics, albeit with a male slant? From the gender differences that form the foundation of the themes of this book, almost as many questions are raised as the book answers.

It is not entirely clear why what would seem to be a shared orientation of Latino male leaders and men of *la gente del pueblo* would not mobilize more Latino men in Boston and other Latino communities. I tentatively suggest several possible reasons. The first is that in Puerto Rico and other Latin countries there seems to be a greater connection between the classes around male political affiliative organizations, possibly because of vestigial paternalistic relationships between the professional/upper-class men and the working-class/lower-class men. Also, as Johvanil (1989) suggests, cultural clubs and sports clubs play an important role in male socialization in Latin countries but are underdeveloped in both their socialization and political roles in Boston.

The second reason Latino male activists may not have more success at mobilizing Latino men, despite shared politicization patterns, stems from the gender-related constraints on participation discussed in the previous chapter. Men like Luis Hernández, among others, want leaders to come into the community, and Tito Morales demonstrates that maintaining connections (within a male-style hierarchical structure) can be effective. The expectation of *personalismo* is thwarted, however, when male Latino leaders, due to their greater access to "good jobs" in the mostly Anglo government, move up the success ladder of government appointments, leaving behind a vacuum. Juan Maldonado, for example, believes being political means formal affiliations, political structures, and, especially, positions in government. He nevertheless voices the negative impact of Latino male leaders moving into new jobs: "There was a down side because none of these leaders had the time or the vision to basically nurture other leadership, or mentor other leadership to take their place. So Nelson leaves—vacuum! Manuel leaves—vacuum! Julio dies—vacuum!" Previous research on Chicana politics suggests that, while some women are constrained by their multiple roles as workers, mothers, and family members, Latina women develop politically in the context of these roles. They cannot go off to a "good job" and leave family responsibilities behind: these responsibilities stimulate a search for change, a connection with others, and an integration of informal and formal community action. For this reason, Latina women may transmit and maintain cultural traditions (including political traditions) in ways that are difficult for the Latino men who have achieved (somewhat limited) access to the power structure. Community ties blend the politics of culture, class, and gender.

In addition, Latino men's sense that the way they contribute to the community is by being role models does not translate into either the concrete benefits or the personal connections needed (because of *personalismo*) for Latino men to feel part of the political system. In other words, Latino men who are of *la gente del pueblo*, like Latina women in general, may require politics to be built upon personal connections—in the case of men, within formal structures like political parties and clubs—but Latino male leaders, having moved into the Anglo power structure, may fail in, or be constrained from, building or maintaining those connections.

While a few men like Tito Morales integrate the need for concrete benefits and cultural expectations into a male version of personal politics, he is outnumbered by the large number of Latina women who draw others into political events by their emphasis on connection, collectivity, and political consciousness. Women like Josefina Ortega, María Luisa Soto, Inez Martínez, Julia Santiago, and Marta Correa represent a blending of culture and politics and constitute an important political resource for successful mobilization in the Latino community.

Finally, is it not possible that on a smaller scale Latino politics mirrors American politics? Is it not possible that, contrary to the implicit ideological bias of the politi-

cal-culture school (and class bias of the progressive movement), *all* people want personal politics?—that what Latinos want from politics reflects a universal need? I have
already discussed the view that the decline of American political participation since
the early part of the century was due, in great part, to the decline in the political
party and the demise of the political machine. What these structural changes really
involved, however, was the simultaneous decline in politics as an interactive *process*.
It may be that what Latinos want from politics is a model for what Americans in
general want from their political system.

It is time for the voices of Latina women to be heard. Latina women have long been
a source of strength in the Latino community. Their skills at building networks,
their experiences blending culture, personal relationships, and political participation
have too long been ignored. Latino political empowerment begins in the community; it depends on the engagement of large numbers of Latino people. Many of
those who can engage Latinos—who can make connections, work collectively, build
community, and raise political consciousness within Latino communities, are Latina
women. As Ivelisse Rodríguez and Luis Hernández said so simply, *"Hay que escu-
char."* It *is* time to listen to the women.

✳   ✳   ✳

QUESTIONS

1. What are the implications of arguing that the private and public spheres of life are or are not separate?
2. Discuss the differences between "power over" and "power to."
3. Are you persuaded that, despite the dangers of establishing *essential* differences between men's and women's senses of politics, there are good reasons to follow this line of reasoning?
4. What is the relation between culture, class, and gender in the study of Latino politics?
5. Does it make sense to draw the conclusion from the above text that there is a politics that is unique to Latinos?

✳ 3 ✳
REFLECTIONS ON LATINO/AS AND PUBLIC CITIZENSHIP

Francisco Hernández Vázquez

In this article, Francisco explores the emergence of Latino/a's quest for public citizenship from a set of
seemingly paradoxical relations of power. One is the history of Latino/a political thought—*the people's* relation
with the state and their struggles for self-determination, and at the same time, the demand for the just

application of the law to eliminate political and economic exclusionary practices that devalue the bodies of the people and their self-respect. Then there are power relations that pressure Latino/as to shed their differences and become part of the proverbial melting pot, forces that at the same time magnify these differences, divide people, and thus divert the power of the civil society. What emerges is a call for the construction of public citizenship as a genuinely democratic practice based on the needs of human bodies: on human rights and not on the interests of states or dominant classes. If we put Francisco's message on a bumper sticker it would say: "It's the materiality of language."

※   ※   ※

> Wherever the *polis* exists with its notion of the equality of the tribes and its standards of justice based on that equality, Zeus, Apollo, and Athene are present. And wherever people [*ethnos*] have imagined, thought, and acted for the sake of blood-related kinship, the Furies are present.
>
> —James Hersh

> The biggest difference I have noticed is that the supervisors are thinking about what they say before they say it. I think they are starting to view us as people who are worth something.
>
> —Francisco Ortiz, Gallo Vineyards worker

> Justice will be done.
> When?
> When the living know what the dead suffered.
>
> —John Berger, *Pig Earth*

A significant aspect of Latino/a political thought is the question of citizenship and the nature of *belonging* to and in the United States. Tracing the course of events that first made Latino/as involuntary, territorial, or cultural citizens reveals a power that begins with a **political technology** in the eighteenth century, grows economically, and in the process of developing into a world leader, appropriates Mexican, Cuban, and Puerto Rican territory and citizens in the nineteenth century and turns them (along with human bodies from all over the world) into commodities that serve the political and economic needs of the state. It is not just a story of Latino/as as victims of the Colossus of the North. In the next one hundred years this political economy expanded all over the world to such an extent that by the twenty-first century it was no longer subject to any authority and had turned all aspects of life itself into a **commodity** for the sake of profit making.

> Even the movements of subatomic particles, the genetic codes of germ plasms, the information of human discovery, the unconscious regions of the id, and the reaches of human technology towards the stars are appropriated for money-profit rule. *Any opposition to this rule is perceived as heresy and condemned as a threat to freedom.*[1]

Ironically, Latino/a and Anglo Americans started off on an equal basis: fighting for freedom against the Divine Right of the King and Queen. Inspired by the

Enlightenment, these patriots shed their blood, sacrificed their families and their lives to obtain liberty for the royal subjects, now categorized as "the people," as entities that were created equal. Let us be clear that these American revolutionary wars promised not only freedom and equality, but justice. While these goals may have been achieved for the few, the vast majority of human bodies continue to struggle to be included in these noble categories. They were subjected instead to the exclusive category of the Other: the uncivilized, indigenous, dark-skinned, women, propertyless, *el pelado*, the meaner sort.[2] It is within this long and continuing struggle that a Latino/a quest for public citizenship becomes also a moral and economic imperative for all. As we reach the limits of growth, it would help make a smoother transition into a sustainable society and prevent the religious, race, or ethnic wars predicted by some.[3]

Looking specifically at the United States of America, human bodies have been placed

> into a bewildering range of categories, including not just birthright and naturalized citizens and state and U.S. citizens but also nonvoting citizens, "jurisdictional" citizens, "commercial" citizens, citizens subject to incarceration or deportation without due process owning to their race, denizens, U.S. nationals, and even colonial subjects.[4]

Here are some examples. We find the same wording in the U.S. treaty with France for the acquisition of Louisiana in 1803, the treaty for the acquisition of Florida from Spain in 1819, and the treaty for the acquisition of much of northern Mexico in 1848 (to replace article IX of the Treaty of Guadalupe Hidalgo proposed by Mexico). To wit:

> The inhabitants of the ceded territory will be incorporated in the union of the United States and admitted as soon as possible according to the principles of the Federal constitution, to the *enjoyment of all the rights, advantages and immunities of citizens of the United States.*[5]

The treaty with Russia for Alaska, however, excludes certain categories of human bodies: "the inhabitants of the ceded territory . . . *with the exception of uncivilized native tribes,* shall be admitted to the enjoyment of all the rights" (emphasis added). Not only are human bodies classified as "natives" excluded from public citizenship, in the case of Puerto Rico a new form of *territorial exclusion* is invented. Compare the statement of the joint congressional resolution of 1898 incorporating Hawaii ("the said Hawaiian Island and their dependencies be and are hereby *annexed as a part of the territory of the United States*"; emphasis added) with the treaty with Spain in 1898 that made Puerto Rico an unincorporated territory ("the civil rights and political status of the native inhabitants . . . *shall be determined by the Congress*"; emphasis added). Furthermore, the Foraker Act of 1900 provided that the former Spanish subjects "will be deemed and held to be *citizens of Puerto Rico.*"[6] As of today, Puerto Ricans are U.S. citizens but cannot vote in presidential elections and have no representation in Congress.[7] Indeed, it "is striking that Americans structure access to their civic identity via terminology and institutions that hark back to political systems their Revolution was meant to overthrow."[8]

Exclusive citizenship was practiced, however, even if initially the wording was inclusive. Take the Treaty of Guadalupe Hidalgo, which ended the war with Mexico, as an example. Under Mexican law, black and indigenous peoples were citizens. According to article IX of the treaty, those who did not choose to remain Mexican citizens would be considered "to have elected" to become U.S. citizens. The California delegates to the state constitutional convention, including six native Californios, constructed a category that would exclude blacks and Indians from citizenship while including "Mexicans." Suffrage was extended to "every white, male citizen of Mexico who shall have elected to become a citizen of the United States."[9] The people residing in New Mexico, following the pattern established under the Northwest Ordinance of 1787 and the Wisconsin Organic Act of 1836, were "citizens-in-waiting." (For Puerto Ricans, their waiting is forever.) For white Mexicans in New Mexico, full U.S. citizenship rights came with statehood in 1912. Indian Mexican citizens, like the Pueblo Indians, lost their rights in 1848. They did not get full American citizenship until 1953.[10] Even Latino/as who were "whites of a different color,"[11] who considered themselves part of the privileged "we the people," who were part of the discourse of progress, civilization, and the U.S. American Dream, like the elites in northern Mexico, Cuba, and Puerto Rico, eventually found themselves dispossessed of property, respect, and political status.[12]

California in 1849 exemplifies the bloody, even genocidal consequences of the combination of an incipient global economy and a citizenship that rests on weak or nonexistent juridical protection, as hordes of "forty-niners" from all over the world, in their desperate search for gold, stabbed, extorted, or lynched native Californios, primarily the dark-skinned ones. It is precisely in this sort of historical experience that one locates the birth of a quest for a public citizenship that privileges the rights of human bodies over exclusive categories that benefit the interests of states and/or the free global market. As efforts to change the U.S. Constitution to curtail the rights of citizenship continue today (as they usually do in response to economic crisis), this becomes an increasingly urgent task.[13]

We are back to a situation somewhat similar to what the patriots faced two hundred years ago. Now, however, it is the "moral absolutism" of a global market, portrayed as "freedom,"[14] that poses the "[t]win totalitarianisms [of] . . . the dictatorships of consumer society and obligatory injustice."[15] When confronted with these new forms of subjectification that provide freedom but not justice, how does one protect the rights of *all* peoples, of *all* human bodies? How does one construct a public citizenship?

The Latino/a political experience may shed some light on these questions. Mexicans have been portrayed as "greasers" and foreigners in their own land and subjected to periodic deportations and repatriations; Puerto Rico became a possession but Puerto Ricans are not yet equal citizens under the U.S. Constitution; and Cubans were subjected to political and economic intervention and are now split by the security interests of two nation-states. To explain these events there are the usual theories and analyses: imperialism, capitalism, sexism, and racism.[16] And there is always the abused notion of human agency or lack of it (Latino/as don't try hard enough) and deficiency theories based on biological or cultural determinism (it's their genes or their culture that is to blame).[17] Given the persistence of injustice, at a later point we will need to question the assumptions behind these analyses about the nature of power and language.

Making use of these analytical tools, Latino/as have indeed organized anticolonial, antiracist, anticlass, and antisexist struggles to fight against these oppressive circumstances. The political history of Latino/as reveals a series of defensive struggles based on the Right of Self-Preservation: uprisings, including guerrilla warfare and social banditry; mutual aid societies and unions to care for the human bodies that the political and economic system has used and discarded; and more recently, a movement for civil rights. Cubans had a revolution to oust the U.S.-backed dictator Batista and many later turned against the revolution. And some Puerto Rican independentistas continue to engage in insurgent or terrorist activities (depending on who is doing the defining). All the while, the vast majority of Latino/as have also been proactive, attempting to exercise their duties of citizenship through productive activities, such as hard work; social, cultural, religious, civic activities; participation in the armed forces; and the electoral process (in the United States as well as in their countries of origin, with which through migration they retain strong ties).

No matter how hard they work and try to be part of the American way of life, however, Latino/as get no respect. Many Latino/as, whether they are U.S. citizens or immigrants, do not feel fully included and accepted by U.S. Americans. This is the consensus found by a recent major research project in New York, Texas, and Los Angeles. Consequently, the authors of the study call for cultural citizenship, that is, the creation of a sociopolitical space to accept cultural differences alongside citizenship.[18] While necessary, it is not enough for public citizenship, however, to assert or claim the right to cultural space and practices. The individual, the human body if you will, is subjected in different, even conflicting ways: by his own self-definition, by the identity imposed by the Latino/a and dominant civil societies, and by the state, its institutions, its judicial procedures. There is indeed a very complex ongoing process of making and unmaking both citizens and "criteria of belonging" for human bodies.[19] At the same time, it is important to note that *respect* is considered the key component in a just society.[20]

This complex process appears as reflecting paradoxes that bring the question of public citizenship to the foreground. On one side, the state and the global economy insist that everyone is Equal, the Same: they either tend to turn ethnic/cultural differences into commodities or to deny them. The goal is to erase, homogenize, normalize differences and create loyal citizen/consumers. Yet the State and the Market also categorize people according to their Differences; here the goal is to define, fragment, divide peoples as Others. This serves to divert the power of a unified civil society and preserve private, white-nationalist, and/or class interests, or to create niche markets!

On the other side, the peoples, *ethnos*, or nations want a just life, one that guarantees their well-being or at least safety and survival. So they work at integrating, even assimilating themselves into the poleis that best serve that purpose (this is an important distinction that will be amplified shortly). They want to be treated as Equals, with the Same respect as everyone else. This is their quest for justice, for public citizenship. Yet they also assert their cultural Differences, sometimes through nationalist and even separatist movements. They may *resist* and even refuse citizenship if it provides no justice or security, or if threatens their identity and self-respect.

As if she has been consorting with the **Furies,** Anzaldúa appropriately states:

> I am visible—see this Indian face—yet I am invisible. I blind them with my beak nose and am their blind spot. But I exist, we exist. They'd like to think I have melted in the pot. But I haven't, we haven't. . . . The whites in power want us people of color to barricade ourselves behind our separate tribal walls so they can pick us off one at a time with their hidden weapons; so that they can whitewash and distort history. Ignorance splits people, creates prejudices. A misinformed people is a subjugated people.[21]

In the paradoxes and interstices of this play of visibilities and invisibilities, of belonging and prejudices, of hidden weapons and distorted history, the necessity of public citizenship begins to appear.

It is not, obviously, an easy task to untangle the manifold relations of power that appear as a simple "us" (Latino/as) against "them" (whites, and Others). After the hegemonic and counterhegemonic dust has settled, that is, after one looks at the socioeconomic status of Latino/a human bodies, there is much to be desired in terms of the effectiveness of explanations, theories, tactics, and strategies. That leaves plenty of gray areas in the complex struggle for justice and public citizenship. For some marginalized populations, aspects of the U.S. polity have proved beneficial. Puerto Rican women used the U.S. Congress to circumvent the island's patriarchal local government and obtain universal suffrage.[22] Cuban exiles received unprecedented moral and material support (even beyond that given to U.S. citizens) to help them become the "golden minority."[23] Many Latino/a gays, known as "sexiles," migrate to the United States because of the homophobia in their countries of origin.[24] Even Mexicans in Mexico (who are usually portrayed as "prickly" nationalists by the media) would favor becoming part of the United States if that meant better living conditions (59 percent of the people, according to a 1991 survey of Mexican people, supported this position).[25]

This could mean that spaces *can* be constructed in the United States where marginalized people can find some justice. It might even mean that the American Dream is alive and well. Or it might mean that the U.S. and Mexican "governments are similar, and people's attitude[s] to each [are] not all that different. . . . Unlike North Americans, Mexicans *can distinguish between nation and state* and know that the interests of the people and the government do not coincide."[26] For example, in his book on the repatriation of half to one million Mexicans, many of whom were U.S. citizens, Hoffman makes the following statement: "Mexicans who crossed their northern border were *looking for a better life, but not necessarily a better citizenship.*"[27]

From the perspective of public citizenship, this is the crux of the matter: looking for a better life *is* looking for a better citizenship, one that fulfills the desires, the physical and moral needs, of the people. Thus Hoffman finds it paradoxical that Mexicans protected themselves by *not* becoming U.S. citizens. The privileges of U.S. citizenship were meaningless in a society where the dominant belief was that "once a Mexican always a Mexican." By remaining a Mexican citizen, one could call on the Mexican consul for assistance and often secure justice. As a U.S. citizen, a Mexican did not understand the courts and was not able to secure as adequate a hearing as she or he could if she or he was a Mexican citizen. The same dynamics would apply to a U.S. American in Mexico.[28] However, proving that the people know their own interests, during the late 1990s millions of Mexicans became U.S. citizens in order to preserve their economic, health, and educational rights, which were being threatened by propositions such as 187 in California.

Of utmost importance for public citizenship, the distinction between the *nation* and the *state* is not, of course, made only by Mexicans. It resonates at the levels of mythology and collective unconscious, with the notion of the Furies, with their striking imagery and vocabulary. These Greek goddesses are responsible for the *ethnos,* the nation-people, tribe, clan, *familia,* the human bodies, and the elements that support their survival: blood, the earth, nature, the economy of the household, and memories of the past, of "what really happened." They protect and avenge the people against the injustices of the city-state, the *polis,* with its preference for civic duty over family allegiance; its tendency to historical amnesia; its tendency toward a justice based on written contracts, constitutions, and abstract laws that are supposed to guarantee the equality of all peoples; and its demand for order and democratic law for the preservation of the *polis* (from where we get our word "polity" or political system).[29]

This opposition *ethnos/polis* has a bearing on current perceptions of Latino/a conservatism, such as interpretations of why Mexican American and Puerto Rican working classes have not supported nationalist, separatist, or independence movements.[30] One hears charges that present-day or previous generations of Latino/as are assimilated, colonized, ignorant, or have false consciousness.[31] And yet, when the U.S. Republican Party attacked immigration and bilingual education, they provoked a pan-Latino/a movement of sorts that cost them many seats in the 1996 elections, including the presidency. To put it bluntly, is it that Latino/as (in this case, Puerto Ricans) "would rather be exploited with some benefits (as in Curaçao and Martinique) than be exploited without any benefits (as in the Dominican Republic and Haiti)?" This "subversive complicity" is, according to Ramón Grosfoguel, the Puerto Rican people's pragmatic rather than utopian strategy "for the protection, deepening, and expansion of the social and democratic rights"[32] or what this essay calls public citizenship. This helps to clarify that the relationship between an *ethnos*-centered strategy and public citizenship is justice. These issues of the apparent conservatism of the masses, and of the opposition between the nation and the state, point once again to the relationship between human beings, the global economy, and the resistance to becoming a commodity. This is a discussion that is becoming increasingly widespread because of its obvious relevance to the survival of the world as we know it.[33]

As for strategies of survival, John Berger observes that peasant conservatism is "a conservatism not of power but of meaning."[34] "What do peasants have to do with a global economy," he asks, and we might add, with Latino/as? Historically, vast social sectors in Puerto Rico have struggled to remain outside of the market. The law known as Ley Libreta of 1849 was one of the instruments used by landholders and the government to force "idle" peasants to work.[35] On January 1, 1994, Mexican Mayan peasants, the Zapatistas, rose up in arms against the Mexican government and the North American Free Trade Agreement (NAFTA). As Tom Barry writes, "The [Mexican] government's commitment to neoliberal macroeconomic policies and free trade had badly shaken the peasantry. Many have rightly concluded that with the Article 27 reforms and NAFTA they are being deleted from the script for Mexico's future."[36] As we enter into a new millennium, we are witnessing another chapter in the peasant Zapatista revolt in Mexico, with a different government for the first time in almost eight decades. We also need to remember that many displaced peoples, due to intervention by U.S. or economic global capitalism, become the refugees, migrants, or exiles of tomorrow. In fact, despite the undeniable importance of working-class Latino/as, many immigrants from Mexico and Puerto Rico already come from peasant cultures. For the sake of comparison, it is important to note that Cuban exiles are the least peasant of all U.S. Latino/as; the material formation of their cultural identity, of *cubanidad,* has been wrapped up with the notion of progress and civilization since the middle of the nineteenth century.[37] At any rate, what is this conservatism of meaning? It is what McMurtry calls the "civil commons," or the underlying life-organization of society.[38] Berger, sounding very much like the Furies, says that "it represents a depository (a granary) of meaning preserved from lives and generations threatened by continual and inexorable change." This meaning becomes important now that the same forces that threaten the peasants threaten all of us:

> Productivity is not reducing scarcity. The dissemination of knowledge is not leading unequivocally to greater democracy. The advent of leisure has not brought personal fulfillment but greater mass manipulation. The economic and military unification of the world has not brought peace but genocide.[39]

Indeed, Eduardo Galeano in *Upside Down: A Primer for the Looking-glass World,* describes in excruciating detail our present world as one where, just like in *Alice in Wonderland,* values have been turned upside down. The last line of his book ends with a suggestion: "Check your local newspaper for an update."[40] Daily newspapers do, in fact, document the enslavement of women and children, the increasing incarceration of (increasingly younger) citizens (in most of the United States a felony is grounds for disenfranchisement) and increasing numbers of death sentences, the income inequalities, the gentrification of low-income neighborhoods, the school push-out rates, regional and international bloody conflicts, and so on. What remains unseen is the insidious fact that many of these "obligatory injustices" (as Galeano calls them) are carried out in the name of freedom.

Faced with the likely future of the "further extension of world capitalism in all its brutalism" or the uncertain victory of a protracted struggle against it, Berger's bleak conclusion is that the peasant experience of survival may be better adapted than the reformist progressive hope of an ultimate victory. In short, ultimately we are all potential peasants, and this is not necessarily an exaggeration. It remains to be seen what, if any, options remain open for everyone's survival once we are confronted with Earth's vital ecological limits.[41]

Perhaps, though, we have not reached the end of history but its return. We seem to have moved back not only two hundred years to war against totalitarianism and, this time, for justice, but also ten thousand years to reconstruct the relationship between the *ethnos* and the *polis:*

> The global market system is a more totalized regime of prescribing how to live than any in history. Its sweeping demands are imposed on societies around the world on a continuous, twenty-four hour basis. Its threats and punishment for violations of its laws exceed in their severity the most punitive of theological fundamentalisms.[42]

In this scheme of things, Latino/as have played the role of the Furies, demanding justice from a *polis* that has mutated from the state(s) to a Global Economy, unable to serve as arbiters if not the protectors of the *ethnos.* This role is demonstrated by Latino/a historical claims of the Right of Self-Preservation against the manipulation of the Law; in their emphasis for the concrete care of the human bodies; in the economic survival and the dignity of the people, through their social, cultural, worker, and political organizations; in their inclusion of differences into a genetic social and political *mestizaje;* in their concern for the environment. Thus, it is no coincidence that Latino/a critiques of theories of justice coincide with those that emphasize care for "disabled lives."[43] Latino/as are not, as they are usually portrayed, just the victims of a vicious system. From the depths of their historical subjugation comes a demand for justice, for the redress of the "durable inequalities"[44] that have continued to this day. While a more precise definition is needed, this demand is embodied in the quest for public citizenship.

Latino/as question the idea of a social contract in which everyone is assumed to be equal and freedom and rationality are understood as being based on maximizing individual interests as opposed to the common good. These are the assumptions that form the basis for the representation of the global market as an absolute, moral, and metaphysical system beyond any questioning. Parting from feminist conceptions of citizenship, for example, Carol Hardy-Fanta echoes the earlier definition of the *polis* in her discussion of traditional, liberal democratic theory according to which a community is narrowly defined as a collection of individuals on a geographical, ethnic basis or as "merely a group of individual interest maximizers." Consequently, citizenship is narrowly defined to mean legal status bestowed upon the individual by the sovereign state and conferring certain rights within the legal/political system . . . as a social contract between the citizen and the state, [under which] the political expression of citizenship is reduced to a limited set of behaviors.[45]

Feminist theories of citizenship are based instead on equality, mutuality, and consensual, face-to-face relationships to develop collectivity while respecting diversity. A Latina feminist vision also calls for the inclusion of groups commonly excluded from the official definition of citizenship: women and immigrants and, especially, "illegal aliens," or rather "undocumented workers." This is, for obvious reasons, of particular interest to Latino/as who attempt to build community on the basis of diversity and, often, the "illegal" status of many members of the community. The key word used by Hardy-Fanta is that these human bodies "do not so much *belong* to a 'found' (or ascribed) community but seek to create a community." This perspective calls for a state that provides an inclusive citizenship.

In addition to a feminist position, there is a remarkable implicit agreement among Latino/as that illustrates the contours of public citizenship. Some of them extend the concept of inclusion within one state to consider peoples who are caught between two or more states. From a Dominican-American perspective:

I have argued in favor of placing primacy on contextual factors influencing migration processes, such as patterns of residence and the legal and political mechanisms existing in both countries. It is difficult to understand how migrants negotiate their existence between two countries and many cultures without analyzing the ongoing communication and relationships that take place across the border, and the ongoing influences of economic and political conditions in both countries.[46]

From a Cuban American position:

Precisely because diaspora communities have had to negotiate their identities in relation to various states and cultures, our experiences may be critical in developing new ways of thinking about multiple identities in which nations (that is, the souls of communities) can survive and states (the mechanisms that control these souls) are transformed.[47]

And from a more personal Cuban American perspective:

For years I felt that I had neatly put away pieces of my identity in different parts of the world, but, more recently, I have come to understand that I need not accept the categories that divide who I am. Instead, I must construct new categories, new political and emotional spaces, *in which my multiple identities can be one.*[48]

According to a Puerto Rican point of view:

The political practice of a radical democratic project would *privilege the improvement of oppressed subjects' quality of life* in the present rather than in a distant future "paradise."

This movement would include a multiplicity of projects to promote and support the struggles of diverse oppressed subjects such as blacks, women, youth, gays, lesbians, and workers.[49]

A Chicano perspective:

> *[T]he globalization of capital, with its power to penetrate and dominate regional markets and undermine native economies,* obliges the Mexican peasant or Guatemalan worker to ignore certain rules and boundaries *in order to survive.* Sentimental loyalty to a particular nation-state and, by extension, that state's idealized "traditional" culture becomes an impoverishing, even life-threatening luxury. To this extent, then, the lived, transcultural experience of *mestizaje* must also be considered transnational and potentially postnational. And policies such as granting voting status to immigrants in school board elections, for example, represent important ways of granting institutional recognition to Latino *mestizaje.*[50]

Public citizenship, it needs to be said, does not mean tribal anarchy or ethnic wars, but the strengthening of the civil society, the reconstruction of democracy *through a democratic process.* Public citizenship includes the interests of human bodies in whatever categories they are placed, their inclusion in the political process that is decision making. It also takes into consideration the relationship between the political economic system and **mestizaje,** meaning the diverse subjectivities, the political, cultural, and personal identities that are simultaneously imposed and expressed. Insofar as it addresses issues of economic inequalities, the notion of public citizenship must include class analysis. For example, in their discussion of Los Angeles as a "Latino Metropolis," Rodolfo Torres and Victor Valle state, "Enlightened pragmatism, not leftist idealism, requires that present and future Latino leaders fashion an industrial and urban policy that transcends *worn-out discourses* of race relations and identity politics."[51] The particular terminology in their call for a reorientation of Latino/a *political discourse,* toward a coherent, long-term *discursive strategy* and for a *discursive umbrella* under which to build coalitions, points to the increasing centrality of the material nature of language in social analyses (see appendixes 3, 4, and 5). This has important implications for the development of counterhegemonic strategies, but it requires an extensive discussion that cannot be included here. The items in such a discussion would include the following:

1. What is the nature of language according to marxist theory? Stalin argues that it is part of neither the base nor the superstructure.[52] This argument, like most conceptions of language, assumes that language is a transparent entity. Arguably, language can be said to have a material existence (in oral tradition as well as written form), with its own weight, history, and transformations and with which humans establish a dialectical relationship. Some consider it the basis for the "public thing," the civil commons, that which exists outside of market forces (at least so far).[53]

2. Despite the postmodern questioning of the existence of the self, the notion of

the sacredness of all life, of humans as moral entities, is found throughout the history of mankind. It is in the nature of language and perhaps of humanity, however, that as old as this knowledge is, it is never fully practiced, never fully implemented. It is part of the Unsaid and the Invisible, those regions from which come What Is Said and What Is Visible. It is from there that we draw our creativity. Or, as the Tao Te Ching (which dates back to the third century B.C.E.) puts it:

> Tao that can be spoken of,
> Is not the Everlasting Tao.
> Name that can be named,
> Is not the Everlasting name.[54]

3. Truth, once it is articulated, is subject to games of power and becomes part of a Discourse, a commodity in the political economy. This realization has led to the questioning of everything that is, was, or has ever been considered a truth as defined by the Enlightenment. And this is where the confusion arises regarding postmodernism and its usefulness as a political strategy. To be anti-essences, to be against "truths" that exclude human beings from exercising their freedom by categorizing them as Others (disabled, ethnics, minorities, illegals, gays, feminists, colored) does not necessarily mean to be against essences that are inclusive, such as the notion of human beings as moral entities, justice, or the oppression of classes.[55]

4. We are faced with a new form of power based on the Nietzschean/Foucauldian notion of the appropriation of values/discourse. This is what makes it possible to construct the global market as an ethical system that guarantees freedom at the cost of destroying all kinds of life forms and ecological systems. It is this enervating microphysics of power that makes class struggle increasingly difficult (see appendix 5).

The history of Latino/a political thought teaches, and the many authors quoted here seem to agree, that the only hope for survival depends, as always, on the *ethnos*, the people, the subjects of civil society or the civil commons. Strategically, that means a focus on public citizenship and a corresponding reconfiguration of (male? Western?) dominant political/economic theory in such a way that the care of the human body and its ecology become the main objective. Tactically, it means to produce public dialogue among individuals across all levels to sort out the mystification that language brings into any struggle for liberation. This will encourage coalitions such as those in the Latino Metropolis of Los Angeles. The goal is to eliminate exclusive categories that make public interest invisible and therefore impossible to protect. Whether or not the category of class is among the "worn-out discourses of race relations and identity politics" depends on how much it actually contributes to public citizenship. The struggle for justice as the care of human bodies and the preservation of all life demands an imaginative use of existing discourses and the invention of new ones. It should be clear by now that the principle of uncertainty reigns over any notion of immutable physical or social laws. As Nietzsche put it, "What sacred games shall we have to invent?"[56]

NOTES AND SUGGESTED READINGS

These reflections are based on my work on Latino/a political thought during a sabbatical from Sonoma State University in the fall of 2000, specifically on research and writing of contextual framing pieces for an anthology/workbook. They represent an expansion of previous postdoctoral work on *Chicanology,* the Logos of, by, and for Chicanos (Francisco H. Vázquez, "Chicanology: A Postmodern Analysis of Meshicano Discourse," *Perspectives in Mexican American Studies* 3 [1992]: 116–47). Similar to Edward Said's notion of "orientalism" (Said, *Orientalism* [New York: Pantheon Books, 1978]), Chicanology is defined as a corporation of knowledge that uses the control of discourse, including the social sciences and the law, to seduce, oppress, discipline, and normalize the discourse of Chicano/a and Latino/a bodies (see appendixes 3, 4, and 5). This situation appears to limit the fight for self-determination to cyclic political movements and intellectual guerrilla warfare for economic, political, and cultural "truths." While Chicanology defines what Chicano/as and Latino/as in general are struggling against, it leaves out a clear consideration of what they are fighting for. That goal now appears to be a quest for "public citizenship." This means a genuinely democratic citizenship based on the needs of human bodies, on human rights and not on the interests of States or dominant classes.

1. John McMurtry, *Unequal Freedoms: The Global Market As an Ethical System* (West Hartford, Conn.: Kumarian, 1998), 279; emphasis added.

2. Francisco H. Vázquez, chapter 5 of this reader.

3. Samuel P. Huntington, "The Clash of Civilizations," *Foreign Affairs* 72, no. 3 (1993): 22–49.

4. Rogers M. Smith, *Civic Ideals: Conflicting Visions of Citizenship in U.S. History* (New Haven: Yale University Press, 1997), 14.

5. The point is made by Roberta Ann Johnson in *Puerto Rico: Commonwealth or Colony?* (New York: Praeger, 1980), 58; emphasis added.

6. Johnson, *Puerto Rico,* 58–59; emphasis added.

7. One of the last actions of exiting president Bill Clinton was to authorize yet another study of the political status of Puerto Rico.

8. Smith, *Civic Ideals,* 13.

9. Richard Griswold del Castillo, *The Treaty of Guadalupe Hidalgo: A Legacy of Conflict* (Norman: University of Oklahoma Press, 1990), 66–69.

10. Griswold del Castillo, *Treaty,* 70–72.

11. See Matthew Frye Jacobson, *Whiteness of a Different Color: European Immigrants and the Alchemy of Race* (Cambridge, Mass.: Harvard University Press, 1998) for a discussion of the factors involved in the subjectification of human bodies to the category of the color white.

12. Jesus de la Teja, ed., *A Revolution Remembered: The Memoirs and Selected Correspondence of Juan N. Seguín* (Austin, Tex.: State House Press, 1991). Rosaura Sánchez, "Constructs of Ethnicity," *Telling Identities: The Californio Testimonios* (Minneapolis: University of Minnesota Press, 1995). Robert J. Rosenbaum, *Mexicano Resistance in the Southwest: The*

Sacred Right of Self-Preservation (Austin: University of Texas Press, 1981). The familiar feeling of "being a stranger in his own land," as Seguín is often quoted, is also found in the Cuban experience. See Louis A. Pérez, *On Becoming Cuban: Identity, Nationality and Culture* (Chapel Hill: University of North Carolina Press, 1999), 136. Regarding Puerto Ricans, the dispossession of the Puerto Rican coffee and sugar plantation owners was one of the first traumatic experiences Puerto Rico suffered as a possession of the U.S. polity. See, for example, Ronald Fernandez, *The Disenchanted Island* (Westport, Conn.: Praeger, 1996), 4–7.

13. Richard Delgado, "Citizenship," in *Immigrants Out! The New Nativism and the Anti-Immigrant Impulse in the United States,* ed. Juan F. Perea (New York: New York University Press, 1997), 318–23.

14. McMurtry, *Unequal Freedoms,* 279.

15. Eduardo Galeano, *Upside Down: A Primer for the Looking-Glass World,* trans. Mark Fried (New York: Metropolitan Books, 200), 25.

16. Juan Antonio Corretjer, *Albizu Campos and the Ponce Massacre* (New York: World View, 1975); Guillermo Flores and Ronald Bailey, "Internal Colonialism and Racial Minorities in the United States: An Overview," in *Structures of Dependency,* ed. Frank Bonilla and Robert Girling (Stanford, Calif.: privately published, 1973), 149–58; Antonio Rios-Bustamante, *Mexicans in the United States and the National Question: Current Polemics and Organizational Positions* (Santa Barbara, Calif.: Editorial La Causa, 1978); Gloria Anzaldúa, *Borderlands La Frontera: The New Mestiza* (San Francisco: Aunt Lute Foundation Book, 1999); Raymund Paredes, "The Origins of Anti-Mexican Sentiment in the United States," in *New Directions in Chicano Scholarship,* ed. R. Romo and R. Paredes, Chicano Studies Monograph Series (San Diego: University of California, San Diego, 1978).

17. Nick C. Vaca, "The Mexican American in the Social Sciences 1912–1970," *El Grito* 4, no. 1 (1970), 17–51.

18. William V. Flores and Rina Benmayor, eds. *Latino Cultural Citizenship: Claiming Identity, Space and Rights* (Boston: Beacon, 1997).

19. Aihua Ong, "Cultural Citizenship As Subject Making: Immigrants Negotiate Racial and Cultural Boundaries in the United States," in *Race, Identity and Citizenship,* ed. Rodolfo D. Torres, Louis F. Mirón, and Jonathan Xavier Inda (Malden, Mass.: Blackwell, 1999), 262–93.

20. John Rawls, *A Theory of Justice* (Cambridge, Mass.: Harvard University Press, 1971). This remains a potentially valid argument despite the questionable assumptions this theory makes in other areas. See for example, Amartya Sen, "Equality of What?" in his *Choice, Welfare and Measurement* (Cambridge, Mass.: MIT Press, 1982), 353–72; Eva Feder Kittay, *Love's Labor: Essays on Women, Equality, and Dependency* (New York: Routledge, 2000); and McMurtry, *Unequal Freedoms.*

21. Gloria Anzaldúa, "La Conciencia de la Mestiza: Towards a New Consciousness," *Borderlands La Frontera: The New Mestiza* (San Francisco: Aunt Lute Foundation Book, 1999), 108.

22. Gladys M. Jiménez-Muñoz, " 'So We Decided to Come and Ask You Ourselves': The 1928 U.S. Congressional Hearings on Women's Suffrage in Puerto Rico," *Puerto Rican Jam: Rethinking Colonialism and Nationalism,* ed. Frances Negrón-Muntaner and Ramón Grosfoguel (Minneapolis: University of Minnesota Press, 1997); Yamila Azize-Vargas, "The Emergence of Feminism in Puerto Rico, 1870–1930," in *Unequal Sisters,* ed. Vicky L. Ruiz and Ellen Carol DuBois, 2d ed. (New York: Routledge, 1994), 260–67.

23. María Cristina García, *Havana USA* (Berkeley: University of California Press, 1996), 29.

24. Ramón Grosfoguel, Frances Negrón-Muntaner, and Chloé S. Georas, "Beyond Nationalist and Colonialist Discourses: The *Jaiba* Politics of the Puerto Rican Ethno-Nation," *Puerto Rican Jam,* ed. Negrón-Muntaner and Grosfoguel, 26.

25. Roger Bartra, *Oficio Mexicano* (Mexico: Editorial Grijalbo, 1993), 93–97.

26. Juan Gómez-Quiñonez, *On Culture* (Los Angeles: University of California, Los Angeles, Chicano Studies Center Publications, 1977), 10; emphasis added.

27. Abraham Hoffman, *Unwanted Mexican Americans in the Great Depression* (Tucson: University of Arizona Press, 1974), 19; emphasis added. For a more extensive discussion of this event, see also the epilogue in Francisco E. Balderrama and R. Rodríguez, *Decade of Betrayal: Mexican Repatriation in the 1930s* (Albuquerque: University of New Mexico Press, 1995).

28. Hoffman, *Unwanted Mexican Americans,* 20.

29. James Hersh, "From *Ethnos* to *Polis,*" *Spring: An Annual of Archetypal Psychology and Jungian Thought* (1985), 56–73.

30. Fred A. Cervantes, "Chicanos As a Post Colonial Minority: Some Questions Concerning the Adequacy of the Paradigm of Internal Colonialism," *Perspectivas en Chicano Studies,* vol. 1, ed. R. Flores Macias (Los Angeles: University California, Los Angeles, Chicano Studies Center, 1977), 123–35; Ramón Grosfoguel, "The Divorce of Nationalist Discourses from the Puerto Rican People," in *Puerto Rican Jam,* ed. Negrón-Muntaner and Grosfoguel, 57–76; and Mariano Negrón-Portillo, "Puerto Rico: Surviving Colonialism and Nationalism," in *Puerto Rican Jam,* ed. Negrón-Muntaner and Grosfoguel, 39–56.

31. See for example the claims that Latino/as in the past have not been very active, in *El Plan De Santa Barbara,* reprint ed. (Santa Barbara: La Causa, 1971) and *The Spanish Land Grant Question Examined* (Albuquerque, N.Mex.: Alianza de los Pueblos Libres, 1966), reprinted in Wayne Moquin, ed., *A Documentary History of the Mexican Americans* (New York: Bantam Books, 1972), 452–53, and discussions of this issue in José E. Limón, "El Primer Congreso Mexicanista de 1911: A Precursor to Contemporary Chicanismo," *Aztlán* 5, nos. 1 and 2 (1974): 85–117, and Mario T. Garcia, *Mexican Americans: Leadership, Ideology, and Identity, 1930–1960* (New Haven, Conn.: Yale University Press, 1989).

32. Ramón Grosfoguel, "The Divorce of Nationalist Discourses from the Puerto Rican People," *Puerto Rican Jam,* ed. Negrón-Muntaner and Grosfoguel, 68–70 passim.

33. There are several ways to approach the historical event that signals the beginning of patriarchy, the state, and the idea of progress. From a mythological perspective, two of them are based on Aeschylus's trilogy of plays, *The Oresteia.* Riane Eisler in *The Chalice and the Blade* (Cambridge, Mass.: Harper and Row, 1987), 78–85, sees it as the denial of full female participation in all aspects of society. As already noted, James Hersh, in "From *Ethnos* to *Polis,*" sees it as the imposition of state rule over independent peoples. The readable novel by Daniel Quinn, *Story of B: An Adventure of the Mind and Spirit* (New York: Bantam, 1996), suggests that totalitarian agriculture allowed one culture to take over others and to replace their two-hundred-thousand-year-old tribal rules with written constitutions intended to provide justice for the diverse peoples contained within the nation-state. The unintended result, he argues, is the current social injustice and ecological crisis. An academic treatment is provided by Kirkpatrick Sale in *Rebels against the Future: The Luddites and Their War on the Industrial Revolution, Lessons for the Computer Age* (New York: Addison-Wesley, 1995). Sale studies this historical confrontation between the values of the human community and the values of a technological society based on progress in terms of the nineteenth-century war of the Luddites against the industrial revolution and notes that this uprising led to the unprecedented militarization of England.

34. John Berger, *Pig Earth* (New York: Vintage International, 1979), xxiii.

35. Mariano Negrón-Portillo, "Surviving Colonialism and Nationalism," *Puerto Rican Jam,* ed. Negrón-Muntaner and Grosfoguel, 52.

36. Tom Barry, *Zapata's Revenge* (Boston: South End, 1995), 233. The amendment to article 27 of the Mexican Constitution ended the land distribution program and opened the way for *ejido* privatization. *Ejido* is a community-based system of land tenure dating back to preconquest times.

37. Louis A. Pérez, *On Becoming Cuban: Identity, Nationality and Culture* (Chapel Hill: University of North Carolina Press, 1999), especially the first two chapters.

38. McMurtry, *Unequal Freedoms,* 26.

39. Berger, *Pig Earth,* xxii-xxvi passim.

40. Galeano, *Upside Down,* 337.

41. A sober look at this possibility is provided by Donella H. Meadows, Dennis L. Meadows, and Jørgen Randers, *Beyond the Limits: Confronting Global Collapse, Envisioning a Sustainable Future* (White River Junction, Vt.: Chelsea Green, 1992).

42. McMurtry, *Unequal Freedoms,* 279.

43. Martha Nussbaum, "Disabled Lives: Who Cares?" *New York Review of Books* 48, no. 1 (January 11, 2001): 34–37.

44. This phrase refers to Charles Tilly, *Durable Inequality* (Berkeley: University of California Press, 1999): "Categorical inequality, in short, has some very general properties. But one of those properties, paradoxically, is to vary in practical operation with the historically accumulated understandings, practices, and social relations already attached to a given set of distinctions" (12).

45. Carol Hardy-Fanta, *Latina Politics/Latino Politics: Gender, Culture and Political Participation in Boston* (Philadelphia: Temple University Press, 1993), 99.

46. Pamela M. Graham, "The Politics of Incorporation: Dominicans in New York City," *Latino Studies Journal* 9, no. 3 (fall 1998), 59.

47. María de los Angeles Torres, *In the Land of Mirrors: Cuban Exile Politics in the United States* (Ann Arbor: University of Michigan Press, 1999), 196–97.

48. De los Angeles Torres, *In the Land of Mirrors,* 199; emphasis added.

49. Ramón Grosfoguel, "The Divorce of Nationalist Discourses from the Puerto Rican People," *Puerto Rican Jam,* ed. Negrón-Muntaner and Grosfoguel, 73; emphasis added.

50. Victor M. Valle and Rodolfo D. Torres, *Latino Metropolis* (Minneapolis: University of Minnesota Press, 2000), 189–90; emphasis added.

51. Valle and Torres, *Latino Metropolis,* 180; emphasis added.

52. J. V. Stalin, *Marxism and Problems of Linguistics* (Peking: Foreign Language Press, 1972).

53. McMurtry, *Unequal Freedoms,* 26.

54. Ellen M. Chen, *The Tao Te Ching* (New York: Paragon House, 1989).

55. Charles Spinosa and Hubert L. Dreyfus, "Two Kinds of Antiessentialism and Their Consequences," *Critical Inquiry* 22 (summer 1996), 735–63.

56. Friedrich Nietzsche, *The Gay Science,* quoted in Patricia Ewick and Susan S. Silby, *The Common Place of Law: Stories from Everyday Life* (Chicago: University of Chicago Press, 1998), 136.

✳   ✳   ✳

QUESTIONS

1. Are there any problems conceiving of the global market as *one* ethical system that uses the notion of "freedom" as a tool for dominations, as opposed to seeing it as created by business decisions that are innocently made by thousands of business people?

2. If Latino/a and Anglo Americans both started out fighting for independence, freedom, and justice, what conditions allowed the latter to become a world power?

3. Are there any conditions under which democracy should be restricted to certain people within a polis or a society?

4. How appropriate is it to apply mythological concepts like *ethnos* and *polis* to present-day political experiences of Latino/as in the United States?

5. What might the United States (or the world) look like if it was based on the care of human bodies and ecology as opposed to the wedded notions of rationality and self-interest? Under what conditions might a new political system be built?

Carved Out of Language: Literary and Historical Discourses

In the previous section, we discussed three perspectives on Latino/a political thought. While we make no attempt to emphasize one over another, it can be argued that all three involve the materiality of language. As noted in the "Introduction for Students," this means that language, as it intersects power and becomes a discourse, functions much like a mountain, river, or forest. It determines to a large extent what can and cannot be said, where we can and cannot go. Carved out of language, therefore, is our history of struggles against the categories that define us as this or that kind of human being. In the first selection, *I Am Joaquín*, Rodolfo "Corky" Gonzales does precisely that kind of carving. He presents a minihistory of a people's struggle, a material memory that reaches back to Aztecs and the Spanish conquest and brings us back to the present struggle against dehumanization. He also addresses a question that pervades this reader: who are we? It is difficult not to conclude from his poem that we are our best friends and our worst enemies.

The poem ends with the words "I shall endure! I will endure!" These words point to another reality that Francisco H. Vázquez discusses in the next selection, "América's Patriots Then and Now," one that is also carved out of language: an unfulfilled quest, an unkept promise, a contract that remains to be enforced. This contract was about social justice for all the inhabitants of the New World. This was a social contract made by Latino/a Americans as well as English Americans. It is in this context that Eduardo Galeano has said that America has yet to be discovered (in the Latino/a imaginary, "America" refers to the continent, not the United States). Again we deal with the question of who we are: does the concept of "we the people" include human bodies categorized as "pelados" and the "meaner sort"? When we realize that these identities, these subjectivities, also seem to be carved out of language we also confront the magnitude of the struggle for social justice.

✳ 4 ✳
I AM JOAQUÍN: AN EPIC POEM (1967)

Rodolfo "Corky" Gonzales

In the poem *I Am Joaquín*, Corky provides a historical context and illustrates the Mexican experience from the Spanish conquest to the present-day United States. But unwittingly, he does more than that, because the struggle against the Spanish and later against U.S. cultural domination is also an integral part of the political experience of Puerto Ricans and Cubans. Indeed, this poem contains statements of particular relevance to Latino/a political thought. One is on the multiple identities of Joaquín; he is both the oppressed and the oppressor. This statement points to the fact that Latino/as can be found anywhere in the political spectrum and, consequently, that Latino/a political thought can also be found anywhere among extreme **right, left,** or **center.** This is important for understanding Latino/a political thought because there is a tendency to attribute a particular essence to Latino/as. In effect, this reader itself might create the impression that Latino/as are "a bunch of revolutionaries" and discontents or a conservative lot. This suggests another aspect of the poem that is worth discussing. The emphasis of this reader is on the quest for citizenship and the "expectation for a better life" on the part of the masses of Latino/as who, due to historical circumstances, became born-again U.S. Americans. Finally, this poem speaks to the ethnic diversity within the Mexican and Latino/a peoples.

＊　　＊　　＊

I am Joaquín
Lost in a world of confusion,
Caught up in a whirl of a
    gringo society,
Confused by the rules,
Scorned by attitudes,
Suppressed by manipulations,
And destroyed by modern society.
My fathers
    have lost the economic battle
and won
    the struggle of cultural survival.
And now!
    I must choose
Between the paradox of
Victory of the spirit,
despite physical hunger
        Or
    to exist in the grasp
of American social neurosis,
sterilization of the soul
    and a full stomach.
Yes,
I have come a long way to nowhere,
Unwillingly dragged by that
    monstrous, technical
    industrial giant called
        Progress
and Anglo success . . .
    I look at myself.

I watch my brothers.
I shed tears of sorrow.
I sow seeds of hate.
I withdraw to the safety within the
circle of life . . .
MY OWN PEOPLE
I am Cuauhtémoc,
Proud and Noble
Leader of men,
King of an empire,
civilized beyond the dreams
of the Gachupín Cortez.
Who is also the blood,
the image of myself.
I am the Maya Prince.
I am Nezahualcóyotl,
Great leader of the Chichimecas.
I am the sword and flame of Cortez
the despot.
And
I am the Eagle and Serpent of
the Aztec civilization.
I owned the land as far as the eye
could see under the crown of Spain,
and I toiled on my earth
and gave my Indian sweat and blood
for the Spanish master,
Who ruled with tyranny over man and
beast and all that he could trample
But . . .
THE GROUND WAS MINE . . .
I was both tyrant and slave.
As Christian church took its place
in God's good name,
to take and use my Virgin Strength and
Trusting faith,
The priests
both good and bad
took
But
gave a lasting truth that
Spaniard,
Indio,
Mestizo

Were all God's children
And
   from these words grew men
     who prayed and fought
            for
their own worth as human beings
   for
     that
       GOLDEN MOMENT
       of
       FREEDOM.
I was part in blood and spirit
   of that
     courageous village priest
               Hidalgo
in the year eighteen hundred and ten
who rang the bell of independence
and gave out that lasting cry:
   "El Grito de Dolores, Que mueran
   los Guachupines y que viva
   la Virgen de Guadalupe . . ."
I sentenced him
     who was me.
I excommunicated him my blood.
I drove him from the pulpit to lead
   a bloody revolution for him and me . . .
     I killed him.
His head,
   which is mine and all of those
   who have come this way,
I placed on that fortress wall
   to wait for independence.
Morelos!
   Matamoros!
    Guerrero!
All Compañeros in the act,
STOOD AGAINST THAT WALL OF
                  INFAMY
to feel the hot gouge of lead
   which my hand made.
I died with them . . .
   I lived with them
     I lived to see our country free.

Free
   from Spanish rule in
   eighteen-hundred-twenty-one.
     Mexico was free ? ?
The crown was gone
    but
all his parasites remained
       and ruled
       and taught
   with gun and flame and mystic power.
I worked,
I sweated,
I bled,
I prayed
   and
waited silently for life to again
               commence.
I fought and died
     for
    Don Benito Juárez
Guardian of the Constitution.
I was him
  on dusty roads
    on barren land
as he protected his archives
   as Moses did his sacraments.
He held his Mexico
    in his hand
       on
     the most desolate
     and remote ground
     which was his country,
And this Giant
    Little Zapotec
gave
  not one palm's breath
of his country to
   Kings or Monarchs or Presidents
   of foreign powers.
I am Joaquín.
I rode with Pancho Villa,
   crude and warm.
A tornado at full strength,
nourished and inspired

by the passion and the fire
of all his earthy people.
I am Emiliano Zapata.
   "This Land
     This Earth
      is
        OURS"
The Villages
  The Mountains
   The Streams
    belong to the Zapatistas.
     Our Life
Or yours
is the only trade for soft brown earth
and maize.
All of which is our reward,
  A creed that formed a constitution
   for all who dare live free!
"this land is ours . . .
  Father, I give it back to you.
   Mexico must be free . . ."
I ride with Revolutionists
          against myself.
I am Rural
  Coarse and brutal,
I am the mountain Indian,
   superior over all.
The thundering hoofbeats are my horses.
The chattering of machine guns
is death to all of me:
  Yaqui
   Tarahumara
    Chamula
     Zapotec
      Mestizo
       Español
I have been the Bloody Revolution,
The Victor,
The Vanquished,
I have killed
  and been killed.
  I am despots Díaz
  and Huerta
and the apostle of democracy
  Francisco Madero

I am
the black shawled
faithful women
who die with me
or live
depending on the time and place.
I am
  faithful,
    humble,
      Juan Diego
      the Virgin de Guadalupe
Tonantzin, Aztec Goddess too.
I rode the mountains of San Joaquín.
I rode as far East and North
  as the Rocky Mountains
    and
all men feared the guns of
      Joaquín Murrieta.
I killed those men who dared
  to steal my mine,
    who raped and Killed
        my love
        my Wife

Then
I Killed to stay alive.
I was Alfego Baca,
  living my nine lives fully.
I was the Espinosa brothers
  of the Valle de San Luis
All
were added to the number of heads
that
  in the name of civilization
were placed on the wall of independence.
Heads of brave men
who died for cause and principle.
Good or Bad.
    Hidalgo! Zapata!
      Murrieta! Espinosa!
are but a few.
They
dared to face
The force of tyranny
        of men
        who rule
    By farce and hypocrisy

I stand here looking back,
and now I see
        the present
and still
    I am the campesino
    I am the fat political coyote
                    I,
of the same name,
                    Joaquín.
In a country that has wiped out
all my history,
                    stifled all my pride.
In a country that has placed a
different weight of indignity upon
                    my
                    age
                    old
                    burdened back.
            Inferiority
is the new load . . .
    The Indian has endured and still
emerged the winner,
    The Mestizo must yet overcome,
    And the Gauchupín we'll just ignore.
I look at myself
and see part of me
who rejects my father and my mother
and dissolves into the melting pot
    to disappear in shame.
        I sometimes
        sell my brother out
and reclaim him
for my own, when society gives me
    token leadership
        in society's own name.
I am Joaquín,
who bleeds in many ways.
The altars of Moctezuma
                    I stained a bloody red.
    My back of Indian slavery
        was stripped crimson
    from the whips of masters
    who would lose their blood so pure
    when Revolution made them pay

Standing against the walls of
   Retribution.
     Blood . . .
   Has flowed from
     me
on every battlefield
     between
Campesino, Hacendado
   Slave and Master
     and
   Revolution.
I jumped from the tower of Chapultepec
   into the sea of fame;
My country's flag
   my burial shroud;
With Los Niños,
     whose pride and courage
could not surrender
     with indignity
     their country's flag
To strangers . . . in their land.
Now
   I bleed in some smelly cell
     from club,
     or gun,
     or tyranny,
I bleed as the vicious gloves of hunger
   cut my face and eyes,
as I fight my way from stinking Barrios
   to the glamour of the Ring
     and lights of fame
       or mutilated sorrow.
My blood runs pure on the ice caked
hills of the Alaskan Isles,
on the corpse strewn beach of Normandy,
the foreign land of Korea
              and now
              Vietnam.
Here I stand
      before the court of Justice
        Guilty
for all the glory of my Raza
      to be sentenced to despair.
Here I stand
   Poor in money

Arrogant with pride
  Bold with Machismo
  Rich in courage
      and
    Wealthy in spirit and faith.
My knees are caked with mud.
My hands calloused from the hoe.
I have made the Anglo rich
      yet
  Equality is but a word,
  the Treaty of Hidalgo has been broken
  and is but another treacherous promise.
My land is lost
      and stolen,
My culture has been raped,
    I lengthen
  the line at the welfare door
and fill the jails with crime.
    These then
are the rewards
        this society has
For sons of Chiefs
        and Kings
        and bloody Revolutionists.
Who
gave a foreign people
    all their skills and ingenuity
to pave the way with Brains and Blood
for
those hordes of Gold starved
Strangers
Who
changed our language
and plagiarized our deeds
              as feats of valor
              of their own.
They frowned upon our way of life
and took what they could use.
    Our Art
    Our Literature
    Our Music, they ignored
so they left the real things of value
and grabbed at their own destruction
      by their Greed and Avarice

They overlooked that cleansing fountain of
        nature and brotherhood
Which is Joaquín.
    The art of our great señores
        Diego Rivera
        Siqueiros
        Orozco is but
another act of revolution for
the Salvation of mankind.
    Mariachi music, the
    heart and soul
    of the people of the earth,
    the life of child,
    and the happiness of love.
    The Corridos tell the tales
    of life and death,
        of tradition,
    Legends old and new,
    of Joy
        of passion and sorrow
    of the people . . . who I am.
I am in the eyes of woman,
        sheltered beneath
her shawl of black,
        deep and sorrowful
        eyes,
That bear the pain of sons long buried
        or dying,
        Dead
on the battlefield or on the barbed wire
        of social strife.
Her rosary she prays and fingers
endlessly
    like the family
working down a row of beets
        to turn around
        and work
        and work
        There is no end.
Her eyes a mirror of all the warmth
        and all the love for me,
And I am her
And she is me.
    We face life together in sorrow,
    anger, joy, faith and wishful
    thoughts.

I shed tears of anguish
as I see my children disappear
behind a shroud of mediocrity
never to look back to remember me.
I am Joaquín.
     I must fight
     And win this struggle
     for my sons, and they
     must know from me
     Who I am.
Part of the blood that runs deep in me
Could not be vanquished by the Moors.
I defeated them after five hundred years.
and I endured.
     The part of blood that is mine
     has labored endlessly five-hundred
     years under the heel of lustful
        Europeans
        I am still here!
I have endured in the rugged mountains
     of our country.
I have survived the toils and slavery
     of the fields.
        I have existed
in the barrios of the city,
in the suburbs of bigotry,
in the mines of social snobbery,
in the prisons of dejection,
in the muck of exploitation
and
in the fierce heat of racial hatred.
And now the trumpet sounds,
The music of the people stirs the
        Revolution,
Like a sleeping giant it slowly
rears its head
to the sound of
          Tramping feet
         Clamoring voices
        Mariachi strains
      Fiery tequila explosions
    The smell of chile verde and
Soft brown eyes of expectation for a
              better life.

And in all the fertile farm lands,
                    the barren plains,
the mountain villages,
smoke smeared cities
            We start to MOVE.
    La Raza!
Mejicano!
    Español!
        Latino!
            Hispano!
                Chicano!
or whatever I call myself,
            I look the same
            I feel the same
            I Cry
                and
            Sing the same
I am the masses of my people and
I refuse to be absorbed.
            I am Joaquín
The odds are great
but my spirit is strong
                    My faith unbreakable
                    My blood is pure
I am Aztec Prince and Christian Christ.
            I SHALL ENDURE!
            I WILL ENDURE!

            ✳   ✳   ✳

QUESTIONS

1. Are there any images in this poem that represent a particular subjectivity, stereotype, or political position?

2. In what sense is it possible to "lose" the economic battle and "win" the struggle for cultural survival? Is there an assumption here about the definition of culture?

3. Consider the notions the author connects in the passage, "a lasting truth that/ Spaniard/ Indian/ Mestizo/ were all God's children/ And/ from these words grew men/ who prayed and fought/ for/ their own worth as human beings." Is there an implicit assumption here about the connection between religion and politics?

4. After reviewing the history of Mexican human bodies, Joaquín concludes that in the present he has "a different weight of indignity" upon his age-old-burdened back. What different interpretations can be deduced from this statement? In the final analysis, is Joaquín a victim or a victor?

5. According to Joaquín, the social problems experienced by Chicanos also threaten "the salvation of

mankind." What might these threats be and does the poem provide an adequate connection between a concern for a specific group of people and all humans?

✳ 5 ✳
AMÉRICA'S PATRIOTS THEN AND NOW: ANTICOLONIAL STRUGGLES AND LATINO/A POLITICAL THOUGHT

Francisco Hernández Vázquez

In this text, Francisco uses a comparative framework to explore the political evolution of English Americans and Spanish Americans. Both peoples share a common history of struggle, against the British and Spanish crowns, respectively. Concepts like nation, class, **sovereignty,** natural law, will of the people, constitution, and revolution (as in their declarations of independence), as well as political and economic institutions, were used by both peoples to construct their respective national identities. As Americans and as *americanos,* they both fought for freedom and the right for self-determination, but unfortunately their quests did not include justice for all. Today, almost three centuries later, the struggle for social justice continues. It is precisely against this background of anticolonial struggles that one can best appreciate the important political role played by Puerto Ricans, Mexican Americans, Cuban Americans, and other ethnic minorities.

If you are willing to have help of a kind and have no real voice in the government of the nation to which you are appended, why, then, that is one thing. If I were a Puerto Rican that would not satisfy me, just as it did not satisfy Washington, Thomas Jefferson, and Simón Bolívar.

—Senator Millard Tydings, Senate Committee on
Territories and Insular Affairs

Often, writings about U.S. Latinos refer to the relation between the colonizer (the United States) and the colonized (Mexicans, Puerto Ricans, Cubans, and others). There is a story that is helpful to understanding Latino/a political thought as part of a historical struggle for social justice, what we might call a quest for public citizenship. That is the account of how humans in the American continent changed their status from subjects of kings to members (not all necessarily citizens) of nation-states during a very important half century of wars of independence (1775–1825). In other words, how did indigenous people, (sub-Saharan) African slaves, Europeans born in the Americas (or in Europe), and Asians come to share identities as either (U.S.) Americans or (Latin American) *Americano/as*? And how does this process shed light on the understanding of the political experience of Puerto Ricans, Cuban Americans, and Chicano/as? Are the militant members of these ethnic groups modern-day patriots and *insurgentes* who follow the words of the U.S. Declaration of Independence?

> But when a long train of abuses and usurpations, pursuing invariably the same Object, evinces a design to reduce them under absolute Despotism, it is their right, it is their duty, to throw off such Government, and to provide new Guards for their future security.

Or are they rabble-rousers who misjudge "When in the Course of human events, it becomes necessary for one people to dissolve the political bands which have connected them with another"? After all, Cuba broke away from the United States, but Cuban Americans seem content to be American citizens. And who exactly are "one people," or better yet the "We the people" mentioned in the preamble to the U.S. Constitution?

FROM OPPRESSED SUBJECTS TO
ENLIGHTENED CITIZENS

Once upon a time (in the latter part of the eighteenth century) Spanish and English Americans actually had some things in common. They were subjects of their respective monarchs, Fernando VII and George III. And, based on their own political traditions and experiences, they both applied the ideas of the Enlightenment to "shed light" on the tyranny of church and monarchies. Among these ideas are that Law and Rights can be derived from a rational observation of Nature and that our knowledge is not necessarily limited to revelations from God. This belief in natural law led to concepts such as Rights of Man and All Men Are Created Equal (these are the self-evident truths and unalienable rights in the U.S. Declaration of Independence). It also led to the idea of freedom: of political institutions, religion, and trade, the belief in which was then known as liberalism. These concepts had developed over hundreds of years to oppose the notion that God had given the kings or queens the Divine Right to rule over their subjects and do with them (or to them) as they desired.[1]

A key point of liberalism was that sovereignty (the power to control a country, a people, and everything in it) resides in "the will of the people." But if will is not something you can see or touch, how do you embody this will? That is where congresses and assemblies come in; they are "political bodies" that speak for "the people." As you will see in the readings, Mexican Americans, Cubans, and Puerto Ricans also make use of this process of representing the will of the people through political bodies in order to assert their own self-determination or to question the sovereignty of the United States. The problem is one of representation: if sovereignty resides in the people but only one class of people (say property owners) makes up the congress or assembly, then who speaks for the propertyless? If only men, who speaks for women? In some cases, the upper or middle classes have to convince the "lower" classes to fight for the interests of the "ruling" class. Who, then, speaks for the "lower" classes? And if anyone does, how is this "voice" categorized as legitimate or illegitimate? Thus, the definition of the will of the people remains a major problem to this day. At the time of this writing, the fall 2000, one of the key issues in the presidential election in the United States was which candidate represented the interests of the people as opposed to the interests of the corporations.

Not surprisingly, the political thought of the ruling classes is based on practical matters. And here, too, we find similarities among those who assumed the voice of the people in the Spanish and English American colonies. At first, they were loyal to their kings: they both wanted to remain part of their respective empires; they just wanted to be treated as equals with other provinces and peoples within their respective empires. Secondly, what they wanted was to protect their own class interests: they both opposed the increase in taxation and the protection of the Indians by the British or Spanish kings.[2]

However, in a fifty-year period, roughly from 1775 to 1825, these two peoples changed their political status from colonial subjects to sovereign, independent nations with their own qualifications for citizenship. To compare the paths that Spanish and English American revolutionaries took, we will view three key ingredients in nation making: national identity, economic and political institutions, and economic and political processes. As you discover while reading the newspaper, these are at play not only in Latino or U.S. American political thought, but in politics all over the world (including your neighborhood). More specifically, throughout this reader, we will see them playing a role in the making of Chicano, Cuban, and Puerto Rican identities and in discussions of nationalism.

FROM ENGLISH SUBJECTS TO "WE THE PEOPLE"

The demographics of a nation, the number and "kinds" of people, are important not only because they show the relations of power between the rich and the masses (the class structure), but also because they show the contradictions between the ideal that all men are created equal and the reality of women and men who are left with only the quest for equality and justice, that is, for public citizenship. Let us fly to the English colonies in 1665 and see the makeup of the people. If we asked the man in the street, he would say that there are five separate "sorts" of men: (1) the "better sort" (large landholders, crown officials, merchants, and allied lawyers and professionals); (2) the "middling sort" (small landholders, independent artisans, shopkeepers, petty officials, and professional men of lesser pretensions); (3) the "meaner sort" (a category of free but depressed men who were laborers, servants, dependent artisans, sailors, unprosperous farmers, and nondescript drifters; (4) the bonded white servants, an even meaner sort who served some master under an indenture limited in time; (5) and the very lowest elements in society, the freed (sub-Saharan) Africans. Only the first two took part in the process of self-government, due to the belief that only people with property possessed the independence necessary to participate in political life. The best estimate that can be made of the different nationalities living in the colonies in 1765 are English, 65–70 percent; Scots and Scotch-Irish, 12–15 percent; Germans, 6–9 percent; and all others, 3–5 percent. Out of a total population of 1.45 million, four hundred thousand (21 percent) were so-called Negroes or mulattoes.[3]

The concept of "people" did not include all human bodies. Women (bodies without a penis) were not part of the body politic. Another one of these groups was the "Indians" (unlike the French and the Spanish, the English were not interested in converting "Indians" to Christianity or entering into mixed marriages). African slaves were not included, first because they were defined as property, not humans, and later because of their race/color. A fourth group of humans defined as "ethnics" was also excluded. The term "ethnic" initially arose in Puritan writings to signify traits or individuals diverging from the Christian narrative, or for heathens (including not only American Indians but also Dutch and Germans).[4] As this reader illustrates, the exclusion of "ethnics" continues to play an important role in contemporary U.S. politics.

Though made up of diverse groups like the Separatists, the Presbyterians, and the Congregationalists, all Puritans shared the nearly fanatical belief that God had determined the outcome of history and that they were the soldiers of Christ, the chosen people destined to build a society that would serve as an example to the rest of the world.

The year 1775, the beginning of the Revolutionary War, finds the English American colonists enjoying an economic boom and already envisioning their expansion throughout the continent in the coming century as their "manifest destiny." At that time the financial difference between the poorest and richest English/European American was probably the smallest such difference of any in the world. It was easy to move from one class to the next and especially from both directions into the middle. Furthermore, European Americans were beginning to assert the value of individuality over the demands of group identity.[5]

As we will see repeatedly, class structure is very important because it indicates the degree of cohesion and stability of the population in a given nation. In effect, the English American colonists were able to successfully fight a war of independence against England for several reasons. Among these is that the American-born Europeans in the British colonies were the majority of the population. They also did not have to worry about an Indian uprising (the Indians were divided by intertribal hostilities) or, with very few exceptions, a slave rebellion (slaves were 20 percent of the population, 90 percent of whom lived in the South; whites outnumbered blacks in all the colonies except South Carolina, which was next to Spanish Florida, a haven for runaway slaves). The unique class stratification in the English American colonies helps to explain why the concept of class struggle is fairly absent from U.S. political discourse. This does not mean the colonists did not have class conflict.

Political practice and institutions are the third key ingredient in nation making. For the English Americans, a tradition of self-governance, as well as the practice of political opposition, provided a continuation from the British tradition of representative government. English Americans built on these political technologies through strong political participation in colonial government. Although, as we already noted, this participation was limited to those humans who fit the definition of "better" or "middling" sort, that is, those with property, there is an important lesson here about how people become political. John Adams noted in 1766 that, "The people, even to the lowest ranks, have become more attentive to their liberties, more inquisitive about them, and more determined to defend them, than they were ever before known or had occasion to be."[6] Adams attributed this awakened political consciousness among the poor to the English Parliament's Stamp Act, the first direct tax imposed by Britain on its American colonies to help cover the cost of maintaining troops in the colonies. Since the English colonists did not have representation in Parliament, they argued that this was taxation without representation. There are parallels here with Puerto Ricans, who have no voting representation in the U.S. Congress (and thus pay no federal taxes) and U.S. Mexicans in California, who "became more attentive to their liberties" by becoming U.S. citizens after the passing of Proposition 187, which denied benefits to the undocumented.

It is ironic that, after independence, the English Americans still lacked a sense of nationhood. Because of their emphasis on local government, they still thought of themselves as members of thirteen different states, not as "Americans."[7] Instead of developing national institutions, the founding fathers went back to their respective colonies or states. These served as laboratories for political experiments in the form of new political technologies that we now take for granted, like writing down and publishing the contract between the people and the government, that is, the constitution for each state. Here again we see that outside events forced upon them a national political Identity. Among these were difficult relations with Spain, discontent among the colonies, and the 1786 Daniel Shays Rebellion (in which two thousand farmers organized an illegal convention and rebelled against the government of Massachusetts—so there was class struggle!).

While the Declaration of Independence refers to *these* United States, the U.S. Constitution begins with the well-known phrase, "We the People of the United States." Here we have the sense of nationhood, if not nationalism, represented by the U.S. Constitution. But more than a symbol, the Constitution embodies the political institutions, the frameworks that will allow for future power struggles regarding the definition and interpretation of key concepts like "people," "men," "equality," and from the preamble, "justice," "general Welfare," and "Blessings of Liberty," among others. In other words, the Constitution is an institutionalization of the quest for public citizenship as defined by changing political realities, by games of truth. Indeed, to understand political thought, Latino/a or not, you would do well to keep your eye on the making of political institutions. Such institutions were the stepping-stones that led English American revolutionaries to change their status from subjects to citizens and to consolidate their **nation-state** as the United States of America between 1789 and 1830.

FROM SPANISH SUBJECTS TO THE COSMIC RACE

Let us briefly compare the English American political evolution with that of the Spanish colonies in the Americas, with a focus on New Spain (later known as the United States of Mexico) and specifically on northern Mexico.

Unlike the homogeneous, cultural, and racial identity that the English colonists developed through a policy of exclusion during one and a half centuries, the inhabitants of the Spanish colonies had evolved for three hundred years into a multicultural, multiracial society, a "Cosmic Race" according to the Mexican philosopher José Vasconcelos. Humans in New Spain were categorized into different groups. There were *peninsulares* (born in the Iberian Peninsula, that is Spain), **criollos** (Spaniards born in the Americas), indigenous people, and *castas* (descendants of mixed marriages among the three, plus Asians and Africans). In 1793 Mexico, close to the time of the war for independence, there were 3,799,561 inhabitants, of which 61 percent were indigenous, 11 percent mestizos, less than 1 percent blacks, 10 percent mulattoes, less than 1 percent Spanish, and 18 percent criollos (no figures are available for Asian Mexicans).[8] Unlike the English colonies, here only 20 percent were Europeans. And even the criollo category is open to question, because many mestizos obtained *Cédulas de Gracias al Sacar,* or certificates of whiteness. In the rest of Latin America and the Caribbean, the proportion of blacks was much greater than in the United States (half of the Brazilian population and about one third of Cuba, compared with 12 percent for the United States).[9]

What do demographics have to do with politics? Unlike their English American counterparts (who simply excluded Indians and blacks) the Spanish American revolutionaries had to take into account class and race in their struggle for independence. The relationship between demographics and politics also played a major role in the 1820s, when Anglos became the majority in east and central Texas (see chapter 6), and in the year 2000, when Latinos become political players due to their population growth.

In Mexico, in terms of social categories comparable to the English colonies, there were (1) the royal officials (the governing class, considered a foreign elite); (2) the great magnates (the largest merchants and owners of mines, haciendas, and textiles with primary interest in the colony); (3) the secondary elite (well-educated professionals; they also engaged in enterprises like food processing, bakeries, pulque processing plants, cattle raising, and markets); (4) the small bourgeoisie (owners of small ranchos, mule trains, inns, stores; they considered themselves middle class, or *gente decente*); (5) the artisan class (who identified with their social superiors and tended to own very little property other than their tools); (6) the workers (the most numerous, who generally owned no property and relied entirely on their earnings); and (7) the *léperos,* meaning "the destitute and indecent," the homeless and unemployed (a floating criminal class or a marginal labor force depending on your point of view). Keep in mind that all ethnic groups (with the exception of blacks and the royal officials) could be found in each of these social classes.[10] Thus, at this point in history, it appears that the Spanish Americans were more open to diversity than their English American counterparts. But there is more to the story.

The Spanish American colonies were divided into four viceroyalties: New Spain (what is now the Southwest of the United States, Mexico, Central America, Cuba, Puerto Rico, and the rest of the Caribbean), New Granada (what is now Colombia and Panama), Peru, and La Plata (what is now Argentina, Bolivia, Paraguay, and Uruguay). This social and economic diversity and the enormous territory it encompassed (from the tip of South America to what is now the U.S. Southwest) led to three different revolutions. In Mexico, the criollos started the movement toward revolution but did not have economic power or political institutions to maintain it, so they had to appeal to popular support.[11] Consequently, the revolution included the demand for the liberation of the indigenous people and the slaves and for agrarian reform; but due to the circumstances, it later had to compromise with the landowning criollos, the military, and the Church on its demands for social justice. In Greater Colombia, the revolution began as a movement of the upper class criollos. But they had to deal with the mulattoes' demands for social equality and include them in the war for independence in order to win the war. (A similar situation took place in the Cuban revolution almost one hundred years later.) In Chile and Argentina there was no social content of importance in the revolution, which was carried out by the upper classes. They were able to get the support of the masses without making many concessions.[12]

What about Cuba and Puerto Rico? The great South American revolutionary Simón Bolívar had plans to extend the Spanish American wars of independence to them until the U.S. government made clear their opposition to the independence of these countries from Spain.[13] As a result, they continued to be colonies of Spain until 1900, when the United States took them over. Cuba got its freedom with the revolution of Fidel Castro; Puerto Rico remains, in the year 2000, the oldest colony in the world.

The movements for liberation started toward the end of the eighteenth century, when the Spanish king, like his English counterpart, increased taxes to pay for the wars among the European monarchies. This had the same impact on the Spanish colonies as the Stamp Act on the English colonies. To be sure, there was significant economic growth and the king wanted part of it, but there was also a tremendous population growth that created a huge gap between the rich and the poor. This created a dislocation among the castes—the laboring classes—making them more politically conscious and aware of their oppression, and at the same time established their identity as *Americanos*. Under these circumstances, the game of truth for the criollos was to have a revolution that would give them political equality with the peninsulares. But they were afraid that Indians, blacks, and primarily, the mestizos, who were a growing majority, would push the revolution beyond its political goals toward social and economic changes that would negatively impact their own privilege. But there is more to this fear than class-struggle concerns.

Unlike that of their English counterparts, the criollo revolutionary enthusiasm was tempered by reaction to the excesses of the French Revolution known as the

Reign of Terror (1793–94), when French mobs executed thousands of people for political reasons. Closer to home, in 1804 Haiti became the first Latin American colony to gain its independence, when African slaves overthrew the French. This created a fear of black uprisings throughout Latin America, depending on blacks' proportion to the total population. This fear continued to play an important role in the development of national identity in Cuba, where by 1846 the population was 44 percent white and 56 percent black.[14] So once again we are faced with the question of "who are the people?"

Criollos and mestizos in New Spain, who identified themselves as Mexicans, distinguished themselves as historians, scientists, and philosophers who were full participants in the modern age. Politically, they delved into the Spanish legal tradition regarding the consent of the governed (established at the time of the conquest) and notions of natural law and right, liberty, common good, and general welfare.[15] Their objective was to prove that, since the Spanish king had been deposed by Napoleon, sovereignty (the supreme power to rule) reverted to the people. In an assembly called by the viceroy to discuss this very issue, judge Aguirre, a peninsular loyal to the king and against the notion of "power to the people," asked the presenter, lawyer Verdad, what he meant by "people." Verdad hesitated and then answered, "the constituted authorities."

> Then Aguirre, "replying, in turn, that those authorities were not the people, called the attention of the viceroy and of the junta to the original people to whom, upon the principles advanced by the official, the sovereignty ought to revert; but he went no further in clarifying this concept . . . because the governors of the Indian settlements were present, among them a descendant of the emperor Moctezuma.[16]

This incident illustrates the politics of definitions and interpretations that in this reader we call games of truths. El Grito de Independencia (the cry for independence) of September 15, 1810, however, added a new dimension to the question of who are the people. On that day, the Indians, workers, *léperos,* and small bourgeoisie took up arms against Spanish control, and the leader of the uprising, the priest Miguel Hidalgo y Costilla, issued proclamations to free slaves and return the land to the Indians. Unlike with the English Americans, this initial period of the war for independence included goals that would benefit all of the people, including Indians, blacks, and mixed-race people. But these goals were not reached. Though independence from Spain brought fundamental change to the *Americanos,* the criollos used the military, Church, and landownership institutions to maintain their privileges.

We said that the process of building a nation-state requires political institution as well as experience in self-governance, which is usually gained from participation in government affairs. We also noted earlier that for the English Americans property was what allowed individuals the independence to participate in politics. In the Spanish American colonies, this was not the case, because chief administrative posts were restricted to human bodies born in Spain. There was a religious-political hierarchy extending from the king of Spain down to local government, with the exception of the *cabildo* (city council). Office holding had elements of being a royal gift given to favored individuals. So, for the criollos, wealth and social status were based on landownership but not on self-government. Because the Spaniard recognized the rights of the natural leaders of the Indians and, supposedly for their own protection, society was divided into a Republic of the Indians and a Republic of the *Españoles*. The Indian leaders were part of the nobility of Spanish America, but within their own republics they still followed a traditional political system based on paying tribute. In this kind of exclusionary political system, a great deal of politics was conducted outside political office at the personal and informal level, through negotiations or through protests. Petitions could be brought to the viceroy by the Indians or others and he would intercede in their favor. The point is that most people had no access to and therefore no experience in the overall governance of the colonies.

The only political practice in self-government available to criollos was the *cabildos* (city or town councils). Of all the institutions of the Spanish colony the *cabildo* was considered to have a special legitimacy coming from the will of the people, a tradition coming from the Spanish municipalities. However, their function was so rigidly defined by Spanish legislation that the post of *regidor* (councilman) was regarded as largely honorific and by 1556 these positions were sold to the highest bidder. Thus Spanish Americans had no "political training school" to prepare them for democracy after independence. With the expulsion of the Spaniards after the wars of independence, the Spanish Americas had few trained leaders experienced in running national institutions. At the end of the devastating Wars of Independence, each of the four viceroyalties fragmented into several nation-states influenced by the U.S. Constitution but lacking a clearly defined national identity. Soon after independence, for example, the Central American countries broke away from Mexico, as did the Texas territory a dozen years later. A lesson to be learned is that identity alone is not enough to sustain a nation-state; it must have a political and economic system to sustain the national identity.

Unlike the continuity of political thought and practice between England and the English American colonies, the dominant political thought in Mexico led to a rejection of the Spanish colonial legacy as well as the mestizo-centered, multicultural society, and with this rejection came the introduction of a politics of identity. Lucas Alamán and other conservatives maintained that the true national character was to be found within a traditional Spanish heritage. (This is similar to the positions of some conservatives in Puerto Rico and Cuba one hundred years later.) A few nationalists, like Carlos Maria Bustamante, attempted to circumvent the colonial experience by identifying Mexican nationality with the preconquest Aztec state (a position that appears in the discourse of Chicano political thought, i.e., the notion of Aztlán). Others, like José María Luis Mora, asserted that the nation's character must be sought in the "white" race. This was part of a widespread discourse of racism that saw the nonwhite population as a sickness to be cured through ethnic cleansing.[17]

While conservatives longed for an imaginary Spanish past, liberals looked toward foreign political models.[18] As noted before, this included not only the U.S. Constitution, immigrants, capital, and technology, but also European, primarily British investments. Later in the nineteenth century, Cuba also rejected the Spanish legacy and reached out to the United States as a model.

In the Mexican constitutional assembly of 1823, the principal debate was between the centralists and the federalists (similar to the debate held by English Americans at their constitutional convention). Should power be concentrated in Mexico City or distributed among the nineteen states and four territories? With respect to the English thirteen colonies, Fray Servando Teresa de Mier argued:

> They were already separate and independent one from another. They federalized themselves in union against the oppression of England; to federalize ourselves, now united, is to divide ourselves and to bring upon us the very evils they sought to remedy with their federation. They had already lived under a constitution that, when the name of the king was scratched out, brought forth a republic. We buckled for three hundred years under the weight of an absolute monarch, scarcely moving a step toward the study of freedom.[19]

The liberals won and the Constitution of 1824 organized the Estados Unidos Mexicanos along the lines of the U.S. Constitution. But the conservatives won special privileges for the Catholic Church and for the president in times of emergency. The struggle between the liberals (those for freedom, democracy, and federalism) and the conservatives (those for the traditional class and religious privileges) continued for several decades. And it was here that the political economic interests of the English and Latino Americans intersected.

Northern Mexicans in Texas, Nuevo Mexico, and California had been integrally involved in the colonial government, the debates over independence, and the wars for independence, and they now were participants in the centralist/federalist debate.[20] This debate was of particular importance for them, because most of them wanted to have a system that would allow them self-government. It was in this political context that U.S. Americans' economic and cultural penetration of Mexico took place. In fact the economic penetration of all of Spanish America by English and U.S. business interests was possible for two reasons: unlike the English-American Revolutionary War, the Spanish American Wars of Independence devastated the economies of the Spanish colonies and after independence free trade policies opened the borders to foreign economic interests.[21]

What does this history represent in terms of the origins of U.S. Latino/a thought?

1. The dominant political discourse in Latino/a history is based on the same liberal concepts that inspired the founders of the United States of America and continue to serve as a basis to demand inclusion of "different" people into the polity.
2. Mexicans (as well as other Latino/as) have a unique historical experience with a multicultural society based on miscegenation and class struggles and this has played an important role in their political development.

3. Despite the differences between U.S. and Spanish America, before and after independence from England and Spain, we find a similarity: a national identity discourse that masks a system based on class and **pigmentocracy** (an order based on skin color) that benefited primarily the dominant, white, male, European, wealthy, landowning class (whether of Spanish, English, or other European descent). In other words, first a common identity, as *Americano/as,* was used as a convenient weapon to fight against imperial rule; after independence, a nationalist identity was used as a tool to attempt to control certain ideas, classes, Indian nations, and ethnic groups.

In the final analysis, the questions of justice and equal opportunity for people of all social classes, which figured so prominently among English and Spanish American patriots, remain unanswered today.

NOTES AND SUGGESTED READINGS

1. That these ideas were powerful we can tell because they were considered "illegitimate" and therefore dangerous by the king's authorities; the books containing these ideas were banned and periodically burned in France, Rome, and Spain and of course in their colonies.

2. Harold Eugene Davis, "Ideas in the Independence Movements of Mexico and the United States," *Proceedings of the Pacific Coast Council on Latin American Studies* 6 (1977–79): 7, 9.

3. Clinton Rossiter, *The First American Revolution* (New York: Harcourt, Brace & World, 1956), 18, 139, 148. As Rossiter indicates, it is impossible to fix the precise proportions of each nationality, which is why these figures do not add up to 100 percent.

4. Wilson Neate, "Alienism Unashamed," *Latino Studies Journal* 8, no. 2 (spring 1997): 68–91.

5. Rossiter, *First American Revolution,* 179.

6. Rossiter, *First American Revolution,* 237.

7. This is an example of the relation between violence (war in this case) and political consciousness. It was the institution of the army that provided the first traces of an "American consciousness." Similarly, as Mario T. Garcia points out in his discussion of the League of United Latin American Citizens (LULAC), U.S. Mexicans developed a political consciousness as "Americans" through their participation in World War I (*Mexican Americans: Leadership, Ideology, & Identity, 1930–1960* [New Haven: Yale University Press, 1989]).

8. Colin M. MacLachlan and Jaime E. Rodriguez O., *The Forging of the Cosmic Race: A Reinterpretation of Colonial Mexico* (Berkeley: University of California Press, 1990), 197. I converted the figures into percentages.

9. Helen Safa, "Introduction," *Latin American Perspectives* 25, no. 3 (May 1998): 9.

10. Safa, "Introduction," 223–28.

11. For a detailed discussion of the role that different classes played in the wars of independence, see Enrique Semo, *Historia Mexicana: Economía y Lucha de Clases* (Mexico City: Ediciones Era, 1982), 161–99.

12. Charles C. Griffin, "Further Reflections," in *History of Latin American Civilization,* ed. Lewis Hanke (Boston: Little, Brown, 1967), 48–49.

13. José Trias Monge, *Puerto Rico: The Trials of the Oldest Colony in the World* (New Haven, Conn.: Yale University Press, 1997), 22.

14. Lourdes Martínez-Echazábal, "Mestizaje and the Discourse of National/Cultural Identity," *Latin American Perspectives* 25, no. 3 (May 1998): 40.

15. Luis Villoro, "The Ideological Currents of the Epoch of Independence," in *Major Trends in Mexican Philosophy*, ed. Mario de la Cueva et al., trans. A. Robert Caponigri (Notre Dame, Ind.: University of Notre Dame Press, 1966), 185–219.

16. Villoro, "Ideological Currents," 195.

17. Lourdes Martínez-Echazábal, "Mestizaje and the Discourse of National/Cultural Identity," *Latin American Perspectives* 25, no. 3 (May 1998) and Martin, "The Sick Continent and Its Diagnosticians" in Martin Stabb, *In Quest of Identity* (Chapel Hill: University of North Carolina Press, 1967).

18. For thirty years the Porfirio Diaz dictatorship (1876–80, 1884–1911) attempted to make Mexico into a nation-state similar to France culturally and the United States politically and economically. The Mexican Revolution of 1910 returned the country to its mestizo past. Though as Mexican mass media clearly illustrate, a pigmentocracy still dominates the Mexican cultural horizon. See for example Mireya Navarro, "Spanish-Language TV Burgeoning," *Press Democrat*, August 25, 2000. According to this article, television "stars are so blond . . . they seem to hail from Eastern Europe rather than Hispanic countries."

19. *Antologia del pensamiento social y politico de América Latina* (Washington, D.C., 1964), 242–43, quoted in Michael C. Meyer and William L. Sherman, *The Course of Mexican History*, 3d ed. (New York: Oxford University Press, 1987), 314.

20. Juan Gómez-Quiñonez, *Roots of Chicano Politics, 1600–1940* (Albuquerque: University of New Mexico Press, 1994).

21. Eduardo Galeano, *Open Veins of Latin America* (New York: Monthly Review, 1997). Some argue that this was just a new form of colonization (neocolonialism) that deformed the economies of the newborn nations and set the stage for their historical uneven development. Whatever the arguments or theories, the social problems that led to revolution continue to hurt most people to this day.

QUESTIONS

1. Which claim is more persuasive to you: (a) that Laws can be derived from our observation of nature, (b) that Laws are arbitrary social constructions (we just invent them) or (c) that Laws are established by God or religion?

2. Besides voting, how is the will of the people expressed in the United States? Can graffiti be considered part of the expression of the will of the people? Or at least the expression of a political identity?

3. The article observes that Spanish Americans, unlike their English-American counterparts, had no "training schools" to prepare them for democracy after independence. What activities or institutions in which you participate do you consider "training schools" for democracy? How do you express your political will? Your political voice?

4. To be sure, English Americans were against the "sins" of privilege they clearly saw among the English aristocracy, but their objective was to level off the top, not to raise the bottom, of society. In regard to their own privilege over women, indentured servants, or poor whites, slaves, and Indians, were they blind to it or

was it invisible? This is a question of agency, of intention: is it that they *could not* see it or that they *did not want* to see it?

5. Note also that if the American Revolutionary War started because it was a matter of Englishmen wanting to treat other Englishmen as inferiors, "to reduce them under absolute Despotism," does not this then raise the same question of liberty for Americans who treat other Americans as inferiors? In other words, to what extent are Chicano, Puerto Rican, and African American militants two hundred years later in the same position the American patriots were in? Do white Americans treat nonwhite Americans as if they were part of an internal colony to be exploited? Is the key question here one of abuse of power? Of justice?

Seduction and Aggression:
The Birth of Territorial, Involuntary,
and Cultural U.S. Citizens

The seduction: there are some similarities in the way Puerto Ricans, Cubans, and Mexicans were subjugated and colonized by the United States. Vázquez (chapter 5) mentions how Spanish American revolutionaries, the ancestors of today's Latino/as, implemented the U.S. form of government for good reasons: it helped to overthrow the European empires and promised equality to all. Also, in each of the cases under consideration, the countries were politically and economically devastated due to wars against Spain. Under these circumstances, there were increased economic exchanges and a mixing of the native elite with the newcomer elite.

The aggression: then, after a more-or-less subtle courting, came the imposition by force of a new order that divested the native population of their land and subjected their labor to the needs of the dominant government. In the case of Mexico, U.S. troops invaded Mexico City and for a while the U.S. government considered keeping the entire country. Then it realized that it would not be able to assimilate so many Mexican Indians, so it kept only the northern part. In Cuba and Puerto Rico, U.S. troops were sent ostensibly to support the movement for independence from Spain. Troops withdrew once the required documents mentioned below were signed or otherwise approved.

The birth: Mexicans, Puerto Ricans, and Cubans were born as U.S. political or cultural citizens when their "birth certificates" were signed by their respective representative bodies. These "birth certificates" were the Treaty of Guadalupe Hidalgo (1848), the Treaty of Paris (1899), the Foraker Act (1900), the Jones Act (1917), Public Law 600 (1950), and the Platt Amendment (1901).

While there is no room to include all these documents in this reader, we encourage you to read them. Incidentally, students are not the only ones who find the language of the treaties and acts very difficult to understand. But is it not paradoxical that the words in these documents, behind which stand so much bloodshed and wealth of labor and land, are so enigmatic and perplexing? Here is the power to take over half of Mexico, to annex Puerto Rico, and to declare the U.S. right to intervene in Cuba, and these documents might as well be invisible. Who wants to read legal documents? And yet legal documents represent one of the most concrete and durable realities since the invention of the written word. They literally dictate what Must Be, and violation may lead to a death sentence. It helps to consider these documents in light of other documents that exercise power over us on a daily basis, such as federal, state, and city laws and also school policies on how to behave and how to dress. All these are examples of language that contains power to dictate to people what they can or cannot do. These documents represent what was "said" in such a way that the words were carved into everyday reality. These words are not "carried away by the wind," they are backed by military, police, school, or parental authority. These are considered legal documents.

But all births are painful. And reality is much too fluid to be contained by discourse. Who negotiated and signed the treaties and the acts and the amendments? Who opposed them? Once signed, can these documents be challenged? As we see in the sections below, there were many who immediately challenged the **juridical** reality represented by these documents with a violent response against U.S. encroachment. At different times and with varying intensity, tactics, and strategies, they opposed their change of status from "nationals" (members of a polity) to "ethnics" (subordinate members of the United States). And the fight continues today. Some Puerto Ricans are still struggling for independence; some Mexicans feel that the Treaty of Guadalupe Hidalgo violated international law. Julio Chavezmontes argues in *Heridas Que no Cierran*[1] that there is a basis in international law to argue that the takeover of the Mexican North (now the U.S. Southwest) and the resulting Treaty of Guadalupe Hidalgo are illegal and that the Mexican president should demand compensation. There was also the takeover of Catalina Island in southern California by the Brown Berets, who raised a Mexican flag and denounced the violation of the Treaty of Guadalupe Hidalgo agreements by the United States.[2] And of course Fidel Castro challenged U.S. authority over Cuba in 1960 and continues to challenge U.S. presence on Cuban soil (at Guantanamo Bay).

This is the stuff that makes history and politics. The question raised by this reader (and left for you to answer) is whether this Latino/a struggle for justice and self-determination is indeed an instance of separatism or a quest for public citizenship. The following story about Mexicans becoming Chicano/as addresses this point.

NOTES AND SUGGESTED READINGS

1. Julio Chavezmontes, *Heridas Que no Cierran* (México: Editorial Grijalbo, 1988).
2. David Sánchez, *Expedition through Aztlán* (La Puente, Calif.: Perspectiva, 1978).

✳ 6 ✳
THE MAKING OF A TEJANO: THE PERSONAL MEMOIRS OF JOHN N. SEGUÍN

Jesús de la Teja, editor

For the sake of telling a brief yet comprehensive story, the editors chose to print primarily Jesús's narrative on Seguín's life and to weave into it the preface and an excerpt from Seguín's memoirs. We strongly recommend, however, the reading of the entire of Seguín's memoirs and the viewing of the 1979 film, *Seguín*, directed by Jesús S. Treviño. In the film, Juan (born October 27, 1806) dreams of a free and independent Tejas (the original spelling of "Texas") where a multicultural society would thrive, and this leads him to fight against the Mexican government for Texas independence. His dream turns into a nightmare as anti-Mexican sentiment threatens his life and he becomes, as he puts it, "a foreigner in my native land" and is forced to flee to Mexico and fight against the U.S. government.

There is more to the story, however. Texas had become an object of desire within a geopolitical context (as considered by other pieces in this reader, this was also the case in California, Cuba, and Puerto Rico in the course of the century). First, the Louisiana Purchase in 1803 brought into conflict the interests of Spain, France, and the United States and constructed Tejas and Tejanos as a buffer between the ever-expanding Anglo Americans and the rich mines of New Spain. This situation functioned like a magnet, attracting opportunists from all over the world. Then, from 1810 to 1821, Mexicans fought a war for their independence from Spain that economically devastated the country. Within this context (and the context of negative portrayals of the Mexican in the United States), the Mexican government opened the borders to immigrants from the United States. The goal was to populate the area with other "civilized" (read economically developed, light-skinned) bodies who could assist in the economic recovery and in the struggle against the "hostile" indigenous peoples or American Indian nations. Erasmo Seguín, Juan's father, was charged with negotiating an agreement that legally admitted the first three hundred Anglo American colonists under the leadership of Steven Austin. The history of the Seguín family, incidentally, includes involvement by its members in the 1740s Spanish establishment of the Texas territory, the Mexican War of Independence, the Texas secession, the U.S.-Mexico War, as well as the Wars of Reform and the French Intervention in Mexico.

After the battles of the Alamo and San Jacinto, Texas became the Republic of Texas for the next decade. It is cruelly ironic that the U.S. Americans ended up seeing the elite Mexicans as neither white nor civilized. Yet, as told in his memoirs, Seguín's story itself does a certain violence to women and the underclass by rendering *them* invisible. For example, the only piece of information available about Juan's wife (according to Jesús) is that she was fat and illiterate. And there is also mention of a Mexican boy "in Mexican garb, looking more like an Indian than anything else," who joins Seguín's troops. What *is* visible is the struggle of the Tejano/a people to achieve self-determination in the midst of centralist versus federalist conflicts, legal and illegal immigrants and refugees, and a separatist Anglo movement within the newly born Mexican nation-state. Also evident are the conflicting and contradictory politics of self-preservation and economic and cultural seduction among northern Mexicans as well as the microphysics of power (see appendix 5) operating in the takeover of land. These are further illustration of the claim (raised by some of the texts in this reader) that a people's identity and its quest for public citizenship is not constrained by national borders. Incidentally, almost one hundred years later another Mexican, Henry B. Gonzalez, became a political player in Texas politics. A comparison of these two political figures and how they saw themselves as legitimate members of the polity and not as "ethnic" politicians, as they were defined by the dominant culture, would be very instructive.

SEGUÍN'S PREFACE

A native of the city of San Antonio de Béxar, I embraced the cause of Texas at the sound of the first cannon which foretold her liberty, filled an honorable role within the ranks of the conquerors of San Jacinto, and was a member of the legislative body of the Republic. In the very land which in other times bestowed on me such bright and repeated evidences of trust and esteem, I now find myself exposed to the attacks of scribblers and personal enemies who, to serve *political purposes* and engender strife, falsify historical fact with which they are but imperfectly acquainted. I owe it to myself, my children and friends to answer them with a short but true exposition of my acts, from the beginning of my public career up to the time of the return of General Woll from the Rio Grande with the Mexican forces, among which I was then serving.

I address myself to the American people, to that people impetuous as the whirl-wind when aroused by the hypocritical clamors of designing men but just, impartial, and composed whenever men and facts are submitted to their judgment.

I have been the object of the hatred and passionate attacks of a few troublemakers who, for a time, ruled as masters over the poor and oppressed population of San Antonio. Harpy-like, ready to pounce on everything that attracted the notice of their rapacious avarice, I was an obstacle to the execution of their vile designs. They there-fore leagued together to exasperate and ruin me, spread malignant calumnies against me, and made use of odious machinations to sully my honor and tarnish my well earned reputation.

A victim to the wickedness of a few men whose false pretenses were favored because of their origin and recent domination over the country, a foreigner in my native land, could I stoically be expected to endure their outrages and insults? Crushed by sorrow, convinced that only my death would satisfy my enemies, I sought shelter among those against whom I had fought. I separated from my coun-try, parents, family, relatives and friends and, what was more, from the institutions on behalf of which I had drawn my sword with an earnest wish to see Texas free and happy. In that involuntary exile my only ambition was to devote my time, far from the tumult of war, to the support of my family who shared in my sad condition.

Fate, however, had not exhausted its cup of bitterness. Thrown into a prison in a foreign country, I had no alternatives left but to linger in a loathsome confinement or to accept military service.

On one hand, my wife and children, reduced to beggary and separated from me; on the other hand, to turn my arms against my own country. The alternatives were sad, the struggle of feelings violent. At last the father triumphed over the citizen; I seized a sword that pained my hand. (Who among my readers will not understand my situation?) I served Mexico; I served her loyally and faithfully. I was compelled to fight my own countrymen, but I was never guilty of the barbarous and unworthy deeds of which I am accused by my enemies.

Ere the tomb closes over me and my contemporaries, I wish to publicize this stormy period of my life. I do it for my friends as well as for my enemies. I challenge the latter to contest with facts the statements I am about to make, and I confidently leave the decision to those who witnessed the events.

"THE MAKING OF TEJANO" (by de la Teja)

Don Erasmo's son, Juan Nepomuceno Seguín, had been born [October 27, 1806] in a sparsely settled land during very unsettled times. The political and social changes sweeping Mexico and the United States made Texas a crossroads of revolution and an object of desire. The Louisiana Purchase in 1803 brought the United States and Spain together along the Texas border, which the United States now claimed to be the Rio Grande. In Madrid, Paris and Washington, Texas took on a political importance it had not had for almost a century. In its new role as buffer between the ever-expanding Anglo Americans and the rich mines of New Spain, Texas became the destination of royalist troops intent on protecting the frontier, of Spanish and French refugees from Anglo-American Louisiana, and of filibusters from the United States.

Even as an adolescent Juan must have appreciated the importance his father and other prominent Bexareños attached to Stephen Austin and his colonists. The significance of his father's hosting James E. B. Austin, Stephen's brother, for over a year could not have been lost on Juan. The young Tejano also witnessed the growing frustration of Bexareños as they saw the Anglo-American colonies prosper while San Antonio remained stagnant, caught between the political power of Monclova and Saltillo and the economic power of San Felipe, Nacogdoches and the other Anglo-American settlements.

Juan's economic and social development brought about quick political maturity. Despite being just twenty-two years old at the time, Juan was elected as one of two San Antonio *regidores* for 1829, on occasion serving as *alcalde* during the absences of the incumbent, Gaspar Flores. Regarding the young office holder's political skills, the political chief, Ramón Músquiz, confided in Stephen Austin "Don Juan Nepomuceno Segin [Seguín] is very talented for his age, but he needs practice in order to be a good administrator of Justice."[1] During his tenure Juan was asked to perform what could only be considered thankless tasks. His efforts to collect the voluntary contribution for the local primary school proved a failure because of the lack of money in the town. Juan had to suggest to the political chief that the collection be suspended until such time as some hard cash came into town. Only a few days later he found out that he had to enforce a new state law requiring each citizen to contribute the proceeds from three days' labor to the local school. Only slightly less demanding was the compilation of the municipality's annual statistical report, for which he and the other *regidor* were responsible. On occasion he served as judge in minor civil and criminal cases.[2]

His success in handling his first elective office made Juan a prime candidate for future political activities. In the complicated world of post-independence Mexican politics, elections beyond the local level were indirect; the eligible citizens voted for electors who in turn voted for representatives to state and national offices. In 1833 he won twenty-six of thirty-three votes for secretary of the electoral assembly, and was subsequently elected as one of twenty-one electors. The following year he served as president of the electoral assembly.[3]

* * *

Juan's comment in the memoirs that, "we had agreed that the movement should begin in the center of Texas," makes it clear that the Tejanos were not about to expose themselves to Santa Anna's wrath on their own. They were aware of Zacatecas's fate for resisting the new centralist government: a large force composed of local militias had been routed by Santa Anna's army, which sacked the city before withdrawing. Juan and other Tejano leaders also knew that, despite the existence of a "War Party," the commonly held sentiment among the Anglo Americans was against an uprising so long as their own rights were not violated.

The violation, whether orchestrated by war party members or not, came by way of General Cos, who asked that William B. Travis, the leader of a group of settlers who had ousted the customs officer at Anahuac, be delivered to him. Cos also issued arrest orders for a large group of federalists including Samuel Williams, Mosley Baker, Lorenzo de Zavala, and José María Carbajal. At the same time he issued a proclamation advising the settlers that they had nothing to fear from the new government, but made it clear they must accept the changes without recourse. Not only did the Texans refuse to comply with Cos's orders, they violently resisted the army's effort to collect a cannon that had been lent to the town of Gonzales for Indian defense.

This action at Gonzales, which took place on October 2, mobilized the Anglo Texans and the Tejanos. Juan, commissioned "captain of the Federal Army of Texas," raised a company of thirty-seven men. His brother-in-law, Salvador Flores, and Manuel Leal organized another company from the San Antonio ranches. The Mexican settlers from the Victoria area organized themselves into a company of twenty-eight under Placido Benavides's command. Desertions from the San Antonio and Goliad garrisons brought additional Tejanos into the ranks of the Texas Army.[4]

The roles assigned to the Tejanos—foraging, spying, harassments, and raids—clearly aimed at taking advantage of their knowledge of the countryside and their horsemanship. This is not to say that the Tejanos did not take part in the major engagement of the early struggle. There is considerable evidence that at least part of Juan's company, probably including himself, took part in the storming of San Antonio, which began on December 5. Immediately after General Cos's withdrawal from San Antonio, Seguín's company joined Travis's in raiding the Mexican army's horse herd.[5]

By January 1836 the Mexican army had been driven from Texas and Juan's company of mounted volunteers had disbanded. Juan himself had been chosen judge of San Antonio, a position he held until returning to military service in February, when Santa Anna advanced on Texas. Also in January, the government commissioned Juan a captain in the cavalry corps, although there apparently was some confusion regarding the appointment. In any case, Juan was busy acting as intermediary between the Tejanos, the Anglo Texans, and the revolutionary government, as well as attending to town business. Among these activities was a run-in with James Bowie over the latter's unauthorized release of a prisoner. As judge, Juan also was responsible for conducting the election that sent Francisco Ruiz and José Antonio Navarro as the only native-born Texans to the convention that declared Texas independence.[6]

Once Santa Anna arrived in Béxar, Juan withdrew into the Alamo along with an unspecified number of Tejanos. There are a number of reports which suggest that between Santa Anna's arrival on February 23 and March 3, some individuals had an opportunity to withdraw; more probably however, they withdrew between the time Santa Anna was spotted and the time he entered Béxar. Among those who chose not to remain were a number of Tejanos who probably felt it was useless to remain in the fort when Houston was organizing an army in the interior.[7]

Juan left the Alamo as a messenger, probably on the night of February 28. Apparently his knowledge of the area and his Spanish made him the logical choice in an attempt to get through the Mexican lines. He never made it to Goliad, his original destination, for on the road he met one of Colonel James Fannin's officers, who informed him that the Goliad garrison was on its way. Soon, however, Seguín was informed by another of Fannin's men that the colonel had decided to return to Goliad. Juan now headed for Gonzales where, upon his arrival, he found many of the Tejanos who had been in San Antonio until Santa Anna's approach. There he reorganized his company, part of which was ordered by Sam Houston to help protect the evacuation of the San Antonio River valley ranches. Juan specifically sent three men from his unit to help his family leave the area while he and the rest of the company made up the rear-guard of the main body of Houston's army. Before taking up the march, Juan took the time to inform the Bexareño delegates at Washington-on-the-Brazos, Francisco Ruiz and José Antonio Navarro, about the fall of the Alamo.[8]

Juan and his men earned Sam Houston's respect at San Jacinto. Writing a letter of introduction for Juan to the governor of Louisiana, Houston stated: "The Colonel commanded the only Mexican company who fought in the cause of Texas at the Battle of San Jacinto. His chivalrous and estimable conduct in the battle won for him my warmest regard and esteem."[9] Writing to Juan's father some years later, Houston extended his compliments to the company in general, citing Juan's conduct and that of "his brave company in the army of 1836, and his brave and gallant bearing in the battle of San Jacinto, with that of his men."[10]

But Juan earned another kind of notoriety during the war; he was one of the few Tejanos to be singled out by the Mexicans for his participation in the war. For instance, José Enrique de la Peña, a participant in Santa Anna's expedition, published a diary of the campaign in 1836. In it he attacked the ingratitude of the Anglo-American settlers and the credulousness of many Tejanos. But for Juan and two others he reserved the harshest judgment:

> The cry of independence darkened the magic of liberty that had misled some of the less
> careful thinkers . . . there remaining with the colonists only Don Lorenzo de Zavala and

Béjar natives, Don Antonio Navarro and Don Juan N. Seguín, the only intelligent men
who incurred the name of traitor, a label both ugly and deserved.[11]

Juan's command turned out to be full of controversy and turmoil. Felix Huston,
who became commander of the army in October, after Sam Houston's election to
the presidency and Thomas Rusk's appointment as secretary of war, was opposed to
Seguín's holding the command. One of the "American straggling adventurers" of
whom Juan complains in his memoirs, Huston had arrived in Texas well after San
Jacinto with ambitious plans for invading Mexico. The general obviously had little
respect for Juan, complaining in letters to Houston in November 1836 that Seguín
was unfit for command because "he cannot speak our language" and was calling for
the abandonment of Béxar.[12]

When General Huston tried to carry out the evacuation and destruction of San
Antonio at the beginning of 1837, Juan successfully appealed the order to President
Houston. Although Juan's appeal has not surfaced, the tenor of Houston's reply
suggests the Tejano was deeply insulted by the order. After discussing the steps taken
to undo Huston's orders, the president concluded: "You will, I confidently hope, be
satisfied that no intention has been entertained to wound your feelings, or to compromise your honor! You will therefore retain your command, and command of the
post of Bexar." Juan was satisfied, but he apparently made an enemy of Huston and
his associates, who may have been involved in a scheme to buy up land in San Antonio cheaply as a result of the abandonment.[13]

The withdrawal from San Antonio proved propitious, however, for in April Juan
claimed to be in a position both to mount those yet on foot and to return to the
vicinity of Béxar. It would seem, however, that Juan was growing increasingly eager
to take care of personal interests. Confident that the Mexicans would not soon
attack and that his command was on a stable footing, he asked for a month-long
furlough. By the fall of 1837 he was again away from his command, on his way to
New Orleans where he remained until early 1838. When he returned to Béxar in
March he discovered that he had been elected Béxar's senator to the Texas Congress.
Traveling to Houston, then the capital of the young republic, he resigned his commission on May 14, 1838, and four days later obtained his pay in bounty land—
1,280 acres. He also acquired a donation grant of 640 acres of land for his service
at San Jacinto.[14] Having made significant military contributions to the young republic, Juan now turned his talents to the political field, where his efforts were directed
at making the coexistence of Tejano and Texan a reality.

Juan again found himself breaking ground, this time as the only Tejano senator
to serve during the republic. He could not have had much time to formulate an
agenda for himself, however, given the suddenness of the news of his election and
the fact that the Second Congress was nearing the end. But even during the remaining nine days Juan proved to be a man of action. He introduced a bill for the relief
of the widows and orphans of those who died at the Alamo, and even joined in the

debate, though he did so in Spanish. Despite his need for a translator, Juan served during the Third and Fourth Congresses as chair of the Committee on Military Affairs, and had a seat on the Committee of Claims and Accounts.[15]

As the only Tejano in the senate it was clearly up to Juan to represent the interests not only of Bexareños but of all Tejanos. Juan clearly was concerned both that Tejanos understood the new system of government by which they were quickly being overwhelmed and that their interests were properly represented in congress. His only surviving speech, made during the Fourth Congress, came as result of a Treasury report stating that $15,000 had been appropriated for the translation and publication of laws into Spanish. Perhaps Juan noted a growing disregard for the interests of Tejanos, a sense of their increasing isolation within a now overwhelmingly Anglo-American Texas. If so, his comments ring eloquently for the rights of his minority:

> Mr. President, the dearest rights of my constituents as Mexico-Texians are guaranteed by the Constitution and the Laws of the Republic of Texas; and at the formation of the social compact between the Mexicans and the Texians, they had rights guaranteed to them; they also contracted certain legal obligations—of all of which they are ignorant.
> . . . The Mexico-Texians were among the first who sacrificed their all in our glorious Revolution, and the disasters of war weighed heavy upon them, to achieve those blessings which, it appears, [they] are destined to be the last to enjoy.

Juan's interest in instruction extended beyond expanding his constituency's understanding of the law. Given his own educational concerns, it is not surprising that he and José Antonio Navarro (the only Tejano serving in the house of representatives during the Third Congress) attempted to use their offices to obtain academic institutions for San Antonio. As Catholics, they found in Father John Timon, appointed by the bishop of New Orleans in 1838 to assess the Church's state of affairs in Texas, an opportunity to provide Béxar with a preparatory school and college of liberal arts and sciences while at the same time bringing needed reform to the spiritual life of Tejanos. Although Seguín and Navarro offered to endow a Catholic college with four leagues (17,714 acres) of land from the Republic,[16] conditions were not yet right and the plan fell through. Juan was able to influence the religious situation in San Antonio, however. After discussing the improprieties of the San Antonio and Goliad clergy with Father Timon, he provided an affidavit on the subject in January 1839 which contributed to their removal the following year.[17]

Despite Juan's apparent pursuit of his own programs, it was impossible for him not to become embroiled in both local and national political factionalism. Moreover, the emerging schism between Texans and Tejanos was bound, sooner or later, to have an impact on Juan's relationships with San Antonio's growing Anglo population. In the summer of 1838 Launcelot Smithers, an English doctor who settled in San Antonio shortly after independence, declared erroneously: "there is not any 'danger' of Seguín being elected another term to Congress. His conduct has ruined him with the Mexicans: they supported him before thro' fear of his strength and of his resentment."[18] Adjutant General Hugh McLeod was even more blunt about Juan: "Seguine [*sic*] is my enemy, independent of his Houston allegiance, at least so I think, and yet the fellow *smiles and smiles,* but the Navarro family can neutralize him, & I may count upon the Beramendi's."[19] Speaking of a failed 1839 campaign by companies of Anglos and Tejanos against the Comanche, in which Seguín led the Tejanos, Mary Maverick suggested a less than courageous character on Juan's part: "They had been away from San Antonio ten days, when Captain Seguín returned reporting the woods full of Indians and predicting that our men would surely be killed."[20]

The return to San Antonio proved disappointing in another respect, for in January 1841 the first skirmish in Mexico's renewed campaign against Texas took place and Juan was one of its first victims. During a raid on the San Antonio River ranches by a company belonging to the Mexican general Rafael Vázquez's command, Juan lost a number of head of cattle. It was a loss he could not afford at the time, not only because his investment in the Canales Expedition was in jeopardy but because the size of his herd was still small. Juan now set out with Major George T. Howard on a fruitless pursuit of the Mexicans.[21]

Before he left, Juan received a small token of the aldermen's continuing appreciation for him as the mayor of San Antonio, a position which proved a heavy burden, particularly as it brought him into increasingly hostile contact with a growing body of Anglo-American vagrants and adventurers. As early as May of that year the town council found it necessary to formally voice their support for Juan:

RESOLVED BY THIS BOARD OF ALDERMEN, that the Mayor of this City in their opinion is fully authorised [*sic*] and empowered by the Act of incorporating said city to execute and carry into effect all laws passed by this body and they hereby vest him with full Executive Powers to that effect.[22]

Juan's efforts to contain the vagrant problem was seconded by none other than Launcelot Smithers, now a member of the board of aldermen, and a strong critic of Seguín three years before. At the September 9, 1841, meeting of the city council he proposed that all individuals in the city who were not residents of the Republic should register with the mayor, and that anyone harboring a suspicious individual should be fined by the mayor.[23] Considering his previously stated attitude, it is quite possible that Smithers meant "Mexicans" when he referred to suspicious individuals and not the Anglo Americans against whom Seguín directed his efforts.

Juan also faced financial difficulties at this time. Having borrowed over $3,000 to equip the companies he took to Mexico in answer to General Canales's call and having failed to collect on either his investment or his men's salaries, Juan was in need of raising the money by some means. He found an opportunity in the summer of 1841 when Rafael Uribe came to Texas on behalf of General Mariano Arista to discuss cooperating on measures against the Indians who were making assaults on both sides of the border. On his return to Mexico, Juan decided, as he says in the memoirs, to enter "with him into a smuggling operation." Juan mortgaged a sizeable amount of property to Duncan C. Ogden and George T. Howard in order to obtain the goods he took to Mexico: his residence, a house and lot fronting on Flores Street in San Antonio; a house and lot fronting on Main Street on the main plaza; and a league of land adjoining his father's ranch, Casa Blanca.[24]

This trip, though of a strictly private nature for Juan, proved no more successful than his military project of the previous year. Mistaken by General Arista for one of the delegates from the Texas government, Seguín was ordered to leave the country. Juan was now the victim of his previous efforts in support of federalism. In the face of reports that he was recruiting volunteers for a possible revolt by the general against the centralist government in Mexico City, Arista could not afford to have Seguín around. Hoping to make the best of the situation, Juan left his goods behind, only to discover later that his money and remaining goods had been confiscated.

On his return to San Antonio Juan resumed his duties as mayor under a cloud of suspicion, for a rumor arose that he had betrayed the Santa Fe Expedition to the Mexicans. Since President Lamar's ill-advised effort to conquer New Mexico had left only a day before Uribe arrived in Austin, it is clear that Uribe had ample opportunity to learn about the expedition and report to his government. Uribe hurried back to Mexico, and soon after his return "Governor Francisco G. Conde of the Department of Chihuahua published the news of the Texan expedition toward Nuevo México and warned his people against being led astray by the flattering talk of the Texans."[25]

The rumor of Juan's betrayal, in its most eloquent form, is found in the memoirs of Mary Maverick:

> It was strongly believed by many that Juan Nepomicino [*sic*] Seguín, who had held the honorable position of Mayor of San Antonio, and Representative to Congress, from Bexar, and being a man of great pride and ambition, had found himself surpassed by Americans, and somewhat overlooked in official places, had become dissatisfied with the Americans, and had opened communications with the officials of Mexico, exposing the entire plan from its inception as "invading Mexican soil." . . . From this time Seguín was suspected and Padre Garza, a rich and influential priest, was known to carry on traitorous correspondence with the Mexican authorities. Positive proof, however, was not obtained until Padre Garza escaped. Seguín indignantly denied the charge and many suspended judgement.[26]

Judgment was indeed suspended, for Juan not only resumed his duties as mayor, he was reelected at the end of the year.

After reelection Juan had to face the continuing problem of squatters on city property. As early as 1838, Mayor pro-tem Antonio Menchaca wrote to the commissioner of the General Land Office that a number of individuals, including Cornelius Van Ness, John W. Smith, and William Daingerfield among others, were attempting to take possession of land within the corporate boundaries of San Antonio. James

Goodman, the single most visible offender at the time Seguín was mayor, was ousted from the property he claimed by Seguín, acting at the direction of the Board of Aldermen. Dr. Cupples, who settled in San Antonio in 1844, remembered Goodman in an interview he gave William Corner in 1890:

> I knew the man Goodman, you speak of; I remember him well, and the years of trouble he gave the city before he was finally ousted from the property on the Plaza, just opposite where Kalteyer's drug store is now was the location of the property he claimed. I remember he once came near to killing Ed Dwyer over that and other matters.[27]

Despite Juan's best efforts, the squatters problem escaped a solution. All Seguín managed was to make an enemy of Goodman.

The Goodman episode turned out to be one of Seguín's last actions as mayor of San Antonio. In the memoirs, Juan maintains that his efforts to repay the loan of $3,000 for which he had mortgaged his property led him to ask General Rafael Vázquez for a pass so that he might conduct some business. Juan, suspecting an invasion, shared Vázquez's letter of reply with the city council and the citizenry, and wrote President Houston for help on January 30, 1842. The response, which came from Secretary of War George Hockley, proved a disappointment: "I regret exceedingly that [the] impoverished condition of our country renders it almost helpless, and that we must depend upon the patrio[tism] of those who are willing to defend it."

Understanding that he and San Antonio could expect no help from the government, Seguín counseled a withdrawal from San Antonio. Many of the Mexican families began leaving and Juan retired to his ranch. The Anglo Americans, in the meantime, decided to stay and organize a defense. The effort proved useless, however, and when Vázquez arrived in March, the defenders quickly withdrew to the town of Seguin. Although the Mexican forces remained in San Antonio for only two days, from March 5 to 7, they sowed enough suspicion and animosity against Seguín that it became impossible for him to recover.

Despite his joining Captain Jack Hays' company in pursuit of Vázquez, Juan returned to find that he had been branded a traitor. Even enjoying General Edward Burleson's favor—the general refused to hear any charges against Juan but instead ordered him to forage for the army among the ranches of the San Antonio River— Seguín could find no peace. Judging it impossible to remain in the city, Seguín went to the ranches but was constantly harassed. On April 18, 1842, citing "the turbulent state in which this unfortunate county finds itself," he resigned as mayor of San Antonio. By May Juan was on his way to Mexico, "a victim to the wickedness of a few men whose imposture was favored by their origin and recent domination over the country," as he states in the preface to his memoirs. In far-away Nacogdoches Adolphus Sterne wrote in his diary for May 27: "Col. Seguín has joined them, and as is usually the case, when our warm Friends turn against us, they become the most inveterate foes, I am satisfied, that it will be so in this case."[28]

Even aside from the pain of being labeled a traitor, being hounded by the men against whom he had acted as mayor, and being forced to abandon his native land, Juan must have been extremely confused. With the advantage of hindsight, we can sort things out. Vázquez, perhaps hoping to force a break that would bring the Tejanos over to the Mexican side, probably did attempt to discredit Juan and thus further confuse Texans about the loyalty of the Tejano population. Goodman, and the other Anglo-American latecomers with whom Juan had dealt harshly, thus had an opportunity to take their revenge and gain the upper hand over the Bexareños.

AN EXCERPT FROM THE MEMOIRS

What follows are excerpts from Seguín's unedited memoirs so that you can read his own account of this particular event.

On the 30th of April, a friend from San Antonio sent me word that Captain James W. Scott and his company were coming down by the river, burning the ranchos on their way. The inhabitants of the lower ranchos called on us for aid against Scott. With those in my house, and others to the number of about one hundred, I started to lend them aid. I proceeded, observing Scott's movements from the junction of the Medina to Pajaritos. At that place we dispersed and I returned to my wretched life. In those days I could not go to San Antonio without peril for my life.

Matters being in this state, I saw that it was necessary to take some step which would place me in security and save my family from constant wretchedness. I had to leave Texas, abandon all for which I had fought and spent my fortune, to become a wanderer. The ingratitude of those who had assumed onto themselves the right of convicting me, their credulity in declaring me a traitor on the basis of mere rumors, the necessity to defend myself for the loyal patriotism with which I had always served Texas, wounded me deeply.

But before leaving my country, perhaps forever, I determined to consult with all those interested in my welfare. I held a family council. All were in favor of my removing for some time to the interior of Texas. But to accomplish this there were some unavoidable obstacles. I could not take one step from my rancho towards the Brazos without being exposed to the rifle of the first person who might meet me for, throughout the whole country, credit had been given to the rumors against me. To emigrate with my family was impossible as I was a ruined man after the invasion of Santa Anna and our flight to Nacogdoches. Furthermore the country of the Brazos was unhealthier than that of Nacogdoches. What might we not expect to suffer from disease in a new country, without friends or means?

Seeing that all these plans were impracticable, I resolved to seek a refuge among my enemies, braving all dangers. But before taking this step, I sent in my resignation as mayor of the city to the municipality of San Antonio, stating to them that, unable any longer to suffer the persecutions of some ungrateful Americans who strove to murder me, I had determined to free my family and friends from their continual misery on my account, and go and live peaceably in Mexico. That for these reasons I resigned my office, with all my privileges and honors as a Texan.

I left Béxar with no obligation to Texas, my services repaid with persecutions. Exiled and deprived of my privileges as a Texan citizen, I was outside the pale of society in Texas. If Texas could not protect the rights of her citizens, they were privileged to seek protection elsewhere. I had been tried by a rabble, condemned without a hearing, and consequently was at liberty to provide for my own safety.

When I arrived at Laredo the military commander of that place put me in prison, stating that he could not do otherwise until he had consulted with General Arista, whom he advised of my arrest. Arista ordered that I be sent to Monterrey. When I arrived in that city, I earnestly prayed the general to allow me to retire to Saltillo, where I had several relatives who could aid me. General Arista answered that, as he had informed Santa Anna of my imprisonment, he could not comply with my request. Santa Anna directed that I be sent to the City of Mexico but Arista, sympathetic to my unfortunate position, interceded with him in my behalf to have the order revoked. The latter complied, but on condition that I should return to Texas with a company of explorers to attack its citizens and, by spilling my blood, vindicate myself.

Under the orders of General Arista, I proceeded to the Rio Grande to join General Woll, who told me that Santa Anna, at his request, had allowed me to go to Texas with Woll's expedition, but that I should receive no command until my services proved that I was worthy.

I set out with the expedition of General Woll. In the vicinity of San Antonio, on the 10th of September, I received an order to take a company of cavalry and block the exits from the city. By this order the city was blockaded and, consequently, it was difficult for any person to escape. When I returned from complying with this order, at dawn of day, the general determined to enter the city with the infantry and artillery. I was sent to the vanguard with orders to take possession of the Military Square despite all obstacles. I entered the square without opposition and, shortly afterwards, the firing commenced on the Main Square. John Hernández came out of Goodman's shop with a message from him to the effect that if I would pardon him for what he had done against me he would leave his place of concealment and deliver himself up. I sent him word that I had no rancor against him. He delivered himself up, and I placed him under the special charge of Captain Manuel Leal. Those who had made some show of resistance in the Main Square surrendered, and the whole city was in General Woll's possession.

The next day I was ordered, with two hundred men, to take the Gonzales road and approach that town. On the Cibolo I divided my forces, sending one detachment up the creek, another down the creek, and with the main body proceeded on the Gonzales road. The following day, these parties joined the main body. Lieutenant Manuel Carvajal, who commanded one of the parties, reported that he had killed three Texans who would not surrender in the Azufrosa [Sulphur Springs].

I returned to San Antonio. A party of Texans appeared by the Garita road and the troops were taken under arms. The general took one hundred infantry, the cavalry under Cayetano Montero, and one piece of artillery and proceeded towards the Salado. The general ordered one hundred *presidiales* [former garrison soldiers from Texas] to attack. The commander of those forces sent word that the enemy was in an advantageous position and that he required reinforcements. The answer of the general was to send me with orders "to attack at all costs." I obeyed. On the first charge I lost three killed and eight wounded, on the second seven killed and fifteen wounded. I was preparing for a third charge when Colonel José María Carrasco came to relieve me from my command. I returned to the side of the general and made my report, whereupon he ordered the firing to cease.

A new attack was in preparation when the attention of the general was called to some troops on our rear guard. The aides reported them to be enemies and near at hand. Colonel Montero was ordered to attack them with his cavalry. He called on them to surrender to the Mexican Government; they answered with scoffing and bantering. Montero formed his dragoons; the Texans commenced firing, killing two soldiers. Montero dismounted his troops, also began firing, and sent for more ammunition. The general angrily sent him a message asking whether his dragoons had no sabres or lances. Before Montero received this answer he had charged, sabre in hand, ending the engagement in a few minutes. Only some ten or fifteen Texans survived. During this time, I remained by the side of General Woll and was there when Montero made his report and brought in the prisoners. At dusk the troops received orders to return to San Antonio.

In accordance with his orders not to remain over a month on this side of the Rio Grande, General Woll began his retreat by the road he came. The Mexican families who left San Antonio were put under my charge and, consequently, I was not in the affair of "Arroyo Hondo."

Remarks

After General Woll's expedition I did not return to Texas until the treaty of Guadalupe Hidalgo. During my absence nothing occurred that could stamp me as a traitor. My enemies had accomplished their object; they had killed me politically in Texas, and the less they spoke of me, the less risk they incurred of exposing the infamous means they had used to accomplish my ruin.

As to my reputed treason with Vásquez, when we consider that Don Antonio Navarro and I were the only Mexicans of note in western Texas who had taken a prominent part in the war, the interest the Mexican general had in causing us to be distrusted will be seen. Mr. Navarro was then a prisoner. I alone remained, and if they were able to make the Texans distrust me, they gained a point. This is proved by the fact that, after I withdrew from the service, no other regiment of Mexican-

Texans was ever seen. The rumor that I was a traitor was seized avidly by my enemies in San Antonio. Some envied my military position, as held by a *Mexican*; others found in me an obstacle to the accomplishment of their villainous plans. The number of land suits which still encumbers the docket of Bexar County would indicate the nature of these plans, and anyone who has listened to the evidence elicited in cases such as this will readily discover the base means adopted to deprive rightful owners of their property.

But, returning again to the charge of treason. If I had sold myself to Mexico, the bargain would, of course, have been with the government. It would have been in the interest of Mexico to keep the bargain a secret, and not allow inferior officers to know it. So long as I enjoyed the confidence of the Texans, I might have been useful in imparting secrets, *etc.*, but as soon as my fellow citizens distrusted me, I was absolutely useless. And is it not strange that the Mexican officers should have been so anxious to inform the Texans of my treason? General Vásquez took out a paper from his pocket and claimed to Chevallie that it was from me, but when the latter desired to see the letter, Vásquez refused to show it to him.

But I take the expedition of Vásquez to be my best defense. What did Vásquez accomplish in that expedition? The coming into and going out of San Antonio without taking any further steps. Undoubtedly, if I had been allied with him, I would have tried to make his expedition something more than a mere military promenade. Far from doing this, however, I presented the letter that I received from Vásquez to the municipality of San Antonio; I predicted the expedition and counseled such steps as I thought should be taken.

And why, if my treason were so clear, did the patriotic and brave Burleson refuse to subject me to a court of inquiry? Undoubtedly he knew it to be his duty to put me on trial if the slightest suspicion existed as to my character. He refused, and this proved that Burleson and the superior officers were convinced of the shallowness of the charges against me.

During the electoral campaign of August 1855, I was frequently attacked in newspapers and was styled in some "the murderer of the Salado." For some time I had proposed to publish my memoirs, so I thought it useless to enter into a newspaper war, more particularly as the attacks against me were anonymous and were directed with a venom which made me conclude that I owed them to the malevolence of a personal enemy.

I have related my participation in Woll's expedition and have only to say that neither I nor any of my posterity will ever have reason to blush for it.

During my military career, I can proudly assert that I never deviated from the line of duty, that I never shed, or caused to be shed, human blood unnecessarily, that I never insulted a prisoner by word or deed, and that, in the fulfillment of my duty, I always drew a distinction between my obligations as a soldier on the battlefield and as a civilized man after the battle.

I have finished my memoirs; I have neither the capacity nor the desire to adorn my acts with literary phrases. I have attempted a short and clear narrative of my public life in relation to Texas. I publish it without omitting or suppressing anything that I thought of the least interest, and confidently I submit to the public verdict.

Several of those who witnessed the facts I have related are still alive and among us. They can state whether I have falsified the record in any way.

AFTER THE WAR

At this point we return to the story as told by Jesús de la Teja.

The war took its toll on Juan. At forty-three he had little to show for an adult life spent mostly fighting in the saddle. Near the end of the war, he showed up at Presidio Río Grande and made contact with the Texans there. In February 1848 John A. Veatch, captain in the regiment of Texas Mounted Volunteers, informed Mirabeau B. Lamar that "our *Texian-Mexican* Seguín, presented himself a few days since desiring permission to bring his family—which he thinks is in Saltillo—to this place. He says he will return to Texas and risk consiquences [*sic*]. He looks careworn & *threadbare*."[29] Finding his family in Saltillo, Juan determined to return to Texas and wrote in April to Sam Houston, asking for the Texan's "weighty and important recommendation to my former fellow citizens, as also a protection from the President of your Republic." Seguín did not enter into explanations: "You are I think acquainted with the causes which obliged me to leave my country, and as the explanation of them would be long, I defer it till I have the gratification of seeing you." By the end of the year he was back in San Antonio, where he and his family settled down with Erasmo at Casa Blanca.[30]

As public a man as Juan had been throughout his adult life, it proved impossible for him to remain quietly on the ranch for long. In his April 1848 letter to Houston he already hinted at his interest in returning to local politics in San Antonio. In 1852 his interest became reality and Juan won election as Bexar County justice of the peace; he was reelected two years later. He also served as president of his election precinct, which included the ranches along the San Antonio River near his home.[31]

The last important event in Juan's public career was his participation in the establishment of the Democratic Party in Bexar County. The move to found a local Democratic Party stemmed from efforts to offset the growing popularity of the anti-Catholic, anti-masonic, anti-immigration, and anti-naturalization Know-Nothing Party. Although some Tejanos favored the Know-Nothings, many, including Seguín, saw in it the seeds of even worse discrimination against Tejanos. It is a testament to Juan's talents that, despite the presence of other prominent Tejanos in the community who had never been accused of disloyalty, particularly José Antonio Navarro, it was Seguín who became the featured Tejano in the Democratic Party, and Samuel Maverick, the local party president, named Juan to the platform writing committee. Juan also became a member of the Democratic committee of the "Mexican Texan citizens of Bexar County."[32]

His acceptance by Tejanos and Anglo Texans gave Seguín a new sense of responsibility. It did not come without a price, however. His political activities brought
renewed personal attacks from which he had to defend himself. Juan looked upon
the memoirs, which he wrote in 1858, not only as a defense against "the barbarous
and unworthy deeds" of which he was accused but as a means of keeping alive the
possibility of future public service.

His belief that he could once again act as intermediary between Texas and Mexico
surfaced that same year when, perhaps fearing designs floating about Texas and
Washington, D.C., regarding an American annexation of Mexico, Juan offered his
services to Governor Santiago Vidaurri of Nuevo León. Sam Houston, then a member of the United States Senate, offered a bill calling for the United States to establish a protectorate over Mexico and Central America.[33] Juan, who traveled to
Monterrey with his wife in the fall of 1858, returned to Texas with a special commission from Governor Vidaurri; he wrote Texas governor Hardin R. Runnels in January 1859 that Vidaurri wished to enter into a treaty with Texas "for the extradition
of fugitive slaves, peons, robbers, murderers and incendiaries."[34] Governor Vidaurri
thus thought to defuse the Texans' hostility by offering to eliminate their more
important grievances against Mexico.

At this point, it becomes necessary to discuss what for historians has been the
most confusing aspect of Juan's life. According to some students of Seguín, he participated in the 1850s and 1860s wars of the Reform and French Intervention and
later on in Porfirio Díaz's 1871 revolt against Benito Juarez.[35] There is evidence,
however, indicating that the Seguín who participated in these wars was not Juan but
Juan Jr. For instance, at the very time Seguín and his wife made their trip to Monterrey in 1858, Santiago Vidaurri received word that a Juan N. Seguín and his cousin
Miguel Zaragoza (General Ignacio Zaragoza's brother) were on their way to San
Antonio with a mule train.[36] A biography of General Zaragoza makes the following
claim in a genealogical note regarding the Seguín-Zaragoza family: "Juan N. Seguín,
born in 1833, who was the one who accompanied Zaragoza during the War of
the Reform with the rank of colonel and who was his third cousin." Moreover,
Seguín would have been sixty-five years old in 1871, the year Díaz rebelled against
Juárez.

Texas did not entirely forget Juan, nor did Texans view him in an unfavorable light
during the last years of his life. During his return to Texas in 1874 to apply for his
pension, Edward Miles, secretary of the Texas Veterans Association, asked Juan to
write some reminiscences for a "Log Cabin History of Texas," a work that was never
published. In 1882 the San Antonio *Light* reported that the Seguín family, "one of
the oldest and most respected of San Antonio" was visiting from Mexico. Five years
later the Clarksville *Northern Standard* published a premature and quite odd obituary of him: "Capt. JUAN N. SEGUIN, of Laredo, the last surviving captain of the battle
of San Jacinto, died in London, England, a few days since. The flag over the capitol
building in Austin was run down to half mast on the 9th in his honor." In the last

eighteen months of his life Juan also answered requests for information from Texans regarding his activities during the War of Independence.[37]

What is remarkable about these late communications is that there is no sense of hostility, bitterness or regret in Juan's words. His 1887 interview with a reporter from the Laredo *Times,* which was reprinted in other Texas newspapers, evidences a man at peace with himself and with the world around him. Even allowing for some literary license, Juan's questions regarding his former compatriots and their descendants, naming John J. and Edward Linn, John S. Menefee, Thomas O'Connor, and others, suggests that he had many fond memories. This was especially true of Houston: "The old veteran recalled with evidences of pride and pleasure the fact of Houston's friendship, and even partiality, for him, saying that 'Old Sam' was wont to call him his son."

Death came for Juan on August 27, 1890, at age eighty-three. This time there were no obituaries, no ceremonies, no notice of his passing. His memoirs have long remained his only epitaph, yet his achievements and travails have not permitted Texas to forget him. As Tejanos rediscover their contributions to Texas history, as they overcome the barriers that separate Texan and Tejano, Juan Seguín has again returned to serve as intermediary between the two.

NOTES

1. Músquiz to Austin, January 22, 1829, AP, II: 9.

2. Election returns, December 21, 1828, BA; Cuaderno borrador of Gaspar Flores and Juan N. Seguín, June 5, 1829, ibid.; Juan to Jefe Político, June 7 and 20, 1829, ibid.; Resumen general, August 10, 1829, ibid.

3. Election of electoral assembly officers, February 13, 1832, BA; Minutes of the electoral assembly, March 1, 1833, ibid.; Minutes of the electoral assembly, February 9, 1834, ibid.

4. Paul Lack, "Los Tejanos: Texas Mexicans in the Revolution," MSS chapter in forthcoming book on Texas War of Independence, 451–52.

5. Lack, "Los Tejanos," 453–54; Antonio Cruz, Audited Military Claims, TSL; Juan Rodríguez, Republic Pension Applications, ibid.

6. Nicolás Flores to Juan, January 23, 1836, BA; [San Antonio Meeting], January 26, 1836; Jenkins, *Papers of the Revolution,* 4:153–55; J. J. Baugh to Henry Smith, February 13, 1836, ibid.; Harbert Davenport, "Captain Jesus Cuellar, Texas Cavalry, Otherwise Comanche," SWHQ 30 (July 1926): 58; Antonio Menchaca, *Memoirs* (San Antonio: Yanaguana Press, 1937), 23.

7. "Alamo's Only Survivor," San Antonio *Express,* May 12, 1907; Menchaca, *Memoirs,* 23; José María Rodríguez, *Rodriguez Memoirs of Early Texas* (reprint, San Antonio: Standard Printing Company, 1961); Lack, "Los Tejanos," 478.

8. Juan Rodríguez, Republic Pension Applications, TSL; Lack, "Los Tejanos," 479–80; William F. Gray, *From Virginia to Texas* (Houston: Gray, Dillaye & Company, 1909), 131.

9. Houston to E. D. White, October 31, 1837, James Grizzard Collection, TSL.

10. Houston to Erasmo, July 6, 1842, *The Writings of Sam Houston, 1813–1863,* ed. Ame-

lia W. Williams and Eugene C. Barker (10 vols., Austin: University of Texas Press, 1938–1943), 4:125.

11. José Enrique de la Peña, *With Santa Anna in Texas: A Personal Narrative of the Revolution* (College Station: Texas A&M University Press, 1975), 4.

12. Felix Huston to Sam Houston, November 14, 1836, Houston Collection, Catholic Archives of Texas.

13. Jack C. Butterfield, "Juan N. Seguín: A Vindication" (MSS, DRT, n.d.), 12–14.

14. Refugio B-5 and Fannin B-440, Original Land Grant Collection, GLO; Juan N. Seguín, Audited Civil Service Claims, Comptroller's Records, TSL.

15. *Telegraph and Texas Register,* May 19, 1838; Ida Vernon, "Activities of the Seguíns in Early Texas History" (West Texas Historical Association Year Book 25, 1949), 28; Joseph M. Nance, *After San Jacinto: The Texas Mexican Frontier, 1836–1841* (Austin: University of Texas Press, 1963), 281.

16. Unable to afford the expenses of public colleges, Congress promoted the establishment of private institutions through grants of public land.

17. Charles E. Castañeda, *Our Catholic Heritage in Texas, 1519–1936* (New York: Arno, 1976), 7:25–27.

18. Smithers to John P. Borden, July 13, 1838, Early Letters Received, GLO (microfilm).

19. McLeod to Lamar, August 24, 1840, Lamar Papers, TSL.

20. *Memoirs of Mary A. Maverick,* 29.

21. Benjamin Gillam to Hugh McLeod, January 10, 1841, Army Papers, Adjutant General's Records, TSL; White, *The 1840 Census of the Republic of Texas,* 16; Nance, *After San Jacinto,* 409.

22. Journal A, Records of the City of San Antonio from 1837 to 1849, Material from Various Sources, BHC, vol. 815:79.

23. Journal A, Records of the City of San Antonio, vol. 815: 87, 89, BHC; Vernon, "Activities of the Seguíns," 31–32.

24. Journal A, Records of the City of San Antonio, BHC, vol. 815: 82; Juan and Gertrudis Seguín to Howard and Ogden, July 2, 1841, Deed Records of Bexar County, vol. A-2: 447–48; Nance, *After San Jacinto,* 431–34.

25. Nance, *After San Jacinto,* 434.

26. *Memoirs of Mary A. Maverick,* 59.

27. Corner, *San Antonio,* 113.

28. Harriet Smither, ed., "Diary of Adolphus Sterne," Part XV, SWHQ 33 (April 1930): 318.

29. Veatch to Lamar, February 23, 1848, Lamar Papers, doc. 2377, TSL.

30. Vernon, "Activities of the Seguíns," 36; 1850 Census of the United States, Bexar County (microfilm), #146, TSL.

31. *El Bejareño,* July 7, 1855; Santos, "Juan Nepomuceno Seguín," 563.

32. *El Bejareño,* July 21, 1855.

33. Santos, "Juan Nepomuceno Seguín," 564–65; Llerena Friend, *Sam Houston: The Great Designer* (reprint, Austin: University of Texas Press, 1969), 298–300.

34. Juan to Hardin R. Runnels, January 8, 1859, Hardin Richard Runnels Correspondence, Governors Papers, TSL.

35. Jack Jackson, *Los Tejanos* (Stamford: Fantagraphics Press, 1982), 121; Santos, in "Juan Nepomuceno Seguín," 565 (fn. 44), 566, cites the Archivo de la Defensa Nacional, where he examined a folder on "Juan N. Seguín." The author could not consult this folder as it is now unavailable.

36. *La Voz de Zaragoza*, 1 (December 1961): 27; Guillermo Colin Sánchez, *Ignacio Zaragoza*: *Evocación de un héroe* (Mexico: Editorial Porrúa, 1963), 41.

37. San Antonio *Light*, November 13, 1882; Clarksville *Northern Standard*, August 18, 1887.

❋   ❋   ❋

QUESTIONS

1. According to Seguín, why and by whom is he being persecuted? How might his own perception of who he is differ from the subjectivities constructed by Chicanos, Anglos, and Mexicans?

2. On what grounds can we argue that geopolitical forces justify (or do not justify) the subjugation of indigenous people by others more economically, technologically, and militarily more powerful?

3. In what ways does or does not "The Making of a Tejano" seem to fit with U.S. American stereotypes of "Mexicans"?

4. What might be alternative constructions of Indian subjectivities, presented in this text as "hostile attackers of peaceful settlements"?

5. About the representation of Others: this is primarily a male story and, therefore, the status of women, slaves, the working class, and Indians is made obvious by their own invisibility. What voices are not being heard (in addition to Gertrudis Seguín and Juan López, the orphan who "looked like an Indian")?

❋ 7 ❋

LETTER FROM JAMES BUCHANAN AND THE
TREATY OF GUADALUPE HIDALGO

As you read the following treaty, formally titled the Treaty of Peace, Friendship, Limits, and Settlement between the United States and Mexico, you may be wondering "Why did the war between the United States and Mexico happen?" You may recall from previous readings that, after three hundred years of Spanish domination, the nation-state of Mexico was born in 1821 out of the War of Independence in a precarious position, with a devastated economy, warring political factions, and public debt, and soon was dismembered (losing Texas and Central America). Meanwhile, the United States was fulfilling its desire for economic and territorial expansion through the Louisiana Purchase and the acquisition of Texas. As can be expected in a game of truth where the stakes are so high, there are at least five interpretations of who was responsible for the war. One has already been mentioned: manifest destiny, the imperial expansion of the United States. From a purely economic perspective, commercial interests, New England merchants especially, are another explanation. Similarly, a third explanation blames sectional interests, like the Old South's attempt to extend slavery or the West's desire for further expansion. But if we want to blame individuals, the most likely character to blame in a fourth interpretation has been President James K. Polk. Finally, others put responsibility generally on one nation or the other, Mexico or the United States.[1]

In the case of Texas and the Seguín family, we already saw the process of an economic, political, and social seduction that promised to fulfill the desires of the Tejano elite. This same process was repeated throughout the northern provinces of Mexico, with General Mariano Vallejo in California and Governor Manuel Armijo in New Mexico; later it occurred in Cuba and Puerto Rico, creating what Louis A. Pérez calls "binding familiarities" (referring to early Cuban-U.S. relations). Besides the geopolitical perspective, however, it is helpful to gaze at the microphysics of power (see appendix 5) by which this seduction anticipates military intervention and the signing of treaties. As soon as Mexico became independent from Spain (1821), an enterprising William Beck-nell put together a trading party and traveled eight hundred miles from Franklin, Missouri, to what was then the Mexican border, Santa Fé, Nuevo México, where he was welcomed by Spanish-born Governor Facundo Melgares to sell his wares at a princely profit. As David Weber recounts,

> New Mexicans traded bullion, horses, and mules for American manufactured goods, becoming economically depen-
> dent upon the Americans. American trappers and merchants made New Mexico their permanent home . . . becoming
> Roman Catholics and citizens, learning Spanish, and marrying or living with New Mexican women. . . . New
> Mexicans learned that the "gringos," although often unpleasant, were not devils and that American rule over the
> territory would not be intolerable. At the same time, the Americans learned enough of local customs and of the
> power structure to serve as an effective fifth column when war erupted between the United States and Mexico.[2]

The Santa Fe Trail was soon connected to California via the Old Spanish Trail (which had never been used by the Spaniards) and a two-way trade of commodities flowed from the United States, through the northern provinces, and into the interior of Mexico. Thus, as in Texas, the geopolitical dimensions of this process pointed to the interior of Mexico; arguably, it is the same process of economic seduction that more recently led to the signing of the North American Free Trade Agreement (NAFTA).[3] Then as now, not all Mexicans welcomed the U.S. Americans and the disagreement was usually along class lines, with the wealthy supporting relations with the Anglo neighbors. This is similar to the case of Cuba, though in Puerto Rico we find the elite opposing and the poor supporting U.S. intervention. Two final points need to be made here: one is that when it comes to an object of desire all parties become conspirators; the other point is that in this game of truth the voice of the poor people had been deflected.

Below are two kinds of texts. First is Secretary of State James Buchanan's letter to the minister of foreign relations of Mexico, explaining the U.S. Senate amendments to the treaty. Secondly, from the twenty-three articles of the Treaty of Guadalupe Hidalgo we have selected articles VIII–XV, which affect the Mexicans who ended up in the territories taken over by the United States. To allow a comparison, we include copies of articles IX and X, before they were amended (they deal with questions of landownership in the newly conquered territory and also in Texas).

With these documents, Mexicans living in the conquered territories became territorial, involuntary citizens of the United States (although they were given a choice, in one way or another, they became subjects of the government). Unlike Cubans and Puerto Ricans, Mexicans received citizenship at the time of their military conquest. (The term "Mexicans," however, applied to "white" Mexicans and not to Mexican Indians, who were considered Mexican citizens according to Mexican law.) With these documents, Mexico lost half of its territory, including California, New Mexico, Arizona, and parts of Nevada, Wyoming, Kansas, Oklahoma, Colo-rado, and Utah, for which it received an indemnity of $15 million. For purposes of comparison, this same year President Polk offered Spain $100 million for Cuba. This is the harshest treaty in two hundred years of U.S. territorial acquisition, and the only U.S. national document addressing Mexican Americans.[4]

NOTES AND SUGGESTED READINGS

1. Ramón Eduardo Ruiz, *The Mexican War: Was It Manifest Destiny?* (Hinsdale, Ill.: Dryden, 1963).

2. David J. Weber, *Foreigners in Their Native Land* (Albuquerque: University of New Mexico Press, 1973), 56. Governor Manuel Armijo sent word in 1827 to Mexico City "that every day the foreigners are becoming more influential over the miserable inhabitants of this Territory" and warning of an "evil of great consequence" should the foreigners not be dealt with. The new nation, however, lacked the resources to defend its northern frontier, so ultimately Armijo followed the example of other New Mexican oligarchs, formed a trading partnership with an American, and began importing goods from the United States. From Texas to California, Mexicans with capital welcomed the opportunity to trade with foreigners, due to the low cost of U.S. manufactured goods compared with the outrageous prices the Spanish had charged. And though the threat of invasion was very real, as Weber points out, "ideology and diplomacy were not nearly as important as low-cost merchandise and the end of isolation" (135).

3. For a recent analysis on the negotiation of NAFTA, see Maxwell A. Cameron and Brian W. Tomlin, *The Making of NAFTA* (Ithaca, N.Y.: Cornell University Press, 2000).

4. Juan Gómez-Quiñonez, *Roots of Chicano Politics, 1600–1940* (Albuquerque: University of New Mexico Press, 1994), 188–89.

LETTER FROM JAMES BUCHANAN TO THE MINISTER OF FOREIGN RELATIONS OF MEXICO[1]

To His Excellency, the Minister of Foreign Relations
of the Mexican Republic.

Sir: Two years have nearly passed away since our Republics have been engaged in war. Causes, which it would now be vain if not hurtful to recapitulate, have produced this calamity. Under the blessing of a kind Providence, this war, I trust, is about to terminate, and, hereafter, instead of the two nations doing each other all the harm they can, their mutual energies will be devoted to promote each other's welfare by the pursuits of peace and of commerce. I most cordially congratulate you on the cheering prospect. This will become a reality as soon as the Mexican Government shall approve the treaty of peace between the two nations concluded at Guadalupe Hidalgo on the 2nd February, last, with the amendments thereto which have been adopted by the Senate of the United States.

The President, in the exercise of his constitutional discretion, a few days after this treaty was received, submitted it to the Senate for their consideration and advice as to its ratification. Your Excellency is doubtless aware that under the Constitution of the United States, "the advice and consent of the Senate" is necessary to the validity of all treaties and that this must be given by a majority of two thirds of the Senators present. Every Treaty must receive the sanction of this august Executive Council in the manner prescribed by the Constitution, before it can be binding on the United States.

The Senate commenced their deliberations on this Treaty on the 23rd February, last, and continued to discuss its provisions until the 10th instant (March) when they finally advised and consented to its ratification by a majority of 38 to 14. Your

Excellency will perceive that a change of 4 votes taken from the majority and added to the minority would have defeated the Treaty.

I have now the honor to transmit you a printed copy of the Treaty with a copy, in manuscript, of the amendments and final proceedings of the Senate upon it. This is done to hasten with as little delay as practicable the blessed consummation of peace by placing in the possession of the Mexican Government at as early a period as possible all the information which they may require to guide their deliberations.

In recurring to the amendments adopted by the Senate, it affords me sincere satisfaction to observe that none of the leading features of the Treaty have been changed. Neither the delineation of the boundaries between the two Republics—nor the consideration to be paid to Mexico for the extension of the boundaries of the United States—nor the obligation of the latter to restrain the Indians within their limits from committing hostilities on the territories of Mexico nor, indeed, any other stipulation of national importance to either of the parties, has been stricken out from the Treaty by the Senate. In all its important features, it remains substantially as it was when it came from the hands of the negotiators.

The first amendment adopted by the Senate is to insert in Article 3 after the words "Mexican Republic" where they first occur, the words, *"and the Ratifications exchanged."*

Under this article, as it originally stood, the blockades were to cease and the troops of the United States were to commence the evacuation of the Mexican territory immediately upon the ratification of the Treaty by both Governments. The amendment requires in addition that these ratifications shall have been first exchanged.

The object of this amendment doubtless was to provide against the possibility that the American Senate and the Mexican Congress might ratify the Treaty, the first in its amended and the latter in its original form: in which event peace would not thereby be concluded. Besides, it was known that this amendment could produce no delay, as under the amendment of the Senate to the 23rd article, the ratification of the Treaty may be exchanged at the seat of Government of Mexico the moment after the Mexican Government and Congress shall have accepted the Treaty as amended by the Senate of the United States.

The second amendment of the Senate is to strike out the 9th Article and insert the following in lieu thereof.

[Here follows the English version of Article 9]

This article is substantially the same with the original 9th article; but it avoids unnecessary prolixity and accords with the former safe precedents of this Government in the Treaties by which we acquired Louisiana from France and Florida from Spain.

The Louisiana Treaty of the 30th April, 1803 [Document 28], contains the following article.

ARTICLE 3

The inhabitants of the ceded territory shall be incorporated in the union of the United States, and admitted as soon us possible, according to the principles of the

Federal Constitution, to the enjoyment of all the rights, advantages and immunities of citizens of the United States, and in the mean time they shall be maintained and protected in the free enjoyment of their liberty, property, and the religion which they profess.

Again, in the Florida Treaty of 22nd February, 1819 [Document 41], the following articles are contained.

ARTICLE 5

The inhabitants of the ceded Territories shall be secured in the free exercise of their religion, without any restriction; and all those who may desire to remove to the Spanish Dominions, shall be permitted to sell or export their effects, at any time whatever, without being subject, in either case, to duties.

ARTICLE 6

The inhabitants of the territories which His Catholic Majesty cedes to the United States, by his Treaty, shall be incorporated in the Union of the United States, as soon as may be consistent with the principles of the Federal Constitution, and admitted to the enjoyment of all the privileges, rights and immunities of the citizens of the United States.

Under these Treaties with France and Spain, the free and flourishing States of Louisiana, Missouri, Arkansas, Iowa and Florida have been admitted into the Union; and no complaint has ever been made by the original or other inhabitants that their civil or religious rights have not been amply protected. The property belonging to the different churches in the United States is held as sacred by our Constitution and laws as the property of individuals, and every individual enjoys the inalienable right of worshipping his God according to the dictates of his own conscience. The Catholic Church in this country would not, if they could, change their position in this particular.

After the successful experience of nearly half a century, the Senate did not deem it advisable to adopt any new form for the 9th Article of the Treaty; and surely the Mexican Government ought to be content with an article similar to those which have proved satisfactory to the Governments of France and Spain and to all the inhabitants of Louisiana and Florida, both of which were Catholic provinces.

I ought perhaps here to note a modification in the 9th article, as adopted by the Senate, of the analogous articles of the Louisiana and Florida Treaties. Under this modification, the inhabitants of the ceded territories are to be admitted into the Union, "at the proper time (to be judged of by the Congress of the United States") &c.

Congress, under all circumstances and under all Treaties are the sole judges of this proper time, because they and they alone, under the Federal Constitution, have power to admit new States into the Union. That they will always exercise this power as soon as the condition of the inhabitants of any acquired territory may render it proper, cannot be doubted. By this means the Federal Treasury can alone be relieved from the expense of supporting territorial Governments. Besides, Congress will never lend a deaf ear to a people anxious to enjoy the privilege of self government. Their application to become a State or States of the Union will be granted the moment this can be done with safety.

The third amendment of the Senate strikes from the Treaty the 10th Article.

It is truly unaccountable how this article should have found a place in the Treaty. That portion of it in regard to lands in Texas did not receive a single vote in the Senate. If it were adopted, it would be a mere nullity on the face of the Treaty, and the Judges of our Courts would be compelled to disregard it. It is our glory that no human power exists in this country which can deprive one individual of his property without his consent and transfer it to another. If grantees of lands in Texas, under the Mexican Government, possess valid titles, they can maintain their claims before our Courts of Justice. If they have forfeited their grants by not complying with the conditions on which they were made, it is beyond the power of this Government, in any mode of action, to render these titles valid either against Texas or any individual proprietor. To resuscitate such grants and to allow the grantees the same period after the exchange of the ratifications of this Treaty to which they were originally entitled for the purpose of performing the conditions on which these grants had been made, even if this could be accomplished by the power of the government of the United States, would work manifold injustice.

These Mexican grants, it is understood, cover nearly the whole sea coast and a large portion of the interior of Texas. They embrace thriving villages and a great number of cultivated farms, the proprietors of which have acquired them honestly by purchase from the State of Texas. These proprietors are now dwelling in peace and security. To revive dead titles and suffer the inhabitants of Texas to be ejected under them from their possessions, would be an act of flagrant injustice if not wanton cruelty. Fortunately this Government possesses no power to adopt such a proceeding.

The same observations equally apply to such grantees in New Mexico and Upper California.

The present Treaty provides amply and specifically in its 8th and 9th Articles for the security of property of every kind belonging to Mexicans, whether acquired under Mexican grants or otherwise in the acquired territory. The property of foreigners under our Constitution and laws, will be equally secure without any Treaty stipulation. The tenth article could have no effect upon such grantees as had forfeited their claims, but that of involving them in endless litigation under the vain hope that a Treaty might cure the defects in their titles against honest purchasers and owners of the soil.

And here it may be worthy of observation that if no stipulation whatever were contained in the Treaty to secure to the Mexican inhabitants and all others protection in the free enjoyment of their liberty, property and the religion which they profess, these would be amply guaranteed by the Constitution and laws of the United States. These invaluable blessings, under our form of Government, do not result from Treaty stipulations, but from the very nature and character of our institutions. . . .

James Buchanan
Department of State
Washington, 18th March, 1848

THE TREATY OF GUADALUPE HIDALGO: ARTICLES 8–15[2]

Article VIII

Mexicans now established in territories previously belonging to Mexico, and which remain for the future within the limits of the United States, as defined by the present treaty, shall be free to continue where they now reside, or to remove at any time to the Mexican Republic, retaining the property which they possess in the said territories, or disposing thereof, and removing the proceeds wherever they please, without their being subjected, on this account, to any contribution, tax or charge whatever.

Those who shall prefer to remain in the said territories, may either retain the title and rights of Mexican citizens, or acquire those of citizens of the United States. But they shall be under the obligation to make their election within one year from the date of the exchange of ratifications of this treaty: and those who shall remain in the said territories, after the expiration of that year without having declared their intention to retain the character of Mexicans, shall be considered to have elected to become citizens of the United States.

In the said territories, property of every kind, now belonging to Mexicans, not established there, shall be inviolably respected. The present owners, the heirs of these and all Mexicans who may hereafter acquire said property by contract, shall enjoy with respect to it, guarantees equally ample as if the same belonged to citizens of the United States.

Article IX

The Mexicans who, in the territories aforesaid, shall not preserve the character of citizens of the Mexican Republic, conformably with what is stipulated in the preceding article, shall be incorporated into the Union of the United States and be admitted, at the proper time (to be judged of by the Congress of the United States) to the enjoyment of all the rights of citizens of the United States according to the principles of the Constitution; and in the mean time shall be maintained and protected in the free enjoyment of their liberty and property, and secured in the free exercise of their region without restriction.

[*One of the amendments of the Senate struck out Article 10.*]

Article XI

Considering that a great part of the territories which, by the present Treaty, are to be comprehended for the future within the limits of the United States, is now occupied by savage tribes, who will hereafter be under the exclusive control of the Government of the United States, and whose incursions within the territory of Mexico would be prejudicial in the extreme; it is solemnly agreed that all such incursions shall be forcibly restrained by the Government of the United States, whensoever this may be necessary; and that when they cannot be prevented, they shall be punished by the said Government, and satisfaction for the same shall be exacted, all in the same way, and with equal diligence and energy, as if the same incursions were meditated or committed within its own territory against its own citizens.

It shall not be lawful, under any pretext whatever, for any inhabitant of the United States, to purchase or acquire any Mexican or any foreigner residing in Mexico, who may have been captured by Indians inhabiting the territory of either of the two Republics, nor to purchase or acquire horses, mules, cattle or property of any kind, stolen within Mexican territory by such Indians.

And, in the event of any person or persons, captured within Mexican Territory by Indians, being carried into the territory of the United States, the Government of the latter engages and binds itself in the most solemn manner, so soon as it shall know of such captives being within its territory, and shall be able so to do, through the faithful exercise of its influence and power, to rescue them and return them to their country, or deliver them to the agent or representative of the Mexican Government. The Mexican Authorities will, as far as practicable, give to the Government of the United States notice of such captures; and its agent shall pay the expenses incurred in the maintenance and transmission of the rescued captives; who, in the mean time, shall be treated with the utmost hospitality by the American authorities at the place where they may be. But if the Government of the United States, before receiving such notice from Mexico, should obtain intelligence through any other channel, of the existence of Mexican captives within its territory, it will proceed forthwith to effect their release and delivery to the Mexican agent, as above stipulated.

For the purpose of giving to these stipulations the fullest possible efficacy, thereby affording the security and redress demanded by their true spirit and intent, the Government of the United States will now and hereafter pass, without unnecessary delay, and always vigilantly enforce, such laws as the nature of the subject may require. And finally, the sacredness of this obligation shall never be lost sight of by the said Government, when providing for the removal of the Indians from any portion of the said territories, or for its being settled by citizens of the United States; but on the contrary special care shall then be taken not to place its Indian occupants under the necessity of seeking new homes, by committing those invasions which the United States have solemnly obliged themselves to restrain.

Article XII

In consideration of the extension acquired by the boundaries of the United States, as defined in the fifth Article of the present Treaty, the Government of the United

States engages to pay to that of the Mexican Republic the sum of fifteen Millions of Dollars.

Immediately after this treaty shall have been duly ratified by the Government of the Mexican Republic, the sum of three millions of dollars shall be paid to the said Government by that of the United States at the city of Mexico, in the gold or silver coin of Mexico. The remaining twelve millions of dollars shall be paid at the same place and in the same coin, in annual installments of three millions of dollars each, together with interest on the same at the rate of six per centum per annum. This interest shall begin to run upon the whole sum of twelve millions, from the day of the ratification of the present treaty by the Mexican Government, and the first of the installments shall be paid at the expiration of one year from the same day. Together with each annual installment, as it falls due, the whole interest accruing on such installment from the beginning shall also be paid.

Article XIII

The United States engage moreover, to assume and pay to the claimants all amounts now due them, and those hereafter to become due, by reason of the claims already liquidated and decided against the Mexican Republic, under the conventions between the two Republics severally concluded on the eleventh day of April eighteen hundred and thirty-nine, and on the thirtieth day of January eighteen hundred and forty-three: so that the Mexican Republic shall be absolutely exempt for the future, from all expense whatever on account of the said claims.

Article XIV

The United States do furthermore discharge the Mexican Republic from all claims of citizens of the United States, not heretofore decided against the Mexican Government, which may have arisen previously to the date of the signature of this treaty: which discharge shall be final and perpetual, whether the said claims be rejected or be allowed by the Board of Commissioners provided for in the following Article, and whatever shall be the total amount of those allowed.

Article XV

The United States, exonerating Mexico from all demands on account of the claims of their citizens mentioned in the preceding Article, and considering them entirely and forever cancelled, whatever their amount may be, undertake to make satisfaction for the same, to an amount not exceeding three and one quarter millions of Dollars. To ascertain the validity and amount of those claims, a Board of Commissioners shall be established by the Government of the United States, who awards shall be final and conclusive: provided that in deciding upon the validity of each claim, the board shall be guided and governed By the principles and rules of decision prescribed by the first and fifth Articles of the unratified convention, concluded at the

City of Mexico on the twentieth day of November, one thousand eight hundred and forty-three; and in no case shall an award be made in favour of any claim not embraced by these principles and rules.

If, in the opinion of the said Board of Commissioners, or of the claimants, any books, records or documents in the possession or power of the Government of the Mexican Republic, shall be deemed necessary to the just decision of any claim, the Commissioners or the claimants, through them, shall, within such period as Congress may designate, make an application in writing for the same, addressed to the Mexican Minister for Foreign Affairs, to be transmitted by the Secretary of State of the United States; and the Mexican Government engages, at the earliest possible moment after the receipt of such demand, to cause any of the books, records or documents, so specified, which shall be in their possession or power (or authenticated Copies or extracts of the same) to be transmitted to the said Secretary of State, who shall immediately deliver them over to the said Board of Commissioners: provided that no such application shall be made, by, or at the instance of, any claimant, until the facts which it is expected to prove by such books, records or documents, shall have been stated under oath or affirmation.

THE TREATY OF GUADALUPE HIDALGO: ARTICLES 9 AND 10 BEFORE SENATE AMENDMENT[3]

Article IX

The Mexicans who, in the territories aforesaid, shall not preserve the character of citizens of the Mexican Republic, conformably with what is stipulated in the preceding Article, shall be incorporated into the Union of the United States, and admitted as soon as possible, according to the principles of the Federal Constitution, to the enjoyment of all the rights of citizens of the United States. In the mean time, they shall be maintained and protected in the enjoyment of their liberty, their property, and the civil rights now vested in them according to the Mexican laws. With respect to political rights, their condition shall be on an equality with that of the inhabitants of the other territories of the United States; and at least equally good as that of the inhabitants of Louisiana and the Floridas, when these provinces, by transfer from the French Republic and the Crown of Spain, became territories of the United States.

The same most ample guaranty shall be enjoyed by all ecclesiastics and religious corporations or communities, as well in the discharge of the offices of their ministry, as in the enjoyment of their property of every kind, whether individual or corporate. This guaranty shall embrace all temples, houses and edifices dedicated to the Roman Catholic worship; as well as all property destined to its support, or to that of schools, hospitals and other foundations for charitable or beneficent purposes. No property of this nature shall be considered as having become the property of the American Government, or as subject to be, by it, disposed of or diverted to other uses.

Finally, the relations and communication between the Catholics living in the territories aforesaid, and their respective ecclesiastical authorities, shall be open, free and exempt from all hindrance whatever, even although such authorities should reside within the limits of the Mexican Republic, as defined by this treaty; and this freedom shall continue, so long as a new demarcation of ecclesiastical districts shall not have been made, conformably with the laws of the Roman Catholic Church.

Article X

All grants of land made by the Mexican Government or by the competent authorities, in territories previously appertaining to Mexico, and remaining for the future within the limits of the United States, shall be respected as valid, to the same extent that the same grants would be valid, if the said territories had remained within the limits of Mexico. But the grantees of lands in Texas, put in possession thereof, who, by reason of the circumstances of the country since the beginning of the troubles between Texas and the Mexican Government, may have been prevented from fulfilling all the conditions of their grants, shall be under the obligation to fulfill the said conditions within the periods limited in the same respectively; such periods to be now counted from the date of the exchange of ratifications of this treaty: in default of which the said grants shall not be obligatory upon the State of Texas, in virtue of the stipulations contained in this Article.

The foregoing stipulation in regard to grantees of land in Texas, is extended to all grantees of land in the territories aforesaid, elsewhere than in Texas, put in possession under such grants; and, in default of the fulfillment of the conditions of any such grant, within the new period, which, as is above stipulated, begins with the day of the exchange of ratifications of this treaty, the same shall be null and void.

The Mexican Government declares that no grant whatever of lands in Texas has been made since the second day of March one thousand eight hundred and thirty-six; and that no grant whatever of lands in any of the territories aforesaid has been made since the thirteenth day of May one thousand eight hundred and forty-six.

NOTES

1. Reprinted from Hunter Miller, ed., *Treaties and Other International Acts of the United States of America*, Vol. 5 (Washington, D.C.: Government Printing Office, 1937), pp. 253–57.

2. Reprinted from Miller, ed., *Treaties and Other International Acts of the United States of America*.

3. Reprinted from Miller, ed., *Treaties and Other International Acts of the United States of America*.

✳   ✳   ✳

QUESTIONS

1. What is your impression of the tone of Buchanan's letter?

2. Do you agree with Buchanan that the problem with the original article IX was "unnecessary prolixity"?

3. How might a Puerto Rican react to Buchanan's claim that "Congress will never lend a deaf ear to a people anxious to enjoy the privilege of self government. Their application to become a State or States of the Union will be granted the moment this can be done with safety"?

4. Again, according to Buchanan, "no human power exists in this country which can deprive one individual of his property without his consent and transfer it to another." A similar sentiment is expressed in article IX. What might have happened, then, that by 1923 most propertied Mexicans who remained in the United States had become destitute?

5. How can one explain the different perceptions regarding article X?

FROM SPANISH COLONIES, TO INDEPENDENCE, TO U.S. AMERICAN COLONIES: THE TREATY OF PARIS

What led to the Treaty of Paris of April 11, 1898? What caused this "splendid little war" (so called by then Secretary of State John Hay)? Not surprisingly, there are different explanations. The United States declared war on Spain when the warship USS *Maine*, which had been sent to protect American citizens, mysteriously exploded in Havana harbor. To protect Americans citizens from what? From the war that Cubans had been fighting against the Spaniards. One view is that the United States needed to control these countries for strategic reasons and provoked the war when it was clear that these countries were about to become independent. Others say that the U.S. economy needed expansion. And still others argue that the United States was just responding to the cries for help on the part of oppressed peoples. The larger historical context is that Cubans, Puerto Ricans, and Filipinos were engaged in the latest round of struggles against European imperialism started by the Haitian African slaves on May 6, 1794 (leading to Haiti's independence from France) and continued by Hidalgo, Sucre, San Martín, and Bolívar in the following three decades (see Vázquez, chapter 5).

The Spanish-American War was fought mostly on Cuban soil, from April to August 1898, and it won for the United States, Puerto Rico, Guam, the Marianas, Samoa, Panamá, the Philippine Islands (until 1946), and Cuba (until 1959, when Fidel Castro took over). This was a violation of these countries' expectations to be completely free and independent, not only from Spain but also from any other power, including the United States. The Treaty of Paris also marks the time that the United States itself was "born" as a twentieth-century world power. What strikes as ironic is the discontinuity of a revolutionary discourse. In other words, U.S. Americans, in this shift to an imperial power, seem to have forgotten their own revolutionary roots, their own struggle against oppression. Now they turned against those compatriots who struggled for freedom. Even though this war took place a little over one hundred years ago, the implications for Puerto Ricans and Cubans are very much alive today. Will Puerto Rico remain a colony, become independent, or become the fifty-first state of the United States? Will Cuba continue to be independent or will Cuban Americans, given the opportunity, attempt to make Cuba part of the United States? But we are getting ahead of the story.

U.S. AMERICANS AND CUBANS: RELATIONS OF MUTUAL DESIRE

In many ways, Cubans were the first Latinos to become American cultural citizens. Cubans were conceived as Cuban Americans as early as 1848, when U.S. president Polk offered Spain $100 million for the island. (The same year, the United States paid Mexico $15 million for half of Mexico and as a war settlement.) Four years later President Franklin Pierce upped the offer to $130 million, without success. As for the Cuban people, their experience of the United States can be traced to the early 1850s. At a time when northern Mexicans were attempting to cope with the consequences of being new, involuntary U.S. citizens, when the United States itself was undergoing fundamental geopolitical and economic changes, Cubans in the United States and on the island were searching for ways to give expression to their own sense of nationality. Louis A. Pérez makes several key observations worth mentioning here.[1] Over three successive generations, Cubans of all classes and ages, men and women, black and white, emigrated to the Unites States to escape life in colonial Cuba and to plot the revolution against Spain. These included the people who would play a major role in the construction of *cubanismo,* of Cuban identity and nationality. More incisively, "they early developed the type of familiarity [with U.S. Americans] often reserved for a people of the same nation."[2] These events illustrate a particular aspect of a process of acquiring "cultural citizenship" discussed by Vázquez in chapter 3.

As an alternative to Spanish rule, Cubans contemplated a life similar to the one they had experienced in the United States. Consequently, their sense of self and of nation, and many of their values, such as the affirmation of modernity, progress, and above all civilization, were adopted from the United States. "At some point late in the nineteenth century," Pérez writes, "it became all but impossible for Cubans to contemplate their future, especially their future well-being, without pausing first to reflect on their relationship to North Americans." These circumstances paved "the way for the subsequent arrival of North Americans as bearers of more of the same truths after the U.S. intervention in 1898."[3] There are important implications here.

An important difference from the conquest of northern Mexicans, of all classes, is that while economic and political elements were obviously (and necessarily) involved, in the case of Cubans, it was more a case of cultural seduction. Pérez's thesis is, in effect, that "Cuban participation was indispensable to the success of U.S. hegemony and that Cubans bore some responsibility for their own domination, although it must be emphasized that few at the time would have remotely construed their condition as one of 'subjugation.'"[4] The same judgment may be said to apply to the Mexican elites from northern Mexico. And yet coercion and violence, low wages, and racism were also a part of the relationship. Consequently, as with any political relation, the possibility for conflict is always there, ready to erupt when the economic and political conditions are ripe, such as they were in the late 1950s with the arrival of Fidel Castro on the scene. The following two articles describe a particular aspect of the U.S.-Cuban relations of mutual desire.

NOTES AND SUGGESTED READINGS

1. Louis A. Pérez, *On Becoming Cuban: Identity, Nationality and Culture* (Chapel Hill: University of North Carolina Press, 1999).

2. Pérez, *On Becoming Cuban,* 6.

3. Pérez, *On Becoming Cuban,* 7.

4. Pérez, *On Becoming Cuban,* 10.

✳ 8 ✳
MEANINGS IN TRANSITION

Louis A. Pérez

The material conditions that set the stage for eventual colonization included commercial trade unique to each countries' needs and a transfer of technology (steamships, railroads, telegraph) that led to the need for U.S.-trained personnel. U.S. Americans began to arrive in great numbers (doubling their numbers between 1846 and 1862) and to dominate the local economy. Incidentally, many of the newcomers to Cuba were transients on their way to the California gold rush. The reaction of the Spanish authorities was similar to that of the Mexican authorities with respect to Texas: to consider restricting the acquisition of land by U.S. Americans. To the chagrin of many Cubans, the English language also began to spread throughout the island. As in the case of northern Mexico, among the U.S. Americans settling in Cuba were drifters, deserters, fugitives, and escaped convicts.

In the following text, we see the other side of the two-way traffic between the United States and Cuba: Cubanization of the United States. This piece provides details regarding the tens of thousands who went for tourism, for education, for employment, to escape political repression, or to plot the revolution and describes the many levels of their integration into U.S. society. Most importantly, it discusses how the emigration served to forge many vital elements of Cuban nationality. The discourse on nation benefited from the freedom to discuss, communicate, and publish. The discourse on nation also expanded from the *criollo* elite to include statements from the working class and the poor and also extended to include the role of women. We consider this as a further illustration of a quest for public citizenship.

Throughout the nineteenth century Cubans went to the United States by the tens of thousands, as tourists and travelers, vacationers and visitors, for education and employment, to escape political repression and plot colonial revolution. They represented a broad population: planters, merchants, manufacturers, workers, and members of the middle class, including attorneys, engineers, physicians, dentists, journalists, teachers, publishers, writers, and students. Among them were intellectuals José Antonio Saco and Rafael María Mendive; journalists Carmela Nieto de Herrera, Víctor Muñoz, Enrique Piñeyro, Julio Villoldo, Rafael Serra, and Raimundo Cabrera; labor leaders Carlos Baliño and Diego Vicente Tejera; historian Pedro José Guiteras; painter Leopoldo Romañach; poets Miguel Teurbe Tolón and Bonifacio Byrne; and novelists Cirilo Villaverde, Miguel de Carrión, Carlos Loveira, and Luis Rodríguez Embil.

Cubans integrated themselves at all levels of North American society. They attended school, obtained jobs, set up households, and raised families in communities across the United States. They established medical and dental practices and opened law offices. They engaged in all types of commercial activities. Many operated small business enterprises and retail stores. They adapted to North American ways of doing business, used local newspapers to advertise their goods and services, and learned that good business meant prompt service and competitive pricing. In local advertisements Antonio López, who owned the United States Laundry in Key West, assured prospective customers of "promptness in delivery and moderation in price [that] will prove satisfactory to all."[1] Luis M. Arredondo, who graduated from Manhattan College in 1882 subsequently worked as an interpreter for various New York hotels. The number of Cuban-owned hotels and boardinghouses increased throughout the nineteenth century; many served as the point of entry for newly arrived émigrés.[2]

Cubans bought countless retail stores, cafes and restaurants, pharmacies, barbershops, and *bodegas* (general stores). In New York, Manuel García Cuervo owned the Bodega Cubana and sold products of Cuba and *sanwiches* of all types. Julián Moreno was proprietor of the Restaurant Cubano, where "the food is Cuban, it's good, and moderately priced." Emiliano Pérez operated the barbershop in the lobby of Central Hotel. José Guillermo Díaz, who identified himself as an "ex-professor of the Faculty of Pharmacy at the University of Havana," operated the Columbia Pharmacy on Lexington and Eighty-seven Street. Echemendía and Company was a Cuban-owned publishing house. Néstor Ponce de León and Ignacio Mora owned bookstores. *Patria*'s roster of Cuban advertisers in New York between 1892 and 1895 listed forty cigar manufacturers, thirty-five physicians, twenty-five merchants, twenty attorneys, fifteen music teachers, six dentists, five bodegas, four restaurants, three drugstores, and two colegios.[3] In Key West, Gabriel Ayala owned the Nuevo Siglo grocery store, J. Avelino Delgado operated the Singer Sewing Machine agency, and D. Báez and Company managed a popular dry goods store. In Tampa, the Valdés Brothers operated a successful dry goods establishment. Manuel Moreno de la Torre, proprietor of El Bazar Americano, sold shoes, hats, and "Cuban style clothing"; Manuel Viñas's La María bakery sold "Cuban and American style bread." Marcos I. Sánchez operated a real estate office, Francisco Ysern was the proprietor of the Salón Central liquor store, and Antonio Salazar managed El Central restaurant.

Cubans were appointed to government positions and elected to political office at the municipal, state, and federal levels. In Key West, Alejandro Mendoza, Enrique Esquinaldo, Rogelio Gómez, and Juan María Reyes served as justices of the peace; Alfredo Reynoso was chief of police, and Juan Busto, Delio Cobo, Marcos Mesa, Juan Carbonell, Manuel Varela, and José Valdés were members of the city council. Isaac Carrillo received a federal appointment as southern district attorney, and Carlos Manuel de Céspedes and Manuel Govín were installed as officers in the U.S. customhouse in Key West. Céspedes subsequently won the mayoral seat in Key West, and Govín served as postmaster of Jacksonville. José Alejandro Huau was elected to four terms on the Jacksonville city council. Celestino Cañizares became mayor of Ocala. Manuel Moreno, Manuel Patricio Delgado, José Gonzalo Pompés, and Fernando Figueredo Socarrás were sent to the Florida legislature. Figueredo Socarrás, a Rensselaer graduate, served as superintendent of schools in Hillsborough County and mayor of West Tampa. The first West Tampa city council included

Vidal Cruz, S. Fleitas, Martín Herrera, J. D. Silva, and R. Someillán. In 1874 Aniceto G. Menocal was appointed chief engineer in the U.S. Navy and supervised all canal surveys in Panama and Nicaragua. He later designed the naval gun plant in Washington, D.C., and helped establish the naval base in the Philippines before retiring with the rank of commander. Joaquín Castillo Duany held a commission in the U.S. Navy and was assigned as surgeon to the 1881 Polar expedition. José Primelles Agramonte, who in 1887 graduated from Columbia University with a degree in civil engineering, obtained employment with the New York City Streets Department. Juan Guiteras served a tour of duty as a physician in the U.S. Army and subsequently joined the staff of the Marine Hospital Service. Charles Hernández was raised in Brockton, Massachusetts, where he attended public school, worked for the Brockton Electric Light Works, and served nearly a decade in the Massachusetts National Guard. Sotero E. Escarza graduated in civil engineering from Rensselaer in 1894 and for the next five years worked in the Pennsylvania Railroad Division of Bridges. José Agustín Quintero received a law degree from Harvard in 1849 and settled in New Orleans, where he was a member of the editorial staff of the *Picayune*. During the Civil War he served in the Confederate diplomatic corps in Latin America.

Still others fully integrated themselves into North American society, acquiring new identities and new careers, and went back to Cuba as representatives of U.S. interests. Pedro Bustillo graduated from the New York Business College, obtained U.S. citizenship, and returned to Havana in 1883 as the general agent of the Equitable Life Assurance Society. Another Business College graduate, Felipe Estrada, directed the Departamento Hispano Americano of the New York Life Insurance Company, also in Havana. Hipólito Dumois from Santiago de Cuba was educated at St. John's College in New York before taking a job with the American Ore Dressing Company copper mines in Oriente. Joaquín Chalons earned an engineering degree in North America, then returned to work for the Steel Ore Company in Santiago de Cuba. Esteban Duque Estrada graduated from the Stevens Institute of Technology in Hoboken, New Jersey, and in 1883 joined the Bethlehem Iron Company to supervise railroad construction in Santiago de Cuba. In Heredia's *Leonela*, John Valdespina studied engineering at William Penn College in Pennsylvania before returning to Cuba as chief engineer on the railroad construction project for Smithson Brothers.

Cubans found employment as educators and taught a generation of North Americans in a variety of fields. Luis A. Baralt Peoli and Antonio Franchi taught Spanish at Columbia University. Others included Mariano Cubí y Soler (Louisiana State University), Calixto Guiteras (Girard College), and Luis Felipe Mantilla (New York University). Federico Edelman Pinto served on the New York Board of Education and taught evening classes at DeWitt Clinton High School. Professors of medicine included Carlos J. Finlay (Columbia) and Juan Guiteras (University of Pennsylvania Medical School). Manuel González Echeverría was a professor of mental diseases at the State University of New York and founded the first asylum for epileptics and the mentally ill in the state. Gonzalo Núñez advertised his services as "professor of piano." Pianist Pablo Desvernine emigrated to New York in 1869 and taught piano to young adults, the most famous of whom was Edward MacDowell. Juan de Valera, the son of a sugar planter, earned a living teaching piano in New York, where he met and married Irish immigrant Catherine Coll. He died shortly after the birth of their son Eduardo, and Catherine returned to Ireland; she then gave the boy's name its Gaelic form: Eamon.

Some Cubans established private schools. In 1885 Tomás Estrada Palma founded a college preparatory school, Instituto Estrada Palma, in Central Valley, New York. Eduardo Pla directed an elementary school in Sussex County, New Jersey. Also in New York, Carlos de la Torre established El Progreso elementary school, Demetrio Castillo Duany opened a business school, Inocencio Casanova organized the Instituto Casanova, and N. A. Carbó and J. R. Parras operated the Academia de Idiomas. In Tampa, Cirilo Pouble founded the Academia Pouble.

A generation of Cuban musicians and performers spent their most productive years in the United States. In 1875 pianist Ignacio Cervantes, a student of Louis Gottschalk, arrived in New York, where his recitals earned him critical acclaim. Shortly after emigrating to New York in 1889, soprano Ana Aguardo was appointed soloist at the San Francisco Xavier Church. Opera singer Rosalía Díaz de Herrera performed on the Philadelphia and Washington stage under the professional name of Rosalía Chalía. Flutist Guillermo M. Tomás developed a following in New York during the 1880s and 1890s. Concert pianist Emilio Agramonte established the New York School of Opera and Oratory in 1893 and served as director of the Eight O'Clock Musical Club and conductor of the Gounod Choral Society of New Haven.

The emigration served as the crucible of nation, for many vital elements of Cuban nationality were forged and acquired definitive form in North America. Some of the most important leaders of independence emerged from this community. Martín Morúa Delgado, Enrique José Varona, Rafael Serra, Manuel Sanguily, Diego Vicente Tejera, Francisco Vicente Aguilera, and José Morales Lemus all lived in the United States. Néstor Ponce de León resided in New York for thirty years before returning to the island in 1899. José Martí lived most of his adult life in the North. The principal leaders of the Cuban Revolutionary Party (PRC), Tomás Estrada Palma and Gonzalo de Quesada, were U.S. citizens and longtime residents of New York. Quesada received a law degree from Columbia.

Some of the most prominent military chieftains of the Liberation Army also emerged from this community. General Francisco Carrillo, commander of the Fourth Army Corps, and Colonel Julio Sanguily were U.S. citizens. General Pedro Betancourt, commander of the Matanzas division, was a U.S. citizen and a graduate of the University of Pennsylvania Medical School. Chief of Expeditions General Emilio Núñez, a naturalized U.S. citizen, and General Carlos García Velez both graduated from Penn in dentistry. General José Ramón Villalón, who served on the staff of Antonio Maceo, received an engineering degree from Lehigh University. General Eugenio Sánchez Argamonte (Fordham) was chief of the medical corps. General Carlos Roloff, a naturalized U.S. citizen, had previously worked for Bishop and Company in Caibarién. Colonel José Miguel Tarafa (New York Business College) was chief of staff for General Javier Vega of the Third Army Corps of Oriente. General Carlos María de Rojas (Harvard) served on the staff of General José María Rodriguez. The staff of General Calixto García was especially well represented with alumni of U.S. schools, including Chief of Staff General Mario G. Menocal (Cornell), Colonel Juan Miguel Portuondo Tamayo (Columbia), and Major Luis Rodolfo Miranda (Packard Business College).

Destierro was a transformative experience. For Cubans absorbed with matters of *patria*, the United States provided an environment in which the evolving discourse on nation was offered up freely at public forums among a vast number of participants. The proliferation of Cuban publications in exile—pamphlets, periodicals, and books, but mostly newspapers—was nothing less than extraordinary. Scores of newspapers, which appeared in almost every émigré community, were devoted primarily to the proposition of Cuba Libre in all of its ideological representations and programmatic manifestations. This was a free and frankly opposition press, defying—if from a distance—Spanish censorship and openly committed to overthrowing Spanish rule.

A mass readership emerged within émigré communities, and what concerned it most was the ongoing debate on nation. Some newspapers, most notably *Patria, El Yara*, and *El Avisador Cubano*, enjoyed national circulation. Many that were smuggled into Cuba were read daily by *lectores* (readers) to thousands of workers on hundreds of cigar factory floors.

The émigré press contributed to consciousness of nationality by creating open fields of exchange and expanding the modes of communication. These were local newspapers, to be sure, a source of local news and advertisements. But local news was also news of the nation and fostered community out of neighborhood, constituency out of community, and nationality out of constituency. This was a long-standing process of integration and inclusion, a narrative on nation that engaged Cubans of all social classes, men and women, black and white, conducted openly and in public.

The press contributed directly to a unified and informed constituency. Much of the exchange took place in editorials, letters to the editor, petitions, and public meetings—almost all of which would have been inconceivable inside Cuba. In expatriate communities from New Orleans to New York, the text of émigré newspapers resonated with renderings of nation. These were important conduits of the competing versions of patria debated in countless meeting halls and back rooms, on front porches and sidewalks, at factories and in homes, in barbershops and bodegas, in cafés and restaurants, and at hundreds of political clubs and patriotic *juntas*.

These were decisive developments, for the very process by which national identity formed was in large measure by way of discourse sustained outside Cuba by huge numbers of people who were daily subjected to North American influences, large and small, and who in the ordinary course of events drew on their environment to advance the cause of Cuba Libre. The circumstance of exile thus had a major impact on the elements used to define and defend patria. That these forms could themselves affect the character of identity was not readily apparent at the time, but increasingly the methods used to create nation also shaped the content of nationality.

The development of the émigré press was very much a product of this condition. Newspapers were in transition in the United States, as technological innovations reduced production costs and increased circulation. Improvements in communications by telegraph, cable, and telephone, as well as advances in transportation by road, rail, and sea, made for efficient collection of news and rapid distribution of newspapers. The cylinder presses that replaced the manually powered flatbed presses of the 1850s further reduced costs and increased efficiency. During the 1860s inexpensive newsprint made from wood pulp supplanted costly rag paper. These were the years, too, of the cheap penny press, popular urban-based newspapers focusing on social and economic issues, directed at specific readerships, and on which the émigré press was modeled.[4] Timing and circumstances made a network of émigré newspapers possible, allowing Cubans to publish at low cost for mass distribution at cheap prices.

That political dissidents could emigrate to the United States and enjoy comparative freedom of action all but guaranteed that much of the opposition to Spain would move to the North. The United States soon became the principal base from which to organize and sustain rebellion. The political leadership of almost all separatist uprisings between 1868 and 1898 was headquartered in New York. Indeed, often it was actually easier for Cubans in the western end of the island to join an insurrection in the eastern end by traveling north. The narrator of Raimundo Cabrera's partly autobiographical novel *Sombras que pasan* (1916) recalled the Ten Years War: "To conspire in Havana in 1870 and 1871 was a dangerous activity and all but absolutely impossible. More than an armed camp, the capital was a prison. On each street corner, a sentry post of armed guards; the cafés and grocery stores were under the surveillance of Volunteers; in every door way, a guard, an armed gate-keeper. In the homes, every Cuban man with a policeman near by. Three Cubans could not get together on a street corner or on the plazas without arousing suspicions."[5] Gustavo Robreño's historical novel *La acera del Louvre* (1925) similarly recalled the days when many Cubans "traveled abroad on the pretense of vacation or business" as a way to reach the rebellion. The "strict vigilance exercised by colonial authorities in the capital," Robreño remembered, "made it impossible for *habaneros* to join the insurrection and it was absolutely indispensable to go abroad, to return as members of an expedition."[6]

Much in Cuban political culture thus developed around the use of the United States as a surrogate site of opposition from which to plot conspiracies and plan for war, to raise funds and organize resistance, to publish opposition newspapers, and to establish hundreds of revolutionary clubs, patriotic juntas, and political associations. Inevitably, in the search for allies and assistance, Cubans involved North Americans in their affairs. And this also became a permanent feature of the Cuban practice of politics.

The circumstance of exile produced new ways to articulate discontent and to assemble power. Such mobilization for change, frankly subversive and revolutionary, could not have developed inside Cuba in the same way. Previous challenges to Spanish rule had originated from clandestine plots organized by small groups of conspirators, limited largely to representatives of creole elites.

The exile experience opened the discourse on nation to the participation of thousands of Cubans, for the discursive process itself functioned as a means of mobilization. The political base of the *independentista* constituency broadened, acquiring greater social diversity and ideological range, and eventually assumed the proportions of a populist mass-based movement. The incorporation of new social groupings guaranteed that the final rendering of patria, the one that would serve as the call to action, addressed the concerns of a vast and heterogeneous constituency. It was in exile that definition of national community broadened and the meaning of patria was transformed, the point at which a moral imperative insinuated itself into the final representation of patria. Nation was subsequently conceived in programmatic terms as national identity expanded to incorporate an explicit ideological content to free Cuba. These were not altogether new tendencies, of course. Much in these formulations had antecedents earlier in the nineteenth century. What was different after 1868, however, was a matter of degree, and eventually the difference in degree was sufficiently great to create a distinction in kind.

During the North American exile the meaning of national community expanded to include the working class, the poor—in the formulation of José Martí, *los humildes* and *los pobres de la tierra*. Martí understood the importance of incorporating los humildes into the separatist coalition; he also recognized that only by addressing working-class concerns explicitly as a function of nation could workers respond to patria. Indeed, Martí required the allegiance of workers to legitimize the construct of Cuba Libre as a representation of the whole nation and could plausibly find this endorsement only among the cigar workers of Florida. He detected in the Floridian communities the fullness of the ideal of nation: cigar workers organized in peculiarly North American small-town fashion—in Key West, Tampa, Jacksonville, and Ocala: entire townships of Cubans united by a vision of nation and governed by officials elected from among their own ranks. The creation of the Cuban Revolutionary Party in Tampa and Key West in 1892 gave institutional structure and political form to the inclusion of workers in the definition of nation. By 1892 Martí could proclaim that "the working people" were the "backbone of our coalition."[7]

The North was also the place where the process of nation formation was open to women. They shared with men many of the same patriotic concerns, often articulated in similar fashion, most of which had to do with the central issues of independence and sovereignty. Many enrolled in separatist ranks in response to opportunity, much of which arrived in the form of modernity. Women entered into the process of national liberation as a means of personal liberation and vice versa. In this period of transition and rapid change, old gender boundaries were difficult to sustain. For instance, in Wenceslao Gálvez's novel *Nicotina* (1898), set in Tampa during the early 1890s, Lucrecia contemplates the imminence of a new separatist war and regrets "not being a man so I too can go and fight." Reprimanded by her father—"Don't speak of those things, child, for women should not get involved in politics, that is unseemly"—Lucrecia retorts: "And why not? Those are backward views!"[8]

Women in exile became "involved in politics" at all levels—as fund-raisers, political organizers, and community leaders. They sponsored bazaars, picnics, and dances; organized theater groups; and collected clothing and medicine for insurgent forces in Cuba. Carolina Rodríguez, Emilia Casanova, Ana Aguardo de Tomás, María Josefa de Moya, Rosalía Hernández, Carmen Miyares, Magdalena Mayorga, and Paulina Pedrosa were only the most prominent women associated with the cause of Cuba Libre. Hundreds more served on the patriotic juntas and in the revolutionary clubs that were established in émigré communities. In sum, forty-nine women's clubs joined the PRC, representing more than 1,500 women, approximately 40 percent of the PRC delegates.[9]

The integration of women in the mobilization of patria introduced different issues about the nature of nationality, about who could participate and under what circumstances, much of which passed directly into the programmatic construct of nation. Although these developments were not entirely new, never before had conditions so favored the discussion of gender issues explicitly as a facet of nation. Patria may still have implied patriarchy, but it was no less true that women in exile contributed in fundamentally new ways to the assumptions from which the formulation and meaning of nation were derived. One émigré *programa político* in 1890 called for universal suffrage and "the progressive emancipation of women with the right to vote and to hold public and official positions." In 1897 Edelmira Guerra de Dauval, founder of Club Esperanza del Valle, issued a manifesto demanding equal rights for women, "the vote for single women and widows over the age of twenty-five, divorce for just cause, and access to public office in accordance with physiological and social laws."[10]

Destierro could be highly disruptive, for even the most commonplace assumptions were challenged daily, especially assumptions about gender roles. In many households the boundaries of production and "public," associated with men, and reproduction and "private," related to women, were blurred as the dislocation incurred by exile reduced the space between "work" and "home." It was but a short step from "public" in pursuit of patria to "public" in the pursuit of livelihood.

The position of bourgeois and middle-class women was particularly complex. They were deprived of status and experienced declining living standards. The same conditions that undermined the traditional male roles of husbands and fathers also transformed the traditional female roles of wives and mothers. Women formerly of comfortable means obtained work outside the home—in the factories, in sales positions, in service sectors. Large numbers of émigré households were headed by women, as men remained in Cuba to fight in a war or were killed or imprisoned. Men preparing to join an insurrection often relocated their families in the United States and then returned to Cuba on an expedition. Women themselves emigrated, often alone or with small children, as widows or after abandonment, in search of opportunities to support their families. Newly widowed Concha Agramonte, like many other women during the Ten Years War, immigrated to New York with her nine children and subsequently obtained work as a seamstress. Juan Pérez Rolo recalled his mother taking the four children to Key West in 1869 on the death of his father to find a job and security.[11]

Throughout the 1880s and 1890s increasing numbers of women joined the wage labor force in the United States. "There were Havana families . . . ," Juan Manuel Planas recounted of Key West, "who accepted the most humble employment in order to live. Housewives worked as laundresses and the daughters of good families were seamstresses or cooks." Data on employment patterns in the Florida cigar factories are incomplete but suggestive. Between 1887 and 1893 nearly 20 percent of the labor force in Key West (3,000 out of 15,000 workers) and Tampa (1,100 out of 5,900) were women.[12]

Criollas in the United States could not help but note the freedom of movement enjoyed by North American women, the ease and liberty with which they traveled alone, strolled, and shopped unaccompanied. These things were not done in Cuba, certainly not by white women with any real or pretended social status. "When we old-timers were children," Alvaro de la Iglesia remembered, "one never saw a lady on the streets unless she was in her carriage." North American travelers to Cuba were slightly bewildered by the proscription against women in public. Women from the United States on Havana streets alone, observed one U.S. tourist, "were greeted in their progress by the half-suppressed exclamations of the astonished Habaneros, who seemed as much surprised to see a lady walk through their streets, as a Persian would to see one unveiled in his."[13]

These observations, of course, suggested larger issues. The encounter with the North could not but challenge the premises and the propriety of the constraints of women of the colony. The experience contributed to new ways by which women came to reject the assumptions of the colonial condition and develop expectations of a new nationality. Certainly nothing caught the attention of criollas so quickly as the sight of North American women appearing alone in public. "What a pleasure it is to see women here driving their own carriages, often alone, sometimes with a girl friend or young daughter," exclaimed Aurelia Castillo de González, "to see also women alternate with their husbands, sometimes with her in the passenger seat, and sometimes him!" All this occurred without the reputation of the man "suffering in the slightest," commented Castillo de González, without anyone "caring about what they were doing, free and happy," in sharp contrast to those countries of "reclusion and preoccupation."[14]

These were customs that many women adapted to easily and, by implication, customs to which men adapted. Cuban men did not object to their wives and daughters traveling alone on North American city streets. One of the pleasures provided by family travel in the North was the opportunity for women to go out unaccompanied to shop, sightsee, and dine with other women. In New York, men conducted business, visited factories and banks, observed Eusebio Guiteras; their women shopped, attended the theater, and visited Central Park. These ways took hold among many Cuban women who lived in the United States. Carlos Loveira, who had himself spent many years in residence there, would write in *Generales y doctores* (1920) of "girls intoxicated with the feminine freedom that is inhaled in the North" and of the many criollas who "adopted American liberty, roots and all."[15]

These developments suggested other possibilities. Women found in the United States opportunities that were scarcely imaginable in Cuba, including education, professional training, and career possibilities. Few who traveled north failed to notice them. "Women in the United States," Eusebio Guiteras noted in 1883, "who receive a very complete education, have many options available to them to make a living." Aurelia Castillo de González made a similar observation. As in "every civilized country," she wrote, North American women are "formed by physical and intellectual education that create possibilities for an infinite number of lucrative occupations." Castillo de González marveled at conditions designed to assist women in their "campaign of emancipation," central to which was the opportunity for a "complete education."[16]

Women in exile did indeed pursue a variety of professional careers and business opportunities. The three daughters of Dr. Juan Fermín Figueroa and Angela Socarrás Varona graduated from pharmacy school in New York and opened the city's first pharmacy owned by women. Adela Campo de Grillo was the only female pharmacist in Key West. After graduating from the New York College of Pharmacy, María Dolores de Figueroa returned home and became the first woman licensed pharmacist in Cuba. Flora and Leopoldina Quesada ran a school for girls. Ana Otero and Isabel Salazar were self-employed music teachers. Herminia Andrade de Benech in New York advertised her skills as a seamstress of the "latest fashions," Dionisia Estrada in Tampa opened a dressmaking business, and Gertrudis Heredia de Serra operated the "Midwife Clinic of Havana" in New York. The Estenoz sisters ran a *casa de familia*, advertising "Cuban food, Cuban hospitality." After years of education and residence in New York, Camagüey-born Rita Dunau returned to Havana and offered instruction in fencing, cycling, and riding as well as classes in French and English. Julia Martínez completed her secondary education at Notre Dame in Baltimore and subsequently received her doctorate in pedagogy at the University of Havana. María Josefa Granados, who lived in Key West and Tampa between 1886 and 1898, eventually went back to Cuba to establish the weekly *El Sufragista* of the Partido Sufragista Cubano in 1913 and subsequently participated in the founding of the Partido Femenista de Cuba.[17]

Samuel Hazard later told of women in Cuba looking "upon the United States as a country to be dreamed of as a fairy vision, where life and liberty are to be really enjoyed." Hazard recounted one conversation with "one sweet innocent": "'Everyone is free there now, Señor?' 'Oh yes,' I replied; 'we have no negro slaves there now.' 'No, no! Señor, you don't understand me. I mean the women, too—are they not free?' to which I was compelled to reply they were. . . . 'Es may bueno, Señor; it is not so here.'"[18]

NOTES

1. *Daily Equator-Democrat*, March 26, 1889, p. 3.
2. In New York, these included the Hotel Central owned by Gervasio Pérez, Nuevo

Boarding Cubano of Alfredo Du-Bouchet, Leopoldo Ortiz's Hotel Habana, Hotel Fénix owned and operated by F. Ferrer, Hotel América owned by Bernardo Pérez, Gran Boarding Cubano, Troncoso House, and Casa de Huéspedes Cubana. In Saratoga, Pedro M. Suárez owned the Everett House, offering "special arrangements for families," and Luis Baralt operated the Congress Park House—advertised as "a Cuban family hotel located at the best site in Saratoga." In Tampa, Miguel Montejo was proprietor of the Hotel Victoria, and the Hotel de La Habana passed through several ownerships before burning down in the early 1900s; in Key West, Martín Herrera owned the Hotel Monroe.

3. *Patria*, October 22, 1892, p. 4.

4. See Michael Schudson, *Discovering the News: A Social History of American Newspapers* (New York, 1978), pp. 31–42; Robert A. Rutand, *The Newsmongers: Journalism in the Life of the Nation, 1690–1972* (New York, 1973), pp. 240–62; and Sidney Kobre, *Foundations of American Journalism*, 2d ed. (Westport, Conn., 1970), pp. 300–307.

5. Raimundo Cabrera, *Sombras que pasan* (1916; reprint, Havana, 1984), p. 109.

6. Gustavo Robreño, *La acera del Louvre* (Havana, 1925), p. 245.

7. José Martí, "El Partido Revolucionario Cubano," April 3, 1892, in Martí, *Obras completas*, ed. Jorge Quintana, 5 vols. (Caracas, 1964), 1, pt 2:303–7, and "La proclamación del Partido Revolucionario Cubano, el 10 de Abril," ibid., 1, pt. 2:307–13.

8. Wenceslao Gálvez, "Nicotina," *Revista Bimestre Cubana* 29 (May–June 1932): 409–10.

9. The juntas and clubs included: in New York, Liga de las Hijas de Cuba, Club Mercedes de Varona; in Tampa, Club Estrella Solitaria, Discípulas de Martí, Club Gonzalo de Quesada, Club Justo Carrillo; in Key West, Club Hospitalarias Cubanas, Grupo Alegórico del Cayo, Protectoras de la Patria, Club A. Díaz-Marcano, Club Mariana Grajales de Maceo, Hijas de la Libertad, and Hermanas de Ruis Rivera. For the activities of women's clubs in Key West, see Raoul Alpízar Poyo, *Cayo Hueso y José Dolores Poyo* (Havana, 1947), pp. 26, 43–44; *Revista de Cayo Hueso*, May 19, 1897, pp. 1–2; and K. Lynn Stoner, *From House to Streets: The Cuban Woman's Movement for Legal Reform, 1898–1940* (Durham, 1991), p. 24.

10. José Mayner y Ros, *Cuba y sus partidos políticos* (Kingston, Jamaica, 1890), p. 78; María Collado, "La evolución femenina en Cuba," *Bohemia*, December 11, 1927, p. 58.

11. Francisco Díaz Vólero, *Amor, patria y deber* (Havana, 1921), p. 87; Juan Pérez Rolo, *Mis recuerdos* (Key West, 1928), pp. 6–9.

12. Juan Manuel Planas, *La corriente del golfo* (Havana, 1920); U.S. Congress, House of Representatives, *Tenth Annual Report of the Commissioner of Labor, 1894*, 54th Cong., 1st sess., H. Doc. 339, 2 vols. (Washington, D.C., 1896), 1:138–49.

13. Alvaro de la Iglesia, *Cosas de antaño* (Havana, 1917), p. 180; A Physician, *Notes on Cuba*, p. 42.

14. Aurelia Castillo de González, *Un paseo por América: Cartas de Méjico y de Chicago* (Havana, 1895), pp. 63–64.

15. Eusebio Guiteras, *Un invierno en Nueva York* (Barcelona, 1883), pp. 134–40; Carlos Loveira, *Generales y doctores* (Havana, 1920), pp. 189–200.

16. Guiteras, *Un invierno en Nueva York*, p. 88; Castillo de González, *Un paseo por América*, p. 64; and "Cartes de Aurelia Castillo," *Revista Cubana* 21 (April 1895): 307–29.

17. *Revista de Cayo Hueso*, March 27, 1898, p. 7; "Farmacia cubana en Nueva York," *Carteles*, September 18, 1955, p. 117; *El Fígaro*, March 3, 1895, p. 117; Ana Núñez Machín, *La otra María* (Havana, 1975), pp. 24–110.

18. Samuel Hazard, *Cuba with Pen and Pencil* (Hartford, Conn., 1871), pp. 84–85.

✳ ✳ ✳

QUESTIONS

Several material conditions support the construction of Cuban subjectivities as U.S. cultural citizens. In other words, Cubans became integral members of the U.S. body politic through economic, political, and social channels.

1. To what extent are these conditions indications of a quest for U.S. cultural (and legal) citizenship and/or a desire to maintain a "Cuban" identity?

2. How do these conditions differ from those of Mexican Americans? Puerto Ricans?

3. How does one explain the paradox of a Cuban dual identity as U.S. citizens and, at the same time, Cuban revolutionaries developing a sense of *cubanidad,* of Cuban nationality?

4. Why would the exile experience promote the inclusion of diverse classes into the independence movement?

5. How does the exile experience affect the status of women? Are these circumstances similar to those Apodaca (see chapter 1) describes for Chicanas in terms of forces of production and social relations?

☀ 9 ☀
THE PLATT AMENDMENT (1901)[1]

Unlike Mexico, which became independent in 1821, Cuba and Puerto Rico remained colonies of Spain throughout the nineteenth century. Before the Spanish-American War, which led to U.S. control of Cuba, there were several decades of Cuban rebellion and Spanish repression. First there was the Ten Years War (1868–78), then the Little War (1879–80), and finally the War of Independence (1895–98). This last one took José Martí's life. By 1898 it was clear to all that the Cuban insurgents were about to defeat the Spanish forces and gain independence. But there was another game of truth going on here. The United States and the Cuban elite class had for a long time feared an independent Cuba because they believed that with the large number of Afro-Cubans, the country would experience political instability, social conflict, and economic chaos (as they saw happen in Haiti). By the 1850s, *criollos* were 44 percent and blacks were 56 percent of the population. That is why the U.S. government had actually supported Spain in their war against Cuban *independentistas*. It was another game of truth in which heroes turn into villains at the snap of a finger.

In April 1898 President William McKinley requested congressional authority to intervene militarily in Cuba, supposedly to serve as a neutral party to stop the fighting between Cubans and Spaniards. But the Cuban revolutionary leaders considered this military intervention a declaration of war against them and vowed to fight against the United States. An agreement was worked out through the Teller Amendment, which promised "to leave the government and control of the island to its people."[2] The Cuban war for independence turned into the Spanish-American War when the USS *Maine* mysteriously exploded. The Cuban revolutionaries were forced to take a back seat, not only in the conduct of the war but also in the negotiations for the Treaty of Paris. The United States' next move in this game of truth was to have the old colonial elite that supported U.S. intervention take charge of the government. But the *independentistas* were much too popular and their candidates kept on winning majorities of seats in the constitutional conventions.

Frustrated, U.S. officials resorted to a reinterpretation of the Teller Amendment. Now it was read as asserting the need for the United States to make sure that Cuba had a stable government. This interpretation led to the interventionist Platt Amendment, named after U.S. Senator Orville H. Platt, which was enacted into law by the U.S. Congress in February 1901 and imposed on the Cuban Constitutional Assembly. Protests were held throughout the island and there was talk of taking up arms against the United States. The Cuban Constitutional Assembly balked at enacting the amendment as part of their constitution. But the threat of continued military intervention prevailed and the Platt Amendment was accepted as an appendix to the new 1901 constitution by a sixteen to eleven vote.

Unlike Puerto Rico, which was outright annexed, Cuba became part of the United States by virtue of the Platt Amendment, which gave the United States the right to intervene anytime it deemed it necessary (under the pretense of the need "to maintain stability in the island"). Unlike Puerto Ricans, Cubans remained citizens of their country. As indicated in other readings on Cuba, however, Cubans had become "cultural citizens" of the United States through what Pérez calls "binding familiarities." This process is similar to the experience of northern Mexicans with the United States that started with the Santa Fe Trail. Unlike Puerto Ricans, Cubans had some freedom to elect their own political representatives (as long as they did not threaten U.S. interests). The Platt Amendment was abrogated on May 29, 1934, but the United States kept the Guantánamo naval station (which as of the year 2001 Fidel Castro is still trying to get back). A reciprocal trade agreement that reestablished U.S. hegemony over the Cuban economy was signed the same year.

NOTES AND SUGGESTED READINGS

1. This summary is based on Louis A. Pérez, "Intervention and Occupation," in *Cuba and the United States: Ties of Singular Intimacy* (Athens: University of Georgia Press, 1990), 82–112.

2. Pérez, *Cuba and the United States,* 96.

I. That the government of Cuba shall never enter into any treaty or other compact with any foreign power or powers which will impair or tend to impair the independence of Cuba, or in any manner authorize or permit any foreign power or powers to obtain by colonization or, for military or naval purposes or otherwise, lodgment in or control over any portion of said island.

II. That said government shall not assume or contract any public debt, to pay the interest upon which, and to make reasonable sinking fund provision for the ultimate discharge of which, the ordinary revenues of the island, after defraying the current expenses of government shall be inadequate.

III. That the government of Cuba consents that the United States may exercise the right to intervene for the preservation of Cuban independence, the maintenance of a government adequate for the protection of life, property, and individual liberty, and for discharging the obligations with respect to Cuba imposed by the Treaty of Paris on the United States, now to be assumed and undertaken by the government of Cuba.

IV. That all Acts of the United States in Cuba during its military occupancy thereof are ratified and validated, and all lawful rights acquired thereunder shall be maintained and protected.

V. That the government of Cuba will execute and as far as necessary extend, the plans already devised or other plans to be mutually agreed upon, for the sanitation of the cities of the island, to the end that a recurrence of epidemic and infectious diseases may be prevented, thereby assuring protection to the people and commerce of Cuba, as well as to the commerce of the southern ports of the United States and of the people residing therein.

VI. That the Isle of Pines shall be omitted from the proposed constitutional boundaries of Cuba, the title thereto being left to future adjustment by treaty.

VII. That to enable the United States to maintain the independence of Cuba, and to protect the people thereof, as well as for its own defense, the government of Cuba will sell or lease to the United States land necessary for coaling or naval stations at certain specified points, to be agreed upon with the President of the United States.

VIII. That by way of further assurance the government of Cuba will embody the foregoing provisions in a permanent treaty with the United States.[1]

NOTE

1. U.S. Statutes at Large 21, 897–98.

QUESTIONS

1. Did class struggle make Cubans really incapable of self-government?
2. Even if this was the case, was the United States justified in imposing its will over Cubans?
3. Can we separate good intentions from hegemonic ones?

PUERTO RICANS: POLITICAL STATUS IN SUSPENDED ANIMATION

Of all Spanish colonial possessions in the Americas, Puerto Rico is the only territory that has never gained its independence. In fact, it is the oldest colony in the world. Many of the same internal and geopolitical dynamics that we saw affecting Cuba during the last quarter of the nineteenth century are involved here. The island's value to U.S. policy makers was as an outlet for excess manufactured goods and as a key naval station in the Caribbean. One important difference, however, is that Puerto Rico did not have the benefit of technological modernization. The railroads, for example, were operating in Cuba by 1837, but Puerto Rican construction had barely begun by 1878. When the U.S. Americans conquered the island they saw trains pulled by oxen; no one had capital to buy locomotives.[1] This difference in material conditions is a key factor in the difference in the relations of these two groups with the U.S. government and the dominant society.

By the 1830s the United States had begun to emerge as an important potential market for Puerto Rican products, and the inescapable presence of the "Colossus of the North" inevitably influenced Puerto Rican political thinking and established some of the "binding familiarities" that Pérez identifies in the early U.S.-Cuban relationship and that we also saw operating in U.S. relations with northern Mexicans. The rural population relegated to the mountainous areas barely lived at a subsistence level. It is from these rural highland folk that the term *jíbaro* originated. This term functions variously as an image, stereotype, or symbol of either all that is great or all that is wrong about the people of Puerto Rico, depending on your political orientation (similar to the term "Chicano" for U.S. Mexicans). In the Indian language, *"jíbaro"* means "being free."

More and more after 1850, Puerto Rican political opinion failed to divide simply into two camps—for Spain and for autonomy—and the political issues were complicated by the differing stakes of various groups on the island. There were those fundamentally loyal to Spain and essentially accepting of Puerto Rico's dependent status under the Crown; there were others who desired greater autonomy, the abolition of slavery, and a stronger orientation to the United States; finally, there were the separatists, who sought in varying degrees an autonomous or independent Puerto Rico. By 1867, Puerto Rico had 656,328 inhabitants, with 346,437 recorded as whites and 309,891 as "of color" (which included blacks, mulattoes, and mestizos). Out of this heterogeneity, a sense of national culture had been established, as represented in music, the arts, colloquial language, and architecture.

Frustrated by the lack of political and economic freedom, and enraged by the continuing Spanish repression on the island, a pro-independence movement staged an armed rebellion in 1868. The "Grito de Lares" broke in September 23, 1868. The rebellion was planned by a group, led by Dr. Ramón Emeterio Betances and Segundo Ruiz Belvis, who on January 6, 1868, founded the Comité Revolucionario de Puerto Rico from their exile in the Dominican Republic. Between 1869 and 1873, the establishment of a liberal government in Spain led to ample liberties in the Caribbean, including the rights of Puerto Ricans and Cubans to send representatives to the Spanish Cortes. The liberal reforms extended to the island included granting of the status of *diputación provincial* (making the island a province of Spain) and paved the way for the establishment of the first national political parties.

Toward the end of the 1880s, the island's population suffered from a severe economic crisis. Consequently, there were many violent incidents, particularly looting and arson, against Spanish commercial establishments. The government and its Civil Guard responded with a series of raids and imprisonments, applying severe torture measures that became known as "compontes." The social conditions of the island were also critical to events during this period. In addition to a lack of civil liberties, approximately 85 percent of the population remained illiterate. Malnutrition and extreme poverty were widespread. Puerto Ricans and Cubans finally were granted self-government by Spain when the Carta Autonómica (a form of constitutional autonomy) was approved by the Spanish Cortes on November 25, 1897. But by the time of the first elections in March 1898, tensions were already building between Spain and the United States, and the freedoms for which Puerto Ricans and Cubans had fought for four hundred years would come to an abrupt end one month later with the advent of the Spanish-American War.

Although Spanish surrender was certain by July 1898, the United States soon occupied Puerto Rico in an effort to secure a presence on the island prior to the initial discussions of a peace settlement. On July 18, General Nelson A. Miles and eighteen thousand U.S. troops landed at Guánica Bay and immediately moved to the city of Ponce and other towns on the southern part of the island. Many Puerto Ricans welcomed U.S. troops, *trusting* that they would end colonialism. The U.S. troops then proceeded north toward San Juan, Puerto Rico's capital and the main military post of Spanish forces on the island. But before they could reach San Juan, Spain agreed on August 13 to sign a peace treaty, putting an end to all military hostilities. The formal transfer of Puerto Rico to the United States took two months, from August 13 to October 18, when the last Spanish troops sailed back to Spain and the U.S. flag was raised in most public buildings on the island. Incidentally, Miles decided to make the islanders spell the name of their country "Porto Rico" though the word "porto" does not exist in the Spanish language.[2] It took an act of the U.S. Congress on May 7, 1932, to change the name back to Puerto Rico. A military government was established in 1898 under the command of General John R. Brooke. This was replaced by a civilian government under the Foraker Act (1900) discussed by José Trías Monge in chapter 10.

Later, the Jones Act (1917) provided U.S. citizenship and Public Law 600 (1950) allowed Puerto Rico to have its own constitution. These documents construct a peculiar, ambiguous, and contradictory political identity for the Puerto Rican nation and a conflicting and paradoxical subjectivity for the human bodies that inhabited not only the island but also the mainland United States. This discrepant construction is reflected in the Puerto Rican reaction to the annexation. Beginning with the distinguished Puerto Rican scholar Eugenio María de Hostos, there was a movement for independence; but there was also support for U.S. occupation. The sugar plantation owners and the professional classes as well as individuals from the left, such as Santiago Iglesias and his Socialist Party, were relentless advocates for statehood. And so was Luisa Capetillo, the feminist and anarchist popularly known as the first woman in Puerto Rico to wear pants in public.[3]

NOTES AND SUGGESTED READINGS

1. Ronald Fernandez, *The Disenchanted Island*, 2d ed. (Westport, Conn.: Praeger, 1996), 30.
2. Fernandez, *Disenchanted Island*, 9.
3. Juan Gonzalez, *Harvest of Empire* (New York: Viking, 2000), 61.

✳ 10 ✳
THE SHAPING OF A COLONIAL POLICY

José Trías Monge

In previous discussions, we made reference to the construction of individual or group subjectivities. In this piece, José illustrates the construction of a national subjectivity, that is to say, the fabrication of the Puerto Rican nation as a Frankensteinesque political body. Obviously, this text does not represent all Puerto Rican political thought, but it does represent the political structure within which Puerto Ricans exercise their political rights. We are dealing here with a game of truth that includes the usual issues of representation of "the people," citizenship, the right of consent of the governed, race, and economic issues. Paradoxically, by becoming part of U.S. democracy, Puerto Ricans have seen their quest for public citizenship frustrated. But this game of truth also includes a still unresolved issue regarding the right of the United States to possess *any* people and its territory in the world without extending to them full constitutional rights. The direct implication for Puerto Ricans is that, since Puerto Rico is "foreign to the United States in a domestic sense," Puerto Ricans are in the dubious position of being "separate but equal." This is precisely what the Foraker Act entails.

✳   ✳   ✳

Many sources influenced the shaping of a colonial policy and the establishment of civil government for Puerto Rico. In this chapter I will look at the welter of opinions concerning what should have been done at the time and how the executive branch and later Congress finally approved the Foraker Act of 1900, followed by the reaction of the United States Supreme Court.

In 1898, President McKinley sent Reverend Henry K. Carroll, a distinguished leader of the Methodist Episcopal Church, to Puerto Rico to report on island conditions. Carroll held hearings and advised McKinley of the importance of granting Puerto Ricans a high degree of self-government. He stated in his report: "They expect under American sovereignty that the wrongs of centuries will be righted. . . . They may be poor, but they are proud and sensitive, and would be bitterly disappointed if they found that they had been delivered from an oppressive yoke to be put under a tutelage which proclaimed their inferiority. . . . They will learn the art of governing the only possible way—by having its responsibilities laid upon them."[1]

Carroll recommended a legislature composed of two chambers, both fully elected by universal male suffrage, the grant of American citizenship, the extension of the U.S. Constitution, elective mayors, free trade, and the right to elect a Delegate to Congress. Few of his recommendations would find their way into the first organic act for Puerto Rico.

The Secretary of War, the official in charge of Puerto Rican affairs for many decades, sent his own Insular Commission to Puerto Rico early in 1899. Its report, issued in May, advised that the people of Puerto Rico wanted nothing but American laws, leaving no trace of Spanish legislation. "The only exception to this view," the commission added sarcastically, "comes only from those few who believe they have an inherent right to hold the offices and dictate the laws and policy of the Island, which they call self-government."[2]

The Insular Commission did not favor a local legislature of any kind, even one composed of appointed members only. In testifying before Congress on the report, Judge H. G. Curtis, a member of the commission, stated that the President himself should legislate for Puerto Rico, at the recommendation of the Governor to be appointed by him.[3] The commission also opposed the extension of American citizenship. The commission recommended not one, but three federal courts, one each in San Juan, Ponce, and Mayagüez. Their decisions would not be appealable to any mainland American court, but to the President himself.[4]

General Davis also disagreed with Carroll. In his view, Puerto Rico should be a "Dependency" of the United States under the control of the President, exercised through the Secretary of State. There should be an Executive Council, composed of seven department heads to be appointed by the President, and four persons selected by the Governor from among the members of the legislature. Contrary to the Insular Commission, Davis favored an elected legislature composed of a single chamber. Suffrage should be limited to those men who could read and write or pay taxes.[5] Davis recommended that the justices of the Supreme Court be appointed by the President. There should be a federal court and free trade, but Puerto Ricans should not have American citizenship or representation of any kind in Congress, not even through a delegate.

By that time, the commission that had been set up to recommend a government for Hawaii advised that the Hawaiians should enjoy American citizenship, an elected legislature, a cabinet appointed by the Governor, a Delegate to Congress, and other attributes of full territorial government—all of which Congress soon provided.[6] Davis warned that Puerto Rico should not have such a degree of self-government. According to him, the British Crown colony type of government provided a better model.

Elihu Root, a distinguished New York attorney who served as Secretary of War from 1899 to 1904 and as Secretary of State from 1905 to 1909, awarded the Nobel Prize for Peace in 1912, who much later would come to favor the status of an American protectorate for a free Puerto Rico, did not believe at the time that Puerto Ricans were ready for much self-government. After studying the views described so far, he reported to Congress: "The people have not yet been educated in the art of self-government, or any really honest government. . . . A form of government should be provided for Porto Rico which will assure the kind of administration to which we are accustomed with just as much participation on the part of Porto Ricans as is possible without enabling their inexperience to make it ineffective, and with opportunity for them to demonstrate their increasing capacity to govern themselves with less and less assistance."[7]

Root therefore recommended that the Governor and his cabinet be appointed by the President, with the advice and consent of the Senate. The idea of an Executive Council to assist the Governor, as recommended by Davis, was unacceptable to him. He did not favor the establishment of a legislature, as suggested by Carroll and Davis, either. He recommended instead a Legislative Council, in the English colonial fashion, composed of the department heads and a minority of members appointed by the President. Laws were to be subject to veto by the President and also by Congress.

Root opposed universal male suffrage for Puerto Rico, as well as the grant of American citizenship. He also believed that United States laws should not apply in Puerto Rico, except in matters specifically to be enumerated by Congress.

The administration's theory as to the power to govern the new possessions was devised chiefly by Root. He thought that the Constitution did not apply automatically, *ex proprio vigore,* to the new dependencies and that they were accordingly subject "to the complete sovereignty of [Congress], controlled by no legal limitations except those which may be found in the treaty of cession."[8] Root did add that government officials could hardly be delegated power to act, for example, without due process of law, but he put this forward as a moral, rather than a legal limitation. In his message to Congress prior to presentation of the Foraker bill, McKinley basically adopted the position developed by his Secretary of War.

Prior to the Spanish-American War, since the Northwest Ordinance of 1787, a different view held. Territories were acquired with a view to eventual admission to the Union. They were part of the United States in both the domestic and the international sense. The Constitution followed the flag and accordingly applied in all of them, only they were governed under the plenary powers granted Congress by the so-called territorial clause of the Constitution. The inhabitants were made citizens of the United States.

The acquisition of the new colonies—the start of an empire—led the administration to devise a policy different from the established territorial one from the mass of theories within it, some of them conflicting. Its fundamental tenets would be that the people of Puerto Rico were not ready for self-government; a learning period, of unspecified duration, was necessary before self-government could be extended; the eventual status should be neither statehood nor independence, but a self-governing dependency, subject to the plenary power of Congress; the learning process required a policy of political and cultural assimilation, which necessarily involved the extension of United States laws, institutions, and language to the island; and living conditions should be improved to the extent possible. This colonial policy, still incipient at that moment, would prove to be a hardy one once it jelled. Parts of it still plague the relationship between the United States and Puerto Rico.

There were both sharp criticism and unstinting praise of the emerging policy on the part of distinguished academicians. William Graham Sumner, professor of political and social sciences at Yale University, wrote in a biting article entitled "The Conquest of the United States by Spain":

> There are plenty of people in the United States today who regard Negroes as human beings, perhaps, but of a different order from white men, so that the ideas and social arrangements of white men cannot be applied to them with propriety. Others feel the same way about Indians. . . . The doctrine that all men are equal has come to stand as one of the cornerstones of the temple of justice and truth. It was set up as a bar to just this notion that we are so much better than others that it is liberty for them to be governed by us. . . .
>
> The Americans have been committed from the outset to the doctrine that all men arc created equal. . . . It is an astonishing event that we have lived to see American arms carry this domestic dogma out where it must be tested in its application to uncivilized and half-civilized peoples. At the first touch of the test we throw the doctrine away and adopt the Spanish doctrine. We are told by the imperialists that these people are not fit for liberty and self-government; that it is rebellion for them to resist our beneficence; that we must send fleets and armies to kill them if they do it; that we must devise a government for them and administer it ourselves; that we may buy them or sell them as we please, and dispose of their "trade" for our own advantage. What is that but the policy of Spain to her dependencies?[9]

Sumner's views would be echoed by many Democratic Congressmen and Senators in the course of the debates on the Foraker bill. Sumner and those members of Congress, if alive today, would be surprised to hear that administration officials and many in Congress still cling to the notion that the United States has plenary power to govern Puerto Rico as it pleases and that the limited self-governing powers of

Puerto Rico are subject to sufferance by the Congress under the territorial clause of the United States Constitution.

Other distinguished professors backed the administration. James Bradley Thayer, of Harvard Law School, criticized Sumner's position and wrote, in impeccable colonialese, about "the childish literalness which has crept into our notions of these principles, as if all men, however savage and however unfit to govern themselves, were oppressed when other people governed them; as if self-government were not often a curse; and as if the great nation does not often owe its people, or some part of them, as its chief duty, that of governing them from the outside instead of giving them immediate control of themselves."[10] In another article, Simeon E. Baldwin, of Yale Law School, wrote: "Our Constitution was made by a civilized and educated people. It provides guaranties of personal security which seem ill-adapted to the conditions of society that prevail in many parts of our new possessions. To give the half-civilized Moros of the Philippines, or the ignorant and lawless brigands that infest Puerto Rico . . . the benefit of such immunities from the sharp and sudden justice—or injustice—which they have been hitherto accustomed to expect, would, of course, be a serious obstacle to the maintenance there of an efficient government."[11] The strong brew of imperialism, with its deadly ingredients of Manifest Destiny, the white man's burden, and other powerful additives, also affected the judgment of the good professors.

Senator Joseph Benson Foraker presented his first bill to provide a civil government for Puerto Rico in January 1900.[12] Foraker, born in 1846, had been a judge in Cincinnati, twice Governor of Ohio, and Republican Senator for Ohio since 1897. His bill was much less restrictive than the one recommended by the President and the Secretary of War. The bill granted American citizenship to all the inhabitants of Puerto Rico who chose to accept it and extended the United States Constitution to Puerto Rico. It provided for an elected House of Delegates as recommended by Davis. A bill would also be presented in the House.[13]

Puerto Rico's leaders did not attend the Congressional hearings. The sole voice from Puerto Rico critical of what had happened so far was that of Dr. Julio Henna, a fighter for independence in Spanish times, who stated at the end of his testimony, which had been fairly conciliatory in tone: "The occupation has been a perfect failure. We have suffered everything. No liberty, no rights, absolutely no protection. . . . We are Mr. Nobody from Nowhere. We have no political status, no civil rights."[14]

General Davis testified twice. The second time around he changed his mind about the readiness of Puerto Ricans to have a legislature.

The Senate Committee report reflected the views of the administration concerning the constitutionality of holding colonies, a topic on which a debate was then raging in Congress, newspapers, and academic journals. The Constitution did not follow the flag, the committee held. Colonies could be acquired and governed by the United States without regard to the strictures of the Constitution. As the report put it, without mincing words:

If we should acquire territory populated by an intelligent, capable and law-abiding people, to whom the right of self-government could be safely conceded, we might at once, with propriety and certainly within the scope of our constitutional power, incorporate that territory and people into the Union as an integral part of the United States, and . . . extend to them at once the Constitution of the United States; but if the territory should be inhabited by a people of wholly different character, illiterate, and unacquainted with our institutions, and incapable of exercising the rights and privileges guaranteed by the Constitution to the States of the Union, it would be competent for Congress to withhold from such people the operation of the Constitution and the laws of the United States, and, continuing to hold the territory as a mere possession of the United States to govern the people thereof as their situation and the necessities of the case may require.[15]

Behind the abstruse debate as to whether the Constitution applied in full to the new possessions there were, of course, realities of a different order. The doctrine of the selective, nonautomatic applicability of the Constitution and the consequent plenary powers of Congress to govern the new possessions was essential to two types of protectionists: the opponents of free trade, who feared the influx of Puerto Rican and Philippine products to the United States market; and the noneconomic protectionists, who wanted to prevent the extension of American citizenship to peoples of a different race and, with even greater intensity, forestall any move toward eventual statehood. The proponents of free trade, who comprised the sugar refiners, the wheat producers, and the manufacturers interested in new markets for their products, favored the automatic application of the whole Constitution. In 1900, destitute Puerto Rico was the fifth largest market for American products in Latin America and twenty-seventh in the world. By 1910 it was fourth in Latin America and eleventh in the world.

The committee did favor the extension of American citizenship, the establishment of a legislature as recommended in the Foraker bill, the election of a Delegate to Congress, limited suffrage, and the imposition of a 25 percent tariff on products imported to the United States from Puerto Rico.

Senator Orville H. Platt, from Connecticut—then an important tobacco state—proposed a tariff of 80 percent on all products. Senator McEnery, from Louisiana, was happy with just 50 percent. Senator Fairbanks, from Indiana, proposed another type of amendment to the bill: the application of the immigration laws to Puerto Rico. Some Republicans, bothered by the accusations of imperialism hurled at them by the Democrats, favored a resolution to the effect that the United States would not govern a people without their consent. The Democratic opposition largely contended that the United States had no power to acquire territories for the purpose of governing them as colonies.

The debate on the tariff imperiled passage of the bill. A compromise was reached which allowed two amendments suggested by McKinley to go through in the House by the narrow margin of eleven votes: a tariff of 15 percent would be imposed on Puerto Rican products, but the provision would last only for two years, unless extended by Congress. The amendments, of course, constituted an assertion of Congressional power to tax commerce with the new possessions, a statement sought by those whose main preoccupation was the Philippines, rather than Puerto Rico.

Opposition to the grant of American citizenship was so powerful that Foraker was forced to give up this provision, though it was backed by the administration. The measure granting Puerto Rico a nonvoting delegate in Congress also had to be discarded. Instead, Puerto Rico would have a Resident Commissioner in Washington, with no legal right as such to sit in Congress. In 1902 an amendment to the House rules allowed the Resident Commissioner to participate in Congressional deliberations, but without power to vote on any matter. The extension of the Constitution likewise fell by the wayside. Efforts failed to give Puerto Rico a wholly elected legislature and the rights to adopt its own constitution and to be consulted as to whether they favored the annexation. The bill passed the Senate, 40–31, and the House, 161–153. President McKinley signed the Foraker Act into law on April 12, 1900.[16]

The Foraker Act, or first organic act, called for a Governor appointed by the President of the United States, with the advice and consent of the Senate, for a four-year term, but removable by the President at will. There were to be six departments, the heads of which were also to be appointed by the President, with the advice of the Senate. Together with five citizens, who had to be born in Puerto Rico, they composed the Executive Council, which functioned as a second legislative chamber. The other chamber of the Legislative Assembly was a House of Delegates, constituted by thirty-five elected members for a term of two years. The members had to be able to read and write either English or Spanish and had to own property subject to taxation. Universal male suffrage would not apply unless the legislature so decided, which meant that such a move could be prevented by the Executive Council and the Governor. As a further precautionary measure, the Congress retained the capacity to annul at any time any law approved by the Puerto Rican legislature. A Resident Commissioner would be elected every two years to represent Puerto Rico before the executive departments. No provision was made for representation in Congress.

The judicial power was vested in a Supreme Court of Puerto Rico, whose members were to be appointed by the President, with the advice and consent of the Senate, and in the courts created during the time of military government. The Governor would appoint the lower court judges, with the advice and consent of the Executive Council. Decisions by the Supreme Court of Puerto Rico could be appealed to the United States Supreme Court. A federal court was also established, as under the occupation, and all proceedings therein had to be conducted in English.

Senator Foraker's initial proposal to extend American citizenship to Puerto Ricans was rejected. The inhabitants of the island were declared to be "citizens of Puerto Rico." The act was silent as to their right to travel to the United States, a matter which later would be decided in the affirmative by the courts. There was no Bill of Rights.

There would be a customs union between the United States and Puerto Rico, but Puerto Rico would not participate in the process of approving the tariffs, as in Spanish times. The coastwise shipping laws, prohibiting less expensive foreign carriers from carrying cargo between Puerto Rico and the United States, were specifically made applicable to the island, with severe economic consequences through the years.

All United States laws were extended to Puerto Rico, unless found to be locally inapplicable; no federal law has ever been found to be locally inapplicable to Puerto Rico.

The Foraker Act did away with most of the liberties that Puerto Rico was able to achieve with such difficulty in the course of four hundred years of Spanish rule. Puerto Ricans lost equality of citizenship with the metropolitan country; full representation in the metropolitan legislature; the right to universal male suffrage; a parliament of its own, composed of a fully elected lower house and a majority of elected members in the upper chamber and with far greater powers of legislation; the right to impose its own tariffs and to enter into commercial treaties; and several other rights described in chapter 1. Above all, Puerto Rico lost the right to government by consent of the governed: the Autonomic Charter was not amendable except at the request of the insular parliament, while the Foraker Act was subject to the unilateral will of Congress.

The Foraker Act was supposed to be a temporary measure to provide a civil government for Puerto Rico, which fact was expressed in its title, but it has never been repealed. Although parts of it have been replaced, some of its sections live to this day as part of the Federal Relations Act.

The controversy about the right of the United States to acquire territory for purposes of empire and to govern it without being subject to the full limitations of the Constitution soon reached the courts. Between 1901 and 1905 the Supreme Court decided a number of controversies concerning the status of the new possessions which came to be known as the Insular Cases.

After the approval of the Foraker Act, the matter of self-governance continued to be the subject of intense public and academic debate. The Democratic party platform in 1900 endorsed the principle of government by consent of the governed and stated that the Constitution applied wherever the American flag flew.[17] Many other voices condemned the holding of colonies and the plenary powers theory, including Republican leaders like John Sherman, former Secretary of State under McKinley, Senator George F. Hoar and Thomas B. Reed, the former Speaker, as well as former President Cleveland, Charles Eliot (president of Harvard), William James, Jane Addams, Samuel Gompers, Mark Twain, and Andrew Carnegie.[18]

The constitutional controversy naturally engaged the interest of many academicians. All shades of opinion were represented, foreshadowing the basic views set forth by various justices in the Insular Cases. Dean Langdell of Harvard Law School was a fervent advocate of the plenary powers doctrine, while opposing the possibility of statehood for the islands.[19]

A second group, part of the so-called Anti-Imperialists, upheld the *ex proprio vigore* doctrine—the theory that the Constitution followed the flag, that new territories could be acquired by conquest or cession, but only to be governed subject to the full limitations of the Constitution and solely with the purpose of eventually admitting them to the Union in equality with other states. Many of the Anti-Imperialists were, however, against the admission to the American Union of societies with a different racial and cultural background and therefore opposed the annexation of the islands.[20]

Professor Abbott Lawrence Lowell of Harvard, later its president, was the principal exponent of a third view, the one espoused by the administration, with somewhat less precision, and eventually adopted by the Supreme Court. Lowell thought that the Constitution allowed for two kinds of territories: those that were part of the United States and those that were not part of but were instead possessions of the United States. The Constitution did not extend completely to the latter, but there were certain provisions embodying certain rights that limited the otherwise plenary powers of Congress.[21]

Downes v. Bidwell, decided in 1901, was the most important of the Insular Cases.[22] *Downes* is essential to the proper understanding of the political status to which Puerto Rico was to be relegated. The case was brought by an importer of oranges sent from San Juan to New York, who complained about the 15 percent duty levied on the product. He claimed that the imposition violated the clause of the United States Constitution that commands that "all duties, imposts and excises shall be uniform throughout the United States." This claim effectively put into question the right of the United States to establish a colonial empire, to own territory to which the Constitution would not extend. Five opinions were issued by the Court, none commanding a majority, but three of them upholding the administration's power to govern territory acquired by conquest or treaty without the restraints imposed by the Constitution.

The Fuller Court, as it was known, was not a distinguished court. This was the court that sanctioned racial discrimination in the United States in the notorious *Plessy v. Ferguson* case of 1896; justified the use of injunctions against labor unions and upheld the imprisonment of its leaders for conduct later considered to be protected by the Constitution; frequently employed the due process clause to annul progressive social legislation, such as that of limiting daily working hours; considerably reduced state power to regulate the tariffs charged by public service companies; and exempted the American Sugar Refining Company, which controlled 98 percent of the sugar sold and refined in the United States, from the strictures of antitrust legislation.

Six of the justices had been appointed by Republican Presidents: John M. Harlan, Horace Gray, David J. Brewer, Henry B. Brown, George Shiras, and Joseph McKenna. The three Democrats were Chief Justice Melville W. Fuller, Edward D. White, and Rufus W. Peckham. The majority in *Downes* was composed of four Republicans (Brown, McKenna, Shiras, and Gray) and a Southern Democrat (White). Two Republicans (Harlan and Brewer) joined two Democratic appointees (Fuller and Peckham) to form the minority. The three opinions that favored the position of the administration were written by Brown, White, and Gray. White's theory eventually would prevail in the Insular Cases and beyond. Fuller and Harlan wrote the dissenting opinions. Let us take a closer look at the dramatis personae, beginning with the writers of the opinions that made the majority.

Brown served with little distinction in the Court from 1891 to 1903. He was notoriously insensitive to questions of racial equality. His best-known opinion was the majority opinion in *Plessy v. Ferguson,* where he stated: "We consider the underlying fallacy of the plaintiff's argument to consist in the assumption that the enforced separation of the two races stamps the colored race with a badge of inferiority. If this be so, it is not by reason of anything found in the act, but solely because the colored race chooses to put that construction upon it. . . . If one race be inferior to the other socially, the Constitution of the United States cannot put them upon the same plane."[23] Brown's opinion in *Downes* reveals his deep preoccupation with the supposedly grave consequences of making Puerto Ricans and Filipinos citizens of the United States and extending the United States Constitution to strange peoples and lands.

White was an ardent protectionist from Louisiana, where he served briefly on the state supreme court and later became a Senator. Oliver Wendell Holmes, who served with him on the United States Supreme Court for nineteen years, said that White was "built rather for a politician than a judge."[24] A subsequent critic wrote: "What impresses later generations in White's opinions is less their substance than their extraordinary form. He moved portentously across the thinnest of ice, confident that a lifeline of adverbs—'inevitably,' 'irresistibly,' 'clearly,' and 'necessarily'—was supporting him in his progress."[25]

Gray, the author of the third majority opinion, had perhaps the best professional credentials prior to his appointment. A reputable Boston lawyer, he had served for a creditable number of years in the Massachusetts Supreme Court. Although deriving from the same cultural and social milieu as Holmes, his record in civil rights cases was dismal. He voted with the majority in the Civil Rights Cases, in which the Court annulled the federal 1875 Civil Rights Act, which required equal treatment for every American citizen, regardless of color, in any place under the jurisdiction of the federal government. He also authored the opinions that denied United States citizenship to American Indians and severely limited the human rights of foreigners residing in the United States.

The fourth member of the majority, Shiras, was a railroad lawyer from Pittsburgh, ultraconservative in matters of social legislation but with a liberal bent in civil rights issues.

The fifth member, McKenna, was the sole McKinley appointee to the Court. He was a former Congressman from California, identified with the political machine of the railroad magnate Leland Stanford. His lack of professional preparation has often been commented upon: "His mind uncluttered by the complex dicta of legal scholarship, McKenna tended to decide each case individually as it came before the Court, mostly on the basis of the application of 'common sense.' The net result of his erratic empiricism is a series of frequently conflicting opinions and votes. . . . The quilted pattern of McKenna's legal decisions largely defies logical analysis."[26]

Among the dissenters, Fuller was a Grover Cleveland appointee and a vigorous critic of the extension of the national powers, contrary to the nationalist inclination of the majority of his court. Although his civil rights record was not good, he had written several dissents defending minorities from the use of arbitrary power.

Harlan, the author of the second dissenting opinion in *Downes,* had and still deservedly has a considerable reputation. Defeated in his bid to be Governor of Kentucky, he was later considered as a vice presidential candidate. He dissented in *Plessy v. Ferguson,* the Civil Rights Cases, *Lochner* (the maximum hours case), and many others.

Finally, Brewer was the most conservative judge of the Court in 1901. His strong disapproval of government intervention in individual economic activities did make him at times, however, a defender of personal liberty in other fields. He was also fundamentally at odds with the expansionism that characterized the age.

Brown's position was, in brief, that the Constitution applies only to the states and to territories where Congress decided to extend the Constitution. There could be territories subject to the jurisdiction of the United States, but to which the Constitution did not apply, except to the extent that certain of its provisions restricted the powers of Congress. Evidencing his concern about different races, the author of the majority opinion in *Plessy* wrote in *Downes:*

> We are . . . of the opinion that the power to acquire territory by treaty implies, not only the power to govern such territory, but to prescribe upon what terms the United States shall receive its inhabitants, and what their status shall be in what Chief Justice Marshall termed the "American empire." There seems to be no middle ground between this position and the doctrine that if their inhabitants do not become, immediately upon annexation, citizens of the United States, their children thereafter born, whether savages or civilized, are such, and entitled to all the rights, privileges, and immunities of citizens. If such be their status, the consequences will be extremely serious. Indeed, it is doubtful if Congress would ever assent to the annexation of territory upon the condition that its inhabitants, however foreign they may be to our habits, traditions, and modes of life, shall become at once citizens of the United States.[27]

Brown's theories fit nicely with the position backed by the administration.

White, whose opinion would eventually triumph, reached the same result as Brown through different semantics. He held that there were two types of territories, both subject to the jurisdiction of the United States: those incorporated to the nation and those that were not. The Constitution extended to the first group, but not to the second, except those parts of the Constitution that referred to principles that could be termed fundamental. White firmly rejected the view that the United States could not constitutionally acquire colonies: "While no particular provision of the Constitution is referred to, to sustain the argument that it is impossible to acquire territory by treaty without immediate and absolute incorporation, it is said that the spirit of the Constitution excludes the conception of property or dependencies possessed by the United States and which are not so completely incorporated as to be in all respects a part of the United States. . . . But this reasoning is based on political, and not judicial, considerations."[28]

White considered that the acquiring country had unrestricted power to determine what rights to concede to the acquired territory. To say otherwise, he ruled, would be "to say that the United States is helpless in the family of nations, and does not possess the authority which has at all times been treated as an incident of the right to acquire."[29] Puerto Rico's constitutional status was therefore thus defined: "While in an international sense Porto Rico was not a foreign country, since it was subject to the sovereignty of and was owned by the United States, it was foreign to the United States in a domestic sense, because the island has not been incorporated into the United States, but was merely appurtenant thereto as a possession."[30]

The nature of this holding is not generally known in either the United States or Puerto Rico. The typical American or Puerto Rican is shocked to learn that Puerto Rico has never been part of the United States in the domestic sense. It should also be unsettling to know that it is the prevalent position of the United States government, even at present, that Congress still has plenary powers over Puerto Rico, to the full extent declared in *Downes,* and that, accordingly, Puerto Rico is still a territory, possession, or chattel of the United States.

Gray's position was that, until it was ready to establish a complete government for Puerto Rico, Congress could provide a temporary government. Gray did not reach the issue of whether the United States could under the Constitution possess permanent colonies, but in practice Gray went further than Brown or White in defining the extent of United States power over Puerto Rico. He thought that the temporary civil government established by Congress could exercise powers as great as those wielded by the military government, and he was the only justice to abstain from holding that Congressional power over the new territories was limited by certain fundamental or natural rights.

Fuller held in his dissenting opinion that the United States could be composed only of states and territories, to all of which the Constitution applied. To his mind, the Constitution did not allow political entities to be subject to the absolute will of the Congress. He thus summarized the contrary contention:

> The contention seems to be that, if an organized and settled province of another sovereignty is acquired by the United States, Congress has the power to keep it, like a disembodied shade, in an intermediate state of ambiguous existence for an indefinite period; and, more than that, that after it has been called from that limbo, commerce with it is absolutely subject to the will of Congress, irrespective of constitutional provisions. . . .
>
> That theory assumes that the Constitution created a government empowered to acquire countries throughout the world, to be governed by different rules than those obtaining in the original states and territories, and substitutes for the present system of republican government a system of domination over distant provinces in the exercise of unrestricted power.[31]

Fuller accordingly held that the Constitution applied *ex proprio vigore* to Puerto Rico, dismissing as political the argument about the dire consequences of extending the totality of the Constitution to the new territories. The Chief Justice, however, did not believe that extension of the Constitution to the new territories entailed immediate acquisition of American citizenship. While indicating that the issue was not before the Court, he stated: "Doubtless the subjects of the former sovereign are brought by the transfer under the protection of the acquiring power, and are so far impressed with its nationality, but it does not follow that they necessarily acquire the full status of citizens."[32]

Harlan's dissent was a vigorous indictment of the theory that the United States could establish a colonial system. He wrote:

> In my opinion, Congress has no existence and can exercise no authority outside the Constitution. Still less is it true that Congress can deal with new territories just as other nations have done or may do with their new territories. This nation is under the control of a written constitution, the supreme law of the land and the only source of the powers which our government, or any branch or officer of it, may exert at any time or at any place. Monarchical and despotic governments, unrestrained by written constitutions, may do with newly acquired territories what this government may not do consistently with our fundamental law. To say otherwise is to concede that Congress may, by action taken outside of the Constitution, engraft upon our republican institutions a colonial system such as it exists under monarchical governments. Surely such a result was never contemplated by the fathers of the Constitution. . . . The idea that this country may acquire territories anywhere upon the earth, by conquest or treaty, and hold them as mere colonies or provinces,—the people inhabiting them to enjoy only such rights as Congress chooses to accord them—is wholly inconsistent with the spirit and genius, as well as with the words, of the Constitution.[33]

Thus, by a one-vote margin, the Supreme Court, reflecting the deep division at the time in the body politic itself, confirmed Puerto Rico's status as a colony of the United States.

Yet *Downes* actually opened up the possibility of a different treatment of Puerto Rico under a regime of special laws. After federal taxation started in 1913, Puerto Rico could safely be left outside its scope, although Congress remained free to change its mind. On the other hand, many critics of the present condition of Puerto Rico point to *Downes* and the rest of the Insular Cases as allowing unequal treatment of Puerto Rico in many ways, such as its exclusion from the right to vote for President, full or meaningful representation in Congress, and equal participation in federal aid programs.

The treatment of Hawaii at the same time was quite different. After its annexation in 1898 through the Newlands Resolution, Hawaii's organic act, passed shortly after the Foraker Act in 1900, made Hawaii part of the United States and started it on the path to statehood. That incorporation of Hawaii by Congress had taken place, contrary to what happened to Puerto Rico, was confirmed in 1903 in the *Mankichi* case (another of the Insular Cases).[34] By 1905, in the *Rasmussen* case, the Supreme Court decided that Alaska was also an incorporated territory where the Constitution applied.[35] White's incorporation doctrine commanded a majority of the Court, although it was not until 1922 in the *Balzac* case, where the Court unanimously ruled that the extension of American citizenship to Puerto Ricans did not make Puerto Rico part of the United States.[36]

The Insular Cases, in sum, left the government of the United States free to pursue the policies that had started taking shape during the military government. The main legal assumptions of the imperialists were confirmed: formation of a colonial empire was possible; Puerto Rico was not part of the United States as other territories had been, but instead was a dependency or possession; and Puerto Rico could accordingly be held and governed indefinitely, without the restrictions of the Constitution, except those relating to certain undefined human rights of a fundamental nature. The other elements of the United States' new colonial policy were consequently left undisturbed, and it could hardly be otherwise, given the limitations of judicial power: the cautious extension of limited self-governing powers, as conditions would dictate, but without any promise, explicit or implicit, of eventual independence or statehood; cultural assimilation, considered a necessary part of the Puerto Rican people's education in the art of self-government; and enlightened economic treatment of the island, as the term was understood in those laissez-faire days, long before vast governmental aid programs were launched.

NOTES

1. Carroll, Henry K., *Report on the Island of Porto Rico,* Washington, D.C., Government Printing Office, 1899, pp. 56–58.

2. *Report of the Insular Commission of the Secretary of War Upon Investigations Made into the Civil Affairs of the Island of Porto Rico,* Washington, D.C., Government Printing Office, 1899, p. 61.

3. U.S. Congress, *Senate Hearings before the Committee on Pacific Islands and Porto Rico of the United States Senate on S. 2264,* 56th Cong., 1st Sess., Senate Document (hereafter S. Doc.) 147, Washington, D.C., Government Printing Office, 1900, p. 96.

4. Ibid., 97.

5. Davis's views are expressed in U.S. Congress, House of Representatives, *Reports of Brig. Gen. George W. Davis on Civil Affairs in Porto Rico,* 56th Cong., 1st Sess., H. Doc. 2.

6. U.S. Congress, Senate, *Report of the Hawaiian Commission,* 56th Cong., 3rd Sess., S. Doc. 16, Washington, D.C., Government Printing Office, 1898.

7. U.S. Congress, House of Representatives, *Report of the Secretary of War, 1899,* 56th Cong., 1st Sess., H. R. Doc. 21, pp. 26–29.

8. Ibid., 24.

9. Sumner, W. B., "The Conquest of the United States by Spain," 8 *Yale L. J.* 176–77 (1899).

10. Thayer, J. B., "Our New Possessions," 12 *Harv. L. Rev.* 464, 475 (1899).

11. Baldwin, S. E., "The Constitutional Questions Incident to the Acquisition and Government by the United States of Island Territory," 12 *Harv. L. Rev.* 392, 415 (1899).

12. S. 2016, 56th Cong., 1st Sess. The later version, on which hearings were held, was S. 2264.

13. H. R. 6883, 56th Cong., 1st Sess.

14. U.S. Congress, House of Representatives, *Hearings on H.R. 6883,* House Committee on Insular Affairs, January 8 and 10, 1900, Washington, D.C., Government Printing Office, 1900, p. 103.

15. S. Rep. 249, 56th Cong., 1st Sess., pp. 8–9.

16. 31 Stat. 77.

17. Porter, K. H., and Johnson, D. B., *National Party Platforms (1840–1964),* Urbana, University of Illinois Press, 1966, pp. 112–13.

18. Morison, S. E., and Commager, H. S., *The Growth of the American Republic*, New York, Oxford University Press, 1962, vol. 2, p. 430.

19. Langdell, C. C., "The Status of Our New Possessions," 12 *Harv. L. Rev.* 365, 386 (1899).

20. See, for example, Adams, E. B., "The Causes and Results of Our War with Spain from a Legal Standpoint," 8 *Yale L. J.* 119 (1899); Randolph, C. F., "Constitutional Aspects of Annexation," 12 *Harv. L. Rev.* 291, 314–15 (1898).

21. Lowell, A. L. "The Status of Our New Possessions—A Third View," 13 *Harv. L. Rev.* 155 (1899).

22. 182 U.S. 244 (1901).

23. *Plessy v. Ferguson*, 163 U.S. 537, 551–52 (1896).

24. Freund, Sutherland, Howe, Mark and Brown, *Constitutional Law*, 4th ed., Boston, Little, Brown, 1967, vol. I, p. xlv.

25. Ibid., pp. xlv, xlvi.

26. Watts, J. F., Jr., in L. Friedman and F. L. Israel, *The Justices of the United States Supreme Court, 1789–1969*, vol. III, pp. 1471, 1479.

27. 182 U.S. 244, 279–80 (1901).

28. Ibid., pp. 311–12.

29. Ibid., p. 306.

30. Ibid., pp. 341–42.

31. Ibid., p. 373.

32. Ibid., p. 369.

33. Ibid., p. 380.

34. *Hawaii v. Mankichi*, 190 U.S. 197 (1903).

35. *Rasmussen v. United States*, 197 U.S. 516 (1905).

36. *Balzac v. People of Porto Rico*, 258 U.S. 298 (1922).

QUESTIONS

1. Are you convinced by the reason given in the text why some people found it necessary to deviate from established procedures regarding the acquisition of territories when it came to Puerto Rico?

2. What rationale do you imagine can be provided to explain why the consent of the governed is not necessary in the case of Puerto Rico and why it was acceptable to extend the full U.S. constitutional rights to Hawaii and Alaska, but not to Puerto Rico?

3. According to the civil government structure established by the Foraker Act, who are the Puerto Rican people who are given a voice? On what basis might one judge that a people are not ready to govern themselves?

4. Behind the legal arguments that led to the signing of the Foraker Act, is it possible to detect politics, economics, or racism (or something else) as a predominant factor?

5. What, if anything, is the significance of the fact that Puerto Rico's name was changed to "Porto Rico" and it took an act of Congress to give the country back its real name?

Summary and Conclusion

SUMMARY

In the preceding readings, we discussed conceptual tools for understanding Latino/a politics as the quest for public citizenship. One explanation of this struggle is based on class struggle for the control of economic production, which is basic to our survival as physical beings. Another focuses on exclusive and inclusive conceptions of politics alongside masculine and feminine genders, respectively. A third claims that the relations of power and desire are deployed through discourses and may adopt either class struggle, patriarchal, or other forms in a never-ending struggle waged between domination and liberation within the possibilities set by material conditions. We have also encountered examples of discourses that produce and reproduce nationalist, ethnic, gender, patriotic, inclusive, and exclusive identities. These texts also exemplify the archeological effort to "dig out" and "re-cognize" illegitimate struggles, silenced voices, and invisible subjectivities so that they too can be included in the politics of the present.

Through a process of military aggression, economic and political seduction, even willful participation as well as manipulation of the law, thousands of Latino/as became U.S. political or cultural citizens, while others became subjects of the U.S. empire. The fate of citizens and subjects was and remains sealed in a particular discourse set in stone, that is, in the form of treaties, acts, laws, and amendments that symbolize their birth certificates as new members of the polity. The key institutions at play in this game of truth are the expanding economy, the military capability to defeat Mexico and Spain, and the resistance/acceptance of the new territorial and cultural citizens. They speak concepts like manifest destiny, *independencia,* and the right of self-preservation.

Some subjective positions have clear boundaries: you are either conquered or conqueror, man or woman. In others, hegemony is subtle and seductive, human bodies become enchanted by domination. Identities are constructed along the lines of nationalist or ethnic struggles as well as clearly defined gender roles. Political enemies and positions seem clear: liberals or conservatives, pro- or anti-U.S., in favor of the poor and the working class or in favor of the rich and the capitalists. Central in these foundations of Latino/a political thought are the human bodies that reveal in their flesh the consequences of belonging to particular political categories. Under these conditions, the response of the human beings caught up in these new political circumstances was tactical rather than strategic; that is, individually or collectively they mostly engaged in local uprisings.

CONCLUSION

Neither northern Mexicans nor Puerto Ricans nor Cubans (even though the latter two collaborated in their struggle against Spain) organized an overall strategy to repel the invading U.S. armed forces. (Others, like the

Philippines, did engage in armed struggle for many years.) The reasons, as the readings indicate, are very complex and unique to each Latino/a group. However, we have seen that economic and therefore political considerations—class, mixed marriages between elite and invaders, nationalism, nationality, ethnicity, and racism—are elements in the games of truth. The one success in the national struggle against U.S. encroachment is Cuba under the leadership of Fidel Castro. Cuban human bodies inside and outside of Cuba, unfortunately, continue to pay a heavy social, economic, and political price for this liberation from U.S. hegemony.

On this, as in all political issues, there are many perspectives. Here we attempt to follow a nonessentializing analysis. There are many Latino/as who are convinced that the U.S. hegemony is the best thing that could have happened to them. There are others who have dedicated their lives to fighting it. The one undeniable reality is manifested by the human bodies themselves that are afflicted by poor social conditions. But even the privileged ones are subjected to disciplinary, normalizing, and therefore, alienating practices. This bio-power is exercised not only in the most powerful and wealthiest nation the world has ever seen and upon bodies categorized as Latino/as, Native Americans, African Americans, Asians, and others. It is also inherent in the nature of relations of power and desire. But so is the quest for a public citizenship, a just life, and a sense of belonging, acceptance, and respect.

Last-Mambo-in-Miami

Gustavo Pérez-Firmat

Soy un ajiaco de contradicciones.
I have mixed feelings about everything.
Name your tema, I'll hedge;
name your cerca, I'll straddle it
like a cubano.

I have mixed feelings about everything.
Soy un ajiaco de contradicciones.
Vexed, hexed, complexed,
hyphenated, oxygenated, illegally alienated,
psycho soy, cantando voy:
You say tomato,
I say tu madre;
You say potato,
I say Pototo.
Let's call the hole
un hueco, the thing
a cosa, and if the cosa
goes into the hueco,
consider yourself en casa,
consider yourself part of the family.

(Cuban-American mí:
I singo therefore I am, sí.)

Soy un ajiaco de contradicciones,
un puré de impurezas,
a little square from Rubik's Cuba,
que nadie nunca acoplará.
(Cha-cha-chá.)

PART II

LIFE WITHIN THE EMPIRE: (DE)CONSTRUCTING POLITICAL POSITIONS AND IDENTITIES

IN PART I WE WITNESSED THE NINETEENTH-CENTURY expansion of U.S. territory and of the United States' international political status from an isolationist country into an empire, as it appropriated Mexican, Puerto Rican, and Cuban bodies (among many others). Through war, violence, and political resistance, these new members of the U.S. political body were subjectified as secondary citizens, as *ethnos*. These events took place within the global context of an industrial revolution that caused mass migrations and political-economic realignments all over the world. For example, between 1820 and 1920 an estimated sixty million people, or the equivalent to the total U.S. population in 1890, moved from rural to urban areas. During this same period, thirty million Europeans migrated to the United States. Almost half of these arrived between 1890 and 1914.

Part II consists of two sections that traverse the twentieth century. In the first section, the readings explore the political adjustments of the newly adopted members, their resistance to and negotiations with the U.S. polity during the first six decades of the century. Here we provide extensive introductory discussions to contextualize the texts that address the following three topics: (1) the Puerto Rican's conflicting status as a U.S. citizen, (2) the Cuban (American?) attempt at self-determination while under the influence of the United States, and (3) the fragile political status of the Mexican American.

A map of the power relations that construct Latino/a political thought during the first half of the century would have to include the continually expanding U.S. forces of production and the social, political, and economic consequences these had on the inhabitants of Mexico, Cuba, and Puerto Rico. Indeed, industrialization and its craving for human bodies, as well as World War I, led to immigration to the United States, not only from Europe but also from Asia, Mexico, Cuba, and Puerto Rico, and to a lesser extent, from other Latin American countries. Within the United States, the relocation was from rural to urban, from south to north, and from east to west. The material conditions of industrialization also constructed political identities, subjectivities caught in games of truth that assigned human bodies a relative value in the U.S. polis depending on the usual categories of skin pigmentation, nationality, class, and gender. As might be deduced from these conditions, during this period there was a very strong nativist, antiethnic, anti-immigrant movement in the United States (more fully discussed in the section "The Fragile Political Status of Mexican Americans," later in part II). Nevertheless, in their quest for public citizenship these human bodies continued their political, economic, and cultural struggles using a variety of tactics and strategies.

In the section "Manifold Identities and Struggles," we include texts that illustrate some of the diverse and manifold political struggles that emerge from roughly the

1960s to the present. Some are repetitions or continuations of past struggles, such as those of the Mexican and Filipino farmworkers and the Puerto Rican *independentistas*. Others, as indicated in the chart of world-historical social movements (see appendix 1A), shift their tactics to the arenas of public space and everyday life: feminism, new forms of being political, grassroots organization, the taboo subject of pigmentocracy among Latinos. And still others in their quest for public citizenship carve out a space where, paradoxically, others are excluded.

As always, we need to keep in mind that this proliferation of discourses, of identities and forms of struggles, is an integral part of a corresponding proliferation of global economic relations that have increased since World War II. They are hidden, illegal, invisible discourses that address variant forms of subjectification, of oppression, but also the possibilities for liberation. This is the postmodern condition that the texts address in part IV.

Resistance and Negotiation
(ca. 1900 to 1960s)

PUERTO RICAN RESISTANCE TO, AND
INSISTENCE ON, U.S. CITIZENSHIP

English and Spanish American patriots fought against their respective rulers to give a voice to the will of the people. History repeated itself in the Puerto Rican struggle for one right enjoyed by democratic societies: government by the consent of the people. In this case it is not a battle of the Rights of (Hu)Man against the Divine Right of the King/Queen. It is a charge against "a pathological insistence on keeping Puerto Rico on parole, with electronic devices on hands and feet to forewarn of any suspicious movement, claiming that the self-governing powers so far granted could at any time be unceremoniously taken away."[1] This may appear to be an epic story of a struggle between good and evil, between two nations, one of which keeps the other under submission. Perhaps this is why *independentista* revolutionary statements figure so prominently in this discourse of liberation. Games of truth and the quest for public citizenship, however, go beyond good and evil.

In part I, the texts provided a historical background for the birth of Puerto Ricans as U.S. Americans, with the Foraker Act symbolizing a birth certificate. Other texts represent the limits within which Puerto Rican political discourse has been articulated for over one hundred years. On one side are the legal documents (not included in the reader), such as the Jones Act, which grants U.S. citizenship to Puerto Ricans, and Public Law 600, which grants Puerto Rico the status of commonwealth. Texts at the other limit, at the threshold of illegality, may be in the form of revolutionary activity and/or physical violence by or against Puerto Rican *independentistas,* as represented in the pieces by Rafael Cancel Miranda and Patricia Guadalupe. Both of these are essentialized discourses: one is adamant about not fully accepting Puerto Ricans into U.S. society or letting them go free and the other is resolute about the Right of Self-determination through independence. One manifestation of this particular exercise of power through the control of discourse is *la Mordaza,* the gag law signed in 1948 by Jesús Piñero, the first Puerto Rican governor. *La Mordaza* makes it a felony to engage in any act that could lead to Puerto Rico's independence, which would necessarily involve the overthrow of the U.S.-controlled Puerto Rican government. It is a felony to "print, publish, edit, circulate, sell, distribute, or publicly exhibit any writing or publication which encourages, pleads, advises, or preaches the necessity, desirability, or suitability of overthrowing the insular government."[2]

Now, within the colonial and *independentista* or national discourses, there is a wide spectrum of political positions that more properly represent the diversity of Puerto Rican political thought and quest for public citizenship. This is illustrated by José Trías Monge's legal analysis, Carol Hardy-Fanta's feminist approach ("Latina vs. Latino politics"), and Ramón Grosfoguel's nonessentialist description ("subversive complicity"). But the key political issue is silencing the voice, denying the will of the people, ignoring the consent of the governed, the countless ways they struggle outside our current understanding of "politics." The focus is on what is not visible. How often are we exposed to the actual words of official documents that dictate the limits of a nation's political status and therefore structure the political behavior of over six and a half million bodies? How often are we presented with the opportunity to reflect on the violence that is inherent in the colonial relationship represented by these documents? And what about the women and men who find it necessary to voice their opposition to colonialism by putting their own bodies, their lives, on the line? Are they patriots or terrorists?

Yamila Azize-Vargas goes beyond the essence of colonialism and nationalism to discuss other discourses deployed in the construction of a Puerto Rican political identity but tending to remain invisible. These involve a more subtle and insidious sort of abuse in the form of prejudice toward and exclusion of female and Puerto Rican human bodies. But which of these bodies actually qualify for that special political category of "the people"? And how many of them are there?

As a consequence of increasing rates of migration, by 1960, 42 percent (one million) of all Puerto Ricans lived on the mainland United States. By the year 2000, 46 percent (2.8 million), of all Puerto Ricans lived on the mainland and 3.8 million remained on the island.[3] This adds up to a total of 6.6 million Puerto Ricans in both the United States and Puerto Rico.

Earlier we said that the Foraker Act constructs the political status of the Puerto Rican nation. In effect, colonialism produces an identity not only for the nation but also for its citizens. Grosfoguel, Negrón-Muntaner, and Georas indicate, for example, that military, economic, and symbolic U.S. interests were deployed for over a century to create not only the entity we know today as Puerto Rico but also, more problematically, an "ethno-nation" that encompasses the mainland United States as well as Puerto Rico.[4] As María de los Angeles Torres points out (in chapter 26, part IV), in an increasingly interconnected world this transnational political and cultural identity is practiced by many immigrant peoples, including U.S. Cubans and Mexicans.

This is not necessarily a new phenomenon, however. The Puerto Rican insistence on self-determination at any cost is not unlike that of some Tejanos, who desired self-government within or without the Mexican state. These ambivalent political positions appear confusing unless we see them as quests for public citizenship. For example, almost immediately after annexation the Union Party, under the leadership of Luis Muñoz Rivera, insisted on having a "government founded on the will of the governed" and that this could be achieved through either statehood or independence (even if it was obtained under a protectorate status). The central point of contention was (and continues to be one hundred years later) that the Puerto Rican people have never been given the right to vote (other than symbolically) on the relationship they want to have with the United States. Supposedly, on the other side of the political spectrum, the Puerto Rican Republican Party, under the leadership of Afro-Puerto Rican José Barbosa, welcomed U.S. annexation and even statehood. But from 1920s to 1950s the party expressed ambivalence about the issue and eventually questioned statehood after repeated rejections from Washington. These major parties represented the propertied classes leaving the workers outside of traditional politics, until Spanish-born Santiago Iglesias in 1915 founded the Socialist Party, which clearly supported statehood. This ambivalent discourse continues in the twenty-first century; it is represented, among others, by the Popular Democratic Party, which backs continued commonwealth status (Public Law 600), and the New Progressive Party, which supports statehood for Puerto Rico.

In addition to the obsessive concern with status, the political battles in the first fifteen years included a criticism of the imposition of the U.S. educational system (including requiring instruction in the English language); the concentration of power in the hands of U.S. individuals, as opposed to institutions that represented the various segments of the Puerto Rican people; and the Americanization of Puerto Rican law, which was a powerful force in the drive toward assimilation. There is a cruel paradox in this game of truth: the more politically active Puerto Ricans became in the exercise of and demand for full political rights, the more they were portrayed by U.S. politicians as incapable of self-government. (This is not to say that the Puerto Rican political leadership always acted in a responsible manner.) The response of U.S. officials was to establish a connection between granting citizenship and the impossibility of independence. This in turn sparked *indepen-*

dentista movements.[5] In other words, after being rejected, rebuffed, repudiated, refused, spurned, and ridiculed, even the most ardent pro-U.S. elite, capitalist Puerto Rican Republicans began to think about independence. As Ronald Fernández puts it:

> Four hundred years of Spanish rule and no colonial government had ever managed to create a serious and wide-spread push for independence. But within fifteen years of taking over the island, Americans produced such a desire for independence that Congress gave the islanders U.S. citizenship to permanently eliminate their then ardent desire for a divorce.[6]

It is in this context that we must consider Puerto Ricans' ambivalence toward the collective (as opposed to individual) U.S. citizenship imposed on them by the Jones Act. Such citizenship was opposed by many Puerto Ricans during the House and Senate debates.

This ambivalence helps to define the space where the quest for citizenship is constructed. From the U.S. perspective, granting citizenship was an act that appeared to be within its egalitarian tradition; it also helped to clarify the status of Puerto Rico as a *possession* for those *independentistas* who wanted self-government, while the act was also seen as an extension of the benevolent effort to Americanize Puerto Ricans. At the same time, the act was ambivalent: it confirmed that such citizenship would not lead to Puerto Rico's ever becoming *a legitimate part of the United States*. For many if not most Puerto Ricans, U.S. citizenship meant obtaining the respect that the Foraker Act had denied them. It was also an implied promise for future rights and freedoms. And since Puerto Ricans had once enjoyed the privilege of being citizens of Spain, they desired to regain the respect this status had offered. Their ambivalence comes with the fear of cultural assimilation.[7] If this was a personal relationship it could be dramatized in the following conversation:

> "You belong to me but we can never have a serious relationship. Furthermore, you are not acceptable the way you are, therefore, you must become like me."
>
> "Right now I don't have a choice about belonging to you. Regarding a serious relationship, we will just have to see what happens. But I can never stop being who I am. I can never be you."

We are dealing here with the exercise of colonial power, an attempt at total and absolute oppression. We are also dealing with a manifold counterhegemonic battle against it.[8] Note also that U.S. Mexicans, who historically have preferred to remain Mexican citizens, have done so because they have had more access to justice through the Mexican consulates. For the same reason, a U.S. American living in Mexico might prefer to remain a U.S. citizen.[9] Individuals in both cases have the option of an appeal to their respective nation-states of origin; that is, their claim to justice, their quest for public citizenship, is based on their respective nationalities. In the case of Puerto Ricans, their quest for public citizenship cannot be an appeal to their nation-state of origin (they are colonial subjects); therefore, cultural nationalism becomes the counterhegemonic force to challenge the United States. In fact, overt demonstrations of Puerto Rican cultural identity were once regarded as subversive.[10] Thus, culture becomes a very important site of struggles, some of which are overtly "political" and others of which are not obviously so, as with Puerto Rican *jaiba* politics or the *choteo* in Cuba, or with *cantinflismos* in México.[11] Many such forms of political struggle remain invisible in terms of our understanding of their particular tactics and strategies. There are still illegitimate knowledges that we continue to excavate (involving subalterns such as Afro-Latino/as, the elderly, gays, lesbians, women, workers, and youth).

Ultimately, though, these hidden and not so hidden political relations are manifested by the Puerto Rican bodies on both the island and the mainland. The conditions of these bodies are the only "real politics" at work here. It must be acknowledged that some improvements in living conditions and/or the status of women (as described by Yamila Azize-Vargas) did take place during the first forty years in which Puerto Rico was a U.S. colony. The economy of the island nevertheless remained in a shambles and social conditions were little better than at the end of the nineteenth century.[12] Almost one hundred years later, Puerto Rico's level of poverty is atrocious, having fallen below that of several other Caribbean countries; unemployment is between two and four times that of the United States; the high school dropout rate is 30 percent; and the homicide rate is 27.5 per 100,000 residents, as opposed to 9 percent for the mainland United States.[13] As in the case of Cuba, the poor social conditions are the result of economic relations with the United States and, more recently, of the restructuring of the global economy. Mass migrations to the mainland United States, a severe dislocation of human bodies, have resulted.

Meanwhile, other than the election of Sila Calderón of the Popular Democratic Party, a woman governor, in the November 2000 elections; the demonstration in Vieques; and the rise in labor organizing, it is mostly politics as usual. The referendums in 1963, 1993, and 1998 indicate an increasing preference for maintaining the status quo (about 48 percent in 1998) over statehood (about 46 percent) and a decreasing percentage (4 percent and 2.5 percent in the last two referendums) for independence. The reasons for this are discussed by Ramón Grosfoguel.

We conclude with a statement that points to the quest for public citizenship: "Above all, they [the Puerto Rican *independentistas*] must finally learn that it is not independence per se that the masses are after, but a political status that will clearly fulfill their aspirations to a better life."[14] From another perspective, though, the nationalists are like the Furies, the three Greek goddesses who, regardless of the wrongdoer's motivation, punished wrongs committed against blood relatives and that had escaped detection or public justice.

NOTES AND SUGGESTED READINGS

1. José Trías Monge, *Puerto Rico: The Trials of the Oldest Colony in the World* (New York: Yale University Press, 1997), 120.

2. Ronald Fernández, *The Disenchanted Island* (Westport, Conn.: Praeger, 1996), 178.

3. Juan Gonzalez, *Harvest of Empire* (New York: Viking, 2000), 81.

4. Ramón Grosfoguel, Frances Negrón-Muntaner, and Chloé Georas, "Beyond Nationalist and Colonialist Discourses: The *Jaiba* Politics of the Puerto Rican Ethno-Nation" in *Puerto Rican Jam: Rethinking Colonialism and Nationalism*, ed., Frances Negrón-Muntaner and Ramón Grosfoguel (Minneapolis: University of Minnesota Press, 1997), 17.

5. Trías Monge, *Puerto Rico*, 53–66 passim.

6. Fernández, *Disenchanted Island*, 33.

7. Trías Monge, *Puerto Rico*, 61.

8. This struggle is illustrated by J. Gómez-Quiñonez, "Toward a Concept of Culture," *Revista Chicano-Riqueña*, 5, no. 2 (1977): 29–47; and William V. Flores and Rina Benmayor, eds., *Latino Cultural Citizenship: Claiming Identity, Space and Rights* (Boston: Beacon Press, 1997).

9. Abraham Hoffman, *Unwanted Mexican Americans in the Great Depression* (Tucson: University of Arizona Press, 1974), 20.

10. Arlene Davila, *Sponsored Identities* (Philadelphia: Temple University Press, 1997), 1.

11. Ramón Grosfoguel et al, "Beyond Nationalist and Colonialist Discourses," 26. The terms *jaiba, choteo,* and *cantinflismos* refer to the practice of mocking authority and power as a counterhegemonic tactic, that is, a tactic against domination.

12. Trías Monge, *Puerto Rico*, 98.

13. Trías Monge, *Puerto Rico*, 160.

14. Wilfredo Mattos-Cintrón, "The Struggle for Independence: The Long March to the Twenty-first Century," *Colonial Dilemma*, ed., Edwin Meléndez and Edgardo Meléndez (Boston: South End, 1993), 214.

✳ 11 ✳
THE EMERGENCE OF FEMINISM IN PUERTO RICO, 1870–1930

Yamila Azize-Vargas

As indicated by Yamila in this text, U.S. military intervention had a major impact on Puerto Riqueñas. Echoing Apodaca's analysis of the relationship between economic production and the status of women, she notes that "[w]omen's work outside the home and their access to more education contributed to creating the conditions for the emergence of feminism in Puerto Rico." Women in the United States struggled for over a century before getting the right to vote in 1919. Since Puerto Rican women had become U.S. citizens in 1917, one would think that they also would be able to vote in 1919. But this particular "truth" enters into a political game in which Puerto Rican feminists side with the Socialist Party *and* the U.S. Congress against the Puerto Rican legislature and the Catholic Church. This is but one of the many instances in which gender equality comes up against nationalism. An important fact left out in this excerpt is that universal suffrage was finally given to Puerto Rican women in 1935.

Without a doubt, the twentieth century can be named the Century of Feminism. Economic, political, and social transformations interacted to significantly change women's status. Puerto Rico was no exception. Here I discuss the principal factors and events that were fundamental to improving women's situation during the first three decades of the twentieth century.

First I give a brief summary of women's education in Puerto Rico during the nineteenth century and then contrast it with the historical changes brought about by the U.S. invasion of Puerto Rico in 1898. U.S. military intervention had a major impact on women's work, particularly with the establishment of the tobacco and needlework industries, which employed thousands of women between 1900 and 1930 in Puerto Rico.

Women's work outside the home and their access to more education contributed to creating the conditions for the emergence of feminism in Puerto Rico. Two major groups emerged: one consisting of working class women, and the second of formally educated and more affluent women. Here I discuss their conflicts and struggles to achieve recognition for women in Puerto Rican society.

SPANISH COLONIALISM AND EDUCATION

Education stands out as one of the most important forces that molded women's lives. There is little to be said about formal education during the first half of the nineteenth century. The Spanish government was not interested in providing any education to women. What efforts were undertaken were made possible by private institutions and individuals. A very small number of privileged girls were taught exclusively by women professors. Men were prohibited from teaching at or visiting girls' schools. There were very few women professors or girls' schools. In 1860, for example, there were 122 schools for boys and tweny-five for girls. Ten years later, in 1870, the unequal proportion of schools still persisted: 246 schools for boys, sixty-seven for girls.[1]

The quality of women's education was very poor. As Cuesta Mendoza, a historian of this period, has said; "Education for Puerto Rican women in the nineteenth century condemned them to living between saucepans and sewing cases for the rest of their lives."[2] Several prominent Puerto Rican intellectuals spoke out on this issue, among them intellectuals like Eugenio María de Hostos, Salvador Brau, Manuel Fernández Juncos, and Alejandro Tapia y Rivera. Eugenio María de Hostos was one of the very first to endorse educational equity, not only in Puerto Rico, but also in Latin America. In a speech entitled "Scientific Education for Women," Hostos argued that women's inferiority was caused by "social, intellectual and moral restraints" together with "men's monopoly of social power." He proposed that society give women a "scientific" education; that is the only way women "will be emancipated from error and slavery." Exiled from Puerto Rico for political reasons, he worked in Chile and the Dominican Republic to establish educational institutions for women.[3]

AFTER THE UNITED STATES INVASION

The end of the century brought significant changes to Puerto Rico and to women's education and status. After the United States Army invasion in 1898, education became one of the priorities of the metropolitan power. Education was envisioned as an instrument to Americanize the population.[4] More schools were opened, and the number of students and teachers in public education increased dramatically. Coeducation was established and more girls attended school, but their education remained quite different from the boys'. Women's educational inequality was imposed and planned by the United States government, based on U.S. economic interests and needs. World War I was also a determinant factor in implementing educational policy for women.

During the first two decades of the twentieth century, a significant transformation of the Puerto Rican economy took place. The devaluation of the Spanish "peso" immediately after the U.S. invasion created a serious economic crisis on the island. Poor women were forced into jobs based on their traditional education and skills; female employment increased significantly in the needlework and tobacco industries, and in professions such as nursing and teaching. By 1910, women made up more than half the labor force in the field of education and the tobacco industry. In 1919, more than thirty-five thousand women did needlework at home.[5]

World War I severely interrupted commercial relations between the U.S. and the Philippines, the garment industry's main supplier. Puerto Rico, the new colony, provided a new source of cheap labor to the garment industry. There was a desperate need for jobs on the island and, given the critical economic situation, workers' wages were extremely low. Garment firms started to train people, mainly women who traditionally had learned this kind of sewing at home. The training then became institutionalized, as home economics became part of the public school's curriculum for all girls. They were enrolled in home economics programs taught by North Americans. Several commercial needlework corporations, interested in establishing their developing businesses in Puerto Rico, financed these programs or opened their own schools. By 1918, according to the Commissioner of Education, home economics was "so popular" that courses in embroidery and drawn work became part of the curriculum in all Puerto Rican schools.[6]

Along with needlework, U.S. investment was concentrated in tobacco. In contrast to needlework, tobacco production revolved around the factory.[7] Thus, while women's work in the tobacco industry, like needlework, capitalized on their supposed manual abilities, women in the tobacco industry faced quite a different work experience. They had to leave their homes, work with other women and men in a common space, and deal with terrible working conditions.

Women experienced various kinds of discrimination in the needlework and tobacco industries, as well as in education and the other occupations in which they were concentrated. They were paid less than men even when they did the same kind of work. Historical testimonies document women complaining about sexual harassment from their male bosses. The Puerto Rico Employment Bureau reported and denounced the inhumane working conditions in the garment industry. In the teaching profession, where they constituted a majority, women were forbidden to be members of, or even vote for, the School Board.

Women's oppression in the needlework and tobacco industries contributed to the conditions for the emergence of class and feminist consciousness. Women faced double exploitation: as workers and as women. They were paid less than men, while they continued to be responsible for their households.

WOMEN'S STRUGGLES AND THE *FEDERACIÓN LIBRE DE TRABAJADORES* (FREE WORKERS' UNION)

The first clear signs of protest came from women who worked in the tobacco industry. From the beginning of the twentieth century, newspapers published women's testimonies demanding help from the leaders of the *Federación Libre de Trabajadores* (FLT), then the main labor organization in Puerto Rico. Women demanded the right to organize, to be educated and to be protected from discrimination and harassment. The FLT's first response was rejection. But despite opposition from several male leaders, the women began their organizing drive. By 1904, there were eight women's unions with more than five hundred members.[8] In 1906 and 1907, newspapers reported several strikes by women in the tobacco industry.[9]

The presence of the "lector" (reader) in the tobacco factories played a significant role in the process of women's growing awareness and organization. The reader, paid by the workers, read daily newspapers and major literary works to workers in the factory. Oral testimonies and research document that this "lector" was an agitator who promoted unionization among the tobacco workers.

The high point of these struggles came in 1908, when two women delegates to the Fifth Annual Congress of the FLT presented a resolution demanding an official campaign to promote the unionization of working women in Puerto Rico. Other resolutions approved in that meeting dealt with the right to education, to better working conditions and *the first formal demand for women's suffage.*[10] The leaders of the tobacco unions, who years before had complained about women's participation in the industry, finally recognized that "they couldn't do anything to stop women in the industry . . . we must then, help them to get organized in unions, to get education; they can't be our enemies, they have to be our allies."[11] Soon after, women also became part of the Board of Directors of the *Federación Libre de Traba-jadores.*[12]

LUISA CAPETILLO

One of the most outstanding women leaders in this movement was Luisa Capetillo. Born in Arecibo, of a Spanish father and French mother, she received a liberal education. Her involvement in the labor movement began in 1907 when she became a "lectora" in one of the tobacco factories. She became actively involved in meetings and strikes, and then worked as a reporter for *Unión Obrera,* the main labor newspaper in Puerto Rico at the time. As a writer she published several books: *Ensayos libertarios (Libertarian Essays, 1907), La humanidad del futuro (The Humanity of the Future, 1910), Mi opinión sobre las libertades, derechos y deberes de la mujer (My Opinion about Women's Freedom, Rights and Duties, 1911)* and her last, *Influencia de las ideas modernas (The Influence of Modern Ideas, 1916).* She wrote on education and the importance of women working outside the home, on the benefits of a communist society free from oppression and religion, on love, and on the future of society. In all her writings she insisted on her affiliation with socialism, on her support for women's liberation, and particularly her defense of "free love." She never married, and had three children in open relationships. Ms. Capetillo traveled to New York, Cuba, the Dominican Republic and Florida, and published the feminist magazine, *La Mujer.* She was arrested in Cuba for wearing slacks. In Puerto Rico she is remembered in a popular song that says: "Dona Luisa Capetillo, intentionally or not, has created a tremendous uproar because of her culottes."[13]

THE SUFFRAGIST MOVEMENT

Several years after the working women's feminist campaigns, another group of women organized the *Liga Femínea de Puerto Rico* (Puerto Rican Feminine League).

Founded in 1917 by Ana Roqué de Duprey, its main objective was to fight for women's right to vote. Ana Roqué's commitment to women's rights had begun at the end of the nineteenth century. As the founder and editor of several feminist newspapers, she consistently demanded the right to vote, to education and to the active participation of women in society.[14]

In contrast to the feminist working women, the suffragists from *Liga Femínea* demanded the *restricted* vote. This meant that only those women twenty-one years old and over who knew how to read and write could participate in general elections. In Puerto Rico only one sixth of the female population met those requirements. The suffragist organization, though contemporary with the working women's organization, had a different ideology and different strategies. Working women in labor unions were active in strikes, demanded universal suffrage, and discussed issues affecting the working class as a whole. In contrast, the majority of the suffragists who favored the restricted vote did not share working women's problems or situation, and avoided involvement in militant demonstrations like strikes or other kinds of protests.[15]

THE NINETEENTH AMENDMENT: COLONIALISM, FEMINISM, AND THE FIGHT FOR UNIVERSAL SUFFRAGE

As early as 1908, the impact of feminist polemics was evident in the political arena. Nemesio Canales, writer and legislator, expressed his solidarity with the resolutions approved at the *Federación Libre de Trabajadores* assembly, and presented a bill demanding "legal emancipation for Puerto Rican women," including universal suffrage. The bill was not approved.[16] This was the first of a series of twelve different bills presented over a twenty-year period.

Besides male opposition, an additional obstacle to women's suffrage involved Puerto Rico's colonial status. Given Puerto Rico's subordination to the United States, several suffragists expected that the Nineteenth Amendment to the U.S. Constitution (passed in 1919, granting *universal* suffrage to all U.S. women citizens twenty-one years or over) would extend to Puerto Rico. Since Puerto Ricans were granted U.S. citizenship in 1917, there was a legal basis for this expectation.

Events were, however, more complicated. Once Congress approved the law, the Puerto Rican Legislature was uncertain about its validity in Puerto Rico. The confusion over the amendment's applicability was clarified by a solitary but militant action by one woman: Genera Pagán.

Born in San Juan at the end of the nineteenth century, Genera Pagán became a tobacco stripper in one of the largest tobacco factories. As a working woman, she faced miserable wages and terrible working conditions. Like other women, Genera realized the importance of syndicalism and militancy to achieve social change. She emerged as a leader during a working women's strike in 1914. Years later, after losing her husband in World War I, she emigrated to New York, where she worked in the garment industry. The feminist movement in the United States was at its height, particularly around the issue of universal suffrage. Shortly after the approval of the Nineteenth Amendment, Genera became involved in the fight for the extension of the new law to Puerto Rico. When she learned about the confusion over the new law, she decided to go back to Puerto Rico and fight for women's rights.[17]

Genera Pagán believed that as a U.S. citizen, the 1919 law applied to her and all Puerto Rican women. Thus, she attempted to register to vote. The Puerto Rican government did not know what to do, so it requested an opinion from the Bureau of Insular Affairs in Washington, D.C. Several months later, the Bureau of Insular Affairs decided that the Nineteenth Amendment was not applicable to Puerto Rico.[18]

Several considerations shaped this outcome. As Ana Roqué pointed out in 1920, in one of the last issues of her feminist newspaper, Puerto Rican legislators feared approving universal suffrage in Puerto Rico for three hundred thousand women. The majority of women were poor, and potential supporters of the Socialist Party, the first political party to support both suffrage for women and working women's labor struggles. Several legislators were quoted in a few newspapers saying that they were afraid of a possible victory by the Socialist Party due to women's electoral support. This explains why Ana Roqué wrote in her newspaper: ". . . if you (the legislators) are afraid of the political power the illiterate class could gain with the vote, *you should restrict the right to vote to literate women.*" Several years later her statement became a prophecy.[19]

The challenge raised by Genera Pagán showed that suffragists were overconfident about the extension of the Nineteenth Amendment to Puerto Rico. Disillusioned with the negotiations, their militancy decreased significantly. *Liga Feminea* disappeared and its leader, Ana Roqué, announced in 1920 that she was temporarily quitting, proclaiming that the "only hope in the universal suffrage struggle lay with working women's organizations." Mercedes Solá, another distinguished suffragist writer and leader, also recognized the importance of solid organizations "like the one built by working women in the struggle for women's rights."[20]

WORKING WOMEN'S STRUGGLE
FOR UNIVERSAL SUFFRAGE

Working women were, again, the first to raise the banner of feminism at the beginning of the new decade. By 1920, the Socialist Party organized the *Asociación Feminista Popular* (AFP Popular Feminist Association). One of its first activities was a mass rally with special guest speaker, Betty Hall, a very well-known North American suffragist.[21] This liaison between Puerto Rican and North American feminists was an important precedent, which influenced future feminist strategies.

Several months after the foundation of the AFP, the suffragists decided to reorganize. A new organization, *Liga Social Sufragista* (Suffragist Social League), was founded. Milagros Benet Newton, an active suffragist who held more conservative views than prior leaders, was elected president. She disapproved of Genera Pagán's defiant acts, and stood in favor of the restricted vote.[22] Her presidency, however, did not last long. She was followed by Ricarda López, one of the founders of the Teachers Federation, who brought significant changes to the League, particularly the defense of universal suffrage.

Subsequently, women's struggles for universal suffrage gained momentum. Two other suffragist groups were organized: *Asociación Puertorriqueña de Mujeres Sufragistas* (Puerto Rican Association of Suffragist Women) and *Liga Panamericana de Mujeres Votantes* (Pan-American Women's League), which followed the conservative direction promoted by Benet Newton. These new organizations took a firm stand in favor of *restricted* suffrage. The majority of the legislators shared this conservative position. Thus, of the eleven proposals presented for legislation, none was as liberal and comprehensive as the one that had been presented by the legislator, Nemesio Canales, in 1908. The majority asked for *restricted* suffrage, fearing the party preference of poor women—the Socialist Party. The Liberal Party, the party in power, of course opposed universal suffrage for women.

The political battle was on, and the debate reached other institutions: civic and religious associations, magazines, and newspapers. For example, cartoons appeared in popular magazines like *El Carnaval* and *El Diluvio,* mocking women's demand for suffrage.[23] The Catholic Church leaders opposed women's vote because it "could interrupt women's destiny, according to God and Nature, to be mothers and housewives."[24] *El Mundo,* one of the leading newspapers at that time, conducted a survey in which the majority of people who responded favored universal suffrage for women.[25] The Teachers Federation approved a resolution demanding women's suffrage.

BUILDING SOLIDARITY WITH NORTH AMERICAN FEMINISTS AND THE PRESSURE FROM WASHINGTON, D.C.

Over the following years, suffrage was one of the most widely discussed issues in the political arena. By 1927, there was a general consensus among several important civic, professional, and political organizations favoring women's right to vote, but the debate over universal versus restricted suffrage constituted a major obstacle to passing legislation. This debate initially divided the politicians and the feminists. A temporary coalition was formed between the conservative suffragist groups, which supported restricted suffrage, and feminist working women from both the Socialist Party and labor unions, which defended and insisted on universal suffrage. But the issue of restricted versus universal suffrage dissolved this united front. However, liberal suffragists in the *Liga Social Sufragista,* who supported universal suffrage, created a different strategy: lobbying in Washington, D.C.[26]

These liberal suffragists developed an ongoing relationship with the National Woman's Party. (It should be pointed out, however, that before the *Liga* began to seek help from North American suffragists, working women from the Socialist Party had contacted them.) Through their North American contacts, the Puerto Rican suffragists were able to lobby several congressmen. Their efforts paid off; they were able to convince two congressmen to present legislation. In January 1929, the bill moved up to the Committee for Insular Possessions and Territories of the United States Congress, which gave it a favorable recommendation.[27] This legislation then put pressure on the Puerto Rican Legislature to approve women's suffrage. Several months later a new bill, Number 12, was presented in Puerto Rico. If this bill was not approved soon, the U.S. legislation would be enacted. The bill was approved— granting *restricted* suffrage for women. Protests arose immediately. Leaders of the Suffragist Social League,[28] the Socialist Party, and other groups vigorously attacked the discriminatory law.

In 1932, approximately fifty thousand women participated in general elections, the first elections in which a group of women exercised their right to vote. Ironically, María Luisa Arcelay, who was not a feminist and was not involved in feminist struggles, was the first woman elected to the legislature. She had economic power as an owner of several needlework factories, and thus her record as a legislator who lacked interest in feminist issues, and in some instances opposed women's interests. For example, she did not support a bill to raise wages for women in the needlework industry, and did not initiate the bill to grant universal suffrage to women. It was clear that when she had to take sides, she defended her personal economic interests.

Feminist struggles waned during the period following the passage of the suffrage bill. This was also the trend in other countries. Thirty years passed before we witnessed a new wave of feminist activism.

CONCLUSION

One of the major achievements of contemporary feminist movements has been the rediscovery of their forgotten history. Women can learn many lessons from their predecessors' fights. The history of women's struggles, as this essay on Puerto Rican feminism shows, widens the discussions and perspectives on the current situation for women. Three major issues should be underlined: first, the inexorable relationship between feminism and social class, evident for example in the restricted versus universal suffrage polemic and the selection of María Luisa Arcelay as the first "token woman" in the Puerto Rican Legislature; second, the tremendous importance of international solidarity among women, as was demonstrated by the support and collaboration between Puerto Rican and U.S. feminists; third, women's obtaining of rights and equality where they unite and organize, when they develop a collective commitment to struggle for their rights.[29]

NOTES

The present essay is a summary of the author's book *La mujer en la lucha* (Cultural, P.R. 1985)—*Women in Struggle*—which discusses the history of feminism in Puerto Rico from the 1870s to the 1930s.

1. For more information on the history of women's education in Puerto Rico, see Cayetano Coll y Toste, *Historia de la instrucción pública en Puerto Rico hasta el año 1898* (*History of Puerto Rican Public Education up to 1898*) (Editorial Vasco Americana, Spain 1970). Statistics quoted were taken from Juan José Osuna, *A History of Education in Puerto Rico* (Editorial U.P.R. 1949), p. 56.

2. Cuesta Mendoza, A. *Historia de la educación en el Puerto Rico colonial de 1821–1898* (*History of Education in Colonial Puerto Rico from 1821–1898*), vols. I and II (Imprenta Arte y Cine, República Dominicana, 1948).

3. For more information on Hostos see *Hostos en Santo Domingo, Homenaje de la República Dominicana con motivo del Centenario de Eugenio María de Hostos* (*Hostos in Santo Domingo, Dominican Republic's Homage to Eugenio María de Hostos*), ed. E. Rodríguez Demoncci, 1939, pp. 214–215; Eugenio María de Hostos, "La educación científica de la mujer," *Páginas Escogidas* ("Scientific Education for Women" *Selected Pages*) (Colección Estrada, Argentina, 1952), p. 81.

4. Negrón de Montilla, Aida. *Americanization in Puerto Rico and the Public School System 1900–1930* (Editorial Edil, P.R. 1971).

5. "Major Female Occupations in Puerto Rico, 1899–1930." United States Department of Labor, *The Employment of Women in Puerto Rico* (Washington, D.C.: Government Printing Office, 1934).

6. Report of the Governor of Puerto Rico, *Informe del Comisionado de Instrucción* (*Report of the Education Commissioner*). Años 1911, p. 175; 1917, p. 467; Reyes de Martínez Ana. L. *El Desarrollo del programa de economía doméstica en Puerto Rico 1903–1964* (*The Development of the Home Economics Program in Puerto Rico from 1903 to 1964*) (Departamento de Instrucción Pública, Junta Estatal de Instrucción Vocacional, P.R. 1964).

7. Quintero Rivera Angel. "Socialista y tabaquero: La proletización de los artesanos." ("The Socialist and Tobacco Worker: The Proletarization of the Artisans") *Sin Nombre* (January–March, 1978), p. 13, P.R.

8. Iglesias, Igualdad. *El obrerismo en Puerto Rico* (*Workmanship in Puerto Rico*). "La mujer en la organización obrera" ("Women in the Workers' Organizations") (Ed. Juan Ponce de León, España, 1973), pp. 323–327.

9. *Unión obrera* (periódico) (*Workers' Union,* Newspaper) (September 1, 1910; September 26, 1910; August 26, 1911; July 14, 1911).

10. Federación Libre de Trabajadores, editor (Free Workers Union). *Procedimientos de Sexto Congreso de la Federación Libre de Trabajadores de Puerto Rico* (*Procedures of the 6th Conference of the Free Workers Union of Puerto Rico*) (San Juan, P.R. 1910).

11. Torres, A. *Espíritu de clase* (*Class Spirit*) (Imprenta F.L.T., San Juan, P.R. 1917), pp. 43–44.

12. *Unión Obrera* (*Workers' Union*) (September 1, 1906).

13. Valle, N. *Luisa Capetillo* (San Juan, P.R. 1975).

14. For more information on Ana Roqué see Negrón Muñoz A. *Mujeres de Puerto Rico* (*Women in Puerto Rico*) (Imprenta Venezuela, San Juan, Puerto Rico 1935); Meléndez, C. "Ana Roqué de Duprey: Biografía en cuatro tiempos," *Figuraciones de Puerto Rico* (Instituto de Cultura Puertorriqueña, San Juan, 1958).

15. For more information on the suffragist organizations, see several of their newspapers: *Pluma de mujer* (1915); *Album puertorriqueño* (1918).

16. Canales, N., *Paliques* (Edit Coquí, San Juan, P.R. 1968).

17. *El Mundo* (September 3, 1920).

18. *El Mundo* (September 17, 1920; January 6, 1921).

19. *Heraldo de la mujer* (October 1919), Author's Emphasis.

20. Solá, M. *Feminismo* (Imprenta Cantero, P.R. 1922).

21. *Unión Obrera* (December 14, 1920).

22. *El Mundo* (September 3, 1920).

23. *El Carnaval* (September 12, 1920), cartoon entitled "Cuando las mujeres voten"; (September 19, 1920), "Cosas del sufragio femenino"; (September 26, 1920), "Y quieren que uno las apoye."

24. *El Mundo* (September 4, 1920).

25. *El Mundo* (March, April and May 1923).

26. *El Mundo* (November 28, 1927).

27. "Confer the right to vote to women of Porto Rico," House of Representatives, Report #1895, 70th Congress, May 1928; "Conferring the Right to Vote upon Porto Rican Women," Senate, Report #1454, 70th Congress, January 18, 1929.

28. *El Mundo* (May 29, 1929).

29. For more information on the history of feminism in Puerto Rico see Azize, Y. *La mujer en la lucha. Historia del feminismo en Puerto Rico 1898–1930* (*Women's Struggles. History of Feminism in Puerto Rico 1898–1930*). (Editorial Cultural, San Juan, Puerto Rico, 1985); Azize, Y., ed. *La mujer en Puerto Rico. Ensayos de investigación* (*Woman in Puerto Rico, Research Essays*) (Editorial Huracán, P.R. 1987).

＊   ＊   ＊

QUESTIONS

1. Yamila claims that the U.S. government imposed and planned women's educational inequality based on its own economic interests. Can this claim also be made regarding all women in the mainland United States? Or regarding all workers regardless of gender?

2. What different interpretations can be made regarding (a) the devaluation of the peso, (b) the economic crisis and the desperate need for jobs, (c) the garment and tobacco industries providing jobs, and (d) a school curriculum that trains workers for these jobs?

3. What explanations are there for the divisions among workers (rejecting women as union members) and among women (universal vs. restricted suffrage)?

4. What are the implications for the struggle for women's equality when the first woman to be elected to the Puerto Rican legislature is actually against universal suffrage and for her own economic interests?

＊ 12 ＊
WE CAME OUT OF PRISON STANDING, NOT ON OUR KNEES

Martín Koppel with Rollande Girard and Jacob Perasso

The following is an interview with Rafael Cancel Miranda, one of the five nationalists involved in the attacks on the House of Representatives in 1954 and the Blair House, President Harry Truman's temporary residence, in 1950. Rafael was a member of the Nationalist Party and had been engaged in political and armed struggle against U.S. imperialism since he was a high-school student. He is considered both a patriot and a terrorist and was imprisoned for over twenty-five years.

*   *   *

Rafael Cancel Miranda, a leader of the struggle for Puerto Rico's independence, is one of a group of five Nationalists who in the early 1950s conducted armed protests in Washington, D.C., against U.S. colonial policy. Cancel Miranda, together with Lolita Lebrón, Andrés Figueroa Cordero, and Irving Flores, carried out an armed demonstration in the U.S. House of Representatives in 1954. Oscar Collazo took part in a 1950 attack on Blair House, President Harry Truman's temporary residence.

The five Nationalists spent a quarter century in U.S. prisons for their pro-independence actions. Faced with a growing international defense campaign, the U.S. government finally freed Figueroa Cordero in 1978 and the other four in 1979.

In an interview with *Militant* reporters Rollande Girard and Jacob Perasso, conducted April 27, 1998, in Cabo Rojo, Puerto Rico, and in subsequent discussions with this reporter, Cancel Miranda recounted some of the background to those dramatic events and the political experiences he was part of during his years in jail.

Cancel Miranda became involved in Puerto Rico's independence movement as a youth in the early 1940s in the western city of Mayagüez.

"My father was the president of the Nationalist Party committee in Mayagüez," he said. "I was brought up among Nationalists. I grew up hearing the name of Pedro Albizu Campos. He and my father were comrades-in-arms and friends, and when he would come to speak in Mayagüez he would stay in our home." Albizu Campos was the central leader of the Nationalist Party and the Puerto Rican independence movement for several decades.

On March 21, 1937, Cancel Miranda's father and mother attended a Nationalist Party rally in the city of Ponce that was attacked by the police on orders from Gen. Blanton Winship, the colonial governor. The cops fired on the peaceful gathering, killing twenty-one people and wounding two hundred. "Blanton Winship, an American who had been appointed by Franklin Delano Roosevelt, was praised for 'defending democracy' by slaughtering our people," said Cancel Miranda, who at the time was six years old.

"My parents survived the massacre. My mother went there dressed in white and returned dressed in red, covered in the blood of the dead, whose bodies she had to crawl over as the bullets flew overhead." He would never forget that image.

A couple days later, he refused to pledge allegiance to the U.S. flag in his first-grade class, and was promptly sent home.

As he grew up, Cancel Miranda found out more and more about the truth behind the Ponce massacre and other brutal realities of U.S. colonial rule in Puerto Rico. "As the years went by I began to seek out the root of the problem, and the ideas advocated by my father and my Nationalist friends, who were serious and noble people. I wanted to be like them.

"While in school, I learned that the Yankees had bombed San Juan and killed Puerto Ricans from U.S. ships on May 12, 1898, and that they had invaded us on July 25 of that year. I learned this and other facts, and came to the conclusion that my parents and the Nationalists were right. Through my own convictions I became a Nationalist and partisan of Puerto Rico's independence.

"As a teenager, I and others organized nationalist youth committees in different towns. We had a radio program and a small newspaper."

Cancel Miranda recalls meeting Albizu Campos in December 1947 when the Nationalist Party leader returned from the United States after serving out a ten-year prison sentence—first in the U.S. penitentiary in Atlanta, then in New York—on charges of conspiracy to overthrow the U.S. government and "inciting rebellion" against it. "I went to welcome him as part of the Cadets of the Republic. The Cadets were the military section of the Nationalist Party. We wore black shirts and white pants."

JAILED FOR REFUSING U.S. DRAFT

Following World War II, widespread resistance to Washington's attempt to impose English as the main language of instruction in Puerto Rico's schools forced the U.S. government to drop that effort. Cancel Miranda relates that "in high school, when they tried to make us all speak English in class, we organized a student strike in defense of our language, and I along with others was accused of organizing it. They kicked me out of school for a year and barred me from studying in my town. I had to go to San Juan to finish school, even though I had only about two months to go before graduating."

Washington also had a hard time convincing Puerto Rican youth to join the army of the colonial master that occupied their homeland. During World War II, scores of Puerto Rican youth had been jailed for refusing to serve in the U.S. armed forces. During the 1950–53 Korean War, some one hundred thousand youth on the island refused to be drafted. In 1948 Cancel Miranda, then eighteen, was one of those who said no to the U.S. draft.

"One day," he recounts, "I was walking to school in San Juan with other students, and there was a car with four men sitting at the corner. I saw their faces and knew they weren't Puerto Ricans. They were four FBI agents. I handed my books to the other students to take them to the place where I was living, because I figured I might not return. They arrested me and charged me with refusing the U.S. draft. Later they arrested another six or eight youths.

"To me it didn't make sense to be in the same army that invades your country and massacres your people. If you're going to fight, you should fight *them*.

"The U.S. court here in Puerto Rico—they call it federal but it's a foreign court—sentenced me to two years and one day in prison. They put me on a plane along with five or six of us and sent us to the U.S. prison in Tallahassee, Florida."

There Cancel Miranda soon ran into trouble with the jailers for confronting racist segregation inside prison walls. Under Jim Crow legislation at the time, the prison dormitories were segregated.

"For some reason they put me in the dormitories for whites," he notes. "In the dining hall, Blacks and whites were supposed to eat in different sections, but I would go eat with the Black prisoners whenever I wanted to. There were Puerto Ricans who, because they were a little darker-skinned than me, were put in the dormitories for Blacks. One prison guard, by the name of Haynes, used a racist term against one of us who was darker-skinned. I told him in my thoughts, 'When you do that to me, I'm going to do something to you.'

"One day, when he did something to me I punched the racist guard. So I lost the five months of good time I had earned. They put me in the 'hole,' in solitary confinement, and I had to serve out the entire two-year-and-one-day sentence."

Cancel Miranda was in jail in Tallahassee when Washington launched its war of aggression against Korea in 1950. That same year, the Nationalist Party led an armed rebellion in Puerto Rico, which the colonial regime brutally crushed. Thousands were arrested, including Cancel Miranda's father.

"When I returned from prison in 1951 I got married," he continues. "But just eleven days later, they wanted to lock me up again for refusing the draft. My wife Carmen and my sister Zoraida told me: don't let yourself get arrested!

"So I went to Cuba under a different name and lived there for fourteen months. In Havana I landed a job in the construction of the tunnel under the Almendares river. I worked that job several months. Later, the dictator Fulgencio Batista, who was a U.S. puppet, put me in jail and deported me to Puerto Rico." Batista had come to power through a military coup in March 1952.

A short time later Cancel Miranda moved to Brooklyn, where he joined his wife. There he got involved in the effort to oppose Washington's attempts to prevent Puerto Rico's colonial status from being discussed at the United Nations.

ARMED PROTEST IN U.S. CONGRESS

"From the end of World War II until 1952, the U.S. government had to report to the United Nations on Puerto Rico," he explains. "There was a UN committee on territories that were not independent, and Puerto Rico was on that list as a colony. The U.S. government wanted to take Puerto Rico off the list so it wouldn't have to report and show its warts to the world. In 1953 they took their case to the United Nations, claiming that in 1952 we had by a sovereign, free vote become a 'commonwealth.' They claimed we were happy and content.

"I got involved in lobbying at the United Nations. A couple of times my wife went with me to speak to the ambassador of India, a friend of Puerto Rico who fought for our position at the United Nations. But the Yankees won a victory and got Puerto Rico taken off the list of non-sovereign countries. They presented us to the world as satisfied slaves." Washington even engineered the expulsion of the official observer the Nationalist Party had had at the United Nations since 1945.

In response, Cancel Miranda said, he and three other Nationalists living in New York "decided to carry out a demonstration that would draw the world's attention to the truth about Puerto Rico, that would tell the world that there were Puerto Ricans who were willing to die for our independence and that the U.S. government was fooling the United Nations and the world—including my people—with this so-called commonwealth."

The other three were Andrés Figueroa Cordero, Irving Flores, and Lolita Lebrón. At the time, Cancel Miranda, twenty three years old, was a press operator in a shoe factory in New York. Figueroa Cordero was working in a butcher shop, Flores in a furniture factory, and Lebrón in a garment shop as a sewing machine operator.

The U.S. rulers, Cancel Miranda stated, "had the money and the arms, but we had the moral force. We went to Washington to carry out an armed demonstration—we knew that if we went with signs we weren't going to get attention. There we fired inside the U.S. Capitol on March 1, 1954." The shots, fired from the spectators' gallery, wounded five congressmen.

"They put us on trial in Washington, D.C. They sentenced the three men to seventy-five years and Lolita to fifty years. Then they took us to New York, where we were tried for 'conspiracy to overthrow the government by force and violence' and sentenced to six more years. Can you imagine us thinking we could overthrow the U.S. government with little pistols? I wish I could!"

The four Nationalists were shipped off to different prisons. Figueroa Cordero was sent to the federal penitentiary in Atlanta; Lebrón to the women's prison in Alderson, West Virginia; and Flores to Leavenworth, Kansas, where Oscar Collazo, veteran of the 1950 Blair House action, was incarcerated. Cancel Miranda was sent to Alcatraz, the island prison in the San Francisco Bay.

"I've got the honor of being the only Nationalist who has ever been in Alcatraz, the worst prison they had," he says. "They thought they were humiliating me, but actually they were honoring me. It was like giving me a big medal. If they said, 'You're a good boy,' it would mean I wasn't fighting for my people.

"I was in Alcatraz for six years. There they didn't allow me to see my children for the entire six years. A couple of times my wife and I got to talk through a glass in the visiting room, using a phone. And you had to talk in English.

"Afterward they took me to Leavenworth, where I spent ten years. Andrés, Irving, Oscar, and I were in Leavenworth together for several years.

"In 1970 we started a strike at Leavenworth because the guards had committed abuses against some of us. We stopped working. They charged me with organizing the strike and put me in the hole for five months."

Later that year, Cancel Miranda was transferred to Marion federal prison in Illinois, where he was held until his release in 1979. "A big strike took place in Marion too," he recounted, "because the guards had blackjacked a Mexican prisoner. They put me in isolation for eighteen months. This time they put me in the 'behavior modification program' of the Control Unit. They gave us all kinds of drugs. When that didn't work they used the big stick."

The kind of treatment the Nationalists were routinely subjected to increasingly became public knowledge and fueled the campaign for their release. When Cancel Miranda's father died in 1977, his supporters campaigned to allow him to attend the funeral. "I was in Puerto Rico for seven hours for my father's funeral," he related. "But my people jumped with anger when they learned that at the St. Louis airport, on the way to Puerto Rico, they put me in a dog cage. While waiting for the next plane, they took the dog out and put me in. I had mentioned it casually to people, because I had been in prison for years and it was a normal thing to me, but to them it was unimaginable."

For years, Cancel Miranda remarked, "I kept thinking up escape plans, because I wasn't resigned to die in prison of old age. When the campaign for our release began, that's when I stopped thinking about escaping because the campaign became political work for us."

POLITICAL ACTIVITY BEHIND BARS

The broad and growing worldwide campaign for the release of the Puerto Rican Nationalists was the product of, and part of, the deep political radicalization in the United States during the 1960s and 1970s. It was fed by the victorious mass struggle by African Americans that brought down the Jim Crow segregation system, by the anti-imperialist audacity of the Cuban revolution, by the deepening opposition to the U.S. rulers' attempts to crush the Vietnamese national liberation struggle, and by the resurgence of the Puerto Rican independence movement. In Puerto Rico itself, defiance of the draft became so massive despite scores of arrests that the U.S. government eventually decided to drop most prosecutions of resisters on the island.

This social and political upheaval found expression behind prison bars as well. By the late 1960s, there were increasing numbers of prisoners engaged in political activity, and Cancel Miranda joined with them.

The Cuban revolution had a profound impact on him. "As I heard more and more about Cuba," he noted, "I realized it was not just another military coup like so many others in Latin America, but a true social transformation. I internalized it to the point that the Cuban revolution has become as important to me as the fight for the freedom of my people."

When the Chicano struggle developed in the United States, "in prison I became involved in that fight, including the defense of Corky Gonzales and the Crusade for Justice," he said. Gonzales and the Chicano rights organization he led, the Denver Crusade for Justice, were the target of a government frame-up in the early 1970s.

Every September 16, Cancel Miranda would join the Mexican and Chicano prisoners in marking Mexico's independence day with a work stoppage. "I also got involved in the Black struggle. We did many other things, even producing newspapers like the Chicano prisoners' paper *Aztlán*. I also wrote a couple of articles for the *Militant*.

"In other words, I was never really imprisoned. I never felt defeated. I kept fighting inside prison and always had the hope of getting out—one way or another. When you resign yourself to the idea that you're not going to get out, that's when you become a convict. The prison becomes your world. But none of us resigned ourselves."

In the early years there was no campaign for the release of the Nationalist political prisoners. "For fifteen years or more we were buried in oblivion, in silence," Cancel Miranda commented. "Circumstances at that time were different. Maybe sometimes you might have heard a little voice somewhere asking: 'I wonder what happened to those four young Nationalists?' It was later that the campaign for our freedom began. It began in Chicago, through two young American lawyers, Michael Deutsch and Mara Siegel from the People's Law Office."

INTERNATIONAL DEFENSE CAMPAIGN

"I was locked up in the Control Unit after the big strike in Marion. This was in 1972. There was an Afro-American, Ed Johnson, or Akinsiyu, as he preferred to be called, who knew the People's Law Office. He was from the group called Republic of New Africa, and was in prison for his political ideas. Akinsiyu wrote the young lawyer, Michael Deutsch, and asked him to visit us, explaining that there were one hundred of us in the Control Unit. He said there was a Puerto Rican locked up with him who could also tell him the truth about what was happening.

"The Puerto Rican community in Chicago started the campaign. Then it grew. It spread to New York, then to Puerto Rico. In the United States, people of all kinds took part in the campaign."

The campaign spread to other countries too, especially in Latin America. The revolutionary government of Cuba was one of the most vocal defenders of the five Nationalist prisoners.

"There were committees working for our freedom in Venezuela and other countries. Even the UN Committee on Decolonization passed a resolution asking for our release," he notes.

"Thanks to thousands of people everywhere who supported us, we won a victory in 1979. We came out of prison standing, not on our knees."

Under international pressure, President James Carter released Figueroa Cordero in 1978, as he was dying of cancer. The other four were freed in September of the following year.

Some voices in U.S. big-business circles immediately protested the release of the four Nationalists, whom they labeled terrorists. "Two days after our release," Cancel Miranda recalls, "a newspaper in Chicago asked how it could be that in Puerto Rico thousands of people were waiting for us, holding Puerto Rican flags. And a few days before, in Chicago and New York, thousands of people from the Puerto Rican communities had welcomed us too.

"They could not understand how these people, who had shot up 'our' congressmen, could be welcomed as heroes by our people.

"But they were also incapable of understanding the Vietnamese people, how the Vietnamese people were able to fight for their homeland and defeat them."

QUESTIONS

1. Are there ways to justify Puerto Rican youth refusing the draft?

2. In what ways could Cancel Miranda's sense of justice, of what is right, be interpreted as "troublemaking"?

3. Are there circumstances in which "moral force" and the willingness to die are necessary in order to draw the world's attention to a particular truth about injustice? Is such appropriation of discourse intended to achieve political and social change?

CUBAN SELF-DETERMINATION UNDER U.S. HEGEMONY

In part I, we learned that in the second half of the nineteenth century Cubans established "ties of mutual desire" with the United States and that this relationship was used as a weapon in their fight for independence from the Spanish empire. This cultural and economic seduction of the Cuban people was a very complex set of power relations that constructed Cubans as Cuban Americans long before the mass exodus to the United States in the 1960s.

At the turn of the twentieth century the United States carved its hegemony in the very constitution of Cuba. So how does a country function when it has been forced, militarily, to accept the hegemony of another country? In this case, capitalism dictated the behavior of Cuban political institutions. We have here a case of a repetition that shatters the illusion of a linear progress. As in Puerto Rico, during the first decades Cuba was under the power of the United States, the lives of the people of "Cuba Libre" resembled in many ways their situation during the last decades under Spain.[1] Who were "the people"? As usual, it helps to look at the people according to their position in the class structure. The old colonial elite and the middle class became part of the economic and cultural structures of the United States. This dependency was manifested at all levels of everyday life, "through ties of sentiment and persuasion, by habits and self-interest."[2] Afro-Cubans, local manufacturers and industrialists, peasant farmers, small *colonos* (tenant farmers), and workers did not fare as well as the local elites. Racial discrimination, business failure due to unfair competition, loss of land, and displacement by U.S. corporations or colonists was the most common experience for the former groups. The Cuban government served the interests of the United States and offered no protection from exclusionary racism, economic protection, or labor policies.[3]

In a familiar pattern throughout Latin America and other parts of the world, U.S. political and economic intervention led to waves of political and economic refugees leaving Cuba. This movement of human bodies was related to the ups and downs of the cigar and sugar industries, and there were also social and political struggles that created political exiles. These struggles also continued to influence the unfolding of events in the

Cuban émigré community, which also grew over time. The prerevolutionary Cuban population in the United States, however, was no more than thirty thousand.[4]

For many years Cubans lived under the illusion of a public citizenship that combined a dedication to the ideal of Cuba Libre and a yearning for the United States. They felt equal to U.S. Americans. In fact, they were particularly optimistic about their future because they had achieved a decade of political stability after many years of cultural, political, economic, and class struggles. The event that shattered this image of Cuba as a modern, civilized nation was the U.S. support of a coup d' état (an illegal seizure of government) on March 10, 1952, by General Fulgencio Batista and the wave of political repression and persecution that followed. As Louis A. Pérez describes "the lengthening shadows" of the days before the Castro revolution, the will of the Cuban people was ignored at a great cost in terms of human suffering; and that was just the beginning. To fully understand this situation, however, we need to look at the contradictions generated by a growing population and a local economy based on the production of sugar and structurally dependent on, and therefore limited by, the U.S. economy. Once again we have here an illustration not only of the interaction between the forces of production and social relations but also of the production of a nationalist discourse.

After Fidel Castro's forces defeated the dictator Batista and took over the Cuban government in December 1959, the United States reacted with hostility to his modest reforms designed to help the working classes. Thus the political center (made up of Cubans who were trained in the United States and committed to democracy) was eliminated, facilitating the further radicalization of the revolution. Castro, however, was unable to forge an inclusive governing structure to accommodate the diverse groups that supported the revolution. As indicated by María de los Angeles Torres, U.S. and Cuban national security interests provoked a massive Cuban exodus. Almost immediately after Castro's takeover, the first of three waves of Cuban exiles to the United States was under way, and it lasted until the end of the Cuban missile crisis of October 1962. The wave of 248,070 Cuban human bodies was quite homogeneous: 94 percent white, they were an average of thirty-four years old, and had an average of fourteen years of schooling. Their political values were also homogeneous and similar to those of the conservatives in the American Republican Party.[5] The second wave of exiles began in 1965, when the U.S. and Cuban governments negotiated an air bridge to transport the exiles, legally, from Camarioca, Cuba, to Miami, and lasted until 1973. While whites were still in the majority, out of the 297,318 human bodies, 24 percent were of African, Chinese, Jewish, or mulatto ancestry. Though educated people still predominated, there were many members of the working class.[6]

In terms of public citizenship and subjectivities attributed to human bodies, it is important to note that the Eisenhower and Kennedy administrations added institutional support and millions of dollars of federal assistance to the already significant effort of a wide range of private social and charity institutions that offered relief programs to the Cuban exiles. The exiles received more support in terms of food, money, training, education, and relocation programs than was available to U.S. citizens. They also received special treatment from the U.S. Congress and the Immigration and Naturalization Service. In this particular game of truth, African Americans in Miami "watched in disbelief as Cuban black and mulatto children attended 'white schools.'"[7]

Between April and September 1980, the third wave brought 124,776 additional Cubans to the United States. These Cubans differed from those of the previous two waves in several ways. Forty-two percent were single males or females, there was a large number of homosexuals, and there were also many "street people" (prostitutes, petty thieves, con men, pimps), some with criminal records.[8] Consequently, their subjectivity was constructed differently from that of previous exiles. This means their differences made them "undesirables"; they did not get as warm a reception from the U.S. government or the Cuban exile community as previous Cuban refugees did.

García does not delve much into the specifics of racial relations among Cuban Americans in her book,

Havana USA. She is not alone, for the topic of racial relations among Latinos owes its invisibility to the historical attempt to subsume racial questions under nationalism. Still, we could also argue that *marielitos,* those who came to the United States in the third wave, were not "desirable" because of their racial makeup (15–40 percent were Afro Cubans, compared to 3 percent of the 1959–1973 migration). At the same time, we cannot ignore the centrality of the forces of production: the *marielitos* arrived in the United States at a time of economic recession and consequent political turmoil.

What is not left out of García's discussion, however, is the violence perpetrated upon Cuban bodies on both sides of the conflict. Cuban exiles engaged in killings under orders of the U.S. government or on their own, to the extent that Miami became known to the FBI as "the terrorist capital of the United States."[9] With reference to discourses that remain invisible or unsaid, and to Hardy-Fanta's notion of feminist politics, it is pertinent to mention here an important point that is not included in the texts below. Even though a consistent, major concern of the entire exiled community has been the political prisoners in Cuba, women political prisoners in Cuba have received less attention than the men. In fact, the "roster of women who served time in prison for counterrevolutionary activities or ideological diversionism has never been fully tabulated and it was not until the late 1980s that the women's experience even began to be told in the exile press in Miami."[10] This despite the fact that Dr. Elena Mederos established Of Human Rights at Georgetown University in Washington, D.C., to monitor human rights abuses in Cuba, and despite the fact that women played a crucial role in that organization's campaign, since it was their husbands, fathers and sons, and sisters and daughters who were held prisoner.

By 1990 there were 1,043,932 exiled bodies living in the United States, or 10 percent of Cuba's entire population. In a game of truth that continues into the twenty-first century, Cubans continue to migrate to the United States under the Cuban Adjustment Act, which grants Cubans—and only Cubans—the right to legal residency, to a work permit, and to citizenship one year after arriving. In order to regularize Cuban migration, this act was amended in 1994, and now it applies only if Cuban refugees reach dry land; those caught at sea who cannot prove political persecution by the Castro regime are returned. The amendment to the act includes the Cuban government agreement to allow twenty thousand people to come to the United States every year through a visa lottery system.[11] As a demonstration of the principle of uncertainty in power relations, it is pertinent to note that, in Miami, the Cuban American quest for public citizenship apparently has become a quest for exclusivity. This is not a question of culture or ethnic "essence," but an exercise of power that needs to be confronted as any other hegemonic practice.

At any rate, the Cuban **diaspora** (as well as that of Puerto Rico, Mexico, and an increasing number of other countries) calls for the redefinition of the concepts of nation, state, and citizenship so as to include the needs and desires of human bodies according to the realities of a global economy.

NOTES AND SUGGESTED READINGS

1. Louis A. Pérez, *Cuba and the United States* (Athens: University of Georgia Press, 1990), 147.
2. Pérez, *Cuba and the United States,* 148.
3. Pérez, *Cuba and the United States,* 148.
4. Alejandro Portes and Robert L. Bach, *Latin Journey: Cuban and Mexican Immigrants in the United States* (Berkeley: University of California Press, 1985), 84.
5. José Llanes, *Cuban Americans: Masters of Survival* (Cambridge, Mass.: Abt Books, 1982), 8–9.
6. José Llanes, *Cuban Americans,* 98.
7. Maria Cristina García, *Havana USA* (Berkeley: University of California Press, 1996), 20–29.

8. Llanes, *Cuban Americans,* 183.

9. García, *Havanna USA,* 141.

10. García, *Havanna USA,* 159.

11. Derek Reveron, "Elian's Policy Legacy," *Hispanic Business Review* (October 2000).

* 13 *

EL EXILIO: NATIONAL SECURITY INTERESTS AND THE ORIGINS OF THE CUBAN EXILE ENCLAVE

María de los Angeles Torres

In previous readings, we learned that the Cuban quest for inclusiveness in the U.S. polity became exhausted in the 1950s and that the result was the Cuban revolution led by Fidel Castro. In this piece, María illustrates a game of truth that constructs a new Cuban American subjectivity. Going beyond one-dimensional analyses, she considers three different players: the United States and Cuba and their respective national security interests as well as El Exilio, the exiled community, and its dynamics.

In terms of Cuban human bodies, it is of interest to note the many identities to which they are subjected (subjectivities). They support the revolution but, feeling excluded from it, become exiled and find themselves defined as enemies of the state, nonpersons in their own country. Once they leave Cuba, they receive special immigrant status and "fulfill the military, propagandistic, and symbolic needs of the United States." These bodies are trained for covert military operations (like the famous Bay of Pigs) under terrible conditions, but are defined as "untrustworthy." They are useful as exiles, that is, as long as they are not part of the United States; when U.S. policy changes, their subjectivity changes from exiled/soldier/militant to "terrorist."

Prior to the revolutionaries' triumph in 1959, an estimated 124,000 Cubans had emigrated to the United States. Throughout the 1950s economic and political conditions on the island had spurred an exodus. A common practice among U.S. corporations was to recruit trained personnel straight from Cuban universities. Nor was it out of the ordinary for political refugees to enter the United States illegally. Yet, as much as postrevolutionary emigration represented a continuation of these trends, this exodus and the exile community, El Exilio, it created emerged from a unique set of circumstances.[1]

The origins of the postrevolution exile must first be understood in the context of the revolution itself and the dynamics it introduced on the island and abroad. Second, an analysis of the exodus and the subsequent communities it spawned must survey the international involvement of the United States as well as its domestic environment in the early 1960s. Finally, the exile community emerges from a society at war with itself, a war that had been carried out through battle with a foreign state. The community contributes to the shaping of its own politics and identity, which in turn influences the subsequent flow of émigrés, just as these successors leave their imprint on the politics and identity of the exile community.

Studies of Cuba and the Cuban community have been marked by some of the same ideological fault lines created by the cold war.[2] Although many factors have influenced the development of the community, studies of Cuban exile politics and identity have usually emphasized only one of many factors. In the early 1960s, with rare exception,[3] studies of the exile community had an island-based perspective. In studying the reasons why people left, scholars who had recently left Cuba explained that repressive conditions had spurred the massive exodus.[4] These analyses usually omitted U.S. policies as factors contributing to the exodus. In the 1970s, Cuban exile academics who were trained in the United States shifted the point of reference to the United States. These studies looked at the community as a minority group and emphasized the role that émigrés fulfilled for the U.S. state.[5] Unlike other Latinos, Cubans were seen as a privileged minority who had been afforded special immigration status because of their symbolic value in the cold war. Other studies looked at U.S. immigration policies as a determining factor in the development of the exile community.[6]

In the early 1980s, island-based academics linked to intelligence-gathering policy centers began to study the community that until then had been offficially censured as an area of inquiry. Indeed, those studying the Cuban exile community were monitored closely. Internationally renowned sociologist Oscar Lewis was expelled from Cuba when, as part of his study of a Cuban family on the island, he interviewed family members who had emigrated to Miami. Officially sanctioned Cuban academics emphasized the part the United States played in fomenting immigration, claiming that the U.S. role had been an effort to sabotage the revolution while ignoring Cuban policies as well as the role of the community.[7]

While all these factors have contributed to the emergence and development of the Cuban exile community, our understanding of this community, particularly its origins, has been fragmented by the same ideological divide that so definitively demarcated people's political loyalties; it was either Cuba's fault or that of the United States. In this chapter I attempt a more comprehensive understanding of this period, beginning with an examination of the moment of rupture, taking into account the links between the opposition to Batista and Castro. I continue by looking at the role of the United States in facilitating and defining the movement and development of communities in the United States. I conclude by looking at the politics and identity of Cubans in the United States in the early years. Throughout this chapter I try to understand the unfolding of events within a context I assume has multiple players and states.

This is a difficult task. The fault line of the cold war is not just a theoretical proposition for people whose lives were ruptured by these historical events. For those of us who were young at the time of exile the memory of these early years is intricately interwoven with our childhood. The sharp contrast between our island existence and our U.S. existence has burned powerful images into our memories. The Cuban revolution stands as a monumental event in our lives, making it difficult to decipher the powerful myths it engendered. Many of our families were ardent supporters of the revolution, as was the vast majority of *el pueblo cubano*. U.S. government officials reacted in ways that facilitated the concentration of power on the island under the leadership of one man. This new leadership proved incapable of sustaining a governing structure that included the diverse groups that had supported the revolution. One of the consequences of this failure was the mass exodus of almost 300,000 Cubans in the two years following the revolution.

REVOLUTION AND ITS OPPOSITION

During the 1950s Cubans of all social classes organized into several coalitions demanding political change. Politicians willing to support change through an electoral process clustered around two parties, Los Auténticos and Los Ortodoxos. But this strategy lost its viability after Fulgencio Batista, a mulatto army sergeant, led a military coup in 1952 against President Carlos Prío Socarrás with the support of the United States.[8] On July 26, 1953, armed men attacked military barracks in Santiago de Cuba, signaling the commencement of an armed struggle against the island's military regime. This act represented frustration over the inability to achieve political change through peaceful means.[9]

The revolutionary movement was composed of many organizations and sectors. It included a faction of the Auténticos that had gone underground after President Prío Socarrás had been deposed. El Directorio Revolucionario, composed mainly of university students heavily influenced by progressive Catholic thought, organized in Havana and advocated a strategy of *golpear arriba* (strike at the top). Their most dramatic act was a failed attempt to take over the presidential palace on March 13, 1957.[10] Fidel Castro's Movimiento 26 de Julio (M-26–7), named after the date of the assault on the Moncada military barracks, amalgamated an array of sectors that had settled on a strategy of guerrilla warfare in the countryside. The Partido Socialista Popular, Cuba's Communist Party, condemned the actions of both El Directorio and the M-26–7.

Seven anti-Batista organizations signed a unity pact in November 1957 forming a Cuban Liberation Council. Within a month Fidel had resigned from the council, claiming that it had not been sufficiently opposed to foreign intervention; years later he admitted that he did not believe that his group could control that many organizations.[11] Diverse ideologies, future visions, and strategies were included in this broad coalition, but all were united in their commitment to restore the Constitution of 1940 and to hold elections. The organizations opposed to Batista included:[12]

- Los Auténticos: Ramón Grau San Martin, Carlos Prío Socarrás (elected president in 1948 and 1952), removed by Batista military coup; initially advocated peaceful change but later financed various underground armed movements.

- Partido del Pueblo Cubano Ortodoxo (Los Ortodoxos): Offshoot of Los Orto-doxos, founded in 1947 by Eduardo Chíbas, congressman and later senator, who shot himself during his radio program in 1951.
- Movimento Nacional Revolucionario: Offshoot of Los Ortodoxos, headed by Rafael García Barcena, professor at the University of Havana and La Escuela Superior de Guerra; advocated armed coup led by military officers.
- Movimiento 26 de Julio (M-26–7): Headed by Fidel Castro, formally of Los Ortodoxos; armed movement focused on rural and mountain actions, named after its failed attempted takeover of a military barracks on July 26, 1953.
- Directorio Revolucionario: Founded in 1955 by members of the Federación de Estudiantes Universitarios (sole governing body of university students); headed by Antonio Echeverria; focused on urban armed actions, specifically at "hitting the top"; entered into a coalition with M-26–7 in 1956. Most of its leaders were killed in an attack on the presidential palace on March 13, 1957.
- Cuban Liberation Council: Formed on November 1, 1957; included, among others, M-26–7, Directorio, and Auténticos; Fidel Castro pulled out a month later.
- Segundo Frente del Escambray: Offshoot of El Directorio, headed by Eloy Gutiérrez Menoyo (other members of El Directorio joined M-26–7).
- Legion Acción Revolucionaria: Small group headed by Manuel Artime.
- Civic Resistance Movement: Civic group allied with M-26–7.
- Agrupación Católica: Headed by Juan Manuel Salvat and other Catholic students.

Despite the broad popular support enjoyed by these organizations, all met with brutal repression, resulting in an estimated twenty thousand deaths, according to *New York Times* correspondent R. Hart Phillips.[13] For Cubans of all walks of life the struggle was to regain the nation and the dignity they had lost at the hands of the military dictatorship. On January 1, 1959, Fidel Castro declared victory after a pro-tracted guerrilla struggle in the mountains and began a march across the island that ended in Havana a week later. This marked the end of the movement that resulted in the ousting of Batista.

Disregarding the decisive participation of many organizations and sectors in the struggle against Batista, Castro quickly consolidated power under his command and his organization, the 26th of July Movement.[14] At first this was done by eliminating Batista supporters and bringing in representatives of the various sectors that had supported the revolution. A fairly representative cabinet was put in place in the early part of 1959, but before long it became evident that Castro would not tolerate dif-ferences in his government and an intense power struggle began. Frequent political purges characterized the new regime's administrative style. To the chagrin of many who had fought against Batista, Fidel began promoting members of the Partido Socialista Popular, the Cuban Communist Party, which had not supported the revo-lution and had advocated accommodation with Cuba's dictators since the 1930s.

Rapid and often unexpected political changes added to the daily turmoil.[15] Legal changes had the effect of concentrating power in the executive. A law passed by the cabinet in February vested legislative power in the cabinet.[16] Formal political institutions were bypassed as Castro overturned court decisions, often announcing his dictates on national television. In one renowned case a court in Santiago acquitted forty-four of Batista s airmen, only to have the case dismissed and a new trial ordered by Fidel.[17] Another major point of contention were elections that had been promised during the revolution but were never held.

In addition, the revolution caused a restructuring of power and class relations that led to a redistribution of land and resources. Once in power the government became increasingly radical. Initial reforms aimed at nationalizing large landholdings were extended to landowners with only moderate holdings. The Instituto de Reforma Agraria (Agrarian Reform Institute) became one of the institutional mechanisms through which Fidel and *los rebeldes* (the rebels) consolidated their power. Economic changes, such as the urban reform that included limits on the numbers of housing units that could be rented, also contributed to unrest.

Opposition to the new government grew. Fissures were evident in many sectors, and there were high-level defections. When Huber Matos, a former commander of the 26th of July Movement, tried to resign from his post with the Instituto de Reforma Agraria, he was arrested for counterrevolutionary activities and sentenced to twenty years in jail. Manuel Artime, who had been part of Agrupación Católica and later headed an armed group against Batista—and who would later play a leadership role in both the political and armed opposition to Fidel—resigned from the Agrarian Reform Institute and left the country before he could be arrested. Pedro Díaz Lanz defected from the air force, and many liberals started to resign from government, including Manuel Urrutia, who had been named provisional president; José Miró Cardona, prime minister; Elena Mederos, minister of social welfare; and later Manuel Ray, minister of public works.

Many of the organizations and sectors that had supported the revolutionary movement opposed the direction taken by Fidel Castro and his supporters. They resented his new alliance with the communists, whom they considered opportunists. They fought back by going underground and again taking up the arms they had used against Batista. The Auténticos regrouped under an organization named Rescate Revolucionario headed by Manual Antonio (Tony) de Varona and Ramón and Polita Grau. Agrupación Católica began publishing a newspaper titled *Trinchera*. Its members were closely allied with El Directorio Estudiantil headed by Juan Manuel Salvat and Alberto Müller. Manuel Artime went on to head El Movimiento de Recuperación Revolucionaria. All had varying degrees of contact with the United States.

By the middle of 1960 the various political and military organizations that had emerged following Castro's rise to power announced the formation of a coalition in Mexico City called the Frente Democrático Revolucionario. By then these groups were receiving help from the CIA in response to U.S. concerns about communist participation in the government but also for a series of other reasons that had little to do with Cuba. Under the auspices of the CIA the underground was organized under the banner of Unidad Revolucionaria.[18]

Repression and Exodus

For many who had supported the revolutionary movement it was the repressiveness of the new government that made them feel betrayed. Arrests, trials, and firing squads first used against Batista's former henchmen were now turned against anyone who was critical of Fidel. Arrests increased and revolutionary justice was quickly dispensed.

The day before the Bay of Pigs invasion the Cuban government made a massive series of arrests. Many adolescent boys were detained in collective jails for days. Detention and incarceration of political opponents became common practice.[19] Prisoners were summarily executed by firing squads. In a particularly dramatic case two young students, Virgilio Campaneria and Alberto Tapia Ruana, were executed on April 17, 1961.[20] Their execution drove a deep wedge into the broad support previously enjoyed by the revolution; the reason many people had joined the movement against Batista was because they rejected the arbitrary and repressive methods of his regime.

There was generalized uncertainty about what would happen next. Most people thought that the U.S. government would not sit by and let the situation continue. Rumors of invasion had begun to be heard as early as 1960, and many Cubans wanted to be outside the country when it happened. Cubans had begun leaving the island early in 1959. Most of these departures were undertaken without much fanfare. According to an analysis of the situation in Santiago de Cuba written by a consulate official, the demand for visas was increasing for a variety of reasons:

> Some wish to get away from the possibility of another revolution, others . . . "in case."
> Others think that the government is going to place further restrictions on travel, despite
> official denials. Still others are leaving because of the economic squeeze as a result of
> revolutionary laws . . . Some persons are going to considerable length to make trips
> appear casual, e.g., splitting up families or going by different routes to the U.S. or other
> countries. This, and leaving without publicity, are attempted because they do not want
> to attract attention which they think might bring intervention or confiscation of their
> properties.[21]

The exodus accelerated in response to one government action in particular. The government announced that all private schools would be closed, setting off panic among the middle class. This added fuel to rumors that the government was going to take over the *patria potestad* (legal authority) over children. The Catholic Church was particularly vehement in defending its right to provide private education. Priests in Cuba who had lived through the Spanish Civil War and witnessed the separation of families and children voiced their fears that the same would occur in Cuba. For parents whose children attended Catholic schools, this was a sure sign that they would lose power over what happened to their children. Simultaneously, the government initiated a literacy campaign to send all those who could read to the country-side to teach peasants how to read and write, further separating families and dispersing educated people. The rush to get out of Cuba grew. This is when many parents, including my own, decided to send their children—fourteen thousand of them—to the United States.

To Stay or Leave? Patriot or Traitor?

The issue of leaving or remaining in Cuba provided the new government with a political rallying point it could use to mobilize support for the revolution.[22] Leaving or staying, as well as one's position toward those who left, became a litmus test for loyalty to the revolution. For instance, when a great number of professionals began leaving and the loss started to have a noticeable impact on Cuba's economy, a political campaign was launched to link the act of remaining on the island with patriotism. During a rally at the University of Havana, Cuban president Osvaldo Dorticós asked those present to stand and take an oath that they would stay and give their services to the nation.[23] Those present complied. But pledging one's loyalty was not enough: revolutionary cadres were discouraged from staying in contact with relatives who had left the island. Party militants were explicitly prohibited from writing to relatives. In fact, writing to relatives was one of the criteria used to deny students entrance into the university.

In 1960 Raul Castro, Fidel Castro's younger brother and head of the Cuban Armed Forces, presented outgoing migration as "the normal exodus that takes place when the people take the power in their own hands and liquidate exploitation and the privileged classes. Their departure does not damage the revolution, but fortifies it as it is a spontaneous purification."[24]

Others had a much harsher view of the exiles. In the early days of the revolution Fidel Castro said, "Those who escape their duty, taking the road to the north, have lost the right to be worthy sons of *la patria*."[25] From the beginning the Cuban revolution considered leaving the island a treasonous act; the punishment was to strip the person who left of his or her national identity. People who left were called *gusanos* (worms), a reference to the duffel bags they carried with them.

Dissent was interpreted by Cuba's leadership as a threat to the nation's security. The closing of political space for peaceful or legal dissent meant that those on the island had few options for registering disagreement other than risk imprisonment or leave the country. For many leaving became a way of dissenting. Leaving thus acquired a symbolic value as a political act of defiance, which, in turn, reinforced the idea that those who left were enemies of the state. Furthermore, most Cubans who emigrated went to the United States—a host country that historically had been antagonistic to the homeland. Indeed, the participants in the 1961 U.S.-backed invasion of the island were Cuban émigrés. Thus, the concept of exile and enemy of the state were fused.

For a nationalist revolution the unrelenting exodus of people was indicative of profound systemic political and ideological problems. The revolution, which had been won precisely through the support of broad sectors of the nation, failed to remain inclusive when it came time to govern. Moreover, massive outgoing migration represented a tremendous loss of human resources. Externalizing dissent also had a high cost in that it led to a process of denationalization—the opposite of the goal of a nationalist revolution. In essence the exodus represented a crisis of legitimacy.

The painful rupture that accompanied leaving the country was extremely difficult to reconcile with the immediate past experience of many Cubans, who had been accustomed to being able to take a ferry from Cuba to Florida, honeymoon in Miami, and maintain a close relationship with friends and relations in the United States. Suddenly a trip that had been an easy weekend holiday had become a bureaucratic and political nightmare.

Eventually, the reaction of Cuba's leaders toward those who left was institutionalized in a series of policies that were enforced by government structures whose function was to guard the security of the nation. As early as 1961, a law was passed that authorized the Ministry of the Interior to grant exit and reentry permits to those wishing to leave the country. If a person had not returned by the date on the reentry permit, his or her leave was considered a "definitive abandonment" of the country and the state had the right to confiscate all of his or her property.[26] A law had been passed in 1959 calling for the confiscation of properties of those involved in counter-revolutionary activities, but the law of definitive abandonment included any person who overstayed the sixty-day limit.[27] Those who left the island were not allowed to return, even to visit. These policies marked a radical break with legal precedent, as Cuban law had guaranteed free travel to and from the island for all citizens. The use of exit and reentry permits and loss of property rights were justified by the government on the grounds of national security.[28] The effect was that those who left became classic exiles: nonpersons in their own country.

While the Cuban practice of exile has roots in its colonial past (Spain, too, had used it as a form of punishment), it contradicted contemporary immigration law that had been put into effect by a U.S. military governor in 1901. This law—an exact copy of U.S. immigration law at the time—does not *recognize* dual citizenship. Everyone born in Cuba or descended from a parent born in Cuba is defined as Cuban regardless of where they live. When traveling to Cuba, they must do so on a Cuban passport. Every Cuban constitution of this century also has stipulated, however, that anyone who acquires the citizenship of another country loses his or her Cuban citizenship. The law leaves room for regulations that define exactly how this is to occur. These regulations require that each case be processed individually; in other words, automatic stripping of citizenship is not allowed. In effect, there is a contradiction between law and practice, for a Cuban passport is required of any Cuban even if he or she has obtained citizenship in another country. Many of us in the Cuban diaspora now have two passports. But, while we may have Cuban passports, because of the postrevolutionary law of definitive abandonment, we have no property or social rights in Cuba.

Another major contradiction has tugged at Cuba's policy toward dissidents and émigrés. While the revolutionary government has maintained publicly that the construction of socialism is "una tarea de hombres libres" (a task of free men), it simultaneously set up legal mechanisms to punish those who left without authorization. In fact, departures not authorized by the government were considered political crimes. Leaving legally, even when the United States allowed massive immigration, has been very difficult. Once Cuban citizens filed the required papers at the Ministry of the Interior declaring their intent to leave the country, they generally lost their jobs, their property was inventoried, and their children were expelled from special educational programs.

Because of the politicization of emigration, Cuban émigrés have fulfilled several functions for the Cuban state. They have provided the government with ideological ammunition with which to rally their forces. For example, leaflets showing "lazy gusanos" were used to mobilize workers to cut sugar cane. Emigration also became the vehicle through which the government could rid itself of political opponents and consolidate power. If dissenters were externalized, competition for power would be reduced. State structures were created and often expanded to implement these governmental goals.

Massive emigration exacted a high toll on the state. It was living proof that the Cuban government could not effectively incorporate all parts of the nation. In addition, the sporadic and abrupt ways in which Cubans have left the country presented a security threat because these departures could ignite a rebellion against the government.

Once abroad, the ever-present threat of the counterrevolution from *el exilio* helped rationalize the need for strong national security agencies within Cuba charged with protecting the revolution. The conflict between the United States and Cuba required an expansion of Cuba's governmental capabilities to meet an external threat—an expansion that mirrored the post–World War II growth in the U.S. intelligence apparatus.[29] The expansion of the Cuban national security apparatus has been especially pronounced for those agencies dealing with Cubans who leave the island. Among the most important of these is the Ministry of the Interior, which encompassed both immigration services and the nation's internal and external intelligence agencies. Rapid growth has also been the case for offices within other departments, such as the Ministry of Foreign Affairs, the Cuban Communist Party, and the Instituto de Amistad Con los Pueblos (the Institute of Friendship with Other Countries),[30] an organization that supports solidarity with revolutionary movements throughout the world.

The violent postrevolutionary social rupture within Cuban society and the reaction of the United States to these events have found expression in Cuba's domestic and foreign policies. These policies have been conceived and developed in the realm of national security. In terms of foreign policy the overriding concerns are defense of territory and maintenance of sovereignty. In terms of the domestic agenda the preoccupation has been with economic and political stability.[31]

U.S. NATIONAL SECURITY INTERESTS
AND CUBAN EXILES

During the first years following the Cuban revolution U.S. policymakers operated with the unquestioned assumption that the leadership that had assumed power on the island would not last. The initial transfer of Cubans to the United States was not a mass movement of refugees but, rather, a response to military needs. U.S. government agencies involved in the fight against the Castro government needed ways to evacuate agents working for the underground opposition and their families. The story of how these programs evolved to become unprecedented immigration and relocation programs traverses the Eisenhower, Kennedy, and Johnson administrations; a contentious Congress; and a local and national backlash to unbridled immigration from the island to the United States. Furthermore, these years were marked by the failed invasion of the island and events that led to the brink of a nuclear war. Throughout the period Cuban exiles came to fulfill symbolic and political roles for the U.S. government as well as for the Cuban government—roles that in strange ways mirrored each other.

U.S. involvement in Cuban affairs was nothing new, and neither was the presence of Cubans in the United States. During the revolution the official U.S. representative in Havana, Earl Smith, had opted against supporting the popular will, choosing instead to try to help Batista until it became evident that his days were numbered.[32] After Batista was toppled, the Eisenhower administration reacted with hostility to the modest agrarian and urban reforms sponsored by the new Cuban revolutionary leadership.[33] Unlike interventions prior to World War II, however, U.S. reactions to the Cuban revolution were cast through the lens of the cold war and became intermeshed with the new crusade to stop communism from spreading in the Western hemisphere.[34]

Unquestionably, the Cuban revolution challenged U.S. hegemony in the Caribbean. It called for a reordering of political power to protect Cuban national interests rather than U.S. interests. It also called for exporting the revolution to other countries in Latin America. In the McCarthyite mood of the late 1950s, in which anticommunist hysteria permeated American public opinion, it was easy to see a revolutionary movement on an island ninety miles offshore as a test of wills between the United States and the Soviet Union. The immediate U.S. response was to attempt to remove the revolutionary leadership from power using military, political, and economic means.

But, unlike past incursions into Cuban affairs, a new mode of intervention was implemented—a foreign state-sponsored social movement.[35] Cuban émigrés became the conduit through which U.S. foreign policies were implemented. Used to try to overthrow and discredit the Cuban revolution,[36] these émigrés came to fulfill the military, propagandistic, and symbolic needs of the United States. The resulting relationship between the émigrés and their host country was forged within the evolving national security state.

Exiles: A Cover for U.S. Intervention

As early as spring 1959, during a National Security Council meeting, Vice President Richard Nixon proposed arming and otherwise supporting an exile force for direct military intervention against Fidel Castro.[37] He also succeeded in getting CIA and FBI approval of his recommendation.[38] On March 17, 1960, President Dwight Eisenhower approved a CIA policy paper that outlined the steps to be taken to "bring about the replacement of the Castro regime with one more devoted to the true interests of the Cuban people and more acceptable to the U.S. in such a manner as to avoid any appearance of U.S. intervention."[39] The document recommended a series of steps that could be taken, including the formation of an "exile" opposition whose slogan could be to "Restore the Revolution," which, it was to claim, had been lost to a "new dictatorship of Cuba subject to strong Sino-Soviet influence." It also included the provisions that individual freedoms must be restored and collectivism in commerce and education eliminated. The formation of a political opposition was to be accompanied by a military and propaganda operation.

Yet there were several concerns that needed to be addressed. One was the reaction of other Latin American countries to U.S. efforts to overthrow Castro. U.S. policymakers had been stung by Latin American protests, as evidenced among other things by CIA director Allen Dulles's testimony to a Senate Committee on Foreign Relations in 1958 regarding Nixon's tour of Latin America that year.[40] Thomas Mann, the assistant secretary for Interamerican affairs, wanted thoroughly to conceal U.S. sponsorship.[41] The White House and the CIA were also concerned about reactions from the press and other agencies (such as the State and Justice Departments) to the CIA's violation of its own charter by its anti-Castro activities in Miami.[42] When President John F. Kennedy took office he wanted to make sure that, if intervention in Cuba failed, it would not be perceived as his fault but, rather, that of the Cuban exiles directly involved; "plausible deniability," the ability to hide the CIA's direct involvement, was critical.[43]

The CIA promoted multiple organizations at the same time that it tried to get these organizations to form a united front. There were disagreements within the bureaucracy and Congress about the appropriate nature of the organizations that should be supported, with some promoting less ideologically driven politicians and others the more liberal and nationalist groups. But agreements were finally reached, and by early 1960 the CIA had facilitated a meeting of organizations it deemed necessary for a united front. Whether or not this coalition would be considered a government in exile was a point hotly contested by the State Department's lawyers, who were concerned about formal recognition because the United States still had full diplomatic relations with the Castro government. In addition, official recognition would break with past policy in that it would recognize a "government" that existed outside national territory and one that did not control the state apparatus.[44] Nonetheless, the Frente (Front), as it was first called, was formed in the spring of 1960 at a meeting at New York's Statler Hotel hosted by CIA agent Frank Bender.[45] The formation of the group was announced publicly in Mexico City on June 21,

1960; it included the following men, described to the president by the State Department as follows:[46]

- Manuel Antonio de Varona, leader of a large faction of the Auténticos, the official political party during the administration of Ramón Grau San Martin and Carlos Prío Socarrás (1944–52);
- Justo Carrillo, head of the Montecristi Group formed in 1952 by wealthy professionals and businessmen in opposition to the Batista dictatorship;
- José Ignacio Rasco, head of the Christian Democratic Movement (MDC) formed in late 1959 by young Catholic groups in opposition to the Castro regime;
- Manuel Artime, nominal head of the Movimiento Recuperacion Revolucionaria, an underground anti-Castro movement formed in 1959 whose members consisted principally of defectors from the July 26 Movement; and
- Rafael Sardiña Sanchez, former vice president of the Asociación de Colonos Cubanos (Cuban Association of Sugar Cane Cutters). (He is not identified as a member of this group in any lists.)

The fifth member of the group was Aureliano Sanchez Arango, a member of the United Front of National Liberation who had served as minister of education and state in the Prío administration. Both his closeness to the communists and his attitude—he was described by the Americans as a prima donna—made him a controversial figure in Washington.[47] Curiously, one of the CIA operators on the Cuban case listed Antonio Maceo, the grandson of one of the generals of the War of Independence, as the fifth person. Apparently, there was either confusion or disagreement (or both) within the U.S. bureaucracy regarding the composition of the group.

At the same time, military training had begun two months earlier, when President Eisenhower authorized the CIA to attempt to overthrow the Castro government. Cuban émigrés provided the human resources to implement a military strategy against Cuba that would appear to be Cuban in origin. Estimates of the number of Cubans who received military training from the United States range from two thousand to fifteen thousand.[48] The most dramatic action would be an invasion, training for which took place in the United States, Guatemala, and Nicaragua. Operatives received a monthly pension from the U.S. government for themselves and their families: $175 for themselves, $50 for the first child, and $25 for each additional child.[49]

Conditions were terrible for those in training. Kept in the dark about the political maneuvering taking place behind the scenes in Washington and Miami, the men in the camps, many of whom had fought for the revolution, felt underrepresented and marginalized. One of their concerns was that the more liberal sectors of the opposition had been excluded from the political organization. Conflicts erupted, and the men went on strike. On March 18, 1961, Tony de Varona and Manuel Ray, at one time described as the Frente's coordinators for the island,[50] met to negotiate the expansion of the Frente and agree on a spokesman. The strike had resulted in the dissolution of the Frente and the formation of a new civic political structure called El Consejo Revolucionario Cubano (Cuban Revolutionary Council).[51]

This expansion was also supported by liberals in the Kennedy administration such as Arthur Schlesinger Jr., whose candidate, José Miró Cardona, former law professor and the first prime minister of the revolutionary government, was elected as coordinator over Felipe Pazos, Ray's candidate.[52] Tracey Barnes of the CIA described the members' political leanings, underlining the names of the original members of the Frente; there was a discrepancy about Aureliano Sanchez Arango, who at the time did not join the Consejo in protest over the inclusion of former politicians in a provisional government (see table 13.1).[53]

The group's platform consisted of twelve points, including the reestablishment of the 1940 Constitution as well as a commitment to hold elections within eighteen months.[54] The new organization, however, had its opponents in the U.S. government, among them Senator Thomas Dodd from Connecticut, at the time vice chairman of the Internal Security Subcommittee. On March 23, 1961, he wrote to Secretary of State Dean Rusk about his concerns that José Miró Cardona, Manuel Ray, and Felipe Pazos were anti-American and had socialist leanings, calling them left-wing turncoats. In addition, he was extremely concerned about the amount of money being paid to the various organizations directly under the control of the CIA, saying that, "this operation meant that some Cubans had never had it so good as during exile and consequently acquired a financial interest in preserving the Castro regime."[55]

After months of training, the Bay of Pigs invasion was launched.[56] Despite the demand from the soldiers that Cuban exile political organizations and not the CIA be in charge of the operation, the role of the exile organizations continued to be essentially propagandistic. On April 17, 1961, the day of the invasion, the members of El Consejo were locked in barracks at a military camp in Opa-Locka, Florida, unable to communicate with "their" soldiers; in fact, they were not even told that the invasion was under way. This, however, was not surprising given the CIA's view that Cubans were not to be trusted. The CIA's psychological profile of Cubans described them as follows:

> From a management point of view the Cuban may seem disappointing in long-range performance and at the same time overly sensitive to criticism. . . . The biggest problem

Table 13.1. Exile Groups

Left	Left of Center	Center	Right
Carrillo	Artime	Varona Rasco	Maceo
Jesus Fernandez	Collada	Fernandez Travieso	Vargas Gómez
(Labor, 30 November)	(Labor for Fraginals)	(students for Müller)	Carlos Hevia
		Alverez Díaz	Goar Mestre
		Sergio Carbo	
		Pepin Bosch	

appears to be that of long-term loyalty and control. Essentially, the Cuban is loyal only to himself.[57]

Disregard for the exiles was again apparent when council members tried to see the president after the invasion had failed. Arthur Schlesinger Jr. was worried about the impact of such a visit and warned in a memo:

> Exiles who see the President are likely to try to make capital of this when they return to the Cuban community. FBI clearance is not enough. If this should turn out to be a responsible and representative group, I see no objection. Indeed such a presentation might help in composing the feelings of the Cuban exile community. We do not, however, regard this as a high priority.[58]

Schlesinger did, however, urge the president to call Dr. Miró Cardona, who was afraid that his son, captured in the invasion, would be executed. "The feeling is that his anguish would be relieved if you were to call him and express sympathy." His concern with negative press is reflected in the postscript: "Cardona is holding a press conference from 11:30 to 12:30."[59]

The U.S. attempt to hide its military actions behind a Cuban exile screen failed. But the consequences of having trained a secret army would be felt throughout the next decade. The CIA now had highly specialized small teams with which to carry out a covert war against Castro and other governments.[60] The military actions had their influence on politics as well.

Foreign Policy Contours of Exile Politics

The *origins* of the Cuban exile are anchored in both the foreign policy objectives of the U.S. state and the internal policies of the Cuban state. Exiles provide the United States with military resources and ideological cannon fodder. As long as Cuban émigrés were exiles and not a part of the United States, the administrations in Washington could deny involvement in the military actions taken by them against the revolution. Because of their exile status, they provided plausible deniability to the CIA and other agencies involved in the covert war against the Castro regime. Exiles also fulfilled the ideological functions of providing evidence that communism is a repressive system; they had shown that they preferred to flee to a free country. Legal definitions within the United States as well as U.S. aid to the exile community contributed to this distinct exile identity. These international, bureaucratic, and political concerns all contributed to institutionalizing practices that in effect *created* Cuban exiles and turned Miami, where most exiles landed, into a foreign city on U.S. soil.

Cuban state policies also influenced the formation of the exile community. By equating fleeing with treason, the Cuban government used (and continues to use) the exiles as a rallying point. Externalizing opposition allows the Cuban government to get rid of its dissidents in a way that renders them impotent to launch legitimate challenges to the government.

Such has been the case for most exiles of the twentieth century, including those from the Spanish Civil War, Vietnamese, and Chileans.[61] Often home country governments equate abandoning the regime with treason, and thus the process of exodus becomes one of delegitimation. This is particularly effective if the host country is at war with or is antagonistic to the home country. A force tied to one of the nation's historical enemies has little chance of mounting a popular claim against the government. The Cuban revolution delegitimized those who left by defining their exit as "definitive." They were no longer considered part of the nation. Worse, they migrated to the United States, a host country that was a historical as well as a contemporary enemy of Cuba. The revolution fueled an exile that, in the short run, may have externalized opposition but, in the long run, institutionalized exile as a persistent feature of the Cuban and American landscape.

The interaction between U.S. foreign policy objectives and Cuban domestic security policies fueled the creation of a Cuban community abroad in exile. The close interaction of national security agencies within Cuba and the United States created political organizations and ideologies that were then consolidated within the community. In effect, Cuba's need to divide the opposition and the U.S. need to control it may have contributed to the proliferation of the many groups operating in exile.

From 1960 on the CIA's strategy to defeat Castro relied on military action.[62] These actions institutionalized a series of practices that cemented the military functions Cuban émigrés continued to fulfill for the United States. On the one hand, Cuban émigrés were part of U.S. foreign policy, since they received monies and training from the CIA and carried out orders. On the other hand, émigrés were kept away from the centers of power and treated as nationals of another state. Through this distancing, the United States could avoid taking responsibility for the émigrés' actions. The militarization of this opposition by the United States and the promotion of hard-line policies on both sides of the Florida Straits encouraged antidemocratic tendencies within the community and contributed to the politics of intolerance.[63] This had a negative influence on the political culture of the exile.

Once outside national territory and without links to the internal opposition, exile activism became exaggerated and out of touch with the internal dynamics of the island. The United States promoted the exile/soldier as a militant, but, when the United States disengaged from active opposition to the Castro regime, the militant activist came to be considered a terrorist.[64]

Politics is articulated through political organizations. In the case of post-revolutionary Cubans in the United States it was the national security apparatus and policies that had a dominant influence on exile politics. U.S. foreign policies directed at overthrowing and discrediting the Cuban revolution were implemented in part by Cuban émigrés. Having arrived in the United States, many Cuban émigrés participated in military actions backed by the United States, such as the Bay of Pigs invasion in 1961. Through these dynamics the U.S. intelligence network gave life to the first political organizations and leaders in the Cuban community. This connection continued after the failure of Bay of Pigs as the U.S. government again tried to engage exiles in its war against Castro.

NOTES

1. "Analysis of the Opposition Movement to the Castro Regime," Foreign Service Dispatch, American Embassy, Havana, December 6, 1960; reported by W. C. Bowdlering.

2. For an extensive review of the debates about Cuban studies, see Marifeli Perez-Stable, "The Field of Cuban Studies," *Latin American Research Review* 26, no. 1 (1991): 239–50.

3. An exception to this was the seminal study of Cuban exile political attitudes by Richard Fagen, Richard Brody, and Thomas J. O'Leary, *Cubans in Exile: Disaffection and the Revolution* (Stanford: Stanford University Press, 1968).

4. See the work of Juan Clark, "The Exodus from Revolutionary Cuba (1959–1974): A Sociological Analysis" (Ph.D. diss., Dept. of Sociology, University of Florida, 1975).

5. I include my own work in this, along with that of Lourdes Argüelles, "Cuban Miami: The Roots, Development, and Everyday Life of an Émigré Enclave in the National Security State," *Contemporary Marxism* 5 (summer 1982): 27–44; as well as Pedraza-Bailey, *Political and Economic Migrants*, 146.

6. Jorge Domínguez, *Cuba: Order and Revolution* (Cambridge, MA: Belknap Press, Harvard University, 1978), 140.

7. Rafael Hernández, "La política imigratoria de Estados Unidos y la revolución cubana" (Centro de Estudios Sobre America, La Habana, Serie Avances de Investigacione no. 3, 1980).

8. For a detailed account of the various attempts to hold elections, see both Hugh Thomas, *The Cuban Revolution* (New York: Harper and Row, 1971); and Thomas G. Paterson, *Contesting Castro: The United States and the Triumph of the Cuban Revolution* (New York: Oxford University Press, 1994).

9. Marifeli Pérez-Stable, *The Cuban Revolution: Origins, Course, and Legacy* (New York: Oxford University Press, 1993), has an excellent account of the emergence of the armed struggle strategy.

10. Jaime Suchlicki, *University Students and Revolution in Cuba, 1920–1968* (Miami: University of Miami Press, 1969).

11. Ibid., 84.

12. Composed with information from ibid.; Thomas, *Cuban Revolution.*

13. R. Hart Phillips, *Cuba: Island of Paradox* (New York: McDowell, Oblensky, 1957), quoted this figure although the numbers have been contested and may be as low as eight thousand.

14. After the early 1960s, few references to the revolutionary movement include any organization except Movimiento 26 de Julio. In fact, Jesús Díaz's fictional film, *Cladestino,* caused quite a stir in Havana upon its release because it legitimized the urban struggle.

15. See Domínguez, *Cuba,* chap. 6.

16. Thomas, *Cuban Revolution,* 416.

17. Ibid., 423.

18. Jay Mallin Sr., *Covering Castro: Rise and Decline of Cuba's Communist Dictator* (New Brunswick: Transaction Publishers, 1994).

19. Estimates of the number of political prisoners vary widely depending on the method of counting "political" crimes, but they range from 10,000 to 20,000. See María Cristina

García, *Havana, USA: Cuban Exiles and Cuban Americans in South Florida* (Berkeley: University of California Press, 1996), 156–57.

20. Tomas Fernández-Travieso, "Los ocho fusilados," *El Nuevo Herald,* April 17, 1991, p. 4.

21. Foreign Service Dispatch no. 100, April 21, 1960.

22. For an extensive review of the literature of postrevolutionary immigration, see Lisandro Pérez, "Migration from Socialist Cuba: A Critical Analysis of the Literature," in Miren Uriarte and Jorge Cañas, eds., *Cubans in the United States* (Boston: Center for the Study of the Cuban Community, 1984), 12–22.

23. In Pedraza-Bailey, *Political and Economic Migrants,* 151.

24. Quoted in ibid., 150; from *New York Times,* July 23, 1961.

25. Quoted in ibid., 149; from *New York Times,* November 12, 1960.

26. Law no. 989, *Gaceta Oficial de la Republica de Cuba,* miercoles, December 1, 1962, 23705.

27. Abel Enrique Hart Santamaría, *Delitos contra la seguridad del estado* (Havana: Editorial de Ciencias Sociuales, 1988), 76.

28. See the work of Hugo Azcuy, "Los derechos fundamentales de los Cubanos y la cuestion de la emigracion en las relaciones Cuba-Estado Unidos" (paper presented at the Latin American Studies Association, Cuban-Community Research group meeting, Chicago, April 1995).

29. Domínguez, *Cuba,* 37.

30. Rex A. Hudson, "Castro's America Department" (Washington, DC: Cuban-American National Foundation, Departamento de las Americas pamphlet, 1991).

31. Santamaría, *Delitos contra la seguridad del estado,* 171.

32. Earl Smith, *El Cuarto Piso: Relato sobre la revolucion comunista de Castro* (Santo Domingo: Editora Corripio, 1983).

33. Fidel Castro, *La historia me absolvera* (speech given at his trial after the failed assault on the military garrison, Moncada, 1953), (Havana: Editorial Ciencias Sociales, 1973).

34. Barnet, *Roots of War;* and Saul Landau, *The Dangerous Doctrine: National Security and U.S. Foreign Policy* (Boulder: Westview Press, 1988).

35. Carlos Forment, "Caribbean Geopolitics and Foreign State Sponsored Social Movements: The Case of Cuban Exiles Militancy, 1959–1979," in Uriarte-Gaston and Canas, *Cubans in the United States,* 65–102.

36. Argüelles, "Cuban Miami," 27–44.

37. Philip Brenner, *From Confrontation to Negotiations: U.S. Cuba Relations* (Boulder: Westview Press, 1988), 12.

38. William Appleman Williams, *The United States, Cuba, and Castro* (New York: Monthly Review Press, 1962), 122.

39. CIA document entitled "A Program of Covert Action against the Castro Regime," March 16, 1960, 1 (approved for release June 18, 1988, MR Care No. 88–21).

40. U.S. Congress, Senate Committee on Foreign Relations Executive Sessions of the Senate Foreign Relations Committee (Historical Series), vol. 10, 85th Cong., 2d sess., 1958, in Lars Schoultz, *National Security and the United States Policy toward Latin America* (Princeton: Princeton University Press, 1987), 16.

41. Peter Wyden, *Bay of Pigs: The Untold Story* (New York: Touchstone, 1979), 100.

42. Ibid., 76.

43. Williams, in *United States, Cuba, and Castro,* adds that "he was also concerned for his

power, his externalization of evil, and his urge to control the future while still in the present" (152).

44. Correspondence between Joseph Scott, December 2, 1960, and Mr. Hager, December 7, 1960, addressed to Mr. Merchant; obtained from the State Department's Freedom of Information Office, identified as being from the State Department's Cuba file, 1960, 737.00/ 12/2/60.

45. Haynes Johnson, with Manuel Artime, José Pérez San Román, Erneido Oliva, and Enriquez Ruíz-Williams, *The Bay of Pigs: The Leaders Story of Brigade 2506* (New York: W. W. Norton, 1964), 29.

46. A memo to the secretary from Mr. Mann on the subject of the President's Inquiry Regarding Cuban Opposition groups, dated October 28, 1960; obtained from State Department's Freedom of Information Office.

47. Department of State, Memorandum of Conversation, Cuba Series; participants, Ambassador Philip Bonsal and Dr. Aureliano Sanchez Arango, February 3, 1961, 737.00/ 2–361.

48. Argüelles "Cuban Miami," 31.

49. Wyden, *Bay of Pigs,* 49.

50. Johnson et al., *Bay of Pigs,* 62.

51. Department of State, Cuba Series, Foreign Service Dispatch no. 397, American Embassy, Mexico, D.F., October 1960, Report of Conversation with Jose (Pepin) Bosch reported by R. G. Cushing and J. J. Montilor, 737.00/10–1160.

52. Department of State, Cuba Series, Memorandum of Conversation, February 4, 1961; participants, Carlos Piad and Ambassador Philip W. Bonsal, 737.00/2–461.

53. Memorandum for director of Central Intelligence Agency from Tracy Barnes, March 21, 1961, John F. Kennedy (JFK) Presidential Library, National Security Council Files, Cuba, box 48.

54. Ibid.

55. Report sent to Dean Rusk, secretary of state, from the Department of State, Cuba Series, March 23, 1961, 737.00/3–2361.

56. Johnson et al., *Bay of Pigs,* 62.

57. Andrew Wilson, "Portrait of a Cuban Refugee," Central Intelligence Agency, *Studies in Intelligence* (summer 1964): 35–41.

58. Arthur Schlesinger Jr., memorandum for Kenneth O'Donnell, May 8, 1961, JFK Presidential Library, White House Papers, Arthur Schlesinger Jr. files, box 5.

59. Arthur Schlesinger Jr., April 21, 1961, box 115, Presidential Papers, JFK Presidential Library.

60. "Alleged Assassination Plots Involving Foreign Leaders: An Interim Report of the Select Committee to Study Governmental Operations with Respect to Intelligence Activities," United States Senate, 94th Cong., November 20, 1975, report no. 94–465.

61. Shain, *Frontiers of Loyalty,* 23.

62. Paterson, *Contesting Castro.*

63. Forment, "Caribbean Geopolitics."

64. Ibid., 66.

QUESTIONS

1. If the political conditions in the 60s, 70s, and 80s affected the studies of Cuba and the Cuban community, what can be said about the political conditions affecting Torres's own study?

2. In what ways did U.S. government officials facilitate "the concentration of power on the island under the leadership of one man"? To what extent is this a case of unintended consequences?

3. With so many organizations involved in the ousting of the dictator Batista, how was Castro able to consolidate power? To what extent can we say that Castro intended to create a dictatorship if his original objective was to restore the Constitution of 1940 and to hold elections? To what extent can we say he was a victim of circumstances?

4. The political situation in the 60s allowed the formation of a Cuban American exiled community. Were Cubans justified in leaving Cuba?

5. Imagine that Cubans had been not been accepted into the United States. Would Cubans have migrated to other countries in the same numbers? How might the history of Cuba be written if that was the case?

THE FRAGILE POLITICAL STATUS OF MEXICAN AMERICANS

In the fifty years after the U.S. conquest of northern Mexico, the political status of Mexicans in these territories as a dominant, governing, stratified people was deconstructed to that of an excluded, disenfranchised, property-less, and despised minority ethnic group. In terms of actual human bodies, the Mexican population in what was now the United States grew from 116,000 in 1848 to 500,000 in 1900. But due to massive immigration from Europe, this amounted to less than 1 percent of the country. Numerically and in many other ways, by 1900, Mexican human bodies in the U.S. polity were nearly insignificant.[1]

During the first half of the twentieth century, each major economic and political transformation had specific consequences for the reconstruction of a persistently tenuous political and demographic presence: If you have major economic development in the Southwest of the United States, then you create a tremendous demand for labor from Mexico. If U.S. investments promote economic development in Mexico and you increase the connection between the two economies, then this stimulates the displacement and migration of human bodies to where the jobs are. To intensify this situation, all you need is the first major social upheaval of the twentieth century: the Mexican Revolution (see Apodaca for a personal account). If you want to rev up all the previous conditions, then just add the economic stimulus and labor demands of World War I. The result was that, by the beginning of World War II, the U.S. Mexican population had increased fivefold, to 2.5 million (although it remained about 2 percent of the U.S. population). Now, if the conditions change, as they did during the 1930s Great Depression, then you have to get rid of the bodies. Just send them back to Mexico. It does not matter if many of them are U.S. citizens. But if you have inhuman living and working conditions, for those who manage to remain in the United States, the consequence is increased political and labor organizing activity throughout Mexican American communities.

It is within the interplay of these material, objective conditions that Latino/a, specifically U.S. Mexican, political thought was constructed. And it is to these same conditions that U.S. Mexican bodies owe their fragile political status. Who are these people and how did they pursue their quest for public citizenship, for a just life? The political activity of these bodies reflected the diversity of their historical and intellectual formation, for it included aspects of immigration, labor exploitation and repression, rural-urban dichotomies, cultural reaffirmation, deculturalization, educational segregation, increased politicization, labor conflict, intracommunity factionalism, and transborder politics.[2] It was a discourse, as Octavio Romano puts it, in which an individual or a family "could be living three histories at once"[3] (a rather postmodern experience!).

As discussed by the pieces in this section, U.S. Mexican political struggles are characterized by at least three **dialectical** relationships. One is the preservation of cultural integrity, although this takes place within an ambivalent U.S. American discourse regarding "ethnic people." This is reflected in two ways: one is in the Repatriation Program and the other is in the subjectification of the U.S. Mexican as biologically or culturally deficient by the social sciences. A second dialectical relationship involved U.S. Mexicans' response to the lack of support by U.S. institutions, and their consequent development of their own institutions, such as the Congreso Mexicanista (see chapter 15) and the oldest Latino/a organization, the influential League of United Latin American Citizens (LULAC).[4] The third dialectical relationship involves the consistent participation in labor struggles, despite union and judicial exclusionary practices.

In a larger context, the ambivalent desire for, and denial of, ethnicity is a key aspect of the U.S. nationalist discourse that can be traced through the formation of the early colonies, the revolutionary period, the invitation and then exclusion of the Chinese in the nineteenth century and other legislative measures. Wilson Neate refers to these "troubled legislative efforts," noting that the "confused 1917 Immigration Act, detailed thirty categories [of immigrants] to be refused admission and ten classes of exceptions."[5] Mexicans were exempted from the literacy test and head tax, for example, when their labor was needed. There was also the 1924 National Origins Act, which denied entrance to human beings from Central, Eastern, and Southern Europe (because they were deemed racially inferior), but tried to maintain "the American character" by facilitating continued Northwestern European immigration. The notion of a melting pot process itself includes the conflicting tension between the inclusion of ethnicity but its exclusion through assimilation. This phenomenon is especially obvious in Mexican immigration to the United States, a process that is compared to a faucet that is turned on or off depending on the needs of the U.S. economy. This is a major factor in the construction of a fragile political status for Mexican Americans and it is nowhere more amply illustrated than by the Repatriation Program of 1929–39, which expelled one half to one million U.S. Mexicans during what is known as the "decade of betrayal." Though ironic, it is not surprising to learn that some repatriates arrived at their destination only to find labor contractors recruiting workers to pick cotton and other crops in Texas and Arizona![6] In the 1950s "Operation Wetback" rounded up and deported over one million Mexicans and U.S. Mexicans. And most recently, Proposition 187 in California attempted to turn every government official, including teachers and doctors, into official immigration agents for reporting the "undocumented" (a code word for "Mexicans") who may be using educational and health benefits reserved for U.S. citizens.

The dialectical relationship with institutions is dramatized by the fact that, unlike the first two waves of Cuban exiles, Mexican immigrants did not receive support from U.S. institutions. Though U.S. Mexican bodies belonged to categories such as "Catholics," "workers," "students," and "U.S. citizens," their quest for inclusivity was not supported by the corresponding institutions, such as the Catholic Church, the American Federation of Labor, schools, or English-language newspapers. Protestant churches did try to help but only by demanding that U.S. Mexicans adopt Anglo customs. Philanthropic institutions cared little for the welfare of U.S. Mexican bodies. In the final analysis, the effects of power during the first half of the twentieth century are evident in the bodies of the many U.S. Mexicans who were subjected "to terrorism, coercion, and murder in its most brutal form, lynching."[7]

Contrary to the stereotype of the illiterate, apathetic, passive Mexican, the people survived through their own institutions, such as the mutual aid societies and labor and political organizations, and through the abundant production of discourse through Spanish-language newspapers, music, corridos, and theater. Since the nineteenth century, Mexicans have engaged in resistance and radical movements as well as in organized labor, Masonic groups, and religious groups. The most prevalent and persistent were the cultural societies, the rudimentary unions and *mutualistas,* groups that are also found among Puerto Ricans and Cuban Americans (the latter refer to them as *municipios*). In effect, one of the key institutions at play in this particular game of truth is the *mutualista,* a mutual-aid group that contributed to the organizing efforts of community forums, trade unions, and social and political associations, such as the Congreso Mexicanista, discussed in chapter 15. Present in almost every barrio in the Southwest, *mutualistas* maintained close links to other institutions, such as the Mexican consulate, and tried to use Mexican consulate services for lodging complaints against Anglo authorities. *Mutualistas* also played an economic function: in return for dues, member families received a payment upon the death of the wage earner and some unemployment benefits were also available. Members were from the working and the lower-middle classes, with new immigrants making up a large number.[8]

The dialectical relationship with U.S. unions is evident in the political discourse of the *mutualistas*. One of their goals was to encourage U.S. Mexican workers to organize and protest because of low wages, poor treatment, and the desire for self-improvement. They also promoted solidarity with Anglo workers, who in most cases did not want to be associated with them. Non-Mexican workers defined power in terms of ethnocentric solidarity, exclusion of minorities, and identification with the Anglo middle class. Often, white workers, not employers, persecuted nonwhite workers. U.S. Mexicans were often ineligible for union membership and, on union-dominated jobs, often no Mexicans were hired. This led to the practice of organizing separately.[9] These events illustrate how Mexicans struggled for inclusion in the life of the nation, only to be rejected, and the necessary retreat into an ethnic discourse and their own communities.

A further illustration underlines U.S. Mexican workers' desires to be active citizens. Since they were mostly involved in agricultural work, they did not play a major role in industrial areas. And yet many U.S. Mexicans were significant participants in labor struggles in the South and the Midwest of the United States, even where they were systematically excluded from leadership or from union membership by exclusionist unions, such as the American Federation of Labor. Indeed a major chapter in Latino/a political thought is the important and often leading role of U.S. Mexican workers through the Partido Liberal Mexicano (PLM), especially in the more militant sectors of the U.S. labor movement, such as the Industrial Workers of the World (IWW).[10] The Partido Liberal Mexicano, led by Ricardo Flores Magón, "represents an innovation in the political history of the Mexican people in the U.S. and in Mexico. It was an international, revolutionary, ideological, and clandestine party that fought for the destruction of the dictatorship in Mexico and capitalism in general."[11] It had significant ties to U.S. American radicals, especially the IWW. In some ways it can be compared to the Cuban Revolutionary Party, which under the leadership of José Martí operated in the United States to overthrow the Spaniards from Cuba. This active political discourse of U.S. Mexican workers was adversely affected not only by the Repatriation, but also by laws that were specifically used to deter militancy in the Mexican community. The Taft-Hartley Act of 1947 allowed the U.S. president to order workers to go back to their jobs, gave states the right to eliminate union membership as a prerequisite for many jobs, and required union officials to sign affidavits pledging no Communist affiliation. The McCarran International Security Act of 1950, among other provisions, makes a distinction between naturalized and native citizens; it was used to deport citizens for political reasons—such as labor organizing.[12]

Paradoxically, the increased demand for Mexican labor from Mexico was matched by the exclusionary disregard for the well-being of those same human bodies once they were on U.S. soil, once they became U.S. Mexicans. These are political struggles for and about the human body (its categorization according to class, pigment of skin, nationality, ethnicity, and "desirability"—desirable citizen versus undesirable alien) for the purpose of the extraction of its labor and the preservation of a particular image of what constitutes the United States of America. This paradox represents a poorly understood dynamic that leads many people to believe that U.S. Mexicans prefer to have their own separate communities. On the contrary, their quest in the early part of the twentieth century illustrates a Mexican American political practice to include others in the struggle for public citizenship. This quest, however, has been confronted by a constant discourse of exclusion, animosity, and exploitation that elsewhere has been termed "Chicanology."[13] These are the power relations that construct a fragile political status for the Mexican American.

NOTES AND SUGGESTED READINGS

1. To differentiate them from "Mexicans" from Mexico, we use here the term "U.S. Mexicans."

2. Juan Gómez-Quiñonez, *Roots of Chicano Politics, 1600–1940* (Albuquerque: University of New Mexico Press, 1994), 296.

3. Romano, I. R.-V., "The Historical and Intellectual Presence of Mexican Americans," *El Grito* (winter 1969): 32–46.

4. For a contextualized exposition, see Mario T. Garcia, *Mexican Americans: Leadership, Ideology, and Identity, 1930–1960* (New Haven, Conn.: Yale University Press, 1989), 25–61.

5. Wilson Neate, "Alienism Unashamed," *Latino Studies Journal* 8, no. 2 (spring 1997): 68–91.

6. Balderrama, Francisco E., and R. Rodríguez, *Decade of Betrayal: Mexican Repatriation in the 1930s* (Albuquerque: University of New Mexico Press, 1995), 118.

7. Gómez-Quiñonez, *Roots of Chicano Politics*, 299.

8. Juan Gómez-Quiñonez, *Mexican American Labor, 1790–1990* (Albuquerque: University of New Mexico Press, 1994), 57.

9. Gómez-Quiñonez, *Mexican American Labor*, 57–61.

10. Gómez-Quiñonez, *Roots of Chicano Politics*, 300.

11. Gómez-Quiñonez, *Roots of Chicano Politics*, 342.

12. Gómez-Quiñonez, *Mexican American Labor*, 174.

13. Francisco H. Vázquez, "Chicanology: A Postmodern Analysis of Meshicano Discourse," *Perspectives in Mexican American Studies* 3 (1992): 116–47.

✳ 14 ✳
OUR FEMINIST HERITAGE

Marta Cotera

Though much work remains to be done to recognize the participation of women at all levels of social struggle, to write "Chicanas into history" and "decolonize the imaginary," as Emma Pérez puts it, it helps to at least have a map of this history. This is what Marta provides in the following piece, which started as a speech in 1973 and later was published in her anthology *The Chicana Feminist.*

Because Mexican women had participated valiantly in the 1810 War for Independence and the subsequent wars for reform, they were not expressively excluded from voting and holding office by the 1857 Constitution. Unfortunately, subsequent election laws did restrict suffrage to males. Suffrage and feminist activities in Mexico in the 1880s were advocated primarily by socialists who spoke in favor of women's rights. As early as 1878 *La International* published a 12-point program in which number 7 called for the emancipation, rehabilitation and education of women. In the 1880s and 1890s during the Porfirio Díaz regime Mexican women were admitted to institutions of higher learning and by the end of last century, Mexico had women professionals in law, medicine, pharmacy, and the teaching professions. The social and economic upheavals which deposed the Díaz regime and produced the 1910 revolution gave Mexican feminists yet another arena for action. Revolutionary supporters established women's organizations like the Hijas de Cuauhtémoc and newspapers like *Vesper* which helped the cause and raised women's consciousness about their own status. Juana Belen Gutiérrez de Mendoza was an outstanding feminist and journalist of the period.

In terms of women's rights, the Mexican revolution of 1910 had enormous impact. During the revolution men and women developed relationships of partnership and mutual regard very seldom seen in most societies. Through their activities as clerks, secretaries, smugglers, telegraphers, journalists, financiers, and soldiers, women had a rare opportunity to develop their potential on a large scale, beside the men, and won their respect and recognition as partners. Perhaps within the Mexican culture this phenomenon was only to be repeated in the U.S. with the Chicano farmworker and civil rights struggles of the twentieth century.

Mexicanas built on this relationship to press for more representation in the nation's public life during the revolutionary years and during the formulation of public policies following the revolution. President Francisco I. Madero, through the influence of his wife and Soledad González, his assistant, became deeply interested in women's rights. His brief term in office precluded any action on this matter.

President Venustiano Carranza had as a close aide Hermila Galindo, an early champion of women's rights in Mexico. Through various [plans] and reforms Carranza changed the legal status of women, although their political status remained unchanged. His aide, Hermila Galindo, continued to spread feminist propaganda in Veracruz, Tabasco, Campeche, Yucatán, San Luis Potosí, Coahuila, and Nuevo León. Hermila's activities no doubt also helped propagandize Carranza's Constitutionalist cause among women.

From September, 1915, to 1919 Hermila Galindo, Artemisa Saenz Rayo and other women published a feminist journal, *La Mujer Moderna*, which advocated women's rights. They also worked to organize Mexico's first International Congress of Women which was held in Merida, Yucatán, in January, 1916. This congress included more than 700 delegates nationwide. Activities included reports on the status of women on an international scale and resolutions on the protection of women and children.

Although women had sacrificed fortunes, families, and lives during the revolution, their social and political status remained unchanged when the 1917 constitution was drawn up and adopted.

There are indications that even as early as 1917 the radicals and liberals feared traditional church influence over women if women were allowed to vote in national and state elections. Feminist victories during this period included a "law concerning family relations" which gave women the right of divorce, the right to alimony, and to management and ownership of property. But again, the national election law of June, 1918, ignored women and specified that "all Mexican males 18 years of age or over if they are married and 21 years or over if they are not, who enjoy full political rights and whose names have been duly registered in their municipalities are eligible to vote."

Another feminist congress met in Mexico City in 1921 and by 1922, Yucatán passed the first of a series of state laws granting the vote to women in the state.

Mexicanas continued to press for women's rights and suffrage through a multitude of organizations such as the Mexican Y.W.C.A., the Liga Feminista, and the Asociación Panamericana.

During this period women's groups also worked towards the obliteration of poverty, the equitable distribution of land, and improvements in the lives of all women and children in Mexico.

Although states like Chiapas and San Luis Potosí provided suffrage to women, both states were forced to rescind their decisions. Women continued through the 20s and 30s to press for suffrage until 1959 when the right to vote was finally granted them.

Historians for this period and leading to 1959 indicate that during sessions of Congress, women attorneys, judges, orators, journalists, and activists showed up daily to demand the right to vote. Politicians always waved them aside for a more propitious time. But the Mexicanas did not desist until that day, July 7, 1959, when Mexican women voted for the first time.

And the sky did not fall in and no Catholic Bishop has been elected President, as the men had predicted.

Because of the human migration between borders it is difficult to separate some developments of the Mexicana's suffragist activities from Chicana history and development.

In many instances Chicana feminism followed separate but similar courses to Mexican feminism. In most instances Chicana feminist activities have been intricately interwoven with the entire fabric of the Chicano civil rights movement from 1848 to the present.

From Frances Swadesh's research on southwestern cultures we know that *mestizas* in the southwest enjoyed a very liberalized existence as compared to Mexico and other parts of the United States in the 1850s. Women like pony rider mail carrier Candelaria Mestas and "La Tules" in New Mexico blew the Chicana stereotypes. In the 1880s socialist and labor organizer Lucy Gonzales Parsons was actively organizing women workers in Chicago. Her very presence and activity as a leader in the labor movement for thirty years propelled both the feminist and labor causes.

Other feminist activities within the Chicano community included the activity of Mexicanas and Chicanas within the Partido Liberal Mexicano from 1905 to approximately 1917. Hundreds of women worked with the revolutionary exiles Enrique and Ricardo Flores Magón to achieve rights for all workers, men and women. The

P.L.M. and its publication *Regeneración* became important vehicles for the espousal of women's rights in the U.S. within the Chicano community.

Other important events in Chicana feminist history include:

- The activities of Jovita Idar and Soledad Peña who advocated women's development and helped form the Liga Femenil Mexicanista on October 15, 1911, in Laredo, Texas.
- María L. Hernández' civil rights activities as early as 1923 in Texas.
- Chicana activities in labor organizing in the 1930s in the Monte Berry strike, the Pecan Shellers strike, and the concurrent national conferences. Chicanas active in the period were Emma Tenayuca, Luisa Moreno, and Manuela Sager. Many relatives of present day campesinas like Raquel Orendain were also involved.
- Isabel Malagran González' political activism in Colorado in the 1930s and 1940s and her outspoken stance on the involvement and development of Chicanas.
- The filming of *Salt of the Earth* in 1953 on the role and courage of Chicanas.

In the 1960s the historical cycle was completed and Chicanas picked up the feminist threads introduced by the radical Club Liberal de San Antonio and the autonomous Liga Mexicanista Femenil of the 1920s. Both organizations, unlike GI Forum, Ladies LULAC, and Chicana groups working within predominantly male groups, were feminist and autonomous. Chicanas had come of age. They have been willing in the seventies, as before, to participate in community and male-dominated organizations. But in addition, they recalled part of themselves, part of their energies, to participate in newly formed all-women caucuses and organizations.

The recurring rationale for this action has been expressed in Chicana feminist ideology and in position statements from coast to coast. It centers around these issues identified by Chicanas:

- Chicanas have realized that in terms of socio-economic status and prospects for improvement, they are at the bottom of the social heap in this country.
- Chicanas realize that there is always room for recruiting more women into social action and advocacy, and that women can be successfully recruited if concentrated attention is given to this matter. Chicanas welcomed the opportunity to shoulder at least 50 percent of the burden for development and improvement of the community.
- Women have some very special and unique concerns in areas such as sex education, child care, rape, Chicana studies or university and public school nonsexist ethnic studies, which they can effectively identify and clarify. In these areas, mixed groups have not always been as effective advocates as all-women organizations.
- Male-dominated organizations have provided limited opportunity for leader-

ship experiences to women. In all-female organizations, all positions are available to women.

- Women sometimes can be more successfully involved in all-women organizations than in mixed groups. From the entry point in a woman's organization, they can be introduced to other community advocacy efforts.
- Chicanas realized that Anglo women were advocating for greater rights and privileges and prioritizing of programs on women's issues; as a good strategy, special-purpose Chicana organizations/institutions need to be instituted to benefit from the government's attention to women.

The 70s has seen an upsurge in activity and development for Chicanas without parallel. Chicanas have made enormous contributions in the fields of education, journalism, politics and labor. They have certainly added depth and new dimension to feminist philosophy and literature in this country.

Feminists within the Chicano ranks have not had an easy time, first of all because most of them received the label unintentionally for doing what they had been doing for decades and for merely reminding males that women had egos, too and needs; and secondly, because a women's movement happened to come on the scene when Chicanas were ready to take the step towards stronger development and realistic approaches to family problems.

Nevertheless, the evidence is available in Chicano journals that women have not been frightened by the challenge. They have met it head-on, and if feminism or a women's liberation movement continues its activities in this country, Chicanas seem ready to make certain it is a multicultural movement, especially in educational institutions and in the political and socio-economic arena.

NOTE

Cotera gave this as a speech in 1973 and then published it in her anthology, *The Chicana Feminist* (Austin: Information System Development, 1977: pp. 1–7).

QUESTIONS

1. How might one attempt to explain that (a) on one hand Mexican women were accepted into higher education by the end of the last century and "men and women developed relationships of partnership and mutual regard very seldom seen in most societies," which continued through the Mexican Revolution and the U.S. Chicano/a farmworker and civil rights movements, and (b) on the other hand, machismo as male supremacy is characterized as a dominant trait among Mexicanos and Chicanos?

2. Cotera argues that Mexicanas have been feminists all along and were given the label in the 1970s, when it became a fashionable word. To what extent does the historical record of struggles for suffrage support her argument?

＊ 15 ＊
EL PRIMER CONGRESO MEXICANISTA DE 1911:
A PRECURSOR TO CONTEMPORARY CHICANISMO

José E. Limón

At the turn of the century we find a deterioration of the economic situation; a noticeable loss of the Mexican culture and the Spanish language; general social discrimination, particularly in education; and a pattern of officially tolerated lynching of U.S. Mexicans. It is particularly the unpunished brutality against the bodies of U.S. Mexicans that leads to this particular aspect of Latino thought represented by the Congreso Mexicanista de 1911. As the title of José's article indicates, these ideas are part of a radical, antiassimilationist discourse of resistance that reappeared sixty years later. No wonder some Chicanos believed that they had invented this particular kind of radical resistance. Even before the advent of a global society, the Congreso also illustrated a discourse of transnational political and cultural identities discussed by María de los Angeles Torres in part IV, chapter 26.

As exemplified by the League of United Latin American Citizens (LULAC), the tactics change in the 1920s.[1] But even then, a continuity in Latino/a political thought was maintained by the economic, physical, social, or psychic violence carried against Latino/a children, women, and men. There are similarities between the Congreso and the Cuban Patriotic League of Tampa.[2] A particularly invisible thread in Latino/a political thought is the presence of **Freemasonry** (a secret society) among many of the liberation groups discussed in these readings.[3] This system of lodges as a primary organizational base is also described by the Mason Benjamin Franklin in his autobiography. Another point of commonality between the Congreso, the Puerto Rican *independentistas,* the Cuban revolution, and the Chicano movement is the notion of separatism. After much human suffering there are indications that Latino/as got to the point where, as the U.S. Declaration of Independence states, "it becomes necessary for one people to dissolve the political bands which have connected them with another."

NOTES AND SUGGESTED READINGS

1. Mario T. Garcia, *Mexican Americans: Leadership, Ideology, and Identity, 1930–1960* (New Haven, Conn.: Yale University Press, 1989), 25–61.

2. Enrique Collazo Pérez, "José Martí, the Cuban Patriotic League of Tampa and the Cuban Revolutionary Party," trans. and ed. K. Lynn Stoner, in *José Martí in the United States: The Florida Experience,* ed., Louis A. Pérez, 71–80 (Tempe: Arizona State University, Center for Latin American Studies, 1995).

3. The role of Masons in Latino/a political thought has yet to be discussed comprehensively. Juan Gómez-Quiñonez, an authority on Chicano history, in his *Roots of Chicano Politics, 1600–1940* (Albuquerque: University of New Mexico Press, 1994), lists only one bibliographical entry on this topic: José Maria Mateos, *Historia de la Masonería en México desde 1806 hasta 1884* (Mexico City: 1884). One helpful source on Freemasonry in general is Stephen Knight, *The Brotherhood* (Dorset Press, 1986).

＊   ＊   ＊

In its struggle for social change on behalf of the Chicano community, the contemporary Chicano movement has developed a broad coherent ideology to guide and legitimize its activity in the areas of schooling, labor, and organized politics. At least five major themes form the ideology that distinguishes this movement, composed largely of student groups such as MECHA and MAYO. This ideology consists of: (1) a critical attack on the social subordination of Chicanos as a holistic phenomenon; (2) a personal, artistic, and institutional affirmation of the special variant of Mexican culture found in the U.S.; (3) the assertion of a feminist position within the larger movement; (4) the search for a unified political solution to Chicano problems including at least a partial acceptance of radical politics; and (5) the somewhat unclear projection of a quasi-separate nation state as the final goal for this movement.[1]

Finding no adequate historical precedents within the community, scholars attribute a seeming novelty to this ideology. One influential study labels the 1848–1921 period as "apolitical." According to Alfredo Cuéllar, this period of organizational and ideological inactivity is followed by a series of organizations such as the Order Sons of America (1921), LULAC (1929) and the American G.I. Forum (1948). However, these groups follow an ideology of adaptation and accommodation to Anglo American society—a practice not substantially altered by later groups such as MAPA (1959) and PASSO (1960). As such the 1921–1960 groups stand in marked contrast to the contemporary Chicano movement of the mid sixties and its new ideology of Chicanismo.[2] Or, as Cuéllar put it in 1970:

> Until recently no Mexican-American had tried to define the problems of the community in any terms except those of assimilation. It is precisely these ideas of assimilation and social "adjustment" that the Chicano militant rejects. As a new alternative, Chicanismo represents a conception of an autonomous and self determining social life for Mexican-Americans.
>
> It is interesting to note that it was not until the 1960's that the Chicano leaders emerged to question some of the oldest and most fundamental assumptions of Mexicans in American society.[3]

This history of ideologies needs to be revised on the basis of new evidence furnished by *El Primer Congreso Mexicanista de 1911*. In the present study I will argue that this early congress and its social milieu anticipate many of the major themes that define the supposedly new ideology of Chicanismo.

BACKGROUND OF THE CONGRESO

El Primer Congreso Mexicanista was a political conference held in Laredo, Texas, on September 14–22, 1911.[4] It was convened by Texas-Mexicans to express and act upon a variety of social grievances which were the culmination of an encroaching Anglo-American domination of Texas-Mexicans during the latter half of the nineteenth century and into the early twentieth. This period was marked by the transfer of almost all Texas-Mexican land into Anglo-Texan hands through various legal and

illegal means.[5] Coupled with an intensifying Mexican immigration, this loss of economic position started the conversion of the Texas-Mexican population into a cheap
labor pool for the developing Anglo-Texan ranching and farming interests.[6] Protected by his nearly exclusive control of the political order and reinforced by his
visible economic dominance, the Anglo-Texan, with his embedded sense of racial
and cultural superiority, created a pattern of local, officially sanctioned segregation
between the two peoples.[7] Finally, by suppressing acts of native resistance such as
those of Juan Cortina and Catarino Garza and physically intimidating the Texas-
Mexican population as a whole, law enforcement and military authorities reflected
and supported the new socio-economic order.[8] In response to this developing climate of social oppression, Sr. Nicasio Idar and his family initiated a campaign of
journalistic resistance that eventually led to El Primer Congreso Mexicanista.

THE IDAR FAMILY AND *LA CRÓNICA*

Born in Point Isabel, Texas, near Brownsville on December 26, 1853, Nicasio Idar
moved to Laredo, Texas, in 1880, after living in Corpus Christi and attending
schools there. He was primarily a journalist and commercial printer, although he
also served as an Assistant City Marshall and a Justice of the Peace in Laredo. As
a journalist he published *La Revista,* a Masonic review, and *La Crónica,* a weekly
independent newspaper dedicated "al beneficio de la raza méxico-texana." In addition to his affiliation with the Mexican Masonry, he also belonged to the Sociedad
Mutualista Benito Juárez in Laredo and was a vice president of a Mexican and Texas-
Mexican fraternal lodge system known as La Orden Caballeros de Honor. According
to his obituary he had also been active in labor organizing "haste lograr la fundación
de la primera associación de ferrocarrileros mexicanos . . . La Alianza Suprema de
Ferrocarrileros Mexicanos." He died on April 7, 1914, leaving his widow Jovita and
eight children, one of whom eulogized him as a man who left a legacy of ideas
"sanas, nobles, benéfices, que forman un tesoro inacabable, pródigo siempre en
beneficios y enseñanzas."[9]
     At least three children had shared, not only their father's ideas, but his enthusiasm
and zeal in defending the rights of the Texas-Mexican community. Jovita (named
after her mother), Clemente and Eduardo joined their father in his work as editor
and publisher of *La Crónica.* This remarkable newspaper covered local and area
news, México, and worldwide affairs, although it was centrally dedicated to "el progreso y desarrollo industrial, moral e intelectual de los habitantes mexicanos en
Texas."[10] Eduardo covered Brownsville and the lower Rio Grande Valley as a traveling correspondent, while Jovita and Clemente served in a general capacity including
considerable staff writing.[11] There were other writers for *La Crónica* including guest
writers and the newspaper reprinted significant articles appearing elsewhere. It began
publication sometime in the 1890s with Nicasio Idar as editor, although it is likely
that he did not become its owner and publisher until 1910.[12]

LA CRÓNICA AND SOCIAL OPPRESSION

Throughout the period 1910–1911, *La Crónica* launched a series of attacks on particular manifestations of the social conditions oppressing Texas-Mexicans. Five issues drew the Idar's interest and formed the immediate social context of El Primer Congreso Mexicanista: (1) the deteriorating Texas-Mexican economic condition; (2) the already perceptible loss of Mexican culture and the Spanish language; (3) general social discrimination; (4) the particular problem of educational discrimination; and (5) the pattern of officially tolerated lynchings of Texas-Mexicans. The latter two drew their principal attention.

On November 2, 1910, Antonio Rodriguez, probably a Mexican national, was arrested by sheriff's deputies near Rocksprings, Texas, and accused of having murdered an Anglo-American woman on a ranch near town. His guilt or innocence will never be known, because within hours a mob took him from the Rocksprings jail, tied him to a tree and burned him to death. The local coroner returned a verdict of death "at the hands of persons unknown."[13] A later investigation by the Texas Rangers would show that "the recent burning of the Mexican there was done entirely by Americans. . . ."[14] This atrocity had an impact on U.S.-Mexican relations and on the Texas-Mexican community.[15] *La Crónica* bitterly attacked the burning as a barbaric act, and denounced the inaction of the local authorities.[16]

On June 19, 1911, Antonio Gómez, age 14, was asked to leave a place of business in Thorndale, Texas. He refused, a fight ensued and a Texas-German was left dead with a wound from Gómez's knife. Gómez was arrested, but was taken from the authorities by a group of men who beat him to death and dragged his body around town with a buggy. *La Crónica* commented on this particular lynching and on the general condition of injustice:

> Este hecho bárbaro fue communicado á todo el mundo civilizado causando la consternación consiguiente. Se espera saber que hará el Gobierno de Texas pero hay que suponer que se encausará a los lynchadores y se les dejará libres bajo fianza y despues de cansar la opinión pública con simulacros de juicios, se desechará completamente la causa; pues hasta ahora no recordamos de americano alguno que haya sido castigado por el lynchamiento de un mexicano, á pesar de que se han cometido algunas.

La Crónica saw this incident as a particular case of the general racial hatred and contempt felt by most Anglo-Texans toward Mexicans.[17] In a later article, *La Crónica* attacked the Mexican consuls for timidity in entering the case and, noting that Thorndale Mexicans were retaliating by boycotting Anglo merchants, concluded:

> . . . no queda a los mexicanos mas que un remedio; el que han adoptado los hombres de todas las razas para hacerse respetar: La asociación.[18]

Later that month *La Crónica* took note of an Orden Caballeros de Honor meeting held in Bay City on the Texas Gulf Coast to discuss the Thorndale matter and the need to unify Texas-Mexicans. In attendance were delegates from Matagorda, Rock-eye, Wharton, and Runge.[19]

La Crónica took interest in a third criminal case. León Cárdenas Martínez was arrested and tried for allegedly murdering two Anglo women near Reeves, Texas, in July, 1911. According to George Estes, his lawyer, a mob forced Martínez to confess at gunpoint. A single jury member who dissented on the "guilty" vote was threatened, and Martínez was finally sentenced to death. Under personal threats to his own life, Estes appealed the case and the death sentence was reduced to thirty years in the penitentiary.[20] Texas-Mexicans had sent several letters, including one from *La Crónica*, to Governor O. B. Colquitt asking for clemency for the 16 year old Martínez.[21] Governor Colquitt received pressure from the other side as well:

> . . . a petition said to bear the signature of nearly every Caucasian in Reeves County has been sent to Governor Colquitt asking him not to commute the Mexican's sentence.[22]

The Martínez case would receive attention at the Congreso.

The judicial injustices committed against Mexicans were a logical result of the general climate of social discrimination. According to *La Crónica*, even the *Houston Post* noted the effect of the Alamo syndrome on juries trying Mexicans. The *Post* concluded that there was very little sympathy for the "greaser" in this country. J. J. Mercado, the translator of the *Post* article commented:

> Lo sabíamos ya nosotros antes de que el Post nos lo dijera y lo hemos sabido siempre, que millares de fallos judiciales en los tribunales de Texas en contra del Mexicano, han sido inspirados en la sangrienta venganza que entraña el grito "Remember de Alamo" y en el concepto de "greaser" que naciera de la eterna predisposición contra la raza mexicana.[23]

Earlier in the year *La Crónica* had noted the general climate of racial discrimination particularly in central Texas where signs such as "No lots sold to Mexicans" and "No Mexicans admitted" were prevalent, and where, in Austin, State Representative J. T. Canales was called "the greaser from Brownsville" during a session of the legislature.[24]

The "greaser" concept particularly affected the educational process. Toward the end of 1910 and on through early 1911 Clemente Idar wrote a series of articles exposing glaring discrimination in Texas public schools, particularly in upper southern Texas. He argued that Texas-Mexicans paid school taxes, but were not permitted to participate in the educational system. The Mexican consul in Laredo was asked to investigate, but confined his investigation to the largely Mexican counties of Webb, Starr, and Zapata and concluded there was no discrimination in Texas. Idar urged him to visit the rest of southern and central Texas as he himself had done, but this was never done. Idar continued to attack specific counties: Val Verde, Hays, González, Atascosa, Medina, Frío, La Salle, Dimmit, McMullen, Uvalde, and Wilson, and also the towns of Pearsal, Devine, Kingsville, Asherton, Kyle and Del Rio.

In one significant article he interpreted this pattern of discrimination as a violation of the Treaty of Guadalupe Hidalgo. As a result of this extensive series *La Crónica* began to receive letters from its readers all over Texas confirming the existence of segregation in their communities.[25]

However, *La Crónica* also recognized that even in inferior and segregated schools, an ethnocentric educational process was starting to anglicize Texas-Mexican children. It expressed deep concern about the loss of the Spanish language and Mexican history and culture, and in a strikingly modern tone, argued for bilingual education:

> Con profunda pena hemos visto á maestros mexicanos enseñando inglés á niños de su raza, sin tomar para nada en cuenta el idioma materno que cada día se va olvidando más y cada día van sufriendo adulteraciones y cambios que hieren materlalmente al oído de cualquier mexicano por poco versado que este en la idioma de Cervantes.[26]

English should also be learned, but Spanish was fundamental:

> . . . lo que quisimos significar simplemente es que no debe desatenderse el idioma nacional, porque es el sello caracteristico de las razas y las castas se hunden cuando se olvida la lengua nacional . . . No decimos que no se enseñe el ingles a la niñez mexico-texana, sea en hora buena, decimos que no se olviden de enseñarles el castellano.[27]

A second consequence of such mis-education would be a progressive cultural apathy and indifference:

> . . . si en la escuela americana á que concurren nuestros niños se les enseña la Biografía de Washington y no la de Hidalgo y en vez de hechas gloriosas de Juárez se le refieren las hazañas de Lincoln, por mas que estas sean nobles y justas, no conocerá ese niño las glorias de su Patria, no la amará y haste verá con indiferencia a los coterranos de sus padres.[28]

Late in 1910, *La Crónica* had proposed a dramatic solution for the cultural problem created by ethnocentric Anglo-U.S. schools: the creation of a separate school system staffed by imported Mexican teachers where the primary language of instruction would be Spanish. The expenses for such a school system were to be borne by the Texas-Mexican community.[29] Replying to a Texas-Mexican critic of this radical idea, *La Crónica* approvingly pointed to educational efforts of this kind already underway within the community:

> . . . en las cuales se propone la creación de escuelas donde se instruya á la juventud mexicana exclusivamente en la idioma de Cervantes, como una medida eficaz para que no pierda terreno y siga siendo todo el tiempo la hija de 'labradores pobres' y por tanto la bestia del trabajo, triste condición á la que se le quiere condenar . . .[30]

This was a strikingly modern linkage between the non-use of the child's native language and his progressive failure in the schools and in society. The notion of community created schools would appear again a month before the Congreso:

La niñez mexicana en Texas necesita instruirse. Ni nuestro gobierno ni el de EEUU pueden hacer nada por ella, y no queda otro recurso que el de hacerlo por nuestro propio impulso á trueque de no seguir despreciados y vejados por los extranjeros que nos rodean.[31]

Another area of concern for the Idars was the steadily deteriorating economic position of Texas-Mexicans. They urged the people not to sell their land to the growing wave of,

. . . agentes y compradores de terrenos, que hacen sus mejores especulaciones comprando propiedades de mexicanos á precios infimos, para traspasarlas á manos de otros individuos que nada tienen en común con nosotros, y el resultado lógico de esa actividad, inevitablemente será que en muy pocos años el numero de nuestros hombres acandalados de hoy se habrá reducido en grande proporciones, y entonces, sus descendientes y sus hermanos serán los que sufren las consequencias de su imprevisión.[32]

Idar felt now was the time to reverse the tide and hold on to the land. Only in this way could Texas-Mexicans reach "el no lejano y glorioso provenir que espera á nuestra raza heróica y viril."[33] As a result of this host of issues, the Idars begin making plans for El Primer Congreso Mexicanista.

EL PRIMER CONGRESO
MEXICANISTA—ORGANIZATIONAL TECHNIQUES

The Idars were active members in the Orden Caballeros de Honor (OCH) a Texas-Mexican and Mexican fraternal lodge, and they utilized the Texas wide system of lodges as a primary organizational base. The largest groups were in Brownsville (200), Corpus Christi (80) and Laredo (90).[34] In January, 1911 through *La Crónica* the Idars began calling for a convention of the various lodges and special guests— "los mexicanos mas ilustrados en las letras, residentes en Texas, a todos los periodistas mexicanos de Texas, y a todos los cónsules Mexicanos." This convention to be held in Laredo, was to take up the questions of: (1) school discrimination; (2) the need for teaching Spanish in community controlled schools with Mexican teachers; (3) the Mexican consular system; (4) ways and means to protect Mexican lives and interests in Texas; (5) the role of the Orden; (6) formation of women's groups under the auspices of the Orden; (7) the need for Texas-Mexicans to acquire land and hold on to that which they had; and (8) organizing a future meeting to be known as El Primer Congreso Mexicanista.[35]

By February, 1911, the Idars changed their minds and asked each OCH lodge to send a special delegation to the OCH conventions. These special delegations would convene separately as El Primer Congreso Mexicanista so that immediate steps would be taken toward solving the Texas-Mexican problems. Arguing that Texas-Mexicans could not depend on change in the Anglo-Texan community or on external help from Mexico, *La Crónica* urged organization, unification, and education of the Mexican masses as the only solution to "los problemas que afectan las vidas y los intereses de nuestros hermanos." An open invitation was extended to all Texas-Mexican organizations, "que en algo se preocupen por nuestro bienestar." A special invitation was extended to the Texas-Mexican Masonic Lodges. Indeed, *La Crónica* urged Texas-Mexicans to organize themselves locally for the purpose of sending a delegation to the meetings.[36]

In the March 16th issue of the newspaper, the Idars printed letters of support from prominent individuals in various groups. They also received the support of the very important sociedades mutualistas. These self-help social groups existed extensively throughout Texas primarily to provide an insurance service, a place for socializing and an organizational base for the celebration of Mexican holidays in Texas. During this month the decision was also made to hold the dual convention during the week of September 14–22, 1911. The symbolic value of the date is, of course obvious, but *La Crónica* also took note of the tactical advantages—lower holiday train fares and the presence of large numbers of visitors in Laredo to celebrate las fiestas patrias.[37]

In July the proposed Congreso received the support of the Agrupación Protectora Mexicana of San Antonio, led by Doneciano Dávila and Emilio Flores and dedicated to the defense of Texas-Mexicans especially on the issue of lynchings. Dávila and Flores called for a nation-wide political unification of all Mexicans in the U.S. so that,

> . . . unidos todos bajo los vinculos más estrechos de compañerismo y con fraternidad nos pongamos á cubierto de los limites de la ley, de todo genero de infamias é injustícias que con nosotros se pretenda cometer.

Nicasio Idar thanked them for their support noting their previous efforts on behalf of Texas-Mexicans, particularly "en el asunto de Cortez" in obvious reference to the legal defense of Gregorio Cortez.[38] In this same month the Idars published the first estimate of the expected attendance at the meetings. We are told that "la asistencia será de 300–400 personas."[39] In August we learn that a Mesa Directiva was to be elected by a majority of those present and that after the Congreso, chapters were to be established "en todos las poblaciones mexicanas" under the central Mesa Directiva that would function as "el centro de protección de todos los mexicanos de Texas, por medio de él se demandará justicia cuando sea necesario . . ."[40] In early September, *La Crónica* also took note of growing local support in the form of financial contributions.[41] And, on the morning of the Congreso, *La Crónica* announced the presence of additional delegations from the Agrupación Protectora Mexicana of Houston and a Masonic lodge in México City.[42] That same morning a terse announcement entitled, "Otra Víctima del Odio Yankee" appeared in the paper:

> El lunes último fue muerto en Corpus Christi por un americano, el laborioso y digno mexicano José Olivares, hermano por parte materna del Sr. Nicasio Idar . . .[43]

No further explanation was given of this incident personally affecting the Idar family.

EL PRIMER CONGRESO MEXICANISTA—THE MEETINGS

On September 14, 1911 the delegates finally met on the second floor of a building in the town square known as Los Altos del Mercado. Roughly about this time the city of Laredo, located on the Rio Grande border approximately 200 miles from the Gulf port of Brownsville, was described in these terms:

> . . . a healthy and pleasant climate, an industrious and law abiding population, abundant and cheap labor, supplied with all the modern appliances for comfort, water works, electric lights, telephone exchange, costly public buildings, churches, schools, and private residences, smelters, and scapling works, ice factories, machine and car shops . . . a population of 15,000 souls and a taxable wealth of $3,000,000.[44]

More importantly a general review of Laredo newspapers from this time period tells us of a city whose political, educational, and cultural life were significantly influenced, if not dominated, by Texas-Mexicans—a situation which continues to the present.

As the Congreso met, a journalist covering the events would articulate the fundamental reason for the meetings:

> Estar en tierra extraña, vivir á merced de la majoria que son los habitantes de la tierra en que están y no unirse y defenderse mutuamente es estar a merced de ellos, es entregarse manistados al primer explotador de conciencia elástica, pero unirse entre sí, formar una sola liga defensiva ofensiva es ser invulnerables, es triunfar en el campo de la razón y de la justicia.[45]

We do not have an exact count of the persons in attendance, although we do know the Idars were successful in gathering two delegates from each OCH lodge in twenty-four Texas localities. We can add to this an unspecified number of representatives from Masonic lodges, sociedades mutualistas, agrupaciones protectoras, other types of social groups such as El Club Internacional of Laredo, special visitors such as the delegations from México, the press, and of course an unspecified number of ordinary visitors.[46] The secretary of the Congreso spoke of "una gran multitud" present at the sessions.[47] After a welcoming address by Nicasio Idar, the convention moved to elect a Mesa Directiva for the Congreso and to express its gratitude to Clemente Idar for his leadership role in organizing the Congreso. The Mesa was composed of: José P. Reyes, President (Brownsville), Nicasio Idar, Vice President (Laredo), Lisandro Peña, Secretary (Laredo), and as vocales J. A. Garza (unknown), Isidro G. Garza (Kingsville) and Timoteo F. Gloria (Rio Grande).[48]

Unfortunately we do not have a detailed day to day account of the Congreso proceedings. We do have a program of events, short general descriptions of the sessions, and most importantly, a collection of the major speeches (see footnote 47). The remainder of the study will be based on this data.

The Congreso was composed of formal discursos rendered in a high oratorical style together with discusiones and conferencias or what we might call workshops. Music was used extensively and the Congreso opened with a chorus of children singing patriotic songs and the recitation of a patriotic poem by a young boy. The poem, and all of the major speeches are replete with extensive allusions to México and Mexican history and culture. This pervasive nationalistic style is one of the major themes of the Congreso. [49]

Eight other ideas emerged in the speeches. The call for unity against the oppressor was repeated again and again. Lisandro Peña, for example, exhorted the people so oppressed in the past to unite and claim that which was theirs in the face of "malvados y tiranos."[50] J. M. Mora also called for Unity:

> . . . cuando se hayan establecido relaciones de alianza y fraternidad en todas las sociedades mexicanas del Estado de Texas, será una liga tan fuerte y poderosa, revistiendo un carácter tan imponente ante el cual doblegarían la cerviz los políticos más astutos de la época, y sobre todo tendría gran representación social tanto aquí como en México, que llamaría la atención del mundo.[51]

A third major idea is a radical working class ideology again expressed by Mora representing la Sociedad de Obreros Igualdad y Progreso:

> En esta ciudad existió no hace mucho, una gran organización, y vimos como el capital persiguió a los obreros, hasta exterminarlos. El Capital como los políticos, ven un peligro amenazador para sus intereses cuando se trata, como en el asunto que nos ocupa, de unir el elemento obrero. Urge, pues, unir a la clase obrera y principalmente a los mexicanos que residimos en este país.[52]

A fourth idea was language and culture. S. G. Domínguez proposed the establishment of schools to teach both English and Spanish.[53] The Houston delegation sought discussion on the question of whether or not it makes more pedagogical sense to teach children in their native language first.[54] On the program we also find discursos and conferencias on topics such as "Mexicanismo" and "Orígen y Civilización Azteca."[55]

Several speakers addressed themselves to the question of criminal justice and bitterly denounced the lynchings.[56] They were, in fact, seen as one of the motivating reasons for the Congreso.[57] Hortencia Moncayo spoke explicitly on this issue and was congratulated by the Agrupación Protectora of San Antonio who saw her and other active women as "las descendientes de Doña Josefa Ortiz de Domínguez, la Correjidora de Querétero y de Doña Leona Vicario."[58]

Texas-Mexican women and their particular social problems received the attention of the Congreso. A special invitation had been extended to women in the Laredo area.[59] The education of women was a topic on the program and Prof. S. G. Domínguez supported the idea:

... lo absolutamente indispensable es educar a la mujer de nuestra raza para que amolde la tierna inteligencia de sus hijos . . .[60]

Soledad Flores de Peña pursued this idea in addressing the assembly:

... es necesario comprender bien los dedeberes de cada uno y obrar según ellos: yo, como vosotros creo, que el mejor medio para conseguirlo es educar á la mujer, instruirla, darle ánimo a la vez que respetarla.

In return, she promised, women would be true to the tradition of Mexican heroines and develop strength, pride, and intelligence in their children.[61]

A seventh major theme was the social discrimination experienced by Texas-Mexicans. A letter read at the meetings expressed this view:

Dia a dia se ve cruzar el Rio Bravo por grandes grupos de mexicanos que ansiosos de mejor salario para el sostenimiento de la familia van a Texas, y si bien es cierto que consiguen comer y vestir mejor . . . tambien es cierto que con frecuencia son tratados con un vergonzoso desprecio de parte de loa americanos trantandolos como a raza degenerada o inculta . . .[62]

And, with regard to the particular case of school discrimination, the Houston delegation urged the Congreso to make a formal protest to the State Superintendent of Schools.[63]

Finally Telésforo Macías of Laredo urged Texas-Mexicans to practice sound economics so that the community would not find it necessary to go "de rodillas a poner en el mercado de los traficantes del trabajo ajeno, nuestro sudor, nuestro esfuerzo y nuestras energias en publica subasta."[64] Macías also eloquently summarized all of the Texas-Mexican concerns that prompted the Congreso including the lack of criminal justice, discrimination, labor exploitation, cultural retention, and the need for unity.[65]

On September 20, 1911, this first state wide gathering of Texas-Mexicans took a first small step in response to their social grievances. Appropriately enough, it donated $17.35 to the legal defense of León Cárdenas Martínez.[66]

THE ROLE OF LAREDO

The success of the Congreso required at least four elements: dedicated organizers, a medium of communication, money and a protected environment. The Idars and their newspaper provided the first two. The City of Laredo contributed the others. Financial contributions totaling $118.77 had been obtained from small Texas-Mexican merchants in the city and these funds were used to pay for chairs, hall rental, decorations, music and printed materials.[67] The availability of funds, however, only revealed a more fundamental characteristic of the city. The Texas-Mexican influence in its political, social and cultural life provided a supportive context that would have been extremely difficult to obtain elsewhere in 1911 with the possible exception of Brownsville. Laredo's distinctive characteristics had been noted in a March issue of *La Crónica*.[68]

RECEPTION IN THE PRESS

This narrative would not be complete without a discussion of the available newspaper coverage given to the Congreso. According to *La Crónica*, Spanish language newspapers such as *El Demócrata Fronterizo* (Laredo), *El Imparcial* (San Antonio), *El Gallo* (Falfurrias), *El Hachero* (Eagle Pass) and *El Porvenir* (Brownsville) supported the Congreso and its aims.[69] The Anglo-American press reacted somewhat differently, if we can judge this reaction using two major newspapers from the area. The *San Antonio Express* and the *Laredo Weekly Times* reported the general factual details of the Congreso such as the time and place of the meetings and the names of the speakers, but deliberately or otherwise, they missed or misrepresented the tone and content of the meetings.[70]

Throughout both newspapers we find the redundant use of the term *interesting* to describe the speeches. Almost nothing was said about their content and what was expressed does not correspond with the evidence presented in this study. According to the small notices buried in the back pages of both newspapers, the Congreso gathered to celebrate the "Mexican holidays" and to develop education and citizenship programs designed to elevate the "Mexican race." According to the *Express*, José Reyes, the president of the Congreso,

> . . . made an interesting speech in which he said the objects of the Mexican congress were of an uplifting character and that its principal work will be the enlightenment and elevation of the Mexican element in the State of Texas with a view of making them more desirable and better citizens and a credit to the Texas cities in which they make their homes. Several other addresses were made along similar lines and the Congreso seems determined in the work it has undertaken.[71]

The *Laredo Weekly Times* reported that J. M. Mora spoke on ways to relieve Mexican misery and,

> . . . maintained that the best way to bring about this condition was by the carrying out of moral and elevating ideas among the Mexican people, the bettering of their social positions by their own individual efforts to thereby obtain from them a position among the people with whom they make their homes.[72]

Unfortunately we do not have a text of José Reyes' speech, but it would seem improbable that a man expressing such views would have been elected to the presidency of a Congreso gathered to discuss lynchings, discrimination, the loss of land, labor exploitation and cultural nationalism. Mora, as I have shown, clearly spoke of the need for Mexican labor to unite itself over and against capital interests.

POST CONGRESO DEVELOPMENTS

In an effort to provide a continuous long range solution to the multiplicity of Texas-Mexican problems, the Congreso decided to create an on-going state wide organization with local chapters, According to its constitution, la Gran Liga Mexicanista de Beneficiencia y Protección would have these objectives: (1) carry out culture and moral instruction among its members; (2) protect its members when treated unjustly by authorities; (3) protect them against unlawful acts by other persons; (4) create a fund for the organization; and (5) prevent the exclusion of Mexican children from Anglo-American schools, and its motto would be "Por la Raza y Para la Raza."[73] Structurally, la Gran Liga would be composed of a central governing mesa directiva and local chapters each with their own mesa. The central and local mesa would have the same official structure: Director, Vice Director, Secretary, Treasurer, and a Master of Ceremonies. The central mesa was to be elected annually by delegates from the local ligas to the annual convention on September 16th. The central mesa had only the power to carry out those policies already written into the constitution or adopted at the conventions, including the power to hire agents to start local ligas in places of its own choosing, although each delegate was supposed to carry out the task in his local community.[74] The rest of the constitution spelled out the requirements for membership and the rights and obligations of the members. The organization was not limited to U.S. citizens or to males. [75] The first Mesa Directiva of La Gran Liga Mexicanista was composed of: Nicasio Idar, Presidente (Laredo), Basilio Soto, Vice Presidente, (San Antonio), Gerónimo Jiménez, Tesorero (Laredo), Lisandro Peña, Secretario (Laredo). A Master of Ceremonies was not elected and all of the delegates were named as vocales.[76]

This was not the only organization produced by the Congreso. The women were to be heard from again. On October 15, 1911,

> Un grupo de damas tan respetables como bellas se reunieron el domingo como a las diez de la mañana en el Salon de la Respetable Sociedad de Obreros "Igualdad y Progreso" y bajo los auspicios del Congreso Mexicanista organizaron la primera Liga Femenil Mexicanista con el ardiente anhelo de luchar ellas tambien POR LA RAZA Y PARA LA RAZA.[77]

A debate was held to select a more specific name for this women's group and the biographies of several Mexican heroines were read including those of Josefa Ortiz de Domínguez, Leona Vicario, and Doña Manuela Aguado de Abasolo. Apparently no name was chosen. The officers of the new organization were: Presidenta: Jovita Idar, Vice Presidenta: Profa. M. de J. de León, Secretaria: Profa. Soledad F. de Peña, Tesorera: Profa. María Rentería, Consejera General: María Villarreal, Vocales: Sritas. Profas. Luisa Cabrera, Rita Tarvin, Aurelia Peña y Sra. de Silva.[78] Since a number of these women were teachers, the organization immediately undertook a project to provide free instruction for poor Mexican children who could not afford to attend school.[79]

This is as much as we presently know about El Primer Congreso Mexicanista and its offspring organizations. They do not appear to have met again in 1912. The issues of *La Crónica* that I have been able to locate run through December, 1911 with a single issue from April, 1914. No mention is made of the Congreso in this latter issue, nor is it mentioned in other local available newspapers from 1912 to1913. Although there were limited, scattered reports of efforts to organize ligas in a few communities, we must presume that La Gran Liga Mexicanista did not thrive.[80]

ANALYSIS

The data presented permits us to argue that El Primer Congreso Mexicanista de 1911 represents an early organizational effort that anticipated many of the major themes of contemporary Chicanismo. Clearly we have the same pervasive concern for the socio-economic plight of Chicanos. To take three examples: (1) although far more subtle, the problem of social discrimination, particularly in the schools, continues to be a matter of intense interest to Chicanos; (2) the restoration of the land, particularly in Nuevo México, and the plight of Chicano labor, continue to attract contemporary attention; and (3) present day protest against police brutality in Chicano communities echoes the Congreso's denunciations of officially tolerated lynchings in 1910–1911. Yet taken by itself, the common concern with the subordinate socioeconomic position of Chicanos would not alone argue for the Congreso as a precursor to the Chicano movement. In their own way the post 1921 accomodationist groups, Order Sons of America, the LULACS, and the American G.I. Forum, were also generally committed to this basic cause.

The particularly firm and unique ideological parallels between the Congreso and the contemporary period are to be found in their mutual interest in cultural retention and a rejection of assimilation, the rights of women and political unification. Like today's insistence on a personal and institutional commitment to bilingual and bicultural education, the Congreso was equally dedicated to the teaching of the Spanish language and of Mexican history and culture. Indeed we can even find in the Congreso milieu a tendency toward alternative school systems controlled by the community bringing to mind contemporary Chicano efforts in Colorado, the lower Rio Grande Valley and Crystal City, Texas. Similarly today's activist Chicanas can find strong historical precedent for their work in the activity of the Congreso women and la Liga Femenil Mexicanista. Finally the cry for political unity can still be heard. The apparent failure of la Gran Liga Mexicanista to achieve the latter in no way diminishes its importance as an effort that anticipated the current struggle of the Raza Unida Party to provide a single unified Chicano political vehicle for obtaining the same basic goals of the Congreso.[81] The opening remarks of this study referred to the contemporary vision of a quasi-separate nation-state for Chicanos.[82] The Congreso did not evoke a utopian ideal paralleling the contemporary notion of Aztlán. Yet, given their insistence on cultural nationalism and a pure ethnic organization together with the developing Texas-Mexican numerical majority in south Texas, it seems likely that their hypothetical success would have led to a political and cultural Texas-Mexican domination of the area. If not Aztlán, at least a reasonable portion of that vision.

These common interests, the socioeconomic position of Chicanos, cultural retention, women's rights and the unity of the people, argue for the precursory character of El Primer Congreso Mexicanista de 1911. This relationship can perhaps be seen with greater clarity if approached with a conceptual framework.

Professor Ralph Guzmán has provided a simple and useful scheme for categorizing historical Chicano political organizations according to two variables— participation in the U.S. political system and intention to assimilate (see figure 15.1).[83] The data and analysis in the present study permit us to fill in some of the vacancies in his conceptual grid. All of the evidence gathered so far points to an extremely low almost non-existent assimilative intent in the Congreso and the ligas. The U.S. when mentioned was perceived as a problem, an obstacle, an enemy. Learning English, when it was mildly favored, if at all, was a purely utilitarian matter and seemed to have no intrinsic positive value as did the use of Spanish. Indeed we should note the exclusive use of Spanish in the Congreso and in *La Crónica*. Finally, we have a constant appeal to the Mexican cultural past.

The potential and the organizational structure for political participation were clearly present in the Congreso and the ligas. Yet apparently they did not have the opportunity to participate directly in U.S. electoral politics. For these reasons they are characterized as "medium" in terms of this variable. Using low assimilative intent and medium political participation, the Congreso has been located in the appropriate square in a revised version of Guzmán's scheme (see figure 15.2).

Figure 15.1. Social and Political Intent of Chicano Organizations as Posited by Ralph Guzmán

Social Intent (Assimilation)

		High	Medium	Low
Political Intent (Participation)	High		Mexican-American Political Association (MAPA), 1959 Political Association of Spanish-Speaking Organizations (PASSO), 1960	
	Medium	League of United Latin American Citizens (LULAC), 1927 The Order of the Sons of America (OSA), 1920	Community Service Organization (CSO), 1947 American G.I. Forum, 1948	
	Low			Mexican Liberal Party (MLP), 1906

Figure 15.2. Revision of Social and Political Intent of Chicano Organizations

Social Intent (Assimilation)

		High	Medium	Low
Political Intent (Participation)	High		MAPA, 1960 PASSO, 1960	Gran Liga Mexicanista, 1991 Raza Unida Party, 1970
	Medium	LULAC, 1927 OSA, 1920	CSO, 1947 American G.I. Forum, 1948	Primer Congreso Mexicanista, 1910–11 Chicano Movement 1965–70
	Low			MLP, 1906

In both respects the Congreso and its milieu greatly resemble the 1967–70 Chicano movement ideologically, particularly in Texas. They were both phenomena marked by a strong sense of cultural nationalism, and, therefore, a low assimilative intent. Neither, however, actively and fully participated in the political process. On the same two criteria, the contemporary movement has been located in the same conceptual category with the Congreso.[84] Had la Gran Liga Mexicanista developed and participated in the U.S. political process on the same ideological grounds as the Congreso, it probably would have resembled the contemporary Raza Unida Party in Texas which developed directly from the Chicano movement.[85] Like Raza Unida, la Gran Liga would have been the institutionalized agency resulting from a formative ideological, organizational phase. The actual Texas Raza Unida Party and a hypothetically successful Gran Liga Mexicanista are conjoined in figure 15.2.

CONCLUSIONS

These findings permit us to fill in previously empty historical and conceptual slots thereby altering the political history of Chicanos in a significant manner. Whereas before it was probably correct to speak of a pre 1921 apolitical period and of a unique and novel post 1965 period, we now have to contend with an organized, militant, nationalist, pro-feminist social movement appearing in 1911.

The Congreso's scholarly importance is clear, but in arguing its precursory relationship to the contemporary scene, this study perhaps has accomplished more than a scholarly exercise. Professor Juan Gómez-Quiñones has called for a "union of history as discipline and history as action on behalf of a community in its struggle for survival."[86] If this new knowledge of historical ideological precedents lends moral and intellectual support to the contemporary struggle, this work has responded adequately to this call.

NOTES

My appreciation to Linda X. Jiménez for her research assistance on this project.

1. Alfredo Cuéllar, "Perspective on Politics" in *Mexican Americans.* Joan Moore, ed. (Englewood Cliffs, N.J.: Prentice Hall, 1970), pp. 137–158. See also Rodolfo Acuña, *Occupied America: The Chicano's Struggle Toward Liberation* (San Francisco: Canfield Press, 1972) particularly chps. 9–10, and Armando Rendón, *Chicano Manifesto* (New York: Macmillan, 1971).

2. Cuéllar, pp. 137–156. For broader yet similar analyses, see Rodolfo Alvarez, "The Psycho-Historical and Socioeconomic Development of the Chicano Community in the United States," *Social Science Quarterly,* Vol. 53, No. 4 (March, 1973), pp. 920–942; Jesús Chavarria, "A Precise and Tentative Bibilography on Chicano History," *Aztlán,* Vol. I, No. 1 (Spring, 1970), pp. 133–141; Juan Gómez-Q. "Toward a Perspective on Chicano History," *Aztlán,* Vol. II, No. 2 (Fall, 1971), pp. 1–49: Ralph Guzmán, "Politics and Policies of the Mexican-American Community," in *California Politics and Policies,* Eugene P. Dvorin, ed. (Palo Alto, Cal.: Addison Wesley, 1966), pp. 350–385, and Miguel D. Tirado, "Mexican-American Community Political Organization, the Key to Chicano Political Power," *Aztlán,* Vol. I, No. 1 (Spring, 1970), pp. 53–78. Carey McWilliams' useful but incomplete *North From Mexico* has been superceded by Rodolfo Acuña's *Occupied America: The Chicano's Struggle Toward Liberation* (San Francisco: Canfield Press, 1972) and Matt Meir and Feliciano Rivera, *The Chicanos: A History of Mexican Americans* (New York: Hill and Wang, 1972). Neither of these general histories departs significantly from the analysis cited above. A study that sees cultural retention as a basic concern of the so-called assimilationist period is Charles Ray Chandler's, "The Mexican-American Protest Movement In Texas," Ph.D. dissertation, Department of Sociology, Tulane University, 1968. However, Chandler does not deal with the contemporary Chicano movement.

3. Cuéllar, pg. 155.

4. Prof. David J. Weber has published a speech from the Congreso and a brief commentary. See "Por La Raza y Para La Raza—Congreso Mexicanista, 1911," in *Foreigners in Their Native Land: Historical Roots of the Mexican American* (Albuquerque: University of New Mexico Press, 1973), pp. 248–251. This publication appeared independently and somewhat after my research note "El Primer Congreso Mexicanista de 1911: A Note on Research in Progress," *Aztlán,* Vol. III, No. 1 (Spring, 1972), pg. 171. Weber's commentary misses some important issues discussed at the Congreso and incorrectly identifies León Cárdenas Martínes as the victim of the Thorndale lynching. (See pp. 223–24 of this study.) To my knowledge this is the only scholarly work on the Congreso.

5. D. W. Meinig, *Imperial Texas: An Interpretive Essay in Cultural Geography.* (Austin: University of Texas Press, 1969), pp. 54–56.

6. Victor Nelson-Cisneros, "La Clase Trabajadora en Texas, 1920–1940," (Unpublished Ms., Center for Mexican-American Studies, University of Texas at Austin), pp. 3–4.

7. Meinig, pp. 98–101.

8. Américo Paredes, *With His Pistol in His Hand* (Austin: University of Texas Press, 1971), pp. 31–32. See also Carey McWillams, *North From Mexico* (New York: Greenwood, 1968), pp. 112–114.

9. *La Crónica,* April 18, 1914, pp. 1–2.

10. See any masthead of *La Crónica* (1910–1911), Texas Newspaper Collection, University of Texas at Austin.

11. "El Primer Año de Vida" *La Crónica* (Jan. 1, 1910), pg. 1. The author is currently at work on the preliminary research for a collective biography of this remarkable family whose members continue to be active participants in Chicano affairs today.

12. *The Chaparral*, (Feb. 18, 1899), pg. 3. "Mr. N. Idar, Assistant City Marshall and Editor of *La Crónica*, we regret to state has been quite sick the early part of this week." See "Progreso de 'La Crónica,'" LC (Sept. 3, 1910), pg. 1.

> Con elementos propios principiamos in publicación de nuestro semanario *La Crónica* en Enero del año pasado, viniendo a ser la segunda época de su existencia.
> Nunca creimos que llegaría en un año de vida a sentar la reputación y popularidad de que hoy goza tanto en la frontera Norte de México como en Texas, California, Arizona, y Nuevo México.

13. *San Antonio Light and Gazette* (Nov. 4, 1910), pg. 1.

14. "All Quiet in Edwards County—Lynching at Rock Springs Done By Americans, Says Ranger Captain." *San Antonio Daily Express* (Nov. 22, 1910), pg. 10.

15. Stanley R. Ross, *Francisco I. Madero: Apostle of Democracy* (New York: Columbia University Press, 1955), pg. 137.

16. "Barbarismos" *La Crónica* (Nov. 12, 1910), pg. 1.

17. "Cobarde Infame e Inhumano Lynchamiento de un Jovencito Mexicano en Thorndale, Milam Co., Texas," *La Crónica* (June 29, 1911), pg. 1. The accused were found not guilty. See "Lo Mismo de Siempre" *La Crónica* (Nov. 16, 1911), pg. 1.

18. "Valiente Cobardia de los Linchadores de Thorndale, Texas, Los Estados Unidos y Mexico Nada Pueden Hacer Para El Castigo de los Criminales—Represalias Unica Solución Posible," *La Crónica* (July 13, 1911), pg. 1.

19. "Junta de Indignacion—El Infame hecho de Thorndale gita á los Mexicanos de Bay City" *La Crónica* (July 20, 1911), pg. 6.

20. "Traducción: Integra de la narración que hizo el Lic. George Estes á alungos periodicos como Defensor del niño Leén Cárdenas Martínez, Jr., en el Proceso que se le enstruyo en Pecos, Texas el 29 de Julio de 1911." *La Crónica* (Oct. 26, 1911), pg. 2.

21. "Solicitud de Indulto," *La Crónica* (Aug. 24, 1911), pg. 1.

22. "Claim Mexican Lad is Not Murderer" *San Antonio Light* (Sept. 12, 1911), pg. 1.

23. J. J. Mercado, "Facultad de Perdonar—Traducción" *La Crónica* (Sept. 21, 1911), pg. 4.

24. "La Labor de *La Crónica*" (March 2, 1911), pg. 5.

25. "Los Niños Mexicanos en Texas" *La Crónica* (Nov. 26, 1910), pg. 3; "La Exclusión de los Niños Mexicanos en la Mayor Parte de las Escuelas Oficiales de Texas es Positiva." (Dec. 17, 1910), pg. 1; "Tanto los Niños Mexicanos como los Mexico-Americanos son excluídos de las Escuelas Oficiales—¿ya se Olvidaron los Tratados de Guadalupe?" (Dec. 24, 1910), pg. 1; "La Exclusión en el Condado de Guadalupe," and "Los Mexicanos de San Angelo Demandan a Los Sindicos de las Escuelas Públicas" (Dec. 31, 1970), pg. 1; "La Exclusión de los Niños Mexicanos de la Escuelas Americanas En Algunas Partes de Texas" (Jan. 26, 1911), pg. 3; "La Exclusión en las Escuelas de los Condados de Frio, Bee, Hays, Bastrop, Comal, Caldwell, Blanco, etc. etc." (Feb. 9, 1911), pg. 1.

26. A. V. Negra, "Por La Raza—La Niñez Mexicana en Texas," *La Crónica* (Aug. 10, 1911), pg. 1. (See also J. J. Mercado, "El Mexicano en Texas" *La Crónica* (Sept. 14, 1911), pg. 2 expressing concern for the linguistic deterioration already underway.)

27. A. V. Negra, "La Conservación del Nacionalismo," *La Crónica* (Aug. 17, 1911), pg. 1.

28. Ibid.

29. "En Pro de la Raza Mexicana del Estado de Texas," *La Crónica* (Nov. 26, 1910), pg. 1.

30. "A 'El Imparcial de Texas'," *La Crónica* (Dec. 10, 1910), pg. 4.

31. A. V. Negra, "Por la Raza—La Niñez Mexicana en Texas," *La Crónica* (Aug. 10, 1911), pg. 1.

32. Clemente Idar, "Nuestro Deber en Este País: Solidaridad y Altruismo," *La Crónica* (Dec. 24, 1910), pg. 1.

33. Ibid.

34. "Excitativa del Gran Concillo de la Orden Caballeros de Honor á la raza Mexicana," *La Crónica* (Dec. 17, 1910) oja suelta inserted in newspaper.

35. "A la Orden Caballeros de Honor de Brownsville, Texas," *La Crónica* (Jan. 12, 1911), pg. 3.

36. "Un Gran Excitativo Al Gran Concilio de la Orden Caballeros de Honor," *La Crónica* (Feb. 2, 1911), pg. 1.

37. "Los Elementos Mas Conspicuous de Laredo Influyen Cerca del G. Concilio de la Orden Caballeros de Honor," *La Crónica* (March 16, 1911).

38. Nicasio Idar, "Agrupación Protectora Mexicana," *La Crónica* (July 13, 1911), pg. 2. See Américo Paredes, *With His Pistol in His Hand*, (Austin: University of Texas Press, 1958) for the full account of Gregorio Cortez.

39. "Una Gran Convención Se Reúne en Laredo," *La Crónica* (Jul. 27, 1911), pg. 4.

40. "El Congreso Mexicanista. ¿Qué Es y Qué se Propone?" *La Crónica* (Aug. 24, 1911), pg. 2.

41. "Para El Congreso Mexicanista" *La Crónica* (Sept. 7, 1911), pg. 4.

42. "Mas Delegados" *La Crónica* (Sept. 14, 1911), pg. 1.

43. "Otra Victima del Odio Yankee" *La Crónica* (Sept. 14, 1911), pg. 4.

44. E. R. Tarver, *Laredo, the Gateway Between the United States and Mexico*, Laredo Immigration Society (1889), pg. 1.

45. "El Congreso Mexicanista" *Fiat Lux* (Sept. 15, 1911), pg. 1.

46. That morning a general invitation to the public had appeared In *La Crónica*. "Invitación" *La Crónica* (Sept. 14, 1911), pg. 1.

47. *Primer Congreso Mexicanista, Verificado en Laredo, Texas, EEUU de A. Los Dias 14 al 22 de Septiembre de 1911. Discursos y Conferencias Por la Raza y Para la Raza*. Tipografia de N. Idar (1912), pg. 1.

48. Ibid., pg. 5. We have no evidence concerning voting procedures and privileges.

49. Ibid., pp. 3–5, 10–13. *The San Antonio Express* (Sept. 17, 1911), pg. 6 reports a number of patriotic speeches, the display of Mexican flags and shouts of "¡Viva Mexico!" and "¡Viva Hidalgo" during the meetings on the 16th.

50. Ibid., pg. 13.

51. Ibid., pg. 17.

52. Ibid., pg. 16.

53. Ibid., pg. 19.

54. Ibid., pg. 31.

55. Ibid., pg. 4.

56. Ibid., pg. 26.

57. Ibid., pg. 1.

58. Ibid., pp. 26–27.

59. "A La Mujer Mexicana de Ambos Laredos" *La Crónica* (Sept. 14, 1911), pg. 1.

60. *Primer Congreso Mexicanista*, pg. 20.

61. Ibid., pg. 24.

62. Ibid., pg. 14.

63. Ibid., pg. 31.

64. Ibid., pg. 34.

65. Ibid., pp. 28–30.

66. "Al Beneficio de León Cárdenas Martínez," *La Crónica* (Sept. 21, 1911), pg. 1.

67. "Corte de Caja," *La Crónica* (Sept. 28, 1911), pg. 4.

68. "La Labor de *La Crónica*," *La Crónica* (March 2, 1911), pg. 5.

69. See "La Convención de los Caballeros de Honor y El Primer Congreso Mexicanista," *El Demócrata Fronterizo* (Sept. 23, 1911), pg. 4, "Congreso de Mexicanistas" *La Crónica* (April 20, 1911), pg. 4, and "Comentarios de la Prensa Sobre el Congreso Mexicanista," *La Crónica* (Sept. 28, 1911), pg. 3.

70. There was only one exception. "Mexicans May Protest Against Separate Schools. Matter Is Placed Before Congreso Mexicanista in Session Now at Laredo" *San Antonio Express* (Sept. 17, 1911), pg. 16.

71. "Form New Organization, Congreso Mexicanista Is Brought Into Existence" *San Antonio Express* (Sept. 16, 1911), pg. 9. See also the *Express* for Sept. 15, 1911 (pg. 9), Sept. 18, 1911 (pg. 7), Sept. 19, 1911 (pg. 2), and Sept. 20, 1911 (pg. 7).

72. "The Mexican Congress—Interesting Subject Discussed" *Laredo Weekly Times* (Sept. 24, 1911), pg. 4. See also the *Times* for Sept. 17, 1911 (pg. 10) and Sept. 24, 1911 (pp. 6, 8, 10).

73. "Constitución de la Gran Liga Mexicanista de Beneficiencia y Proteccion" in *Primer Congreso Mexicanista*, pg. 39.

74. "Constitución . . . ," pp. 39–42.

75. "Constitución . . . ," pp. 39–40, particularly Cap. II, Art. 3 on pg. 39.

76. "Para Constituyentes de la Comisión Consejera Del Congreso Mexicanista" *La Crónica* (Sept. 28, 1911) pg. 4.

77. "Liga Femenil Mexicanista" *La Crónica* (Oct. 19, 1911) pg. 1.

78. Ibid., pg. 1.

79. "La Liga Femenil Mexicanista" *La Crónica* (Dec. 7, 1911) pg. 1.

80. See "*La Crónica* publicará Semanariamente Los Progresos del Congreso Mexicanista" *La Crónica* (Sept. 28, 1911) pg. 4 and "Liga Mexicanista, No. 2" *La Crónica* (Oct. 12, 1911) pg. 1.

81. Rodolfo Acuña, *Occupied America: The Chicano's Struggle Toward Liberation* (San Francisco: Canfield Press, 1972), pp. 236–237.

82. Armando Rendón, *Chicano Manifesto* (New York: Macmillan, 1971), pg. 168.

83. Ralph Guzmán, "Politics and Policies of the Mexican American Community," in *California Politics and Policies,* Eugene P. Dvorin, ed., (Palo Alto, Cal.: Addison-Wesley, 1966), pg. 374.

84. There are also strong similarities in the social-behavioral determinants of these phenomena as social movements. The author is currently at work on a study of these relationships.

85. Acuña, pp. 234–236.

86. Juan Gómez-Quiñones "Toward a Perspective on Chicano History" *Aztlán*, Vol. 4 No. 2 (Fall, 1971), pg. 39.

QUESTIONS

1. In notes 4 and 5, Limón lists the many studies that see the Chicano movement as a new phenomenon. What can be said about such a game of truth? What are the political benefits/disadvantages of such "invisible" knowledge?

2. What is the process by which U.S. criminal, educational, and civil laws become tools for the oppression of a particular set of human bodies? Why would Texas Mexicans still demand "justice" and plan to have a nationwide political association to place themselves "under the protection of the law"?

3. How is the voice of the Texas Mexicans appropriated and suppressed? How is it invested with power and institutionalized to impact social reality?

4. Are there any hidden assumptions revealed in the description of the Mexican by the Anglo press?

5. After reading the articles about the Chicano movement, do you agree with Limón that the Congreso anticipated its major themes? In particular, is it reasonable to argue that either one or both advocates separatism or, on the contrary, requesting equal treatment under the law or what we call public citizenship?

* 16 *

EPILOGUE FROM *DECADE OF BETRAYAL*

Francisco E. Balderrama and Raymond Rodríguez

Repatriation is a game of truth whereby certain members of the U.S. body politic are expelled. As is to be expected, questions of who, why, and how many are a matter of politics, not science, but what is important is that this event illustrates the fragility of the political status of being a "Mexican" in the United States. If you were a Mexican entering the United States prior to 1908, there were no regulations on border crossing; in fact, there was no one to keep a record of your entry. If you entered before 1917 you were not required to pay a head tax or to pass a literacy test (unless your labor was needed, in which case you were exempt). If you entered before 1924 (when the Border Patrol was created) it was not even a crime to enter the United States "illegally." After 1924, however, these new laws would be applied retroactively and make you an "illegal" (or a "communist" if you were involved in union or social causes) and subject you to deportation or repatriation.[1]

How many Mexican human bodies were in the United States by the time of the Repatriation and the 1930s depression, whose concurrence was not coincidental? Here we must confront an impossible task, precisely because of the fragile subjectivity of the U.S. Mexican. In the 1920s, the U.S. Census Bureau counted U.S. Mexicans as members of the white population. In the 1930 census, however, Mexicans were defined as a separate "race," even as efforts were made to separate recent arrivals from those who were "territorial citizens." According to the census of 1930, there were 1,422,533 Mexicans in the United States. This number does not include undocumented Mexicans and it is also marred by the thousands who were already on the move due to Repatriation pressures. One calculation is that an additional one million Mexicans entered the United States without the proper documentation.[2] And how many were deported? Anywhere between one half and one million Mexicans, many of whom were born in the United States and therefore were U.S. citizens. The actual bodies repatriated belonged in many categories: laborers, craftsmen, business people, merchants, shopkeepers, farmers, property owners, women (widows, single, abandoned), children, teenagers, children in county orphanages, the old and infirm, bedridden and terminally ill patients, the mentally ill. The methods used ranged from seduction and inducement to threats of bodily harm, terrorism, and scare tactics.[3] By defining people along ethnic and cultural as opposed to national lines, U.S. officials deprived American children of Mexican descent of rights guaranteed them by the U.S. Constitution.

In these games of racial truths, even the undesirable Mexican, "who had no idea of becoming a citizen or a menace" (i.e., they were deportable), was preferred over the undeportable "Porto Rican Negro."[4] Indeed, most U.S. Mexicans did not become U.S. citizens, because they would still be viewed and treated as Mexicans anyway, and because as Mexican citizens they could seek the support of the Mexican Consul and secure justice. It is the same reason an American living in Mexico would prefer to remain a U.S. citizen.[5] What we see here is a quest for acceptance and belonging in the society in which one must live.

In terms of the role that institutions play, it is pertinent to note that the Bureau of Immigration was first placed in the U.S. Department of Labor. In 1933 its function was expanded to include naturalization and in 1940 the Immigration and Naturalization Service (INS), as it was by then called, was transferred to the Department of Justice. In effect, the root cause of the Repatriation was the belief that getting rid of "aliens" would free up enough jobs for U.S. Americans. This illustrates the crisis that arises among members of a society when there are economic problems or the impact of the lack of production on social relations (see appendix 6).

What follows is a personal note from editor Vázquez to illustrate the personal dimensions of this event:

> Allow me the liberty to share my personal experience with the Repatriation Program. My mother, born in Colorado in 1926, was repatriated at the age of six, along with her parents and five siblings. She would have had to live in the United States until she was fourteen years old in order for me to get my U.S. citizenship *jus sanguinis* (through bloodline). I argued with the Immigration and Naturalization Service for thirty years that I should be given a certificate of citizenship, because she *would have been here* if she had not been kicked out. After three decades, however, I had to obtain my U.S. citizenship through "naturalization." What strikes me about this event is its invisibility. Neither my grandparents, nor my mother, nor my in-laws ever talked about it. The clerk that dealt with my file told me that in over thirty years that she had worked in INS, she never heard about the Repatriation. How do you hide one million experiences, many of which represent a violation of the civil rights of American citizens?

It is all in the power of a discourse that erases memories that are not in agreement with the image of a freedom-loving country that is incapable of doing wrong. Memories of injustices, however, have a way of coming back. This is illustrated by Francisco E. Balderrama and Raymond Rodriguez's book, from which the following piece is excerpted, and other recent publications and movies such as *Mi Familia/My Family* and *Born in East L.A.* Space limitations, unfortunately, prevent us from including additional personal accounts regarding this apocalyptic event.

In the following text, Francisco and Raymond summarize the main issues, implications, and consequences of the Repatriation. It is a mere glimpse of the trials and tribulations of the human bodies involved in one of the great mass movements in history. Hopefully, it will motivate you to learn more about it.

NOTES AND SUGGESTED READINGS

1. Abraham Hoffman, *Unwanted Mexican Americans in the Great Depression* (Tucson: University of Arizona Press, 1995), 50.

2. Francisco E. Balderrama and Raymond Rodríguez, *Decade of Betrayal: Mexican Repatriation in the 1930s* (Albuquerque: University of New Mexico Press, 1995), 7.

3. Balderrama and Rodríguez, *Decade of Betrayal*, 107–11.

4. Hoffman, *Unwanted Mexican Americans,* 29.

5. Hoffman, *Unwanted Mexican Americans,* 20.

No lloro, pero me acuerdo. [I don't cry, but I remember.]

—*Dicho Mexicano* [Mexican proverb]

The foregoing work chronicles the tragedy of a people who, in spite of being maligned and mistreated by American society, refused to surrender to adversity. Like other immigrant groups, they were proud of the contributions they made to their adopted country. However, during the Great Depression, American society chose to disregard the significant role that Mexicans had played in creating the nation's wealth. Instead, regardless of their place of birth, it became fashionable to blame Mexicans for the country's economic ills. A relentless campaign was launched to get rid of the pariahs by shipping them to Mexico. Since many of the Mexicans had been actively recruited to come and work in the United States, their ruthless expulsion was an ironic twist of fate. The vendetta created the first major contingent of displaced refugees in the twentieth century.

One of the most tragic aspects of the movement was the wholesale violation of basic human rights. When individuals were caught in INS raids, they were summarily deported without being informed of or accorded their legal rights. The wanton disregard of legal constraints in denying deportees their constitutional rights was so flagrant that groups as diverse as the Los Angeles Bar Association, the Wickersham Commission, industrialists, and ranchers felt compelled to condemn the illegal tactics, but to no avail. Protests about the injustice were drowned out by the roar of approval from opportune politicians, labor unions, and civic or patriotic groups. In 1942, another minority group, the Japanese, also learned the bitter lesson that constitutional guarantees are meaningless when mob hysteria is accorded institutional or legal status.

In many instances, the same charges of illegal action can be made regarding the repatriation efforts. As in the days of slavery, when families were split asunder by selling certain members "downriver," Mexican families suffered the same fate. Wives often refused to return to Mexico with their husbands because their children were American born and were entitled to remain in the United States. The situation became truly heart wrenching when older children refused to join their parents on the trek south. Younger children who had no choice but to accompany their parents suffered wholesale violations of their citizenship rights. This accounts for the fact that approximately 60 percent of those summarily expelled were children who had been born in the United States and were legally American citizens.

Lacking concrete or convincing substance were the three facetious claims often used to justify or at least to rationalize banishing the Mexicans: Jobs would be created for "real Americans"; cutting the welfare rolls would save taxpayers money; and "those people" would be better off in Mexico with their "own kind"! In every case, the allegations begged or ignored the question. With unemployment rates in the colonias averaging 50 percent or more, due to decrees forbidding their hiring in government or public projects, the Mexicans had been effectively eliminated as a rival working force. Many private employers were also scare headed by mobs into firing their Mexican workers. Furthermore, since the Mexicans constituted less than 1 percent of the nation's total population, few jobs would have been made available even if all of them had been shipped to Mexico.

The same false claims were made concerning welfare costs and projected savings. Mexican families with American-born children qualified for welfare assistance if the family could meet residency requirements and prove entitlement. However, even in Los Angeles and Detroit, the cities with the largest number of Mexicans on relief, they constituted 10 percent or less of the total number of welfare recipients. In truth, the anticipated savings were impossible to achieve for the simple reason that 85 percent of the approximately twenty million people on welfare were native-born or naturalized Americans. Yet politicians and the media adroitly created and nurtured the impression in the public's mind that Mexicans constituted the overwhelming majority of those on the public dole. The baseless and misleading charges were merely a ploy to inflame an overwrought public's anti-Mexican passions.

Equally inane were repeated attempts to justify the expulsion of the Mexicans by claiming that they would be better off in Mexico among relatives and friends. The irony was that Mexican families residing in barrios or colonias were already living among close relatives and friends. Many of them had resided in the United States for such a long time, often their entire adult life, that they did not have close friends or relatives in Mexico. Bearing the traumatic burden of being shipped "back" to Mexico were those least able to cope with their plight: the children. Shipping them to Mexico so they could be with "their own kind" was absolutely absurd. Although of Mexican ancestry, they considered themselves to be Americans and many of them spoke only a limited amount of Spanish. To them, historically and culturally, Mexico was a totally foreign country.

Nonetheless, welfare authorities reasoned that young children rightfully belonged with their parents and should accompany the family to Mexico. This convenient rationale relieved repatriation authorities of any blame or responsibility for failing to protect the rights of the American-born children. Regretfully, no one seemed to care about what was happening to them. Their personal identity and sense of self-worth were stripped from them without any qualms and hardly a ripple of protest in their behalf. The prevailing attitude was that "a Mexican was a Mexican," regardless of birthright.

The assumption that a Mexican was a Mexican prevailed in both the United States and Mexico, but for different reasons. The Mexican government accorded dual citizenship to children who were born abroad and whose parents were Mexican citizens. This dual citizenship was intended to enable them to move freely between the respective countries. It was also used as an inducement to relocate and settle in Mexico, with all the rights and privileges enjoyed by native-born individuals. It was hoped that they would not only augment Mexico's relatively small population, but would also contribute to the nation's socioeconomic stability.

In American society, the attitude of "once a Mexican, always a Mexican" enabled authorities to take collective action against the entire Spanish-speaking population. They were not hampered by the task of having to differentiate between Mexican Nationals and native-born Mexican Americans. This situation made racial and anti-Mexican propaganda easier to disseminate and more readily acceptable, and created a situation in which people blindly condoned illegal and discriminatory acts against a defenseless minority. The public's support dramatically eased the awesome task of expelling, with complete impunity, hundreds of thousands of people whose only crime was poverty.

Despite the odds arraigned against them, most Mexicans struggled to maintain their self-respect and independence. Three significant examples attest to their dauntless perseverance and their determination to survive. As has been previously stated, the overwhelming majority disdained applying for welfare and attempted to survive by a variety of innovative means. A resourceful lot, they often managed to cope with the relentless and bruising depression better than did their Anglo counterparts. Families who had lost their breadwinners were subjected to prolonged unemployment or were split apart by deportation or repatriation; or they were aided by extended families, friends, and neighbors. In most barrios and colonias, a common bond evolved in order to help each other survive. Families who had always paid their own way were reluctant to admit defeat and seek any type of government assistance. In many instances, that attitude served as the impetus for families who decided to return to Mexico voluntarily.

Disdaining any sort of government interference, the vast majority of Mexicans who lived adjacent to, or within driving distance of, the border simply loaded their personal belongings into the family sedan and headed south. Individuals who owned a truck and were returning to Mexico often found it convenient to take two or three families with them. This enabled the owner either to charge them a small fee or to share the trip's expenses. Women traveling alone or with young children welcomed the opportunity to hitch a ride with family or friends. Given the perilous nature of the journey, it was always best to travel with several companions. The highly individualistic Mexicans found it more to their liking to ignore the bureaucratic red tape on both sides of the border and to make their own arrangements.

The individualistic and philosophical attitude of the Mexicans illustrates the third aspect of their struggle to survive. Even during the darkest days of the Great Depression, they persevered in attempts to overcome racial discrimination, social injustice, segregated schooling, and unfair treatment in the workplace. Protests, demonstrations, and strikes were utilized in attempts to achieve their goals. In pursuing their aims, however, they were often set upon by hoodlums, goon squads, and local police and sheriff's deputies. Despite the beatings inflicted, barrio leaders repeatedly exhorted their compatriots not to abandon the struggle to improve the quality of life for themselves and for their children.

Exacerbating their plight and adding to their dilemma were the routine violations of legal rights by the judicial system. Basic procedural rights were commonly ignored as judges, sworn to uphold the law, turned their chambers into nothing more than kangaroo courts. The news media joined in discrediting the protestors and their goals by accusing them of being un-American or labeling them as communist agitators. With the willing connivance of the Labor Department and the Immigration Service, and the collaboration of police and the court system, trumped-up charges were used to justify deporting Mexicans who advocated ending discrimination, better working conditions, or desegregated schools.

Plagued by such adverse circumstances and envisioning little change for the better, many destitute and desperate Mexicans viewed returning to Mexico, if not as a boon, at least as a change for the better. Official releases on both sides of the border emphasized the benefits to be reaped by those who took advantage of the opportunity to return and colonize productive lands awaiting the plow. Using the work habits and skills acquired in El Norte, they would be able to help Mexico achieve new heights in agricultural and industrial production. The newcomers would also enrich the country's social development by augmenting the nucleus of the emerging middle class. Politically, they could infuse the nation with the ideals of a viable democratic system. Optimistic returnees and government officials envisioned Mexico assuming the role of "los yanquis" of Latin America. With the help of the repatriates, Mexico would be propelled into the twentieth century.

In actuality, the results were radically different from what the repatriates had envisioned. The dreams, hopes, and lofty aspirations failed to materialize. The task of resettling and assimilating the horde of people returning to *la madre patria* overwhelmed the Mexican bureaucracy. The sheer numbers and the enormity and complex nature of the vast undertaking taxed the government's ability to respond effectively. Farmland—vital to successful colonization and the crucial factor on which the nation's prosperity would be based—was not available in sufficient quantities. Despite the government's good intentions and its heroic efforts to build dams and irrigation canals, there were simply too many people who desperately needed help. Unfortunately, official edicts or decrees could not change the climate or the topography.

Lacking the opportunity to colonize and having no place else to go, most repatriates gradually drifted back into their native villages and ranchitos. Some opted to settle in the larger cities in the hope of earning a decent living. For the majority of the newcomers, the scenario they had foreseen when they made up their minds to go back to Mexico remained an illusion. Instead of being welcomed home with open arms, acquiring good land, and regaining their self-respect, they were trapped in a morass of grinding poverty rivaling the one they thought they had left behind in the United States.

Compounding their plight and adding to their misery was the fact that their status and well-being were issues that often became expedient political footballs. Politicos were aware that efforts to aid the resettlement of repatriates did not set well with rank-and-file Mexicans. Despite official policy, many politicians and their supporters believed that the nation's fiscal and material resources should be used to

benefit loyal sons and daughters who had stayed home. Repatriates accused antago-
nists of conveniently overlooking the financial remuneration consisting of millions
of dollars that they had remitted to families and relatives in Mexico during more
prosperous times. Each group viewed the other as a bunch of ingrates.

Many Mexicans felt that the expectations and demands of the repatriates were
unwarranted and that they should stop badgering the Mexican government, who
could ill afford to grant them the aid they so desperately needed. Mexicanos believed
those forced to return to Mexico should have exhausted all legal means available to
them before succumbing to their fate. Instead, the repatriates had readily acquiesced
in their own expatriation. By doing so, they had completely absolved the United
States of any responsibility for their well-being, and this was especially true for those
with American-born children. The children were deemed to be the responsibility of
the American, rather than the Mexican, government.

In hindsight, the protestors were undoubtedly correct. The callous attitude of
American authorities exposed the repatriated children to a cruel and virtually unten-
able fate. Ultimately, it was the children who bore the brunt of rejection and discrimination. They were neither Americans nor Mexicans as defined by their
respective cultures. In the U.S. they were unilaterally classified as Mexicans, regardless of birthright. In Mexico they were regarded as *pochos, tejanos,* or even *gringos.*
For teenagers, adjustment was especially difficult and they constantly badgered their
parents to return to the United States.

The Mexican press reacted with hostility toward "ingrates" who sought to leave.
Their departure was viewed as a slap in the face to Mexico's generous hospitality.
The media failed to understand the urge that tormented the young repatriates and
compelled them to return to their rightful homeland. The predictable reaction was
an example of the perverse dilemma that beset the Mexican press. Failure to support
and expound the government's official policy could have dire consequences. In com-
menting on the problems associated with the repatriates, the press had to be careful
to absolve the government of any responsibility for the deplorable situation. While
lauding the government's efforts, it unmercifully castigated the United States for its
inhumane and racist actions.

Although not faced with the constraints that hindered the Mexican press, few
English-language newspapers in the United States protested the injustices perpetrated against Mexican Nationals or against American citizens who happened to be
of Mexican ancestry. While legal justification could be made for getting rid of
unwanted aliens, it was an entirely different matter to deprive American citizens of
their constitutional rights solely because of the accident of birth. Instead of protest-
ing, the media acquiesced in the despicable action by commending authorities for
their zeal and success in getting rid of as many Mexicans as possible. The failure to
speak out in behalf of the Mexican community remains a black, irredeemable blot
on the record of the American press.

In assessing the treatment accorded repatriation and deportation by the media, it
must be borne in mind that neither the American nor the Mexican government was
anxious to have its role in the tragedy publicly disclosed. The United States feared

that the massive repatriation and deportation efforts could have negative repercussions upon its relations with countries in Latin America. It did not want to exacerbate the situation at a time when it was seeking to curtail immigration from the Western Hemisphere. To counter the adverse publicity, emissaries were sent abroad to convey assurances of America's goodwill. The United States was zealous in its efforts not to be perceived as a heartless society that turned its back on indigent immigrants in their hour of need.

The Mexican government also sought to minimize the repatriation issue in order not to alarm its own people about the magnitude of the problem. It diligently sought to avoid any embarrassment due to its inability to cope with the situation. Additionally, the Mexican government was caught between the horns of the proverbial dilemma: Since it was pursuing its own policy of expulsion against the Chinese and other unwanted individuals, it was not in a position to protest the expulsion of its Nationals from the United States. Mexico judiciously supported the right of every nation to determine who would be allowed to reside within its borders.

Obviously, authorities in both countries would have been acutely embarrassed if an accurate record of the number of Mexicans shipped to Mexico had been kept. However, a definitive body count is not essential to the essence of the tragic experience. Of greater importance were the consequences suffered by those forced to depart as well as those who remained behind. The loss of approximately one-third of the Mexican population in the United States augured an uncertain future for residents of *México de afuera*. Barrios and colonias were not only physically gutted; they lost a large cadre of dedicated community leaders. More significantly, they suffered the loss of a generation of young, intelligent minds.

The loss effectively stifled the socioeconomic development of Mexican colonias in the United States. Seemingly, the community had to await the coming of age of a new generation unencumbered by the stifling experience of a decade of betrayal before recovering from the ordeal. That may help to explain why the "Chicano movement" did not occur until twenty-five years after the end of the ominous decade. One can only speculate what might have been achieved in the intervening period if the Mexican community had not been devastated by the massive travesty unleashed against it. In truth, that may well constitute the ultimate tragedy of the anti-Mexican movement during the Great Depression.

Decade of Betrayal recounts what must be considered as the most significant and crucial event to befall *México de afuera* residents during the twentieth century. No other phenomenon, not even the issue of illegal immigration in the 1990s, has had such a far-reaching impact on the community. Following the tradition of Paul Taylor, Manuel Gamio, and Emory Bogardus, the work adds a new dimension to the study of Mexican Nationals and Mexican Americans in the United States. It delineates the consequences of deportation and repatriation on both sides of the border, from both the Mexican and American perspectives. However, the uniqueness of *Decade of Betrayal* lies in its focus on the calamitous experiences of the people who underwent the ordeal of the betrayal. This particular aspect constitutes an important historical contribution and a valuable insight for historians, students, and lay readers.

Yet the lessons of history appear to be lost in the turmoil besetting the question of legal and illegal immigration in the 1990s. Since massive repatriation is not a feasible alternative, other ingenious means are being proposed to halt the unwanted immigrant influx. It is suggested that steel walls, moats, fences, floodlights, and a beefed-up and well-equipped border patrol be deployed along the U.S.–Mexico border to deter entry from Mexico and Central America.

For those already in the United States, it is proposed that services encouraging people to emigrate be severely curtailed or totally eliminated. These services would include medical services, welfare eligibility, educational opportunities, drivers licenses, and similar benefits. Some states, including California, Texas, and New York, are contemplating or have sued the federal government in order to recover the billions of dollars they claim are being spent to serve the immigrant horde.

As in the 1930s, events beyond political control may again end the controversy. In this instance, rather than the ravages of war, it will be the ravages of old age. The population of the United States over sixty-five is aging twice as fast as the general population. That fact, and the nation's low birthrate, means that as the twenty-first century unfolds the United States will be forced to import a labor force, as it has done traditionally in the past. Eventually, the tide will turn and immigrants again will be welcomed as a prime resource. As Mexicans are fond of saying about "what the fickle and unpredictable fates" have in store: "Dios sabrá, Qué será, será!"

QUESTIONS

1. Are there ever justifiable reasons to expel members of a particular society?

2. Is there an assumption regarding culture hidden under the phrase, "Once a Mexican always a Mexican"?

3. Consider the statement, "They were neither American nor Mexican as defined by their particular cultures." What are the implications of this statement for the present reality that a person has rights only when accorded by a particular state?

4. Are there any similarities between U.S. Mexicans' status and the status of Cuban Americans and Puerto Ricans?

5. How do the state interests of the United States and Mexico contribute to the construction of the Mexican American/Chicano subjectivity and its subsequent political economic development? Are there any similarities with the U.S./Cuban construction of El Exilio described by Torres?

Manifold Identities and Struggles
(ca. 1960s to Present)

This section is all about **paradigm** shifts, a new form to contest power: contestation of public space and everyday life as opposed to seizure of power (see appendix 1A). In 1968 French students almost toppled the government when they were joined by mass media workers and eventually by industrial workers. This event placed the production of knowledge at the center of political struggle.[1] When the status of truth itself was questioned, we witnessed several transformations: the civil rights movement and protests against the war in Vietnam began, Negroes became blacks, Mexicans and Mexican Americans became Chicanos, "chicks" became feminists. In retrospect, these social movements pointed to a demand for public citizenship, a demand for justice.

The texts of this section discuss continuing identities, like the farmworkers and the Puerto Rican *independentistas,* and issues such as pigmentocracy and the status of Afro-Latinos, as well as new definitions of being political, such as through gay liberation or, in the case of Cuban Americans, through the status of "ethnic minority." The texts also illustrate that we keep repeating ourselves, we keep reconstructing structures of domination even as we fight for liberation. The sporadic violence of Puerto Rican and Cuban militants (but not Chicanos?) indicates that the Furies are always lurking there, coercing us to remedy a past injustice. Furthermore, the fact that Cubans in Miami engage in exclusionary practices that affect African and Anglo Americans as well as non-Cuban Latinos is a further indication that the quest for public citizenship is not question of ethnicity or gender but a manifestation of power relations.

NOTE

1. George Katsiaficas, *The Imagination of the New Left* (Boston: South End, 1987).

✳ 17 ✳
THE ORGANIZER'S TALE

César E. Chávez

Largely invisible in the political memory of many people is the fact that U.S. workers fought long and hard for their right to speak collectively and negotiate with the bosses for what we now take for granted, such as the eight-hour work day, the elimination of child labor, and worker's compensation. It surprises many to learn that the right to organize into unions was not guaranteed until 1935, with the passing of the National Labor Relations Act. After learning this, it amazes some to learn that farmworkers were not included in this act. So we must begin this particular story with the understanding that "labor unions and strikes in U.S. agriculture have been, for the most part, sporadic and scattered, except among Mexicans, who have waged strikes unmatched in scope, intensity or continuity for nearly one hundred years."[1] One example from the 1880s is their participation in the Knights of Labor.

While we cannot review the entire history of the farmworker struggle for economic democracy, to understand the endurance of a quest for equality it is important to mention two labor institutions that preceded the United Farm Worker's union (UFW), organized by César E. Chávez. While they were not successful in improving the working conditions of the farmworkers, the National Farm Labor Union (NFLU), founded in 1946, and the Agricultural Workers' Organizing Committee (AWOC), begun in 1960, served as training grounds for many future labor leaders, such as Chávez and Dolores Huerta. This story is told by Ernesto Galarza in *Spiders in the House and Workers in the Field*. In the words of Gómez-Quiñonez:

> In spite of all the union and governmental activity throughout the twentieth century, by the 1960s the socioeconomic condition of farm workers was still horrendous. Farm workers historically have labored in the most hazardous, dehumanizing, and oppressive conditions, and farm work has been the third most dangerous occupation in the United States because of accidents. While other workers have made gains, the situation for agricultural workers has remained the same. There was no minimum wage. Their wages provided for only the basic necessities of life and often even less than that. Thousands of impoverished laborers have been exploited, with low pay, abominable working conditions, lack of decent food, and continuous discrimination. The majority of farm workers have had no personal savings to fall back on in times of emergency, economic crisis, or layoffs. They have had no opportunity to make up lost wages, no fringe benefits, no basic insurance guarantees, and no retirement security.[2]

At this time César E. Chávez entered into the story. To help place the following piece by César in a chronological context, it will help to remember that he was born in Arizona on March 31, 1927. He joined the navy at seventeen and served in the South Pacific at the end of World War II. At the age of nineteen, he joined the agricultural workers' effort at Corcoran, California, and became involved in strike activities. Although the 1946 strike was for the most part unsuccessful, Chávez gained organizing experience. In the late 1940s, when the National Farm Labor Union was formed, he became an active member. In the following piece, César begins his tale in 1950, describing how he had joined the Community Service Organization. The Battle of the Corcoran Farm Camp, an event he refers to as "thirty years ago" (meaning in October 1933), entailed one of the high points of California worker militancy and grower violence. In Pixley, the farmers opened fire on the striking farmworkers, killing two and injuring eight.[3] Finally, the date when the NFLU and AWOC joined in a strike in Delano was Monday, September 20, 1965. The new union would be the UFW, which would be based on a "humanist" rather than a "business" basis. There is as yet no happy ending, however; this approach has apparently brought another set of problems.[4]

NOTES AND SUGGESTED READINGS

1. Juan Gómez-Quiñonez, *Mexican American Labor, 1790–1900* (Albuquerque: University of New Mexico Press, 1994), 129.

2. Gómez-Quiñonez, *Mexican American Labor*, 242.

3. Ronald B. Taylor, *Chávez and the Farm Workers* (Boston: Beacon, 1975), 52–57.

4. Theo J. Majka and Linda C. Majka, "Decline of the Farm Labor Movement in California: Organizational Crisis and Political Change," *Critical Sociology* 19, no. 3 (1993): 11–36.

It really started for me 16 years ago in San Jose California, when I was working on an apricot farm. We figured he was just another social worker doing a study of farm conditions, and I kept refusing to meet with him. But he was persistent. Finally, I got together some of the rough element in San Jose. We were going to have a little reception for him to teach the *gringo* a little bit of how we felt. There were about 30 of us in the house, young guys mostly. I was supposed to give them a signal— change my cigarette from my right hand to my left, and then we were going to give him a lot of hell. But he started talking and the more he talked, the more wide-eyed I became and the less inclined I was to give the signal. A couple of guys who were pretty drunk at the time still wanted to give the *gringo* the business, but we got rid of them. This fellow was making a lot of sense, and I wanted to hear what he had to say.

His name was Fred Ross, and he was an organizer for the Community Service Organization (CSO) which was working with Mexican-Americans in the cities. I became immediately really involved. Before long I was heading a voter registration drive. All the time I was observing the things Fred did, secretly, because I wanted to learn how to organize, to see how it was done. I was impressed with his patience and understanding of people. I thought this was a tool, one of the greatest things he had.

It was pretty rough for me at first. I was changing and had to take a lot of ridicule from the kids my age, the rough characters I worked with in the fields. They would say, "Hey, big shot. Now that you're a *politico,* why are you working here for 65 cents an hour?" I might add that our neighborhood had the highest percentage of San Quentin graduates. It was a game among the *pachucos* in the sense that we defended ourselves from outsiders, although inside the neighborhood there was not a lot of fighting.

After six months of working every night in San Jose, Fred assigned me to take over the CSO chapter in Decoto. It was a tough spot to fill. I would suggest something, and people would say, "No, let's wait till Fred gets back," or "Fred wouldn't do it that way." This is pretty much a pattern with people, I discovered, whether I was put in Fred's position, or later, when someone else was put in my position. After the Decoto assignment I was sent to start a new chapter in Oakland. Before I left, Fred came to a place in San Jose called the Hole-in-the-Wall and we talked for half an hour over coffee. He was in a rush to leave, but I wanted to keep him talking; I was that scared of my assignment.

There were hard times in Oakland. First of all, it was a big city and I'd get lost every time I went anywhere. Then I arranged a series of house meetings. I would get to the meeting early and drive back and forth past the house, too nervous to go in and face the people. Finally I would force myself to go inside and sit in a corner. I was quite thin then, and young, and most of the people were middle-aged. Someone would say, "Where's the organizer?" And I would pipe up, "Here I am." Then they would say in Spanish—these were very poor people and we hardly spoke anything but Spanish—"Ha! This *kid?*" Most of them said they were interested, but the hardest part was to get them to start pushing themselves, on their own initiative.

The idea was to set up a meeting and then get each attending person to call his own house meeting, inviting new people—a sort of chain letter effect. After a house meeting I would lie awake going over the whole thing, playing the tape back, trying to see why people laughed at one point, or why they were for one thing and against another. I was also learning to read and write, those late evenings. I had left school in the 7th grade after attending 67 different schools, and my reading wasn't the best.

At our first organizing meeting we had 368 people: I'll never forget it because it was very important to me. You eat your heart out; the meeting is called for 7 o'clock and you start to worry about 4. You wait. Will they show up? Then the first one arrives. By 7 there are only 20 people, you have everything in order, you have to look calm. But little by little they filter in and at a certain point you know it will be a success.

After four months in Oakland, I was transferred. The chapter was beginning to move on its own, so Fred assigned me to organize the San Joaquin Valley. Over the months I developed what I used to call schemes or tricks—now I call them techniques—of making initial contacts. The main thing in convincing someone is to spend time with him. It doesn't matter if he can read, write or even speak well. What is important is that he is a man and second, that he has shown some initial interest. One good way to develop leadership is to take a man with you in your car. And it works a lot better if you're doing the driving; that way you are in charge. You drive, he sits there, and you talk. These little things were very important to me; I was caught in a big game by then, figuring out what makes people work. I found that if you work hard enough you can usually shake people into working too, those who are concerned. You work harder and they work harder still, up to a point and then they pass you. Then, of course, they're on their own.

I also learned to keep away from the established groups and so-called leaders, and to guard against philosophizing. Working with low-income people is very different from working with the professionals, who like to sit around talking about how to play politics. When you're trying to recruit a farmworker, you have to paint a little picture, and then you have to color the picture in. We found out that the harder a guy is to convince, the better leader or member he becomes. When you exert yourself to convince him, you have his confidence and he has good motivation. A lot of people who say OK right away wind up hanging around the office, taking up the workers' time.

During the McCarthy era in one Valley town, I was subjected to a lot of redbaiting. We had been recruiting people for citizenship classes at the high school when we got into a quarrel with the naturalization examiner. He was rejecting people on the grounds that they were just parroting what they learned in citizenship class. One day we had a meeting about it in Fresno, and I took along some of the leaders of our local chapter. Some redbaiting official gave us a hard time, and the people got scared and took his side. They did it because it seemed easy at the moment, even though they knew that sticking with me was the right thing to do. It was disgusting. When we left the building they walked by themselves ahead of me as if I had some kind of communicable disease. I had been working with these people for three months and I was very sad to see that. It taught me a great lesson.

That night I learned that the chapter officers were holding a meeting to review my letters and printed materials to see if I really was a Communist. So I drove out there and walked right in on their meeting. I said, "I hear you've been discussing me, and I thought it would be nice if I was here to defend myself. Not that it matters that much to you or even to me, because as far as I am concerned you are a bunch of cowards." At that they began to apologize. "Let's forget it," they said. "You're a nice guy." But I didn't want apologies. I wanted a full discussion. I told them I didn't give a damn, but that they had to learn to distinguish fact from what appeared to be a fact because of fear. I kept them there till two in the morning. Some of the women cried. I don't know if they investigated me any further, but I stayed on another few months and things worked out.

This was not an isolated case. Often when we'd leave people to themselves they would get frightened and draw back into their shells where they had been all the years. And I learned quickly that there is no real appreciation. Whatever you do, and no matter what reasons you may give to others, you do it because you want to see it done, or maybe because you want power. And there shouldn't be any appreciation, understandably. I know good organizers who were destroyed, washed out, because they expected people to appreciate what they'd done. Anyone who comes in with the idea that farmworkers are free of sin and that the growers are all bastards, either has never dealt with the situation or is an idealist of the first order. Things don't work that way.

For more than 10 years I worked for the CSO. As the organization grew, we found ourselves meeting in fancier and fancier motels and holding expensive conventions. Doctors, lawyers and politicians began joining. They would get elected to some office in the organization and then, for all practical purposes, leave. Intent on using the CSO for their own prestige purposes, these "leaders," many of them, lacked the urgency we had to have. When I became general director I began to press for a program to organize farmworkers into a union, an idea most of the leadership opposed. So I started a revolt within the CSO. I refused to sit at the head table at meetings, refused to wear a suit and tie, and finally I even refused to shave and cut my hair. It used to embarrass some of the professionals. At every meeting I got up and gave my standard speech: we shouldn't meet in fancy motels, we were getting away from the people, farmworkers had to be organized. But nothing happened. In March of '62 I resigned and came to Delano to begin organizing the Valley on my own.

By hand I drew a map of all the towns between Arvin and Stockton—86 of them, including farming camps—and decided to hit them all to get a small nucleus of people working in each. For six months I traveled around, planting an idea. We had a simple questionnaire, a little card with space for name, address and how much the worker thought he ought to be paid. My wife, Helen, mimeographed them, and we took our kids for two or three day jaunts to these towns, distributing the cards door-to-door and to camps and groceries.

Some 80,000 cards were sent back from eight Valley counties. I got a lot of contacts that way, but I was shocked at the wages the people were asking. The growers were paying $1 and $1.15 and maybe 95 per cent of the people thought they should be getting only $1.25. Sometimes people scribbled messages on the cards: "I hope to God we win" or "Do you think we can win?" or "I'd like to know more." So I separated the cards with the pencilled notes, got in my car and went to those people.

We didn't have any money at all in those days, none for gas and hardly any for food. So I went to people and started asking for food. It turned out to be about the best thing I could have done, although at first it's hard on your pride. Some of our best members came in that way. If people give you their food, they'll give you their hearts. Several months and many meetings later we had a working organization, and this time the leaders were the people.

None of the farmworkers had collective bargaining contracts, and I thought it would take ten years before we got that first contract. I wanted desperately to get some color into the movement, to give people something they could identify with, like a flag. I was reading some books about how various leaders discovered what colors contrasted and stood out the best. The Egyptians had found that a red field with a white circle and a black emblem in the center crashed into your eyes like nothing else. I wanted to use the Aztec eagle in the center, as on the Mexican flag. So I told my cousin Manuel, "Draw an Aztec Eagle." Manuel had a little trouble with it, so we modified the eagle to make it easier for people to draw.

The first big meeting of what we decided to call the National Farm Workers Association was held in September 1962, at Fresno, with 287 people. We had our huge red flag on the wall, with paper tacked over it. When the time came, Manuel pulled a cord ripping the paper off the flag and all of a sudden it hit the people. Some of them wondered if it was a Communist flag, and I said it probably looked more like a neo-Nazi emblem than anything else. But they wanted an explanation. So Manuel got up and said, "When that damn eagle flies—that's when the farmworkers' problems are going to be solved."

One of the first things I decided was that outside money wasn't going to organize people, at least not in the beginning. I even turned down a grant from a private group—$50,000 to go directly to organize farmworkers—for just this reason. Even when there are no strings attached, you are still compromised because you feel you have to produce immediate results. This is bad, because it takes a long time to build a movement, and your organization suffers if you get too far ahead of the people it belongs to. We set the dues at $42 a year per family, really a meaningful dues, but of the 212 we got to pay, only 12 remained by June of '63. We were discouraged at that, but not enough to make us quit.

Money was always a problem. Once we were facing a $180 gas bill on a credit card I'd got a long time ago and was about to lose. And we *had* to keep that credit card. One day my wife and I were picking cotton, pulling bolls, to make a little money to live on. Helen said to me, "Do you put all this in the bag, or just the cotton?" I thought she was kidding and told her to throw the whole boll in so that she had nothing but a sack of bolls at the weighing. The man said, "Whose sack is this?" I said, well, my wife's, and he told us we were fired. "Look at all that crap you brought in," he said. Helen and I started laughing. We were going anyway. We took the $4 we had earned and spent it at a grocery store where they were giving away a $100 prize. Each time you shopped they'd give you one of the letters of M-O-N-E-Y or a flag: you had to have M-O-N-E-Y plus the flag to win. Helen had already collected the letters and just needed the flag. Anyway, they gave her the ticket. She screamed, "A flag? I don't believe it," ran in and got the $100. She said, "Now we're going to eat steak." But I said no, we're going to pay the gas bill. I don't know if she cried, but I think she did.

It was rough in those early years. Helen was having babies and I was not there when she was at the hospital. But if you haven't got your wife behind you, you can't do many things. There's got to be peace at home. So I did, I think, a fairly good job of organizing her. When we were kids, she lived in Delano and I came to town as a migrant. Once on a date we had a bad experience about segregation at a movie theater, and I put up a fight. We were together then, and still are. I think I'm more of a pacifist than she is. Her father, Fabela, was a colonel with Pancho Villa in the Mexican Revolution. Sometimes she gets angry and tells me, "These scabs—you should deal with them sternly," and I kid her, "It must be too much of that Fabela blood in you."

The movement really caught on in '64. By August we had a thousand members. We'd had a beautiful 90-day drive in Corcoran, where they had the Battle of the Corcoran Farm Camp 30 years ago, and by November we had assets of $25,000 in our credit union, which helped to stabilize the membership. I had gone without pay the whole of 1963. The next year the members voted me a $40 a week salary, after Helen had to quit working in the fields to manage the credit union.

Our first strike was in May of '65, a small one but it prepared us for the big one. A farmworker from McFarland named Epifanio Camacho came to see me. He said he was sick and tired of how people working the roses were being treated, and he was willing to "go the limit." I assigned Manuel and Gilbert Padilla to hold meetings at Camacho's house. The people wanted union recognition, but the real issue, as in most cases when you begin, was wages. They were promised $9 a thousand, but they were actually getting $6.50 and $7 for grafting roses. Most of them signed cards giving us the right to bargain for them. We chose the biggest company, with about 85 employees, not counting the irrigators and supervisors, and we held a series of meetings to prepare the strike and call the vote. There would be no picket line; everyone pledged on their honor not to break the strike.

Early on the first morning of the strike, we sent out 10 cars to check the people's homes. We found lights in five or six homes and knocked on the doors. The men were getting up and we'd say, "Where are you going?" They would dodge, "Oh, uh . . . I was just getting up, you know," We'd say, "Well, you're not going to work, are you?" And they'd say no. Dolores Huerta, who was driving the green panel truck, saw a light in one house where four rose-workers lived. They told her they were going to work, even after she reminded them of their pledge. So she moved the truck so it blocked their driveway, turned off the key, put it in her purse and sat there alone.

That morning the company foreman was madder than hell and refused to talk to us. None of the grafters had shown up for work. At 10:30 we started to go to the company office, but it occurred to us that maybe a woman would have a better chance. So Dolores knocked on the office door, saying, "I'm Dolores Huerta from the National Farm Workers Association." "Get out!" the man said, "you Communist. Get out." I guess they were expecting us, because as Dolores stood arguing with him the cops came and told her to leave. She left.

For two days the fields were idle. On Wednesday they recruited a group of Filipinos from out of town who knew nothing of the strike, maybe 35 of them. They drove through escorted by three sheriff's patrol cars, one in front, one in the middle and one at the rear with a dog. We didn't have a picket line, but we parked across the street and just watched them go through, not saying a word. All but seven stopped working after half an hour, and the rest had quit by mid-afternoon.

The company made an offer the evening of the fourth day, a package deal that amounted to a 120 per cent wage increase, but no contract. We wanted to hold out for a contract and more benefits, but a majority of the rose-workers wanted to accept the offer and go back. We are a democratic union so we had to support what they wanted to do. They had a meeting and voted to settle. Then we had a problem with a few militants who wanted to hold out. We had to convince them to go back to work, as a united front, because otherwise they would be canned. So we worked—Tony Orendain and I, Dolores and Gilbert, Jim Drake and all the organizers—knocking on doors till two in the morning, telling people, "You have to go back or you'll lose your job." And they did. They worked.

Our second strike, and our last before the big one at Delano, was in the grapes at Martin's Ranch last summer. The people were getting a raw deal there, being pushed around pretty badly. Gilbert went out to the field, climbed on top of a car and took a strike vote. They voted unanimously to go out. Right away they started bringing in strikebreakers, so we launched a tough attack on the labor contractors, distributed leaflets portraying them as really low characters. We attacked one—Luis Campos—so badly that he just gave up the job, and he took 27 of his men out with him. All he asked was that we distribute another leaflet reinstating him in the community. And we did. What was unusual was that the grower would talk to us. The grower kept saying, "I can't pay. I just haven't got the money." I guess he must have found the money somewhere, because we were asking $1.40 and we got it.

We had just finished the Martin strike when the Agricultural Workers Organizing Committee (AFL-CIO) started a strike against the grape growers, Digiorgio, Schenley liquors and small growers, asking $1.40 an hour and 25 cents a box. There was a lot of pressure from our members for us to join the strike but we had some misgivings. We didn't feel ready for a big strike like this one, one that was sure to last a long time. Having no money—just $87 in the strike fund—meant we'd have to depend on God knows who.

Eight days after the strike started—it takes time to get 1,200 people together from all over the Valley—we held a meeting in Delano and voted to go out. I asked the membership to release us from the pledge not to accept outside money, because we'd need it now, a lot of it. The help came. It started because of the close, and I would say even beautiful relationship that we've had with the Migrant Ministry for some years. They were the first to come to our rescue, financially and in every other way, and they spread the word to other benefactors.

We had planned, before, to start a labor school in November. It never happened, but we have the best labor school we could ever have, in the strike. The strike is only a temporary condition, however. We have over 3,000 members spread out over a wide area, and we have to service them when they have problems. We get letters from New Mexico, Colorado, Texas, California, from farmworkers saying, "We're getting together and we need an organizer." It kills you when you haven't got the personnel and resources. You feel badly about not sending an organizer because you look back and remember all the difficulty you had in getting two or three people together, and here *they're* together. Of course, we're training organizers, many of them younger than I was when I started in CSO. They can work 20 hours a day, sleep four, and be ready to hit it again; when you get to 39 it's a different story.

The people who took part in the strike and the march have something more than their material interest going for them. If it were only material, they wouldn't have stayed on the strike long enough to win. It is difficult to explain. But it flows out in the ordinary things they say. For instance, some of the younger guys are saying, "Where do you think's going to be the next strike?" I say, "Well, we have to win in Delano." They say, "We'll win, but where do we go next?" I say, "Maybe most of us will be working in the fields." They say, "No, I don't want to go and work in the fields. I want to organize. There are a lot of people that need our help." So I say, "You're going to be pretty poor then, because when you strike you don't have much money." They say they don't care about that.

And others are saying, "I have friends who are working in Texas. If we could only help them." It is bigger, certainly, than just a strike. And if this spirit grows within the farm labor movement, one day we can use the force that we have to help correct a lot of things that are wrong in this society. But that is for the future. Before you can run, you have to learn to walk.

There are vivid memories from my childhood—what we had to go through because of low wages and the conditions, basically because there was no union. I suppose if I wanted to be fair I could say that I'm trying to settle a personal score. I could dramatize it by saying that I want to bring social justice to farmworkers. But the truth is that I went through a lot of hell, and a lot of people did. If we can even the score a little for the workers then we are doing something. Besides, I don't know any other work I like to do better than this. I really don't, you know.

✳ 18 ✳

QUEER AZTLÁN: THE RE-FORMATION OF CHICANO TRIBE

Cherríe Moraga

According to Cherríe, "Chicanos are an occupied nation within a nation, and women and women's sexuality are occupied within [a] Chicano nation." Indeed, if the quest for cultural citizenship means being accepted by the dominant culture, what happens when the dominant culture is "your own culture" and, moreover, a traditional, patriarchal, and homophobic culture? Once again we are confronted by the question: who are the people? In this essay, Cherríe addresses one of the frontiers of political identity in Latino/a culture. When El Plan de Aztlán was conceived, "lesbians and gay men were not envisioned as members of the 'house.'" They were, and still are, considered illegitimate children of the Chicano family. As we have discussed, this position deploys a particular set of desire relations, "a critical position to address those areas within our cultural family that need to change." Cherríe also touches on issues of bio-power: human bodies who are denied their rights as moral entities, who are raped physically and psychologically and exposed to violence and illness. She raises a variety of critical questions about the degree of radicalism and acceptance of the Other, even within those who see themselves as oppressed; the good and the bad of Chicano and other nationalisms; relations with Native Americans; sovereignty; and separatism.

How will our lands be free if our bodies aren't?

—Ricardo Bracho

At the height of the Chicano Movement in 1968, I was a closeted, light-skinned, mixed-blood Mexican-American, disguised in my father's English last name. Since I seldom opened my mouth, few people questioned my Anglo credentials. But my eyes were open and thirsty and drank in images of students my age, of vatos and viejitas, who could have primos, or tíos, or abuelitas raising their collective fists into a smoggy East Los Angeles skyline. Although I could not express how at the time, I knew I had a place in that Movement that was spilling out of barrio high schools and onto police-barricaded streets just ten minutes from my tree-lined working class neighborhood in San Gabriel. What I didn't know then was that it would take me another ten years to fully traverse that ten-minute drive and to bring all the parts of me—Chicana, lesbiana, half-breed, and poeta—to the revolution, wherever it was.

My real politicization began, not through the Chicano Movement, but through the bold recognition of my lesbianism. Coming to terms with that fact meant the radical restructuring of everything I thought I held sacred. It meant acting on my woman-centered desire and against anything that stood in its way, including my Church, my family, and my "country." It meant acting in spite of the fact that I had learned from my Mexican culture and the dominant culture that my womanhood was, if not despised, certainly deficient and hardly worth the loving of another woman in bed. But act I did, because not acting would have meant my death by despair.

That was twenty years ago. In those twenty years I traversed territory that extends well beyond the ten-minute trip between East Los Angeles and San Gabriel. In those twenty years, I experienced the racism of the Women's Movement, the elitism of the Gay and Lesbian Movement, the homophobia and sexism of the Chicano Movement, and the benign cultural imperialism of the Latin American Solidarity Movement. I also witnessed the emergence of national Chicana feminista consciousness and a literature, art, and activism to support it. I've seen the growth of a lesbian-of-color movement, the founding of an independent national Latino/a lesbian and gay men's organization, and the flourishing of Indigenous people's international campaigns for human and land rights.

A quarter of a century after those school walk-outs in 1968, I can write, without reservation, that I have found a sense of place among la Chicanada. It is not always a safe place, but it is unequivocally the original familial place from which I am compelled to write, which I reach toward in my audiences, and which serves as my source of inspiration, voice, and lucha. How we Chicanos define that struggle has always been the subject of debate and is ultimately the subject of this essay.

"Queer Aztlán" had been forming in my mind for over three years and began to take concrete shape a year ago in a conversation with poet Ricardo Bracho. We discussed the limitations of "Queer Nation," whose leather-jacketed, shaved-headed white radicals and accompanying anglo-centricity were an "alien-nation" to most lesbians and gay men of color. We also spoke of Chicano Nationalism, which never accepted openly gay men and lesbians among its ranks. Ricardo half-jokingly concluded, "What we need, Cherríe, is a 'Queer Aztlán.'" Of course. A Chicano homeland that could embrace all its people, including its jotería.[1]

Everything I read these days tells me that the Chicano Movement is dead. In Earl Shorris' *Latinos*, the Anglo author insists that the Chicano *him*self is dead. He writes, "The Chicano generation began in the late 1960s and lasted about six or eight years, dying slowly through the seventies." He goes on to say that Chicanismo has been reduced to no more than a "handshake practiced by middle-aged men." Chicano sociologists seem to be suggesting the same when they tell us that by the third generation, the majority of Chicanos have lost their Spanish fluency, and nearly a third have married non-Chicanos and have moved out of the Chicano community. Were immigration from México to stop, they say, Chicanos could be virtually indistinguishable from the rest of the population within a few generations. My nieces and nephews are living testimony to these faceless facts.

I mourn the dissolution of an active Chicano Movement possibly more strongly than my generational counterparts because during its "classic period," I was unable to act publicly. But more deeply, I mourn it because its ghost haunts me daily in the blonde hair of my sister's children, the gradual hispanicization of Chicano students, the senselessness of barrio violence, and the poisoning of la frontera from

Tijuana to Tejas. In 1992, we have no organized national movement to respond to our losses. For me, "El Movimiento" has never been a thing of the past, it has retreated into subterranean uncontaminated soils awaiting resurrection in a "queerer," more feminist generation.

What was right about Chicano Nationalism was its commitment to preserving the integrity of the Chicano people. A generation ago, there were cultural, economic, and political programs to develop Chicano consciousness, autonomy, and self-determination. What was wrong about Chicano Nationalism was its institutionalized heterosexism, its inbred machismo, and its lack of a cohesive national political strategy.[2]

Over the years, I have witnessed plenty of progressive nationalisms: Chicano nationalism, Black nationalism, Puerto Rican Independence (still viable as evidenced in the recent mass protest on the Island against the establishment of English as an official language), the "Lesbian Nation" and its lesbian separatist movement, and, of course, the most recent "Queer Nation." What I admired about each was its righteous radicalism, its unabashed anti-assimilationism, and its rebeldía. I recognize the dangers of nationalism as a strategy for political change. Its tendency toward separatism can run dangerously close to biological determinism and a kind of fascism. We are all horrified by the concentration and rape camps in Bosnia, falsely justified by the Serbian call for "ethnic cleansing." We are bitterly sobered by the nazism espoused by Pat Buchanan at the 1992 Republican Convention in which only heterosexual white middle-class voting Amerikans have the right to citizenship and heaven. Over and over again we are reminded that sex and race do not define a person's politics. Margaret Thatcher is a woman and enforces the policies of the Imperial whiteman and Clarence Thomas is Black and follows suit. But it is historically evident that the female body, like the Chicano people, has been colonized. And any movement to decolonize them must be culturally and sexually specific.

Chicanos are an occupied nation within a nation, and women and women's sexuality are occupied within Chicano nation. If women's bodies and those of men and women who transgress their gender roles have been historically regarded as territories to be conquered, they are also territories to be liberated. Feminism has taught us this. The nationalism I seek is one that decolonizes the brown and female body as it decolonizes the brown and female earth. It is a new nationalism in which la Chicana Indígena stands at the center, and heterosexism and homophobia are no longer the cultural order of the day. I cling to the word "nation" because without the specific naming of the nation, the nation will be lost (as when feminism is reduced to humanism, the woman is subsumed). Let us retain our radical naming but expand it to meet a broader and wiser revolution.

TIERRA SAGRADA: THE ROOTS OF A REVOLUTION

Aztlán. I don't remember when I first heard the word, but I remember it took my heart by surprise to learn of that place—that "sacred landscape" wholly evident en las playas, los llanos, y en las montañas of the North American Southwest. A terrain that I did not completely comprehend at first, but that I continue to try, in my own small way, to fully inhabit and make habitable for its Chicano citizens.

Aztlán gave language to a nameless anhelo inside me. To me, it was never a masculine notion. It had nothing to do with the Aztecs and everything to do with Mexican birds, Mexican beaches, and Mexican babies right here in Califas. I remember once driving through Anza Borrego desert, just east of San Diego, my VW van whipping around corners, climbing. The tape deck set at full blast, every window open, bandana around my forehead. And I think, *this is México, Raza territory*, as I belt out the refrain . . .

> *"Marieta, no seas coqueta*
> *porque los hombres son muy malos*
> *prometen muchos regalos*
> *y lo que dan son puro palos . . ."*

That day I claimed that land in the spin of the worn-out tape, the spin of my balding tires, and the spin of my mind. And just as I wrapped around a rubber-burning curve, I saw it: "A-Z-T-L-A-N," in granite-sized letters etched into the face of the mountainside. Of course, I hadn't been the first. Some other Chicano came this way, too, saw what I saw, felt what I felt. Enough to put a name to it. *Aztlán. Tierra sagrada.*

A term Náhuatl in root, Aztlán was that historical/mythical land where one set of Indian forebears, the Aztecs, were said to have resided 1,000 years ago. Located in the U.S. Southwest, Aztlán fueled a nationalist struggle twenty years ago, which encompassed much of the pueblo Chicano from Chicago to the borders of Chihuahua. In the late sixties and early seventies, Chicano nationalism meant the right to control our own resources, language, and cultural traditions, rights guaranteed us by the Treaty of Guadalupe Hidalgo signed in 1848 when the Southwest was "annexed" to the United States at the end of the Mexican-American War. At its most radical, Chicano nationalism expressed itself in militant action. In the mid-1960s, Reies López Tijerina entered a campaign against the Department of the Interior to reclaim land grants for New Mexicans, resulting in his eventual imprisonment. In 1968, nearly 10,000 Chicano students walked out of their high schools to protest the lack of quality education in Los Angeles barrio schools. The same period also saw the rise of the Brown Berets, a para-military style youth organization regularly harassed by law enforcement agencies throughout the Southwest These are highlights in Chicano Movement history. To most, however, El Movimiento, practically applied, simply meant fair and equitable representation on the city council, in the union halls, and on the school board.

I've often wondered why Chicano nationalism never really sustained the same level of militancy witnessed in the Puerto Rican, Black, and Native American Movements. Certainly violence, especially police violence, was visited upon Chicanos in response to our public protests, the murder of journalist Rubén Salazar during the National Chicano Moratorium of 1970 being the most noted instance. And like other liberation movements, the Chicano movement had its share of FBI infiltrators.

In 1969, El Plan de Aztlán was drawn up at the First Annual Chicano Youth Conference in Denver, Colorado, calling for a Chicano program of economic self-determination, self-defense, and land reclamation, and including an autonomous taxation and judicial system. By the mid-1970s, such radical plans had gradually eroded in the face of a formidable opponent—the United States government—and Chicano nationalism as a political strategy began to express itself more in the cultural arena than in direct militant confrontation with the government.

Another reason for the brevity of a unified militant movement may be the heterogeneity of the Chicano population. Chicanos are not easily organized as a racial/political entity. Is our land the México of today or the México of a century and a half ago, covering thousands of miles of what is now the Southwestern United States? Unlike the island of Puerto Rico whose "homeland" is clearly defined by ocean on all sides, Aztlán at times seems more *meta*physical than physical territory.

As a mestizo people living in the United States, our relationship to this country has been ambivalent at best. Our birth certificates since the invasion of Aztlán identify us as white. Our treatment by Anglo-Americans brand us "colored." In the history of African Americans, when the white slave owner raped a Black woman, the mixed-blood offspring inherited the mother's enslaved status. Over a century later, mixed-raced African Americans overwhelmingly identify as Black, not as mixed-blood. But the history of Mexicans/Chicanos follows a different pattern. The "Spanish-American" Conquest was secured through rape, intermarriage, the African slave trade, and the spread of Catholicism and disease. It gave birth to a third "mestizo" race that included Indian, African, and European blood. During colonial times, "Spanish-America" maintained a rigid and elaborate caste system that privileged the pure-blood Spaniard and his children over the mestizo. The pure blood indio and africano remained on the bottom rungs of society. The remnants of such class/race stratification are still evident throughout Latin America.

Chicano Nation is a mestizo nation conceived in a double-rape: first, by the Spanish and then by the Gringo. In the mid-19th century, Anglo-America took possession of one-third of México's territory. A new English-speaking oppressor assumed control over the Spanish, Mestizo, and Indian people inhabiting those lands. There was no denying that the United States had stolen Aztlán from México, but it had been initially stolen from the Indians by the Spanish some 300 years earlier. To make alliances with other nationalist struggles taking place throughout the country in the late sixties, there was no room for Chicano ambivalence about being Indians, for it was our Indian blood and history of resistance against both Spanish and Anglo invaders that made us rightful inheritors of Aztlán. After centuries of discrimination against our Indian-ness, which forced mestizos into denial, many Mexican-Americans found the sudden affirmation of our indigenismo difficult to accept. And yet the Chicano Indigenous movement was not without historical precedence. Little more than fifty years earlier, México witnessed a campesino- and Indian-led agrarian and labor movement spreading into the Southwest that had the potential of eclipsing the Russian Revolution in its vision. Political corruption, of course, followed. Today, the pending Free Trade Agreement with the United States and Canada marks the

ultimate betrayal of the Mexican revolution: the final surrender of the Mexican people's sovereign rights to land and livelihood.

Radicalization among people of Mexican ancestry in this country most often occurs
when the Mexican ceases to be a Mexican and becomes a Chicano. I have observed
this in my Chicano Studies students (first, second, and third generation, some of
whose families are indigenous to Aztlán) from the barrios of East Los Angeles,
Fresno, and all the neighboring Central Valley towns of California—Selma, Visalia,
Sanger, the barrios of Oakland, Sanjo, etc. They are the ones most often in protest,
draping their bodies in front of freeway on-ramps and trans-bay bridges, blocking
entrances to University administration buildings. They are the ones who, like their
Black, Asian, and Native American counterparts, doubt the "American dream"
because even if *they* got to UC Berkeley, their brother is still on crack in Boyle
Heights, their sister had three kids before she's twenty, and *sorry but they can't finish
the last week of the semester cuz Tío Ignacio just got shot in front of a liquor store.* My
working-class and middle-class Mexican immigrant students,[3] on the other hand,
have not yet had their self-esteem nor that of their parents and grandparents worn
away by North American racism. For them, the "American dream" still looms as a
possibility on the horizon. Their Mexican pride sustains them through the daily
assaults on their intelligence, integrity, and humanity. They maintain a determined
individualism and their families still dream of returning home one day.
   A new generation of future Chicanos arrives everyday with every Mexican immigrant. Some may find their American dream and forget their origins, but the majority of México's descendants soon comprehend the political meaning of the disparity
between their lives and those of the gringo. Certainly the Mexican women cannery
workers of Watsonville who maintained a two-year victorious strike against Green
Giant in the mid-eighties, and farm workers organized by César Chávez's UFW in
the late sixties and early seventies are testimony to the political militancy of the Mexican immigrant worker. More recently, there are the examples of the Mothers of
East Los Angeles and the women of Kettleman City who have organized against the
toxic contamination proposed for their communities. In the process, the Mexicana
becomes a Chicana (or at least a Mechicana); that is, she becomes a citizen of this
country, not by virtue of a green card, but by virtue of the collective voice she
assumes in staking her claim to this land and its resources.

PLUMAS PLANCHADAS: THE DE-FORMATION
OF THE MOVEMENT

> With our heart in our hands and our hands in the soil, we declare the indepen-
> dence of our mestizo nation.
>
> —"El Plan Espiritual de Aztlán"

El Movimiento did not die out in the seventies, as most of its critics claim; it was
only deformed by the machismo and homophobia of that era and co-opted by "hispanicization" of the eighties.[4] In reaction against Anglo-America's emasculation of

Chicano men, the male-dominated Chicano Movement embraced the most patriarchal aspects of its Mexican heritage. For a generation, nationalist leaders used a kind of "selective memory," drawing exclusively from those aspects of Mexican and Native cultures that served the interests of male heterosexuals. At times, they took the worst of Mexican machismo and Aztec warrior bravado, combined it with some of the most oppressive male-conceived idealizations of "traditional" Mexican womanhood and called that cultural integrity. They subscribed to a machista view of women, based on the centuries-old virgin-whore paradigm of la Virgen de Guadalupe and Malintzin Tenepal. Guadalupe represented the Mexican ideal of "la madre sufrida," the long-suffering desexualized Indian mother, and Malinche was "la chingada," sexually stigmatized by her transgression of "sleeping with the enemy," Hernán Cortez. Deemed traitor by Mexican tradition, the figure of Malinche was invoked to keep Movimiento women silent, sexually passive, and "Indian" in the colonial sense of the word.

The preservation of the Chicano familia became the Movimiento's mandate and within this constricted "familia" structure, Chicano políticos ensured that the patriarchal father figure remained in charge both in their private and political lives.[5] Women were, at most, allowed to serve as modern-day "Adelitas," performing the "three fs" as a Chicana colleague calls them: "feeding, fighting, and fucking." In the name of this "culturally correct" familia, certain topics were censored both in cultural and political spheres as not "socially relevant" to Chicanos and typically not sanctioned in the Mexican household. These issues included female sexuality generally and male homosexuality and lesbianism specifically, as well as incest and violence against women—all of which are still relevant between the sheets and within the walls of many Chicano families. In the process, the Chicano Movement forfeited the participation and vision of some very significant female and gay leaders and never achieved the kind of harmonious Chicano "familia" they ostensibly sought.

To this day, although lip service is given to "gender issues" in academic and political circles, no serious examination of male supremacy within the Chicano community has taken place among heterosexual men. Veteranos of Chicano nationalism are some of the worst offenders. Twenty years later, they move into "elderhood" without having seriously grappled with the fact that their leadership in El Movimiento was made possible by all those women who kept their "plumas planchadas"[6] at every political event.

A DIVIDED NATION: A CHICANA LÉSBICA CRITIQUE

> We are free and sovereign to determine those tasks which are justly called for by our house, our land, the sweat of our brows, and by our hearts. Aztlán belongs to those who plant the seeds, water the fields, and gather the crops and not to the foreign Europeans. We do not recognize capricious frontiers on the bronze continent.
>
> —From "El Plan Espiritual de Aztlán"

When "El Plan Espiritual de Aztlán" was conceived a generation ago, lesbians and gay men were not envisioned as members of the "house"; we were not recognized as the sister planting the seeds, the brother gathering the crops. We were not counted as members of the "bronze continent."

In the last decade, through the efforts of Chicana feministas, Chicanismo has undergone a serious critique. Feminist critics are committed to the preservation of Chicano culture, but we know that our culture will not survive marital rape, battering, incest, drug and alcohol abuse, AIDS, and the marginalization of lesbian daughters and gay sons. Some of the most outspoken criticism of the Chicano Movement's sexism and some of the most impassioned activism in the area of Chicana liberation (including work on sexual abuse, domestic violence, immigrant rights, Indigenous women's issues, health care, etc.) have been advanced by lesbians.

Since lesbians and gay men have often been forced out of our blood families, and since our love and sexual desire are not housed within the traditional family, we are in a critical position to address those areas within our cultural family that need to change. Further, in order to understand and defend our lovers and our same-sex loving, lesbians and gay men must come to terms with how homophobia, gender roles, and sexuality are learned and expressed in Chicano culture. As Ricardo Bracho writes: "To speak of my desire, to find voice in my brown flesh, I needed to confront my male mirror." As a lesbian, I don't pretend to understand the intricacies or intimacies of Chicano gay desire, but we do share the fact that our "homosexuality"— our feelings about sex, sexual power and domination, femininity and masculinity, family, loyalty, and morality—has been shaped by heterosexist culture and society. As such, we have plenty to tell heterosexuals about themselves.

When we are moved sexually toward someone, there is a profound opportunity to observe the microcosm of all human relations, to understand power dynamics both obvious and subtle, and to meditate on the core creative impulse of all desire. Desire is never politically correct. In sex, gender roles, race relations, and our collective histories of oppression and human connection are enacted. Since the early 1980s, Chicana lesbian feminists have explored these traditionally "dangerous" topics in both critical and creative writings. Chicana lesbian-identified writers such as Ana Castillo, Gloria Anzaldúa, and Naomi Littlebear Moreno were among the first to articulate a Chicana feminism, which included a radical woman-centered critique of sexism *and sexuality* from which both lesbian and heterosexual women benefited.

In the last few years, Chicano gay men have also begun to openly examine Chicano sexuality. I suspect heterosexual Chicanos will have the world to learn from their gay brothers about their shared masculinity, but they will have the most to learn from the "queens," the "maricones." Because they are deemed "inferior" for not fulfilling the traditional role of men, they are more marginalized from mainstream heterosexual society than other gay men and are especially vulnerable to male violence. Over the years, I have been shocked to discover how many femme gay men have grown up regularly experiencing rape and sexual abuse. The rapist is always heterosexual and usually Chicano like themselves. What has the Gay Movement done for these brothers? What has the Chicano Movement done? What do these young and once-young men have to tell us about misogyny and male violence? Like women, they see the macho's desire to dominate the feminine, but even more intimately because they both desire men and share manhood with their oppressors. They may be jotos, but they are still men, and are bound by their racial and sexual identification to men (Bracho's "male mirror").

Until recently, Chicano gay men have been silent over the Chicano Movement's male heterosexual hegemony. As much as I see a potential alliance with gay men in our shared experience of homophobia, the majority of gay men still cling to what privileges they can. I have often been severely disappointed and hurt by the misogyny of gay Chicanos. Separation from one's brothers is a painful thing. Being gay does not preclude gay men from harboring the same sexism evident in heterosexual men. It's like white people and racism, sexism goes with the (male) territory.

On some level our brothers—gay and straight—have got to give up being "men." I don't mean give up their genitals, their unique expression of desire, or the rich and intimate manner in which men can bond together. Men have to give up their subscription to male superiority. I remember during the Civil Rights Movement seeing newsreel footage of young Black men carrying protest signs reading, "I AM A MAN." It was a powerful statement, publicly declaring their humanness in a society that daily told them otherwise. But they didn't write "I AM HUMAN," they wrote "MAN." Conceiving of their liberation in male terms, they were unwittingly demanding the right to share the whiteman's position of male dominance. This demand would become consciously articulated with the emergence of the male-dominated Black Nationalist Movement. The liberation of Black women per se was not part of the program, except to the extent that better conditions for the race in general might benefit Black women as well. How differently Sojourner Truth's "Ain't I a Woman" speech resonates for me. Unable to choose between suffrage and abolition, between her womanhood and her Blackness, Truth's 19th-century call for a free Black womanhood in a Black- and woman-hating society required the freedom of all enslaved land disenfranchised peoples. As the Black feminist Combahee River Collective stated in 1977, "If Black women were free, it would mean that everyone else would have to be free since our freedom would necessitate the destruction of all the systems of oppression." No progressive movement can succeed while any member of the population remains in submission.

Chicano gay men have been reluctant to recognize and acknowledge that their freedom is intricately connected to the freedom of women. As long as they insist on remaining "men" in the socially and culturally constructed sense of the word, they will never achieve the full liberation they desire. There will always be jotos getting raped and beaten. Within people of color communities, violence against women, gay bashing, sterilization abuse, AIDS and AIDS discrimination, gay substance abuse, and gay teen suicide emerge from the same source—a racist and misogynist social and economic system that dominates, punishes, and abuses all things colored, female, or perceived as female-like. By openly confronting Chicano sexuality and sexism, gay men can do their own part to unravel how both men *and* women have been formed and deformed by racist Amerika and our misogynist/catholic/colonized mechicanidad; and we can come that much closer to healing those fissures that have divided us as a people.

The AIDS epidemic has seriously shaken the foundation of the Chicano gay community, and gay men seem more willing than ever to explore those areas of political change that will ensure their survival. In their fight against AIDS, they have been rejected and neglected by both the white gay male establishment and the Latino heterosexual health-care community. They also have witnessed direct support by Latina lesbians.[7] Unlike the "queens" who have always been open about their sexuality, "passing" gay men have learned in a visceral way that being in "the closet" and preserving their "manly" image will not protect them, it will only make their dying more secret. I remember my friend Arturo Islas, the novelist. I think of how his writing begged to boldly announce his gayness. Instead, we learned it through vague references about "sinners" and tortured alcoholic characters who wanted nothing more than to "die dancing" beneath a lightning-charged sky just before a thunderstorm. Islas died of AIDS-related illness in 1990, having barely begun to examine the complexity of Chicano sexuality in his writing. I also think of essayist Richard Rodríguez, who, with so much death surrounding him, has recently begun to publicly address the subject of homosexuality; and yet, even ten years ago we all knew "Mr. Secrets" was gay from his assimilationist *Hunger of Memory*.[8] Had he "come out" in 1982, the white establishment would have been far less willing to promote him as the "Hispanic" anti-affirmative action spokesperson. He would have lost a lot of validity . . . and opportunity. But how many lives are lost each time we cling to privileges that make other people's lives more vulnerable to violence?

At this point in history, lesbians and gay men can make a significant contribution to the creation of a new Chicano movement, one passionately committed to saving lives. As we are forced to struggle for our right to love free of disease and discrimination, "Aztlán" as our imagined homeland begins to take on renewed importance. Without the dream of a free world, a free world will never be realized. Chicana lesbians and gay men do not merely seek inclusion in the Chicano nation; we seek a nation strong enough to embrace a full range of racial diversities, human sexualities, and expressions of gender. We seek a culture that can allow for the natural expression of our femaleness and maleness and our love without prejudice or punishment. In a "queer" Aztlán, there would be no freaks, no "others" to point one's finger at. My Native American friends tell me that in some Native American tribes, gay men and lesbians were traditionally regarded as "two-spirited" people. Displaying both masculine and feminine aspects, they were highly respected members of their community, and were thought to possess a higher spiritual development.[9] Hearing of such traditions gives historical validation for what Chicana lesbians and gay men have always recognized—that lesbians and gay men play a significant spiritual, cultural, and political role within the Chicano community. Somos activistas, académicos y artistas, parteras y políticos, curanderas y campesinos. With or without heterosexual acknowledgement, lesbians and gay men have continued to actively redefine familia, cultura, and comunidad. We have formed circles of support and survival, often drawing from the more egalitarian models of Indigenous communities.

INDIGENISMO: THE RE-TRIBALIZATION OF OUR PEOPLE

In recent years, for gay and straight Chicanos alike, our indigenismo has increased in importance as we witness the ultimate failure of Anglo-Americanism to bring harmony to our lives. In Ward Churchill's *Struggle for the Land*, he describes an "Indigenist" as someone who "takes the rights of indigenous peoples as the highest priority," and who "draws upon the traditions . . . of native peoples the world over." Many Chicanos would by this definition consider themselves Indigenists, subscribing to an indigenismo that is derived specifically from the traditions of mechicano indio peoples. Since the early seventies, Chicanos have worked in coalition with other Native American tribes and have participated in inter-tribal gatherings, political-prisoner campaigns, land-rights struggles, and religious ceremonies. Chicano Nation has been varyingly accepted as a tribe by other Native American peoples, usually more in the honorary sense than in any official capacity. The Indigenous Women's Network, for example, has included Chicanas since its inception in 1984.

Most Chicanos can claim, through physical traits alone, that we are of Native blood (we often joke that Chicanos are usually the most Indian-looking people in a room full of "skins"). The majority of us, however, has been denied direct information regarding our tribal affiliations. Since our origins are usually in the Southwest and México, Chicanos' Indian roots encompass a range of nations including Apache, Yaqui, Papago, Navajo, and Tarahumara from the border regions, as well as dozens of Native tribes throughout México. Regardless of verifiable genealogy, many Chicanos have recently begun to experience a kind of collective longing to return to our culture's traditional indigenous beliefs and ways of constructing community in order to find concrete solutions for the myriad problems confronting us, from the toxic dump sites in our neighborhoods to rape.

"Tribe," based on the traditional models of Native Americans, is an alternative socioeconomic structure that holds considerable appeal for those of us who recognize the weaknesses of the isolated patriarchal capitalist family structure. This is not to say that all Native Americans subscribe to the same tribal structures or that contemporary Indians fully practice traditional tribal ways. Few Native peoples today are allowed real political autonomy and self-determination. Tribal governments are corrupted by U.S. interference through the Bureau of Indian Affairs, the U.S. military, the FBI, and the U.S. Department of Energy. In essence, however, the tribal model is a form of community-building that can accommodate socialism, feminism, and environmental protection. In an ideal world, tribal members are responsive and responsible to one another and the natural environment. Cooperation is rewarded over competition. Acts of violence against women and children do not occur in secret and perpetrators are held accountable to the rest of the community. "Familia" is not dependent upon male-dominance or heterosexual coupling. Elders are respected and women's leadership is fostered, not feared.

But it is not an ideal world. Any Indian on or off the reservation can tell you about the obstacles to following traditional ways. The reservation is not indigenous to Native Americans; it is a colonial model invented to disempower Native peoples.

The rates of alcoholism, suicide, and domestic violence are testimony to the effectiveness of that system. Chicanos, living in the colony of the U.S. barrio, have the same scars: AIDS, drugs, brown-on-brown murder, poverty, and environmental contamination. Nevertheless, the present-day values and organized struggles of traditional Native communities throughout the Americas represent real hope for halting the quickly accelerating level of destruction affecting all life on this continent.

MADRE TIERRA/MADRE MUJER: THE STRUGGLE FOR LAND[10]

Journal Entry

I sit in a hotel room. A fancy hotel room with two walls of pure glass and pure Vancouver night skyline filling them. I sit on top of the bed and eat Japanese takeout. The Canadian t.v. news takes us east to the province of Quebec, to some desolate area with no plumbing or sewage, no running water, where a group of Inuit people have been displaced. To some desolate area where Inuit children stick their faces into bags and sniff gas fumes for the high, the rush, the trip, for the escape out of this hell-hole that is their life. One young boy gives the finger to the t.v. camera. "They're angry," an Inuit leader states. "I'm angry, too." At thirty, he is already an old man. And I hate this Canada as much as I hate these dis-United States.

But I go on eating my Japanese meal that has somehow turned rotten on my tongue and my bloody culpability mixes with the texture of dead fish flesh and no wonder I stand on the very edge of the balcony on the 26th floor of this hotel looking down on restaurant-row Vancouver and imagine how easy and impossible it would be to leap in protest for the gas-guzzling Inuit children.

The primary struggle for Native peoples across the globe is the struggle for land. In 1992, 500 years after the arrival of Columbus, on the heels of the Gulf War and the dissolution of the Soviet Union, the entire world is reconstructing itself. No longer frozen into the Soviet/Yanqui paradigm of a "Cold" and invented "War," Indigenous peoples are responding en masse to the threat of a global capitalist "monoculture" defended by the "hired guns" of the U.S. military. Five hundred years after Columbus' arrival, they are spearheading an international movement with the goal of sovereignty for all Indigenous nations.

Increasingly, the struggles on this planet are not for "nation-states," but for nations of people, bound together by spirit, land, language, history, and blood.[11] This is evident from the intifada of the Palestinians residing within Israel's stolen borders and the resistance of the Cree and Inuit Indians in northern Quebec. The Kurds of the Persian Gulf region understand this, as do the Ukrainians of what was once the Soviet Union. Chicanos are also a nation of people, internally colonized within the borders of the U.S. nation-state.

Few Chicanos really believe we can wrest Aztlán away from Anglo-America. And yet, residing in those Southwestern territories, especially those areas not completely appropriated by gringolandia, we instinctively remember it as Mexican Indian land and can still imagine it as a distinct nation. In our most private moments, we ask ourselves, *If the Soviet Union could dissolve, why can't the United States?*

Dreams of the disintegration of the United States as we know it are not so private among North American Indians. The dissolution of the Soviet Union has given renewed impetus to seccessionist thinking by Indians here in the United States. One plan, the "North American Union of Indigenous Nations," described in Ward Churchill's book, calls for the reunification of Indian peoples and territories to comprise a full third of continental United States, including much of Aztlán. Not surprisingly, Chicano Nation is not mentioned as part of this new confederacy, which speaks to the still tenuous alliance between Chicano and Native American peoples. Nevertheless, the spirit of the plan is very much in accord with Chicano nationalists' most revolutionary dreams of reclaiming a homeland, side by side with other Indian Nations.

If the material basis of every nationalist movement is land, then the reacquisition, defense, and protection of Native land and its natural resources are the basis for rebuilding Chicano nation. Without the sovereignty of Native peoples, including Chicanos, and support for our land-based struggles, the world will be lost to North American greed, and our culturas lost with it. The "last frontier" for Northern capitalists lies buried in coal and uranium-rich reservation lands and in the remaining rainforests of the Amazon. The inhabitants of these territories—the Diné, the North Cheyenne, the Kayapó, etc.—are the very people who in 1992 offer the world community "living models" of ways to live in balance with nature and safeguard the earth as we know it. The great historical irony is that 500 years after the Conquest, the conqueror must now turn to the conquered for salvation.

We are speaking of bottom-line considerations. I can't understand when in 1992 with 100 acres of rainforest disappearing every minute, with global warming, with babies being born without brains in South Tejas, with street kids in Río sniffing glue to stifle their hunger, with Mohawk women's breast milk being contaminated by the poisoned waters of the Great Lakes Basin, how we as people of color, as people of Indian blood, as people with the same last names as our Latin American counterparts, are not alarmed by the destruction of Indigenous and mestizo peoples. How is it Chicanos cannot see ourselves as victims of the same destruction, already in its advanced stages? Why do we not collectively experience the urgency for alternatives based not on what our oppressors advise, but on the advice of elders and ancestors who may now speak to us only in dreams?

What they are telling us is very clear. The road to the future is the road from our past. Traditional Indigenous communities (our Indian "past" that too many Chicanos have rejected) provide practical answers for our survival. At the Earth Summit in Río de Janeiro in June 1992, representatives from "developing countries," and grassroots, Indigenous, and people-of-color organizations joined together to demand the economic programs necessary to create their own sustainable ecologically sound communities. In a world where eighty-five percent of all the income, largely generated from the natural resources of Indigenous lands and "Third World" countries, goes to twenty-three percent of the people, Fidel Castro said it best: "Let the ecological debt be paid, not the foreign debt."

And here all the connecting concerns begin to coalesce. Here the Marxist meets the ecologist. We need look no further than the North American Free Trade Agreement (NAFTA) to understand the connection between global ecological devastation and the United States' relentless drive to expand its markets. NAFTA is no more than a 21st-century plot to continue the North's exploitation of the cheap labor, lax environmental policies, and the natural resources of the South. The United States has no intention of responding to the environmental crisis. George Bush's decision to "stand alone on principle" and refuse to sign the Bio-Diversity Treaty said it all. Profit over people. Profit over protection. No sustainable development is possible in the Americas if the United States continues to demand hamburgers, Chrysler automobiles, and refrigerators from hungry, barefoot, and energy-starved nations. There is simply not enough to go around, no new burial ground for toxic waste that isn't sacred, no untapped energy source that doesn't suck the earth dry. Except for the sun . . . except for the wind, which are infinite in their generosity and virtually ignored.

The earth is female. Whether myth, metaphor, or memory, she is called "Mother" by all peoples of all times. *Madre Tierra.* Like woman, Madre Tierra has been raped, exploited for her resources, rendered inert, passive, and speechless. Her cries manifested in earthquakes, tidal waves, hurricanes, volcanic eruptions are not heeded. But the Indians take note and so do the women, the women with the capacity to remember.

Native religions have traditionally honored the female alongside the male. Religions that grow exclusively from the patriarchal capitalist imagination, instead of the requirements of nature, enslave the female body. The only religion we need is one based on the good sense of living in harmony with nature. Religion should serve as a justification against greed, not for it. Bring back the rain gods, corn gods, father sun, and mother moon and keep those gods happy. Whether we recognize it or not, those gods are today, this day, punishing us for our excess. What humankind has destroyed will wreak havoc on the destroyer. Fried skin from holes in the ozone is only one example.

The earth is female. It is no accident then that the main grassroots activists defending the earth, along with Native peoples, are women of all races and cultures. Regardless of the so-called "advances" of Western "civilization," women remain the chief caretakers, nurturers, and providers for our children and our elders. These are the mothers of East Los Angeles, McFarland, and Kettleman City, fighting toxic dumps, local incinerators and pesticide poisoning, women who experience the earth's contamination in the deformation and death occurring within their very wombs. We do not have to be mothers to know this. Most women know what it is to be seen as the Earth is seen—a receptacle for male violence and greed. Over half the agricultural workers in the world are women who receive less training and less protection than their male counterparts. We do not control how we produce and reproduce, how we labor and love. And *how will our lands be free if our bodies aren't?*

Land remains the common ground for all radical action. But land is more than the rocks and trees, the animal and plant life that make up the territory of Aztlán or Navajo Nation or Maya Mesoamerica. For immigrant and native alike, land is also the factories where we work, the water our children drink, and the housing project where we live. For women, lesbians, and gay men, land is that physical mass called our bodies. Throughout las Américas, all these "lands" remain under occupation by an Anglocentric, patriarchal, imperialist United States.

LA CAUSA CHICANA: ENTERING THE NEXT MILLENNIUM

As a Chicana lesbian, I know that the struggle I share with all Chicanos and Indigenous peoples is truly one of sovereignty, the sovereign right to wholly inhabit oneself (*cuerpo y alma*) and one's territory (*pan y tierra*). I don't know if we can ever take back Aztlán from Anglo-America, but in the name of a new Chicano nationalism we can work to defend remaining Indian territories. We can work to teach one another that our freedom as a people is mutually dependent and cannot be parceled out—class before race before sex before sexuality. A new Chicano nationalism calls for the integration of both the traditional and the revolutionary, the ancient and the contemporary. It requires a serious reckoning with the weaknesses in our mestizo culture, and a reaffirmation of what has preserved and sustained us as a people. I am clear about one thing: fear has not sustained us. Fear of action, fear of speaking, fear of women, fear of queers.

As these 500 years come to a close, I look forward to a new América, where the only "discovery" to be made is the rediscovery of ourselves as members of the global community. Nature will be our teacher, for she alone knows no prejudice. Possibly as we ask men to give up being "men," we must ask humans to give up being "human," or at least to give up the human capacity for greed. Simply, we must give back to the earth what we take from it. We must submit to a higher "natural" authority, as we invent new ways of making culture, making tribe, to survive and flourish as members of the world community in the next millennium.

NOTES

An earlier version of this essay was first presented at the First National LLEGO (Latino/a Lesbian and Gay Organization) Conference in Houston, Texas, on May 22, 1992. A later version was presented at a Quincentenary Conference at the University of Texas in Austin on October 31, 1992.

1. Chicano term for "queer" folk.

2. To this day, there are still pockets of Chicano nationalists—mostly artists, poets, and cultural workers—who continue to work on a local and regional level.

3. UC Berkeley's Chicano/Latino immigrant students have not generally encountered the same degree of poverty and exploitation experienced by undocumented Mexican and Central American immigrants.

4. Further discussion of the "hispanicization" of the U.S. Latino can be found in the essay, "Art in América con Acento" in *The Last Generation,* Cherríe Moraga (Cambridge, Mass.: South End Press).

5. The twenty-five-year-old Chicano Teatro Movement is an apt example. Initiated by Luis Valdez' Teatro Campesino, the teatro movement has been notorious for its male dominance even within its so-called collective structures. Over eighty percent of the Chicano Theatres across the country are directed by men. No affirmative-action policies have been instituted to encourage the development of Chicana playwrights, technicians, or directors. In recent years, however, there has been some progress in this area with the production of a handful of Chicana playwrights, including Josefina López, Evelina Fernández, Edit Villareal, and this author. To this day, gay and lesbian images and feminist criticism are considered taboo in most Chicano theatres.

6. The image alludes to Chicano cultural nationalists who during the seventies neoindigenist period sometimes wore feathers (plumas) and other Indian attire at cultural events.

7. In contrast to the overwhelming response by lesbians to the AIDS crisis, breast cancer, which has disproportionately affected the lesbian community, has received little attention from the gay men's community in particular, and the public at large. And yet, the statistics are devastating. One out of every nine women in the United States will get breast cancer: 44,500 U.S. women will die of breast cancer this year (*Boston Globe,* November 5, 1991).

8. See Rodríguez' essay "Late Victorians" in his most recent collection, *Days of Obligation: An Argument with My Mexican Father.*

9. This was not the case among all tribes nor is homosexuality generally condoned in contemporary Indian societies. See "Must We Deracinate Indians to Find Gay Roots?" by Ramón A. Gutiérrez in *Outlook: National Lesbian and Gay Quarterly,* Winter 1989.

10. I wish to thank Marsha Gómez, the Indigenous Women's Network, and the Alma de Mujer Center for Social Change in Austin, Texas, for providing me with statistical and other current information about Indigenous peoples' struggles for environmental safety and sovereignty, as well as published materials on the '92 Earth Summit in Brazil.

11. The dissolution of what was heretofore the nation-state of Yugoslavia, composed of Serbs, Slovenes, Croats, Albanians, and Macedonians, including the Muslim and Orthodox religions, represents the rise of bitter nationalist sentiment gone awry. It is a horror story of ethnic and cultural nationalism turned into nazism and serves as a painful warning against fascist extremism in nationalist campaigns.

✳   ✳   ✳

QUESTIONS

1. Moraga claims that at the height of the Chicano movement in 1968 she was "a closeted, light-skinned, mixed-blood Mexican-American, disguised in [her] father's English last name." She also claims that she began her politicization, not through the Chicano movement, but through "the bold recognition of [her] lesbianism." This led to a "radical re-structuring of everything [she] thought [she] held sacred." And this, in turn, delivered her to political action "because not acting would have meant [her] death by despair."

a. Is there some kind of connection between political action and despair?

b. Do you recall other examples in which despair led to political action?

c. Have you ever been confronted by some kind of realization that forces you to reexamine your most sacred beliefs?

d. Have you ever felt that you must hide your beliefs (about anything) in front of your family or friends, as if you were wearing a "political disguise"?

2. It took Moraga a quarter of a century after the walkouts in 1968 to find a place "among la Chicanada" (the Chicano people). Though not a safe place, this is the "original familial place" from which she is compelled to write, to reach her audience, and which serves as a source of inspiration, voice, and struggle. Do you have or can you imagine a place that serves as a cradle for your thoughts and feelings and voice?

✳ 19 ✳

RECONSTRUCTING RACIAL IDENTITY: ETHNICITY, COLOR, AND CLASS AMONG DOMINICANS IN THE UNITED STATES AND PUERTO RICO

Jorge Duany

In this piece, Jorge further illustrates the manifold identities and struggles to which Latino/a human bodies are subjected depending on the dictates of the nation-states they inhabit. Jorge discusses the fourth largest Latino/a group in the United States: the Dominican immigrants to the mainland United States and Puerto Rico. He argues, specifically, that the massive migration from the Dominican Republic has culturally redefined the migrant's racial identity, causing a "traumatic racial experience." There is a contradiction between the public perception and the self concept of Dominican immigrants and this is a key problem for their adaptation to U.S. society. There is also an apparent paradox: though Puerto Rico's racial classification is different from that of the United States and similar to that of the Dominican Republic, Dominicans in Puerto Rico are viewed as black or colored.

When people move across state borders, they enter not only a different labor market and political structure but also a new system of social stratification by class, race, ethnicity, and gender. Migrants bring their own cultural conceptions of their identity, which often do not coincide with the ideological constructions of the receiving societies. As a mulatto Dominican colleague told me recently, she "discovered" that she was black only when she first came to the United States; until then she had thought of herself as an *india clara* (literally, a light Indian) in a country whose aboriginal population was practically exterminated in the 16th century.

For most Caribbean immigrants in the United States, race and color have played a crucial role in the formation of their cultural identities. Two different models of racial hegemony are juxtaposed in the process of moving from the Caribbean to the United States. On one hand, Caribbean migrants—especially those coming from the Spanish-speaking countries of Cuba, the Dominican Republic, and Puerto Rico—tend to use three main racial categories—black, white, and mixed—based primarily on skin color and other physical characteristics such as facial features and hair texture (Seda Bonilla, 1980). On the other hand, the dominant system of racial classification in the United States emphasizes a two-tiered division between whites and nonwhites deriving from the rule of hypodescent—the assignment of the off-spring of mixed races to the subordinate group (Harris, 1964; Winant, 1994). This clear-cut opposition between two cultural conceptions of racial identity is ripe for social and psychological conflict among Caribbean migrants, many of whom are of African or mixed background and are therefore defined as black or colored in the United States (Kasinitz, 1992; Safa, 1983).

I will argue that the massive exodus from the Dominican Republic has culturally redefined the migrants' racial identity. Whereas North Americans classify most Caribbean immigrants as black, Dominicans tend to perceive themselves as white, Hispanic, or other (including the folk term *indio,* to be discussed later). This contradiction between the public perception and the self-concept of Dominican migrants is one of their key problems in adapting to North American society. In Puerto Rico, although the traditional system of racial classification is similar to that of the Dominican Republic, most Dominican immigrants are viewed as blacks or colored (in local lore, *prietos, morenos,* and *trigueños*). Thus, in both receiving countries, Dominicans face the intense stigmatization, stereotyping, prejudice, and discrimination to which all people of African origin are subjected.

The argument is organized in four main parts. [Only the first part is included below.—*Ed.*] First, I will briefly review the extensive literature on race relations in the Caribbean and the United States, with special attention to the Dominican Republic and Puerto Rico. This background will help to clarify the different ideological constructions of racial identity in the sending and receiving countries. Second, I will summarize two field studies I directed among Dominican immigrants in the United States and in Puerto Rico. These studies will provide empirical support for the claim that migration has restructured the cultural conceptions of racial identity among Dominicans living abroad. Third, I will compare the Dominican communities of Washington Heights in New York City and Santurce, Puerto Rico. The data will reveal different patterns of racial and ethnic segregation, prejudice and discrimination, cultural adaptation, and identity, despite the similarity of many of the migrants' socioeconomic characteristics. Finally, I will assess the incorporation of Dominicans into North American and Puerto Rican societies and its potential impact on the Dominican Republic. My main thesis is that the racialization of Dominican immigrants in the United States and Puerto Rico has reinforced the persistence of an ethnic identity against the prevailing racial order and has largely confined them to the secondary segment of the labor and housing markets.

The theoretical framework for my argument owes much to the discussion of the racial formation of the United States by Michael Omi and Howard Winant (1994).

According to these writers, race is not a fixed essence, a concrete and objective entity, but rather a set of socially constructed meanings subject to change and contestation through power relations and social movements. Hence, racial identity is historically flexible and culturally variable, embedded in a particular social context (see Winant, 1994, for a recent attempt to reconceptualize the study of race relations from a Gramscian and poststructuralist perspective). I would argue that the dominant racial ideologies in the United States, the Dominican Republic, and Puerto Rico categorize and interpret race in different ways. Consequently, Dominican immigrants in the United States and Puerto Rico tend to be treated as blacks, although most of them do not define themselves as such.

My comparative analysis of the Dominican diaspora is also informed by recent thinking on transnationalism (Basch, Schiller, and Szanton Blanc, 1994; Schiller, Basch, and Blanc-Szanton, 1992; Rouse, 1991). For present purposes, Schiller, Basch, and Blanc-Szanton (1992) provide the most useful definition of transnationalism as the process whereby migrants establish and maintain sociocultural connections across geopolitical borders. The migrants' social relations, cultural values, economic resources, and political activities span at least two nation-states. Such transnational links are often sustained by a constant back-and-forth movement of people facilitated by rapid transportation and communications systems. As a result, migrants have multiple identities that link them simultaneously to more than one nation. Transnationalism interacts with ethnicity, race, class, gender, and other variables, complicating the process of identity formation. Among other consequences, transnational migration often transforms the cultural definition of racial identity.

In this context, the wider significance of the Dominican experience in the United States and Puerto Rico is twofold. On one hand, the reconstruction of racial identity among Dominican immigrants confirms that all systems of racial classification are arbitrary and contingent on varying forms of cultural representation. As a terrain of ideological contestation, the perceived racial identity of individuals and groups does not necessarily coincide with their self-perception (Omi and Winant, 1994). On the other hand, the racialization of Dominicans in the United States and Puerto Rico is part of a larger phenomenon affecting Caribbean communities in the diaspora. The prevailing definition of these migrants as black and colored tends to exclude them as biologically different from and culturally alien to the receiving societies (Basch, Schiller, and Szanton Blanc, 1994). To the extent that Caribbean migrants are racialized, their efforts to become integrated into the host countries face more obstacles than those of other ethnic groups that are not so labeled.

CARIBBEAN VERSUS U.S. RACIAL DISCOURSES

Much of the academic literature on Caribbean race relations is now several decades old (but see Oostindie, 1996, and Carrión, 1997, for recent collections revisiting the topic). The pioneering essays of the 1950s (Wagley, 1958), 1960s (Harris, 1964; Hoetink, 1967), and 1970s (Lowenthal, 1972; Mintz, 1974) contrasted the social construction of race in the Caribbean, the United States, and other countries of the Americas. The clearest picture emerging from these classic studies is that Caribbean societies tend to be stratified in terms of both class status and color gradations ranging from white to brown to black. Color distinctions in the Caribbean involve a complex inventory of physical traits such as skin pigmentation, hair form, and facial structure (Lowenthal, 1972; see also Smith, 1984). Phenotype and social status rather than biological descent define a person's racial identity, especially in the Spanish-speaking countries.

The Dominican Republic

Historians have shown that the present-day population of the Dominican Republic is the result of the intense mixture of peoples of European, African, and, to a lesser extent, Amerindian origin. By the end of the 18th century, the majority of Dominicans were classified as colored—that is, mulattos and blacks or, in contemporary parlance, *pardos* and *morenos*. Free blacks and mulattos displaced creole whites, African slaves, and Taíno as the leading sector of the colony of Hispaniola (Moya Pons, 1986; Franco, 1989). Today, informed sources agree that approximately 75 percent of the Dominican population consists of mulattos, with about 10 percent black and 15 percent white (compare Encyclopaedia Britannica, 1994; Ferguson, 1992; Black, 1986; Wiarda and Kryzanek, 1982). Like all racial statistics, these estimates reveal more about the official views of race than about the actual extent of racial mixture or the presence of blacks in the country.

Regardless of the exact demographic composition of the Dominican Republic, the dominant discourse on national identity defines it as white, Hispanic, and Catholic. Scholars have traced the origins and development of a racist and xenophobic ideology in the Dominican Republic since the mid-19th century. This ideology has produced an idealized view of the indigenous elements in Dominican culture, a systematic neglect of the contribution of African slaves and their descendants, increasing animosity toward Haitians and other black immigrants (such as the so-called *cocolos* from the eastern Caribbean), and a marked preference for Hispanic customs and traditions (Hoetink, 1994; Sagás, 1993; 1997; Alcántara Almánzar, 1987). As in other Hispanic Caribbean countries, racial prejudice and discrimination have been central features of the conventional wisdom on Dominican identity.

Under Rafael Trujillo's dictatorship (1930–1961), the pro-Hispanic and anti-Haitian discourse became the official ideology of the Dominican state. The Cibao region—with its traditional peasantry, popular music, Hispanic folklore, and "white" physical appearance—became the romantic symbol of an "authentic" Dominican culture (Hoetink, 1994). Thus, the Dominican merengue, particularly in its Cibao variant, became a powerful icon of national identity (Duany, 1994a). Meanwhile, Dominican politicians and intellectuals associated with the Trujillo regime defined Haiti as the antithesis of the Dominican Republic. If Dominicans were supposed to be white, Haitians were black; if Dominicans were Hispanic, Haitians were African; if Dominicans spoke Spanish, Haitians spoke Créole; and if Dominicans were Catholic, Haitians were voodoo practitioners. This binary opposition represented Haitians as the other—as inferior, foreign, and savage. The category "black" disappeared altogether from the official and popular discourses on race in the Dominican Republic, except in reference to foreigners (Baud, 1996; Charles, 1992; del Castillo, 1984).

Nowadays, even the darkest-skinned Dominican is considered not black but *indio oscuro* (dark Indian) or *trigueño*. As a result of this cultural conception, most Dominicans are declared to be white (*blanco*), Indian (indio), or a mixture of the two races (*mestizo*); only Haitians are considered "pure" blacks. A recent essay by Peter Roberts (1997) has analyzed the importance of the concept of indio for the construction of national identity in the Dominican Republic, as well as in Cuba and Puerto Rico. Stressing the indigenous roots of the Dominican nation helped to distinguish it from the Spanish metropolis as well as from neighboring Haiti. According to Ernesto Sagás (1993), the Dominican government now classifies the majority of Dominican citizens as indios. Thus, the term has become an official racial category in the Dominican Republic. The equivalent term *mulato,* referring to a mixture of white and black, is rarely used.

The academic literature contains numerous studies on the hostile relations between the Dominican Republic and Haiti (see the extensive bibliography in Lozano, 1992). The key historiographic issue has been the impact of the Haitian occupation of Santo Domingo (1822–1844) on the formation of the Dominican nation-state (Moya Pons, 1992; Franco, 1989). Whereas most historians traditionally considered this period a traumatic collective experience, Harry Hoetink (1971) emphasized the positive impact of the Haitian occupation on Dominican race relations and cultural identity. One of the recurring themes of the sociological literature is the massive migration of Haitians to the Dominican Republic and their slavelike working conditions on the sugar and coffee plantations (see Báez Evertsz, 1986; Lozano and Báez Evertsz, 1992). An invidious system of occupational segregation has isolated Haitians in the worst-paid and least desirable jobs, such as cane cutting and construction work. In both instances, directing racial and ethnic prejudice at a foreign enemy—Haitians—helped to define and consolidate a Dominican nationalist project conceived by the dominant elite and filtered down to the popular sectors.

Although many Dominican intellectuals in the post-Trujillo era have rejected the myth of Haitian inferiority, the popular sectors continue to repudiate Haitian immigrants and Haiti in general. Lower-class Dominicans attribute all kinds of social problems and negative situations to the Haitian "invasion," including racial "degeneration." According to a young Dominican cook living in Puerto Rico, "All Dominicans were blonde and blue eyed before they got dark and mixed with the Haitians." The Haitian has acquired a mysterious and legendary status in Dominican folklore as a practitioner of obscure rites such as black magic and cannibalism. It will take time to eradicate firmly held beliefs and practices that exclude Haitians (and, by extension, blacks) from the accepted definition of national identity in the Dominican Republic (see Torres-Saillant, 1992–1993; 1997; Sagás, 1993; 1997). Anti-Haitianism pervades the dominant discourse on Dominican identity, from popular religion, music, and literature to economic affairs, public policies, and party politics. One of the main problems faced by the presidential candidate of the Dominican Revolutionary party, José Francisco Peña Gómez, has been his Haitian origin and black appearance. Although racism was not the only reason for Peña Gómez's defeat in 1996, it played a key role in the electoral campaign.

In sum, the Dominican system of racial classification has two peculiar features in a comparative Caribbean context. First, it does not identify local blacks as a separate category within the color spectrum but instead reserves that category for Haitians. Second, it blurs the distinctions among creole whites, light coloreds, and mulattos, thereby creating the impression of a predominantly white and Indian population. Through these discursive strategies, the system fosters the racial and cultural homogenization of the Dominican Republic vis-à-vis Haiti. Thus, the social construction of race and ethnicity is characterized by a strong reactive or oppositional identity. It is this sense of national pride and rejection of their own negritude that many Dominican migrants bring with them and must reevaluate when they confront the U.S. model of racial stratification.

Puerto Rico

The best empirical study of Puerto Rican race relations remains Eduardo Seda Bonilla's pioneering fieldwork, conducted in the late 1950s and 1960s, although several essays have dealt with the racial question on the island and the U.S. mainland since then (see Sagrera, 1973; Zenón Cruz, 1974; Ginorio, 1979; Picó de Hernández et al., 1985; Díaz Quiñones, 1985; Rodríguez-Morazzani, 1996; V. Rodríguez, 1997). Seda Bonilla (1973) argued convincingly that most Puerto Ricans use phenotype rather than hypodescent as the main criterion for racial identity. Puerto Ricans tend to think of three main physical types—white, black, and mulatto—defined primarily by skin color, facial features, and hair texture (see also C. Rodríguez, 1989). Furthermore, whereas North Americans pay close attention to national origin in defining a person's ethnic identity, Puerto Ricans give a higher priority to birthplace and cultural orientation.

Thus, when Puerto Ricans move to the U.S. mainland, they confront a different construction of their racial identity (Seda Bonilla, 1980). In the United States, Puerto Ricans are often grouped together with black and colored people. Those with mixed racial backgrounds lose their intermediate status in a white-nonwhite dichotomy. Light-skinned immigrants are sometimes called "white Puerto Ricans," whereas dark-skinned immigrants are often treated like African Americans. Most are simply classified as "Pororicans" as if this were a distinct racial category. Like other ethnic minorities, Puerto Ricans in the United States have been thoroughly racialized (see V. Rodríguez, 1997; Rodríguez-Morazzani, 1996).

Statistically, the majority of the Puerto Rican population is white by local standards. Estimates of the white group on the island range from 73 percent (Seda Bonilla, 1980) to 80 percent of the population (Encyclopaedia Britannica, 1994), with an additional 8 percent black and 19 percent mulatto in Seda Bonilla's count. These statistics are open to debate because of the fluid definition of racial groups as well as the lack of recent official data on the island's racial composition. (In 1970, the Census Bureau dropped the racial identification question for Puerto Rico.) However, the available figures confirm that most Puerto Ricans perceive themselves as white rather than as black or mulatto.

In any case, study after study has shown that blacks are a stigmatized minority on the island, that they suffer from persistent prejudice and discrimination, that they tend to occupy the lower rungs of the class structure, and that they are subject to an ideology of progressive whitening (*blanqueamiento*) through intermarriage with lighter-skinned groups and a denial of their cultural heritage and physical characteristics (Seda Bonilla, 1973; Zenón Cruz, 1974; Picó de Hernández et al., 1985). Thus, the main difference between the Puerto Rican and North American models of racial stratification is not the treatment of blacks—who are accorded a subordinate status in both societies—but rather the mixed group. In Puerto Rico, light mulattos often pass for whites, whereas in the United States, this intermediate racial category does not even exist officially. The symbolic boundaries among whites, mulattos, and blacks seem more porous in Puerto Rico than in the United States.

New York–based Puerto Rican sociologist Clara Rodríguez reports that many members of the so-called Neo-Rican community resist being classified as either black or white and prefer to identify themselves as "other." In the 1980 Census, 48 percent of New York's Puerto Rican population chose this category, including alternative ethnic labels such as Hispanic, Spanish, and Boricua (C. Rodríguez, 1989; 1992; Rodríguez and Cordero-Guzmán, 1992). Hence, many Puerto Rican migrants and their descendants continue to employ a tripartite rather than a bipolar system of racial classification. Contrary to Seda Bonilla's (1980) prediction that the Neo-Rican community would split along color lines, most migrants reject their indiscriminate labeling as members of a single race (see also Ginorio, 1979). Rather than dividing themselves into white or black, most Puerto Ricans recognize that they are a multiracial or—to use Rodríguez's (1989) apt image—a "rainbow" people.

In sum, the Puerto Rican model of race relations has several distinguishing features. In contrast to North Americans, most Puerto Ricans consider racial identity not primarily a question of biological descent but rather one of physical appearance. As a result, a person of mixed racial background is not automatically assigned to the black group in Puerto Rico. Rather, racial classification depends largely on skin color and other visible characteristics such as the shape of the mouth, nose, and hair. Puerto Ricans have developed an elaborate racist vocabulary for referring to these characteristics. Socioeconomic variables such as occupation and education can also affect a person's racial identity. Furthermore, Puerto Ricans usually distinguish between blacks and mulattos, whereas North Americans tend to view both groups as colored or nonwhite. Finally, because of the proliferation of multiple and fluid physical types, Puerto Rico has not established a two-tiered institutionalized system of racial discrimination such as that of the United States. For example, neither the occupational nor the residential structures of Puerto Rican society segregate its members exclusively by color. As we shall see, the island's system of racial classification has distinct implications for the racial identity of Dominican migrants.

The United States

The preceding discussion has already alluded to the key features of the dominant model of racial formation in the United States. Scholars have debated whether this model resembles a caste system, especially as it operated in the Old South prior to the abolition of the Jim Crow laws in the 1950s. In any case, the North American system is unusual (comparable to South Africa's apartheid) in its terminological simplicity and intense separation between subordinate "racial" minorities and dominant ethnic groups. Historically, the black/white division has been rigidly defined in the United States through the rule of hypodescent (Omi and Winant, 1994). North American race relations have been characterized by institutionalized discrimination against so-called racial minorities such as African Americans, Native Americans, Latinos, and Asians, defined partly by their skin color and partly by their geographic origin.

The dominant racial discourse in the United States assigns an upper status to white groups of European origin and a lower status to black and brown groups from other regions, including the Caribbean and Latin America. Racial minorities such as Haitians and Chinese are stereotyped and marginalized more acutely than other ethnic groups in North American society. As a result, the social distance between such groups is much greater than that between, say, the Irish or Italians and English or Germans, who are all defined as "white ethnics." The racialization of Caribbean immigrants has slowed their structural and cultural assimilation into North American society. Recent studies have coined the terms "segmented assimilation" and "oppositional identity" to refer to the fate of racially defined minorities in the contemporary United States (see Portes, 1994, for a conceptual discussion and empirical data focusing on second-generation immigrants).

Residential segregation is a fundamental aspect of racial and ethnic relations in the United States (Massey and Denton, 1993). Black Americans have been subjected to the highest degree of racial segregation in major urban centers over the past five decades, and so have most Caribbean immigrants, who tend to be considered black or colored (Kasinitz, 1992). Recent studies have shown that Latinos, especially Puerto Ricans and dark-skinned immigrants, suffer from a similar disadvantage in the housing market of metropolitan areas such as New York, Philadelphia, Chicago, and Hartford (Santiago and Wilder, 1991; Santiago, 1992). Some scholars have even predicted that Latinos will become a "middle race" between whites and blacks in the United States (Domínguez, 1973).

Until now, no empirical study has systematically examined the impact of the North American system of racial stratification on the Dominican diaspora. The major publications have neglected the cultural redefinition of the migrants' racial identity in the United States (see Guarnizo, 1994; Grasmuck and Pessar, 1991; Portes and Guarnizo, 1991; Georges, 1990; Georges et al., 1989; del Castillo and

Mitchell, 1987). An exception to this trend is Virginia Domínguez's (1973; 1978) comparative assessment of Cubans, Dominicans, and Puerto Ricans in Washington Heights during the 1960s. One reason for this oversight may be that researchers have usually focused on Dominican migrants as lower-class workers rather than as members of a "racial" minority. Most studies have underestimated a key variable in the incorporation of Dominican immigrants into the secondary segment of the U.S. labor and housing markets: their public perception as blacks, colored, or nonwhite. . . .

CONCLUSION

Transnational migration often calls into question immigrants' conceptions of ethnic, racial, and national identities. In the Dominican Republic, most people perceive themselves as dark-skinned whites or light mulattos; only Haitians are considered black. The Dominican system of racial classification, labeling people along a wide color continuum ranging from black to white, clashes with the racial dualism prevalent in the United States. For most Dominican migrants, who have some degree of racial mixture, the rule of hypodescent means that they are considered black, nonwhite, or colored. Through a profound ideological transformation, the so-called indios suddenly become black, Hispanic, or "other." The data presented here suggest that most of the Dominicans who identify themselves as blacks in New York would probably call themselves indios in their home country. This process of self-redefinition is, in Frank Moya Pons's (1986: 247) graphic expression, a "traumatic racial experience."

Dominicans in Puerto Rico encounter less cognitive dissonance regarding their racial identity than in the United States. Immigrant Dominicans, like native Puerto Ricans, are classified in terms of a complex system that takes into account skin pigmentation, hair texture, facial features, and social class. This cultural conception does not automatically assume that all Dominicans are black or that they can be divided neatly along color lines. Rather, Puerto Ricans traditionally adopt a flexible definition that recognizes multiple and heterogeneous racial groups, especially among intermediate types. Still, the dark skin color and other "African" features of most Dominican immigrants, together with their low occupational status, place them at the bottom of the Puerto Rican stratification system.

The racialization of Dominican immigrants has been a prime obstacle to their successful incorporation into the labor and housing markets of the United States and Puerto Rico. Although many Dominicans oppose their classification as colored, some have become increasingly aware of themselves as an Afro-Caribbean people. Migrants' general response to external labels has been to emphasize racial diversity within their community as well as the cultural bonds of solidarity among Dominicans of different skin colors. The persistence of a Dominican identity in the United States may be interpreted in part as resistance to the prevailing racial order.

The incorporation of Dominican immigrants into Puerto Rican society has been hampered by their class composition as well as their racial identity. Xenophobia and racism have increased with Dominican immigration over the past three decades. The age-old stereotypes of black Puerto Ricans are now extended to Dominican immigrants, who in turn attribute them to Haitians—for example, stupidity, uncleanliness, and ugliness (see Zenón Cruz, 1974, for a complete catalogue of racial infamies in Puerto Rico). The social construction of race and ethnicity in contemporary Puerto Rico increasingly conflates black with Dominican. Still, Puerto Rican society segregates Dominicans not primarily by skin color or national origin but by social class. Barrio Gandul is neither a black ghetto like Harlem nor an ethnic neighborhood like Washington Heights.

The theoretical implications of this comparative case study are numerous, but I can only underline three of them here. First, transnational migrants face different, often conflicting, definitions of their racial identity in the sending and receiving societies. This ideological discrepancy confirms the absence of any essential characteristics or fixed meanings in racial discourses and focuses attention on the socially constructed and invented nature of racial classification systems. Second, regardless of their imaginary and arbitrary character, cultural conceptions of racial identity have a practical and material impact when they are applied to concrete groups and individuals in social interaction. The racialization of Caribbean immigrants in the United States and elsewhere places them in a disadvantageous position in the labor and housing markets and excludes them from the hegemonic cultural practices of the receiving nation-states. Finally, the immigrants' lower-class standing reinforces their public perception as ethnic and racial outsiders. This intersection of ethnicity, color, and class makes it harder for Caribbean diaspora communities to shed their multiple stigmas.

At this point, it is difficult to assess the impact of the cultural redefinition of the migrants' racial identity on the Dominican Republic. A decade ago, the distinguished Dominican historian Frank Moya Pons (1986) claimed that massive migration had not eroded the island's sense of identity. More recently, the New York–based Dominican literary critic Silvio Torres-Saillant (1992–1993) went beyond this to propose that Dominican identity is reasserted in the diaspora against a backdrop of ethnic and racial oppression. In my view, increasing numbers of Dominicans in the United States and Puerto Rico are being forced to confront racially exclusive conceptions and practices, framed in the language either of biological descent or of physical appearance.

By and large, the Dominican diaspora has actively resisted its subordination as a racialized other and attempted to redefine the terms of its incorporation into the host societies. Whether this effort results in asserting that Dominicans are part of a middle race such as Latinos or Hispanics (Domínguez, 1973), making common cause with African Americans on the basis of their colored status, or embracing a wider pan-Caribbean identity that includes Haitians has yet to be determined. For the moment, transnational migration has transformed the cultural conceptions of racial identity among Dominicans in the United States and Puerto Rico. For many racially mixed immigrants, coming to America has meant coming to terms with their own, partially suppressed, sometimes painful, but always liberating sense of negritude.

NOTE

Jorge Duany is an associate professor of anthropology and director of the *Revista de Ciencias Sociales* at the University of Puerto Rico in Río Piedras. He has published widely on Caribbean migration, ethnic identity, and popular culture and has recently coauthored (with José A. Cobas) *Cubans in Puerto Rico: Ethnic Economy and Cultural Identity* (1997) and (with Luisa Hernández Angeira and César E. Rey) *El Barrio Gandul: Economía subterránea y migración indocumentada en Puerto Rico* (Caracas: Nueva Sociedad, 1995). The author thanks Ramona Hernández, Helen Safa, Carlos Severino, Constance Sutton, Emelio Betances, and Jeff Tobin for useful comments on earlier drafts. The Puerto Rican study was conducted with the collaboration of César A. Rey and Luisa Hernández and cosponsored by the U.S. Census Bureau and the University of the Sacred Heart in Santurce, Puerto Rico. The New York study was sponsored by the Dominican Studies Institute of the City University of New York, under the direction of Silvio Torres-Saillant. The author is grateful for his colleagues' intellectual support and for the financial support of these institutions.

REFERENCES

Alcántara Almánzar, José
    1987 "Black images in Dominican literature." *New West Indian Guide* 61(3–4): 161–173.
Báez Evertsz, Franc
    1986 *Braceros haitianos en la República Dominicana.* 2nd ed. Santo Domingo: Instituto
        Dominicano de Investigaciones Sociales.
Báez Evertsz, Franc and Frank D'Oleo Ramírez
    1986 *La emigración de dominicanos a Estados Unidos: determinantes socio-económicos y consecuencias.* Santo Domingo: Fundación Friedrich Ebert.
Basch, Linda, Nina Glick Schiller, and Cristina Szanton Blanc
    1994 *Nations Unbound: Transnational Projects, Postcolonial Predicaments, and Deterritorialized States.* Basel: Gordon and Breach.
Baud, Michiel
    1996 "'Constitutionally white': the forging of a national identity in the Dominican Republic," pp. 121–151 in Gert Oostindie (ed.), *Ethnicity in the Caribbean: Essays in Honor of Harry Hoetink.* London: Macmillan Caribbean.
Black, Jan Knippers
    1986 *The Dominican Republic: Politics and Development in an Unsovereign State.* Boston: Allen and Unwin.
Brownrigg, Leslie A.
    1990 "1990 guidelines for the alternative enumeration. Part 1. Geography and physical space." Washington, DC: Center for Survey Methods Research, Bureau of the Census.
Brownrigg, Leslie A. and Elaine Fansler
    1990 "1990 guidelines for the alternative enumeration. Part 3. Behavioral observations." Washington, DC: Center for Survey Methods Research, Bureau of the Census.

Carrión, Juan Manuel (ed.)
    1997 *Ethnicity, Race, and Nationality in the Caribbean.* San Juan: Institute of Caribbean Studies, University of Puerto Rico.

Charles, Carolle
    1992 "La raza: una categoría significativa en el proceso de inserción de los trabajadores haitianos en República Dominicana," pp. 145–168 in Wilfredo Lozano (ed.), *La cuestión haitiana en Santo Domingo: migración internacional, desarrollo y relaciones inter-estatales entre Haití y República Dominicana.* Santo Domingo: Facultad Latinoamericana de Ciencias Sociales.

del Castillo, José
    1984 *Ensayos de sociologia dominicana.* Santo Domingo: Taller.

del Castillo, José, and Christopher Mitchell (eds.)
    1987 *La inmigración dominicana en los Estados Unidos.* Santo Domingo: CENAPEC.

Diaz Quiñones, Arcadio
    1985 "Tomás Blanco: Racismo, historia, esclavitud," pp. 13–91 in *El prejuicio racial en Puerto Rico.* Río Piedras: Huracán.

Domínguez, Virginia
    1973 "Spanish-speaking Caribbeans in New York: 'The middle race.'" *Revista/Review Interamericana* 3(2): 135–142.
    1978 "Show your colors: Ethnic divisiveness among Hispanic Caribbean migrants." *Migration Today* 6(1): 5–9.

Duany, Jorge
    1994a "Ethnicity, identity, and music: An anthropological analysis of the Dominican merengue," pp. 65–98 in Gerard Béhague (ed.), *Music and Black Ethnicity: The Caribbean and South America.* Miami: North-South Center, University of Miami.
    1994b *Quisqueya on the Hudson: The Transnational Identity of Dominicans in Washington Heights.* New York: Dominican Studies Institute, City University of New York.

Duany, Jorge (ed.)
    1990 *Los dominicanos en Puerto Rico: migración en la semi-periferia.* Río Piedras: Huracán.

Duany, Jorge, Luisa Hernández Angueira, and César A. Rey
    1995 *El Barrio Gandul: economía subterránea y migración indocumentada en Puerto Rico.* Caracas: Nueva Sociedad.

Encyclopaedia Britannica
    1994 "1994 Britannica World Data," in *1994 Book of the Year.* Chicago: Encyclopaedia Britannica.

Ferguson, James
    1992 *Dominican Republic: Beyond the Lighthouse.* London: Latin America Bureau.

Franco, Franklin J.
    1989 *Los negros, los mulatos y la nación dominicana.* 8th ed. Santo Domingo: Editora Nacional.

Georges, Eugenia
    1984 *New Immigrants and the Political Process: Dominicans in New York.* Center for Latin American and Caribbean Studies, New York University, Occasional Paper 45.
    1990 *The Making of a Transnational Community: Migration, Development, and Cultural Change in the Dominican Republic.* New York: Columbia University Press.

Georges, Eugenia, Eric M. Larson, Sara J. Mahler, Christopher Mitchell, Patricia R. Pessar, Teresa A. Sullivan, and Robert Warren
    1989 *Dominicanos ausentes: Cifras, políticas, condiciones sociales.* Santo Domingo: Fundación Friedrich Ebert.

Ginorio, Angela Beatriz
    1979 "A comparison of Puerto Ricans in New York with native Puerto Ricans and Native Americans on two measures of acculturation: Gender role and racial identification." Ph.D. diss., Fordham University.
Grasmuck, Sherri and Patricia R. Pessar
    1991 *Between Two Islands: Dominican International Migration.* Berkeley: University of California Press.
Guarnizo, Luis E.
    1994 *"Los dominicanyorks:* The making of a binational society." *Annals of the American Academy of Political and Social Science* 533: 70–86.
Harris, Marvin
    1964 *Patterns of Race in the Americas.* New York: Norton.
Hernández, Ramona, Francisco Rivera-Batiz, and Roberto Agodini
    1995 *Dominican New Yorkers: A Socioeconomic Profile.* New York: Dominican Studies Institute, City University of New York.
Hoetink, Harry
    1967 *Caribbean Race Relations: A Study of Two Variants.* London: Oxford University Press.
    1971 "The Dominican Republic in the 19th century: some notes on stratification, immigration, and race," pp. 96–121 in Magnus Mörner (ed.), *Race and Class in Latin America.* New York: Columbia University Press.
    1994 *Santo Domingo y el Caribe: Ensayos sobre cultura y sociedad.* Santo Domingo: Fundación Cultural Dominicana.
Iturrondo, Milagros
    1994 "'San Ignacio de la Yola' . . . y los dominicanos (en Puerto Rico)." *Homines* 17 (1–2): 234–240.
Kasinitz, Philip
    1992 *Caribbean New York: Black Immigrants and the Politics of Race.* Ithaca: Cornell University Press.
Lowenthal, David
    1972 *West Indian Societies.* New York: Oxford University Press.
Lozano, Wilfredo (ed.)
    1992 *La cuestión haitiana en Santo Domingo: migración internacional, desarrollo y relaciones inter-estatales entre Haití y Republica Dominicana.* Santo Domingo: Facultad Latinoamericana de Ciencias Sociales.
Lozano, Wilfredo and Franc Báez Evertsz
    1992 *Migración internacional y economia cafetalera: estudio sobre la migración estacional de trabajadores haitianos a la cosecha cafetalera en la República Dominicana.* 2nd ed. Santo Domingo: Centro de Planificación y Acción Ecuménica.
Massey, Douglas S. and Nancy A. Denton
    1993 *American Apartheid: Segregation and the Making of the Underclass.* Cambridge: Harvard University Press.
Mejía Pardo, Diana María
    1993 "Macroestructuras, superestructuras y proposiciones de opiniones en 17 relatos puertorriqueños acerca de dominicanos." Master's thesis, University of Puerto Rico, Río Piedras.
Mintz, Sidney W.
    1974 *Caribbean Transformations.* Chicago: Aldine.

Moya Pons, Frank
1986 *El pasado dominicano.* Santo Domingo: Fundación J. A. Caro Alvarez.
1992 "Las tres fronteras: Introducción a la frontera domínico-haitiana," pp. 17–32 in Wilfredo Lozano (ed.), *La cuestión haitiana: Migración internacional, desarrollo y relaciones inter-estatales entre Haití y República Dominicana.* Santo Domingo: Facultad Latinoamericana de Ciencias Sociales.

New York Newsday
1993 "Trying to make sense of census." June 24.

New York Times
1993 "Immigrants forgoing citizenship while pursuing American dream." July 25.

Omi, Michael and Howard Winant
1994 *Racial Formation in the United States: From the 1960s to the 1990s.* 2nd ed. New York: Routledge.

Oostindie, Gert (ed.)
1996 *Ethnicity in the Caribbean: Essays in Honor of Harry Hoetink.* London: Macmillan Caribbean.

Picó de Hernández, Isabel, Marcia Rivera, Carmen Parrilla, Jeannette Ramos de Sanchez Villela, and Isabelo Zenón
1985 *Discrimen por color, sexo y origen nacional en Puerto Rico.* Río Piedras: Centro de Investigaciones Sociales, Universidad de Puerto Rico.

Portes, Alejandro (ed.)
1994 *The New Second Generation. International Migration Review* 28(4).

Portes, Alejandro and Luis E. Guarnizo
1991 *Capitalistas del trópico: La inmigración en los Estados Unidos y el desarrollo de la pequeña empresa en la República Dominicana.* Santo Domingo: Facultad Latinoamericana de Ciencias Sociales.

Roberts, Peter
1997 "The (re)construction of the concept of 'indio' in the national identities of Cuba, the Dominican Republic, and Puerto Rico," pp. 99–120 in Lowell Fiet and Janette Becerra (eds.), *Caribe 2000: Definiciones, identidades y culturas regionales y/o nacionales.* Río Piedras: Facultad de Humanidades, Universidad de Puerto Rico.

Rodríguez, Clara E.
1989 *Puerto Ricans: Born in the U.S.A.* Boston: Unwin Hyman.
1992 "Race, culture, and Latino 'otherness' in the 1980 census." *Social Science Quarterly* 73(4): 930–937.

Rodríguez, Clara E. and Héctor Cordero-Guzmán
1992 "Placing race in context." *Ethnic and Racial Studies* 15(4): 523–542.

Rodríguez, Víctor M.
1997 "The racialization of Puerto Rican ethnicity in the United States," pp. 233–273 in Juan Manuel Carrión (ed.), *Ethnicity, Race, and Nationality in the Caribbean.* San Juan: Institute of Caribbean Studies, University of Puerto Rico.

Rodríguez-Morazzani, Roberto P.
1996 "Beyond the rainbow: mapping the discourse on Puerto Ricans and 'race.'" *Centro* 8(1–2):151–169.

Rouse, Roger
1991 "Mexican migration and the social space of postmodernism." *Diaspora* 1(1): 8–23.

Safa, Helen I.
  1983 "Caribbean migration to the United States: Cultural identity and the process of assimilation," pp. 47–73 in Edgar Gumbert (ed.), *Different People: Studies in Ethnicity and Education*. Atlanta: Center for Cross-Cultural Education, Georgia State University.
Sagás, Ernesto
  1993 "A case of mistaken identity: *antihaitianismo* in the Dominican Republic." *Latin-americanist* 29(1): 1–5.
  1997 "The development of *antihaitianismo* into a dominant ideology during the Trujillo era," pp. 96–121 in Juan Manuel Carrión (ed.), *Ethnicity, Race, and Nationality in the Caribbean*. San Juan: Institute of Caribbean Studies, University of Puerto Rico.
Sagrera, Martín
  1973 *Racismo y política en Puerto Rico: la desintegración interna y externa de un pueblo*. Río Piedras: Edil.
Santiago, Anne M.
  1992 "Patterns of Puerto Rican segregation and mobility." *Hispanic Journal of Behavioral Sciences* 14(1): 107–133.
Santiago, Anne and Margaret G. Wilder
  1991 "Residential segregation and links to minority poverty: The case of Latinos in the United States." *Social Problems* 38(4): 492–515.
Schiller, Nina Glick, Linda Basch, and Cristina Blanc-Szanton (eds.)
  1992 *Towards a Transnational Perspective on Migration: Race, Ethnicity, and Nationalism Reconsidered*. New York: New York Academy of Sciences.
Seda Bonilla, Eduardo
  1973 *Los derechos civiles en la cultura puertorriqueña*. 2nd ed. Río Piedras: Bayoán.
  1980 *Réquiem para una cultura*. 4th ed. Río Piedras: Bayoán.
Smith, M. G.
  1984 *Culture, Race, and Class in the Commonwealth Caribbean*. Mona, Jamaica: Department of Extra-Mural Studies, University of the West Indies.
Torres-Saillant, Silvio
  1992–1993 "Cuestión haitiana y supervivencia moral dominicana." *Punto y Coma* 4(2): 195–206.
  1997 "Hacia una identidad racial alternativa en la sociedad dominicana." *Op. Cit.: Revista del Centro de Investigaciones Históricas* (University of Puerto Rico, Río Piedras) 9: 235–252.
U.S. Department of Commerce, Bureau of the Census
  1994 *1990 Census of Population and Housing: Population and Housing Characteristics of Census Tracts and Block Numbering Areas, San Juan-Caguas, PR CMSA*. Washington, DC: Government Printing Office.
Wagley, Charles
  1958 *Minorities in the New World*. New York: Columbia University Press.
Waters, Mary C.
  1994 "Ethnic and racial identities of second-generation black immigrants in New York City," pp. 795–820 in Alejandro Portes (ed.), *The New Second Generation*.
Wiarda, Howard H. and Michael Kryzanek
  1982 *The Dominican Republic: A Caribbean Crucible*. Boulder: Westview.
Winant, Howard
  1994 *Racial Conditions: Politics, Theory, Comparisons*. Minneapolis: University of Minnesota Press.

Zenón Cruz, Isabelo
   1974 *Narciso descubre su trasero: El negro en la cultura puertorriqueña.* 2 vols. Humacao:
   Furidi.

QUESTIONS

1. How is it possible to adopt an identity of "white," "indio" or "mestizo" if in fact you are a *mulato,* of African descent? What are the processes involved in the creation of such a fictional identity?

2. If, as it is claimed, U.S. white identity is dependent on U.S. black identity, to what extent is Dominican "nonblack" identity dependent on Haitian black identity? What are the implications of this comparison for the definition of race?

3. Which human bodies can be said to benefit from the different racial classifications in Puerto Rico and the United States? How do these benefits shift as these bodies cross national or territorial (U.S./Puerto Rican) borders? How does class affect these "benefits" in different nations or territories?

4. In terms of the impact on the socioeconomic status of human bodies, what difference does it make to consider racial identity a question of biological descent as opposed to physical appearance?

5. While admittedly a matter of speculation, given the factors for the construction of ethnic and racial identities discussed in this and other articles in this book, do you believe that Dominicans will (a) become a part of a Latino/Hispanic "middle race" in the United States; (b) join the African American identity; or (c) embrace a pan-Caribbean identity? Why?

✳ 20 ✳

NO REGRETS: THE TOUGH CHOICE BETWEEN FREEDOM AND CONVICTIONS FACED BY JAILED PUERTO RICAN ACTIVISTS

Patricia Guadalupe

Though not a social movement—it is not characterized by a mass following—there is a Puerto Rican discursive regularity, a tradition of militancy. It is a militancy against the exercise of power on Puerto Rican people, against what Muñoz Marín poetically calls "a festering sore in the human spirit." In the following brief article, we find a continuation of patriotic insurgency or terrorism, depending on where you stand on the political spectrum. This discourse is anchored by **institutions** that contain memories of previous struggles in names such as Rafael Cancel Miranda Puerto Rican High School in Chicago (renamed Dr. Pedro Albizu Campos) and the Juan Antonio Corretjer Puerto Rican Cultural Center. Patricia tells the story of Lucy and Alicia, two sisters, one born in Puerto Rico and the other in Chicago, who carry on the oldest fight against colonialism.

✳   ✳   ✳

Ida Luz "Lucy" Rodríguez and her younger sister Alicia, and all the others, are trying to put their lives back together again. They've spent almost twenty years locked up in prison for what they and their supporters say is merely an ideological conviction.

The Rodríguez sisters are among the eleven Puerto Rican *independentistas* who last year were granted conditional clemency by President Clinton. The clemency comes with several big strings attached. Now that they are out, the sisters are lying low, distrusting anything that could call attention to their situation while the U.S. government still has the power to yank them back from freedom.

"They're now in Puerto Rico, taking art classes and other types of classes, trying to lead a quiet life," says their mother, Josefina, a friendly Chicago housewife who spends most of her time nowadays tending to her ailing husband. "It hasn't been easy, you know, after being locked up for so long, but I think they are adapting well. The community in Puerto Rico has been an enormous help in their rehabilitation process. I'm just so happy they are out."

Was it worth it? "Absolutely," she adds. "It was hard for me and my husband. As a mother it is painful to have children in jail, but I am very proud that they stood their ground and were willing to go as far as they did for their convictions. Not many people do that."

Of the eleven who accepted the clemency offer, nine opted to live on the island. The sisters have been living in Puerto Rico since last September, where they have been welcomed as heroes almost twenty years after being arrested for their activities seeking independence for Puerto Rico.

Lucy, the oldest, was born in the small Puerto Rican town of Las Marias, in 1950. When she was two the family moved to Chicago, and she eventually studied at Northeastern Illinois University, majoring in psychology and sociology with plans to become a teacher.

"I had no idea they were involved in the sorts of activities the government accuses her and her sister of doing in college and afterwards," Doña Josefina says. "They did the usual things people in college do, like protest and get involved in the Committee to Free the Five Puerto Rican Nationalists. The group was pressing for a presidential pardon for the five *independentistas* who in 1954 opened fire on the U.S. House of Representatives. The five had also tried to assassinate President Harry Truman by firing on a building across the street from the White House where they mistakenly thought he was staying. They were eventually pardoned by President Jimmy Carter in 1979.

According to the FBI, Lucy Rodríguez was also part of the Fuerzas Armadas de Liberación Nacional (FALN), a militant group that advocated independence for Puerto Rico by any means necessary, including force. In the mid-1970's, several bombings in New York and Chicago had been attributed to the FALN, although rumors ran rampant in U.S. Puerto Rican communities and on the island that the FBI had been involved as part of a disinformation campaign to scare the population against independence for the island.

In 1976, as the bombings increased and the law enforcement crackdown on Puerto Rican nationalist activities stepped up, Lucy and several others, including her companion, Oscar López Rivera, went underground. "I was very worried when she went into hiding, especially since I didn't know all that they were doing. I really had no idea," says Josefina Rodríguez. "It was very scary and I feared for her safety, but I felt I had to support her for supporting independence for Puerto Rico. Doing that is a hard thing to do. People are scared to, and we have to back those who do, because so few are willing to do it publicly."

Lucy's sister Alicia, who was born in Chicago in 1954, once said she got involved in *independentista* movement activities because, even though she was born in the United States, she felt that her heritage, language and culture were considered foreign and different—and therefore not good—by her teachers and classmates. Her first visit to Puerto Rico, when she was already in college at the University of Chicago, was a turning point in her life, and it made her determined, as she puts it, to combat the root of the island's problems: colonialism.

Her plans and those of her sister came crashing down on the afternoon of April 4, 1980, when law enforcement officials arrested them and nine others in the Chicago suburb of Evanston. They were immediately accused of being members of the FALN. The police found maps, bomb-making devices and other paraphernalia they said pointed to the group's plans to use force. By ten that night, the Rodríguez sisters and the others had declared themselves "prisoners of war" and refused to recognize U.S. jurisdiction over their cases. They refused to be represented and did not speak up in their defense during their trials. The federal government used a little-known law that dates back to the Civil War, seditious conspiracy to overthrow the U.S. government, to convict the group on a variety of charges, including bomb making and weapons possession. None were accused or convicted of direct participation in the bombings, which by then numbered more than one hundred in New York, Chicago and Puerto Rico. Their sentences were severe—Alicia received eighty-five years, Lucy, eighty. The others fared similarly.

The sentences were decried by family members and community supporters as excessive, and they went to work trying to free the incarcerated *independentistas.* The efforts were stepped up when President Clinton was reelected to his second term. The group's supporters figured that they would have a friendlier ear with a lame-duck Democrat rather than during the twelve years of Reagan-Bush.

Supporters held rallies and meetings on the island and in several U.S. cities, and the White House was inundated with postcards in support of a pardon.

"Believe it or not, the Monica Lewinsky situation delayed it for us," the elder Rodríguez muses. "We had been involved in real intense dialogue with the Clinton administration, and the president was prepared to let them go in 1998, but then they had to deal with the Lewinsky situation. That held it up for almost a year."

When President Clinton granted clemency in August 1999, the conditions included severing ties with independence movement activities and each other, and renouncing violence as a means to achieve political goals. The group was willing to accept the second condition, but were having problems with cutting ties to their political activities, and more importantly, to each other. While those are common parole conditions, it seemed to them and their families a hard pill to swallow. The group was also concerned that their parole would be overseen by the same agencies and officials that vehemently opposed their release, and would therefore not be the unbiased observers that parole officers are supposed to be.

"Severing ties with each other was unfair," said Josefina Rodríguez. "I was hoping that there would be no conditions attached, just like the other [1976] pardon. Imagine telling two sisters you can't see each other, especially since they were jailed together. That condition was almost unbelievable. But I urged them to accept the conditions because it was better than nothing, especially as the weeks passed and there was all that negative publicity about the pardon. And when the First Lady [spoke out against the pardon], I imagined it was going to get worse. I figured we could work something out later on. I wanted them to come out."

But not all the *independentistas* are out.

Oscar López is one of those who refused the clemency conditions and remains behind bars. Born in Puerto Rico in 1943, he arrived in Chicago with his family at the age of fourteen. He was later drafted in the Army and served in Vietnam, for which he was awarded the Bronze Star. López became involved in community activities after returning from Vietnam, and was a founding member of the Juan Antonio Corretjer Puerto Rican Cultural Center in Chicago and the Miranda high school. Additionally, he was a community organizer for the national Latino youth group ASPIRA, among others. When he was convicted, López was sentenced to fifty-five years. In 1988 he had another fifteen years attached for conspiracy to escape.

His brother José, executive director of the cultural center in Chicago and a local college professor, says he remains optimistic about his brother's eventual release. He says that Oscar does not regret his decision to refuse the conditions.

"Oscar is a very principled person and he believes that he could not in good conscience accept the terms. He feels that the independence cause for Puerto Rico is a principled struggle against colonialism and a colonial power that is imposing its will on a people, and to accept the terms would have meant to go against what his own principles are." López adds that his brother does not berate others who have accepted the terms. "Everyone has their reasons to do it."

"There were people who told us none of them would ever get out—and look, some are out already. We [the López family] always hold out hope and support Oscar. We understood why he refused to take the commutation. He has his convictions and he is fighting for freedom for Puerto Rico and against colonialism."

"Colonialism is the enemy and the United States represents that. He had to stand up for himself and we support him.

López adds that one of the positive aspects of the clemency has been a greater awareness of Puerto Rico politics. "At least all this has created more of consciousness and a new sense of involvement in the civil society on the island and here in the United States about [the prisoners'] situation and the island's political status. I have faith that change will come. Look who opened up China to the Western world: that virulently anti-communist Nixon. So anything's possible."

✳   ✳   ✳

QUESTIONS

1. Alicia Rodríguez says she joined the Puerto Rican patriots "because even though she was born in the United States, her heritage, language and culture were considered foreign and different—and therefore not good—by her teachers and classmates." Taking this explanation at face value, why don't thousands of Puerto Rican students who are treated in the same way become militants?

2. To what extent is it or is it not "fair" to impose the condition that two sisters do not see each other?

3. Patricia Rodríguez also tells about Oscar López Rivera, who could not "in good conscience" accept the clemency conditions and, consequently, remains in prison. What is the political significance of this position?

✳ 21 ✳
HAVANA USA

María Cristina García

In the following chapter, María Cristina explains the unique political and economic processes by which the Cuban American quest for public citizenship was achieved for many if not all of the exiles. In terms of their politics, she provides an account of a transition period in Cuban American politics from terrorism to working within the political system of the host country. She also gives us a peek at the future relations between Cuba and the Cuban American community and at how the quest for public citizenship may turn into a practice of exclusivity and intolerance. We are left with conjectures: Will Cuba remain independent or will it be annexed by the United States? If the latter, will it be annexed Puerto Rican style or Hawaiian style? Or will it be annexed by the United States as requested by one group of exiles?[1]

NOTE

1. María Cristina García, *Havana USA* (Berkeley: University of California Press, 1996), 165.

THE EMERGENCE OF A CUBAN AMERICAN IDENTITY

As early as the 1970s, there was evidence of a shift in the emigré community, as Cubans began to perceive themselves as permanent residents rather than temporary visitors, as immigrants rather than refugees. This shift in consciousness— attributable, in part, to the termination of the freedom flights, which forced many emigrés to come to terms with their status in the United States—was especially evident in three areas: the economic success of the Cuban community in south Florida;

the growing number of exiles seeking naturalization; and their new involvement in domestic politics and civic affairs.

As the Cubans bought homes, built businesses, paid taxes, and sent their children to school, they established ties to their communities in spite of their original intentions. In south Florida they created a thriving economic enclave that absorbed each new wave of immigration from Cuba as well as from elsewhere in Latin America.[1] By 1980, emigrés in Dade County generated close to $2.5 billion in income each year. Forty-four percent of the nearly five hundred thousand Cubans living in greater Miami were professionals, company managers, business owners, skilled craftsmen, or retail sales and clerical personnel, and eighteen thousand businesses were Cuban-owned. Sixty-three percent of emigrés owned their own homes.[2] The figures improved with each year, and by the early 1990s over twenty-five thousand businesses in Dade County were Latino-owned, making south Florida home to the most prosperous Latino community in the United States.[3] In both the 1980 and 1990 censuses, Cubans also exhibited the highest income and educational levels of the three major Latino groups, levels only slightly below the national average—a notable accomplishment for a community of first-generation immigrants.[4]

The Cubans' success could be attributed to several factors. Cuban women had a high rate of participation in the labor force; as early as 1970, they constituted the largest proportionate group of working women in the United States.[5] Women expanded their roles to include wage-earning not as a response to the feminist movement or the social currents of the 1960s but to ensure the economic survival of their families. The structure of the Cuban household, with three generations living under one roof, also ensured success because it encouraged economic cooperation.[6] The elderly contributed to the family's economic well-being both directly, with salaries, refugee aid, and Social Security checks, or indirectly, by raising children and assuming household responsibilities. These factors, along with the Cubans' low fertility rates and high levels of school completion, facilitated the family's structural assimilation.

In the community, the Cubans created prosperous businesses, built with the skills and capital of the middle- and upper-class emigrés who comprised the first wave of immigrants. The wealthy elite had money invested in American banks at the time of the revolution, and when they settled in Miami they invested that capital in new business ventures. The middle-class emigrés lacked that kind of capital, but they did have the skills and business know-how with which to create lucrative businesses. They identified the needs in the community and built businesses catering to those needs, with the assistance of loans from local banks or the Small Business Administration and long hours of work by family members. As their businesses expanded, these emigrés took on additional employees, almost always their compatriots. Thus, south Florida became home to a thriving business community that provided job opportunities for the new immigrants who arrived each year, easing their assimilation into the economic mainstream.[7]

The Cuban presence attracted international investment and helped convert Miami into a major trade and commercial center linking North and South America.

By 1980, thirteen major banks and over one hundred multinational corporations had established regional offices in the Miami area. Between 1977 and 1980 the port of Miami, which had already replaced New Orleans as the chief port of trade with Latin America, tripled its ship passenger traffic. From 1975 to 1980, air passenger traffic at Miami International Airport increased 100 percent and air cargo traffic 250 percent, making it the ninth busiest airport in the world in passenger traffic and sixth busiest in cargo traffic. During the same period, exports and imports increased by close to 150 percent.[8]

As early as the 1960s, the national news media, particularly popular magazines such as *Life, Fortune,* and *Newsweek,* celebrated the Cubans' business acumen and mythologized the "Cuban success story." Articles with titles like "To Miami, Refugees Spell P-R-O-S-P-E-R-I-T-Y" and "Cuban Refugees Write a U.S. Success Story" proclaimed the Cubans to be "golden immigrants" and the newest Horatio Algers.[9] In an era of social upheaval and disillusionment, when Americans questioned and discarded old values and perspectives, the Cubans seemed to prove that the American Dream was strong and intact. News of the Cubans' apparent success helped ease any misgivings Americans might have had about giving these people asylum or spending millions of taxpayers' dollars on refugee aid.

The "Cuban success story," however, overlooked the fact that many Cubans did not share in the community's wealth, as well as the fact that their success, while substantial, was less spectacular than the rags-to-riches stories promoted by the popular media.[10] Despite the large middle and upper classes and the comprehensive federal assistance pumped into the community, Cuban income still remained below the national average (albeit slightly) and a significant percentage of Cubans lived in poverty.[11] Working class emigrés, like other Americans, struggled for better wages, benefits, and working conditions, as well as job security, particularly if they were women. Black Cubans experienced discrimination from both their white compatriots and the larger society, and as late as 1990 their income lagged behind that of white Cubans by almost 40 percent.[12] As one editorial in an exile newspaper said:

> Many think that all exiles are rich; and it's not that way. . . . Ninety percent of exiles in Miami work in the factories or other such workplaces. They are all workers—some at a higher rank—but they are all workers. It is for these people that we publish our newspaper, so that they will learn American laws and realize that they don't have to be exploited . . . and many of them are exploited, especially by Cuban bosses.[13]

Nevertheless, the Cuban success story enjoyed wide circulation within the exile community: the Cubans made the story an essential element of their collective identity. Rather than focusing on those who had not assimilated economically, they focused on those who had—and there *were* plenty Horatio Algers in the community. To do otherwise would have been to give Fidel Castro propaganda to use against them. They wanted to prove to their compatriots back home what could be accomplished. That the community had accomplished so much in so little time, they argued, was a testimony to the old-fashioned values of thrift, hard work, and perseverance, and a symbol that God was on their side. The U.S. news media celebrated the Cubans' adoption of the Puritan work ethic, but for the emigrés it was simply the exile work ethic. Their strong anticommunism and their economic prosperity were the two characteristics they took the most pride in and promoted about themselves. Their success within the American mainstream was an indictment of the revolution, the best revenge a *gusano* could have.

But not all Cubans were comfortable with the community's success. Some emigrés accused their countrymen of sacrificing *la causa cubana* for the comforts of exile: if they had invested as much time in assisting the counterrevolution as they had in climbing the economic ladder, went the argument, they could have all returned to Cuba within a matter of years. "The dollar sign has destroyed the patriotic values of many," lamented one editorial.[14] Another warned that economic success was "prostituting the combative spirit of the exile community . . . distracting our youth from working on behalf of our slave country."[15] Yet another editor wrote, "We exchanged the committed, militant exile of [1961] for the present apathetic exile, committed only to dances and festivities."[16] For these and other exiles, the economic success of the community signified a denial of their responsibilities toward Cuba.

Nowhere was the theme of national allegiance more evident than in the debate over naturalization, a debate carried out in homes and offices, in newspapers and on the radio, throughout the 1960s and 1970s. Many Cubans were completely opposed to the idea of applying for U.S. citizenship. Some even resented that their children were forced to swear allegiance to the American flag at school. Many Cubans believed that becoming an American citizen meant assuming a new identity, emotionally erasing any memory of life prior to taking the oath of citizenship. The oath was a symbolic act by which they renounced allegiance to their homeland, their heritage, and their people; as one individual wrote, "How can I ever forget my language, my customs, my folklore? How can I honestly forget my past?"[17] Becoming a citizen meant that they had failed *la causa cubana* and compromised their ideals. They would no longer be exiles but rather ethnic Americans. In an effort to remind exiles of their responsibilities, the *periodiquitos* dedicated a number of issues in the early 1970s to defining the concepts of *patria* (nation) and *cubanidad.*

College students were particularly caught up in this debate over identity and national allegiance. Many had left Cuba as teenagers, and they were acutely aware that they straddled two cultures. At the University of Miami, Miami-Dade Community College, the University of Florida at Gainesville, and other universities around the country, Cuban students joined organizations such as the Federación de Estudiantes Cubanos and the Agrupación Estudiantil Abdala (known more commonly as Abdala)[18] to discuss issues of nationality, identity, culture, and their responsibilities toward Cuba. They tried to define *cubanidad* for themselves. "Young people who wish to identify themselves as Cuban face many difficulties in exile," wrote one student in *Antorcha,* the Cuban Students Federation publication at the University of Miami:

I am not referring to the obvious problem of having to choose whether one is Cuban or American, but rather to a more subtle (and perhaps more dangerous) conflict, which is distinguishing between *cubanía* and being Cuban-like. It is one thing to be concerned about the people who share one's language and origin, to be genuinely concerned with Cuba. It is quite another thing to think that one is Cuban simply because one likes *arroz con frijoles* or reads a Spanish-language newspaper in the afternoons. It is best to do both.[19]

Some students became more staunchly nationalistic than their parents, and they castigated the community for forfeiting its ideals. One editorial in *Antorcha* challenged its readers: "We must ask ourselves why we came to Miami. To contribute to its growth? To become involved in its politics? To make money? Did we leave Cuba as emigrants? . . . While we should be proud of being Cubans we should be ashamed of not having a country."[20] Others appealed to their compatriots' sense of *cubanidad,* warning them that the traditions and values they took most pride in would eventually die in the United States. "The Cuban family will be destroyed on foreign soil. . . . It is only in Cuba that we can preserve her."[21] Not surprisingly, many students, particularly those affiliated with Abdala, became more deeply involved in the war against Castro.

Many Cubans, however, saw no contradiction in being both exiles and citizens of the United States. Tangible legal, professional, and economic benefits could be derived from U.S. citizenship; Cuban professionals in particular realized that in order to practice their careers they had to meet state licensing requirements, and permanent residency or citizenship was always a prerequisite. But it was more than just economic considerations that led many Cubans to apply for citizenship. As they resigned themselves to a lengthy stay in the United States, they developed a sense of loyalty to the country that gave them refuge, and citizenship seemed a logical step.

The *Miami Herald* reported in 1974 that approximately two hundred thousand Cubans had sought U.S. citizenship.[22] In late 1975, Cuban professionals, led by media personality Manolo Reyes initiated a citizenship drive, the Cubans for American Citizenship Campaign, with the goal of registering ten thousand new citizens in celebration of the United States Bicentennial. Members of the steering committee recruited exiles, helped them fill out the necessary papers, and taught courses in schools to help them prepare for the examinations. The campaign surpassed its goal: on just one day—July 4, 1976—more than sixty-five hundred Cubans swore the oath of citizenship, and by the end of the year 26,275 exiles had become U.S. citizens.[23] The campaign continued throughout the late 1970s. By 1980, 55 percent of the eligible Cubans in Dade County were American citizens, compared to just 25 percent in 1970.[24] Even with their new legal status, however, these new citizens continued to regard themselves as Cuban exiles—and they would always maintain this dual identity. Their ties to Cuba were unseverable.

During the 1970s, the local news media, and in particular the *Miami Herald,* monitored the sentiments of the exile community. In the aftermath of the Civil Rights Movement, the media tried to reflect the concerns of ethnic minorities and to study the relationships between the different groups in the community. The *Herald* commissioned various polls and surveys to determine how well the Cubans were adapting to life in the United States. Did they feel accepted? Did they want to return to Cuba? Did they object to the reestablishment of diplomatic relations with the Castro government? Many of the surveys yielded surprising results: a 1972 poll revealed that while 97 percent of the Cubans interviewed felt that they had been accepted in Miami, 62 percent were less satisfied with their lives in the U.S. than with the lives they had led in Cuba.[25] The termination of the freedom flights, however, proved to be a turning point in the exiles' attitudes toward Cuba and the United States. A study by sociologists Clark and Mendoza in 1972 showed that close to 79 percent of the Cubans interviewed wanted to return to Cuba once Castro was overthrown, but two years later, less than half expressed the same desire.[26] Another study by Portes and Mozo yielded similar results: in 1973, 60 percent of those interviewed reported plans to return to Cuba once Fidel Castro fell, but by 1979 less than one-fourth wanted to return.[27]

The Cubans' growing involvement in civic affairs and local politics also revealed a shift in consciousness. In 1965, seventeen Cuban businessmen created the Cámara de Comercio Latina (Latin American Chamber of Commerce), or *CAMACOL,* to lobby on behalf of Dade's Latino business community before the Metro-Dade County Commission and the state legislature. In 1970, emigrés created the Cuban National Planning Council to study domestic (U.S.) issues that were important to Cubans, including language, education, health care, and employment. A Cuban ran for the mayoral seat as early as 1967, two ran for the city commission in 1969, and another five ran for various public offices in 1971. All were unsuccessful, but in 1973 two veterans of the Bay of Pigs invasion were elected to public office, Manolo Reboso to the City Commission and Alfredo Duran to the Dade County School Board. The city of Sweetwater also became the first city in south Florida to elect a Cuban-born mayor.

Another example of the Cubans' growing influence in Dade County was the Bilingual-Bicultural Ordinance of April 1973. The resolution designated Spanish as the county's second official language and called for the establishment of a Department of Bilingual and Bicultural Affairs, the translation of county documents into Spanish, and increased efforts to recruit Latinos to county jobs.[28] The passage of such an ordinance by a board comprised entirely of non-Latinos demonstrated a recognition of the role Cubans and other Latinos were playing in the local community, and would play in the years to come. As the resolution declared, "Our Spanish-speaking population has earned, through its ever increasing share of the tax burden, and active participation in community affairs, the right to be serviced and heard at all levels of government."[29] (The resolution was repealed in 1980 in the aftermath of Mariel, but reinstated in 1993.)

Over the next decade, the Cubans' political accomplishments were even more impressive. Cubans came to occupy positions in the local, state, and national government, as well as key positions in the key institutions of Miami and Dade County. At the same time, they continued to be actively concerned with the political affairs of their homeland just ninety miles away. Whether they called themselves Cuban exiles or Cuban Americans, it was clear that the emigrés had carved a niche for themselves in their country of refuge and were satisfactorily resolving the question of identity—at least for themselves.

THE 1970s: A TRANSITION PERIOD

During the 1970s, the exile community in south Florida seemed to be developing along parallel courses, one of adjustment and acceptance, the other of increasing militance and desperation. It was a decade of social and economic progress. The number of emigrés seeking American citizenship increased. The Latino business community of Dade County became one of the most productive in the nation. Emigrés became involved in domestic politics: by 1976, they comprised 8 percent of registered voters in Dade County and occupied important elected offices in city and county governments. There was an indication that some Cubans were developing an ethnic (as opposed to purely national) identity, as seen by their growing membership in pan-Latino organizations such as the League of United Latin American Citizens (LULAC) as well as in the creation of groups such as the Cuban National Planning Council, the Spanish American League Against Discrimination (SALAD), and the National Coalition of Cuban Americans, which focused on voting rights, employment, housing, education, health, and other domestic concerns. All signs seemed to indicate that the emigrés had psychologically unpacked their bags and settled into their new society.

Alongside newspaper headlines celebrating the emigrés' success, however, was news that the war against Castro had taken a menacing turn. Propaganda and paramilitary groups decreased in number in the late 1960s, victims of a lack of funding and growing apathy in the community—an apathy generated, in part, by suspicions that many of these political groups were embezzling funds. But at the same time, new, more militant organizations emerged, committed to overthrowing Castro at whatever the cost. Most had no specific political vision for Cuba, no particular leader they wanted to see occupy the presidency; their goal was simply to eliminate Castro. As these groups became desperate their tactics became more radical, drawing international attention to the exile community in south Florida and polarizing emigrés further.

A shift in American foreign policy catalyzed this radicalism. Under the guidance of Secretary of State Henry Kissinger, the Nixon and Ford administrations adopted a policy of detente. Negotiations concentrated on the Soviet Union and China, but the U.S. government also turned its attention to improving relations with Cuba. In 1973, both countries signed an antihijacking treaty. In 1975, the United States supported the OAS's vote to lift the eleven-year-old embargo of Cuba. For the first time, the U.S. government also allowed subsidiaries of U.S. corporations in foreign countries to trade with the island.

During the Carter administration, the United States and Cuba moved further towards rapprochement. The countries negotiated a fishing rights agreement and a maritime boundary agreement. The U.S. lifted its ban on transferring American currency to Cuba as well as on using an American passport to travel there. In April 1978, the first commercial flight between Miami and Havana in sixteen years departed from Miami International Airport, and the federal government also granted visas to Cubans to come to the U.S. on a temporary basis.[30] An unprecedented number of scholars, artists, writers, and scientists traveled to and from Cuba in the interest of cultural and scholarly exchange. The Cuban government also allowed a group of fifty-five young Cuban exiles of the Brigada Antonio Maceo to witness first-hand the accomplishments of the revolution—the first exiles since the revolution to be permitted to return to the island. The most important development, however, was the creation of American and Cuban "interests sections," which provided limited diplomatic representation.

Many emigrés of course were enraged by this new climate of tolerance. Polls conducted by the *Miami Herald* showed that more than 53 percent remained opposed to reestablishing diplomatic and trade relations with Cuba and felt betrayed by the U.S. government.[31] Emigrés expressed their anger in the exile news media and staged rallies and demonstrations in Miami, Union City, Washington, and other cities. A "Congress Against Coexistence" was held in San Juan, Puerto Rico, in 1974, attended by representatives from some seventy exile organizations. When the OAS announced that member nations would debate the lifting of sanctions against Cuba, emigrés traveled to the meeting as a protest lobby, and in Miami emigrés destroyed the Torch of Friendship, a monument to hemispheric solidarity at Bayfront Park. When the sanctions were finally lifted a year later, in 1975, exile organizations organized a "Liberty Caravan," a thousand-car parade through Little Havana culminating in a boisterous rally at the Orange Bowl condemning the OAS's action.[32]

At the same time, polls indicated that a growing number of emigrés supported some type of rapprochement with the Castro regime. A 1975 *Herald* poll, for example, revealed that 49.5 percent of Cuban emigrés were at least willing to visit the island; a surprising revelation to hardliners in the community. Letters to newspaper editors revealed that some favored reestablishing diplomatic and trade relations— not for the idealistic goal of furthering world peace but for more practical considerations: the normalization of relations would allow them the opportunity to visit their family and friends in Cuba. Many questioned the value of the U.S. embargo, which instead of weakening Cuba's revolutionary fervor only seemed to tighten its ties to the Soviet Union. Polls revealed a generational difference in attitudes: Cubans raised and educated in the United States were more likely to approve of some form of rapprochement than their elders were. While they shared their parents' suspicion of—perhaps even their contempt for—the Castro regime, they tended to favor a diplomatic solution to the problems in Cuba rather than continued military or economic aggression.

A handful of organizations emerged during the 1970s to lobby for the diplomatic approach, among them the Cuban Christians for Justice and Freedom, the National Union of Cuban Americans, and the Cuban American Committee. In 1979, the latter group sent a petition with over ten thousand signatures to President Jimmy Carter requesting that the United States normalize relations with the Castro government.[33] A few individuals established careers as advocates of a new diplomacy, the most controversial being the Reverend Manuel Espinosa, pastor of the Evangelical Church in Hialeah. Espinosa, a former captain in Castro's military and a former member of several anti-Castro organizations, used his weekly sermons to preach reconciliation and to advocate the normalization of diplomatic relations with Cuba.

The number of emigrés that joined these organizations, or who supported these activists, was not significant enough to serve as an effective lobby—at least during the 1970s. Those who favored the normalization of relations kept silent, for the most part, because they feared being branded *comunistas*. In this politically conservative community, such a tag inevitably affected careers, businesses, relationships, and even lives. Espinosa's activism brought him a severe beating at the hands of militant Cuban exiles in 1975, and other activists had their businesses boycotted, their homes vandalized, their families harassed, and their reputations ruined.[34]

Many emigrés believed that an accommodation of the Cuban government was an endorsement of Castro-communism. They could not understand why *exilados* would even speak to the individuals who had tortured, imprisoned, and executed tens of thousands of their compatriots. As one exile wrote, "Those who speak of coexistence demonstrate that they have forgotten our language."[35] Another had harsher words: "Those who physically or intellectually support the Castro regime are traitors, as are those who support a *fidelismo sin Fidel,* a nationalist communism, or who surreptitiously plant the idea of coexistence. Those who forgive, accept, or befriend the traitors are also traitors. Yes, one can be a Cuban by birth, but if one's heart is not Cuban one is a traitor."[36] When Manuel Espinosa publicly admitted (years later, in 1980) that he was an agent for the Cuban government, most emigrés were not surprised; his admission simply confirmed the popular belief that active supporters of renewed relations with Cuba had to be in some way connected to the regime.

Even the shipment via third countries of medicine and food parcels to Cuba was considered by hardliners to be an accommodation of the Castro government.[37] Radio talk show hosts attributed Castro's continued hold on Cuba to the "economic subsidies" Cubans received in the form of packages from the exile community—estimated at hundreds of thousands of dollars a year. If exiles stopped sending their relatives food, clothing, and medicines, they argued, discontent on the island would grow and ultimately lead to Castro's overthrow. For those emigrés who had elderly relatives or children in Cuba, though, maintaining a hard line against Cuba came at great personal and psychological cost. Those who sent packages to Cuba preferred to keep it secret, to avoid censure.

Angered by the new developments in American foreign policy and what they perceived to be a growing complacency in the exile community, the militant extremists escalated the war against Castro. As one militant explained: "It is to be expected that after eighteen years in exile a frustrated generation would emerge whose impatience would lead them to use extreme methods."[38] Their methods were so extreme that even the exile community feared to speak out against them. Groups such as El Condor, Comandante Zero, Movimiento Neo-Revolucionario Cubano-Pragmatista,

Coordinación de Organizaciones Revolucionarias Unidas (CORU), Poder Cubano, Acción Cubana, M-17, the Frente de Liberación Nacional de Cuba, and Omega 7 bombed Cuban embassies and consulates around the world, murdered Cuban diplomatic employees, harassed and threatened individuals and institutions alleged to have ties to the Castro government, and placed bombs aboard planes heading for Cuba.

1976 was a particularly violent year. As thousands of emigrés celebrated the U.S. Bicentennial by taking the oath of citizenship, others waged war against Cuba. In April, commandos attacked two Cuban fishing boats, killing one fisherman, and bombed the Cuban Embassy in Portugal, killing two persons. In July, bombs exploded at the Cuban mission at the United Nations, at the offices of the British West Indian Airways of Barbados (which represented Cubana Airlines, the national airline), and inside a suitcase that was about to be loaded onto a Cuban jet in Kingston, Jamaica. Later that summer, two employees of the Cuban Embassy in Buenos Aires disappeared; the Cuban consul in Mérida, Mexico, was almost kidnapped; and a bomb exploded in the Cubana Airlines office in Panama. In October, bombs exploded on a Cuban jet minutes after it left Barbados; all 73 passengers died. In November, a bomb destroyed the Madrid office of Cubana Airlines.[39] The violence increased further in 1977 and 1978 as a result of the Carter administration's new policies towards Cuba and the *diálogo*.

While the paramilitary organizations of the 1960s had limited their actions to Cuba and its allies, the militant extremists targeted all those they perceived to be their enemies, including members of their own community, and many did not care how many innocent victims got in the way. They bombed Little Havana travel agencies, shipping companies, and pharmacies that conducted commercial transactions with Cuba. They harassed and threatened all who favored political coexistence. Extremists bombed the offices of *Réplica,* a popular Spanish-language news magazine, because its editor, Max Leznick, advocated lifting the trade embargo.[40] They harassed and ultimately murdered crane operator Luciano Nieves and Hialeah boatbuilder Ramón Donestevez because of their suspected ties to the Castro government.[41] In 1973, they assassinated Cuban exile leader José de la Torriente, who was suspected of embezzling funds from a liberation effort he had established, the Plan Torriente.[42] From 1973 to 1976, more than one hundred bombs exploded in the Miami area alone, and the FBI nicknamed Miami "the terrorist capital of the United States";[43] but the groups also operated in (and out of) New York, Union City, Los Angeles, Madrid, Santo Domingo, Mexico City, and Caracas. During the late 1970s, a Cuban exile tabloid in Puerto Rico, *La Crónica*, published interviews with the controversial leaders of these militant groups, whose identities were disguised. They warned the exile community to watch their backs.

Many emigrés spoke out against the terrorism of their compatriots, condemning these acts not only as immoral but also as tactically stupid. "They are politically and militarily incapable of producing a change in the regime," wrote a former member of the CRC of the terrorists: "[They will] cost human lives, create immense anxiety in the community, and, more importantly, discredit the exile community before

U.S. public opinion. . . . Whether one likes it or not, these acts do not serve the liberation cause but, rather, serve subversive Marxist elements in this country."[44]

Sadly, many who spoke out against the terrorism became victims themselves. In 1976, extremists murdered José Peruyero, president of the Brigade 2506 Veterans Association, because he condemned the participation of Brigade veterans in terrorist activities.[45] Journalists became popular targets; they were frequently threatened and their homes and offices vandalized. Three months after Peruyero's death, a bomb exploded in the car of WQBA news and program director Emilio Milián. Milián, who denounced acts of terrorism on his radio program *Habla el pueblo,* miraculously survived the explosion, but he lost both his legs. A few weeks later, he courageously returned to his job at WQBA and resumed his critical editorials, but a year later he was fired by the station because his editorials were allegedly too incendiary.[46]

A joint committee of local, state, and federal agencies investigating these terrorist acts learned that membership in the terrorist groups interlocked—that is, those who committed acts of violence often worked on behalf of three or four different groups. Organizations frequently disbanded and their members created splinter groups, giving the impression that there were more terrorists than there actually were. When a congressional subcommittee asked the Dade County Public Safety Department to identify the number of groups operating in the Miami area, one investigator revealed the frustration of tracking these organizations: "I can say that we have more than 10 militant groups with hard-core militants. . . . those 10 groups may be 12 tomorrow, and next week there may be 50. And then week after next it may be [down] to eight, because there is a constant change in the staffing of these groups and there is constant exchange."[47]

While the terrorist groups received some funding from sympathetic individuals in the community, more often than not they resorted to extortion, threatening wealthier emigrés with death or property damage if they did not supply the necessary funds.[48] A few militants received financial assistance from foreign agents—agents who later used the Cubans in their own domestic plots. The Chilean state police, for example, reportedly hired Cubans to assassinate the former Chilean ambassador Orlando Letelier in Washington in 1976.[49]

Investigations were made especially difficult by the Cuban intelligence network in Miami. American law enforcement agencies had to determine whether the violence and terrorism were actually committed by emigrés or by *infiltrados* who tried to destroy exile organizations by framing them. The Castro government had reportedly infiltrated hundreds of spies into Miami, most of them arriving in the U.S. as small-boat escapees, "fence-jumpers" at the U.S. base at Guantánamo, or immigrants arriving from third countries.[50] So extensive was this network that Castro's spies often served as the FBI's informants on the emigrés' illegal activities: when Alpha 66, for example, hired a gunman to assassinate Fidel Castro during a planned speech at the United Nations, Cuban spies uncovered the plot and notified American authorities.[51] Interviews in the Cuban press with emigrés who defected back to Cuba also revealed the inner workings of the top militant groups operating in south Florida.[52]

Emigrés hotly debated who was responsible for the wave of terror. Most preferred to interpret it as a Castro plot to divide and demoralize the community,[53] arguing that these acts of terrorism were too professional to be done by the "weekend warriors." Castro also stood to gain the most by the campaign of intimidation, which divided and silenced his opponents. In the meantime, while Justice Department officials tried to track down the culprits, emigrés with unpopular views or in visible positions took extra precautions. The exile press carried advertisements for security devices, including remote-control gadgets that could start cars from a distance of one hundred meters.

The FBI eventually tracked down fifteen terrorists associated with the New Jersey–based Omega 7, regarded as the most dangerous of the organizations; all fifteen were ultimately convicted. The FBI also arrested dozens of other militants, including five emigrés accused of assassinating Letelier.[54] Many cases, however, remain unsolved.

The wave of violence that rocked the community during the 1970s arose in part out of the secret war of the 1960s. Several of those convicted for terrorism and government espionage were former CIA protégés. The skills they had learned to destabilize and overthrow the Castro government were now used against their own community and their host society. According to some newspaper accounts, some of the Cubans involved in organized crime in south Florida, particularly in drug trafficking, also had CIA connections. Three of the Watergate burglars, Bernard Barker, Virgilio González, and Eugenio Martínez, were Cuban exiles with ties to the CIA.[55]

Some in the emigré community regarded the extremists as heroes and *patriotas*. One editor of a *periodiquito* wrote:

> I know there are many Cubans who don't like these tactics and criticize them, but I have to ask myself, "What have these compatriots done all these past years, and what has been their contribution to the struggle for liberation?" Most of them have simply enjoyed the comforts of living in the land of liberty. . . . No, my friends. A Cuban is not merely someone who was born in Cuba. A Cuban is someone who thinks about the seven million compatriots who are living as slaves.[56]

A well-known journalist wrote, "The realities of world politics leave no alternative but to use violence. Only when the exiles destroy the lives and interests of our enemies will Washington, Moscow, the OAS, or whoever take our views into account."[57]

Some exiles raised funds to help the militants in their cause—and later in their legal defense.[58] In 1974, Cuban radio stations in Miami helped raise over twelve thousand dollars for the families of two militants associated with the Frente de Liberación Nacional de Cuba who had been injured while constructing a bomb.[59] In 1978, *La Crónica* printed an advertisement for the Cuban Defense League, Inc., which raised funds for the legal defense of "Cuban political prisoners in the United States, Mexico, and Venezuela."[60] That same year, a New York–based publication entitled *Desde las Prisiones* began publishing articles by or in support of the "Cuban freedom fighters." The White House and the Department of Justice frequently received letters and petitions asking the government to commute sentences. In August 1979, for example, a Chicago exile coalition called the Federación de Organizaciones Cubanas de Illinois wrote Attorney General Benjamin Civiletti on behalf of ten men detained for various acts. "Now that the Cuban Communist authorities are releasing political prisoners," they wrote, ". . . we believe the United States Department of Justice should also grant benevolent concessions to the exile patriots incarcerated in this country, who acted according to the best interest of what traditionally has been a struggle to restore freedom and democracy in Cuba."[61]

The most famous militant was Orlando Bosch, a Miami pediatrician who in 1968 was sentenced to ten years in prison for firing on a Polish freighter with a bazooka. Released on parole after four years in a federal penitentiary, Bosch fled the country in 1974 when he became a chief suspect in the assassination of Cuban exile leader José Elias de la Torriente. Over the next two years, he served as leader of the militant group Acción Cubana, which claimed responsibility for the bombings of several Cuban embassies and consulates throughout Latin America. In 1976, the government of Venezuela charged Bosch with conspiracy in the Cubana Airlines bombing that killed seventy-three people, including the entire Cuban national fencing team. Although a Venezuelan judge found insufficient evidence to charge him in the bombing, Bosch remained in prison while his case was reviewed in civil and military courts.[62] Although he was acquitted two more times, he was not released from prison until 1987.

Over the years, Bosch's supporters staged marches and demonstrations to protest his incarceration. They organized exhibitions of his drawings in art galleries in Little Havana, Tampa, Union City, Chicago, and New York City to raise money for his defense and to assist his family. Miami mayoral candidates, hoping to garner a few votes, even visited Bosch in prison in Caracas. The emigré press in particular rallied to his defense. "[Bosch] has done some things which the U.S. government could call terrorism," said WQBA news director Tomás García Fusté, "but he is fighting for the liberation of our country. It is not terrorism but self-defense. We, the Cubans, are at war with Fidel Castro."[63]

Not all emigrés regarded Bosch as a hero, of course. When Miami City Commissioner Demetrio Pérez introduced a resolution in 1983 for an Orlando Bosch Day, both his office and the *Miami Herald* were swamped with letters, as many opposed to the motion as in favor of it. "I am a Cuban, and proud of it," wrote one woman, ". . . but I do not support someone whose idea of patriotism is to attack a Polish freighter, who has violated parole in the United States, and who has been accused of killing 73 innocent people."[64] The federal government was also unsympathetic. When Bosch returned to the United States in February 1988 following his release from prison, he was arrested by U.S. marshals for having violated his parole. Deportation proceedings were begun, but the Justice Department was unable to find any country willing to grant Bosch entry. Finally, in late 1990, he was placed under house arrest.

For many emigrés, the wave of violence posed a moral dilemma that forced them to seriously reconsider their heroes as well as the methods they considered acceptable in the war against Castro. They learned that the line that divided revolutionary activities from terrorist activities could be a very thin one. The violence of the 1970s, then, led some emigrés to disassociate themselves completely, in fear or disgust, from exile politics. For others the negative media attention focused on the community, plus the realization that even the militant groups were impotent in bringing about change, forced them to reevaluate strategy, and slowly they realized that if they wanted to evoke meaningful change in Cuba they had to work within the political machinery of their host country. The war against Castro took a new direction in the 1980s, and the election of Ronald Reagan facilitated that redirection.

CONCLUSION

Those intrigued by the community of Cuban exiles and Cuban Americans in south Florida frequently ask what will happen in Miami once there is a changing of the guard in Cuba. Will the emigrés return to their homeland? Or will thousands more Cubans immigrate to the United States? The answer is yes—to both questions. Once Fidel Castro is no longer in office (for whatever reason)—and assuming that democratic reforms are enacted—some percentage of the community will return to Cuba. The numbers are difficult to predict: a poll conducted in 1993 by Florida International University revealed that 29 percent of Cuban-born heads of households wanted to return to live permanently in Cuba, while a similar poll conducted in 1990 showed that only 14 percent would actually return.[65] Among those born or raised in the United States the percentages are probably much lower. The emigrés talk a great deal about returning to their homeland, but few will actually pack up and leave when the opportunity arises. As several interviewees told me, "Why uproot yourself twice in one lifetime? The first time was hard enough." They have invested time and hard work in the United States. They have rebuilt their lives and careers; they bought homes and raised their children here. They have developed ties to the United States in spite of their original intentions. Most do not want to start all over again, especially in a society that will undoubtedly experience social, economic, and political turmoil in the post-Castro years.

The length of time spent in the United States and family ties in the two countries are the principal factors that will influence the decision to stay or to return. For Cubans who grew up in the U.S., "returning" to Cuba would be akin to moving to a foreign country, notwithstanding the culture they claim to share with those on the island. The emigrés most likely to return will be the elderly, eager to spend their remaining years in their homeland. Also likely to return are those who feel alienated in the U.S. and have found it impossible to adapt. The majority of emigrés, however, will want to stay close to their families. Many of the first generation are now grandparents and even great-grandparents; they will not want to move too far away from their children.

Nevertheless, Cubans in south Florida will always maintain an interest and play a role in the affairs of Cuba. Cuba is closer to Miami than Tampa, Orlando, or the state capital at Tallahassee, and the interest in Cuba is as much geopolitical as cultural. South Florida, like the rest of the Caribbean, has a stake in the political and economic stability of the island, and thus Cuba will play a role in public debate on the streets of Havana USA as well as in the corridors of Tallahassee and Washington.

Travel back and forth across the Florida Straits will be guaranteed. Emigrés who remain in the U.S. will want to travel to Cuba to visit relatives, or for a vacation, or for a variety of other reasons. In much the same way that former refugees from Eastern Europe and the Baltic states are presently investing in their homelands, the more entrepreneurial among the emigrés will want to invest in or establish businesses in Cuba—both to help their former country and to increase their own fortunes. In the early 1990s, U.S. airline and shipping companies were already plotting ways to corner this new travel market. According to the *Miami Herald*, some companies were even drafting models for hydrofoils that might transport people back and forth in a couple of hours. It is conceivable that some emigrés might divide their time between the two countries, working in one country and making their homes in another, much as many Americans commute between, say, New York and Connecticut, or as others commute back and forth across the U.S.-Mexico border. The first generation's dual citizenship will facilitate this development.

Migration from Cuba will continue regardless of what happens in Cuba. In September 1994, in order to force the Cuban government to curtail the traffic of homemade rafts across the Florida Straits, the Clinton administration agreed to allow the immigration of a minimum of twenty thousand Cubans each year, not including the immediate relatives of United States citizens.[66] Even with the installation of a more democratic government, migration from Cuba will continue. Some Cubans will choose to emigrate to be reunited with their families in the United States, while others, impatient with the sluggish Cuban economy, will want to try their luck in the U.S. The number of migrants in such a scenario will depend as much on U.S. immigration policy as on the political and economic conditions in Cuba; but whatever the number, the influx of immigrants will continually revitalize Cuban identity and culture in the United States. Cuban American culture in south Florida will continue to define itself in relation to two countries and two cultures.

The most difficult challenge in the post-Castro era, both on the island and in Florida, will be learning to forgive. The exile community remains divided thirty-five years after the revolution by political differences. Emigrés are unable to forgive each other for their role (or lack thereof) in the revolution and later the counterrevolution. From the comfort of exile, they criticize their compatriots on the island for allowing the government of Fidel Castro to endure, and while they applaud the *balseros* for taking to the seas to escape Castro's Cuba, many wonder suspiciously why they didn't do it sooner. Conversely, many Cubans on the island continue to regard the emigrés as *gusanos* and cannot forgive them for exploiting, and later abandoning, their country. A great deal of cooperation (and, perhaps, time) is needed before Cuban societies on opposite sides of the Florida Straits are tolerant, peaceful, and democratic.

The Cubans of south Florida will play a major role in the civic, cultural, and political life of the area in the years to come. Their principal challenge will be to share their power base with the many different groups that call south Florida home. Over the past three decades, a growing tension—even hostility—has emerged in south Florida, the product of rapid demographic transformation and the perceived dominance of Cubans in the local economy and local politics. The 1990 U.S. census revealed that Latinos comprised 49.2 percent of Dade County's total population of 1.9 million. In the city of Miami, 62.5 percent of the population was of Latino origin; in Hialeah, 88 percent.[67] Despite a near-doubling in total population over the past thirty years, the percentage of non-Latino whites had fallen from 80 percent in 1960 to 37 percent in 1990. Such measures as the 1980 English Only amendment ultimately proved unsuccessful in controlling the Latino population (and in May 1993, voters overturned the 1980 ruling).[68] Unable to compete in a bilingual economy and angered by the cultural changes in south Florida, many non-Latino whites have moved to the counties immediately north of Dade, where they can maintain their cultural and political dominance.

The non-Latino black population has remained more rooted to the area, but blacks, too, are resentful. For thirty-five years, they have watched Cubans grow wealthier and more powerful. They resent the federal government's early assistance to the refugees—the grants and loans that helped them go to school or start small businesses, the remedial education and job retraining programs, the health benefits. Blacks resent that these non-English-speaking foreigners could receive so much while the native-born were overlooked. These benefits helped the Cubans assert their economic and political power. By 1990, three of the five members of the Miami City Commission, including the mayor, were Cuban; by contrast, only one member was African American. Blacks in Dade County have fared better economically than their counterparts elsewhere around the state—in part because of the economic transformation brought on by Cuban immigration—but many feel that they have been shut out from the most important local institutions.[69]

This resentment was obvious as early as 1968, when blacks rioted during the Republican National Convention in Miami Beach. Riots took place again in 1980, 1982, and 1989, each spurred by a specific incident involving police brutality, but each also an expression of the deep-seated resentment towards whites and Latinos.[70] In the wake of the riots the city created an antidiscrimination coalition entitled Greater Miami United to address the concerns of the various racial and ethnic communities. There are many ill feelings, however, and groups from the Nation of Islam to the Ku Klux Klan have tried to capitalize on the tension in the community.

The class, racial, ethnic, and national diversity within the Latino community is also the source of much tension. While the Cubans helped produce the economic prosperity that attracted large-scale immigration from the Caribbean and Latin America, the newer immigrants resent the Cubans' dominance in local institutions, from the Spanish-language media to city hall. Latinos complain of Cuban powerbrokers who refuse to allow others into their inner circle, of the neverending anti-Castro diatribes on the radio, and of the media's lack of sensitivity to issues that are important to them. "They think they're the only Hispanics in Miami," said one disgruntled Puerto Rican. Many of the complaints filed with the FCC in the past decade have been filed by Latinos who perceive the Cuban radio shows to be bigoted.[71] At times, Latino resentment has been expressed through violence—as in December 1990, when Puerto Ricans in the Wynwood neighborhood rioted. Like the black riots of the 1980s, the episode was a reaction to a specific case of police brutality; but it too was a manifestation of the larger ethnic and racial tensions in south Florida.[72]

Latinos also express concern about the climate of censorship in Miami, a concern shared by whites and blacks as well. Individuals who support Fidel Castro or the Sandinistas or who favor tolerance and dialogue are branded *comunistas* and suffer discrimination, and sometimes even verbal or physical abuse. In past years, Latin American entertainers who have performed in Cuba have been banned from appearing at the annual Festival de la Calle Ocho because the organizers claim that to allow them to perform would be to risk a confrontation, endangering the two million people who attend the weeklong festivities. In December 1990, under pressure from the Cuban community, the city of Miami withdrew its official welcoming of Nelson Mandela because of his support of Fidel Castro. In January 1991, Miami city commissioners told members of the local Haitian community that they could celebrate the inauguration of their country's new president at Bayfront Park only if Fidel Castro was not invited to the inauguration in Haiti.[73] For Latinos, Haitians, and others, these incidents are just the most recent examples of the censorship in south Florida that violates their civil rights. Miami, they argue, has become a city where the needs and interests of the dominant group outweigh the needs and interests of the rest of the population.

The Cubans, however, will be forced to make concessions. While they are the largest immigrant group in south Florida, others are growing rapidly. In the early 1990s Central and South Americans, and in particular immigrants from Nicaragua and Colombia, had replaced Cubans as the fastest-growing Latino groups. Emigrés are slowly realizing that it is to their benefit to try to foster a more inclusive vision of community. Just as others accommodated them, they must now accommodate others. Hopefully, the Cuban Americans—particularly the second generation—will play a mediating and conciliatory role in community relations. As the children of emigrés, they can relate to the immigration experience of others; as Americans, they are bound to the local community and to the country that offered them safe haven. They do not share the exile generation's obsession with Cuba; rather, their energies are invested in the hybrid borderland society that produced them. It is the Cuban Americans who will ultimately help determine south Florida's future.

NOTES

1. Among the first to write about the Cuban economic enclave were sociologists Alejandro Portes and Robert L. Bach. They defined the economic enclave as "a distinctive economic formation, characterized by the spatial concentration of immigrants who organize a variety of enterprises to serve their own ethnic market and the general population." According to Portes

and Bach, the enclave economy allowed Cubans to avoid the economic disadvantages that usually accompany segregation. See Alejandro Portes and Robert L. Bach, *Latin Journey: Cuban and Mexican Immigrants in the United States* (Berkeley and Los Angeles: University of California Press, 1985), and Alejandro Portes, "The Social Origins of the Cuban Enclave Economy of Miami," *Sociological Perspectives* 30 (October 1987): 340–71. A study by Portes and Jensen found that ethnic enterprises were effective avenues for economic mobility, particularly for men; although few women were self-employed, they earned higher incomes working within the enclave economy. See Alejandro Portes and Leif Jensen, "The Enclave and the Entrants: Patterns of Ethnic Enterprise in Miami before and after Mariel," *American Sociological Review* 54 (December 1989): 929–49.

For another interpretation of the enclave economy, and more specifically the role of Cubans in the U.S. labor movement, see Guillermo J. Grenier, "The Cuban American Labor Movement in Dade County: An Emerging Immigrant Working Class," in Grenier and Stepick, eds., *Miami Now!* 133–59. Grenier explores the role class-based organizations such as labor unions have played in fostering group solidarity and group consciousness.

2. "Cuban and Haitian Arrivals: Crisis and Response," June 30, 1980, 6, in File "ND16/ CO38 1/20/77-1/20/81" Box ND-42, White House Central File, Subject File: National Security–Defense, Carter Library. See also Carlos Arboleya, *The Cuban Community, 1980: Coming of Age as History Repeats Itself* (Miami, 1980).

3. Carlos Arboleya, *El impacto cubano en la Florida* (Miami, 1985). Arboleya, former president and CEO of Barnett Bank, Miami, periodically published reports on the Cuban community in south Florida. Arboleya's report also included the following statistics for Dade County: over 4,500 Cuban doctors, 500 lawyers, 17 bank presidents and 390 vice presidents, and 25,000 garment workers. See also "Dade Latin Businesses Top U.S.," *Miami Herald,* October 23, 1986, 1A.

4. In 1990, the median family income for Cubans was $33,504, which was higher than the median family income for Latinos in the U.S. ($27,972) but lower than the median national income ($37,403). 18.5 percent of Cubans had four or more years of college education, as compared to 9.7 percent for Latinos and 23.7 percent for the nation as a whole. 21.6 percent of Cuban males and 20 percent of Cuban females were professionals or executives (as compared to the national averages of 26.3 and 27.2 percent). See Alejandro Portes, "¿Quienes somos? ¿Qué pensamos? Los cubanos en Estados Unidos en la década de los noventas," *Cuban Affairs/Asuntos Cubanos* 1, no. 1 (Spring 1994): 5.

For an analysis of the 1980 census, see Lisandro Pérez, "The Cuban Population of the United States: The Results of the 1980 U.S. Census of Population," *Cuban Studies/Estudios Cubanos* 15 (Summer 1985): 1–18; Joan Moore and Harry Pachón, *Hispanics in the United States* (Englewood Cliffs, New Jersey: Prentice-Hall, 1985), 69–78. The 1980 census did not include the Cubans who arrived during the Mariel boatlift.

5. Lisandro Pérez, "Immigrant Economic Adjustment and Family Organization: The Cuban Success Story Re-Examined," *International Migration Review* 20 (Spring 1986): 4–20. See also Pérez, "The Cuban Population of the United States," 8–9. The 1980 census revealed that more Cuban women worked outside the home than any other group, 55.4 percent as compared to the national average of 49.9 percent. For an analysis of Cuban women's roles in the economic, political, and cultural affairs of the community, see García, "Adapting to Exile." For an economic analysis see Myra Marx Ferree, "Employment without Liberation: Cuban Women in the U.S.," *Social Science Quarterly* 60 (January 1979): 35–50. See also Dorita Roca Mariña, "A Theoretical Discussion of What Changes and What Stays the Same in Cuban Immigrant Families," in José Szapocznik and María Cristina Herrera, eds., *Cuban*

Americans: Acculturation, Adjustment, and the Family (Washington: The National Coalition of Hispanic Mental Health and Human Services Organization, 1978).

6. Pérez, "Immigrant Economic Adjustment." See also Portes and Jensen, "The Enclave and the Entrants."

7. Portes and Jensen found that 34 percent of their Mariel respondents (excluding the self-employed) were working for Cuban-owned firms. See Portes and Jensen, "The Enclave and the Entrants."

8. Arboleya, *The Cuban Community, 1980.* See also Raymond A. Mohl, "An Ethnic 'Boiling Pot': Cubans and Haitians in Miami," *Journal of Ethnic Studies* 13 (Summer 1985): 51–74.

9. "To Miami, Refugees Spell P-R-O-S-P-E-R-I-T-Y," *Business Week,* November 3, 1962, 92; "Cuban Refugees Write a U.S. Success Story," *Business Week,* January 11, 1969, 84.

10. In his article "Immigrant Economic Adjustment and Family Organization," Lisandro Pérez challenges the "myth of the golden exile." He concludes that comparisons of economic achievements between Hispanic groups are inconclusive because they ignore the differences in the structural conditions within which economic adjustment takes place. See also Alejandro Portes, "Dilemmas of a Golden Exile: Integration of Cuban Refugee Families in Milwaukee," *American Sociological Review* 34 (August 1969): 505–18.

11. In 1990, 16.9 percent of Cuban Americans lived in poverty, as compared to 13.5 percent of the general population; Portes, "¿Quienes somos?" 5. See also note 60.

12. Alfonso Chardy, "'Invisible Exiles': Black Cubans Don't Find Their Niche in Miami," *Houston Chronicle,* September 12, 1993, 24A.

13. "Temas," *Impacto,* March 11, 1972. Translation mine. The concerns of the Cuban working class are articulated in the exile newspapers *El Trabajador, Trabajo,* and *Impacto.*

14. "Editorial," *Cubanacan: Asociación de Villaclareños en el Exilio,* 9, no. 106 (January 1975), 1. Translation mine.

15. Editorial, *Martiano,* November 1972, 2. Translation mine.

16. "Temas," *Impacto,* May 20, 1973, 2. Translation mine.

17. "Are We to Become Citizens?" *Antorcha,* January 1968, 5.

18. Founded in 1967, Abdala took its name from a fable by the nineteenth-century independence leader José Martí. Abdala, a prince from the imaginary land of Nuvia, renounces all material comforts and pleasures in order to defend his nation. Prince Abdala ultimately dies for his beliefs.

19. "Entre dos banderas," *Antorcha,* April 1973, 2. Translation mine.

20. Editorial, *Antorcha,* October 1969, 1. Translation mine.

21. Editorial, *Antorcha,* December 1969, 1. Translation mine.

22. Roberto Fabricio, "The Cuban Americans: Fifteen Years Later," *Tropic Magazine* (*Miami Herald*), July 14, 1974, 30–36.

23. Miguel Pérez, "10,000 New Americans Is Exile Group's Goal," *Miami Herald,* November 24, 1975, 8B; George Volsky, "Cuban Exiles Now Seek U.S. Citizenship," *New York Times,* July 4, 1976, 19; Helga Silva, "The Cuban Exiles: Landmarks of an Era," *Miami Herald,* April 8, 1979, 22A.

24. Arboleya, *The Cuban Community, 1980,* 3.

25. Roberto Fabricio, "Cubans at Home, but Homesick," *Miami Herald,* October 29, 1972, 1B.

26. Humberto Cruz, "Dade Cubans Won't Return, Study Shows," *Miami Herald,* June 10, 1974. The *Herald* published part of a study by sociologists Juan Clark and Manuel Mendoza of Miami-Dade Community College. Clark and Mendoza conducted interviews with

151 Dade Cubans fifty-five years or older—the group most likely to have failed to adapt to life in the United States—and less than half of these stated that they would return to Cuba if Castro were overthrown.

27. Alejandro Portes and Rafael Mozo, "The Political Adaptation Process of Cubans and Other Ethnic Minorities in the United States: A Preliminary Analysis," *International Migration Review* 19 (March 1985): 35–63.

28. Metro-Dade County, Board of County Commissioners, Resolution no. R.-502–73; Chuck Gómez, "In Cases of Emergency, Latins Can Lose Out," *Miami Herald*, June 3, 1974, 1A.

29. Resolution no. R.-502–73, as cited in Castro, "The Politics of Language in Miami," 116.

30. Myles R. R. Frechette, "Cuban-Soviet Impact on the Western Hemisphere," *Department of State Bulletin* 80 (July 1980): 79–80.

31. *Miami Herald*, December 29, 1975.

32. Roberto Fabricio, "Torch Ruins Show Rising Exile Anger," *Miami Herald*, October 13, 1974, 1B; Roberto Fabricio, "Exiles Protest Lifting of Cuba Sanctions," *Miami Herald*, November 4, 1974, 1B; Roberto Fabricio, "Cubans' OAS Protest Cooled by Downpour," *Miami Herald*, May 11, 1975, 1D.

33. "El exilio pide relaciones entre Cuba y Estados Unidos," *Arcíto* 5, nos. 19–20 (1979): 7–8; "10 mil exiliados piden Carter reanude relaciones con Cuba," *El Mundo*, June 25, 1979, 8.

34. See, for example, the *Miami Herald*, April 2, 1975, July 23, 1975, and August 22, 1978.

35. Editorial in *Martiano*, n.d. Translation mine.

36. Carlos López-Oña, Jr., "Los traidores," *Antorcha*, July 1970, 4. Translation mine.

37. The shipment of food and medicine to Cuba was always hotly debated in the community. See, for example, *¡Fe!*, December 15, 1972, 1. Even burial in Cuba—which was allowed beginning in 1979—was strongly discouraged because such arrangements benefitted the Cuban government financially. Ana E. Santiago, "Más restos cubanos llevados a la isla," *El Nuevo Herald*, April 4, 1991, 1A, 4A.

38. "Desde la cárcel denuncia La Cova al exilio Cubano," *La Nación*, October 15, 1976, 14. Translation mine.

39. "Exiles Say They Planted Bomb on Cuban Airliner," *New York Times*, July 16, 1976, 8; "Terrorism Charged to Cubans in Testimony by Miami Police," *New York Times*, August 23, 1976, 12; "Nine Cuban Refugees Go on Trial in Miami Tomorrow, Putting Focus on Terrorists' Activity in South Florida," *New York Times*, November 28, 1976, 35. See also *Cuba Update* (Center for Cuban Studies) 1, no. 1 (April 1980).

40. Jay Clarke, "Cubans in Miami Fearful," *Washington Post*, May 23, 1976, E1.

41. Edna Buchanan, "Foes Stalked Slain Exile," *Miami Herald*, February 23, 1974, 1B; "Acusa Nieves de agresión a líder pragmatista," *¡Fe!*, April 7, 1973, 3; "No permitiremos que juege con Cuba un puñado de traidores," *¡Fe!*, June 15, 1973, 2. See also Internal Security Hearings, 1976, 615.

42. Hilda Inclán, "Six Cuban Exiles Marked for Death by 'Zero,'" *Miami Herald*, April 15, 1974; "Dara plazo a Torriente," *¡Fe!*, February 24, 1973, 7; "Torriente es el farsante mas grande que ha parido este exilio corrompido y timorato," *¡Fe!*, May 19, 1973, 10.

43. "Nine Cuban Refugees Go on Trial in Miami Tomorrow, Putting Focus on Terrorists' Activities in South Florida," *New York Times*, November 28, 1976, 35.

44. José Ignacio Lasaga, "El terrorismo en Miami," *Krisis* 1 (Spring 1976): 23, 30. Translation mine.

45. On August 31, 1977, a group of men claiming to represent the Brigade 2506 Veterans Association announced that they would continue "all kinds of actions to fight against the communist tyranny."

46. Hilda Inclán, "I Am Not Afraid," *Nuestro,* April 1977, 46–47; Benjamin de la Vega, "Estrepitosa caida de las WQBA en el survey de la Arbitron," *Alerta,* August 1980; Larry Rohter, "Dissenting Voice Fights to Stay on Air," *New York Times,* March 2, 1993, A14. As a side note, Milián organized the first Three Kings Day parade in Little Havana in 1971. See *Miami Herald,* January 7, 1975, 1B.

47. Internal Security Hearings (1976), 615–16.

48. Ibid. 632, 651.

49. Ibid., 652. Letelier, ambassador to the U.S. during Salvador Allende's government, was a vocal critic of the Pinochet military regime. Cuban militants claimed that he was a subversive furthering the cause of international communism. See *El Imparcial,* May 7, 1981, 1.

50. For a sample of newspaper articles dealing with this topic see "El espionaje del G-2 en Miami," *Bohemia Libre,* November 13, 1960, 83; "Lleno el exilio de agentes G-2,"*Patria,* July 25, 1961, 4; "Castro Spies Prowl Miami, Defector Says," *Miami News,* December 18, 1971; Joe Crankshaw, "500 Castro Agents Operate in Miami, Witness Testifies," *Miami Herald,* August 19, 1976; Jim McGee, "Exiles Wage Silent War with Castro Spies," *Miami Herald,* June 19, 1983, 1A. Cuban exile newspapers claimed that the number of spies in Miami was much larger than that supposed by local authorities. One exile newspaper, for example, claimed that as many as seventy-five hundred Cuban spies operated in south Florida. See *Látigo,* January 1979, 10. Most newspapers never explained how they arrived at these figures. The tabloid *Patria* published pictures of suspected G-2 police hiding in exile. See also "Aumento alarmante de infiltrados," *Impacto,* December 30, 1971, 1.

51. McGee, "Exiles Wage Silent War with Castro Spies."

52. For example, a 1974 interview by Prensa Latina with defector Carlos Rivero Collado, (a former *brigadista* and the son of Andrés Rivero Agüero, Batista's chosen successor) discussed his work with the Pragmatistas and the Cuban Nationalist Movement. A Radio Havana interview with 1976 defector Manuel de Armas discussed the alleged involvement of the group Abdala in the assassination of exile leader Rolando Masferrer. Internal Security Hearings (1976) 626–27, 631–32, 649–56.

53. For one such interpretation see Lasaga, "El terrorismo en Miami." See also *El Clarín,* May 27, 1976.

54. In 1990 and 1991, the FBI arrested two more Cubans connected to the plot. Two former Chilean military officials remain in hiding at the time of writing. In July 1991, the Chilean Supreme Court reopened the Letelier case. See Gloria Marina, "Five Cubans and an American Figure in the Letelier Case," *Miami Herald,* May 6, 1978, 11A; and "A investigación aspecto chileno del caso Letelier," *El Nuevo Herald,* September 24, 1990, 1A.

55. Many in the exile community did not understand why Americans were making such a fuss about Watergate, and they continued to support President Nixon in his "struggle against subversion." See Frank Calzón, "El exilio cubano y la crisis norteamericana," *¡Cuba Va!* 1 (Winter 1974): 3–5; Pedro Moreno, "Watergate y los cubanos," *Joven Cuba* 1 (February 1974): 11–12; Roberto Fabricio, "Watergate Had Ironic Twists for Cubans," *Miami Herald,* June 12, 1982, 1B.

56. *Guerra* (New York), November 19, 1976, 3. Translation mine. See also the August/

September 1973 issue of *Abdala,* in which the editors pay tribute to a young Cuban who died while putting together a bomb in his Paris hotel room: "From a very young age he was attracted by his patriotic duty. . . ."

57. Gaston Baquero, "No hay mas alternativa que la violencia," reprinted in *Impacto,* October 14, 1972, 5. Translation mine.

58. *El Imparcial,* May 7, 1981.

59. Internal Security Hearings (1976), 636–37.

60. *La Crónica,* October 10, 1978, 18.

61. Federación de Organizaciones Cubanas de Illinois, "Petition to the United States Department of Justice," Box 17, Staff Offices, Papers of Esteban Torres, Carter Library.

62. Merrill Collett, "Absuelto Bosch en Venezuela," *El Herald,* July 22, 1986, 1A.

63. Reinaldo Ramos, "Exiliados reflexionan sobre Orlando Bosch," *El Herald,* July 27, 1986, 1, 3. Translation mine.

64. Letter to the editor, *Miami Herald,* April 2, 1983, 16A.

65. Deborah Sontag, "The Lasting Exile of Cuban Spirits," *New York Times,* September 11, 1994, 1E.

66. "U.S.-Cuba Joint Communiqué on Migration," *U.S. Department of State Dispatch* 5, no. 37 (September 12, 1994), 603.

67. Richard Wallace, "South Florida Grows to Latin Beat," *Miami Herald,* March 6, 1991, 1A; Sandra Dibble, "New Exiles Flocking to Dade," *Miami Herald,* April 11, 1987, 1D; Celia W. Dugger, "Latin Influx, Crime Prompt 'Flight' North," *Miami Herald,* May 3, 1987, 1B.

68. "Dade County Commission Repeals English-Only Law," *New York Times,* May 19, 1993.

69. Sergio López-Miró, ". . . While Hispanics Become the Area's Scapegoats," *Miami Herald,* October 11, 1990, 27A.

70. Jeffrey Schmalz, "Disorder Erupts Again in Miami on Second Night after Fatal Shooting," *New York Times,* January 18, 1989, 1; Jeffrey Schmalz, "Miami Mayor Apologizes to Police for Actions at Scene of Disorder," *New York Times,* January 19, 1989, 1.

71. Jay Ducassi, "Stations Seldom Face Libel Suits or FCC Action," *Miami Herald,* June 22, 1986, 2B.

72. Steven A. Holmes, "Miami Melting Pot Proves Explosive," *New York Times,* December 9, 1990, E4.

73. Nancy San Martín, "Castro Clause on Inaugural Upsets City's Haitian Leaders," *Miami Herald,* January 31, 1991, 3B.

QUESTIONS

1. To what extent can the status of Cuban Americans as a model Latino minority be attributed to individual drive to succeed and to what extent can it be attributed to the institutional support and material resources provided by the U.S. government?

2. Under what circumstances might we expect other minority groups to become as successful as Cuban Americans if they received the same level of material support? What are the implications for future policy and the nature of social change?

3. Cuba produces the New Men and New Women. The United States produces the Cuban American "golden

immigrants." Given the evidence provided by García, can we say that one system produces a "better" citizen in terms of critical thinking, diversity, and self-motivation?

4. Keeping in mind that during the Revolutionary War English American patriots terrorized their fellow colonists who remained loyal to the king, under what circumstances can we assign Cuban and Puerto Rican "terrorists" the subjectivity of "patriots" or "freedom fighters"?

5. Anglos move out of the area, African American and non-Cuban Latinos riot to protest Cuban-American domination, censorship, and intolerance. To what extent does this situation have to do with the nature of Cuban culture and to what extent does it have to do with the nature of power relations? What are the implications for a pluralistic society?

Summary and Comparative Analysis

At least three stories can be extrapolated from the readings in part II (the variations and alternative interpretations are left to your political imagination). The United States established a special relationship with Puerto Rico: a commonwealth that, according to Public Law 600, is free to govern itself but must check with the U.S. Congress before making any final decisions. Puerto Rican nationalists engage in violent actions to protest this judicial sleight of hand. Class, gender, and pigmentocracy issues, however, lead to the emergence of two majoritarian social movements, one for U.S. statehood and another for keeping the commonwealth status, while support for independence decreases to 4 percent of the electorate.

Cuba and the United States also have an intimate relationship. The relationship became strained due to the weakening of its economic and political colonial structure; it descended into name calling and finally collapsed after sixty years. In the process of getting a divorce and protecting their security interests, these two nation-states gave birth to the Cuban Americans. This group continues a paradoxical Cuban discourse of desire for assimilation into U.S. culture and *cubanidad,* a cultural nationalism that at times reaches extremes of chauvinism and terrorism. At the same time, there is some effort at healing the rupture within the Cuban people, which is presently divided between two rival nation-states.

Mexicans in the United States started off the twentieth century game of truth with a small population. They battled their subjectification as strangers and aliens in their own land and as being genetically or culturally inferior and therefore incapable of progress and inclusion in the U.S. polity. Subjected to political and economic forces in Mexico and the United States that have repeatedly brought their importation and deportation, they have nevertheless used their own social and labor organizations, as well as national and international ones, to build strong, active communities. As is true of other peoples, U.S. Mexicans also struggle within their own communities—against other forms of subjectification and domination based on gender, class, and skin pigmentation.

From these three distinct stories, a comparative analysis may be done on the basis of the following categories.

THE EXERCISE OF U.S. COLONIAL POWER

For Cubans, U.S. colonial power is exercised hegemonically, through the control of the economy and the attempt to control the political system. In Puerto Rico, it is done through Congress and the judiciary. This power has been exercised on these peoples while they remained on their own islands, away from the mainland. For Mexicans, the exercise of colonial power was more violent and coercive because of the struggle for the land and the subjectification of Mexicans as Indians (so that the discourse of extermination was applied to them also). Colonial power was exercised through the state legislatures and courts, vigilantism, and manipulation of the law.

INSTITUTIONAL SUPPORT AND RELATIONS

Education in Cuba remains in Cuban hands. It is imposed on U.S. Mexicans and Puerto Ricans by people who are trained in theories that assume, implicitly at least, the inferiority of these peoples. The Anglo Catholic Church is not particularly helpful to U.S. Mexicans or the majority of Puerto Ricans. Cubans were political refugees at a critical point in a nuclear confrontation, so they received political and economic support even greater than what is provided for U.S. citizens. U.S. Mexicans had to rely on the Mexican consulate offices and mutual aid societies to survive. Puerto Ricans are U.S. citizens and negotiate for the acquisition of benefits that are given to other U.S. citizens.

INCLUSIVE/EXCLUSIVE CITIZENSHIP PRACTICES

Puerto Ricans are U.S. citizens, more or less. Cubans are accepted into the United States with no questions asked and given citizenship as soon as possible. Mexicans are in constant danger of being deported, whether they are U.S. citizens or not.

INTEGRATION INTO (THE ELECTORAL AND OTHER) POLITICS

U.S. Cubans continue their tradition of political involvement, especially because they come primarily from the upper and middle classes. Some engage in terrorism against Castro and their own community. Puerto Ricans participate in politics within the limits imposed by the U.S. Congress and the courts. Those engaged in *independentista* "terrorist" activities are, of course, subjected to persecution by the state. U.S. Mexicans are kept out of the electoral process through a variety of mechanisms, including laws to deport militant workers, literacy standards, and head taxes. At the start of the twenty-first century, however, thirty-two million Latinos in the United States represented 7 percent of the one million votes cast in the November 7, 2000, elections. Approximately two-thirds of these voters were of Mexican descent.

SUBJECTIFICATION AND SUBJECTIVITIES

Cubans arrived in waves and to a particular place, south Florida, mostly from the white upper and middle class, and created an economic, political, and cultural enclave that has supported additional arrivals (also mostly *en masse*), even if they are from working, dark-skinned classes. Cubans are portrayed as the "golden immigrants." In addition to the Mexicans who were already in what is now the United States at the time of the conquest, others arrived in waves, although these waves were more diffuse in terms of time, geography, and class, compared with Cuban exiles. However, most Mexican migration came from peasant stock and this fed the image of "the Mexican" in the United States that still survives today. Puerto Ricans also arrived in waves and, like Cubans, to particular places—New York and New Jersey—and they represent working-class and peasant segments of the population. Cubans have Ricky Ricardo, Puerto Ricans have Maria from *West Side Story*, Mexicans have "Hey Pancho," "Hey Cisco," or "Speedy Gonzalez." An informal survey conducted by the editors show that these are the symbols that most U.S. Americans, across generations, associate with these ethnic groups.

ROLE OF THE U.S. ECONOMY

The United States economy has become increasingly integrated with the Puerto Rican (through Operation Bootstrap), Cuban (until 1960), and Mexican (through NAFTA) economies. Unlike Puerto Ricans and Cuban Americans, who were constructed by issues of national security, the Mexican immigrant population was constructed by the interplay between the U.S. and Mexican political economies. For all three groups, this means subsequent dislocation and movement of human bodies to the United States and back (when they can or when they must). The proliferation of identities and forms of struggles must be understood against the corresponding proliferation of forms of subjectification and oppression created by the globalization of the economy. Such is the postmodern condition.

CULTURAL NATIONALISM

All three peoples have kept their cultures despite or because of the forces of assimilation, or rather "normalization." This is the one constant that underlies the quest for public citizenship. When the going gets rough, it is within the *ethnos,* the extended family, the paisano/as, where we find inclusiveness, respect, and justice.

At what point does cultural nationalism, ethnic identification, and a national consciousness develop into a movement to secede from a nation? This question falls under the jurisdiction of what is known as "the National Question."

PART III

ON THE NATIONAL QUESTION

IN THE PREVIOUS TWO SECTIONS, THE TERMS "nation," "nationality," and "national-ism" have appeared in various contexts. We learned that in the nineteenth century, after being colonies of Spain for three hundred to four hundred years, Mexico, Cuba, and Puerto Rico were newborn countries: they were in the process of consol-idating their identities as nation-states. We uncovered the manifold seduction and conquest of three different nationalities, Mexicans, Cubans, and Puerto Ricans, that led to their "legal adoption" by one nation-state known as the United States of America. We witnessed, vicariously, the transformation of these involuntary, territo-rial, and cultural U.S. citizens from "nationals" to "ethnics." We learned the partic-ulars of the diverse labor, political, economic, cultural, and academic struggles to establish political identities in a quest for public citizenship.

In this section, we attempt to deal with "the national question," a particularly complex game of truths that is central to these issues. Think of the planet Earth as being populated by hundreds of "nations," that is, groups of people who share com-mon customs, origins, histories, and languages. The word comes from the Latin *natio*, which means birth or race; from nasci, *to be born*; literally, "where you are born," your home turf. In the Greek language, the word for "nation" is *ethnos*. So, "nations" are equal to ethnic groups, equal to "tribes," such as the Angles, Saxons (yes, they used to be two different tribes), the Franks, the Navajo, the Maya. There is an implication here of blood ties, of one big family, like with the concept found in discussions of cultural nationalism (as in *familia* Puerto Riqueña, Chicanismo, and *cubanidad*). But when blood ties are involved or imagined, that brings into play the notion of the Furies (the Greek goddesses of vengeance against those who have shed the blood of their blood relatives, when these crimes have escaped detection or public justice). This particular discourse of blood is central to groups like the Nazis (in terms of their notion of "purity"), but it is also present in conflicts all over the world, such as in the Middle East, as well as in rural feuds and among urban gang members.

When some nations reach a particular level of economic and technological devel-opment, they conquer other nations to create kingdoms such as the Aztec, Roman, or British empires. When this happens, the conquered nations may become colonies and they are said to have lost their **sovereignty**, that is, the right to self-determina-tion, the right to make their own decisions; or they may become "integrated" into the dominant nation, the metro-polis (literally, the huge city-state). By the eigh-teenth century, "nation" was being used in the sense of "country" or "nation-state," that is, one that contains other "nations." For example, England ruled over many colonies (formerly independent nations) all over the world, so that the sun never set on the British empire. The United States includes Puerto Rico as a commonwealth, as well as Guam, the Marianas, Samoa, and many Indian nations, such as the Navajo and the Apache.

The relations of domination exercised by one nation over another is what is known as "the national question."[1] But now, we have just added the term **state** to nation: think of the state as the invention of a political machine, a form of government that not only replaced the empire/monarchy in the seventeenth century, but also tended to homogenize populations through the imposition of one language and one culture. This is where a confusion regarding the meaning of nationalism may arise. First of all, the term "nationality" refers to citizenship, to a human body's legal, political identification with a particular nation-state (or vice versa, the nation-states' political definition of human body as *belonging* to it). "Nationalism," however, describes the feelings of loyalty to a particular "nation" or to the "nation-state" that "owns it." Thus, an indigenous person in the Americas may feel her or his first loyalty is to their nation-tribe, not to the Mexican or U.S. nation-state. There are examples all over the world in which particular nations are not happy being owned by nation-states and they want to be independent from them. It is in this sense that we may speak of black, Chicano, Puerto Rican, and Cuban nationalism. But there is another kind of nationalism, like the one that arises in the United States in times of economic distress and leads many U.S. Americans (including blacks, Puerto Ricans, and Mexican Americans) to turn against those who fit the label of "foreigners," "immigrants" that is, those that do not belong to "the Nation." This too is the horizon where the "national question" comes into focus.

The national question may also involve issues of class. Do all U.S. Cubans, Puerto Ricans, and Mexicans feel attached to a political nationalism in the same way? Or are there differences between the wealthy, the middle, and the working classes? Is nationalism just a tool to get political concessions, part of a quest for public citizenship? Who really wants to stay and who wants to go? Or is it a matter of changing the U.S. society? Finally, as noted by Jorge Duany and Cherríe Moraga, the national question may also involve issues of race and gender.[2]

In the case of the United States "adopting" Mexican, Puerto Rican, and Cuban nationals as legal or cultural citizens, several questions may be raised. To which "nation" are they loyal? Or from the perspective of these national groups, if they are being forced into an involuntary political relationship (i.e., through military conquest), if they feel that they are not being integrated into the political life of the country, if they feel they are being exploited because of their national origin, would they be better off breaking away from the United States? We now come to another term that has been used extensively in previous readings, namely, "colonialism." Earlier we said that a nation like England (or the United States) may extend its dominion over other nations and create an empire. At the moment that those nations lose their sovereignty, the right to make their own decisions, they become "colonies" of the empire.

When the feelings of nationalism in a colony reach a particular level of intensity, they may lead to a war of independence. This is what happened when the United States (and later India and many other former colonies) broke away from England

and Latin American countries severed their ties with Spain. It is in this context that some Puerto Ricans want independence from and that Fidel Castro broke relations with the United States.

Cuba and Puerto Rico are islands off the coast of the United States, however, and that provides only one perspective.[3] At the same time, are Native, African, and Mexican Americans also "colonies," but in this case *inside* the United States? Is this a new kind of *internal* colonialism or neocolonialism, as Flores and Bailey argue?[4] Do these involuntary territorial and cultural citizens have a sense of *nationality*, that is, just a "cultural nationalist" identification with their country of origin (with its food, music, dance, fiestas, and other traditions)? Or do they have a sense of *nationalism*, that is, a stronger political loyalty with "their people" than with the "people" of the United States? And if it is the latter, have they reached the point defined in the Declaration of Independence when "it becomes necessary for one people to dissolve the political bands which have connected them with another"? This is, in effect, the claim made in the Brown Beret National Policies. Fred Cervantes, however, makes some critical observations regarding the definition of a Chicano "nation." The same point/counterpoint is provided by the "Young Lords Party 13-Point Program and Platform" and the piece by Ramón Grosfoguel.[5]

NOTES AND SUGGESTED READINGS

1. Juan Gómez-Quiñonez, "Critique on the National Question, Self-Determination and Nationalism," *Latin American Perspectives* 9, no. 2 (spring 1982): 62–83.

2. See also Lillian Manzor-Coats, "Performative Identities: Scenes between Two Cubas," in *Bridges to Cuba/Puentes a Cuba,* ed. Ruth Behar (Ann Arbor: University of Michigan Press, 1995), 253–66.

3. Andres Torres and Victor Rodriguez offer a different perspective on what constitutes a "nation" because, in the case of Puerto Ricans (and Cubans), the people are dispersed between two polities (a colony and a nation-state). See, A. Torres, "Political Radicalism in the Diaspora: The Puerto Rican Experience," in *Despierta Boricua: Voices from the Puerto Rican Movement,* ed. A. Torres and J. E. Velazquez (Philadelphia: Temple University Press, 1999); Victor M. Rodriguez, "Boricuas, African Americans, and Chicanos in the 'Far West': Notes on the Puerto Rican Pro-Independence Movements in California, 1960s–80s," in *Latino Social Movements: Historical and Theoretical Perspectives,* ed. Rodolfo D. Torres and George Katsiaficas (New York: Routledge, 1999), 79–109.

4. G. Flores and R. Bailey, "Internal Colonialism and Racial Minorities in the United States: An Overview," in *Structures of Dependency,* ed. F. Bonilla and R. Girling (Stanford: privately published, 1973), 149–58.

5. For a range of leftist theories attempting to explain why Latino/as in the United States are not on an equal socioeconomic level with other U.S. citizens and what reformist or revolutionary strategies and tactics are proposed to achieve a satisfactory level of equality, see the pamphlet by Antonio Rios-Bustamante, *Mexicans in the United States and the National Question: Current Polemics and Organizational Positions* (Santa Barbara, Calif.: Editorial La Causa, 1978).

✳ 22 ✳
BROWN BERET NATIONAL POLICIES

David Sánchez

The Brown Berets not only provide an example of nationalism in practice, they are the closest that Chicanos have come to creating a formal, nationalist military force.

The context for the Brown Beret National Policies, nevertheless, is arguably symbolic of the quest for citizenship. It is a further illustration that Latino/a political thought is, to a large extent, a reaction to injustice. We begin with the institution of Los Angeles City Hall led by a conservative mayor. The main character in this story is David Sánchez, who in early 1967 occupied the position of president of mayor Sam Yorty's Advisory Commission on Youth, a program that served as Sánchez's political training ground. The story of what happened in that year "clearly demonstrates how the powerful, omnipresent forces of racism can literally transform a young, innocent, politically naive barrio Chicanito with a strong conscience into a fierce, competitive, militant leader fighting for justice for his people."[1] Indeed by the end of the year, David had severed his ties with the mayor's program and founded the Young Citizens for Community Action, which quickly evolved into the Young Chicanos for Community Action, and then into the Brown Berets. As founder and prime minister of the Brown Berets, David channeled young people, many of whom had been gang members or had been in juvenile hall or prison, into a political cause. This blurring of the line between the criminal and the political echoes nineteenth-century Mexicano resistance in the Southwest.

For example, Las Gorras Blancas of New Mexico (U.S. Mexicans who organized guerrilla-style attacks on the properties of wealthy ranchers and later a political party) issued a political platform that has been compared with the Brown Beret National Policies.[2] You may notice the feeling of solidarity with "the people" in general, a feeling that points to a sense of nationhood. We also find the usual governing statements about the abuse of the judiciary and lack of justice, the suffering and persecution of "the people" and the call for social change (see appendix 3). There is also an ambivalence in the call for justice within the existing system and a veiled threat for a violent break from it. Judging from the National Policies, U.S. Mexicans, Chicanos, indeed appear as a nation and (though it is not explicitly stated) a war of liberation is implicit in some of the statements. Among the major actions in which the Brown Berets were involved were the Marcha de la Reconquista, the Chicano Moratorium Marches to protest the Vietnam War (the march of August 29, 1970, witnessed the death of Rubén Salazar), Expedition through Aztlán, and the takeover of Catalina Island. Probably the most significant were the student walkouts in 1968, the largest demonstration by high school students in the history of the United States.

NOTES AND SUGGESTED READINGS

1. David Sánchez, *Expedition through Aztlán* (La Puente, Calif.: Perspectiva, 1978), vii.

2. Sánchez, *Expedition*, vii. See also Robert J. Rosenbaum, *Mexicano Resistance in the Southwest: The Sacred Right of Self-Preservation* (Austin: University of Texas Press, 1981), 111–179. For a novelistic account, see Daniel Aragón y Ulibarrí's *Devil's Hatband* (Santa Fe, N.Mex.: Sunstone, 1999).

✳   ✳   ✳

Let it be known to the universe that these are the policies of the Brown Beret National Organization, and any person who poses to be a Brown Beret and does not follow these policies and principles is not a Brown Beret and should not be respected as one.

For too long individuals have prostituted the good name of the Brown Beret National Organization for their own self advancement, or they have prostituted the Brown Beret name for other movements. And to prevent further foreign agent insurgency, these policies have been created.

ARTICLE I

Let it be recognized that the Brown Beret National Organization is an organization that relates its energies to the historical and geographical situation the Chicano people are within. The situation the Chicano people are within is geographical because the land was stolen from the Chicano, and it is national because the Chicano people are a nation of combined abilities, both survival and cultural, of which we are a nation.

Fifteen million Chicanos are also within a sociological situation, where there is definite discrimination against Chicanos throughout the country. Whereas, wherever a Chicano is discriminated against and no matter where it may be, it is our cause to secure human rights as well as civil rights for all Chicanos.

The existing situation has not only left a people who have lost their land, but also the destruction of our people has taken place which is a detriment to our culture, heritage, and the existence of *la Raza*.

And because of the existing situation, we have created policies to not only create definite strategy, but also to prevent any threat to the coming nation. Whereas, we will halt any type of foreign intervention, by all means necessary.

ARTICLE II: HISTORY

Let it be known to all that the present invasion and occupation of the southwest was not by treaty, annexation, or purchase, as we have been told by the Treaty of Guadalupe Hidalgo of 1848. But, let it be known for historical record that in 1846, Brigadier General Stephen Kearney, along with other U.S. armed forces, took possession of the southwest by force. To prevent further battles between Anglo and Mexican gangs who fought against the occupation, a treaty was resolved in 1848 which guaranteed rights to those who remained in the southwest. And this same treaty of Guadalupe Hidalgo was violated when Rubén Salazar was not given the right of free assembly on August 29, 1970.

The treaty was broken, and two years before 1848, the land was stolen with malicious evil intent and malice. We have suffered, and we will never be free until the land is free from Anglo progress, which has been a detriment to the land, air, and water, as well as to our health.

Because the land purchase negotiations and annexation took place two years after the takeover of the southwest by U.S. forces, we declare the Treaty of Guadalupe Hidalgo invalid as well as its borders and promises. We also declare the invasion of the southwest a mistake, and an historical fraud which calls for attention. We will do all in our power to prove this historical mistake, because in history, the land always returns to the true inhabitants of that land.

ARTICLE III: WE ARE CHICANOS

We do not recognize any party which is affiliated with perpetuating white history. Left wing, right wing, socialists, democrats, and other foreign ideologies have attempted to prostitute the Chicano movement for the purpose of perpetuation of foreign movements. We are neither left wing nor right wing. We are Chicanos, and we denounce all white foreigners who try to put any other label on us, in order to create *la vida nueva de la Raza*.

ARTICLE IV: DEFENSE AGAINST FOREIGN MOVEMENTS

One side of the world is out to destroy the other side. The two great opposing ideologies both solicit nuclear destruction. The whole world is sucked into sick systems, and we wish to have no part in foreign movements. We will do everything in our power to prevent foreign agent persuasion. We are against insurgency by communists or republican parties or any other foreign political intervention.

ARTICLE V: EXPRESSION

Small scattered incidents and mobism in the past has led to lack of organization, turmoil, and some Chicano deaths. Perhaps, at that time, there was no way to control massive demonstrations by *la Raza*, from which we have already suffered not only loss of life, but also suffered at the hands of out-of-control police demonstrations.

Because of this, we wish to demonstrate in an orderly organized fashion with an organized disciplined body of people who can demonstrate without the problems of out-of-control mob violence.

We are on the move to show that we are right and to illustrate to all that anger and frustration can be directed towards constructive change. We will sacrifice our personal freedoms for significance, and to display how far we will go to make social change by the usage of the right of expression; whether that expression is military or otherwise. We have the right through peaceful means to show discontent toward local government by the use of free expression.

ARTICLE VI: PREPARATIONS

We must prepare for the escalation of massive coordination on a national scale, rather than on a local scale, including the development of academies necessary to prepare qualified officers to join our ranks.

All energies and resources must be directed toward preparations.

All education must be directed toward channeling students into a more skilled, technical, and qualified organization of the Brown Beret National Organization.

We must also make shelter and survival possible for Chicanos in case of disaster or evacuation.

ARTICLE VII: ABSOLUTE MILITARISM

In order to create massive organization within a society, and for that organization to control the conditions around it in order to survive conditions, it will take a sacrifice of our personal freedoms for absolute militarism, which is the fastest and strongest way to Chicano power. And in order to create real power for the people, discipline is necessary. We must understand that discipline is necessary in order to secure orderly action which alone can triumph over the seemingly impossible conditions of confrontation against any opposing force.

We must be able to recognize and face fear, because fear is the enemy of discipline. Fear unchecked will lead to panic, and a unit which panics is no longer a disciplined unit but a mob. Absolute militarism is needed to prevent out-of-control mob panic while allowing for effective massive coordination.

ARTICLE VIII: STRATEGY

By strategy, we are creating a movement by design to advance the Chicano movement five to ten years ahead of its time. *La caravana de la reconquista* is a tour and caravan of the southwest which is becoming a continuous migrating mass of people, and this continuous migration will revolve without end. During its travels, officers will be trained on this "Academy on Wheels."

Another strategy will be the reclamation of lands. This will begin first by the control of geographical areas taken place not by force, but rather by forms of occupation.

Further strategy also calls for the development of more chapters which will support the front line of *La caravana de la reconquista,* along with gathering resources from chapters to enforce and support special national projects of the Brown Beret National Organization.

ARTICLE IX: CULTURAL CUSTOMS

We are a nation with a definite culture and with a land that has been stolen. We are a state of *carnalismo,* we are not internationalist, we are nationalist. And those who come, or live in Chicano land must live and do as the Chicanos do.

ARTICLE X: BROWN BERET CHAPTERS

The chapters' first job will be to learn, instruct, and follow the Brown Beret National Policies.

The job of the chapter is one of community service and/or social action for change.

Another responsibility of the local chapter is to educate the *Raza* about these policies as well as getting the community involved with strategies of the Brown Beret National Organization.

Every Brown Beret Chapter is a local reserve organization.

It is also very important that each chapter understand that it is in itself a support office to reinforce the Brown Beret National Organization strategies with funds, reinforcements, and resources for greater national coordination.

ARTICLE XI: STOPPING FOREIGN INSURGENCY

We are a national organization and anyone who has associated himself with any international agency, organization, or other country is automatically terminated.

Anyone who does not accept and practice the Brown Beret National Policy will be terminated.

Any Brown Beret who is associated with the republicans or Anglo controlled Communist Party of the U.S.A., or is associated with the International Communist Party is hereby terminated. Any Brown Beret who identifies as being part of the small scattered incidents of the Chicano Liberation Front is terminated.

ARTICLE XII: SOCIAL SUPPORT

Despite age, profession, or income, it is of upmost importance that all Chicanos back each other in order to raise each other up, so that some Chicanos can have more resources for the purpose of channeling assistance to the Chicano movement.

It is also very important that all lay and professional Chicanos working in offices and organizations use their position as a vehicle to assist the Chicano Movement. Those holding such positions, as well as those without positions must back each other with support for all Chicanos in case anyone should encounter any problems while assisting the movement.

ARTICLE XIII: NEUTRALITY

We are a neutral state, because we have something to offer to the world.

ARTICLE XIV: WE DECLARE A NATION

We the Chicano people of the southwest, hereby declare ourselves a nation, and a nation that has been the subject of a profit-making invasion. We are a nation with a land that has been temporarily occupied.

And we are a nation with the ability to survive. We are a nation with great natural culturability. We are a nation, we who come from different ways, combining ourselves of one nation.

We are the good people who return nature back to its natural balance, and who bring justice to the universe.

ARTICLE XV: CHICANO AND INDIAN

Even though the Indian nation is somewhat unaware of the Chicano as being a people who all hold more than half Indian blood, we are of Indian-Mestizo descent, and we are of one Indian nation with similar and related cultures before the invasion of the primitive white man.

As far as all boundaries within the southwest which was once Mexico, we combine all people of Indian descent as being *ONE,* as well as its borders, boundaries, and perimeters of the southwest.

ARTICLE XVI: FURTHER POLICIES

Part A—Official

1) Anyone who states that he or she is a Brown Beret and does not conduct himself or herself with real discipline is not a Brown Beret.

2) Anyone who states that he or she is a Brown Beret, and does not have loyalty that is responsive to orders as well as ultimate respect towards the Prime Minister's Office, is not a Brown Beret.

3) Anyone who states that he or she is a Brown Beret and does not have loyalty to the National Prime Minister's Office, is not a Brown Beret.

4) Anyone who does not accept the Prime Minister's Office as Executive Chief of the Brown Beret Natural Forces, is not a Brown Beret.

Part B

The Brown Beret National Policy is to create unity within our own *barrios* without the alienation of our own people. We are Chicanos in a struggle for our rights and the eventual return of our land.

Anyone who attempts to apply any other label upon us is in violation of National Policy. The Brown Beret National Organization is based upon years of created organization capital, and anyone who causes a threat to the Foundation is in violation of National Policy.

The Brown Beret National Organization is based upon any funds that can be gathered for communications, transportation, demonstrations, and legal defense. Anyone who receives funds or other materials for the Organization, and does not turn in said funds or materials to the Organization is in violation of National Policy.

Part C

All violators of National Policy are subject to disciplinary action. Rank is for coordination, and those who do not respect rank (which was coordinated for the purpose of massive action) are in violation of National Policy.

During any event or action where there is no leadership in a community emergency situation, a Beret who does not attempt to take the burden of the emergency situation is in violation of National Policy.

Any unit or chapter who titles themselves, or claims affiliation with the name "Brown Beret" but does not actually affiliate with the Brown Beret National Organization, shall be denounced as violators of Brown Beret National Policy.

Any person who states that he or she is a Brown Beret and who is not actually affiliated with a registered chapter or unit, is in violation of National Policy.

Any person who mistreats any *soldado* by applying more stress and danger which is excessive to accomplish duties, is in violation of National Policy.

NOTE

These are the final Brown Beret National Policies adopted in 1972. They appeared in the last Brown Beret newsletter, *La Causa,* Los Angeles, California, 1972, pp. 4–6.

QUESTIONS

1. Is there any basis on which these policies may be construed as a declaration of independence from the United States?

2. Is there any basis on which these policies may be construed as a quest for public citizenship, a demand for justice within the U.S. polity?

3. Are there historical and social contradictions that may be said to explain or to be reflected in the logical inconsistencies of the political positions of the Brown Berets?

4. If you were an American Indian, how would you feel about being included among the Chicano people?

5. Do the writing quality, style, and structure have any political effect of their own?

✳ 23 ✳
CHICANOS AS A POSTCOLONIAL MINORITY:
SOME QUESTIONS CONCERNING THE ADEQUACY OF THE
PARADIGM OF INTERNAL COLONIALISM

Fred A. Cervantes

The following text is a response to the concept that Chicanos and other minorities are an internal colony. Fred begins with a "tribute" in which he underlines the importance of searching for new ways of conceptualizing the reasons ethnic minorities have not achieved the American Dream. Referring to Nick Vaca's efforts to document the social science record of portraying Mexican culture as deficient, Fred notes that there is more to being involved in this effort than playing academic games.[1] He applauds the use of marxist analysis in the new conceptualization of the internal colony, noting the importance of such analysis for those who find themselves at the bottom of the socioeconomic and political ladders. To increase your critical thinking skills, pay particular attention to how he critiques the assumptions implied by the concept of internal colonialism. These assumptions appear in notions such as the legal status of the colonized (citizenship), Mexican American nationalism, postcolonialism, La Raza Unida Party, and pluralism. In place of these ideas, he proposes a strictly marxist analysis that focuses on class struggle. In his view, Chicanos are a national minority seeking multicultural pluralism rather than an anticolonial force seeking national liberation.

Note

1. N. C. Vaca, "The Mexican American in the Social Sciences 1912–1970." *El Grito* 4, no. 1 (1970): 17–51.

Behind the ethereal wall of objective scientific inquiry, traditional social scientists have devoted themselves to the highly normative practice of developing paradigms of assimilation and integration in studying ethnic minorities. With the recognition that not all assimilate well, nor can be accommodated easily within the United States political and social economy, have come a few realizations and some puzzlement. Quite a few notions of social and cultural deviation have been advanced to explain why Chicanos and other "deviants" persist with attitudes and behaviors that have been associated with patterns of futility or failure by the institutions of schooling, politics, penality, and mental and physical health.

Robert Dahl, to cite a relatively innocuous example of traditional political wisdom for the "minority" scholar, suggests that the persistence of ethnic voting patterns is a somewhat puzzling deviation that, surely, will eventually lose its significance.[1] If Dahl just seems to beg important questions, Nick Vaca has identified for us a whole legacy of analysis in the literature of the social sciences that is far more troubling.[2] Vaca notes that over the years the Chicano and his culture have been systematically condemned for creating a set of values that presumably have resulted in social and economic failures because these values were so often diametrically opposed to the acceptable and functionally superior Anglo values. In becoming deviants in their own land, Chicanos have had every thing from their high fertility rate and high school drop-out rates to their family and convict behavior attributed to such "dysfunctional" norm-myths as Machismo and Indian fatalism.

Within the baleful framework of blaming the victim (without really getting normatively involved) there has been little room for the Chicano social scientist. Understandably and commendably we have looked for alternative conceptualizations elsewhere and have been receptive of those that provided a critical framework for looking at historical and institutional forces in terms of their impact on people. There has long persisted a Chicano folkloric tradition that has chronicled the conflicts between Mexicanos and external forces of political and cultural assault. These lessons were hard to come by in the schools of the Southwest. Moreover, Chicanos have shared with Native Americans the distinction of being the special objects of scrutiny by state and federal as well as local law enforcement agencies in the Southwest. Not only have Chicanos been the primary concern of the Texas Rangers since their inception in 1835 to "protect the frontier," but we have known the Immigration and Naturalization Service and U.S. Forest Service as an oppressive controlling force, which is *inter alia*, not to forget the LAPD or the Kern County Sheriffs. So the search for alternative conceptualizations stems from more than an interest in rejecting academic trends in sociology, political science and history.

Out of an identified and professed need for a new perspective, Barrera, Muñoz and Ornelas developed their conception of the barrio as an internal colony.[3] The influence of this model is widely appreciated and is notably represented in its further association with the works of Tomás Almaguer,[4] Guillermo Flores and Ronald Bailey.[5] In their essay, Barrera, Muñoz and Ornelas indicate the limitations of the older "assilationist/accomodationist" view and present the inadequacy of the more recent tendency of explaining Chicano powerlessness as a function of inadequate Chicano leadership. They declare that their model offers a more realistic and effective means of singling out significant aspects of the Chicano "situation."[6]

In applying the model of internal colonialism, previously used by Blauner as an instructive analogy to traditional colonialism, Barrera, Muñoz and Ornelas have gone a step further to urge that the concept of internal colonialism should be regarded as something more than a heuristic device.[7] In this sense, a few Chicano social scientists have braved the U.S. academic waters and shown a consistent willingness to extend an essentially Marxist concept of analysis to U.S. political behavior. To provide an interesting twist to William Appleman Williams' charge against U.S. historians, there has not been a great evasion of Marxist analysis on the part of Chicano political scientists.[8] (Even though I can remember being at a symposium on Chicano politics here in Austin three years ago when it was personally easy and intellectually pragmatic for a Chicano political scientist to wonder out loud about the contemporary and scientific relevance of all this 19th century Marxist stuff he was hearing from Carlos Muñoz.)

As a few voices in the professional disciplines (Williams, Paul Baran, Paul Sweezy and Irving Horowitz) have long suggested, there is much to learn about U.S. society from a Marxist perspective. Moreover, it is a perspective that has become more important to understand for Chicanos and others who find themselves at the bottom of the socio-economic and political ladder in a political economy that has become increasingly multi-national and is straining under new constraints of scarcity and political challenge to its established patterns of capital expansion. Put another way, the Marxist paradigm remains the most significant systematic critique of capitalism as well as being its most important ideological threat.

CRITIQUE

Having noted the importance of the Marxist perspective, it is from this perspective that I would challenge the adequacy of explaining the contemporary Chicano "situation" in terms of the model of internal colonialism.

At different points in their essay, Barrera, Muñoz and Ornelas define internal colonialism as a condition of powerlessness and a condition involving the domination and exploitation of a total population.[9] As they put it: "The essence, then, of being an internal colony means existing in a condition of powerlessness."[10] This essence, however, does not really distinguish internal from external colonialism. Nor, for that matter, does such a definition really distinguish colonialism from the exploitative relationship which exists between the bourgeoisie and the proletariat.

In another broadly inclusive observation, the three authors state that:

> No one disputes that colonialism in its modern usage refers to a relationship in which one group of people dominates and exploits another.[11]

While this can be granted, it really does not take us very far in clearly defining colonialism as a type or system of exploitation distinct, for example, from the mechanisms of class exploitation. In their exposition of colonialism, however, the three authors cite the importance of González-Casanova's idea that a relationship of domination and exploitation of a total population that has distinct classes. Or as Guillermo Flores has noted in citing Memmi's work, colonialism establishes power and privilege for even the poorest colonizer over the colonized.[12]

Restated in a way that further pursues the Aristotelian ideal of understanding a phenomenon's "essence," it can be said that while exploitation and domination are necessary for colonialism to exist, these conditions are not sufficient. Flores suggests the critical importance of understanding colonialism in terms of an institutional control mechanism, which, for me, connotes state and administrative controls capable of clearly and materially elevating even the poorest colonizer to a position of power and privilege over the colonized.

Consequently, a bothersome question arises for me when the three authors assert that:

> The crucial distinguishing characteristic between internal and external colonialism does not appear to be so much the existence of separate territories corresponding to metropolis and colony, but the legal status of the colonized (i.e., whether or not there is a distinct legal status for the colonized).[13]

I would wonder if colonialism can exist at all without a separate legal status for the colonized. According to Barrera, Muñoz and Ornelas, internal colonialism exists if domination or exploitation of a distinct group is maintained even though the colonized have the same formal legal status as the colonizer, whereas external colonialism is said to exist where there are clearly separated legal statuses for the colonized and colonizer. If this distinction is unambiguous it seems arbitrary and, within its own unexplained context, it is dubious if for no other reason than that the distinction violates a coherent understanding of internal and external colonialism based on territoriality. More importantly, what is the conceptual difference between internal colonial and class exploitation according to their schema?

To return to an earlier proposition: for colonialism to exist it is not enough that a pattern of exploitation be identified. Colonialism has been understood as a distinct mechanism of exploitation, noteworthy in its use of economic and legal institutional forms to differentiate the exploited from the exploiters. From a Marxist-Leninist perspective colonialism has been viewed as the material extension of legal administration to politically institutionalize economic inequalities. Even in terms of the concept of neo-colonialism, dependent status is institutionally and jurisdictionally arranged by those who are the alien political administrators or economic exploiters.

The political antidote for both colonialism and neocolonialism in the Third World has been anti-colonial movements of national liberation, that have articulated struggles of national self-determination. Dialectically speaking, this means that the rise of nationalism as a force of political liberation is the negation of colonialism. Consistent with this implication, those who subscribe to the internal colonial model have examined the Chicano movement with a view toward demonstrating the bases of contemporary Chicano nationalism. Indeed, if contemporary Chicano nationalism can be clearly demonstrated it would be a satisfying and satisfactory way to substantiate the existence of colonialism regardless of how well the model of internal colonialism stands up to the analytic scrutiny of traditional Marxist or Stalinist concerns. However, demonstrating that Chicano nationalism is an antithesis of colonialism in contemporary times seems unlikely.

The question of the nature of Chicano nationalism aside for the moment, let us turn to some interesting variations on the internal colonial model advanced by Tomás Almaguer and Guillermo Flores. They challenge us to go beyond Marx, Lenin, Hobson and Stalin while nevertheless submitting their variations on a theme to the dialectical and historical requirements of a nondoctrinaire but coherent Marxist perspective. Moreover, it is instructive to see how their analyses relate to the unresolved questions raised above concerning Chicano nationalism and the definition of internal colonialism.

In the latter part of their essay, Barrera, Muñoz and Ornelas depict racism and stereotyping as both justifications and mechanisms of colonialism, concluding that:

> Of all the mechanisms of domination, the racist mobilization of bias may be the most pervasive and most subtle in its effects.[14]

In his essay entitled "Race and Culture in the Internal Colony; Keeping the Chicano in His Place," Flores picks up where his colleagues left off. He accepts their model and develops his own concept of racial-cultural surplus value, which he views as a major legacy of the colonial past and an operational characteristic of internal colonialism today.[15]

According to Flores the racial-cultural superordinate position enjoyed by the colonizer is part of the surplus value that accrues to all colonizers, presumably without regard to class position—unlike the dynamic end result of economic surplus value which accrues to the bourgeoisie. In the case of racial-cultural surplus value advantage is maintained through a vast ideological apparatus that guarantees racism despite official (political) myths to the contrary. Although dialectical interaction is assumed, there is no clear delineation of substructure and superstructure in this conception of change in which an economic concept, i.e., surplus value, is borrowed to depict attitudes and values without indicating the limits or logic of such an analogy.

Viewing internal colonialism as a "highly fluid system of domination," Flores makes no attempt to determine if racism is more a function of colonialism or an operational part of it.[16] Compatible with the Barrera, Muñoz and Ornelas distinction between internal and external colonialism there is not apparent need to make such an assessment in the Flores model. All forms and manifestations of dependence blend together into colonialism that is bisected only into its internal and external parts by the knife of legal status. If colonialism is nothing more specific than domination and exploitation, however complex, then understandably "internal colonialism is nothing more than the domestic face of world imperialism," as Flores remarks elsewhere (along with Ronald Bailey).[17]

While Flores and Ronald Bailey have stressed the importance of being historical in understanding Chicano colonial status, it is Tomás Almaguer who, in a recent issue of *Aztlán*, has taken us furthest in developing a dialectic of Chicano colonialism.[18] Drawing on European history as a history of competing colonial forces, he brings into dialectical as well as historical perspective the conditions of contemporary Chicano oppression. In his dialectics of racial and class domination, Almaguer sees the expansion of mercantile and industrial capital as driving forces for colonial advantage that were preconditions for the absorption of half of the Mexican territory by the United States in a process of one group of colonizers overwhelming others. He reminds us that the United States was not the only colonizer in the area and that U.S. military and political predominance did not mean a complete cultural and social rout of the Mexicanos, but established a context of struggle and conflict that has in turn, determined the status and struggle of Chicanos today.

In reading Almaguer's account of the complex pattern of colonization that affected the people and area that became the Southwestern United States, I became mindful of the salient importance of Marx's discussions on capital accumulation and Lenin's thesis on imperialism, and recalled William A. Williams instructive survey of *The Making of the American Empire*. But why the legacy of this important colonial experience, which today manifests itself in the racism that we all have known as Chicanos, in the proletarianization of Chicano workers and in other forms of domination and exploitation, should be called internal colonialism is unclear to me—except as a function of an established definition that Almaguer has also assumed.[19]

With a little added help from Marx's writings, Almaguer can be cited to support the suggestion of making the transition from the model of internal colonialism to a model of postcolonialism. He contends that: "The foundation of Chicano oppression is based on the organization of social relations of production,"[20] to which one can add Marx's insight that "Social relations of productions, change, are transformed, with the change and development of the material means of production, the productive forces."[21] This is to say that the means of oppression changes and is transformed by the dialectics of market expansion. It is suggested that colonialism as a form of oppression that defines social relations of production in a particular way changes and may be usefully transformed to a postcolonial means of exploitation once the proletarianization of a dependent people is realized. This pattern of development seems to have been particularly evident in the U.S. with the taking of territories followed by the *selective* granting of statehood.

The point to be made at this juncture is that the contemporary Chicano "situation" can more usefully be conceptualized as being in a state of postcolonial development which, as the term implies, must be understood within the dialectical context of its colonial experience. It is the *legacy* of colonialism that manifests itself in various postcolonial structures of economic and racial-cultural dependencies. As a dialectical process, colonialist oppression of the Mexicano and the Chicano has undergone a series of institutional quantitative changes that has produced a qualitative change that, I suggest, is not usefully or clearly understandable as a different face of colonialism. In addition to the arguments stated above, I would offer a number of other practices and analytic reasons for this shift in conceptual emphasis.

In the first place there is the problem of finding an ideological base in the Chicano movement for the negation of presumed colonialism, i.e., a distinct and salient Chicano nationalism (assuming as I do that nationalism means something more than cultural or ethnic identity). Central to the political nationalism is the idea of the struggle for self-determination not just the right to practice interest group politics equally. In its anti-colonial form, the teleology of nationalism is devoted to the liberation and self-government of a particular oppressed people. The Marxist-Leninist prototype of a model, is specific and rigorous in determining whether or not a distinct community constitutes a nation or potential nation. Stalin prescribes that there must be an "historically constituted" community of people with a common language, a common territory, a common economic life and a common "psychological make-up" that manifests itself in a common culture.[22] According to him a nation does not exist or "ceases to be a nation" if *all* of the features are not apparent. All of the characteristics are regarded as being necessary and sufficient for each other. For the Chicano nation-builder Stalin's is a most demanding model. Stalin can be rejected, of course, for his dogma or his rigor, but final questions concerning the existence of distinct territoriality, separatist politics and economic life must be answered in determining any reasonable concrete measure of Chicano nationalism.

Trapped by having accepted internal colonialism as a definition of Chicano political reality, some of my colleagues, it seems to me, have futilely attempted to interpret reformist politics as Chicano nationalism or, worse, as the power of the Chicano movement to de-colonize the United States.

The lack of political representation is cited as an important example of the political dimensions of internal colonialism by both those who have developed and those who have accepted the model.

The trouble with regarding the lack of representation as a significant aspect of colonialism is that electoral politics can then be logically viewed as an anti-colonialist activity. To stretch this notion to an absurd theoretical conclusion, each new Chicano representative can be cited as an example of the anti-colonial negation of having less or no representation! Regardless of the symbolic significance of the election of two Mexican American governors last year, my common sense tells me that as the number of Chicano elected officials in the Southwest increases, there will be less rather than more evidence of Chicano nationalism working as a force of anti-colonial national liberation. I think it ironic if understandable to admonish Chicanos to intensify their electoral participation as a part of the struggle against internal colonialism.[23]

Even El Partido de La Raza Unida, which has become a factor in Texas electoral politics in the name of justice and equity for Chicanos, finally is not a voice for Chicano nationhood. La Raza Unida, nevertheless, has emerged as a voice against the oppression and domination of Chicanos. Its candidates have sought power through the ballot box and the articulation of Chicano interest, by Chicanos for Chicanos, running for city council, school board seats and state and county offices. While the Partido seeks to redress the political oppression and economic exploitation of Chicanos in Texas and elsewhere, its aim is to reform and make the existing political system serve the interest of Chicanos. The activities of La Raza Unida remind us that one does not have to prove that there is colonialism, internal or external, or practice anti-colonialist politics to demonstrate and tactically respond to the inequities of exploitations.

Flores' conception of internal colonialism as the disparity between our psychological and social ideology on the one hand and our official, i.e., political ideology on the other hand, creates a distinct but related problem. In this schema, reducing the disparities between professed and actual beliefs becomes an anti-colonialist act. The "ideological transformation" that he calls for is, it seems to me, aimed more at making the 18th century promise of "American pluralism" work rather than developing Chicano liberation.[24] His idea of developing critical awareness and consciousness to combat well-developed patterns of psychological exploitation seems to be an approach to the legacy of colonialism rather than a direct anti-colonialist assault. He finds that in its growing sophistication, the Chicano movement increasingly has attacked institutional inequity and decreasingly attacked racist individuals.[25] The awareness that he suggests is developing is an interest group orientation toward gaining access to U.S. institutions.

In viewing the structures of the welfare system as an institutionalization of colonialism as Almaguer for example, does, virtually all poor people are reduced to the status of the colonized. This is problematic for a number of reasons. First of all, this factor tends to equate class status with colonial status, erasing the essential distinction advanced by González-Casanova that colonialism must be understood to level class status for the colonized. Secondly, this factor is not particularly useful for demonstrating the colonization affecting Chicanos in that the largest number of poor people in this country are Anglos. Thirdly, even though Chicanos and Blacks may be disproportionately affected by *some* welfare bureaucracies, we find that the welfare bureaucracy does not govern the lives of most Chicanos and that large numbers of Chicanos have been excluded from the benefits of the welfare state. It is the exclusion of Chicanos, it seems to me, that is a part of the basic oppression and exploitation of the Chicano in relation to the Anglos who have taken relatively much from the public trough. To be sure, a welfare bureaucracy creates dependence. But it is odd to consider welfarism colonialist activity when so much energy in the Chicano movement has been spent on trying to make governmental agencies more responsive to the welfare of Chicanos. Is it colonialism and, if so, who are the anti-colonialists?

Finally, there is something to be learned and questioned in the recent comments of Carlos Muñoz on the politics of protest and Chicano liberation.[26] The most important thing he suggests to me is that we simply do not find ourselves in a colonialist situation. He laments that in the absence of a mass based working class organization, Chicano protest has been effectively channeled into the ongoing political process.[27] Yet he persists in conceptualizing about this phenomena within the framework of the model of internal colonialism asserting that the politics of *Chicano cultural nationalism* has been more of a politics of reform than of radical social change.

To view reformist politics as cultural nationalism I submit, begs an important question and assumes by definition the teleology of Chicano liberation. How novel to regard reformist politics as the stuff of national liberation. I would argue that Muñoz has engaged in reductionism in making trends he has assessed critically conform to an assumed definition of internal colonialism that is as questionable now as it was when it was formulated. Furthermore, I would suggest that the reformist thrust of progressive Chicano politics suggests that Chicano nationalism is not a very important political factor in and of itself.

CONCLUSION AND SUGGESTIONS

Considering the extent of Chicano advocacy of reform and the interest in making pluralism work in this polity, it seems to me we should be ready to close off the dead-ends of the model of internal colonialism but nevertheless extend the main Marxist track on which this theoretical perspective has taken Chicano social scientists. Barrera, Muñoz and Ornelas have demonstrated the need for critical models in our professions and have shown us the essential utility of understanding Chicano politics in relation to the forces of colonialism. Almaguer and Flores have highlighted the importance of casting our analysis of colonialism in a dialectical and historical mold. Following Almaguer and Flores, I underline the importance of setting such questions as the analysis of Chicano nationalism within a context of historical conflict. From this perspective, I am persuaded that we have passed into a postcolonial period in which Chicano progressives have become the leaders of a national minority seeking multicultural pluralism rather than an anti-colonial force seeking national liberation.

To reiterate, colonialism implies a particular pattern of exploitation. Conquest, suppression and separate political administration of an oppressed nation of people offer the clearest example of colonialism. In the case of Chicanos, this kind of colonialism did not abruptly end with the conclusion of the Treaty of Guadalupe-Hidalgo, but the Treaty signalled the beginning of a shift from colonialism to other forms of exploitation. Anglo land barons created the Texas Rangers to keep the Mexican colonized and resist the threats of separatism emanating from Mexican rebels in South Texas until the early part of the 20th century. The notorious "Santa Fe Ring" systematically went about undermining political and economic assurances of the Treaty of Guadalupe-Hidalgo. These are obvious examples of the trauma of U.S. imperialism effecting the Chicano. Moreover, the Rangers are still with us and most of the land of Nuevo México is owned by Anglos and the federal and state governments; and Chicano poverty in Northern Nuevo México and South Texas still suggests the reality of colonialism. But for most of us, this is the legacy of colonialism. Even among the Chicanos of Nuevo México and Texas, where the conditions of exploitation are the worst for large numbers of Chicanos, anti-colonial feelings that would nurture a sense of separate nationalism, it seems have been negated by the reality of reformist politics that seeks redress at the polls or from the courts. However, much of South Texas and Northern Nuevo México have remained in the colonial past. The areas of the Southwest where Anglos first came to clearly outnumber Mexicans were the first to pass into a political postcolonial status.

Territorial status under the U.S. system of government has been roughly equivalent to colonialism. The grant of statehood conversely, was a rough indicator of the beginning of the transition out of colonialism. It was in Texas that the Anglos first came to significantly outnumber Mexicans and first clearly demonstrated their political power in the Southwest—even before the war on México. It was Texas that first became a state in 1845 even before that war. However, the concentration of the Anglo domination of population in the eastern, central, and northern parts of the region created a special problem. It is this distortion of population distribution despite the Anglo numerical superiority that, I would argue, necessitated the maintenance of a quasi-colonialist regime in the southern region of the state while the rest of the state made an early transition to postcolonial status. The difference was that the Anglos could guarantee overall political and economic dominance through their demographic power while they needed to maintain regional colonialism to guarantee exploitation of the Mexicano in South Texas.

In California the number of Mexican and Anglo inhabitants was relatively balanced until after the Gold Rush of 1849—the Indians having been colonized by both. California became a state the next year. Nevada, according to Morison and Commager was "admitted prematurely in 1865 because the Republicans thought they needed its electoral vote."[28] For me the interesting thing about Nevada's admission only four years after it had been reorganized as a territory is that, having been the most extreme example of a mining region it attracted a safe Anglo population majority regardless of its overall size. Colorado had its rush of Anglos after the discovery of gold in the foothills of the Rockies in 1859 and after the development of the railroads in the seventies brought an influx of Anglo farmers. It became a state in 1876.

While having a culturally "safe" (note Utah's late admission date of 1896), and dominant Anglo population may not have been sufficient for statehood, it seems to have been necessary for the political rites of passage to postcolonial status. For Chicanos in the Southwest it was the adverse shift in demographic balance that initiated the beginnings of the postcolonial period. As is generally the case with dialectical conflict, the process of change was uneven. Resistance followed the new material and political reality, particularly in South Texas; but it was eventually quelled and new, more sophisticated forms of exploitation than colonialism were instituted where the scars of colonialism remain.

For us, there remain ample reasons to sustain our probes of U.S. society from the critical perspective that has been introduced by Barrerra, Muñoz, Ornelas, Almaguer, Flores and others. But it is important to relate these concepts more closely to the realities of contemporary Chicano history and politics. For this reason I would advocate conceptualizing the patterns of Chicano resistance, struggle and exploitation as a legacy of colonialism rather than as an example of internal colonialism.

I suggest the importance of looking at topics such as the following as postcolonial phenomena in order to delineate more complex patterns of exploitation, dependence and subordination and superordination: (a) economic dependence, economic entry and racism; (b) restriction of status mobility; (c) the impact of sexism and feminism on Chicanos; (d) cultural suppression of Chicanos; (e) labor market segmentation of Chicanos; (f) the proletarianization and metropolitinization of Chicanos; (g) the imposition of bureaucratic dependence upon Chicanos; (h) symbolic representation of Chicanos and the meaning of Chicano voter participation.

NOTES

1. See Robert Dahl, *Who Governs?* (New Haven: Yale University Press, 1961).

2. Nick Vaca, "The Mexican American in the Social Sciences 1912–1970, Part II: 1936–1970," *El Grito* (Spring 1970).

3. Mario Barrera, Carlos Muñoz and Charles Ornelas, "The Barrio as an Internal Colony" in Harlan Hahn, ed., *People and Politics in Urban Society*, Vol. 6 (Beverly Hills: Sage Publications, 1972), pp. 465–498.

4. Tomás Almaguer, "Historical Notes on Chicano Oppression: The Dialectics of Racial and Class Domination in North America," *Aztlán-IJCSR*, Vol. 5 (Spring/Fall 1974), pp. 27–56.

5. Guillermo Flores and Ronald Bailey, "Internal Colonialism and Racial Minorities in the United States: An Overview" in Frank Bonilla and Robert Gerling, eds., *Structures of Dependency* (1973), pp. 149–160.

6. Barrera, Muñoz and Ornelas, op. cit., pp. 480–482.

7. See Robert Blauner, "Colonized and Immigrant Minorities" in his *Racial Oppression in America* (New York: Harper and Row, 1972) and his "Internal Colonialism and Ghetto Revolt," *Social Problems* (Spring 1969), pp. 393–408.

8. William Appleman Williams, *The Great Evasion* (Chicago: Quadrangle Books, Inc., 1964).

9. Barrera, Muñoz and Ornelas, op.cit., pp. 481–483.

10. Ibid., p. 481.

11. Ibid., p. 482.

12. Guillermo Flores, "Race and Culture in the Internal Colony: Keeping the Chicano in His Place" in Bonilla and Gerling, op.cit., pp. 189–223.

13. Barrera, Muñoz and Ornelas, op. cit., p. 483.

14. Ibid., p. 490.

15. Flores, op.cit.

16. Ibid., p. 201.

17. Flores and Bailey, op. cit., p. 154.

18. Almaguer, op. cit.

19. Ibid., pp. 41–42.

20. Ibid., p. 43.

21. Karl Marx and Frederick Engels, *Selected Works* (New York: International Publisher, 1968), p. 81.

22. J. V. Stalin, *Works* (Moscow: Foreign Languages Publishing House, 1955), Vol. II, pp. 303–307.

23. For a good example of this see: Rodolfo Acuña, *Occupied America, The Chicano's Struggle Toward Liberation* (San Francisco: Canfield Press, 1972)—particularly the last chapter.

24. Flores, op. cit., p. 195.

25. Ibid., p. 215.

26. Carlos Muñoz, "The Politics of Protest and Chicano Liberation: A Case Study of Repression and Cooptation," *Aztlán*, Vol. 5 (Spring/Fall 1974), pp. 119–142.

27. Ibid., pp. 120–121.

28. Samuel Eliot Morison and Henry Steele Commager, *The Growth of the American Republic*, Vol. I (New York: Oxford Press, 1942), p. 703.

QUESTIONS

1. If nationalism is the antithesis of colonialism, what conclusions should we then draw regarding Puerto Rico's *independentista* movement as the antithesis of colonial Puerto Rico? Does this mean that there is no colonial status if there is no nationalist movement?

2. Again in terms of Puerto Rico, if a key event in this transition from colonial to postcolonial is the granting of U.S. statehood to subjugated territories, what are the implications for the current debates on the Puerto Rican political status (keeping the current relationship or not) and the electoral process?

3. Are there any similarities between Cervantes' notion of Chicanos being a national minority seeking multicultural pluralism and the concept of a quest for public citizenship?

4. What truth games, what desires might be involved in the conception and promotion of the internal colony model?

5. By shifting the definition of Chicanos from that of an internal colony to that of a postcolonial status, what might be the implications for devising a political strategy?

* 24 *

YOUNG LORDS PARTY: 13-POINT PROGRAM AND PLATFORM

Edited by Michael Abramson

As the legend goes, until 1967 the Young Lords were a street gang. As with the Brown Berets, they are an example of the blurring of the line between criminal and political activity, between illegitimacy and legitimacy. The emergence of the Young Lords Party (YLP) in 1968 took place within the context of the second generation of Puerto Rican migrants who had achieved some social and economic advances and had started attending college in large numbers. Beyond the legend, though, the YLP was a combination of working-class college students from the Sociedad de Albizu Campos in New York and, yes, gang members. They got their charter from the Chicago Young Lords Organization. Like their Chicano counterparts in the Southwest, the Puerto Rican youth took a militant and aggressive stand. They took a leading part in the demonstrations that shut down the City College of New York in the spring of 1969 and in the militant action at Queens, Brooklyn, and Lehman Colleges that resulted in the establishment of Puerto Rican studies programs. They occupied a church in East Harlem in the spring of 1970, engaged in militant action around Metropolitan and Gouverneur Hospitals, and were involved in aggressive demonstrations around Lincoln Hospital in the Bronx in the autumn of 1970.

The Young Lords Party evolved from an organization with fraternal relations with the Black Panther Party to become a **Maoist** coalition of groups in the early 1970s seeking to create a new, multiracial revolutionary party. By the early 1970s, it had transformed itself into the Puerto Rican Revolutionary Workers Organization. The following document, in English and Spanish, appears as it was originally written in October 1969 and revised in May 1970, when the organization started to grow nationally.

YOUNG LORDS PARTY: 13-POINT
PROGRAM AND PLATFORM

The Young Lords Party is a revolutionary political party fighting for the liberation of all oppressed people.

1. WE WANT SELF-DETERMINATION FOR PUERTO RICANS, LIBERATION ON THE ISLAND AND INSIDE THE UNITED STATES.

For 500 years, first spain and then the united states have colonized our country. Billions of dollars in profits leave our country for the united states every year. In every way we are slaves of the gringo. We want liberation and the Power in the hands of the People, not Puerto Rican exploiters. QUE VIVA PUERTO RICO LIBRE!

2. WE WANT SELF-DETERMINATION FOR ALL LATINOS.

Our Latin Brothers and Sisters, inside and outside the united states, are oppressed by amerikkkan business. The Chicano people built the Southwest, and we support their right to control their lives and their land. The people of Santo Domingo continue to fight against gringo domination and its puppet generals. The armed liberation struggles in Latin America are part of the war of Latinos against imperialism. QUE VIVA LA RAZA!

3. WE WANT LIBERATION OF ALL THIRD WORLD PEOPLE.

Just as Latins first slaved under spain and the yanquis, Black people, Indians, and Asians slaved to build the wealth of this country. For 400 years they have fought for freedom and dignity against racist Babylon. Third World people have led the fight for freedom. All the colored and oppressed peoples of the world are one nation under oppression. NO PUERTO RICAN IS FREE UNTIL ALL PEOPLE ARE FREE!

4. WE ARE REVOLUTIONARY NATIONALISTS AND OPPOSE RACISM.

The Latin, Black, Indian and Asian people inside the u.s. are colonies fighting for liberation. We know that washington, wall street, and city hall will try to make our nationalism into racism, but Puerto Ricans are of all colors and we resist racism. Millions of poor white people are rising up to demand freedom and we support them. These are the ones in the u.s. that are stepped on by the rulers and the government. We each organize our people, but our fights are the same against oppression and we will defeat it together. POWER TO ALL OPPRESSED PEOPLE!

5. WE WANT EQUALITY FOR WOMEN. DOWN WITH MACHISMO AND MALE CHAUVINISM.

Under capitalism, women have been oppressed by both society and our men. The doctrine of machismo has been used by men to take out their frustrations on wives, sisters, mothers, and children. Men must fight along with sisters in the struggle for economic and social equality and must recognize that sisters make up over half of the revolutionary army: sisters and brothers are equals fighting for our people. FORWARD SISTERS IN THE STRUGGLE!

6. WE WANT COMMUNITY CONTROL OF OUR INSTITUTIONS AND LAND.

We want control of our communities by our people and programs to guarantee that all institutions serve the needs of our people. People's control of police, health services, churches, schools, housing, transportation and welfare are needed. We want an end to attacks on our land by urban renewal, highway destruction, and university corporations. LAND BELONGS TO ALL THE PEOPLE!

7. WE WANT A TRUE EDUCATION OF OUR AFRO-INDIO CULTURE AND SPANISH LANGUAGE.

We must learn our long history of fighting against cultural, as well as economic genocide by the spaniards and now the yanquis. Revolutionary culture, culture of our people, is the only true teaching. JIBARO SI, YANQUI NO!

8. WE OPPOSE CAPITALISTS AND ALLIANCES WITH TRAITORS.

Puerto Rican rulers, or puppets of the oppressor, do not help our people. They are paid by the system to lead our people down blind alleys, just like the thousands of poverty pimps who keep our communities peaceful for business, or the street workers who keep gangs divided and blowing each other away. We want a society where the people socialistically control their labor. VENCEREMOS!

9. WE OPPOSE THE AMERIKKKAN MILITARY.

We demand immediate withdrawal of all u.s. military forces and bases from Puerto Rico, VietNam, and all oppressed communities inside and outside the u.s. No Puerto Rican should serve in the u.s. army against his Brothers and Sisters, for the only true army of oppressed people is the People's Liberation Army to fight all rulers. U.S. OUT OF VIETNAM, FREE PUERTO RICO NOW!

10. WE WANT FREEDOM FOR ALL POLITICAL PRISONERS AND PRISONERS OF WAR.

No Puerto Rican should be in jail or prison, first because we are a nation, and amerikkka has no claims on us; second, because we have not been tried by our own people (peers). We also want all freedom fighters out of jail, since they are prisoners of the war for liberation. FREE ALL POLITICAL PRISONERS AND PRISONERS OF WAR!

11. WE ARE INTERNATIONALISTS.

Our people are brainwashed by television, radio, newspapers, schools and books to oppose people in other countries fighting for their freedom. No longer will we believe these lies, because we have learned who the real enemy is and who our real friends are. We will defend our sisters and brothers around the world who fight for justice and are against the rulers of this country. QUE VIVA CHE GUEVARA!

12. WE BELIEVE ARMED SELF-DEFENSE AND ARMED STRUGGLE ARE THE ONLY MEANS TO LIBERATION.

We are opposed to violence—the violence of hungry children, illiterate adults, diseased old people, and the violence of poverty and profit. We have asked, petitioned, gone to courts, demonstrated peacefully, and voted for politicans full of empty promises. But we still ain't free. The time has come to defend the lives of our people against repression and for revolutionary war against the businessmen, politicians, and police. When a government oppresses the people, we have the right to abolish it and create a new one. ARM OURSELVES TO DEFEND OURSELVES!

13. WE WANT A SOCIALIST SOCIETY.

We want liberation, clothing, free food, education, health care, transportation, full employment and peace. We want a society where the needs of the people come first, and where we give solidarity and aid to the people of the world, not oppression and racism. HASTA LA VICTORIA SIEMPRE!

PARTIDO DE LOS YOUNG LORDS
PROGRAMA Y PLATAFORMA DE 13 PUNTOS

El Partido de los Young Lords es un partido politico revolucionario que lucha por la liberacion de todos los pueblos oprimidos.

1. QUEREMOS AUTODETERMINACION PARA TODOS LOS PUERTO-RRIQUENOS—LIBERACION EN LA ISLA Y DENTRO DE LOS ESTADOS UNIDOS.

Hace 500 años que nuestra isla ha estado colonizada: primero por espana y luego por los estados unidos. Billones de dolares en ganancias salen todos los años de nuestra isla hacia los estados unidos. En todo sentido somos esclavos de los yanquis. Nosotros queremos la liberacion y el poder en las manos del pueblo, no en las de explotadores puertorriquenos. ¡QUE VIVA PUERTO RICO LIBRE!

2. QUEREMOS AUTODETERMINACION PARA TODOS LOS LATINOS.

Nuestras hermanas y hermanos Latinos, dentro y fuera de los e.e. u.u., son oprimidos por las empresas norteamerikkkanas. El pueblo Chicano construyo el sur-oeste de este pais, y nosotros apoyamos su derecho a controlar sus vidas y su tierra. El pueblo Dominicano continua su lucha contra la dominacion yanqui y sus generales titeres. La lucha armada en Latinoamerica forma parte de la guerra de todos los Latinos contra el imperialismo. ¡QUE VIVA LA RAZA!

3. QUEREMOS LIBERACION PARA TODOS LOS PUEBLOS DEL TERCER MUNDO.

Tal como los Latinos trabajaron como esclavos, primero bajo espana y luego bajo los e.e. u.u., los pueblos Negros, Indios, y Asiaticos han laborado como esclavos para crear la riqueza de este pais. Por 400 años estos han luchado contra la injusticia y la indignidad impuesta sobre ellos por esta babilonia racista. El Tercer Mundo ha dirigido la lucha por la liberacion. Todos los pueblos oprimidos y de color forman una nacion bajo la opresion. ¡NINGUN PUERTORRIQUENO SERA LIBRE HASTA QUE TODOS LOS PUEBLOS NO SEAN LIBRES!

4. SOMOS NACIONALISTAS REVOLUCIONARIOS Y NOS OPONEMOS AL RACISMO.

Los pueblos Latinos, Negros, Indios, y Asiaticos dentro de los e.e. u.u. son colonias en lucha por la liberacion. Reconocimos que washington, wall street, y city hall trataran de convertir nuestro nacionalismo en racismo, pero los puertorriquenos somos de todos los colores y resistimos el racismo. Millones de personas pobres blancas se estan levantando a exigir su libertad, y a estas tambien nosotros las apoyamos. Son estas las que son pisoteadas por el gobierno y los dirigentes de los e.e. u.u. Cada cual organiza su pueblo, pero la lucha contra la opresion es una y unidos venceremos. ¡PODER A TODOS LOS PUEBLOS OPRIMIDOS!

5. QUEREMOS IGUALDAD PARA LAS MUJERES. ABAJO CON EL MACHISMO Y CON EL CHAUVINISMO MASCULINO.

Bajo el capitalismo, la mujer es oprimida por ambos elementos, la sociedad y el hombre. La doctrina del machismo es usada por el hombre para desenvolver sus frustraciones en las esposas, hermanas, madres, y en los hijos. El hombre debe pelear a lado de sus hermanas en la lucha por la igualdad economica y social y debe reconocer que la mitad del ejercito revolucionario se va a componer de hermanas: las hermanas y los hermanos somos iguales, luchando juntos por nuestro pueblo. ¡ADELANTE HERMANAS EN LA LUCHA!

6. QUEREMOS CONTROL COMUNAL DE TODAS NUESTRAS INSTITUCIONES Y TIERRA.

Queremos que nuestras comunidades sean controladas por el pueblo, y exigimos programas que garantizen que todas las instituciones sirvan a las necesidades del pueblo. Queremos que el pueblo controle las policia, los servicios de salud, las iglesias, las escuelas, las viviendas, el transporte, y el bienestar publico. Queremos que se ponga fin a los asaltos que sobre nuestra tierra llevan a cabo la "eliminacion" urbana, las "destruccion" de carreteras y las universidades y corporaciones. ¡LA TIERRA PERTENECE A TODO EL PUEBLO!

7. QUEREMOS UNA EDUCACION VERDADERA DE NUESTRA CULTURA AFRO-TAINA Y EL USO DEL LENGUAJE ESPANOL.

Tenemos que aprender la historia de nuestra lucha contra el genocidio cultural y economico impuesto sobre nosotros por el yanqui. Cultura revolucionaria, la cultura de nuestro pueblo, es la unica ensenanza verdadera. ¡JIBARO SI, YANQUI NO!

8. NOS OPONEMOS A LOS CAPITALISTAS Y A LAS ALIANZAS CON LOS TRAIDORES.

Los gobernantes puertorriquenos, titeres del opresor, no ayudan al pueblo. Aquellos son pagados por el sistema para que dirijan a nuestro pueblo por callejones sin salida. De las misma manera miles de alcahuetes contra la pobreza son pagados para que apaciguen a nuestras conmunidades para el beneficio de los negociantes. Del mismo modo los trabajadores sociales dividen a nuestras gangas y las mantienen peleandose entre si. Queremos una sociedad en la cual el pueblo controle su labor de un modo socialista. ¡VENCEREMOS!

9. NOS OPONEMOS AL EJERCITO NORTEAMERIKKKANO.

Demandamos la retirada inmediata de las fuerzas militares norteamerikkkanas de

Puerto Rico, Vietnam, y de todas las comunidades oprimidas dentro y fuera de los e.e. u.u. Ningun puertorriqueno debera inscribirse en el ejercito norteamerikkkano para luchar contra sus hermanos y hermanas oprimidas. El verdadero ejercito de un pueblo oprimido es el ejercito popular, el cual combatira a todos los gobernantes. ¡ESTADOS UNIDOS FUERA DE VIETNAM! ¡QUE VIVA PUERTO RICO LIBRE!

10. QUEREMOS LA LIBERTAD DE TODOS LOS PRISIONEROS POLIT-ICOS Y DE TODOS LOS PRISIONEROS DE GUERRA.

Ningun Puertorriqueno debe estar en la carcel, primero porque nosotros somos una nacion y amerikkka no tiene ninguna reclamacion con nosotros; segundo, por-que nosotros no hemos sido tratados por nuestra propia gente (nuestros semejantes). Tambien queremos a todos los luchadores de las libertad fuera de la carcel, porque ellos son prisioneros de la guerra de la liberacion. ¡LIBERTAD A TODOS LOS PRISIONEROS POLITICOS Y PRISIONEROS DE GUERRA!

11. NOSOTROS SOMOS INTERNACIONALISTAS.

Nuestro pueblo es enganado por la television, el radio, los periodicos, las escuelas, y los libros para oponer a nuestra gente en contra de otros pueblos que estan luchando por su liberacion. Muy pronto ya no creeremos estas mentiras que todos estos medios han impuesto en nosotros, porque habremos aprendido quien es el verdadero enemigo y quienes son nuestros verdaderos amigos. Defenderemos a nues-tras hermanas y hermanos alrededor del mundo que luchan por la justicia y que estan en contra de los duenos de este pais. ¡VIVA EL "CHE" GUEVARA!

12. CREEMOS QUE LA AUTO-DEFENSA Y LA LUCHA ARMADA SON LOS UNICOS MEDIOS PARA LOGRAR NUESTRA LIBERACION.

Nos oponemos a la violencia—las violencia de ninos hambrientos, adultos analfa-betos, viejos enfermos, y la violencia de la pobreza y las ganancias. Hemos pedido y peticionado; hemos ido a las cortes; hemos manifestado pacificamente y hemos votado por politicos llenos de promesas falsas. Y todavia no somos libres. Ha llegado el momento en que nos tenemos que defender contra la represion. Tenemos que iniciar una guerra revolucionaria contra el negociante, el politico y el policia. Cuando un gobierno oprime al pueblo, el tiene el derecho de abolirlo y crear un gobierno nuevo. ¡ARMEMONOS PARA DEFENDERNOS!

13. ¡QUEREMOS UNA SOCIEDAD SOCIALISTA!

Queremos liberacion, alimentos gratis, ropas, viviendas, educacion, atencion medica, transporte, servicios de gas, luz y otros servicios y empleos para todos. Que-remos una sociedad en la cual las necesidades del pueblo se antepongan a todo; una sociedad que de a los pueblos del mundo solidaridad y apoyo, no opresion o racismo. ¡HASTA LA VICTORIA SIEMPRE!

✳ ✳ ✳

QUESTIONS

1. Under what conditions does the definition of "nation" fit the statement "All the colored and oppressed peoples of the world are one nation under oppression"?

2. What contradictions do you detect in this platform? How would the Young Lords respond to your observation(s) regarding these contradictions?

3. Was there a feeling among the Young Lords similar to that among Chicanos at the time, that they were charting new ground and had no predecessors?

4. In what ways might or might not the revolutionaries who had been fighting for Puerto Rico's independence be predecessors?

✳ 25 ✳

THE DIVORCE OF NATIONALIST DISCOURSES
FROM THE PUERTO RICAN PEOPLE

Ramón Grosfoguel

In this text, Ramón clarifies the reasons the nationalists are having a difficult time gathering mass support in their political struggle to liberate Puerto Rico from the United States. He is dealing here with a question of bio-power, that is, with those options of the Puerto Rican working class that best guarantee the basics of life, such as the federal minimum wage, food stamps, housing subsidies, unemployment insurance, social security, civil rights, and abortion rights. To become an independent nation-state like Haiti and the Dominican Republic (or Cuba, some will surely point out) may lead into unknown territory at best and dictatorship at worse. To remain associated as a state or a commonwealth, he suggests, does not necessarily imply the elimination of language and culture.[1] He sees the Puerto Rican working class as practicing a political pragmatism, a "subversive complicity" that is not necessarily selling out or a "colonized mentality," but leaves open the possibility for a quest for citizenship or what he calls "a democratization of democracy." Some of the key concepts used here are neocolonialism and (non)essentialist interpretations. The latter is also discussed in the conclusion of Vázquez's "Reflections on Latino/as and Public Citizenship," chapter 3.

NOTE

1. For a similar argument regarding Chicanos, see Mario Barrera, *Beyond Aztlán: Ethnic Autonomy in Comparative Perspective* (New York: Praeger, 1988), 157–76.

The referendum of November 14, 1993, concerning the political status of Puerto Rico provides a critical opportunity to analyze the historically consistent rejection of independence by Puerto Ricans. More than 70 percent of the electorate participated in the referendum. The breakdown of the results by alternatives was as follows: 48 percent voted in favor of maintaining the Commonwealth (the current colonial status), 46 percent voted for statehood, and only 4 percent voted for independence. A significant feature of the outcome was the increase of the pro-statehood vote, which grew by 7 percent, as compared to the 1967 plebiscite where statehood received 39 percent of the vote. There can be no doubt that the great majority of the Puerto Rican people expressed an interest in consolidating some form of "permanent union" with the United States.

Historically, nationalist discourses have put forward several explanations to account for the failure of the independence movement. Certain discourses claim that traditional colonialist leaders have developed a campaign to misinform and instill fear about independence, some blame the "ignorance" of the Puerto Rican people, and still others point to the cultural/ideological colonization by, or assimilation to, the United States as the culprit. Even if we give these arguments the benefit of the doubt, the failure of the pro-independence movement cannot be reduced to a problem of "alienation." Elitist claims that people are "assimilated/alienated" obscure relevant questions such as: Why does independence have minimal support among the Puerto Rican people despite the offer of double citizenship? Why do the overwhelming majority prefer a political status that consolidates the union with the United States? Why has the pro-statehood alternative received massive support among Puerto Ricans despite the "English Only" precondition?

To understand the unpopularity of the independence movements in Puerto Rico, it is important to understand the shifting relationship of Puerto Rico to the United States since 1898. I propose that the United States has made political and economic concessions to working classes in Puerto Rico (which have rarely been made to any other colonial or postcolonial peoples) primarily because of the *military* and *symbolic* strategic importance of the island.

This essay attempts to address these questions and to suggest other ways of articulating the status issue within a radical democratic perspective. The first section consists of a historical overview of Puerto Rico's peculiar modes of incorporation to the United States. The second part critically places the unpopularity of independence discourses within the context of the postwar Caribbean "modern colonies." The last section is an attempt to provide a nonessentialist interpretation of the status alternatives.

PUERTO RICO'S MODES OF INCORPORATION (1898–1995)

The colonization of Puerto Rico by the United States has had three dominant interests, namely, economic, military, and symbolic.[1] Despite the simultaneity of these three interests throughout the century, one interest has acquired priority over the others at times, depending on the historical context. It is important to note that these interests can either reinforce or contradict each other. Contrary to the economic reductionism of some dependency/mode of production approaches, the economic interests did not always dominate the core-periphery relationship between Puerto Rico and the United States. Instead, state geopolitical considerations such as symbolic or military interests have dominated the U.S.-Puerto Rico relations over extensive periods during the twentieth century.[2] The importance of these geopolitical interests was such that in some instances they actually contradicted corporate economic interests of the United States in Puerto Rico.

The economic interests have been embodied by U.S. corporations. The dominant industries have shifted through different historical periods. From 1898 through 1940, U.S. sugar corporations were the dominant economic actors. During the 1947–70 period, labor-intensive light industries (apparel, textile, shoes, etc.) became dominant. As of 1973, U.S. capital-intensive, high-tech, transnational industries (i.e., pharmaceutical and electronic) have controlled the production sphere.

Military interests are represented by the Pentagon. Puerto Rico has served as a beachhead for U.S. invasions and military operations in the Caribbean region. The island has been a naval training ground for joint exercises of NATO and Latin American naval ships. Because of the island's tropical weather, it has served as a training ground for counterinsurgency operations deployed in countries such as Vietnam, Grenada, and Haiti. U.S. military interests in Puerto Rico ruled from 1898 through 1945.

Symbolic interests were inscribed in the actions taken by the State Department and the Department of the Interior. For instance, Puerto Rico became a symbolic showcase of the capitalist model of development that the United States presented to the "Third World" vis-à-vis the competing Soviet model.[3] Thus, Puerto Rico became an international training ground for President Truman's Point Four Program. Through this program, thousands of members of the peripheral countries' elites visited Puerto Rico to receive technical training and learn firsthand the lessons of the first experiment in capital import-export-oriented industrialization. This model of development was based on attracting foreign capital through cheap labor, development of industrial infrastructure, and tax-free incentives for corporations. Billions of dollars in federal aid were transferred from the core state to the colonial administration in order to make Puerto Rico a "success story."[4]

The dialectical dynamics among the interests just outlined are crucial to understanding the specific relationship the United States has with Puerto Rico. For example, as will be discussed later, political concessions to the Puerto Rican population as a result of military or symbolic considerations sometimes clashed with U.S. corporations' economic interests during certain historical periods. Thus, I prefer to conceptualize Puerto Rico's modes of incorporation as the hierarchical articulation (harmonious and/or contradictory) between the economic, military, and symbolic interests of the United States spanning different historical contexts. The consequent periodization of Puerto Rican history during the twentieth century is, then, as follows: a period of agrarian capitalism in which the U.S. military interests predominated (1898–1940), a labor-intensive export-oriented industrialization period in which the U.S. State Department's symbolic interests were dominant (1950–70), a capital-intensive export-oriented industrialization period[5] in which both the transnational corporations and military interests shared the dominant position (1973–90), and an era of overtly economic interest dominating over all geopolitical interests, thus significantly reducing the strategic importance of the island (1991–?). Despite the predominance of one or two actors' interests (the Pentagon, U.S. corporations, the State Department) at a specific historical period, the three have been simultaneously present throughout these periods. The peculiar manifestations of each interest and the articulation among them has, however, changed historically.

EARLY-TWENTIETH-CENTURY PUERTO RICO (1898–1930)

The geopolitical strategies of core countries in the world interstate system have been crucial determinants of the peripheral incorporation of Caribbean societies. The interest of the United States in seizing Cuba and Puerto Rico from Spain in 1898 was a response mainly to state security interests. Several years before the Spanish-American War, American naval strategist Alfred T. Mahan stressed the strategic importance of building a canal in Central America in order to solve a major problem of U.S. mainland defense: the forced division of its naval fleet between the Atlantic and Pacific coasts. A U.S.-controlled canal in Central America would make possible a unified fleet. The fleet would move with greater speed and security from one ocean to the other by way of a canal, thus eliminating the trip around the tip of South America through the Strait of Magellan. Otherwise, 13,000 miles between San Francisco and Florida had to be navigated, taking more than 60 days.[6]

In addition to building and controlling a canal, Mahan added that it would be necessary to control the canal's eastern and western strategic maritime routes before construction. Mahan foresaw that the construction of a canal would attract the interest of other imperial powers, forcing the United States to enter international conflicts. According to Mahan, foreign control of the canal could be used as a beachhead to attack the United States. This foreign control would destroy the major U.S. asset against foreign aggression, namely, its geopolitical isolation.[7] As a means to achieve geopolitical control, he recommended the acquisition of Hawaii and the naval control of four Caribbean maritime routes before building the canal. The four routes were Paso de Yucatán (between Mexico and Cuba), Paso de los Vientos (the principal U.S. access route to the canal between Cuba and Haiti), Paso de Anegada (near St. Thomas, an island off Puerto Rico's eastern coast), and Paso de la Mona (between Puerto Rico and the Dominican Republic).[8] Mahan advised that naval bases be established in each of these zones as necessary steps for the United States to become a superpower. Mahan's influence was strongly felt among key political elites headed by Theodore Roosevelt and Henry Cabot Lodge.[9]

The only islands with access to the four maritime routes mentioned by Mahan were Cuba and Puerto Rico. Moreover, they were more amenable to foreign control when compared to Haiti and the Dominican Republic, which had already become nation-states. Cuba and Puerto Rico were still colonies of Spain, a weak and declining imperial state. Because the United States feared other imperial countries would take advantage of Spain's weakness by seizing its last two colonies in the Western Hemisphere,[10] these islands became targets. At the time, this belief was not far-fetched, because the Germans had a military plan to attack the United States wherein the first step was to seize Puerto Rico.[11] Another strategic consideration in terms of timing was to intervene before Cuban nationalist rebels defeated Spain in their war of independence. A sovereign nation-state could make the negotiation process difficult for the United States.[12] Thus, in the mid-1890s the United States began to plan a conflict with Spain. In 1898, Puerto Rico and Cuba were seized by the United States during the Spanish-American War.

The geopolitical interests of the United States and the local relation of forces in Puerto Rico and Cuba set the conditions for the different modes of incorporation of the two islands. The United States encountered important local differences between Cuba and Puerto Rico. Cuba had a strong nationalist movement pressuring for the departure of the Americans. The negotiations between the United States and Cuba established a protectorate treaty as well as the right of the United States to build a naval base in Guantanamo.

Two salient features of the internal power relations in Puerto Rico affected its mode of incorporation to the United States. First, all political parties supported the annexation of Puerto Rico to the mainland immediately after the 1898 invasion. Shortly after the landing of U.S. troops in Puerto Rico, General Nelson Miles proclaimed that the war against Spain occurred for humanitarian reasons such as justice and freedom.[13]

Second, Puerto Rico did not have a strong nationalist movement at the time of the U.S. invasion. This allowed the United States to make Puerto Rico a colonial possession without difficulties, thus providing the best conditions to safeguard the military strategic use of the island. Accordingly, the U.S. military prescribed that Puerto Rico remain a colonial possession and that a naval base be built off the northeastern coast of Puerto Rico in Culebra.[14]

A few years after the U.S. invasion, the Orthodox Party and Liberal Party exchanged political programs.[15] The Orthodox Party, linked to the sugar landowners who were radical autonomists under Spain, became an annexationist force under U.S. domination. This transition was marked by a name change from the Orthodox Party to the Puerto Rican Republican Party. The Liberal Party, linked to the coffee *hacendados* who were moderate autonomists under Spain, initially assumed an annexationist position with autonomist tendencies, but later, because of the U.S. pro-sugar policies,[16] became a radical autonomist party, ultimately flirting with pro-independence positions. These transitions were marked by name changes from the Liberal Party to the Federal Party and subsequently to the Union Party.

The Union Party represented those social forces with the greatest potential for building a pro-independence movement. However, the local *hacendados* were never supported by the popular classes. Because of the *hacendados'* alliance with the Spanish colonial administration's authoritarian repressive measures against the rights of peasants and workers, many among these sectors perceived the *hacendados* as their class enemies. Workers and peasants associated the *hacendados'* pro-independence positions with a romantic nostalgia for the forms of labor coercion and authoritarianism of the Spanish regime, under which the *hacendados'* social and economic position had not been threatened. Under U.S. domination, on the other hand, many workers saw an opportunity to establish civil and labor rights by pressuring the U.S. government to extend their legislative laws to the island. These sectors adopted the Americanization discourse promoted by the new imperial power as a strategy to weaken the political power of the local *hacendados* and gain democratic rights recognized in the metropolitan constitution. Despite the negative effects on U.S. sugar corporations of extending labor rights to Puerto Rico, the American state extended these rights to the Puerto Rican working class. The U.S. government wanted to gain popular support for the island's colonial incorporation. By extending labor rights to Puerto Rican workers, the pro-annexationist position of the labor movement was strengthened. This encouraged the formation of a pro-colonial bloc, which in turn impeded the possibility of a pro-independence alliance. The U.S. government's extension of civil and labor rights to Puerto Rico proved to be an important deterrent to the development of a collective national demand for self-determination.

The concessions to the Puerto Rican working classes by the U.S. government mark a distinctive feature of Puerto Rico's incorporation. Different from other U.S. military occupations of Caribbean countries such as Cuba, the Dominican Republic, and Haiti, where the U.S. government relied on authoritarian alliances with the landowners and/or the political/military elites to protect its interests, the U.S. strategy in Puerto Rico relied on a populist-democratic alliance with the working classes and progressive liberal middle-class sectors at the expense of the coffee landowners. The extension of democratic rights to the colony precluded the working classes sympathizing with a nationalist solution to the colonial question. The weakening of the *hacendados'* power base also debilitated the pro-autonomy forces and accelerated wage-labor relations in Puerto Rico. By contrast, the U.S. invasion in a country like Haiti relied on a class alliance with the local commercial elites and the coffee landowners, which strengthened noncapitalist forms of labor coercion.[17]

In sum, the evidence suggests that Puerto Rico's re-peripheralization from a Spanish possession to a U.S. colony was predominantly due to the American government's security interests. Puerto Rico's geopolitical location was strategically important for the U.S. government's defense against possible European aggression against the Panama Canal and the U.S. mainland. In contrast to the peripheral incorporation of other countries, where the economic interests in mining or agriculture were predominant, Puerto Rico's incorporation to the United States in the early twentieth century was primarily geopolitical. As illustrated earlier, the secondary status of the economic interests of the United States was such that certain state policies such as the extension of civil and labor rights to the local population contradicted the immediate interests of U.S. corporations investing in the island at the time.

The End of the Sugar Plantations (1930–45)

During the Great Depression, the United States developed the "Good Neighbor" foreign policy toward Latin America. The decline in sugar production, the spread of poverty, unemployment, and hunger throughout Puerto Rico, along with the emerging popularity of pro-independence ideas among many sectors had become shameful examples for U.S. foreign policy in the region. To counteract the impact of Puerto Rico's situation upon its international reputation, the United States extended to Puerto Rico certain New Deal reforms and supported an industrialization program (the Chardón Plan). This change of policy was marked by the transfer of the U.S. colonial administration in Puerto Rico from the Department of War to the Department of the Interior. However, the local power bloc hegemonized by U.S. sugar plantations presented many obstacles for the extension of these reforms. This period in U.S.–Puerto Rico relations (when symbolic interests of the United States dominated Puerto Rico's incorporation) was short-lived because of the imminent possibility of war, which made military interests dominant again.

During the late 1930s and early 1940s, the U.S. government supported a local populist power bloc at the expense of U.S. sugar corporations. The mortal blow to the sugar plantations, however, was the implementation of the 500-acre law in 1941. This law forced U.S. corporations to sell all land exceeding 500 acres to the colonial government. These lands were used to enforce the agrarian reform that eradicated the *agregados* (peasants forced to pay in rent, kind, or labor for living on the landowner's property) and mitigated the housing needs of thousands of peasants.

State military considerations during World War II fundamentally structured these policies. The state understood that a local population angry at the exploitation and abuses of U.S. sugar corporations was completely undesirable because it could represent a security problem for the military use of the island in times of war. The new governor of Puerto Rico in 1941, the reformist liberal Rexford Tugwell, confirms the military priority of Puerto Rico in his memoirs:

> My duty as a representative of my country in Puerto Rico was to shape civil affairs, if I could, so that military bases, which might soon (before they were ready) have to stand the shock of attack, were not isolated in a generally hostile environment.[18]

In short, the U.S. strategy in Puerto Rico was one of exchanging basic democratic rights for Puerto Ricans for the military exploitation of the island.

Postwar Puerto Rico (1945–95)

The U.S. symbolic interest in Puerto Rico gained dominance immediately after World War II. Puerto Rico became a token in the symbolic battleground between the Soviet Union and the United States, particularly in the United Nations. The Soviets claimed that Puerto Rico symbolized U.S. colonialist and imperialist aims in the world. Concerned about the image of the United States in the eyes of newly independent Third World countries, the State Department pressured for concessions to Puerto Rico. These concessions developed into a strategy to make Puerto Rico a showcase of democracy and capitalism during the 1950s and 1960s.[19] The first concession was the appointment of a Puerto Rican as governor in 1946. The right to elect a local governor was established shortly after, in 1948. Following this, the metropolis fostered the creation of a new status called Estado Libre Asociado (Commonwealth), which was approved in 1952. Lastly, a program of industrialization through massive foreign capital investments (i.e., the model of industrialization by invitation) was implemented, thus radically improving the island's infrastructure.

To enable the fulfillment of Puerto Rico's symbolic role and to foster a successful economic program, the U.S. government cooperated with local elites to support a massive labor migration of the marginalized Puerto Rican labor force.[20] The creation of the institutional framework to facilitate migration through the availability of cheap airfares between Puerto Rico and the United States as well as an advertisement campaign for jobs in the United States provided the conditions of possibility for Puerto Rico's "success story" during the 1950s and 1960s.

These transformations allowed the U.S. State Department to designate Puerto Rico in 1950 as the Point Four Program's international training ground for technical development of Third World elites. This program was more ideological than technical to the extent that these elites learned firsthand about the American model of development for "Third World" countries as opposed to the competing Soviet model.

Puerto Rico's important symbolic role during the Cold War explains the massive U.S. federal assistance given to Puerto Rico in areas such as housing, health, and education.[21] Puerto Rico was treated like any other state in need of federal assistance. The main difference between Puerto Rico and other states was that Puerto Rico's residents did not have to pay federal taxes. It is important to note that this "privileged" status was not granted to any other U.S. colonial territories.

Recent events have transformed once again the United States interest in Puerto Rico. The disappearance of the Soviet Union has changed the priorities of the core powers and the articulation among the different global logics. Today, U.S. economic interests have primacy over geopolitical considerations, and domestic economic concerns over foreign policy. As Anthony P. Maingot states in an excellent article about the Caribbean in the post–Cold War era, "geopolitics have given way to geoeconomics."[22] Therefore, the symbolic and military importance of Puerto Rico for the United States has become a secondary concern. In this sense, Puerto Rico is perceived by U.S. political elites more as an expense to the state than as an important military bastion or symbolic showcase. Economic crisis in the United States (such as the huge U.S. public debt) has created the context for Congress to eradicate 936 benefits for U.S. corporations in Puerto Rico, reduce federal transfers, and (among several factions of the U.S. political elites) articulate a sympathetic position toward a more autonomous status for the island. These trends suggest that a change in Puerto Rico's colonial status could result in the formation of a neocolonial relationship with the United States. If Puerto Rico becomes a neocolony, the United States would be relieved from the expenses of a modern colony, creating a "colony without any expenses." Particularly affected by this redefinition are Puerto Rican working classes.

MODERN COLONIES IN THE POSTWAR CARIBBEAN

Modern colonialism is the term that addresses the dramatic change of the colonialism implemented by core countries in the postwar Caribbean.[23] In terms of standard of living and civil rights, postwar Caribbean colonial incorporations to the metropolises have been more beneficial to working classes than neocolonial relationships. This can be illustrated by comparing U.S., French, and Dutch postwar modern colonies to neocolonial republics.

Anticolonial struggles and Cold War geopolitical military and symbolic considerations forced western metropolises to make concessions to their colonies. While certain colonies became nation-states, such as Jamaica, Guyana, and most of the English Caribbean, other territories remained colonial possessions because of their strategic location and/or symbolic/ideological importance. U.S., French, and Dutch colonies such as Puerto Rico, Martinique, and Curaçao, respectively, were granted economic and democratic reforms in order to preclude the success of any potential anticolonial struggles. The benefits enjoyed by these modern colonial populations (vis-à-vis their neocolonial neighbors) include annual transfers of billions of dollars of social capital from the metropolitan state to the modern colony (e.g., food stamps, health, education, and unemployment benefits), constitutional recognition of metropolitan citizenship and democratic/civil rights, the possibility of migration without the risks of illegality, and the extension of Fordist social relations that incorporated the colonial people to metropolitan standards of mass consumption.

Given Puerto Rico's importance as a symbolic showcase and a strategic military location, the United States responded to the 1974 economic crisis with federal assistance aimed to guarantee political stability and the survival of the "industrialization by invitation" model of development. The federal transfers were increased by extending several programs to individuals on the island. Federal transfers to individuals increased from $517 million in 1973, to $2.5 billion in 1980, to $4 billion in 1989. Federal aid represented 8 percent of the GNP in 1973, 23 percent in 1980, and 21 percent in 1989. Federal transfers to individuals were 10 percent of personal income in 1973, 22 percent in 1980, and 21 percent in 1989. While approximately 60 percent of families in Puerto Rico qualified for food stamps, only 11 percent of families in the United States qualified for the same program. This countercyclical "shock absorber" is crucial to understanding how the Puerto Rican lower classes survived the crisis.

These economic benefits account in part for why hardly any significant segment of the population from Puerto Rico, Martinique/Guadeloupe, or Saint Martin/ Curaçao is willing to renounce U.S., French, or Dutch citizenship.[24] The fact that half of the Surinamese population moved to the Netherlands when the Dutch imposed, for economic reasons, the formation of Surinam as a nation-state supports this argument.[25]

There is no doubt that the colonial administration of these modern colonies developed ideological and cultural colonization strategies. The people of these modern colonies, however, are neither passive recipients of colonial policies nor ignorant about what is happening in the region. On the contrary, observing the situation of neighboring neocolonial republics, speaking with immigrants from these countries (e.g., people from the Dominican Republic in Puerto Rico, from Grenada in Curaçao, and from Haiti and Dominica in Guadeloupe), and listening to the authoritarian and elitist discourses of pro-independence leaders, modern colonial peoples of the Caribbean fear the authoritarian and exploitative potential of a nation-state. It is not a coincidence that a constant comment made by Puerto Ricans, Guadeloupeans, and Martinicans in the streets is, "To be independent like Haiti or the Dominican Republic, better to be a colony."

Although authoritarianism is not intrinsic to independence, these issues continue to worry those who enjoy democratic and civil rights under modern colonial arrangements vis-à-vis neocolonial relationships. Their preoccupation should not be underestimated in light of the clientelistic/*caudillista* political traditions and the weak peripheral economies of small Caribbean islands. The possibilities of a dictatorship under these conditions are relatively high, especially considering the long-term dictatorships of Cuba, Haiti, and the Dominican Republic during this century. Moreover, even the recently formed independent Caribbean states like Surinam, Dominica, Guyana, and Grenada have suffered military coups and/or authoritarian regimes.

The anti-independence and pro-permanent union political positions of most modern colonial peoples of the Caribbean should not be caricatured as the product of a "colonized" or "ignorant" people. Given the drastic difference between the situation of working classes in modern colonies and neocolonial nation-states of the region, these people prefer a modern colony that benefits from metropolitan transfers over a neocolonial nation-state with the same colonial exploitation of a modern colony but no benefits from the metropolitan state. Rather than the assumption that modern Caribbean colonial peoples are "alienated" or "assimilated," their position suggests a political pragmatism rooted in conditions where options are extremely limited. In the current Caribbean context there is no space external to U.S. hegemony over the region. Even the most "independent" republic cannot escape U.S. control. Any attempt to subvert this order is militarily or economically destroyed, as occurred in Grenada, Nicaragua, and Jamaica.

The Puerto Rican people's strategy has been pragmatic rather than utopian; that is, they are not struggling to be freed from imperialist oppression (which is highly improbable and perhaps even undesirable under the present circumstances) but are instead attempting to struggle for a milder version of this oppression. They would rather be exploited with some benefits (as in Curaçao and Martinique) than be exploited without any benefits (as in the Dominican Republic and Haiti). In this sense, the unpopularity of the independence movement is a pragmatic rejection of a neocolonial independence. Puerto Rican workers in many instances throughout the century have followed a strategy of *subversive complicity* with the system. This is a subversion from within the dominant discourses. A good example is the use and abuse of the discourse of Americanism by the early-twentieth-century working class movement in Puerto Rico. As a Puerto Rican pro-statehood worker recently stated,

In the name of democratic and civil rights as citizens of the United States we should
struggle for equality by becoming the 51st state. We cannot let the Americans enforce
an independence status on us in order to cut their budget deficit. Through independence they will keep controlling us but without the commitment to extend welfare benefits and civil rights. After destroying our economy and exploiting the best energies of
the Puerto Rican workers during this century, now they want to get rid of us. That is
unacceptable. After the Americans ate the meat, let them now suck the bones.[26]

I am not suggesting that colonialism is the solution to Third World problems
nor that we should stop struggling against colonial oppression. These islands are
no paradise.[27] Instead, I am trying to understand, without resorting to traditional
nationalist moralization or colonialist explanations, why the people from modern
colonies like Puerto Rico, Curaçao, and Martinique prefer a status of permanent
union with the metropolis to independence. Considering the history of imperialist
exploitation and destruction of the local economies, it is legitimate to pose the following questions: On whose shoulders would the sacrifices required by the economic
reconstruction for an independent state fall? Whose salaries and wages would be
reduced for local and transnational industries to compete favorably in the world
economy? Who would be affected by the reduction of state assistance (e.g., food
stamps, housing subsidies) in favor of the republic's economic reconstruction? Obviously, the sacrifice will not be made by the lawyers, merchants, doctors, and professors of the pro-independence leadership but instead will be made by the working
classes. Does the rejection of this scenario imply a "colonized" mentality?

When people ask pro-independence militants how they will survive if Puerto Rico
becomes a nation-state, the response usually refers to the new equality and justice
for all that will be achieved under the republic. This vague response does not address
the legitimate concern that Puerto Rico imports approximately 80 percent of its
food. Those who demand a serious answer are aristocratically accused of being colonized, assimilated, or ignorant. However, people eat neither flags nor hymns; nor do
they outlive the eternity of sacrifices necessary to reach the future "paradise
republic."

The romantic rhetoric of the pro-independence movement cannot conceal the
dire reality awaiting a future republic. In the contemporary world system, where no
space is external to global capitalism,[28] the transition toward an independent nation-
state will entail overwhelming sacrifices for the working classes.

TOWARD A NONESSENTIALIST TREATMENT OF THE
STATUS QUESTION: CHALLENGES AND OPTIONS

Irrespective of whether Puerto Rico becomes an independent republic, a reformed
commonwealth, the fifty-first state, or an associated republic, the island will remain
under U.S. hegemony. Thus, the relevant question is, Which status alternative will
be more favorable to the protection, deepening, and expansion of the social and
democratic rights already recognized under the current colonial status (e.g., federal

minimum wage, unemployment benefits, social security, abortion rights, civil rights)?

The failure of the independence movement in the past referendum (only 4 percent of the votes) manifests the historical divorce between nationalist discourses and the Puerto Rican people. If the pro-independence movement[29] wants to convince the Puerto Rican people of their project, they need to offer a political-economic-ecological-sexual program superior to that of other status alternatives. Their alternative program would have to significantly improve the standard of living and the democratic and civil rights that Puerto Ricans already enjoy. This challenge is difficult to meet, however, within the present context of global capitalism. The free-trade agreement between Mexico and the United States, the increased opening of Cuba, the incorporation of the Central American economies after a decade of civil wars, the absence of a Puerto Rican "national" economy, the island's extreme dependence on federal assistance, and the competition of other low-wage countries in the Caribbean region make the economic viability of an independent Puerto Rico extremely questionable in this historical conjuncture. An independent Puerto Rican nation-state would have to pauperize its population in order to compete in the capitalist world economy by reducing the minimum wage and government transfers to individuals, by submitting to neoliberal policies of the International Monetary Fund to subsidize the trade and balance of payment deficits, and by reducing environmental controls. Thus, given the impossibility in the present historical conjuncture of offering a pro-independence project superior to that of the other status options at this moment in history, the progressive forces within the pro-independence movement have three alternatives. First, they can continue to support the independence project but can speak openly to the people about the necessary sacrifices and risks of a transition to an independent state. Second, they can abandon the independence project and support one of the two remaining status alternatives, submitting to their currently conservative programs and leadership. Third, they can stop understanding the status issue in essentialist terms or as a question of principle. Instead, the movement could struggle for a "democratization of democracy" in all spheres of everyday life, pressure the other parties to develop progressive programs, and open the pragmatic question of which status alternative will do better (or the least evil) in protecting and improving the island's ecology, quality of life, and democracy. This could channel their efforts beyond the limits set by the status debate. Although it is important to assume a position concerning the status issue, progressive forces should not reify it at the expense of democratic struggles. The reification of the status question precludes the emergence of alternative forms of radical politics.

Given the unconvincing platform of the pro-independence movement, the third option, that is, a radical democratic project,[30] could become a more viable alternative than the second alternative, which basically supports the traditional conservative programs and colonialist leadership of the pro-commonwealth and pro-statehood options. The political practice of a radical democratic project would privilege the improvement of oppressed subjects' qualify of life in the present rather than in a distant future "paradise." This movement would include a multiplicity of projects to promote and support the struggles of diverse oppressed subjects such as blacks, women, youth, gays, lesbians, and workers. Coalitions between these groups can only be possible if differences and organizational autonomy are respected without privileging the demands of one group at the expense of another.

Although these demands may not entail the destruction of capitalism, they can at least weaken the power bloc and improve the quality of life of different social groups. I call this strategy subversive complicity with the system against capitalism, patriarchy, racism, heterosexism, and authoritarianism. A meta-narrative (totalizing discourse) articulated to struggle against the system from the vantage point of a utopian space beyond capitalism makes the movement vulnerable to an authoritarian response from the state. By contrast, the strategy of subversive complicity would imply the radical resignification of the symbols of U.S. hegemonic discourses in the Caribbean region such as democracy, civil rights, and equal opportunities. This means using a democratic discourse rather than a socialist discourse but resignifying it in a radical democratic direction.

A radical democratic project in Puerto Rico would "democratize democracy" through the deepening of democratic and civil rights for oppressed subjects and the increasing of their control over the conditions of everyday life. Several struggles could exemplify a radical democratic project:

1. A struggle against environmental pollution. Currently, the colonial government's Junta de Calidad Ambiental (Board of Environmental Control), in alliance with transnational capital, has a pernicious effect on the island's environment. The Junta overlooks pollution increases and allows the destruction of the island's natural resources. A radical democratic project could struggle for the right to a healthy life by demanding legal measures that criminalize harmful industrial practices. The focus would be the democratization of political power over the environment.

2. A struggle for women's rights. Stronger social measures to transform the sexual division of labor that subordinates thousands of women could be developed in the name of equality of opportunities. For instance, the creation of child-care centers combining public and private funds would significantly reduce the amount of work women do in Puerto Rico.

3. Struggles to improve the quality of life. Two measures that would radically improve the quality of life are the construction of a monorail in the major cities and a train route throughout the whole island. This form of transportation would decrease the use of cars (Puerto Rico has one of the highest numbers of cars per capita in the world) and would in turn immediately improve the quality of life by eradicating traffic jams, lowering pollution levels, and indirectly increasing salaries due to the decrease in car expenses (e.g., gas, auto parts, insurance, and loans).

4. A struggle to decrease the crime rate. Most homicides and robberies in Puerto Rico are a result of two factors: unemployment and drugs. First, the legalization of highly addictive drugs (e.g., heroin) and the free distribution of drugs

among the addicted population would eliminate the need to kill or steal to gather the necessary money to maintain a heroin addiction. Experimental programs in England and the Netherlands have had impressive results using this strategy. Second, the reduction of the workday while keeping constant the eight-hour workday salary would increase the job supply, enabling the massive incorporation of unemployed workers in the formal economy. Given the trend toward automation and technological development, global capitalism cannot continue to expand or create new jobs indefinitely. Thus, it is meaningless to plead for the creation of new eight-hour workday jobs. Moreover, these measure would decrease the importance of illegal informal economic activities (e.g., selling drugs) for a large number of unemployed workers. These activities, criminalized by the state, constitute the economy of a large unemployed and underemployed sector of Puerto Rican society.

To gain legitimacy, the Left needs to dissociate itself from essentialist discourses regarding the status issue, namely, to stop defending independence as a matter of principle. Contrary to the discourses and practices of Puerto Rican political culture, status alternatives are not essentially progressive or reactionary. The progressive or reactionary character of a status alternative is contingent on the relation of forces, the strengths or weaknesses of social movements, and the discourses articulating the status options in a specific conjuncture of the global capitalist system. Just as nation-states can be either reactionary or progressive, states or associated republics can be either reactionary or progressive. For instance, compare Hawaii's or Vermont's progressive health-care policies to Pennsylvania's reactionary policies in the United States, or compare the Russian state's authoritarian control over the "autonomous" republics to the democratic autonomous regions of Spain.

The pro-statehood movement in Puerto Rico has been hegemonized by conservative and right-wing factions.[31] However, the statehood alternative is not inherently reactionary. One can imagine an antimilitarist and a radical-democratic pro-statehood movement in Puerto Rico that makes alliances with and defends the democratic struggles of other oppressed groups (e g., Latinos, African Americans, women, gays and lesbians) in the United States. The early-twentieth-century movement of Puerto Rican workers is a good example. This socialist pro-statehood movement built coalitions with U.S. workers' unions and defended Americanism as a strategy to make civil and labor rights recognized in the mainland extend to Puerto Rico.

Similarly, we can imagine an autonomous status, called the Associated Republic, that could eliminate certain federal laws to improve the quality of life of the population instead of pauperizing it. Examples are increased autonomy from federal environmental laws so that stricter regulations could be developed, and the elimination of the federal minimum wage so that it could be increased.

In a more progressive direction, the transformation of the Puerto Rican party system, traditionally organized in terms of status alternatives, presupposes the development of a popular radical democratic movement that defies the boundaries of current debates by undoing the correspondence between status alternatives and political parties. This movement could garner people with diverse political positions regarding the status issue who want to protect and expand the existing democratic, sexual, civil, and social rights. They could struggle for the decolonization of the island by demanding the right of self-determination for the Puerto Rican people without imposing a status option that would unnecessarily divide the movement. This mass democratic movement could struggle against any potential turn toward authoritarianism irrespective of the eventual political status of the island. All in all, the status is not a matter of principle and, consequently, remains secondary in relation to the primacy of radical democratic struggles.

Discourses warning against the threat of losing our "national" identity and language under the actual colonial status or statehood are mainly employed by nationalist groups in Puerto Rico to justify their defense of independence as a matter of principle. To speak Spanish at school and in public administrative life was achieved through the struggles of the Puerto Rican people more than fifty years ago. Moreover, the Quebecois in Canada, the Catalans in Spain, Guadeloupeans under France, and the Curaçaoans under the Netherlands are also "nations" without independent states. These "nations" without nation-states have not lost their languages or their "national cultures" although their cultures and languages have been transformed by the influence of the metropolises. This transformation can be seen, however, as an enrichment rather than a hindrance. Thus, statehood or some other form of union with the metropolis does not necessarily entail cultural or linguistic genocide. Puerto Ricans can be part of the struggle, together with other Latinos, for the recognition of cultural and linguistic diversity in the United States.

The Puerto Rican people share a feeling of nationhood that has not translated into traditional nationalist claims to form a nation-state. Puerto Ricans have formed an "imaginary community" with an imaginary belonging to a territory that spans the island as well as certain areas on the mainland (e.g., South Bronx, Spanish Harlem, North Philadelphia). This imaginary community oscillates between feelings of nationhood and ethnicity; that is, Puerto Ricans simultaneously imagine themselves as a nation and as an ethnic group. Puerto Ricans' self-perception does not fit either the concept of a "nation" or that of an "ethnic group." I believe the concept of "ethno-nation"[32] accommodates the Puerto Ricans' diverse and peculiar subject positions better than that of "nation."

Pro-independence ideologies that attempt to equate the status debate to a matter of principle constitute the political project of a minority seeking to become a national elite and/or bourgeoisie. This movement's emphasis upon the purportedly inevitable cultural and linguistic genocide has precluded a serious discussion of the socioeconomic consequences of independence for working classes today. Their struggles could be more effective if they concentrated on the development of a radical democratic movement that protects, expands, and improves the quality of life and the democratic and civil rights Puerto Ricans have today.

NOTES

1. Ramón Grosfoguel, "World Cities in the Caribbean: The Rise of Miami and San Juan," *Review* (Journal of the Fernand Braudel Center) 17, 3 (summer 1994).

2. Ramón Grosfoguel, "Puerto Rico's Exceptionalism: Industrialization, Migration and Housing Development" (Ph.D. diss., Temple University, 1992).

3. Ibid.

4. Ibid.

5. Public Law 936 (passed in 1976) enabled transnational corporations in Puerto Rico to repatriate their profits to the mainland without paying U.S. federal taxes.

6. María Eugenia Estades Font, *La presencia militar de Estados Unidos en Puerto Rico: 1898–1918* (Río Piedras: Ediciones Huracán, 1988), 27–28.

7. Ibid.

8. Ibid., 29.

9. See Estades Font, *La presencia militar de Estados Unidos en Puerto Rico,* 31; and Jorge Rodríguez-Beruff, *Política militar y dominación* (Río Piedras: Ediciones Huracán, 1988), 149.

10. See Estades Font, *La presencia militar de Estados Unidos en Puerto Rico,* 40.

11. Helger Herwig, *Politics of Frustration: The United States in Naval Planning* (Boston: Little, Brown and Company, 1976), 61–65, 86–87.

12. Wilfredo Mattos Cintrón, *La política y lo político en Puerto Rico* (Mexico: Serie Popular ERA, 1980), 58.

13. See Estades Font, *La presencia militar de Estados Unidos en Puerto Rico,* 89–90.

14. Estades Font, *La presencia militar de Estados Unidos en Puerto Rico,* 36; and Alfred T. Mahan, *Lessons of the War with Spain and Other Articles* (Boston: Little, Brown and Company, 1899), 28–29.

15. Mattos Cintrón, *La política y lo político en Puerto Rico.*

16. Mattos Cintrón, *La política y lo político en Puerto Rico*; Angel Quintero Rivera, *Conflictos de clase y política en Puerto Rico* (Río Piedras: Ediciones Huracán, 1976).

17. Suzy Castor, *La ocupación norteamericana de Haiti y sus consecuencias (1915–1934)* (Mexico: Siglo XXI, 1972).

18. Rexford G. Tugwell, *The Stricken Land* (New York: Doubleday, 1947), 148.

19. Grosfoguel, "Puerto Rico's Exceptionalism."

20. Ramón Grosfoguel, "The Geopolitics of Caribbean Migration: From the Cold War to the Post-Cold War," in *Security Problems and Policies in the Post-Cold War Caribbean,* ed. Jorge Rodriguez-Beruff and Humberto García-Muñiz (London: Macmillan Press, 1996).

21. Grosfoguel, "Puerto Rico's Exceptionalism."

22. Anthony P. Maingot, "Preface," *Annals of the American Academy of Political and Social Sciences* 533 (May 1994): 8–18.

23. Gerald Pierre Charles, *El Caribe Contemporáneo* (Mexico: Siglo XXI, 1981).

24. The most absurd campaign recently pursued by some pro-independence leaders is the rejection of their U.S. citizenship. This "revolutionary" luxury can only be enjoyed by individuals with enough income to sustain their families without working or who do not depend on the welfare state. This campaign shows the elitist character of the pro-independence leadership and their "alienation" from the Puerto Rican people. See also "E.U. impediría ingreso Mari Bras a Puerto Rico," *Claridad,* Feb. 18–24, 1924, 12.

25. Grosfoguel, "The Geopolitics of Caribbean Migration." In a referendum held on Nov. 19, 1993, 76.3 percent of the people of Curaçao voted for the present status. Only 0.5 percent voted for independence.

26. This quote is taken from ethnographic work done by the author in Puerto Rico during the summer of 1990.

27. There has been a cost to this special relationship. In the Puerto Rican case, the high crime rate suggests an acute social polarization.

28. Immanuel Wallerstein, "Dependence in an Interdependent World: The Limited Possi-

bilities of Transformation within the Capitalist World Economy," in *The Capitalist World Economy,* essays by Immanuel Wallerstein (Cambridge and Paris: Cambridge University Press and Editions de la Maison des Sciences de l'Homme, 1979).

29. Although the Left and nationalist movements are not inherently equivalent, they have been linked in Puerto Rico since the founding of the Nationalist Party during the 1920s.

30. Ernesto Laclau and Chantal Mouffe, *Hegemony and Socialist Strategy* (London: Verso, 1985).

31. The only exception has been the socialist pro-statehood movement of the 1910s and early 1920s.

32. For a discussion of the concept of "ethno-nation," see the introduction to *Puerto Rican Jam: Rethinking Colonialism and Nationalism,* edited by Frances Negrón-Muntaner and Ramón Grosfoguel (University of Minnesota Press, 1977).

QUESTIONS

1. How does one explain the lack of widespread nationalism at the time of the U.S. invasion of Puerto Rico and its growth and development in subsequent years?

2. Why did the United States use a strategy of making alliances with the elite among northern Mexicans and Cubans, but not among the Puerto Ricans, preferring instead an alliance with the working class and progressive-liberal middle class?

3. For economic reasons, the Dutch let Surinam become an independent nation-state. According to Grosfoguel, the United States may do that with Puerto Rico if it becomes an "expensive colony." What does he mean by Puerto Rico becoming a neocolony, and what may be some of the consequences?

4. Can Grosfoguel's idea of "subversive complicity" be classified as class analysis or nationalism? In what sense is this analysis a "radical democratic project"?

5. In what ways may or may we not compare the notion of a Puerto Rican "ethno-nation" with that of a Chicano Aztlán?

native of nowhere

Chloé S. Georas

stranded between vanishing islands
floating on an endless sea of receding coasts
my body is my only land
my hands navigate my skin
mapping the currents with my fingers
abysses fields mountains deserts oceans
so many oceans
echoes and cemeteries

transnational orphan
with feet full of memories
of running barefoot along volcanic cliffs
lightning between my breasts
of sitting on hot asphalt in the rain
watching the steam and the fog exchanging masks
of hurting somewhere
deep outside
everywhere

my feet
the corridors to places i lived places i died places i never went places i can't remember
populated by voices of missing people
some dead some i killed some gone some i left behind some i never met
nor did i touch
nor did i caress
people i never traveled

native of nowhere
a ticket to the wind on my back
i swallow hurricanes
my skeleton floats wildly in my body of floods
earthquakes vibrate through my limbs
reconfiguring my desires

my body
a disaster zone of erotic wastes
a white wooden house lies wrecked
my father pulls the curtains

my body is my only land
a land without homes nor hosts
a land of humidity, edges and edges
a land of volcanoes submerged in quicksand
a land of roaming scars

my land
a body from which i remove the earth with each step
i travel that territory called myself
before i become extinct

once again

PART IV
BEYOND THE NATIONAL–COLONIAL DICHOTOMY (HISTORY OF THE PRESENT)

THE ARTICLES IN PART IV COMPLETE THE game of *Serpientes y Escaleras* started in the first section of part I. They also offer operational concepts to understand Latino/a political thought. Part IV is preceded by Georas's poem, which presents images of a native in the process of construction and deconstruction, a "transnational orphan/ with feet full of memories." The images in this poem seem to resonate with the following articles which illustrate the quest for public citizenship. The first article proposes a transnational citizenship to better accommodate the rights of human bodies who must cross the frontiers of nation-states and whose lives are affected by decisions made by more than one state.

Is class the key to social struggle, as some soundly argue?[1] Another article places Latino/a power and politics within the context of class struggle and ethnic relations in Los Angeles. While referring to the lingering invisibility of Latino/as, it points to the increasing political participation of new citizens. This vision of an emerging form of genetic and political *mestizaje* helps to clarify current notions of "race relations."

Going beyond class analysis, a third piece has the ambitious political project to "decolonize otherness." It is an effort to integrate women in history that also illustrates the manifold workings of power and desire in both the oppression and liberation of human bodies. The final brief piece succinctly articulates the questions about language, discourse, and subjectivities that confront not just Latino/as but all beings in the dawn of a new millennium. It addresses a variation of the "who-are-the-people" question we have been raising throughout. The main question, as the author puts it, is, "Who are the remaining we? Who is left to listen and respond to this call?"

In the continuing search for appropriate tools to construct a just society, two perspectives become apparent. While the need for structural, systemic, total change seems necessary in order to eradicate the existing social problems, there seems to be a growing consensus that the struggle at the level of everyday life may also lead to systemic change.

NOTE

1. See also Marta Gimenez, "Latino Politics-Class Struggles: Reflections on the Future of Latino Politics," in *Latino Social Movements: Historical and Theoretical Perspectives,* ed. Rodolfo D. Torres and George Katsiaficas (New York: Routledge, 1999), 165–80.

✳ 26 ✳

TRANSNATIONAL POLITICAL AND CULTURAL IDENTITIES: CROSSING THEORETICAL BORDERS

María de los Angeles Torres

María de los Angeles raises several pertinent questions regarding the need to redefine the concept of citizenship for peoples who "have crossed political borders" or, we might add, who have been crossed by political borders. In terms of subjectification, she notes the political identity that is attached to human bodies who "belong" to a particular state and the games of truth that states can play with those identities. So if you are a human body from a Communist country (say Cuba), you are welcomed as a "refugee," but if you are a human body from a friendly (and non-Communist) country (say Mexico or Haiti), you are expelled as an "illegal alien."

Also in need of redefinition is the concept of assimilation as a desirable and even possible objective. In this context, María de los Angeles considers the nationalist movements (some of them discussed above) as "an affective return to the homeland," but also as something that may be interpreted as a search for inclusion, for belonging, as a quest for dignity and respect.[1] The Latino diaspora, however, did not find inclusivity in their homelands either. Their nation-states of origin have their own exclusive definitions of citizenship. Under these circumstances we see the need to construct a multicultural space in both home and host countries. This has been considered a threat to the idea of the nation-state based on a single culture. We are left facing the monumental task of expanding the concepts of "citizen" and "nation" to accommodate an increasingly global migratory phenomenon.

NOTE

1. The notion of respect is a central issue in the claim for cultural citizenship. See William V. Flores and Rina Benmayor, eds., *Latino Cultural Citizenship: Claiming Identity, Space and Rights* (Boston: Beacon, 1997).

Political borders—a defining feature of nation-states during the twentieth century—are changing, being reinforced at the same time that they are eroding. These increasingly porous frontiers suggest that, like economies, the nature of politics and of political participation may also change.[1] One reason is that people, particularly in diaspora communities, are affected by decisions made by governments in which they have only a limited voice or no voice at all. In home countries, governments make decisions that affect diaspora communities residing beyond the state's geographic jurisdiction. In host countries, diaspora communities often have a restricted role in public affairs because of their newcomer status. Ironically, while some countries are extending voting rights to their communities abroad, most host countries are limiting or even reversing some of the avenues immigrants have used to express their opinions in the past. There are few analytical and legal concepts that go beyond the nation-state as the parameter for political participation, making it difficult to envision immigrant political participation in both host and home countries.

In addition, the cultural identities of diaspora communities are not only informed by the host country, but also have many points of reference to home country culture. Past cultural and familial connections are not severed by crossing political borders. Immigrant flows from home countries have added new layers to existing diaspora communities. Yet the prevailing social science framework used to study the immigrant experience assumes that the nation-state is the principal organizational unit of politics and cultural identity. In this framework, public power is organized and contested within the geographic boundaries of nation-states, which also define the economies and social organization of societies. It is the state that regulates the affairs of the nation.

CITIZENSHIP: WHO IS ENTITLED?

The notion of citizenship is deeply interwoven with the rise of the nation-state. With the formation of nation-states came a new set of conditions that defined the rights of individuals, particularly in relation to the state. These included a definition and legal categorization of who was entitled to these rights. Citizenship became something to be granted or denied by the state. Although there are many legal variations in how citizenship is acquired—for instance, under German law it is passed from parent to child, while under Spanish, French, and British law the place of birth is the determining factor[2]—nation-states make citizenship and residency a requirement of political participation.

Furthermore, citizenship assumes loyalty to a state. In order to acquire U.S. citizenship, for example, emigres must swear an oath of exclusive allegiance to the United States. Yet the identities of many immigrants are too complex to allow this. Diaspora communities often reside in multiple states or have traveled through them. Restricting loyalty to one state flattens immigrants' experiences and limits their political options, particularly when they are affected by the decisions of many states.

The "nation" side of the nation-state concept also carries built-in assumptions. In regard to citizenship, the nation was conceived from the start as socially and culturally homogeneous. Those who are citizens are assumed to have a common cultural base. Even in the United States, where property, gender, and race were used initially to define who was included in the body politic, a romanticized abstraction of the androgynous, raceless citizen prevailed. Naturalized citizens—that is, those not born in the United States—were expected to leave their homeland behind when it came to public affairs.

Those born in other countries are not automatically entitled to U.S. citizenship. The state can choose whether and when to grant this right to those who apply. Moreover, participation in public affairs depends on one's legal status. Undocumented residents and legal residents who are not naturalized are not allowed to vote, nor do they enjoy the same rights as citizens.

THE ASSIMILATION MODEL: POLITICS AND IDENTITY

Assimilation, the prevailing model of immigrant political development, is shaped by a geographically determined definition of political space and agenda. The assimilation model predicts that recent immigrants do not participate in politics immediately after their arrival in the host country because they are still preoccupied with home country issues and with trying to adapt to a new environment. By the second generation, ties to the homeland have weakened. Political involvement begins at the local level, moving to the national level within another generation. By the third generation, the political agenda of immigrant groups may include international issues; by this time the focus of international affairs is not confined to the country of ancestry because the connection with the homeland has effectively been broken. Although there is a distinction between assimilation (becoming the other) and acculturation (adapting to the other), assimilationist views now dominate the public discourse.[3]

This view of political participation fits well within a pluralist framework that conceived of politics as a product of individual and organizational effort. Individuals organized to exert pressure on the political system, which provided outputs needed by the community. This model of politics was based primarily on the experiences of immigrants who came to the United States at the turn of the century—a time of extraordinary industrial growth and relatively weak government structures, particularly at the local level. Communities first became integrated economically, facilitating their political incorporation. (It is not clear whether these earlier immigrant communities genuinely cut their ties to the homeland or whether such ties simply were difficult to maintain. For example, in a study of ethnic Chicago, historians of various immigrant communities noted a persistent interest in homeland issues even at the turn of the century.[4] Models of political development that suggested an assimilationist path to political participation have failed to explain this persistence.)

The assimilation model is less useful in explaining the political development of groups that came to the United States at a time when the economic structure was different and the state had become much more expansive. European immigrants and emigres from countries in neocolonial situations—countries that were politically or economically dominated by the United States, like many in Latin America and the Caribbean—have had different relationships to the United States. When emigre communities did not succeed in achieving formal political incorporation, the unquestioned validity of this model forced social scientists to focus their inquiries not on what was wrong with the model (whose validity was unquestioned), but on what was wrong with these communities. The answer usually was that they resisted assimilation. A group of Latino political scientists set out to disprove this claim by documenting the attitudinal similarities between "Americans" and immigrant groups, such as Mexican-Americans. As a result, for years the study of Latino politics sought to dispel the importance of ethnicity as a factor in political mobilization and to counter the assumption that home country issues were part of the agenda for such immigrant communities.[5]

How is the political identity of diaspora communities evolving in light of changes in the nation-state? Identity is a social construction that requires continuous negotiation among the individual, the community, and the society at large. Social and political identities have at least two important dimensions: how societies construct an individual's or a group's identity, and how the individual or community constructs its own identity.

Social and political identities are closely tied to each other precisely because the nation and the state are coupled. The nation embodies culture, history, and social structures, while political identities are defined and regulated by the state. The concept of citizenship does not exist in a vacuum; rather, it is related to other aspects of a society, particularly when a society is marked and divided by racism and when race and national origin have determined who is awarded citizenship. Nor is the definition of citizenship isolated from questions of politics, as is the case in totalitarian regimes, which demand loyalty not just in return for citizenship, but in return for a national identity. It is in this intersection that social identities, including ethnic and national identities, become critical in understanding who has access to a political system.

The assimilationist view of immigrant identity predicts that, by the second generation, immigrant communities will have lost their affective and cultural ties to their homeland and identify themselves with the host country. In the United States, the second generation will have become "American." However, many first-generation Latinos, their children, and even grandchildren retain a level of interest in home country politics and culture. Like the political assimilation model, the prevalent model of identity assumes a singular identity tied to one geographic space. It also assumes that this identity is fixed and does not change over time.

The notion of assimilation itself assumes not only that integration is desirable, but also that it is possible. Shedding one's ethnicity is taken as a sign of leaving behind that which is old and replacing it with something new. This act suggests that individuals and communities can somehow discard their past and incorporate into a new culture. But this predictive model does not take into consideration the fact that in many host countries, immigrants are neither welcomed nor allowed to assimilate socially or, at times, even legally.

Another serious limitation of the assimilation model is that it cannot explain the persistence and reappearance of ethnicity and the desire to reconnect with the homeland in the sons and daughters of immigrants. These movements may be stronger in the second and third generations, particularly at times when anti-immigrant feelings are on the rise. Such has been the case, for instance, for third-generation Mexican-Americans born on Chicago's South Side. One of the country's strongest and most vibrant neighborhood museums, the Mexican Fine Arts Museum in Chicago's Pilsen neighborhood, was founded by the grandchildren of Mexican immigrants who had come to work in Chicago's steel mills. Their struggles to provide education to the Mexican community included bringing to that community the art and culture of their country of ancestry. (Later on, the museum's goal expanded to include bringing to Mexico culture created by Mexicans in the United States.)

In addition, reconnecting to the identity of one's parents may be more important at certain stages of the life cycle. The passage from adolescence to adulthood is generally accompanied by a reassessment of one's heritage and values. For second-generation immigrants, this can manifest itself as an awakening of interest in the homeland and culture of one's parents.

The prevailing vision of politics and identity insists on a uniform public culture while permitting political pluralism. While a wide array of cultures and even languages is permitted in the private spaces of U.S. society—religious, private educational, and cultural institutions—public (political) discourse demands cultural homogeneity.

The assimilation model itself may be a myth that developed in the United States between the two World Wars. Immigration to the United States from Western Europe was at its peak. When the United States went to war with Europe, patriotism and loyalty to the United States were expected. People rallied publicly under the banner of "Americans." Ethnic communities, particularly those from countries with which the United States was at war, such as Germans, Italians and Japanese, suffered varying degrees of repression. It was during this period that the public myth arose that immigrant communities actually had cut their ties to the homeland and were now as "American" as the native-born. (Curiously, Mussolini's government was the first to develop a state-sponsored project to reach out to Italian communities abroad and encourage them to influence U.S. policies toward their home country.)[6] But racism persisted. For example, after World War II Mexican-Americans formed organizations of veterans to show their loyalty to the United States. But racism was so severe that even Mexican-Americans who had been killed in the war were not buried in the same cemeteries as "white" soldiers. In response to such discrimination, organizations like the GI Forum and the League of United Latin American Citizens (LULAC) began advocating for equality and integration.

THE EMERGENCE OF ALTERNATIVE
VIEWS OF LATINO REALITY

History and Homeland: The 1960s to the Mid-1970s

Integrationist movements of the post–World War II era failed to bring equality and were met with disdain. Although the federal government eventually responded to internal and international pressure to abolish segregationist laws, racism remained entrenched in states and local communities. The persistence of racism contributed to the emergence of more radical movements. In the United States, the civil rights movement of the 1960s led communities that had been excluded from the political process on the basis of race or national origin to demand inclusion on the same grounds. Unlike the integrationist movement of the 1950s, which sought entrance and equality, the movements of the 1960s sought to change the rules of the game as well. This included a vision for transforming the cultural and political spaces in which immigrant communities exist.

Instead of trying to prove that they were loyal Americans, immigrant organizations in the 1960s sought to define their identities in terms of difference. Difference was celebrated in a search for roots that had been severed by oppression and denied by shame. One of the results of this search for identity was an affective return to the homeland. Some groups, such as the Colorado-based Crusade for Justice, founded by Corky González, initially sought a mythical homeland, Aztlán; and even organizations with a U.S.-based agenda, such as Raza Unida, later sought relations with Mexico. In the Cuban exile community, groups like the Antonio Maceo Brigade and Areíto sought connections to Cuba.

At the same time, radical movements in Mexico and Puerto Rico reached out to communities abroad. For example, connections were established between Mexican-Americans and the Mexican left after governmental repression in Mexico forced many political activists to flee to the United States. Organizations like Central de Acción Social Autónoma (CASA) represented the merger of the struggles against repression in Mexico and racism in the United States. Pro–Puerto Rican independence organizations bridged communities on the island and the mainland.

Radical politics in the various Latino communities challenged the prevailing paradigms of identity and politics by crossing borders. Scholars became critical links in this crossing as they began to redefine the paradigms within which the politics and identity of Latinos in the United States were studied. Chicano scholars, for example, played an important role in challenging ahistorical accounts of the origins of the Chicano community.[7] The recovery of history led to a growing awareness in the Southwest of the connections between the Chicano community and Mexico.[8] Alternative frameworks like the internal colonial model looked at the connections between the U.S. conquest of Mexico's northern territory in the mid-1800s and labor exploitation to understand the persistence of poverty and racism in the Southwest.[9]

Parallel critical studies emerged in the Puerto Rican and Cuban exile communities. Studies of Puerto Rican labor migration to the United States examined the connections between the colonization of the island and the migratory response of labor.[10] Cuban exile scholars sought to understand how U.S. foreign policy toward Cuba influenced the formation of Cuban communities in the United States.[11] Yet many of these studies were still bound by nation-state perspectives. An exception was the geopolitical model Carlos Forment suggested to analyze terrorist politics in the Cuban exile community.[12] In this model the unit of analysis is the region, and hegemonic politics finds expression through regional blocs. In the field of sociology, Marisa Alicea's dual-home-base model began to depart from the culturally accepted notion that immigrants have a single "home."[13] (Bi-national experiences were seen under the assimilation model as potentially destructive to the formation of community. Indeed, the ability to move back and forth from the island to the mainland was often cited as the reason for Puerto Ricans' low wages and low voter turnout.)

In addition to the search for homeland, another phenomenon emerged. Various groups of similar national origins began to come together as a means to mobilize community and political resources. Félix Padilla initially documented this phenomenon in Chicago, the first U.S. city to witness the coexistence of communities from several Latin American countries.[14] While retaining its individual ethnic identification, under certain circumstances a community would also adopt the label of "Latino," a broader ethnopolitical identity that coexisted with other ethnic identities.

In 1984 four university-based research centers dedicated to the study of the Latino experience in the United States came together to form the Inter-University Program for Latino Research.[15] This was the first academic endeavor to bring together Latino scholars from different disciplines and communities. Underlying many of its research projects was the assumption that Latino groups in the United States share a common legacy because the United States had intervened in some way in their countries of origin. Yet each group, and each subsequent immigration wave, was unique.

Growing organizational unity at the community level also found expression nationally. Organizations such as the National Association of Latino Elected and Appointed Officials (NALEO) and the Hispanic Institute (the research arm of the Congressional Hispanic Caucus) attempted to present a unified voice in national politics. Since it was harder to find consensus on foreign policy than on domestic issues, these organizations often avoided the former. Other groups, such as Policy Alternatives for the Caribbean and Central America (PACCA), the Southwest Voter Registration and Education Project, and the Cuban American Committee, advocated changes in U.S. policies toward Mexico, Central America, and the Caribbean.[16]

Ambivalent Homelands: The 1970s to the Mid-1980s

Just as attempts to assimilate to the host country encountered limits, so did movements to reconnect with countries of origin. For example, U.S.-based Mexicans experienced a mixed welcome in their homeland, where they were often referred to as *pochos* (wetbacks), and where they found the government's repressive politics intolerable.

Nevertheless, as the number of Mexican-Americans taking part in U.S. political life rose, the Mexican government began to consider the possible implications for its interests in the United States, hoping to create a Chicano lobby similar to the Jewish-American organizations that supported Israel within the United States. In the 1980s, the Mexican government institutionalized this interest in an office dedicated to the *Mexicans de Afuera* (Mexicans Abroad) in its Ministry of Foreign Relations.[17] This office was responsible for developing and maintaining ties with Mexican-American communities in the United States; activities, organized through Mexico's consular offices, included cultural events and arranging for scholarships to study medicine in Mexico.

Cuban exiles, called *gusanos* (worms) in their homeland, had similar experiences with the island government, although this relationship unfolded within a much more politicized climate, both on the island and in the United States. Cuban exiles who tried to return to their homeland were told by government officials that they would better serve the interests of the revolution by remaining abroad and arguing for the lifting of the U.S. embargo imposed on Cuba in the early 1960s.[18] The Ministry of the Interior was put in charge of the Comunidad Cubana el Exterior (COCUEX) project.[19] Like Mexican-Americans, Cuban exiles found that their relationship to the homeland was placed within the context of state interests, particularly foreign and security affairs. Both homeland governments considered those who had left not as nationals, but rather as resources to be used in the "national" interest.

The relationship of Puerto Ricans on the mainland to those on the island was also ambiguous. Although the independence movement at times has been stronger in U.S. cities such as Chicago and New York than in Puerto Rico, those on the island arguing for independence did not support efforts to include Puerto Ricans living in the United States as part of the electorate. On this issue, supporters of independence found allies in the pro-statehood forces, who were also leery of the politics of U.S. Puerto Ricans. When the question of a referendum on the island's status was debated in 1990, groups on the island, including the *independentistas,* lobbied against allowing mainland Puerto Ricans to vote. It became clear that home country governments and political organizations ultimately held a very narrow definition of who was to be considered part of the nation.[20]

The movement to reconnect with homelands failed just as the assimilationist path had. Homeland governments were mainly interested in the political clout, symbolic or otherwise, that their communities abroad could offer. Even when remittances sent home by immigrants began to provide critical economic resources—in some cases becoming the most important or the second most important contribution to the gross national product—communities abroad were still not entirely welcome in the body politic. In many cases, the resentment deepened.

Identity Redefined: The 1980s to the Mid-1990s

Latinos had found that while they shared some common ground with their countries of origin, there were important differences as well. Being in and out of place in both home and host country gave rise to the exploration of border identities. Border identities are unique because they contain elements of various cultures coexisting side by side. Community organizations have played a central role in the creation of border identities, but it is artists and writers—unconstrained by the slow production mode of academia or the structures of the electoral arena—who have redefined the parameters of the debate and offered more radical notions about identity and, consequently, politics.

In the Southwest, Gloria Anzaldúa proposed the notion of border identities, which forced a reexamination of the prevailing rigid categories of ethnicity and gender that had emerged from the 1960s.[21] In Cristina García's novel *Dreaming in Cuban,* Pilar returns for a visit to the forbidden island to reconnect with her grandmother Celia, who gives her the task of remembering not just for the exile community, but for the nation as a whole.[22] This proposition stands in sharp contrast to the passive role ascribed to diaspora communities by most home countries. The same theme is echoed in Guillermo Gómez-Peña's work. Not only does he call for a mutual recognition of home country and diaspora through a radical dialogue, but he also suggests that Mexicans in the United States have developed unique cultural and political skills as a result of the struggles they have had to wage against racism. Furthermore, Gómez-Peña argues, home countries can rely on these skills in developing cultural and political projects that offer an alternative to the pervasive and often popular global market culture.

Rubén Martínez, a Mexican/Central American writer in East Los Angeles, explores the multiple sources of his identity and loyalties in *The Other* Side.[23] For Martínez, *Latinismo* is embodied in himself. He does not suggest, however, that a hybrid identity represents a smooth synthesis; rather it is a continual and sometimes painful process of confrontation where there is always another side with which to contend.

Visual artists also have vividly explored migratory identities. The Puerto Rican artist Bibiana Suárez questions the contradictory images of herself held by her home and host countries through two self-portraits, one in which she is black and another in which she is white. The message is unmistakable: the dominant society in the United States views immigrants from the Caribbean as nonwhite, while on the island her blond hair and green eyes make her *blanquita.* Iñigo Manglano-Ovalle challenges the legitimacy of identities prescribed by political borders in his series on "illegal aliens." Enlarged photographs of detained aliens' thumbprints are accompanied by text containing personal recollections of their journeys to the United States. Included in the exhibit is a resident alien card with the picture and name of Christopher Columbus.

In contrast to the proposition of single nationality (for example, *either* Mexican *or* American), the notion of border identities recognizes the presence and synthesis of many cultures. In this conception, one does not have to deny the existence of the other, and ambiguity is accepted as an essential element of identity. Ambiguity provides flexibility and, consequently, the potential for movement and development. In contrast to the negative notion of ambiguity Richard Rodríguez documents in *Hunger of Memory,*[24] those who emphasize border identity see ambiguity as a fertile zone.

The concept of border identity is also distinct from the hyphenated proposition of ethnicity found, for instance, in Gustavo Pérez-Firmat's *Life on the Hyphen: The Cuban-American Experience.*[25] In this conceptualization, two fixed identities are linked by a hyphen. The direction of change is unilinear, from the identity being left behind to the new American identity, and the emphasis is on the "American"— that is, people supposedly retain some ties to their ethnic background but function as Americans within the society. The hyphenated model complemented the idea that an individual must be loyal to only one state. In contrast, a border identity that is multiple may imply multiple loyalties. Furthermore, the hyphenated model assumed fixed identities on both sides of the equation, while, in reality, home country cultures were becoming more and more "Americanized" at the same time that U.S. culture was becoming more "Latinized."

The cultural border zones that had been so clearly demarcated by political borders eroded as consumer products and cultural images crossed borders with ease. Border identities are ambiguous and constantly changing. They emerge at the margins and define themselves as hybrid creations of distinct forces. The notion of *Chicanismo* is closer to the concept of border identity because it assumes fusion; however, in *Chicanismo* identity was viewed not as a process but as a goal. Indeed, the Chicano movement saw itself as a unique nation in search of a state.

Similar reconstructions of identity have occurred in other Latino communities. The border (in airspace) between New York and San Juan brought forth debates concerning the identity of Puerto Ricans in New York ("Newyoricans") and Puertoriqueños. Fear that U.S. colonization of the island had destroyed its culture contributed to the rejection by island residents of Puerto Ricans who lived in the United States. At the same time, Puerto Ricans were not accepted as "Americans." The response was a hybrid construction ("Am-e-rican") that encompassed both identities and reasserted itself in the eyes of both the host and the home country.[26]

The highly politicized aquatic wall between Cubans in Miami and Havana provoked its own debates. For the island's government, *Cubanía* belonged to those who were committed to the political project of the state. But this rigid notion of who was Cuban was later modified as the Cuban government made moves to open up to its communities abroad. After the collapse of the Soviet Union, exile remittances became the second most important source of cash for the Cuban government, which made efforts to reach out to the exile community at the same time that it continued to exclude it from the homeland. In the meantime, the second generation of Cuban exiles in the United States continued a process of attachment to both host and home country culture nurtured by the unprecedented exodus of artists and intellectuals in the late 1980s who sought a "third option"—a cultural and political space beyond the political borders of the island and the exile community.[27]

The search for a more complex understanding of identity was in part a response to the rigid categories of identity that emerged from the radical movements of the 1960s. It was also a response to the postmodern prediction that, as cultural spaces became increasingly homogenized through easy transportation and communication, all human beings would in effect move toward a single identity. Instead, communities at the "margins" came to witness an accelerated fragmentation of identity. As nation-states eroded, they were not replaced by a homogeneous superstate or a single identity. Rather, societies became more diverse as immigration from one part of the world to another rushed ahead, giving rise to the movement for a recognition of the multicultural character of societies. At the same time, receiving societies became less open. While the 1960s movement for equality—that is, political and civil rights—asked for representation in the host country, and the movements of the 1970s wit-

nessed demands to reconnect with the homeland, the multicultural movement of
the 1980s sought to transform the public spaces in both home and host countries.

INSTITUTIONALIZATION AND BACKLASH

The backlash against the multicultural movement emerged in the late 1980s and
early 1990s at a time when U.S. society was witnessing a major transformation of
its economy as well as its position in the world. The new service-based economy
provided few high-paying and many low-paying jobs, a structure that exacerbates
social inequality. At the same time, an unprecedented number of minorities had
begun to enter what had been previously almost exclusively "white" institutions,
signaling the end of white dominance within them. A backlash ensued, met by newcomers' demands for the transformation of these institutions. Racial and ethnic tension in the United States increased.

Minorities entering U.S. institutions played a critical role in demanding their
transformation. But their demands were met with hostility, even by traditional allies,
such as supporters of the civil rights movement of the 1960s. In universities, for
example, white progressives were insulted when the African-Americans and Latinos
they had helped bring into the academy demanded radical change. For many progressive whites, the question of equality was defined as one of representation, not
necessarily sharing power with minorities.

In some universities, administrators embraced the rhetoric of multiculturalism.
New faculty members were allowed to create courses and even programs devoted to
the study of minority communities, although these generally were not funded at the
same level as traditional programs. Ethnic studies often have been marginalized or
exoticized, with universities and other institutions packaging courses about minorities, women, and gays under the banner of multiculturalism. Instead of mainstream-
ing these topics, this process marginalized these communities further. The reduction
of "otherness" to an exotic location in academia tended to distort the discourse.
Instead of deconstructing "otherness," such strategies reinforced it.

Furthermore, conservatives unleashed a backlash against diversifying the public
sphere. Many conservative intellectuals have questioned whether democratic societies could have a multicultural public space. For example, Richard Bernstein, an
early promoter of the phrase "politically correct," maintains that there should be a
separation between private identities, which can be diverse, and the public realm.[28]
In part, he bases his vision on the need to keep religion and ethnicity out of the
public space, noting that historically (as in the European Jewish experience) when
religion has entered the public discourse, it has been used for repressive purposes.

Arthur Schlesinger, Jr., views the multicultural movement as dangerous to
democracy because it sabotages the unity of the nation. In *The Disuniting of
America*,[29] he presents the argument that democracies need a uniform public identity
in order to grant equal status to all citizens. But while in theory all individuals are
equal, citizens who were not white, rich, and male historically have not had equal

access to the political system. Schlesinger's vision of the United States thus ignores the fact that many communities were never considered part of the unified whole. Similar arguments have been made in Great Britain by John Rex,[30] who sees multiculturalism as incompatible with a democratic state. Like Schlesinger, he equates the public persona to the "citizen," who in theory should have a shared cultural identity, and calls for "privatization" of other aspects of identity.

For proponents of the idea that citizens should share a cultural identity, the basic unit of politics is, again, the nation-state: the public persona is defined as a citizen of a specific nation-state. Individuals who are not born in the nation-state where they reside may or may not be eligible to obtain the status and protections of citizenship.[31]

Many opponents of the multicultural movement also call for the closing of borders, arguing that increased immigration poses a threat to a culturally unified nation. The same forces call for English-only policies. What began as a conservative intellectual backlash in the 1980s found expression at the voting booth a few years later. In the early 1990s, candidates from both the Republican and Democratic parties ran successfully on anti-immigrant platforms with distinctly racial and ethnic overtones. Only mayors of large urban areas like Chicago and New York spoke up in defense of immigrants. In these cities, the undocumented population included significant numbers of European immigrants.

TRANSNATIONAL CULTURAL AND POLITICAL IDENTITIES

The alternative to the notion of a culturally homogeneous public space confined within the border of a nation-state is the multicultural paradigm. In this paradigm, the public space can accommodate many cultures; the teaching of a variety of cultures and languages is encouraged and it is recognized that the imposition of any one culture oppresses the others. Even so, the multicultural paradigm in its first instance proposed a transformation of the public space within the confines of the nation-state, leaving unchallenged the notion of the nation-state itself.

Increased worldwide immigration coupled with ease of transportation has brought people into more direct contact with multiple cultures. In addition, rapid changes in communications and transportation have contributed to a global economic transformation. Political institutions thus far have resisted these changes. Nonetheless, paradigmatic changes in the definition of identity and the resulting vision of politics are taking place.

With increased contact between people and cultures, we may be witnessing the rise of transnational identities. Such identities are likely to be more visible in communities where people have crossed many borders. Diaspora communities where people are grounded in multiple cultures also produce hybrid identities.[32] The notion of a transnational or hybrid identity presents an interesting personal and political vision for diaspora communities. It proposes not only that communities be transformed, but that their host *and* home countries undergo transformation as well. Both home and host countries are often leery of these propositions.[33] This proposition would also encourage a political hybridity that expands not only the objects of politics, but the forms as well.[34] A transnational framework that accepts hybrid cultural formations brings to the forefront questions of what is home and what is exile. It also creates what others have called a "third space" beyond the confines of any one nation-state.[35]

Such a transnational framework also raises the problem of political bi-focality. Purnima Mankekar, for instance, asks "how we conceive of a political space that enables us to subvert the binaries of homeland and diaspora, while simultaneously allowing us to build alliances with struggles for social justices in both places?"[36] Throughout the 1900s, various immigrant communities have participated in both home and host country politics. Sometimes homeland issues have taken priority, while at other times host country problems have dominated the agenda. The contestation of power has crossed borders. The Southwest Voter Registration and Education Project has struggled with this dilemma for years. On questions involving the encroachment of U.S. foreign policy on Mexico and Central America, it has been an ally of the Mexican government; on questions of human rights, it often has challenged that government. In the Southwest, the project's ongoing work to increase voter registration and mobilize Chicano voters has often pitted it against local power structures.

The expansion of the political space to include multiple states suggests that the concept of a citizen bound to a single nation-state also must change. A transnational political identity, or citizenship, would better accommodate the rights of individuals who for a myriad of reasons cross the frontiers of multiple nation-states and whose lives are affected by decisions made by more than one state.

This discussion raises enduring dilemmas. For one, the realm of the political is still organized along the lines of nation-states, and within the international order, some nation-states are more powerful than others. This means that discussion of a global society or a global notion of rights emerging from more powerful nation-states can be read as another form of domination. Nonetheless, regardless of how the language of "globalness" is used by those in power, the reality is that there are human rights that do cross the borders of nation-states, and these need to be protected. Against the backdrop of an interconnected world, it would be shortsighted simply to dismiss any discussion of global rights as impossible to conceptualize. Such a discussion, of course, will involve difficult questions. What is the balance between specific national or ethnic rights and global human rights? Who determines the limits of such rights? Through what institutions are these issues to be discussed and decided upon?

What is clear is that, today, much of what is done in one part of the world affects other parts of it. Because of their transnational experiences, diaspora communities have long struggled against the restrictions of "one identity, one state." The reconceptualization of identity and power emerging from these communities is an important point of departure for a broader discussion that challenges the nature and exercise of power in this century.

NOTES

1. Frank Bonilla, "Migrants, Citizenship, and Social Pacts," in Edwin Meléndez and Edgardo Meléndez, eds., *Colonial Dilemma: Critical Perspectives on Contemporary Puerto Rico* (Boston: South End Press, 1993), pp. 181–88.

2. Douglas B. Klusmeyer, "Aliens, Immigrants and Citizens: The Politics of Inclusion in the Federal Republic of Germany," *Daedalus* 122 (Summer 1993): 84.

3. See, for instance, essays in Laurence Halley, ed., *Ancient Affections: Ethnic Groups and Foreign Policy* (New York: Praeger, 1985); Abdul Aziz Said, *Ethnicity and U.S. Foreign Policy* (New York: Praeger, 1977); Mohammed E. Ahrari, *Ethnic Groups and U.S. Foreign Policy* (New York: Greenwood, 1982).

4. Mervin Holli and Peter d'A. Jones, eds., *Ethnic Chicago* (Grand Rapids: William B. Eerdmans, 1977).

5. See, for example, Rodolfo de la Garza, Robert Winckle, and Jerry Polinard, "Ethnicity and Policy: The Mexican American Perspective," in Chris F. García, ed., *Latinos and the Political System* (Notre Dame: University of Notre Dame, 1988), pp. 426–41.

6. Yossi Shain, *The Frontiers of Loyalty: Political Exiles in the Age of Nation-States* (Middletown: Wellesley University Press, 1992).

7. Juan Gómez-Quiñonez, "On Culture," *Revista Chicano-Riqueña,* 1977, pp. 29–46.

8. See Juan Gómez-Quiñonez, "Notes on the Interpretation of the Relations Between the Mexican Community in the United States and Mexico," and Carlos Zazueta, "Mexican Political Actors in the United States and Mexico: Historical and Political Contexts of a Dialogue," both in Carlos Vasquez and Manuel Garcia y Griego, eds., *Mexican/U.S. Relations: Conflict and Convergence* (Los Angeles: University of California Press, 1983), pp. 417–83.

9. See the work of Tomas Almaguer, "Toward a Study of Chicano Colonialism," in *Aztlán: Chicano Journal of Social Sciences and the Arts* 1 (Fall 1970): 7–21; Rudy Acuna, *Occupied America: A History of Chicanos* (New York: Harper and Row, 1988); and Mario Barrera, *Race and Class in the Southwest* (Notre Dame: University of Notre Dame Press, 1979).

10. History Task Force of the Centro de Estudios Puertorriqueños, *Labor Migration Under Capitalism: The Puerto Rican Experience* (New York: Monthly Review Press, 1979); Manuel Maldonado-Dennis, *The Emigration Dialectic: Puerto Rico and the USA* (New York: International, 1980).

11. See, for example, Lourdes Casal, "Cubans in the United States," in Martin Weinstein, ed., *Revolutionary Cuba in the World Arena* (Philadelphia: Institute for the Study of Human Issues, 1979); Lourdes Argüelles, "Cuban Miami: The Roots, Development and Everyday Life of an Emigre Enclave in the National Security State," *Contemporary Marxism* 5 (Summer 1982): 27–44.

12. Carlos Forment, "Caribbean Geopolitics and Foreign State-Sponsored Movements: The Case of Cuban Exile Militancy 1959–1979," in Miren Uriarte-Gastón and Jorge Canas, eds., *Cubans in the United States* (Boston: Center for the Study of the Cuban Community, 1984), pp. 65–102.

13. Marisa Alicea, "Dual Home Bases: A Reconceptualization of Puerto Rican Migration," *Latino Studies Journal* 1, no. 3 (1990): 78–98.

14. Félix Padilla, *Latino Consciousness: The Case of Mexican Americans and Puerto Ricans in Chicago* (Notre Dame: University of Notre Dame Press, 1985).

15. Frank Bonilla, "Brother Can You Paradigm?" Inter-University Program on Latino Research, Milenio Series, 1997.

16. María de los Angeles Torres, "Latinos and U.S. Policies: Foreign Policy Toward Latin America," *Latino Studies Journal* 1 (September 1990): 3–23.

17. David Ayon and Ricardo Anzaldua Montoya, "Latinos and U.S. Policy," in Abraham F. Lowenthal, ed., *Latin America and the Caribbean Contemporary Record* (Baltimore: Johns Hopkins University Press, 1990).

18. Jesús Díaz, *Del exilio a la Patria* (La Habana: UNEAC, 1977).

19. María de los Angeles Torres, "Encuentros y encontronazos: nación y exilio," *Diaspora: A Journal of Transnational Studies* 4 (1995): 211–39.

20. Angelo Falcón, "A Divided Nation: The Puerto Rican Diaspora in the United States and the Proposed Referendum," in Meléndez and Meléndez, *Colonial Dilemma*, pp. 173–80.

21. Gloria Anzaldúa, *Borderlands = La Frontera: The New Mestiza* (San Francisco: Spinster/Aunt Lute, 1987).

22. Cristina García, *Dreaming in Cuban* (New York: Knopf, 1992).

23. Rubén Martínez, *The Other Side: Fault Lines, Guerrilla Saints and the True Heart of Rock 'n' Roll* (New York: Verso, 1992).

24. Richard Rodríguez, *Hunger of Memory: The Education of Richard Rodriguez, an Autobiography* (Boston: D. R. Godine, 1981).

25. Gustavo Pérez-Firmat, *Life on the Hyphen: The Cuban-American Experience* (Austin: University of Texas Press, 1994).

26. Tato Laviera, *AmeRican* (Houston: Arte Public Press, 1985).

27. Madelin Camara, "The Third Option: Beyond the Border," in Ruth Behar, ed., *Bridges to Cuba* (Ann Arbor: University of Michigan Press, 1995).

28. Richard Bernstein, *Dictatorship of Virtue: Multiculturalism and the Battle for America's Future* (New York: Knopf, 1994).

29. Arthur M. Schlesinger, Jr., *The Disuniting of America: Reflections on a Multicultural Society* (New York: Norton, 1991).

30. John Rex, "Ethnic Identity and the Nation-State: The Political Sociology of Multi-Cultural Societies," *Social Identities* 1, no. 1 (1995): 21–34.

31. Milton Esman, "The Political Fallout of International Migration," *Diaspora: A Journal of Transnational Studies* 2 (1992): 3–38.

32. For an extensive study of transnational communities, see Linda Basch, Nina Glick Schiller, and Cristina Szanton Blanc, *Nations Unbound: Transnational Projects, PostColonial Predicaments and Deterritorialized Nation-States* (Amsterdam: Gordon and Breach, 1994). See also David Skidmore and Valerie M. Hudson, eds., *The Limits of State Autonomy: Societal Groups and Foreign Policy Formulation* (Boulder, Colo.: Westview Press, 1993).

33. David Lipscomb, "Caught in a Strange Middle Ground: Contesting History in Salman Rushdie's *Midnight's Children*," *Diaspora: A Journal of Transnational Studies* 1 (1991): 163–90.

34. Ellen Dorsey, "Expanding the Foreign Policy Discourse: Transnational Social Movements and the Globalization of Citizenship," in Skidmore and Hudson, *Limits of State Autonomy*, pp. 237–67.

35. Homi Bhabha, "The Third Space," in Jonathan Rutherford, ed., *Identity, Community, Culture and Difference* (London: Lawrence & Wishart, 1990), pp. 207–22.

36. Purnima Mankekar, "Reflections on Diasporic Identities: A Prolegomenon to an Analysis of Political Bifocality," *Diaspora: A Journal of Transnational Studies* 3 (1994): 366.

QUESTIONS

1. Does a democracy need both cultural and political pluralism? Why?

2. Can a state or its people (or you?) overcome the fear that some of its citizens may identify with a culture from another country?

3. Regarding multiple political identities: Is it possible to have one political identity that encompasses two different countries? Or does this imply two political identities? Why does this issue arise among some people and not others?

4. What is the balance between specific national or ethnic rights and global human rights?

5. Through what institutions and/or individuals are the definition and implementation of such rights determined?

* 27 *

CLASS AND CULTURE WARS IN THE NEW LATINO POLITICS

Victor Valle and Rodolfo D. Torres

In this piece, Victor and Rudy place Latino/a power and politics within a global and a metropolitan context. Thus they dispel any facile assumptions about a particular ethnic hegemony in Los Angeles. They note, among other things, the incipient political representation and the lingering invisibility to which Latino/as are still subjected. At the same time, they point to the increasing political participation of the "postamnesty" Latino/a voter, a phenomenon that points to the quest for public citizenship. Focusing on the role of the working class, they provide a comprehensive point of view to understand what appears as interethnic or racial conflict. Of particular interest is their notion of genetic, political, and cultural *mestizaje* as a model for future democracy in the United States.

Population trends suggest that Latinos may have to wait until past the midcentury mark before their numerical dominance becomes irresistable. When and if that moment arises, increasing social differentiation and class divisions within the Latino community, complicated by globalisms unforeseen permutations, will make simple notions of ethnic cohesion problematic.

Rather, if Latino power is to have any real constructive and lasting meaning, it should be seen as both the catalyst for and the foundation of a new conception of the multicultural metropolis. Up to this point, we have suggested through our criticism that the only multculturalism worth striving for should not disguise and obscure social inequalities with brotherly platitudes or allow the processes of racialization to continue reproducing themselves behind the benign facade of tolerance. Now we would like to be more explicit and focus our attention upon the immediate future. The Latino community, due to its current social composition, historical experience, and size, has the potential to play a crucial role in the construction of a new cosmopolitanism. Recent events suggest that such a building process is already under way in the political arena.

Spurred on by record levels of Latino voter registration and participation in California, twenty-four Latino and Latina candidates, or one in five members of the state legislature, were elected during the 1998 election cycle, an increase of eighteen over the 1996 election cycle.[1] More important for our study, most of the newly acquired seats were won in Los Angeles County. Yet several factors have distracted many analysts within and outside of the Latino community from grasping simultaneously the political *and* cultural significance of these electoral gains.

For one, dramatic increases in Latino political representation are recent. Not since the nineteenth century has Southern California's Latino community enjoyed such levels of political representation.[2] Still, there is something rather presumptuous about asking whether increased political representation should somehow translate into increased cultural influence. Latinos have viewed themselves as being in the minority for so long that the possibility of becoming the majority seems disorienting. The same goes for Latino leadership. Few Latino scholars have studied politics as an arena for cultural representation because, until relatively recently, it was assumed that, as a politically marginalized group, Latinos enacted their cultural lives in private, or at least in their neighborhoods. Now, however, Latino-elected leaders and their constituents have an opportunity to imagine and enact their cultural lives in public. We intend to show that the opportunities for increased cultural influence offered by enhanced public participation go beyond the simple administrative and legislative remedies available to Latino leadership. The political arena also offers a kind of stage upon which Latinos can construct new public identities. We intend to show that that transition has already been prefigured, and in many ways enabled, by the increasing reach and power of the various forms of Latino media, especially the Spanish-language media. When artists like Los Lobos create music that expresses a profound self-acceptance of their working-class and mestizo roots, when Spanish-language television broadcasters present illegal Latino border crossers as heroic survivors, when Mexican fans fill the Los Angeles Memorial Coliseum to capacity to root for the home team—La Selección Nacional—in a match against the U.S. national team, and when clubs like La Conga Room create a space where Latinos of all national origins can gather to enjoy the best in Afro-Cuban music, via Havana, one can already see the variety of cultural forms from which new public behaviors are being constructed.

As the presidential impeachment scandal of 1999 reminds us, politics is a kind of social practice where subjective, or cultural, forms are produced and circulated for public consumption. It is indeed a cliché of contemporary politics that elections and legislative battles are won or lost in the media. At both the national and the local levels, politicians increasingly debate questions once considered issues of private morality—gay marriage, abortion, adultery, school prayer—in the nation's virtual electronic town squares. And as the country has drifted further to the right, and the national political culture has fallen still more deeply under the sway of the corporate media and corporate dollars, political life, to the degree it is concerned with the production and consumption of moral discourse, is now dominated by the subjective. So it would seem that the same forces that have converted politics into cultural warfare would have further marginalized minority forms of counterrepresentation. Until recently, that judgment would have seemed especially applicable to Latinos, at least at the level of national discourse. Even though African Americans have lost discursive ground in recent decades, they, of all minorities, continue to play the lead role in the national political and cultural dialogue, especially as it concerns urban "race relations." By contrast, and with such notable exceptions as United Farm Workers labor and environmental struggles, Latino contributions to the national political discourse are usually obscured or absorbed by stronger voices. And but for the individual exceptions, it has been more common to conceive of Latino political leaders simply as creatures of their local political enviromnents and not as shapers of the greater political culture.

Not surprisingly—and this is especially true of the practitioners of cultural studies—cultural and social historians have tended to privilege the analysis of marginal spaces and texts to understand how Latinos have contested hegemonic culture or constructed ethnic identities. Hence the recent studies that seek to understand, or read, how Latinos construct their lived cultures, and hence the emphasis on the texts of lived culture, from cookbooks to graffiti to low riders. But recent developments in cities such as Miami and Los Angeles now require a reconceptualization of the way Latinos negotiate the transition from political and cultural minority to political and cultural majority. In Los Angeles, the work of reconceptualization becomes especially urgent as Latino political leadership increases its policymaking role in the transition to an economy based upon cultural production, as evidenced by the explosion of such entertainment projects as the Staples Center, the proposed Dream-Works studio, and the city's first Catholic cathedral. Increased Latino political representation will mean greater access to the levers of government and, as a result, a larger niche in the state's ecology of representation. Now, for the first time since the city's founding, Latinos have the opportunity to acquire the institutional standing to open up what has been a closed dialogue on the matter of race and class.

In a strictly quantitative sense, then, the future already looks promising when considered in the light of recent political history. In the 1970s and 1980s, organizations such as the National Organization of Latino Elected and Appointed Officials measured success by counting electoral victories. Consistent with such thinking, most Latino officeholders replicated mainstream political thinking, making a religion of narrow political pragmatism. As in the major parties, raising money, winning elections, and holding onto political office were their method, objective, and reward. As apathy in the electorate broadened and deepened, ideas and issues played second fiddle to the art of deal making, fund-raising, polling, and media campaigning. Some of this narrowness was understandable. Increases in Latino voter participation had not kept pace with the quickened rate of Latino population growth during the 1970s and 1980s. As a result, Latino candidates remained dependent upon corporate donors, party bosses, and the demands of media campaigning. The dearth of Latino political ideas, however, also reflected weak leadership. The running rivalry between Councilman Richard Alatorre's and Supervisor Gloria Molina's political machines, the decision of Latino elected officials to soften their opposition to Proposition 187 to avoid alienating white voters, and the recent drug scandals engulfing Alatorre and Councilman Mike Hernandez illustrate some of the worst of the past generation of Latino political leadership.[3] By the late 1980s, and continuing until the mid-1990s, Latino population growth, coupled with the consequences of immigration legislation and California's attempt at ethnic cleansing, dramatically altered both the quantity and quality of Latino voter participation in state politics, and, as a consequence, the possibilities for new leadership.

The first tremors of the political earthquake were registered in Orange County when Democrat Loretta Sanchez defeated ultraconservative incumbent Republican Robert Dornan for a seat in the U.S. House of Representatives by a 984-vote margin in 1996. Although Dornan's defeat in the Forty-Sixth Congressional District rocked conservatives where it hurt most, in a seat long considered safe by Republicans, a growing Latino presence in Santa Ana made the upset foreseeable. Groups like La Hermandad Mexicana Nacional, a cross between an old-fashioned Mexican mutual-aid society and a labor and immigrant rights organization, helped translate that presence into votes, an achievement that quickly drew a reactionary response. In the already hostile climate created by the passage of Proposition 187 two years earlier, Dornan played up anti-Latino, anti-immigrant hysteria, accusing La Hermandad of a sinister conspiracy. Meanwhile, the *Los Angeles Times,* according to the *O.C. Weekly,* "manufactured incriminating evidence; declared *Hermandad* guilty months before a grand jury had even convened; and effectively sided with Dornan's laughable accusations that nuns, military men, residents of entire apartment buildings and 'thousands' of noncitizens quietly conspired to unseat him."[4] Local and federal authorities launched investigations, but two years later an Orange County grand jury, citing a lack of evidence, refused to hand down any indictments. In the end, all that could be established with any certainty was that "noncitizens who had passed all immigration tests and who were awaiting formal swearing-in ceremonies" had jumped the gun. They had improperly registered to vote and then exercised their franchise prematurely.[5] The most sinister charge that could be leveled against La Hermandad was that a pair of its voter registration volunteers may have been over-zealous in their efforts to increase Latino political participation.

Ironically, the Dornan-manufactured media panic fueled new efforts to mobilize Latino voters. To protect their families, jobs, and civil liberties from continued Republican-led scapegoating, California's Latino immigrants took advantage of a period of immigration amnesty, became citizens, and then voted in record numbers. Although Latinos remain underrepresented at the polls, the 1996 election results show that newly enfranchised Latino immigrants voted "at a rate exceeding that of the state's voters as a whole." These new voters participated at rates that effectively surpassed the overall voter turnout, with "a little less than two-thirds" of them going to the polls.[6] Los Angeles County, where the 1996 turnout among both new and veteran Latino voters jumped from 11 percent to 18 percent, registered the biggest bounce. In Orange County, the setting for the Dornan-Sanchez race, the Latino vote rose from 6 percent to 9 percent.[7] 1996 elections marked two other historic firsts: Latino voter participation in the Los Angeles mayoral race hit 15 percent, which surpassed African American participation and matched the Westside Jewish turnout.[8] Not surprisingly, several recent studies show that Governor Pete Wilson, the most powerful and aggressive spokesman for the anti-immigrant backlash, did long-term damage to the Republican Party's credibility among new immigrant voters. But the Latino turnout, which rose at a time when Jewish political representation in Los Angeles County's top one hundred political of offices had declined by 30 percent since 1986, also gave the Westside's Democratic establishment much to ponder.[9]

Nativo Lopez, executive director of La Hermandad's Orange County branch, sees the emergence of the "postamnesty" Latino voter as a turning point in Southern California politics. The state's 1.7 million immigration applicants all became eligible to apply for amnesty at the end of 1995.[10] After January, February, and March 1996, these applicants became citizens in increasing numbers, and a growing cohort of high school–aged U.S.-born Latinos began voting thanks to the passage of President Clinton's "motor-voter" law. Equally important, groups such as the Southwest Voter Registration Education Project, La Hermandad, and the Los Angeles County Federation of Labor laid the organizational groundwork that translated legal opportunities into electoral gains. In 1996, their combined efforts succeeded in bringing as many as 1.3 million new potential Latino voters to the California polls.

"Certainly," Lopez said in an interview, "organization was a part of it, not just La Hermandad, but many others spurring people on to obtain their citizenship, and then registering them to vote." La Hermandad takes credit for qualifying anywhere from 175,000 to 180,000 people to enter the amnesty pipeline. "Many are still in the pipeline," Lopez added. "Locally, we have more than 10,000 applicants who have been waiting for twelve months to twenty-four months to get their final citizenship interview." And this trend will continue, "In the Los Angeles INS district," Lopez said, "there are more than a half a million people waiting for citizenship. By the year 2000 that backlog will be eliminated," which will produce another surge in Southern California's Latino vote just in time for the presidential election.[11]

During the 1998 election cycle, eleven Southern California Latino Democrats, most of whom can be classified as pro-labor progressives, rode this confluence of demographic and political forces into the California State Legislature. These victories helped Democrats regain a slim Assembly majority in Sacramento and lifted Antonio Villaraigosa from Assembly majority leader to the powerful position of

Assembly speaker. In yet another portent of Latino political power, Los Angeles City Councilman Richard Alarcon handily won his San Fernando Valley State Senate seat after narrowly defeating former Assemblyman Richard Katz, a Westside political power broker, in a bitter Democratic primary. Other Latino candidates who lost close races in the last election cycle will be back for the next round, Lopez said: "There is no reason why in the year 2000, we shouldn't be close to 30 percent of the state assembly," or in other words, "close to parity with our numbers in the state's population."[12] Even Lopez, despite the onslaught of hostile media coverage, benefited from the postamnesty surge when he was elected president of the Santa Ana Unified School District Board of Education in 1996.

The city of Los Angeles—where Latinos are projected to constitute more than 49 percent of the population by 2001—promises future political opportunities, even though the charter reform movement, various City Council expansion schemes, and the San Fernando Valley secession movement have temporarily clouded that picture.[13] Latinos should continue to gain strength in the Valley, whichever way it goes, and in South-Central Los Angeles, where Latinos already made up 44 percent of the population in 1990.[14] There, Latinos will soon constitute as much as 60 percent of some districts. For the moment, few Latino or African American political leaders will publicly discuss that eventuality. But soon, Lopez said in another interview, "you are going to see Latinos running for those seats that have always been held by African Americans," competition that will increase tensions between Latino and African American political leaders.[15] Some analysts have already predicted that African American council member Rita Walters will be the first to be challenged by a Latino contender.[16] African American political leaders in Los Angeles must negotiate not only changing political demography but the growing fault line that divides a small but thriving African American middle class from the black urban poor. However, Latino office seekers and their supporters should resist the temptation to use ethnic loyalties to exploit the tenuous position of African American political leaders. Although such ploys may yield short-term gains, ethnically targeted appeals reinforce the city's divided political geography while leaving the Latino victors vulnerable to those who would exploit emerging class divisions among their own constituencies. Instead, African American and Latino elected officials representing inner-city districts need to develop strategies that address racialized class inequalities. By acknowledging, rather than obscuring, the class divisions in the Latino and African American communities, a new generation of leaders can build a movement based upon commonalities of class.

The anticipated growth of Latino populations in the suburbs and the unexpected consequences of legislative term limits will mean that "termed-out" Latino legislators will return from Sacramento or Washington to run in city districts both within and outside of the safe barrios now dominated by Latinos. Assembly Speaker Villaraigosa, State Senator Richard Polanco, Assemblyman Gil Cedillo, and Congressman Xavier Becerra, among others, may carpetbag into the seats vacated by Alatorre and Hernandez or run in the South-Central or Hollywood district, potentially doubling the number of Latinos on the City Council from three to six. Even a Villaraigosa mayoral challenge is conceivable if liberals and progressives can construct a viable post-Bradley-era coalition. The next census will also provide the numbers to translate a decade of Latino population growth into district reapportionment that increases Southern California's Latino congressional representation.

For the moment, however, many analysts appear preoccupied with calculating the new political math made possible by increased Latino participation while downplaying the content of the new postamnesty Latino leadership. Conventional political analyses still focus on identifying safe districts, reinforcing the conventional wisdom that the most important divisions in Los Angeles politics are racial or ethnic. Although these analytic prejudices are understandable, given the empiricist bias of professional political science and the racialized representation of the city's social divisions, both tendencies promote the Eastside-versus-Westside turf mentality that reinforces a fragmented status quo. But a closer examination of the postamnesty voter's role in the local and global economy offers important ways of reinterpreting the meaning of Latino voting patterns for the city and county as a whole.

In Nativo Lopez's view, "The most important demographic statistic left out of these discussions is that, in Los Angeles County, Latinos constitute more than 65 to 70 percent of the economically active workforce."[17] When Asian immigrant workers are factored into the equation, the emergence of new Latino and Asian leadership in the local labor movement seems logical. Already, Latino and Asian immigrant workers have begun to revive and expand decaying service sector unions into a new force in Los Angeles politics. The historic victories of the Service Employees International Union bear remembering in this context. An organizing practice that discovers the class interests of Latina, Asian American, and African American female home healthcare workers shows how political alliances can be built across seemingly insurmountable local racialized boundaries.

Such victories, as well as union gains made earlier in the 1990s, have been felt far beyond the county line, providing the kinds of tactical and strategic knowledge that is transforming the AFL-CIO's national policies. At another level, the transformation of Los Angeles unionism bears comparison to the Irish immigrant takeover of New York's labor unions at the beginning of the twentieth century, except that now, Latino and Asian immigrants work under profoundly different economic and cultural circumstances.

Interpreting late capitalism remains tricky, however. The true believers in market solutions still promise that the emerging knowledge-based economy will eventually lift a sufficient number of boats, Latino vessels included, by providing a steady supply of new jobs. But increasing poverty in the midst of so-called full employment has, for the moment, disarmed their glib predictions and fueled postmillennial pessimism. Under the most noirish scenarios, the unequal development fostered by postindustrial society, with its concomitant transition to an information-based, post-Fordist industrial regime, will continue to produce massive economic and social dislocations. At the same time, the complex dialectics of capital, markets, and resources in the developing world will continue to make cities such as Los Angeles the destinations of choice for Latin American, Asian, Near Eastern, and African immigrants, thus creating a future theater of racialized conflict. Worse, during the next economic downturn, the opportunists will attempt to revive the anti-immigrant hysteria of the mid-1990s. Meanwhile, technological innovation will continue to demassify the media and facilitate the emergence of a knowledge elite whose job it will be to create and service the hardware and cultural software of an information/culture-based society. The new knowledge elites, we are told, will emerge as a dominant class of an economic regime based upon post-Fordist production, leaving behind those cultural and social sectors still dependent upon less efficient Fordist modes of production. Under post-Fordism, where information and culture industries emerge as the dominant productive force, the winners will either own or control the production of culture and information in all its economic and political applications. Everyone not owning or participating in these new knowledge-based industries stands to lose social prestige, not to mention financial and political viability. How the Latino community will fare in the ensuing transition to a society organized around digitized information and cultural production is hard to predict. But Latinos—either as members of a working and an incipient owning class—cannot expect to participate in, let alone influence, the knowledge-based industries except as consumers if they remain tied to inefficient Fordist industries. The emergent knowledge elites who serve at the pleasure of post-Fordist capital reserve the best roles for themselves.

Some may take heart in knowing that the *maquiladoras* concentrated along the northern Mexican border and scattered throughout Southern Callfornia's old and new suburbs will at least employ huge numbers of Latinos in the region's post-Fordist industries. The increased earning power of some Latinos has already tempted a few to mistake middle income for middle-class social position. But many middle-income Latinos, the pessimists say, have taken longer to acquire the social privileges and status that come with university-trained professions and upper-management corporate positions. Moreover, the Latinos who have joined the skilled, professional, and university-trained workforce remain in the minority. Most of the highly decentralized industries that employ Latinos do so at the lowest skill levels, offering them the lowest pay, benefits, and opportunities for educational advancement. For example, many of the low-skilled industries that employ Latinos in the Greater Eastside do not appear to have benefited from the globalization that has been so profitable for the knowledge industries, increasing their vulnerability to technological displacement and excess industrial capacity worldwide. The post-NAFTA international trade that has brought new investment and high-salary jobs into places like Santa Monica, Westlake Village, and Beverly Hills has not, according to one study, reached such Greater Eastside cities as Huntington Park, Cudahy, and Maywood, where minimum-wage jobs are plentiful.[18] Nor do the job niches Latinos currently hold in post-Fordist production promise greater access to the means of cultural representation; up to now, Latinos, with a few strategic exceptions, have been excluded from the means of mental production. The retrenchment of anti–affirmative action policies in higher education will act as a further drag on Latino integration in the knowledge-based economy.

Meanwhile, technological innovation will continue to facilitate the breakup of mass-media audiences into smaller, more socially isolated segments, while at the same time promoting the emergence of an information elite whose job it will be to create the information and cultural commodities that service a growing cybereconomy. The information elite will emerge as a dominant economic class of a social regime based upon post-Fordist production, leaving behind those cultural and social sectors still affiliated with Fordist modes of production. Under post-Fordism, where information and culture industries emerge as the dominant productive force, the winners will either own or create the production of knowledge. Everyone else, as Michael Rustin writes, stands to lose social prestige: "Insofar as mental labor does become more central to the production process, it is not surprising that those who live by it gain in social power, just as the depopulation of the countryside earlier had its consequences for class relations."[19]

According to some analysts, the noir scenarios are already visible in the inner city and in Greater L.A.'s aging near-in suburbs. The triple threat of a growing poverty-wage job sector, the steady evaporation of middle-income jobs, and meteoric salary increases for a select few knowledge workers at the top of the employment pyramid has already eroded the tax bases of Los Angeles and the older suburbs that Latinos have recently inherited. The crude inequalities of the new economy deliver the coup de grâce to a post–Proposition 13 history of disinvestment and physical decay in the recently Latinized suburbs. As Mike Davis notes in his latest book, *Ecology of Fear:*

> In addition to the dramatic hemorrhage of jobs and capital over the last decade, aging suburbia also suffers from premature physical obsolescence. Much of what was built in the postwar period (and continues to be built today) is throwaway architecture, with a functional life span of 30 years or less. . . . At best, this stucco junk was designed to be promptly recycled in perennially dynamic housing markets, but such markets have stagnated or died in much of the old suburban fringe.[20]

And as these suburbs decay, white flight—at least for those with the skills to land higher-paying jobs in the knowledge-based and trade-based jobs of the edge suburbs—hastens the loss of tax revenues in the older suburbs.

The noir scenarios may underestimate the role Los Angeles will play in the regional, national, and global economy as well as the Latino community's resolve to salvage places written off as unredeemable, for Latinos will continue to seek social progress wherever they can obtain it. But compared to California's shameless boosters, the noir critique provides a sober corrective to unfounded optimism. For example, some analysts point with pride to increasing Latino household incomes as evidence of a growing Latino middle class. Gregory Rodriguez shows that in 1990 slightly more than 25 percent of Latino households in five Southern California counties earned incomes that exceeded $35,000, which was then the national median income. According to this income standard, slightly more than 25 percent of Latino households in Southern California's five counties were earning 1990 incomes that could be classified as middle-class. Recent immigrants, contrary to the underclass stereotype, constituted a significant portion (34 percent) of the Latino households earning at or above the median income level, registering some of the fastest income increases among Latinos. Latinos, both foreign-born and U.S.-born, showed rates of home ownership second only to Anglos and on par with Asians. Finally, Latino households earning at or above the middle-income level grew faster than the growth of Latino households living in poverty.[21]

Although impressive and important, studies that equate income with social status are nevertheless misleading. Latinos are indeed becoming more socially mobile, but the income numbers also show that 75 percent of Latino households earn below the national median, a proportion that is just as significant if one is interested in understanding the size of a low-wage, low-skilled Latino working class. And even for those Latinos categorized as middle-class, the high number of Latino households with three or more wage earners (more than 52 percent among the foreign-born and more than 25 percent among the U.S.-born, compared to 13.5 percent for U.S.-born whites and 19.4 percent for African Americans) suggests the pooling of several working-class salaries under what would appear to be a single middle-class roof.[22] To be contextualized accurately, studies of Latino social class need to look at per capita earning to understand how middle-income wealth is transmitted between generations. It is also important that researchers account for educational levels of wage earners when attempting to describe Latino social mobility. For example, as Rodriguez correctly notes, only 8.9 percent of foreign-born Latinos classified as middle-class had earned bachelor's degrees. Among U.S.-born Latinos categorized as middle-class, only 15.7 percent had earned bachelor's degrees, compared to more than 40 percent for both U.S.- and foreign-born whites.[23] When per capita income, education levels, and the working-class character of Latino labor force participation are taken into account, Latino movement into the middle class is more ambiguous than the household income figures would suggest. Although one can acknowledge that social mobility is occurring, one can also conclude that that progress is recent and still subject to the reversals produced by the transition to a knowledge-based, post-Fordist economy.

Still other analysts point with optimism to the growing number of Latino entrepreneurs as indicators of social mobility, for what better denotes middle-class social position than business ownership? Again, at first glance, the numbers appear impressive. The number of Latino-owned businesses in the Los Angeles area has grown three times faster than the population in recent years. In 1992, California led the nation in Latino-owned business, and Los Angeles County led the state with 109,104 Latino-owned firms employing 65,000 workers, earning $7.8 billion in revenues. Manufacturers of traditional Mexican and Latin American cheeses, such as Industry-based Cacique, Inc., and Paramount-based Ariza Cheese Co., represent a few of the county's multimillion-dollar successes, employing several hundred employees. The average Latino business owner, however, employed about three-fifths of an employee per business, underscoring the ambiguities of Latino entrepreneurship.[24] According to sociologists Ivan Light and Elizabeth Roach, many of the new Latino businesses were created as a defense against underunemployment, especially among new immigrant arrivals. As employment opportunities for Latinos dropped during the 1990 recession, the number of marginal, unincorporated businesses owned by Latinos tripled to 54,768 from 18,480 in 1980.[25] Most of the unincorporated businesses were started by foreign-born Latinos, many of whom earned slightly below the national median income. In 1990, self-employed Latino entrepreneurs earned an annual mean of $29,599. By contrast, owners of incorporated businesses, most of whom were native-born Latinos, earned a mean of $44,981 a year. Likewise, the foreign-born Lations realized a $4,737 average adjusted benefit for self-employment; native-born Latinos realized a $9,067 average adjusted annual benefit.[26] And although Latino entrepreneurship increased in Los Angeles, as a group Latinos ranked near the bottom, slightly below whites and slightly above African Americans. Self-employment rates among native- and foreign-born Latino males averaged 8 percent, and between 4.5 percent and 6.1 percent for native- and foreign-born Latinas.[27] For Latinos at least, entrepreneurship is not a panacea that will deliver the American Dream, but neither has it failed to produce any rewards. Rather, the truth lies somewhere between these extremes. Light and Roach write that the

> growth of Hispanic entrepreneurs certainly drove down the rewards of business ownership among this group to a greater extent than any other. In a way, however, the Hispanic situation was superior to what the whites faced. They were developing new economic niches in garment manufacturing, gardening, and hotel and restaurant work as whites were losing their comfortable niches. Admittedly, the Hispanics were poorly paid, but getting a bad job may be easier to endure than losing a good one.[28]

Despite notable successes, which the media use to illustrate their model-minority narratives, most Latino businesses manage to employ only their entrepreneurs. Moreover, only a fraction of these entrepreneurs, available data show, have obtained the capital to invest in the knowledge-based businesses of the new economy. As a result, the Latino community cannot afford to put all its faith in market forces, when doing so would risk abandoning those with the least technical skills to combat poverty and despair. In other words, although the benefits of the market economy offer promise for a small but growing minority, the working-class Latino majority must preserve worker-oriented social and political action as a short- and long-term option if it hopes to address present and future structural inequalities. But the meaning of worker-oriented social and political action, as we have attempted to show, must be expanded and reconceptualized to incorporate new forms of struggle.

TOWARD A CLASS-ORIENTED POLITICAL CULTURE

To the degree that immigrant Latino and Asian workers continue taking control of local labor institutions, they will create a power base with the autonomy and human and financial resources to influence the electoral process and further diminish the clout of entrenched party machines. The Los Angeles County Federation of Labor, led by Miguel Contreras, together with immigrant rights groups, demonstrated this fact during Gil Cedillo's 1997 primary bid for the Forty-Sixth Assembly District. The federation, which had identified and canvassed nine thousand newly registered voters in the downtown district, brought an unprecedented 45 percent of these voters to the polls by emphasizing Cedillo's labor-organizing credentials and eagerness to fight Governor Wilson's political agenda.[29] Under Contreras's leadership, the 738,000-member federation also helped the Democrats recapture the State Assembly, enact school bond measures, and pass the living wage ordinance.[30]

Enlightened pragmatism, not leftist idealism, requires that present and future Latino leaders fashion an industrial and urban policy that transcends the worn-out discourses of race relations and identity politics. To achieve this, Latino elected leaders need to broaden and deepen their notions of representation to encompass the class interests of their constituents in the context of the new realities of globalized post-NAFTA Fordist production. The foregoing may sound too theoretical for some, but the post-economic realities that permit Mexican capital to invest in Southern California provide the concrete experiences that underlie these abstractions. Latino immigrant workers, Nativo Lopez explains, are "being employed more and more by other immigrants, other Latinos, and Asian immigrant entrepreneurs who are developing small and medium manufacturing or service plants." As these experiences become commonplace, immigrant workers will see through the mystification of ethnic or racial unity to discover that their "fundamental interests are class interests, not racial interests." At that moment of realization, Lopez argues,

> the possibility of developing multinational, multicultural coalitions will become easier. As a result of NAFTA, the owners of the plants will be Mexicans, and the workers in those plants will be Mexicans. The class lines will be more clearly established for our community. I think that's a very good development for fighting racism, and for fighting economic disadvantage.[31]

And as Latinos begin to make the transition from acting as a class in itself to thinking as a class for itself, they can begin to construct a political culture that represents and advances their interests. Lopez believes this sorting-out process has already begun. Cedillo, for example, received his political training while organizing students against Proposition 187 and leading the Los Angeles County Employees Union. Villaraigosa organized for the United Teachers of Los Angeles and served as president of the ACLU.[32] Becerra, leader of the Congressional Hispanic Caucus, demonstrated political courage by visiting Havana, without making apologies to the Cuban American members of the Congressional Hispanic Caucus, and by voting against moving Israel's capital from Tel Aviv to Jerusalem, without making apologies to Westside Democrats.[33] "This new crop of leaders is better educated, both academically, formally, and in their practical organizing experiences," Lopez said in an interview. "I think that we will have better-quality leadership and a greater ability to mobilize more broadly. I think it's possible, absolutely possible."[34]

Reorienting Latino political discourse toward a deeper appreciation of class issues will require Latino leaders, elected or not, to engage in the culture wars. As the

Republicans recently demonstrated with their Contract with America and family values rhetoric, it is possible for one side to so dominate the political discourse that opponents are forced to speak that faction's language. Likewise, Latino elected leaders must be prepared to reframe the context of political dialogue in ways that are advantageous to their constituents. Whether at Whittier Narrows, in the heartland of the Greater Eastside, or in the newly won jurisdictions of the San Fernando Valley, reframing the political culture of Los Angeles demands a coherent long-term discursive strategy. The conventional functions of representation, such as lawmaking and issue-oriented debate, must be expanded to accommodate new tasks. The bully pulpit, in other words, must be reconceptualized as both political and cultural space. Timid Latino political leaders who cannot capture the cultural space to articulate a transnational human rights agenda, who fail to attack racialized media representations of immigrant workers and to advance an industrial policy that addresses the needs of their predominantly immigrant and working-class constituents, and who fail to utilize Latino-oriented media in a proactive manner risk reinforcing the existing hegemonic order.

Admittedly, the unequal power relations that define the Los Angeles political landscape, particularly the over concentration of media in the hands of local and transnational corporate elites, present formidable obstacles to Latino representation. But recent history also shows that the preamnesty generation of Latino elected leaders often failed to create a discursive umbrella under which coalition building among progressives and Latino-led grassroots organizations could occur. Although they had attained the bully pulpit, this generation of Latino political leaders rarely published or broadcast their ideas outside their districts or legislative chambers. Worse, their poor to mediocre Spanish-speaking skills hindered their ability to utilize the Spanish-language media effectively, which represents a serious failing.

These Latino leaders, particularly those second- and third-generation Mexican Americans with rudimentary Spanish-speaking skills, have been slow to acknowledge the fact that the local and national Spanish-language media, especially radio and television, have permanently changed the political and cultural landscape of Los Angeles. For better or for worse, Spanish-language media, particularly broadcast forms, increasingly function as the space where Latino panethnicity is modified and constructed. And although advertising and marketing decisions play a large role in how the broadcast media construct Latino ethnicity, the narrow marketing focus of these media also creates significant spaces for other forms of political and cultural dialogue to occur. The anecdotal evidence suggests that increases in local and network Spanish-language television news coverage have helped increase Latino political awareness and participation, especially among urban immigrant audiences. In turn, modest increases in news and public affairs coverage have aided urban Latino politicization in at least two ways.

First, although they lack the financial resources of their counterparts in the English-language media, Spanish-language journalists reporting for Spanish speakers in the United States feel a stronger obligation to inform their audiences. Latino journalists' more developed sense of social responsibility stems from pragmatic acknowledgment that their immigrant audiences rely upon their news reports to survive in a new society. But these journalists and their audiences also, even when using empiricized American news formats, expect to be addressed in different discursive forms. Media researcher Virginia Escalante, a former *Los Angeles Times* reporter who is writing a history of Spanish-language newspapers in the United States, argues that Latino-owned newspapers tend to address their readers as citizens, whereas the major English-language newspapers first view their readers as consumers.[35] Whatever factor predominates, economics or culture, recent content studies show a marked discursive difference between English-language and Spanish-language news styles. For example, Spanish-language television news appears to place a greater emphasis upon reporting the social context surrounding crime, which stands in dramatic contrast to the sensational, decontextualized crime-by-crime water torture practiced by English-language television news.[36]

Second, the Spanish-language news media continue to assume an advocacy role on behalf of their audience, but usually within a narrow range of immigration-related and urban issues. In a lucrative, immigrant-supported media market such as Los Angeles, the Spanish-language broadcast media have acquired the economic independence to take bold stances on certain issues, at least compared to their English-language counterparts. Language and narrow marketing focus, in other words, offer Spanish-language news media a degree of discursive freedom not enjoyed by English- language media. Future studies should determine whether this discursive freedom has produced measurable political results. For example, it would not be unreasonable to hypothesize that the Spanish-language broadcast media's coverage of the Proposition 187 policy debates and the televised beating of a truckload of undocumented Latinos by two Riverside police officers helped to mobilize a large Latino voter turnout.[37] The coverage of the Proposition 187 campaign thus represented a kind of discursive victory, one in which the Spanish-language media succeeded in framing the debate from a pro-immigrant perspective. The coverage became so intensely pro-immigrant that Governor Pete Wilson felt compelled at times to complain that he was being "vilified" by the Spanish-language media. By the time the governor had finished his campaigns for Proposition 187 and the anti–affirmative action initiative, the Spanish-language media had effectively transformed Wilson into the Latino community's number-one enemy, which made sense, especially in marketing terms.

Although some Spanish-language media owners contributed funds for and against the Proposition 187 campaign, the news and public affairs coverage rarely forgot which master the owners served: the immigrant audiences that bought the products advertised on their networks. Even the historically conservative Spanish-language newspaper *La Opinión* took a strong stand against the proposition, "running stories of how different segments of the community might be impacted and on the fear 187 was generating." Publisher Monica Lozano also "put a personal stamp on her opposition, reducing ad rates to solicit money for anti–Prop. 187 groups, helping host a fund-raiser for Taxpayers Against 187, and donating $5,000 of her own money."[38] The boost in voter turnout triggered by Proposition 187 pushed Latinos back into the Democratic camp at a time when a shrinking Republican Party most needed new immigrant blood. Latino leaders and pundits, for their part, treated the strong Latino rejection of Wilson's policies as a blessing. The governor and his Republican allies, they argued, had succeeded in mobilizing Latino voters where others had failed. Yet few pundits or scholars credited the role the Spanish-language media played in mobilizing the Latino vote, or in fixing Wilson's racist and anti-immigrant image in the minds of Latino voters.

Still, Spanish-language media, like other media, have maintained a reactive posture to events that limits their discursive independence. The event-oriented focus of daily news coverage is obviously a structuring influence independent of language, as are the symbiotic relations between the media and the state. Another inhibiting factor is the absence of a dynamic Spanish-language print media. La Opinión, still the dominant Spanish-language newspaper in Southern California, remains the weakest link in the city's Latino media ecology. Although the paper continues its historic mission as an important forum for Latin American policy and cultural debates and sports coverage, it has not developed an investigative or political reporting tradition that breaks the major stories that shape policy or precipitate government action. Ideally, a paper like La Opinión should have the resources to do the more complicated stories on local politics, economics, and culture that would influence the news budgets of other local Spanish-language media. Moreover, sustained, aggressive, in-depth print reporting could better prepare Latino readers to increase their levels of civic participation and lay the groundwork for more enterprising Spanish-language broadcast reporting. Many had hoped that La Opinión's impressive circulation gains and the infusion of new capital following Times Mirror Corporation's purchase of a half interest in the paper would have resulted in greater editorial independence and a more pronounced improvement in editorial quality. Recently, however, its growth has stalled. The paper's circulation gains have not been able to go beyond the hundred thousand level. And despite the new energy brought to the paper by Associate Publisher Lozano, the conservative family-run paper has yet to make a significantly larger investment in its editorial product. La Opinión's news staff remains small, low paid, and, some say, demoralized, and the paper's imitation of English-language news formats remains uncritical. Others point to an excessively timid management style hamstrung by corporate interference from Times Mirror.[39] Whatever the reasons, La Opinión remains an underachiever when it comes to local news. And as we saw in the arena policy debate, the local English-language broadcast or print media cannot be relied upon to provide critical coverage for their own target audiences, let alone underserved Latino, African American, or Asian American audiences.

A comparable disconnect also characterizes the Spanish-language broadcast media's weak ties to the more assimilated Latino intellectuals and political leadership. For the latter groups, success in the university, the publishing world, and legislative politics rests on the ability to communicate in English, not in Spanish. Success in one realm has not directly facilitated the Latino intelligentsia's ability to cultivate support in the other. But given the Spanish-language news media's pro-immigrant stance, and its special access to the country's largest Latino community in Los Angeles, Latino leaders and intellectuals must make a systematic effort to bridge this gap. Latino academics can constructively engage the industry by investing more resources in the study and development of Latino-targeted media; by organizing conferences where academics, journalists, and progressives can discuss ways to improve news coverage; and by conducting workshops where community members can acquire media skills. Starting at the most elementary level, such dialogues could help the professional journalists expand their sourcing contacts in the academic community while providing journalists working in Latino-oriented media a chance to impress upon the academics and intellectuals the informational, rhetorical, and linguistic needs of their media. The Latino intelligentsia could also support the efforts of Spanish-language journalists to improve salaries and working conditions. All too often, journalists in the Spanish-language media are treated like second-class professionals; aside from its demoralizing effects, such treatment hinders the development of a Latino critical infrastructure. Addressing the concerns of Latino news editors who say that Spanish-language journalists lack the knowledge, skills, and contacts to cover local government effectively, Latino academics can use their institutional affiliations to organize special workshops on investigating City Hall and development politics. Better ongoing political and economic reporting could help shift the Spanish-language media from a relatively reactive to a more proactive discursive stance. Better coverage of the political economy could help immigrant audiences expand their levels of political participation beyond the immediate survival issues of immigration, health care, and gang violence.

Despite recent political gains, Latino elected officials in Greater Los Angeles represent another weak discursive link, especially when one contrasts them with the creative, vital, and varied Latino union leaders, community arts organizations, individual artists and intellectuals, church and environmental groups, and postamnesty political leaders who have begun to coalesce with non-Latino progressives on a range of issues. Coalitions such as the Los Angeles Alliance for a New Economy (LAANE) and the Bus Riders Union have reached across ethnic, gender, occupational, and neighborhood divisions to build social movements. As previously mentioned, LAANE and organizations like it continue to challenge the social relations of production within the region's largest cultural industry: the combined amusement, sporting, shopping, and multiscreen movie theater complexes packaged as megacultural destinations.[40] In another context, artists have joined forces with workers to engage important cultural empowerment. *Oficios Ocultos/Hidden Labor,* created by Common Threads Artists, stands out as one of the most interesting and creative of these collaborations. Inside department store windows, where displays formerly showed off women's high fashion, a collective of women artists, academics, and garment workers narrated the history of female garment workers in Los Angeles. The display, or rather counterdisplay, illustrated how workers and progressives can expand the arena of contestation by occupying, reinterpreting, and denaturalizing one of the spaces the garment and retail clothing industry has used for fetishizing women's bodies.

Fortunately, some of the discursive preconditions for building a progressive coalition in Los Angeles already exist. Buoyed by the emergence of a Latino and Asian working class in the nation's largest industrial area, the postamnesty Latino leaders are already promoting varying degrees of multiethnic, multigendered, and class-sensitive social justice agendas. This new cadre of leaders will need to develop strategies that reject the racializing identity politics of the present and previous decades and find ways to address Los Angeles residents who believe that their city is fatally fractured, especially for suburban home owners who assume reactionary postures when negotiating their demands for equality with other groups. Obviously, leadership that fails to address the increasing disparity between rich and poor, between racialized inner-city residents and multiethnic suburban home owners, between the landscapes of elite leisure and degraded places of industrial production, cannot expect much success. At the same time, these leaders will have to find ways to deconstruct the elite discourses that promote lopsided, top-down notions of corporate development under the aegis of multicultural tourism and economic empowerment. Moreover, the Latino and Latina leadership of the twenty-first century should begin preparing answers to the divisive, racializing initiatives the next recession is sure to spawn.[41] As LAANE and other groups have begun to demonstrate, an effective progressive agenda can advance simultaneously on political, economic, and cultural fronts because these seemingly distinct spheres are in fact mutually constitutive. So far, these movements have combined an updated class analysis of low-wage immigrant labor and the discourse of multicultural diversity to build tolerance and unity amid ethnic differences. The challenge of integrating class and cultural discourses is more than theoretical.

Latinos, who constitute the majority of industrial workers and residents in both the city of Los Angeles and Los Angeles County, currently endure a symbolic economy that devalues their labor, creativity, and political participation. Patterns of representation have material effects to the degree that they reinforce existing power arrangements. Conventional labor and political organizing alone cannot challenge the cultural discourses that keep immigrant workers isolated and alienated. Moreover, in the first decade of the twenty-first century, Latinos will gain only slim majority margins. And given the still-lagging rates of Latino voter participation and the prevailing class and ethnic divisions that fragment the regional political landscape, no one elite or social sector can attain dominance without building coalitions. The process of weaving a coalition along class lines will help, but it will not overcome the years of socially constructed distrust that divide potential allies along the fault lines of class, ethnicity, gender, and sexual orientation.

DESCONTRUCTING "RACE RELATIONS"

Constructing the Latino metropolis must also demystify the culture industries that construct and reinforce the discourses of race itself. This task requires an understanding of the new linkages between culture industries and the new urban political economy, an understanding of the changing social relations within and between cultural sectors, and a deeper appreciation of the vitality of lived popular culture in the Latino metropolis.

Although Latinos engage the city's culture wars without moral advantages, are clearly susceptible to petty tribalism, and are capable of racializing themselves and others, they nevertheless possess a historic and cultural legacy that can, in the long term, help overturn two particularly divisive aspects of urban "race relations." First, Latinos must elaborate a critical discourse of cultural *mestizaje,* one shorn of essentializing romanticism, to disarm racialized discourses that disguise the economic causes of urban conflict and social inequality. If there is anything the lesson of *mestizaje* teaches, it is that pseudoscientific racial categories are crisscrossed by the actualities of Latino genetic diversity and cultural hybridity. Second, a critical discourse of *mestizaje* grounded in the realities of the global city can be turned against those discourses of cultural production that treat ethnicity and race as commodities of "multicultural" tourism. As the vitality of popular culture continually reminds us, the freeways of cultural appropriation run in two directions. Edward W. Said emphasizes this point when he writes, "Cultural experience or indeed every cultural form is radically, quintessentially hybrid, and if it has been the practice of the West since Immanuel Kant to isolate cultural and aesthetic realms from the worldly domain, it is now time to rejoin them."[42]

What has not become sufficiently evident to Said and other cultural studies scholars, however, are the groundbreaking contributions of Latino intellectuals on the meanings and forms of mestizo hybridity, particularly when the discourse is expressed as one of the earliest critiques of Western colonialism.[43] In fact, Chicana feminist scholars have done some of the most ambitious work on this subject by resituating *mestizaje* in and along the borderlands.[44] The result has been to expand the meanings of *mestizaje* from a cultural to a political metaphor and, in the process, reconceptualize the meaning of culture itself.

Contrary to the construction of the southwestern borderlands and their Latinized cities as a zone of degradations, the Latinos who reside there, argues Renato Rosaldo, occupy one of the world's richest zones of "creative cultural production," which the dominant discourse renders as transitional and empty.

> Similarly, the borders between nations, classes, and cultures were endowed with a curious kind of hybrid invisibility. They seemed to be a little of this and a little of that, and not quite one or the other. Movements between such seemingly fixed entities as nations or social classes were relegated to the analytical dustbin of cultural invisibility. Immigrants and socially mobile individuals appeared culturally invisible because they were no longer what they once were, and not yet what they could become.[45]

In many ways, journalists' nonresponsiveness to multiple Latino identities resembles the academy's attitude toward border regions. Academic institutions maintain "fields" of social science the way the media inscribe the "race relations" discourse—by creating and maintaining boundaries that mutually validate their discursive authority. Under such marginalizing circumstances, political *mestizaje* survives as an outlaw discourse, acknowledged by Latino intellectuals and lived by the Latino community, but ignored by the nation's dominant institutions. Marginalization, however, does not imply the absence of a documented history or discourses. Since the end of the nineteenth century, Latin American writers and intellectuals such as José Martí have translated lived *mestizaje* into written discourse.

Although Latino *mestizaje* in the United States has its antecedents in Mexican and Latin American history, its "lived" experience in the United States has produced discursive innovations. On the U.S. side of the border, immigration accelerates the process through which Latinos simultaneously encounter the First World and other immigrants from the developing world whom they would have been less likely to meet had they stayed at home. On the U.S. side, the meaning and experience of *mestizaje* have also evolved beyond the bounds of official ideology, such as Mexico's ruling PRI, which has historically constructed its meanings so as to maintain a one-party state. Whereas in Mexico the term *mestizaje* have been co-opted to legitimate and integrate the nation's mestizo middle class and regional cultures, in the United States its lived experience occurs beyond official sanction and outside of institutionalized urban "race relations."

In its most mundane form, *mestizaje* on the U.S. side of the border expresses itself as a refusal to prefer one language, one genome, one national or cultural heritage at the expense of others. Culturally speaking, then, *mestizaje* is radically inclusive, a stubborn refusal to make the Sophie's choice between cultural identities and races. At times, its inclusions take the form of a literal transgression of political borders. These transgressions can be, especially when expressed by artists and intellectuals, overtly ideological. Thus, in the manner of Caliban, who uses Prospero's language to blaspheme his colonial enterprise, mestizo hybridity makes a virtue of appropriating elite culture for popular ends. Publishing ethnographies of elite power, for example, represents one way of turning the methods of neocolonialism against the neoliberal global city, in a practice Guillermo Gómez-Peña aptly calls "reverse anthropology."

The day-to-day expressions of *mestizaje,* however, are adaptive. Stated in economic terms, the globalization of capital, with its power to penetrate and dominate regional markets and undermine native economies, obliges the Mexican peasant or Guatemalan worker to ignore certain rules and boundaries in order to survive. Sentimental loyalty to a particular nation-state and, by extension, that state's idealized "traditional" culture becomes an impoverishing, even life-threatening luxury. To this extent, then, the lived transcultural experience of *mestizaje* must also be considered transnational and potentially postnational. And policies such as granting voting status to immigrants in school board elections, for example, represent important ways of granting institutional recognition to Latino political *mestizaje.*

To again borrow Gómez-Peña's phrasing, the border crosser thus operates as a kind of cultural "cross-dresser" who willfully blurs political, racial, or cultural borders in order to survive in an unjustly constructed world. The lived experience of cultural *mestizaje* is not schizoid, nor does it lack the boundedness to produce identity. Instead, Latinos have evolved a countertradition, or anti-aesthetic, of juggling languages, music, clothing styles, foods, gender, anything with which to fashion a more meaningful social and cultural coherence. And it is this aspect of cultural *mestizaje* that allows Latinos to participate in and express the most contemporary manifestations of modernity.

Whatever the terminology, the "styles" of mestizo cultural construction evolve dialectically, generating adaptive responses to changing material conditions and forms of cultural representation. Contrary to the musings of some European postmodernists, who see the multicultural Americas as an orgy of limitless conjunctions, heterodoxy in this hemisphere occurs within materially and culturally defined combinatory systems. Some combinatories are identified with specific cultural spaces— Nuevo Laredo or New Orleans—whereas others, like thousands of migrant Mexican workers, float or migrate, as it were, from place to place, physical or virtual, as individual or communal stylistic expressions. Whether rooted or moving, mestizo border culture coheres, acquires integrity and patterning from its mode of construction, which, depending on the circumstances, may be pragmatic, strategic, or ideological in its orientation to the world. Over time, these strategies take on the appearance of what some would call tradition but could more properly resemble the dialectic between genetics and environment. Like an individual's DNA, cultural *mestizaje* obeys its own rules of inclusion and exclusion, conjunction and disjunction. Whatever internal consistency it achieves is derived over time from the culture's repertoire of responses to a specific landscape, its material conditions and social relations. Latinos may have evolved a particular style of border crossing, but they are not unique in this practice. "All of us," Rosaldo writes, "inhabit an interdependent late-twentieth-century world marked by borrowing and lending across porous national and cultural boundaries that are saturated with inequality, power, and domination."[46] Chicanos who live in the borderlands know this instinctively when they acknowledge their cultural differences and similarities to Mexicans or other Latinos.

However, *mestizaje* is one of many strategic responses to the decline of the imperial West, and is thus symptomatic of a world in flux. The lived cultural experience of more and more people occurs outside the cultural norms idealized by the state and its enabling institutional apparatus. Cultural *mestizaje's* aggressive disregard for boundaries and unexpected inclusions should therefore be appreciated for its political possibilities in a context of global transformations.

Giving political expression to the praxis of mestizo border culture also offers a pragmatic alternative to representations that thwart coalition building in a multicultural city. The news media's reiteration of the "race relations" discourse has framed inner-city life as a competition in which contestants are defined by means of racial taxonomy. For Latinos, whose lived cultural experience spills beyond racialized boundaries, bending to or cooperating with the urban politics framed by the "race relations" discourse only delays the birth of a new political culture. Representations that encapsulate Latinos in essentialized racial or ethnic identities discourage use of the very tool—knowledge of their profound hybridity—with which they can unmask the lie of "race" and build an urban politics based upon commonalities of culture and class. Coalition builders in Los Angeles, Latino or not, will fail in imagining, let alone constructing, a new hegemony if they continue to represent their potential allies and friends in racialized terms and ignore the common interests created by the post-Fordist economy. The failure to deconstruct the discourse of "race relations" may make the attainment of Latino majority status, even when backed by political power, a cruel disappointment. Latino leaders who continue to perpetuate minority thinking by advancing their narrow ethnic interest in fact put off the moment when they might reap the fruits of majority power. Coming to this realization will mark the first step toward political maturity for Latino leadership. Acting upon this realization, by developing appropriate strategy and tactics, represents the second challenge.

Finally, a dialogue between journalists and intellectuals on cultural *mestizaje* could help reinforce certain healthy discursive tendencies already present in Latino journalism. Latino academics should acknowledge those moments when the Spanish-language media effectively counter the mainstream media's racializing representations of Latinos and criticize the Spanish-language media when they reaffirm "race" as an objective reality. Latino intellectuals should encourage the Spanish-language media's efforts to construct a pan-Latino political culture based upon a critical analysis of Latino multiethnicity and criticize those media when they commodify *mestizaje* as a means to mercenary marketing ends.

Constructing a political dialogue that mitigates the weaknesses and exploits the strengths of Latino media becomes all the more crucial if we remember that the discourses of dominance will continue to face crises of signification. Some crises will be triggered by social upheavals caused by the growing disparities of late postindustrial capitalism; whereas others will result from the "multicultural" conflict powered by migration, demographic change, and the continuing communication revolution. The blurring distinction between media programming and computer software will also continue to produce periods of discourse disequilibrium, as will the continuing decline of Fordist mass media and emerging post-Fordist demassified information industries. The atomization of media markets into ever smaller units will provide temporary tactical opportunities for Latino cultural workers to develop innovative progressive programming for economically viable ethnic audiences, but only if they can obtain needed technical assistance. The recent upsurge in computer purchases among Latinos suggests that some of the cultural benefits of Internet access may become more widely available to middle- and working-class Latinos than initially anticipated. In this way, members of the emerging ethnic pluralities in the nation's image-making cities, both as consumers and workers, may acquire the tools with which to mobilize discursive responses when social and cultural upheavals recur. Each moral panic constructed by the state and the media also presents an opportunity for critical analysis and community action when anticipated in the Latino metropolis. The Latino community's success at advancing a political as well as cultural discourse of *mestizaje* can thus acquire strategic significance, both for the community itself and for other communities disappeared by dominant media discourses. Counterdiscourse based upon inclusion, that renders hybridity, ambiguity, and border experience meaningful and empowering, and that makes racialized categories uninhabitable, will provide a nation as heterodox as the United States the acid with which to deconstruct its prisons of race and gender. To the degree a discourse of cultural *mestizaje* is not touted as a new orthodoxy, we believe it represents the greatest contribution Latinos will yet make to the United States. And Los Angeles, the nation's multicultural metropolis, will be the place where that contribution will first become evident.

NOTES

1. George Skelton, "Now Latinos Are Changing the Face of Both Parties," *Los Angeles Times,* November 23, 1998, A1.

2. A recent study by the United Way of Greater Los Angeles found that as of September 1999 there were 240 Latinos holding elective office in L.A. County, most serving in city posts and on school boards. See United Way of Greater Los Angeles, Research Services, *American Dream Makers: Executive Summary* (Los Angeles, January 2000).

3. Gregory Rodriguez, "The Impending Collision of Eastside and Westside," *Los Angeles Times,* August 3, 1997, M1, M3.

4. R. Scott Moxley, "No Hits, One Run, 200 Errors: Hermandad Probes' Central Figure Returns from Mexico," *O.C. Weekly,* August 14–20, 1998, 14.

5. Ibid.

6. Ted Rohrlich, "Latino Voting in State Surged in 1996 Election," *Los Angeles Times,* December 31, 1997, A1.

7. Ibid.

8. Rodriguez, "The Impending Collision," M1, M3.

9. Ibid., B3.

10. Nativo Lopez, interview by Victor Valle, tape recording, Occidental College, Los Angeles, October 14, 1998.

11. Ibid.

12. Ibid.

13. Beth Shuster, "New Latino Political Picture Offers Opportunity," *Los Angeles Times,* October 5, 1998, B12–B13.

14. David M. Grant, Melvin L. Oliver, and Angela D. James, "African Americans: Social and Economic Bifurcation," in *Ethnic Los Angeles,* ed. Roger Waldinger and Mehdi Bozorgmehr (New York: Russell Sage Foundation, 1996), 382.

15. Nativo Lopez, interview by Victor Valle, tape recording, Occidental College, Los Angeles, October 3, 1998.

16. Jim Newton, "Council Size Issue to Be Put to the Voters," *Los Angeles Times,* October 20, 1998, B2.

17. Lopez interview, October 14, 1998.

18. Manuel Pastor Jr., "Advantaging the Disadvantaged through International Trade" (Merril College, University of California, Santa Cruz, July 1998, photocopy), 11–13.

19. Michael Rustin, "The Politics of Post-Fordism; or, The Trouble with 'New Times,'" *New Left Review* 175 (May/June 1989): 66.

20. Mike Davis, *Ecology of Fear: Los Angeles and the Imagination of Disaster* (New York: Metropolitan, 1998), 404.

21. Gregory Rodriguez, "The Emerging Latino Middle Class," Pepperdine University Institute for Public Policy AT&T paper, October 1996, 7–12.

22. Ibid., 12.

23. Ibid., 12–13.

24. Robert A. Rosenblatt and Vicki Torres, "Number of Latino Firms Up 76 Percent in 5 Years; California Has Most," *Los Angeles Times,* July 11, 1996, D1; Lee Romney, "Hispanic Cheese: Haute Item," *Los Angeles Times,* June 16, 1998, A1, A32.

25. Ivan Light and Elizabeth Roach, "Self-Employment: Mobility Ladder or Economic Lifeboat?" in *Ethnic Los Angeles,* ed. Roger Waldinger and Mehdi Bozorgmehr (New York: Russell Sage Foundation, 1996), 198.

26. Ibid, 200–201, see Table 7.2.

27. Ibid., 205, see Table 7.4.

28. Ibid., 209.

29. Rohrlich, "Latino Voting in State Surged," A1.

30. Sandra Hernandez, "Inside Agitators: The City's Most Effective Activists," *L.A. Weekly,* October 2–8, 1998, 38.

31. Lopez, interview, October 3, 1998.

32. Harold Meyerson, "Activists Turned Elected Officials," *L.A. Weekly,* October 2–8, 1998, 30.

33. Rodriguez, "The Impending Collision," M1, M3.

34. Lopez, interview, October 3, 1998.

35. Escalante cited in Melita Marie Garza, "Hola, America! Newsstand 2000," *Media Studies Journal* 8 (summer 1994): 157.

36. Vivian Chavez and Lori Dorfman, "Spanish-Language Television News Portrayals of Youth and Violence in California," *International Quarterly of Community Health Education* 16, no. 2 (1996): 121–38.

37. Unfortunately, the underdeveloped state of Latino media studies means that cause-and-effect correlations between media coverage and political participation can still only be surmised.

38. Sandra Hernandez, "Stuck in Translation: La Opinión Searches for Readers—and a Mission—in the Times' Shadow," *L.A. Weekly,* June 11–17, 1999, 6.

39. Ibid., 2–9.

40. For example, the Bus Riders Union, led by Eric Mann, the labor veteran who in the 1980s battled GM to stop it from shutting down its Van Nuys plant, organized a cross section of Los Angeles's working-class bus riders to launch a civil rights court battle that stopped the MTA from allocating hundreds of millions in public funds for sorely needed bus service to underground rail projects targeted for a tiny minority of suburban, middle-class commuters.

41. Sharon Zukin, *The Culture of Cities* (Cambridge, Mass.: Blackwell, 1995), 263.

42. Edward W. Said, *Culture and Imperialism* (New York: Alfred A. Knopf, 1993), 58.

43. Roberto Gonzalez Echevarria, "Latin America and Comparative Literature," in *Poetics of the Americas: Race, Founding, and Textuality,* ed. Bainard Cowan and Jefferson Humphries (Baton Rouge: Louisiana State University Press, 1997), 50.

44. See, for example, the incisive work of Sonia Saldívar-Hull, *Feminism on the Border: Chicano Gender Politics and Literature* (Berkeley: University of California Press, 2000).

45. Renato Rosaldo, *Culture and Truth: The Remaking of Social Analysis* (Boston: Beacon, 1989), 209.

46. Ibid., 217.

✳ ✳ ✳

QUESTIONS

1. What are the changes that make it necessary to negotiate and reconceptualize the role of Latino/as in the United States?

2. Do the conditions described by Valle and Torres lead to the possibility for Chicanos in southern California to establish regional autonomy?

3. How persuasive is the argument that class interests will override ethnic conflicts between Latino/as, African Americans, Asians, Anglos, and other groups?

4. If the Latino/a community "cannot afford to put all its faith in market forces," what other options are available? And what might be the implications of such options?

5. To what extent do or do not the views in this piece regarding culture and race echo other concepts of "culture"?

* 28 *
THE DECOLONIAL IMAGINARY:
WRITING CHICANAS INTO HISTORY

Emma Pérez

Emma is an archeologist of knowledge and her writings clearly indicate what a complex task it is to explain why people suffer under this or that oppression or, more specifically, what a complex task it is to integrate women into history (see Cherríe Moraga's "Queer Aztlán," chapter 18). This complexity is transferred into the language of the explanation. While challenging to read, this brief excerpt from her book illustrates what we consider the most recent effort in a quest for citizenship. Emma is attempting to break through the rules for the control of discourse and thus to open up spaces for the voices of women to be heard. To do so, she uses Foucault's ideas on the relation between power and knowledge to invent a new category to help us rethink the past in a way that acknowledges the transformative power of Chicana/o agency.

Emma calls this the "decolonial imaginary," a "third space feminist" critique. It is intangible and invisible; "it acts much like a shadow in the dark." Furthermore, the "shadow is the figure between the subject and object on which it is cast, moving and breathing through an in-between space." In other words, it is a power that is effective precisely because it is invisible, one that affects our everyday lives, our behaviors and gestures. "Orientalism," "Chicanology,"[1] and "decolonial imaginary" are terms that acknowledge that categories are insufficient to contain the exuberance of human experience, which like a rhizome appears in the most unlikely crevices. While for some the future of Latino/a politics is in the recognition of its working-class dimension, for Emma the "historian's political project . . . is to write a history that decolonizes otherness." The key question is not class struggle but the liberation of desire from disciplinary power.

NOTE

1. "Chicanology," the Logos of, by, and for Chicanos (Francisco Hernández Vázquez, "Chicanology: A Postmodern Analysis of Meshicano Discourse," *Perspectives in Mexican American Studies* 3 [1992]: 116–47), is similar to Said's notion of *Orientalism* (New York: Pantheon, 1978). It is defined as a corporation of knowledge that uses the control of discourse, including literature, the social sciences, and the law, to seduce, oppress, discipline, and normalize the discourse of Chicano/a Latino/a bodies.

✳   ✳   ✳

MALINCHE, THE PHALLIC MOTHER:
THE CASTRATION FANTASY

In "Sexuality and Discourse: Notes from a Chicana Survivor," I probed the Oedipal arrangement as a metaphor for colonial sexual relations. Freud's Oedipus is generated by repressed desire, produced by a prohibition that can be reduced to the following dictum: "you will not marry your mother, and you will not kill your father."[1] These repressed desires are retained within the unconscious mind and body; the desiring mind and body are therefore sculpted by repression. What would it mean to defy Oedipus in colonial/neo-colonial regions such as the Southwest, where sexualities are dictated and encoded upon the body by the law everywhere, but in specific ways, depending upon regional laws and morals? In *Anti-Oedipus,* Deleuze and Guattari claim that we have been fooled by the Oedipal triangle. Instead, desire and its machines may offer an alternative. They suggest that "desire is revolutionary," while the Oedipal triangle is the entanglement that entraps us. I argued that Oedipus is the Western colonial-sexual prototype imprinted upon the colonial subject who has to enter new psychic terrain in order to resist Oedipus. That new terrain is "desire," with all its potential to disrupt repressive social machines. But can we move beyond Oedipus? Has it been so encoded upon our bodies, their desires, that we are doomed to repetition, a repetition which, I think, recycles a specific Chicano nationalism rooted in patriarchal discourse and activism? Again I contend that sexuality and its discourse is precisely the problem we face in Chicana/o nationalisms and feminisms. The Oedipal triangle reemerges, like the "return of the repressed," to haunt relationships. *Anti-Oedipus* may attempt liberatory relationships and freedom from the Oedipal arrangement, but even they are already inscribed by the past.

That which I attempted in "Sexuality and Discourse" was a prescribed method for deconstructing Chicano/a ideologies and dominant thoughts that have sculpted our histories. Chicano/a history, I claimed in chapter 1 of [my book *Decolonial Imaginary: Writing Chicanas into History* (Bloomington: University of Indiana Press, 1999)], excluded voices that did not conform to a dominant intellectual paradigm being constructed and written. "Sexuality and Discourse" challenged the way "sex" and its language, often silenced, implicitly guide the minds of those writing our histories. By focusing upon Octavio Paz and his denigrations of La Malinche, I devised what I called the Oedipus Conquest Complex to interrogate preconceptions about Indias/mestizas/Chicanas. The corrido, or ballad, about Delgadina also critiques a dominant, all-encompassing patriarchal "order of things" that demands disclosure. In other words, even when unnamed, sexual power relations are present, often hidden and unspoken yet performed between and among people.

But whose desire is enacted? Whose Oedipal moment is privileged? The "nation" becomes the family. Nationalism becomes the "return to the mother," the original place or space. Aztlán is that symbolic original place where the nation will survive again in pre-Oedipal bliss. Women are not allowed to be sexed or to have sex; therefore sexual difference is not possible for Chicanas. They can be only pre-Oedipal, hence pre-sexual, in this scenario of nationalism. Only men may have their Oedipal moment, their castration fantasy, hence their sex. Feminism disrupts this pre-Oedipal space in which the womb symbolizes Aztlán. The nationalist imperative is to move back in time, a regression, a return to the mother, but the mother cannot be Malinche. She must be La Virgen de Guadalupe; she cannot be sexual. She must be pure for the nationalist dream. In this way, Aztlán is not an empirical, internal colony, but an imaginary, a maternal imaginary, while the father's significance is something else. He has many possibilities under patriarchal nationalism; he is many heroes—from Emiliano Zapata to Ruben Salazar. He is not an object; nor is he represented through the "land"; nor is he judged for being whore or virgin. He is always already a hero, a leader—a leader who must lead his people to a land. And the land is maternal; it is pure, virginal; it is where the family will all be safe in the womb. Hence, nationalism becomes a return to the mother—Aztlán—where woman can be only metaphor and object. When she has agency like La Malinche, she is repudiated by the nation as the betrayer, the whore, la chingada. Just as Oedipus is everywhere, always, reinscribing sociosexual and cultural relations, for Indias/mestizas/Chicanas La Malinche is always everywhere, reinscribing women's agency. In Chicano/a myths, histories, tropes, taxonomies, and so on, La Malinche cannot be avoided. La Malinche encodes all sociosexual relations and there is no way out. Well, maybe there has been a way out. Feminists have reinscribed Malinche with new "flesh," with a new imagined history.[2] For Chicana feminists, Malinche has become the powerful mother—not the phallic mother feared by modernist, patriarchal nationalists, but an enduring mother, a cultural survivor who bore a mestizo race.

POWER/DESIRE

To discuss power and desire, I call upon Foucault, who continues to incite and inspire poststructural and postcolonial theorists. His work, encoded with desire, has contested our contemporary society with insights on power/knowledge. His *Technologies of the Self* has guided many, including feminist theorist Teresa de Lauretis, who scrutinizes social construction and its "technologies of gender." In *The Practice of Love,* de Lauretis rereads Freud's theory, a "negative theory of sexuality [in which] perversion appears as the negative or nether side of . . . so-called sexual normality."[3] She elaborates upon "a model of desire that goes beyond the Oedipus complex and in its own way resolves it" for the perverse, intimating lesbians.[4] De Lauretis reads Freud with Foucault's "self-analysis," or technology of the self, to conclude finally how society designs the body, its desires, and more specifically lesbian desire. Foucault began to theorize the inscription of history upon the body, and how the material body itself was engraved with psychic desires that could be realized in any number of ways. That he was so intrigued with sadomasochism as a form of queer liberation also demonstrates how he thought desire moved beyond the moralism and ethics of contemporary Eurowestern "family values." The normal or normative was and has been considered heterosexuality in Europe and in the Americas since the sixteenth century. Any deviation from the "law," from so-called "normal" heterosexuality, was deemed "criminal," and therefore had to be punished or disciplined. Criminals and deviants became one and the same. Both had to be disciplined by "moral engineering," which reconstructed bodies and pleasures to fit society's "natural laws."[5] Lodged in this repressive society is power—power *over* desire, a power to police desire, to remake the deviant into the "normal." In *History of Sexuality*, Foucault aims his discourse at the conflict between power and desire. The question for Foucault, then, is what do we do when the desire for power overwhelms and polices the power of desire?

How do we reinscribe our bodies with the passions of desire when power and desire are so enmeshed? In his preface to *Anti-Oedipus*, Foucault asked,

> How does one keep from being fascist, even (especially) when one believes oneself to be a revolutionary militant? How do we rid our speech and our acts, our hearts and our pleasures, of fascism? How do we ferret out the fascism that is ingrained in our behavior?[6]

A dangerous, fascist militancy is tantamount to a nationalism that repudiates women's voices, intolerant of any differences. That is the space where power polices desire. We are threatened once again by a reemergence of uncompromising nationalist movements in which feminisms are dismissed as bourgeois, in which queer voices are scoffed at as a white thing, in which anyone who does not sustain the "family values" of modernist, patriarchal nationalism is not tolerated and is often silenced. This reemergence *is* the return of the repressed, where a community becomes fascist, staging a revolution that trivializes sexualities, differences, and technologies of desire.

The Mexican Revolution and its nationalism has served as a history lesson for the Chicano/a movement. I attempted to speak to this in part two of [my] book. But the women of the revolution have been so idealized and romanticized that they have come to represent for contemporary Chicano nationalists imagined values and morals to fit a nationalist paradigm. Chicanas are expected to mimic the Adelitas, camp followers who serviced the male soldiers, cooking tortillas and mating with the men. Early-twentieth-century journalist John Reed chronicled the Mexican Revolution and wrote a popular account of soldaderas epitomizing the passive, willing Mexicana eager to be protected by a male soldier, any male soldier. When one partner died, she simply took up with another.[7] Reed interpreted this as passive acceptance, not agency. What Reed also overlooks are the soldaderas who were tortilleras—marimachas, mariconas, and jotas; but of course, historical erasure has not permitted those queer voices to be heard. Elizabeth Salas, in her study *Soldaderas in the Mexican Military*, hints at some of the women who cross-dressed in male uniforms, not only to survive the revolution, but to engineer their own revolution.[8] But women's activism often disappears even when they are weaving their politics differentially in historical movements such as the Mexican Revolution. In chapters 2 and 3, I argued that Mexican feminists during the Revolution of 1910 spoke and acted a feminism-in-nationalism, moving within dominant discourses of nationalism that wanted to relegate them to gender-specific duties. Contemporary nationalist discourses imitate similar demands.

DESIRE AND HISTORY

Will history, its memory, its desire, free us, navigate us through passion where the unthought, the unspoken, shuffle through unidentifiable spaces, moving us out of Oedipus, from the colonial imaginary into identities where power relations that police, whether from above or below, are disrupted by a decolonial imaginary? I have suggested that some answers lie in a psychic terrain, that unseen region where our only hope is a new consciousness, a healing consciousness, where desiring devices can serve to free us and not obstruct, stifle, and limit our identities.

Desire, its historical construction, its discourse, has been repressive, even fascist, in its colonial forms. Silent Tongue and her mestiza daughters, Delgadina, and La Malinche—all had to negotiate colonial desire practiced upon their physical, psychic bodies. Selena, however, represents the move toward decolonial desire. Women's desires have been like archaeological silences. How do we name and theorize the new machines of this revolutionary desire, whether using metaphors of the third space or metaphors as yet unspoken? Desire nonetheless stubbornly occupies the colonial imaginary, where its passion is often caged in political-social institutions where power in its doubling effect works for us and against us. The challenge is to redefine the rules of formation, as I have argued, in historical studies to voice our many differences, to sift out the technologies of decolonial desire, where the colonial object may fantasize her desires to become decolonial subject. Ultimately, the point is to move beyond colonialist history by implementing the decolonial imaginary with a third space feminist critique to arrive finally at postcoloniality, where postnational identities may surface.

Throughout this chapter, I have specified how "Sexuality and Discourse" are relevant to history and its historiographic construction. I recapitulated how history—its stories, narration, studies—is devised through power, through knowledge, through sexuality erased, empowered, silenced, or imposed upon historical bodies. In other words, sexuality and its discourse can be a methodological instrument for historiography, a historiography that witnesses power relations that cannot be avoided—power relations established through sexualities that remain unspoken, unsaid, even avoided, yet always already present. Somewhere between Foucault's archaeology and genealogy, supplemented with a perverse reading of psychoanalysis, may lie new perspectives for understanding the making, or the poetics, of history and its study.

THIRD SPACE FEMINIST (RE)VISION

Forget the Alamo.

—Pilar in *Lone Star*

When Pilar, the mixed-race Chicana in the John Sayles film *Lone Star,* ends the film with a resolute, quiet, matter-of-fact "forget the Alamo," she is reinscribing a colonial imaginary with a decolonial one.[9] At that liberatory moment, the decolonial imaginary is enacted as hope, as love, transcending all that has come before, all that has been inherited only to damage daughters and sons who have fallen heir to a history of conquest, of colonization, of hatred between brown and white. "Let's start from scratch," she pleads to the man she loves, despite just having learned from him that they are half-brother and half-sister, a secret kept from them by Pilar's Mexican mother and Sam's Anglo father, who were clandestine lovers in the small, generically named border town of Frontera, Texas. Sam, Pilar's lover, her half-brother, the post-modern Euroamerican, fragmented in his responsibilities as sheriff in a racist town, nods his head faintly, agreeing. We know by now that his love for Pilar is immutable. For the lovers, to "forget the Alamo" and "start from scratch," as they sit in front of a blank white drive-in movie screen in the light of day, means they have agreed to remake their story, to transcend an inhibiting, treacherous past. The blank screen in front of them represents newness. But Pilar speaks the words, not Sam. If Sam had spoken them, I would have walked away from the theater a cynic, disappointed and angry because one more time, a white man was trying to persuade me to forget a history of brutality and move on. John Sayles, perhaps himself the postmodern man, wrote the script and directed the actors, and he is indeed the white man who once again will attempt to persuade me to erase a history that still brutalizes. But somehow, by placing the words in Pilar's mouth, he has unwittingly compelled me to listen and wonder why I have been so jolted.

I, a tejana by cultural construction, have been trying all my life to forget the Alamo, but ironically I chose history as my profession. As a historian, I cannot forget the Alamo; as a tejana, I am not allowed to forget the Alamo. It is imprinted upon my body, my memories, my childhood. But to hear the words "Forget the Alamo" from a Chicana is, for me, a freeing, a freedom from a history that nags me for revision. I'm anxious to move to another site of remembrance. I am anxious to remake and reclaim another story—stories of love, of compassion, of hope.

I am, however, caught in the time lag between the colonial and the postcolonial, in a decolonial imaginary reinscribing the old with the new. My history of Chicanas, a feminist history, has been written inside a decolonial time lag, with a third space feminist critique, between what has been, what is, and what many of us hope will be. All at once we live the past, present, and future. History itself has encoded upon it a tool for a liberatory consciousness. Marx was probably the first theorist-philosopher to teach this lesson to Chicana/o historians. It has taken Foucault, however, to warn us that power/knowledge disrupts the classic terrain of binaries. We can no longer resort to simple binaries that determine enemies or friends according to their color, class status, gender, sexualities, and any other differences that become our historical bodies. If we choose to enact the tool of history and call it third space feminist consciousness, as I have done throughout [my] book, then we begin to build another story, uncovering the untold to consciously remake the narrative. Third space feminism allows a look to the past through the present always already marked by the coming of that which is still left unsaid, unthought. Moreover, it is in the maneuvering through time to retool and remake subjectivities neglected and ignored that third space feminism claims new histories, Chicana feminist histories that may one day—finally—"forget the Alamo."

NOTES

1. Gilles Deleuze and Felix Guattari, *Anti-Oedipus: Capitalism and Schizophrenia* (Minneapolis: University of Minnesota Press, 1983), 114.

2. La Malinche has been represented in art, poetry, short stories, novels, films, and essays. I provide only a few examples. The following are literary and historical accounts: Norma Alarcón, "Chicana's Feminist Literature: A Re-vision through Malintzin/or, Malintzin: Putting Flesh Back on the Object," in Cherríe Moraga and Gloria Anzaldúa, eds., *This Bridge Called My Back: A Collection of Writings by Radical Women of Color* (Watertown, Mass.: Persephone Press, 1981), 182–90; Deena González, "Malinche as Lesbian: A Reconfiguration of 500 Years of Resistance," *California Sociologist,* Special Issue, 14 (Winter/Summer 1991): 90–97; Sandra Messinger Cypess, *La Malinche in Mexican Literature: From History to Myth* (Austin: University of Texas Press, 1991); Joanne Danaher Chaison, "Mysterious Malinche: A Case of Mistaken Identity," *The Americas* 32 (April 1976), 514–23; Federico Fernández de Castillejo, *El amor de la conquista: Malintzin* (Buenos Aires, 1943); Paz, *The Labyrinth of Solitude;* Gustavo A. Rodriquez, *Doña Marina* (México, 1935). For a poem by a Chicana writer, see Alicia Gaspar de Alba, "Malinchista, a Myth Revised," in *Three Times a Woman* (Tempe, Ariz.: Bilingual Review Press, 1989), 16. For a fascinating short story in which the author plays with time, moving from the conquest to a modern-day Mexico, see Mexican writer Elena Garro, "La culpa es de los tlaxcaltecos," in *La semana de colores* (México, 1987), 11–29.

3. Teresa De Lauretis, *The Practice of Love: Lesbian Sexuality and Perverse Desire* (Bloomington: Indiana University Press, 1994), xi–xii.

4. Ibid., xix.

5. Hayden White, *The Content of the Form* (Baltimore: Johns Hopkins University Press, 1987); see pp. 128–29 for his discussion of "moral engineering." On p. 134 he refers to the "discipline of bodies and pleasures."

6. Deleuze and Guattari, *Anti-Oedipus,* xiii.

7. John Reed, *Insurgent Mexico* (New York: D. Appleton and Co., 1914), 99–109.

8. Elizabeth Salas, *Soldaderas in the Mexican Military: Myth and History* (Austin: University of Texas Press, 1990).

9. When I was growing up in Texas, I remember my father telling me how he would argue with co-workers about history and remind them to forget the Alamo.

QUESTIONS

1. Are there any statements that remain "unsaid" in your everyday life? Are there any thoughts that you feel are forbidden? If you were to dare to think "the unthinkable," what would that be?

2. What feelings, desires do you have that you feel unable to express due to fear of being disciplined either by peer or family pressure or by regulations and laws?

3. In what sense can we say that desire is a political force?

4. Emma claims that "We can no longer resort to simple binaries that determine enemies or friends according to their color, class status, gender, sexualities, and any other differences that become our historical bodies." What impact does this statement have on the notion that, "in the final analysis," class struggle over the means of production is the most important factor?

5. Does Emma have a teleological vision? That is, does she imagine a time in history where we all live happily ever after? What is your own vision in this regard?

* 29 *
A POSTDEMOCRATIC ERA

Guillermo Gómez-Peña

At the tail (or the mouth, depending on your perspective) of the serpent, Guillermo's text raises a very important question, one that we have been trying to figure out from the many identities that are forced upon human bodies: who are we? Appropriately enough, this short text is part of a collection, under the general title *Reflections on the Culture of Despair,* in which Guillermo attempts to articulate the philosophical and political complexities of this decade. In a concise manner, he touches upon the topics covered by previous articles in this collection: the difficulty of finding a language to express our fears or desires, a post-something era in which concern for human bodies is not a government concern or even on the political agenda. In such a world, Guillermo calls for new models of citizen collaboration and multilateral cooperation, or what we have called a quest for public citizenship.

We experience the end of the world . . . and the word, as we know them, and the beginning of a new era. Perhaps our main frustration is our total inability to envision the characteristics and features of the coming age. It's a bit like being drunk in the middle of an earthquake, and not having a language to express our fears. But who are *we* anyway?

We now live in world without theory, without ethics, without ideology. Our spiritual metahorizons are rapidly fading, and so are our geopolitical borders. Nation-states collapse in slow motion before our swelling eyes. As they crumble, they are immediately replaced by multinational macro-communities governed by invisible corporate boards, "trading partners," and media trusts. Composed of cold-blooded technocrats and clean-cut neoliberals who position themselves at the center of the center of nothingness, the new political class believes—or perhaps pretends to believe—that free trade and a healthy economy are the solutions to all our problems, even the cultural and social ones. They have no (visible) blood on their hands. They simply press buttons and computer keys. They silently exchange and transfer capital, products and weapons, from continent to continent.

In this unprecedented "postdemocratic era" (if I may call it that), basic humanistic concerns are no longer part of the agenda for these politicos. Civic, human and labor rights, education, and art are perceived as minor privileges, expendable budget items, and dated concerns. Both the politicians and the media seem to have lost (or willingly abandoned) the ability to address the fundamental issues and ask the crucial questions: with all their rhetoric of globalization, why are the US and Western Europe retrenching to isolationist and xenophobic positions, advocating nativist policies and criminalizing immigrants? Why do they advocate open borders from North to South, and closed borders from South to North? Why is Washington still bombing small nations in the post cold-war era? Why are all types of guns freely available to the citizenry of the US? Why does the death penalty still exist in certain so-called "First World" nations? Why are policemen so rarely punished when they engage in acts of brutality? Why are most educational systems bankrupt and dysfunctional? Why are the homeless living in the streets? Why have the arts been defunded? Why aren't these questions being asked in national forums?

In our crumbling postdemocracies, humanism has become a mere corporate "interest" or "goal," a quaint topic explored by the Discovery Channel, a trendy marketing strategy for computer firms. In this new context, artists and intellectuals don't seem to perform any meaningful role other than that of decorators of the omnipresent *horror vacui* and entertainers of a new, more tolerant and cynical consumer class.

As far as I am concerned, we have no real government looking after the human being. The homeless, the elderly, our children and teens, and the newly arrived immigrants from the South are completely on their own. Alone and abandoned in the virtual jungle of advanced capitalism, it is entirely up to us to figure out what can be the new models of citizen collaboration and multilateral cooperation, the new terms for a new social and cultural contract, the new artistic rituals to give voice to our rage, shape our eclectic spiritualities and our fragmented identities. In this sense, citizen responsibility, community action and the creation of a civilian *logos* have been for me the most crucial issues of the 90s. This presentation is a humble expression of a search for new metaphors and images to begin articulating our new place in a foreign world, as well as a humble call for community action. But the main question remains unanswered: who are the remaining *we*? Who is left to listen and respond to this call?

PART V

CONCLUSION

THIS LONG JOURNEY REVEALS THAT LATINO/A POLITICAL thought was born from the realities of military, economic, and cultural conquest. It has been shaped by the struggle between the self-determination of Latin American nations and peoples and the needs and desires of the U.S. political economy, and it is currently an increasingly audible voice in (inter)national discourse.

There is an obvious need to create structures that protect human bodies: structures that give them a voice in policy making, structures that produce justice. One problem is the durable inequalities, the difference between being wealthy and being rich in financial and social capital terms. This is where the forces of habit and tradition play a role. At the same time, it is a matter of configurations of relations of power that are beyond our control. These blocks of power relations could be in the form of a union of workers, or of women, or of men or gays or dark-skinned people or nationalists, or even of regional blocks such as the Caribbean or transnational blocks such as the European Union and NAFTA. The problem is that the present institutional arrangements do not include certain kinds of human bodies in the sort of arrangements that produce justice. For Latino/as, this means that those with particular historical experiences, such as Mexicans (especially the immigrants and more recent arrivals) and Puerto Ricans, are left out of the dominant discourses. Others, such as Cuban Americans, with different sets of historical experiences, have appropriated discourse in more effective ways. But this is at the general level of ethnic/national identity. Within each of these groupings of human bodies are subjectifications according to class, skin color, and gender that spell out (in)justice for them.

As the notion of authority shifts, as manifested by the postmodern practice of parody that can also be described as attitudes of irreverence and sarcasm, we need to recognize our complicity in the construction of social reality. As Unamuno observed, we must act in order to make the principle true, not because the principle is true. We must come to the realization that power is within each one of us. In this way, we build structures that produce justice. It is vital to realize, however, that individual efforts are necessary but not sufficient; we need to imagine, invent, and fight to institutionalize appropriate relations of power; we need to sculpt, out of the materiality of language, political activities, programs, and institutions that will give a voice to the oppressed. The true (global) *polis* depends on the Furies' call for justice, not only for all tribes, but also for all human bodies and against the categorizations that have made history a bloody and painful nightmare.

APPENDIXES

✳ Appendix 1A ✳
THE DEVELOPMENT OF WORLD HISTORICAL SOCIAL MOVEMENTS

	1776–1789	*1848*	*1905*	*1917*	*1968*
Ascendant Revolutionary Classes	Bourgeoisie	Urban proletariat	Rural proletariat	Urban and rural working class	New working class
Emergent Organizations	Representative assemblies	Insurrectionary parliaments and political parties	Soviets/councils	Vanguard party	Action committees/ collectives
Vision/ Aspirations	Formal democracy; liberty, equality, fraternity	Economic democracy; trade unions; democratic constitutions	Universal suffrage; unions; freedom from empires	Socialism as the "Dictatorship of the Proletariat"; land, bread, and peace	Self-management; all power to the people/ imagination
Tactics	Revolutionary War	Popular insurrections	General strike	Organized seizure of power	Contestation of public space/everyday life

Source: George Katsiaficas, *The Imagination of the New Left* (Boston: South End, 1987).

* Appendix 1B *
COMPARATIVE CHRONOLOGY OF MAJOR EVENTS IN CUBAN, MEXICAN, PUERTO RICAN, AND U.S. POLITICAL HISTORY

Dates	Cuba	Mexico	Puerto Rico	United States	World
1450s–1490s	Arawaks rule	Aztecs rule over tribes in Mesoamerica	Tainos rule Borinquen, Columbus finds island in second trip	Indigenous tribes rule their own regions	Age of "discoveries," Spain is born as a nation after Jews, Arabs kicked out
1500s–1540s	Conquest of Cuba, founding of Santiago and Habana	Spanish conquest, 95% of indigenous people killed by European disease	Founding of Caparra, San Juan becomes capital	Formation of Powhattan Confederacy	Luther launches Protestant Reformation
1550s–1590s	Hapsburgs' policies stifle economic and political growth in all Spanish colonies	Spanish explore and claim what is now the U.S. southwest	British pirates attack	Formation of the League of the Iroquois	Britain defeats Spain's armada
1600s–1640s			Dutch fleet attacks, building of El Morro Fortress	Pilgrims land at Plymouth, slaves arrive at Virginia, white-Indian wars	Russian fur traders on Pacific Coast, English Civil War
1650s–1690s		Hapsburgs' policies stifle economic growth	City of Ponce founded on south coast	Founding of New York and New Jersey	England's Glorious Revolution
1700s–1740s	Bourbons bring more open policies	Bourbons restructure New Spain	Mayaguez is founded on the west coast	English and French move into Ohio valley	British attempt to increase colonial revenues
1750s–1790s	British attack and occupy	California missions established	British attack	Stamp Act riots, Boston Tea Party, Revolutionary War	French Revolution

Dates	Cuba	Mexico	Puerto Rico	United States	World
1800s–1840s	Loyal to Spain during revolutionary wars, U.S. investment and offer to buy for $100 million	Independence from Spain, loss of Texas, war with the United States	Remains loyal to Spain during revolutionary wars	War with England, settlers move into Texas and Oregon, war with Mexico	Congress of Vienna tries to bring stability to Europe, social uprisings occur
1850s–1890s	United States offers to buy for $130 million, Spain grants autonomy, Spanish-American War, Treaty of Paris	Wars of reform: Juárez separates church and state, French Intervention, Porfirio Diaz dictatorship	Grito de Lares, slavery abolished, Spain grants autonomy, Spanish-American War, Treaty of Paris	Civil War, Spanish-American War	Tremendous growth of scientific thought and applications to industry, agriculture, and other areas, Franco-Prussian War as a prelude to World War I
1900s–1950s	Protectorate of the United States, open for political and economic intervention for its own good	Plan de San Diego, Mexican Revolution, LULAC, Repatriation, Bracero Program	Colony of the United States, Foraker Act, Jones Act, Ponce Massacre, allowed to elect own governor	Philippines fight American rule, World War I, Great Depression, World War II, Cold War, economic expansion	First social revolutions in Mexico and Russia, Spanish Civil War
1950s–1990s	Batista's dictatorship backed by United States, Castro's regime, exile community in the United States	Operation Wetback, Bracero Program ends, Chicano Power, Farmworkers union	Free associated state of the United States, Nationalists attack House of Representatives	Korean War, Cold War, missile crisis, man on the moon, Vietnam War, civil rights and Counterculture movements	Fall of Soviet Union, AIDS epidemic, Internet, global warming, genocides in Africa and Eastern Europe
2000s	Cubans try to build bridges, despite Elian Gonzalez incident	First president in seventy years from a party other than PRI	First woman governor elected	Contentious presidential election, government split evenly among parties, attack on United States (September 11, 2001) leads to war against terrorist groups and states that harbor them, to economic decline, and to threat against civil liberties	The global market controls all aspects of life on the planet

❋ Appendix 2A ❋
MEXICO'S NORTHERN TERRITORIES LOST TO CONQUEST
OR BOUGHT BY THE UNITED STATES

❋ Appendix 2B ❋
Puerto Rico and Cuba: Strategic Locations for U.S. Security and for Migration to the United States

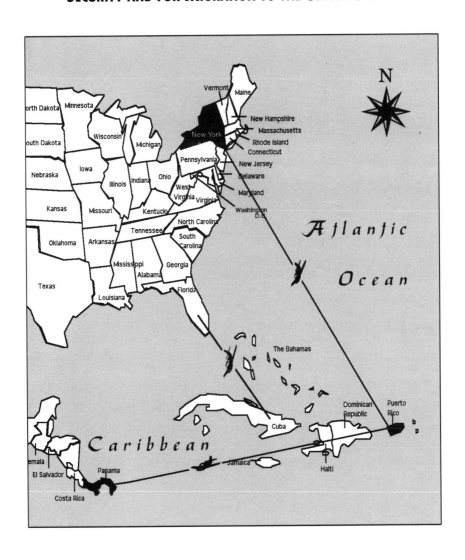

✳ Appendix 3 ✳
CHART OF LATINO/A POLITICAL DISCOURSE AS PRESENTED IN THE READER

These statements are put into operation with the same regularity as the governing statements, but with a regularity that is more delicately articulated, more clearly delimited, and localized through the appearance of new technical improvements and conceptual transformations, and through the rules and procedures for the control and production of discourse.	*Biopower:* Beyond nationalism and colonialism; people's desires against the structures of nation-states and essentialized positions	Part IV: The present, 2000–?
	—	—
	The National Question: How do Latino/as want to be free of U.S. domination?	Part III: A continuing discourse
	Assertion of political identities at the national, local, and interpersonal levels	Part II: 1960–2000
	—	—
	Mexicans under Siege Castro's Cuban revolution Puerto Rican nationalism	Part II: 1900–1960
	—	—
	Puerto Ricans subjectivized as a possession of the U.S. Congress Cubans subjectivized as U.S. cultural citizens Mexicans subjectivized as ethnics	Nineteenth century: 1898 1848
	—	
	Scattered uprisings Treaties that make Mexican, Puerto Rican, and Cuban bodies part of the U.S. Polity	
Governing statements: 　1. Put into operation rules of formation of discourse in their most extended form. 　2. Present the most general possibilities of characterization. 　3. While constituting a strategic choice, leave room for the greatest number of options.	• racial theories • land grab • establishment of the colonial system • physical and psychological violence • justice system • nationalistic attitudes • educational processes • internal divisions (class, gender, color, religion, nationality, youth gangs, etc.) • right of self-preservation	

✳ Appendix 4 ✳
CHART OF DISCURSIVE ANALYSIS

DISCOURSE

OBJECTS	SUBJECTIVITIES	CONCEPTS	INSTITUTIONS	BIOPOWER
Things that draw attention and dominate a field of reality, a regime of truth.	Spaces that open up in a discourse or statement to be occupied or assigned to individuals who claim to speak the truth.	Ideas, theories, ideologies, philosophies, systems of thought that claim to explain what is true and why.	Behaviors, procedures that endure through time; they define social reality by supporting a regime of truth.	The human body as a physical and moral entity: the ultimate test for what is True once all the games of truth and power are played out.
OBJECT	SUBJECTIVITIES	CONCEPTS	INSTITUTIONS	BIOPOWER

STATEMENT

Note: "Discourse" encompasses the five categories above and functions like a paradigm, a model, a pattern, a theory, and a context for statements. When language ("what is said" anywhere, anytime, in any of the categories above) intersects power, it becomes a "Statement." When this occurs on a regular basis, it constitutes a "Discourse." (See the "Introduction for Students" for additional explanation.)

✳ Appendix 5 ✳
RULES AND PROCEDURES FOR THE CONTROL AND PRODUCTION OF DISCOURSE

The rules and procedures for the control of discourse listed and defined here are more fully illustrated, implicitly in this reader's articles and explicitly in the "Introduction for Students: Power/Knowledge, Language, and Everyday Life." These rules and procedures are an integral part of the formation of particular discourses that deploy political, economic, and cultural power relations. The term "microphysics of power" refers to these relations when they are deployed at their most specific level. That includes everyday social and cultural interactions, and legal, political, and economic transactions, such as conversations, courting, rituals, political meetings, going to court, buying, and selling. Something as minute as a facial expression, a look, or the lyrics of a song may be an expression of a microphysics of power. Their ultimate, powerful, impact defines them. The term "bio-power" refers to the notion that knowledge/power always impact human and other forms of life. In the final analysis, it is in this impact where power must be studied.

PROHIBITION

This is perhaps the most obvious procedure. It means you cannot speak, that your voice is completely invalidated, as in "Speak English, you are in America" or *"Tu cállate, tu eres un(a) tonto/a y no sabes nada."*

REASON/MADNESS

There is a more subtle technique of intervention in the control of discourse that is based on the contrast between Reason (usually on the side of the dominant power, as in *la gente de razón)* and Insanity (usually on the side of those who are subjugated).

TRUTH/FALSITY

An even more insidious technique to deny the validity of "what is said" is the assignment of the status of truth to certain events or statements. In other words, the

430

regime of truth appropriates the right to decide the distinction between true and false statements, the correct method to acquire knowledge, and who is qualified to speak the truth. As noted before, this is not a matter of what is true or false, but of what can be made to appear as true or false. The struggle to clarify Puerto Rico's political status represents this sort of game of truth.

ACADEMIC DISCIPLINES

Even in academic disciplines we find procedures of control in the production of truth. Disciplines allow us to build a discourse, but within a narrow framework. They are defined by groups of objects of study, by methods, by a body of propositions considered to be true (the literature), and by the interplay of rules, definitions, techniques, and tools. To speak the truth within a discipline, one must obey the rules of some discursive policy. That is why you hear statements like, "You don't sound like a political scientist."

STATUS OF INTELLECTUALS

There are various methods to limit the number of individuals who are given the charge of speaking the truth. One of these methods is the establishment of the status of the speaking individual through (1) criteria of competence; (2) systems of differentiation and relation with other individuals or groups with the same status; (3) the function of this status in relation to society in general and the Latino/a community in particular; (4) the institutional sites that lend legitimacy to their statements; and (5) the various positions occupied by the speaking individual in information networks. Who are the most influential Latino/as? How do they fulfill the above criteria and how do these criteria define them?

FELLOWSHIPS OF DISCOURSE

More restrictive than academic disciplines is the control of discourse performed by what may be called fellowships of discourse. Their function is to preserve, reproduce, or circulate discourse according to strict regulations and within a closed community (or even a secret society). One thinks of the members of a "good ol' boys network," who keep important information to themselves and their friends, gender, or family. There were also the *Penitentes* of New Mexico, a religious order whose members were, secretly, members of the militant guerrilla group known as Las Gorras Blancas.

DOCTRINE

At first glance, doctrine (religious, political, philosophical) would seem to be the opposite of a fellowship of discourse, for among the latter the number of individuals is, if not fixed, at least limited. It is among this number that discourse is allowed to circulate and be transmitted. Doctrine, on the other hand, tends toward diffusion. It is the holding in common of a discourse on which individuals, as many as possible, can define their reciprocal allegiance. In appearance, the only requisite is the recognition of the same truths and the acceptance of a rule of conformity with these truths. If it were a question of just that, doctrines would be barely different from scientific or academic disciplines. The control of discourse would bear only on the form or content of what was said. But doctrines involve both the speaker and the spoken. Doctrines involve the statements of speakers in the sense that they are permanently the instruments and manifestations of an adherence to a class; a social, ethnic, or racial status; a nationality, a struggle, a revolt. In short, doctrine links individuals to a certain type of statement while consequently barring them from all others. It brings about a dual subjection, that of speaking individuals to discourse and that of discourse to the group of individual speakers.

EDUCATION

On a much broader scale, education can be the social appropriation of discourse. Education is the instrument whereby every individual can gain access to any kind of discourse. But we well know that in its distribution, in what it permits, and in what it prevents it follows the well-defined battle lines of social conflict. Every educational system is a political means of maintaining or modifying the appropriation of discourse, with the knowledge and powers that it carries with it.

Of course, these forms of control of discourse—the status given to individual speakers, fellowships of discourse, doctrinal groups, and social appropriations—are linked together, constituting a corporation that distributes speakers among the different types of discourse. What is an educational system, after all, but the allocation of discourse to specific individual speakers, the constitution of a diffused doctrinal group, a distribution and appropriation of discourse with all its pedagogical powers?

NOTE

Adapted from Michel Foucault, *The Archaeology of Knowledge and the Discourse on Language* (New York: Pantheon Books, 1972), 215–37.

* Appendix 6 *
HISTORICAL MATERIALISM

What follows is a brief introduction to Marxist concepts and terminology that are used by some scholars, in the articles in this reader, and also by common people in most parts of the world. Historical materialism is an essential part of marxian reasoning; it was developed to explain why feudalism gave way to capitalism and why capitalism will give way to socialism. Below, it is presented in abbreviated form, and then each part of the theory is explained in detail.

At any given time, in historical materialism, people in society have a certain level of *productive ability:*

1. In the first place are the *productive forces* or the *material forces of production:* knowledge and skills, technology (computers, machines, tools, draft animals) and the natural environment.
2. This productive ability determines the *social relations of production.* These relations include (1) how people make a living (such as hunting and gathering, farming, working in industry, programming computers, banking) and (2) how people relate to one another in producing and exchanging the means of life (lord/serf, master/slave, capitalist/worker, global economy/consumer).
3. The combination of the productive forces and the social relations of production form the base, or *economic structure,* and it has a complex relationship with what is known as the *superstructure* (people's religious, political, intellectual, artistic, and legal systems).

[It is important to note that language is considered to be part of neither the base nor the superstructure, but as serving all classes at all times. Language is believed to be like a tool for communication but not exactly, because unlike any other "tool" known to humans, language tends to stay very much the same even after a particular base or superstructure disappears.]

THE PRODUCTIVE FORCES

The productive forces are (1) the material means of production that people use to gain a livelihood from nature; (2) the machines, tools, raw materials, and natural

433

resources available; (3) the human beings, their knowledge, talents, aspirations, and needs.

The development of productive forces occurs through labor, activity, and the growth of needs and abilities. As change takes place, people develop further capabilities and desires; thus, people make a living and make themselves at the same time.

People differ from animals in that they engage in purposeful productive activity, that is, they produce their means of subsistence consciously, not instinctively. This is done within a certain mode of production or economic structure. Human nature is determined by the mode of production under which people work to maintain human life—as the mode of production changes, so does human nature.

For example, men and women living under a feudal mode of production have values, aspirations, abilities, and needs that differ from those living under a capitalist mode of production. As feudal men and women designed better tools and altered and controlled the environment, they changed themselves. Thus capitalism succeeded feudalism, not only because of technological changes, but also because, in the process of technological change, people changed their values and skills and their outlook on what was important and so on. Development, then, is not imposed from the outside—we do not adapt passively to social changes; humankind makes itself through purposeful activity.

SOCIAL RELATIONS OF PRODUCTION

The social relations of production form the class structure of a society, which is revealed in the work process (see table A6.1). The productive forces determine the social relations of production and exchange through (1) institutions and practices closely associated with the way goods are produced, exchanged, and distributed; (2) property relations; (3) the way labor is recruited, organized, and compensated; (4) the markets or other means for exchanging the products of labor; and (5) the methods used by the ruling class to capture and dispose of surplus product.

Eventually the developing productive forces come into conflict with the prevailing class structure (or social relations of production). New ways of making a living become incompatible with the old ways. For example, commercial activity in the sixteenth century became incompatible with feudal relations in the countryside and with the guilds in the towns. This is also exemplified by the imposition of the U.S. economic system on northern Mexico's economy. This growing contradiction takes the form of a class struggle between the rising class associated with the new means of production and the old ruling class. Class struggle, under appropriate conditions, intensifies the contradictions between the means of production and the class structure until, as a result of revolution, new relations of production (compatible with the superior forces) are established.

Table A6.1.   The Social Relations of Production in Capitalism versus Feudalism

Capitalism	Feudalism
technical knowledge, sailing ships, new weapons, energy resources, machinery, and factory processes	land rights, control of rural work processes, judicial and military systems

SUPERSTRUCTURE

The economic structure molds the superstructure of social, political, and intellectual life, including sentiments, morality, illusions, modes of thought, principles, and views of life. The superstructure contains the ideas and systems of authority (political, legal, military) that support the class structure, that is, the dominant position of the ruling class. Thus transformation of the economic structure of society eventually changes the character of the superstructure.

Interactions between superstructure and structure are inevitable, numerous, and complex; the way people make a living affects their ideas; ideas, in turn, affect the way people make a living; modes of thought, however, are shaped and limited in the first place by the mode of production. Ideas that become influential in society reflect only the narrow range of the material activities and interests of the dominant class. Many ideas do not gain prestige because they conflict with the real position of the dominant class (for example, current ideas calling for no or even limited growth are incompatible with capitalist aspirations).

Life is not determined by consciousness, but consciousness is determined by life. Revolutionary ideas can exist side by side with conventional ones, but they cannot by themselves overthrow the prevailing class structure that gave rise to the ruling ideas.

The superstructure contains not only ideas, but institutions and activities that support the class structure of society, such as the state, legal institutions, family structure, art forms, and spiritual processes. For example, prehistoric paintings indicate the need of hunters to depict their prey accurately and naturally. Later, geometric pottery designs reflected the more abstract, mysterious forces that determine whether crops live or die. The change from gathering and hunting to agriculture also altered family structures, religions, rules and laws, government bodies, games played, and military organizations.

The religious world is a reflection of the real world, a consolation for the degraded human condition. Friedrich Engels linked some changes in religious views to changes in material life over a period of two thousand years, but he carefully noted that once an ideology (religion) develops, it acquires a certain independence of economic structures.

The state is a product of society at a certain stage of development. It is an institution that, to protect the property and privileges of the ruling class, preserves order among the oppressed and exploited classes. As such, it is an instrument of class rule. But in some cases the power involved in a class struggle may be evenly divided, so that the state acquires some independence from both the capitalist and the working class.

Marx's materialism differs from older definitions of materialism that saw human beings as passive. For Marx, it is a matter of the dialectical relationship between humans and the material world. The dialectical method stresses the following elements:

1. All things are in constant change.
2. The ultimate source of change is within the thing or process itself.
3. This source is the struggle of opposites, the contradiction within each thing.
4. This struggle, at key points, brings about qualitative changes or leaps so that the thing is transformed into something else.
5. Practical-critical activity resolves the contradictions.

NOTE

Robert C. Tucker, ed. *The Marx-Engels Reader* (New York: Norton, 1972).

* Appendix 7 *
MODEL FOR SERVICE LEARNING, COMMUNITY ORGANIZING, RESEARCH, AND POLICY MAKING

The following six appendixes can be integrated into a model for student service learning, community organizing, research, and policy. Depending on the resources available in the community, students can be integrated into the process at the level that is most appropriate. Members of the Latino Student Congress at Sonoma State University, for example, have done seminars in the community and collaborated with the local Industrial Areas Foundation in the staging of "Actions" and citizenship classes. One may begin in the classroom with "Journal and Other Exercises for Critical Thinking and Pedagogy" (appendix 7A) or by inviting the community to participate in journal workshops. Secondly, using the guidelines in appendix 7B on how to conduct a seminar, students can conduct seminars among themselves, in their student organizations, or in the community. The "Interactive Games" (appendix 7C) are very useful not only as "ice-breakers," but also to demonstrate the workings of power and cultural assumptions respectively, and they can be used in the classroom as well as in the community.

The Latino Student Congress (LSC) requires time commitment and resources beyond the class. It helps the students practice their leadership and policy-making skills, and in the process the students promote community organization and political consciousness (appendix 7D). A well-organized LSC, with the assistance of faculty, parents, and community members, can conduct a community assessment study (appendix 7E) that can be used, among other things, to establish a cultural center (appendix 7F).

* * *

✳ Appendix 7A ✳
JOURNAL AND OTHER EXERCISES FOR CRITICAL THINKING AND PEDAGOGY: THOUGHTS AND SUGGESTIONS FOR CLASSROOM USE

There are three interrelated notions for assisting students in increasing their critical thinking skills and seeing the relevance of academics to "the real world": (1) the importance of knowing oneself for the exercise of critical thinking, (2) journal writing as a way to know and govern oneself, and (3) the correlation between personal journal writing and academic writing. The first came to my attention via Said's *Orientalism* and it is in the form of a quote from Antonio Gramsci:

> The starting-point of critical elaboration is the consciousness of what one really is, and is "knowing thyself" as a product of the historical process to date, which has deposited in you an infinity of traces, without leaving an inventory; therefore it is imperative at the outset to compile such an inventory.[1]

This makes it clear that critical thinking is not just a matter of knowing logic or mastering techniques, but that it is necessary to "know thyself" through a process of constant remembering. One way to explore the depths of one's identity is through writing, a practice that has a long history as well as political implications, and this is where the second notion comes in.

According to Greek philosophers, just as no technique, no professional skill can be acquired without exercise, neither can the "Art of Living" be learned without a particular training. This was one of the traditional principles to which the Pythagoreans, the Socratics, and the Cynics for a long time attributed great importance. Among the forms this training took were abstinence, memorization, examinations of conscience, meditations, silence, listening to others, and writing. It seems that writing (the fact of writing for oneself and for others) was a technical innovation that came along quite late to play a sizable role. The use of notebooks, or "Books of Life," as guides for conduct, for personal and administrative purposes, was coming into vogue at Plato's time (400 B.C.E.).

Well over two thousand years later, we are still trying to figure out what the Art of Living is all about. We spend twelve to sixteen years in training for it in educational institutions. But we end up with a diploma instead of a "Book of Life." Today, whether we use a notebook, portfolio, binder, or handheld computer, the objective remains the same: into them go quotations, fragments of works, examples, and actions one has witnessed or read about, reflections or reasonings that one has heard or that have come to mind. These journals help to maintain a material memory of things read, heard, or thought, which become an accumulated treasure for rereading and later meditation. They also form a raw material for more extensive writings in which one entertains arguments and means by which to struggle against personal problems or overcome difficult circumstances. This raw material may also serve as a basis for written assignments like essays, research papers, and reports.

For the Greeks, the objective of the Book of Life was to make the recollection of fragmentary experience (transmitted by teaching, listening, or reading) a means to establish as adequate and as perfect a relationship of oneself to oneself as possible: retiring into oneself, profiting by and enjoying oneself. The notebook was used for the constitution of a sort of permanent political relationship to oneself: one must manage oneself as a governor manages the governed, as a head of an enterprise manages his enterprise, as a head of a household manages his household.[2]

Today, for the same reasons, a journal or a even a portfolio (if it is more than a compilation of work done) remains a useful process and teaching tool to encourage students to take themselves seriously as learners. That means that they are aware of the political dimensions of the relationship between academic subject matter and the issues that affect their personal and socioeconomic realities.

The third notion, therefore, is the importance of complementing personal journal writing with academic writing. In table A7.1, I have used Ira Progoff's particular format and adapted it to mirror assignments from my interdisciplinary courses.[3] This table is intended to show the full range of possibilities for this sort of parallel personal/academic work. Notice this practical matter: I give students a choice to buy a binder and create sections for each of the sixteen categories or to simply collect in a binder the individual journal exercises they do for my class. This is obviously not the appropriate place for an extensive discussion on the use of the entire table or the Progoff journal. Furthermore, there are many methods available for journal keeping and for the implementation of portfolios for teaching and evaluation that faculty and students may prefer. I first provide brief guidelines for using the journal to "know thyself"; second, I provide exercises for interaction with the contents of the "Introduction for Students"; and finally I provide exercises for interaction with the contents of this reader.

To begin a general exploration of the self, use these instructions:

1. Using one or two words, list the ten stepping-stones or key events of your life. Depending on the topic under discussion, "life" may be defined more specifically, such as educational life or political life.

2. Period Log. Where are you in your life now? Of all the overlapping periods or events of your life, describe the beginning, middle, and end of the one that is most intensely present in your mind.

3. Twilight imagery log. What image do you have of where you are in your life now (of the description you just gave in number 2)?

4. To have dialogues (see table A7.1), begin by listing the stepping-stones for the person, event, etc., you are talking to (except not for the inner wisdom dialogue). Make a brief statement about what you want to talk about. You may begin by simply saying, "Hello, Rudy!" Make it a real dialogue, not a disguised monologue.

5. Don't dialogue with "society"; choose a person to represent the social issue you want to explore.

The first four exercises should not take longer than an hour, including for students who may want to read their entries out loud. Students who want to continue the dialogue should be encouraged to do so outside the class. It is important to keep in mind that these life explorations may, and often do, have an emotional impact. All of them can be tailored for almost any class. A more lengthy exploration of the self that includes the depth and life/time dimensions would require some sort of specialized or interdisciplinary course of study. I have used them in a course titled "Discourse and Consciousness."

To explore the personal dimensions of politics, the following four exercises are included in the text of the "Introduction for Students."

EXERCISE #1

(a) List the stepping-stones of your political life.
(b) Write a three- to five-page essay describing the political beliefs, principles, or positions you "inherited" from your parents and ancestors. Include if or how these differ from your own politics or personal policies.
(c) Write a dialogue with one of your parents or ancestors about a political issue.

Table A7.1. Connections between a Personal Journal and Academic Work

Personal Section	Academic Section
1. Daily log—gives you raw material to work with in other categories	Daily newspaper helps to establish connections with your life and studies
Dialogue Dimension	
2. Dialogue with persons	Dialogue with individuals from history or literature
3. . . . projects/works	Dialogue with historical deeds, events, undertakings
4. . . . society	Dialogue with a representative of a specific social issue
5. . . . events, situations, circumstances	Read or write a microhistory or monograph
6. . . . your body	Report on the status of human bodies under specific categories
7. Inner wisdom dialogue (with a spiritual entity)	Religious/spiritual/philosophical beliefs and practices
Symbolic Depth Dimension	*Psychology and the Arts*
8. Dream log	The unconscious
9. Dream enlargements	The archetypal
10. Twilight imagery log	The aesthetic, poetry, visual art, literature
11. Imagery extensions	
Life/Time Dimension	*(Auto)Biography (factual or fictional)*
12. Stepping-stones	Key events in a given life (or arguments in a text)
13. Period log	
14. Life history log—expand your stepping-stones	
15. Intersections—what could have happened but did not	
16. Now: the "Open Moment"	Summary, conclusion, judgment

EXERCISE #2

While mostly reserved for graduate studies and elite or honors programs, seminar discussions can be conducted, even with large classes or outside of class on your own as "study groups." Ask your teachers to hold seminar discussions or form your own seminar with members of your class outside of school. Write a one- to two-page response paper on your observations of the process.

EXERCISE #3

(a) List ten stepping-stones of your "educational life."
(b) Write a dialogue with society (specifically with your school principal or teacher).
(c) Write a three- to five-page essay on your educational experiences using Freire's concepts of education.

EXERCISE #4

Think about the ideas of politics, language, knowledge/power and education as they affect your everyday life. What does your political world look like and what role do you play in it? Referring to the images in this section draw or paint a poster-sized map that illustrates your political realities, the many forces that affect you, and the ways you can affect them in return.

And, finally, to interact with the contents of the reader, on the right-hand side of table A7.1 there are several suggestions for exercises that can be applied specifically to the reader. Here are some examples:

EXERCISE #5

Analyze the representation of Latino/as in newspapers and other media.

EXERCISE #6

Dialogue with an author or historical character; with one of the many events, situations, and circumstances; or with one of the many social issues.

EXERCISE #7

Write a research paper on one of the themes or one of the Latino/a groups using one or more of the frameworks and scaffolds for understanding Latino/a political thought.

EXERCISE #8

Research the areas or voices not covered in the reader, such as Latino/a political thought expressed through the arts: for example, prose, poetry, music, painting, or film.

EXERCISE #9

Write an essay addressing one or more of the polemics or theories raised by the texts.

NOTES

1. Antonio Gramsci, quoted in Edward W. Said, *Orientalism* (New York: Pantheon, 1978), 25. As Said notes, the English translation inexplicably leaves out the second part of

the sentence. Gramsci, *The Prison Notebooks: Selections,* ed. Quintin Hoare and Geoffrey Nowell Smith (New York: International, 1971), 324.

2. Michel Foucault, afterword to Hubert L. Dreyfus and Paul Rabinow, *Michel Foucault: Beyond Structuralism and Hermeneutics* (Chicago: University of Chicago Press, 1983), 246–47 passim.

3. Ira Progroff, *At a Journal Workshop* (New York: Dialogue House Library, 1982).

✳   ✳   ✳

✳ Appendix 7B ✳
INTRODUCTION TO SEMINARING IN THE HUTCHINS SCHOOL OF LIBERAL STUDIES

Wise men characteristically ask interesting questions while experts usually reveal their lack of wisdom by answering them.

—Joseph W. Meeker

A seminar is a contract between people to be prepared—every day—to explore the boundaries of knowledge. A dynamic seminar is one in which the members work together to help each other understand the readings and the questions that develop out of the readings and conversations. There is likely to be nothing more exhilarating in your years at college than the experience of a really good seminar.

The most important part of a seminar is keeping up with, or exceeding, the reading. There is nothing more frustrating than trying to discuss a book in a seminar and realizing that the other members haven't read it.

To participate effectively in a seminar, it is important to be aware of several basic seminar skills. If you do the reading, come to class, and familiarize yourself with the following seminar skills and approaches, you are almost certain to have vibrant, dynamic, and lively seminars:

- Remember that *you* are important—vital—to the seminar.
- Consider yourself as the teacher. What do you want to learn?
- Try to come to class with written-down questions, thoughts, or feelings about the material.
- Don't let the instructor/facilitator answer all of the questions and don't direct your questions at the facilitator; direct them toward each other.
- Take risks. *Take the initiative.*
- Verbalize incomplete thoughts, feelings, or questions. Try.
- Help your fellow students build on incomplete ideas. Don't leave them hanging when they do take risks.

- Be an active listener. Write thoughts down so you don't forget them. *Ask divergent questions* (questions that permit many answers) and attempt to answer them.
- Often, asking a quiet person a question or merely giving her or him an opportunity to talk will evoke a really interesting response and lead to good conversation.
- Be compassionate. To have a good seminar you have to make yourself vulnerable.
- Your feelings are just as important as your thoughts. Often others will feel similarly and good conversation will ensue.
- Don't be afraid of adding some structure at times. Go-rounds and brainstorms can be very useful when conversation is dull or to find out quickly how everyone feels about something.
- Instructors are not perfect. Facilitating a seminar is much harder than giving a lecture. Often instructors will talk too much, either because *you aren't talking* or because they are really enthusiastic about the material. Help them to be sensitive to your needs.
- A seminar is an incredibly unique opportunity to learn how to learn. *Take advantage of it!*
- Have fun.

Many of the above skills and approaches involve some sort of interaction with other people. They are geared toward helping you learn how to develop a line of thought in cooperation with others. The objective is knowledge, not self-gratification. As one Hutchins student said, "The strength of [the seminar] is that it teaches you how to express yourself in a safe environment." A seminar does not supply reinforcement for competitiveness.

It is also important to begin each seminar in a relaxed way. The facilitator might want to give everyone a chance to say how they are feeling, or she/he might just have casual conversations among the participants, whatever it takes to create a safe atmosphere for intensive discussion.

Occasionally certain people will dominate the seminar. Here are some behavior characteristics to watch out for and avoid, in yourself as well as in others.

Hogging the show: talking too much, too long, too loudly.

Problem solver: continually giving the answer or solution before others have had much chance to contribute.

Speaking in capital letters: giving one's own solutions or opinions as the final words on the subject.

Nit-picking: pointing out minor flaws in statements of others and stating the exception to every generality.

Restating: saying in another way what someone else has just said perfectly clearly (not *always* bad).

Self-listening: formulating a response after the first few sentences, not listening to anything from that point on, and leaping in at the first pause.

All of the things mentioned in the two lists are important to be aware of, but don't worry too much about trying to memorize them. The objective of this appendix is to facilitate communication by making you aware of the dynamic that will occur in your seminar. By learning to identify various skills and behaviors, you will be better communicators, both inside and outside the seminar.

Ultimately, "the essence of good communication [is] trusting and being trusted. . . . Trust is at the heart of a program built on a sense of community," and of the seminar.[1]

NOTE

1. Mervyn L. Cadwallader, *Against the Current: Reform and Experimentation in Higher Education* (Cambridge, Mass.: Schenkman, 1984), 356.

✳   ✳   ✳

✳ Appendix 7C ✳
INTERACTIVE GAMES

There are many interactive games available that allow for the simulation of crosscultural or gender/power relations. Two games that are good to use along with this reader or in courses that deal with similar topics are Bafá Bafá and ACCESS. These games are flexible enough to be adjusted for time and numbers. Here we limit ourselves to an introductory description of these interactive games. Your librarian should be able to help you locate them or order them for you.

BAFÁ BAFÁ

In this game, created by R. Garry Shirts, participants live and cope in a "foreign" culture and then discuss and analyze the experience. There are two cultures in the simulation. The Alpha culture is a warm, friendly, patriarchal society with strong in-group and out-group identity. The Beta culture is a foreign-speaking, task-oriented culture. Once the participants learn the rules, customs, and values of "their" culture, they visit the other culture. The most unique feature is probably that the interest and involvement reaches a climax after the simulation. During the discussion, the mysteries of each culture are unraveled and the participants compare perceptions of one another's culture. Are Betans "cold and greedy"? and Alphans "lazy, unfriendly, and sexist"? Below is a sample of what participants report they learned:

1. The outsider must realize that what seems irrational, contradictory, or unimportant to her/him may seem rational, consistent, and terribly important to a person in the other culture.
2. One is likely to seriously misinterpret other cultures if one evaluates them solely in terms of one's own values, expectations, and behavior.
3. Visitors are often "invisible" to people within the culture.
4. There is often a reluctance to explain one's own culture to outsiders until they have "earned" the right to know.

ACCESS

Created by Susan Ebel Arneaud (University of Michigan) and Jean L. Easterly (Oakland University) this game is ostensibly "a simulation which raises a number of issues related to the role of women in western society." In our experience, the game illustrates not only gender relations but also relations of inequality that apply equally to minority groups of any gender that have to survive in a dominant society. The game includes two activities that reward the participants, the Greens and the Reds, on an unequal basis. This is not immediately obvious to the participants, who resort in many cases to different strategies (such as cheating) to "beat the system." When frustration, an uprising, riot, or revolution is about to start, the game ends and the director opens a discussion to explore the relations of power that led to that situation.

Both games are published by Simile II, 218 12th Street, P.O. Box 910, Del Mar, CA 92014.

✳   ✳   ✳

✳ Appendix 7D ✳
THE LATINO STUDENT CONGRESS

WHAT IS A STUDENT CONGRESS?

What if students from high schools in the area had the opportunity to share their perceptions, ideas, thoughts, and emotions with each other? What if they could also share these with college students, other members of their communities, politicians, and other decision makers? This is the simple idea behind a student congress: to enable students of different schools, levels, ages, and status to talk to each other, to talk to others in the community, and to insert their discourse into the fabric of society.

This is how it functions in an ideal situation:

1. Briefly, the Student Congress (SC) is a ten-month leadership program for high school students who meet once a month for two hours at a college (this is preferable to other locations, because it exposes students to an academic setting). Upon graduation from the program, students become alumni of the SC.
   a. During the first hour, the student(s) who represent their high schools in the congress:[1]
      i. report on events taking place in their schools and discuss the issues their constituencies (schoolmates) find in their daily lives,
      ii. explore ways in which these issues can be confronted,
      iii. make specific suggestions to solve the problem(s).
   b. The second hour is allotted to a seminar discussion with the congress staff (see below) and/or an invited guest who is knowledgeable about a particular topic of interest to the students.
      i. Some of these latter meetings may be dedicated to a speaker series in which events are scheduled and advertised ahead of time and are open to the members of the congressional clubs (see below) and to the general public.
2. The duties and responsibilities of congress students are:
   a. in addition to the monthly meetings, attend
      i. biyearly retreats (to learn leadership skills and plan activities),
      ii. an annual conference (to share information with students, parents, and teachers at large),
      iii. a graduation ceremony (to honor and recognize congress students and welcome the new ones);
   b. keep journals of their experiences as congress students;
   c. share the information, decisions, projects, etc. discussed at the congressional meeting with their high schools' congressional clubs and other clubs/ organizations;
   d. make presentations on the Student Congress to teachers, students from other schools, businesses, and social organizations as requested;
   e. promote seminar discussions and activities among students (such as paraprofessional organizations, tutoring, mentoring, and outdoor leadership outings, such as a "ropes course");
   f. participate in major congressional projects such as:
      i. a congressional monthly newsletter,
      ii. a theater play or a video that deals with current youth issues and can be shared with other high school students,

      iii. working as junior researchers in joint projects with college students, teachers, faculty, and others to gather information to address social issues or for the writing of grants.

3. The specific objectives of the Student Congress are:
   a. to find out what works and does not work in terms of educational success;
   b. based on these findings, to make suggestions (policy recommendations) to the appropriate decision makers, parents, teachers, principals, elected officials, etc.;
   c. to provide practical leadership experiences to prepare students to run for student government and eventually for public office or leadership in their community.

4. Students get two units of college credit for participating in the congress. This is the best way to make sure that the schools and the students make the time commitment necessary for this activity; as an outreach effort, it also creates a very real link between universities and high schools.

WHO ELSE IS INVOLVED IN A STUDENT CONGRESS?

1. Every congress student has a congressional staff that includes students from junior college and college, professionals and business people, parents, school teachers, and administrators.[2]
   a. The duties and responsibilities of staff members include the following (depending on whether the congress is starting or is already established):
      i. find out the when/where/who of student meetings at the targeted school;
      ii. contact a principal or faculty sponsor and the appropriate student club president to get permission to serve as a resource person and to attend their meetings (or, if necessary, to distribute applications for membership in the congress);
      iii. attend student meetings at their high schools and keep a record of the meetings for the students and for student newspaper articles;
      iv. participate/facilitate seminars in which students
         (1) read about and discuss the issues that concern them and
         (2) develop the strategies and policies to address those issues;
      v. coordinate financial and human resources to support the projects the students want to conduct;
      vi. submit monthly reports at congressional meetings;
      vii. actively participate in congressional meetings and the planning of retreats, leadership conferences, and other special meetings.
   b. The recruitment of members for a congressional staff may be done as follows:
      i. some students get credit for doing an independent project or a class project based on their participation in the Student Congress (some stu-

        dents may do it on the strength of their commitment, but it is best to have some sort of accountability);

    ii. there are several community members who like to work with young people and some will already be serving as mentors. While mentoring is critical in some cases, perhaps many, one of the problems is that there are not enough community members able to do mentoring for all the students who need it. Those who can commit themselves to being part of the congressional staff for a particular school reach many more students than they would in one-on-one mentoring;

    iii. there are many teachers, administrators, and parents who welcome support from the community and who are also willing to participate in this kind of effort.

2. The Congressional Club consists of students who are interested in social issues and want to participate in leadership activities. This participation is done through:

    a. club meetings in which their congress representative reports to and receives information from his or her classmates;

    b. seminar discussions in which the membership organizes groups (of twelve members each) within the Congressional Club to address specific issues or readings;

    c. membership in the club is decided by the members of each high school's congressional club.

HOW DOES ONE BECOME A MEMBER OF THE STUDENT CONGRESS?

1. Any high school student is eligible to become a congress woman or man and to represent her/his high school in a given county or region, provided that she/he does the following:

    a. fills out an application and submits it by a given deadline with a one-dollar fee;

    b. interviews with congress students and/or the congressional staff; and

    c. shows that she/he is a leader in a strict sense, here defined as being an intellectual warrior; that is, someone who

        i. takes the initiative to do something in the struggle for social justice,

        ii. follows through with her or his commitment and is on time, and

        iii. is informed and prepared to discuss the issues.

2. The recruitment and selection of students is done on a yearly basis:

    a. during May, a leadership conference is held at a local college and applications are distributed and collected there;

    b. if a particular school does not participate in the conference, applications are taken to student clubs, organizations, and/or teachers.[3]

NOTES

1. Whether one or more students are selected as congress students to represent their school depends on how many schools are involved. It is advisable to keep the whole congress to about thirty students. Since the long-range plan is eventually to include junior high and elementary school students, that may affect the number from year to year.

2. While the involvement of many people is desirable, the main thrust is to put the students in contact with people attending junior college or college or practicing a profession. This way, the students feel comfortable knowing that they are getting the information from those who are "in the know."

3. To recruit intellectual warriors to become congress men and women can be a difficult enterprise, because sometimes the leaders who are identified by teachers are not those identified by students. And the leaders elected by students are often not leaders in a strict sense but the winners of a popularity contest. A good way to find potential congress students is to announce that applications are available to all students. Those who take the personal initiative to fill out and return the applications with the one-dollar application fee can then be considered as candidates for membership. The important point is to allow for different styles (and circumstances) of leadership. Organizing a gang, taking care of several younger siblings, or acting as the translator for her/his parents who do not speak English demonstrate as much leadership potential in a student as other more conventional indicators. This situation will vary depending on the time a congress has been in existence and on other circumstances. The most important point to remember is that the initiative must come from the young people. They must be treated as the congress women and men they want to be.

✳   ✳   ✳

✳ Appendix 7E ✳
COMMUNITY ASSESSMENT STUDY TO LEAD TO POLICY-SETTING AGENDA: AN OUTLINE OF THE PROCESS

1. Identify ten community leaders who are conversant—clear—on the issues; have them make a "laundry list" of issues and identify those that are "actionable."

2. Prioritize "actionable issues" and create task forces to address each one.

3. Have the task forces go into the community to discuss these issues and gather information. They will work with the director(s) of the project for one year.

4. Have a full-day meeting with the community, present and discuss a draft of findings.

5. Publish a report, a five-year plan consisting of policies to be implemented.

6. Contract a public policy center to oversee the implementation of these policies.

✳   ✳   ✳

✳ Appendix 7F ✳
GOALS FOR CULTURAL CENTER / *CENTRO CULTURAL*

1. To provide resources for the general population on the culture of Latino/a people (bookstore, gallery, theater, dance, music, literature readings, crafts, films, forums).

2. To promote the production of cultural activities through classes or workshops (in visual arts, theater, dance, crafts, music, etc.).

3. To support the activities of the Latino Student Congress and to monitor Latino/a students from kindergarten through graduation from college.

4. To present special interest workshops on social, political, and economic development (to address health issues, voter registration, how to start your own business, etc).

5. To provide an atmosphere where people can enjoy the aesthetic as well as the culinary aspects of Latino/a culture.

GLOSSARY

center, centrists. See **political spectrum.**

citizenship. A citizen is a member of a legally constituted state who possesses certain rights and privileges, subject to corresponding duties. With certain restrictions, a citizen of the United States has the right to hold and transfer all types of property, to vote, to seek elective office, to hold governmental positions, to receive welfare and social security benefits, and to enjoy the protection of the Constitution and the laws. Some of these rights are denied to aliens, even though they may have been in the United States most of their lives. Both U.S. citizens and permanent resident aliens have the corresponding duties to pay taxes, obey the laws of the United States, and defend it against enemies. Citizens are also subject to jury duty. In most monarchies, including the United Kingdom, citizens are usually referred to as subjects, meaning that they owe their allegiance to the sovereign in return for protection, but not necessarily for rights of self-governance. The term "national" is used, particularly in international agreements, to mean all those who owe allegiance to a state. Nearly all nationals are now citizens, the main exceptions being inhabitants of some colonies who are nationals but not citizens. For the meaning of "public citizenship" as used throughout this reader, see chapters 2 and 3.

commodity. Something useful that can be turned to commercial or other advantage. In some cases it is said that human bodies—people—are used also as commodities.

criollo. A Spaniard born in the Spanish Americas. Politically, she or he did not have the same status as the *peninsulares,* those born in Spain (on the Iberian Peninsula). Not to be confused with "Creole," which includes this definition but also others that do not apply in a Latino/a context.

deductive. The process of reasoning in which a conclusion follows necessarily from the stated premises; inference by reasoning from the general to the specific. See also **inductive.**

dialectics. Simply put, the art or practice of arriving at the truth by the exchange of logical arguments. A method of argument or exposition that systematically weighs contradictory facts or ideas with a view to the resolution of their real or apparent contradictions. More popular is this word's meaning as the contradiction between two conflicting forces viewed as the determining factor in the continuing interaction of those forces. An example is the process of arriving at the truth by stating a thesis, developing a contradictory antithesis, and combining and resolving them into a coherent synthesis. See also "Historical Materialism," appendix 6.

diaspora. Once used to describe Jewish, Greek, and Armenian dispersion, now shares meanings with a larger semantic domain that includes words such as "immigrant," "expatriate," "refugee," "guest worker," "overseas community," and "ethnic community."

enlightenment. Literally to shed light on the darkness of superstition and tyranny, this is a term for the rationalist, liberal, humanitarian, and scientific trend of eighteenth-century Western thought; the period also is sometimes known as the Age of Reason. The enormous scientific and intellectual advancements made in the seventeenth century by the empiricism of Francis Bacon and John Locke, as well as by Descartes, Spinoza, and others, fostered the belief in natural law and universal order, promoted a scientific approach to political and social issues, and gave rise to a sense of human progress and belief in the state as its rational instrument. Representative of the **Enlightenment** are such thinkers as Sor Juana Inéz de la Cruz and Carlos de Sigüenza y Góngora in México; Voltaire, J.-J. Rousseau, Montesquieu, Adam Smith, Swift, Hume, Kant, G. E. Lessing, Beccaria; and in America, Thomas Paine, Thomas Jefferson, and Benjamin Franklin. The social and political ideals such figures presented were enforced by "enlightened despots" such as Holy Roman Emperor Joseph II, Catherine II of Russia, and Frederick II of Prussia. Diderot's *Encyclopédie* and the U.S. Constitution are representative documents of the Age of Reason.

Freemasonry. A tightly knit, all-male society, many of whose members hold very influential positions, all of whom are bound by an oath of secrecy. It is claimed that all presidents of Mexico and the United States (with the exception of John Kennedy) have been masons.

Furies. In Greek mythology, the three Furies—Tisiphone, Megaera, and Alecto— were goddesses of vengeance. Their function was to punish crimes that had escaped detection or public justice. Although their usual abode was Hades, they also pursued the living, as in the story of Orestes. In appearance they were ugly, bat-winged, serpent-haired creatures born of the blood of Uranus when he was mutilated by the sickle of Cronus. In the afterlife, the Furies dispensed justice from the netherworld, where, armed with scourges, they meted out the torments of remorse and other punishments. The Furies, also known as Erinyes, were called the Eumenides in later Greek literature.

inductive. The process of reasoning by which general principles are derived from particular facts or instances.

institutions. A set of behaviors that endure through time: political institutions are for the distribution of power; economic institutions are for the production and distribution of goods and services; cultural institutions involve arts, religion, and traditions; kinship focuses on the family, marriage, and the raising of young.

juridical. Of or relating to the law and its administration.

left, leftist. See **political spectrum.**

Maoist. Marxism-Leninism developed in China, chiefly by Mao Zedong.

mestizaje. The largest mixing of races in the world, which took place in what is now known as Latin America. Also used in a political sense (see chapter 27).

nation-state. See **state** and the introduction to part III.

paradigm. A worldview that dominates how we perceive reality. It can be scientific, social, artistic, or other. For example, in terms of science, the Aristotelian paradigm dominated for over one thousand years; currently the Newtonian paradigm has been superseded by that of Einstein's theory of relativity. The **Enlightenment** and **postmodernism** are two other examples.

pigmentocracy. Relations of power based on skin color. I prefer the term "pigmentocracy" over the more general term of "racism," because the former specifically points to the universal practice of valuing light-skinned human bodies more than dark-skinned human bodies, a practice that occurs not only between blacks and whites but within all ethnic and cultural groups.

political spectrum. This concept includes **centrists** (middle ground, social democrat-liberal-moderate), **leftists** (anywhere from liberal to democratic socialist, socialist, communist, or anarchist), and the **right** wing (anywhere from conservative and neoconservative to reactionary, libertarian, or fascist) and comes from France. Before the French Revolution, there was an Estates General, a parliamentary body like a congress, that was last called together in 1789. In that year, the king sat in the center with moderates, who favored compromise between the conservatives and liberals and the preservation of the monarchy based on concessions to the people. The conservative nobility and clergy, who advocated maintaining the status quo—retaining the monarchy and the privileges of nobility—sat on the king's right. On his left were the liberal and radical representatives of the common people, who advocated the abolishment of the monarchy and the nobility.

political technology. The techniques and tools that are available to govern a society, such as definitions (of who is entitled to rights, obligations, punishment); representation (one [hu]man, one vote, on the basis of the number of people or of geographical areas); division of power into legislature (makes the laws), executive (carries out the dictates of the law), and judiciary (interprets the law); contracts; and processes (who talks first?).

postmodernism. A **paradigm** based on the realization that "Truth," once it is articulated, is subject to political interpretations and becomes part of a discourse, a **commodity** in a political economy. This leads to the questioning of everything that is, was, or ever has been considered "True" and the struggle to account for all the diverse, conflicting, invisible "Truths" that go into constructing what is claimed to be the one and only "Truth." The purpose of postmodernism, however, was to question those categories that in the age of modernism (1700–2000) were considered as unchangeable *essences* and therefore obstacles to social justice. Take, for example, categories such as the "Divine Right of Kings" or the "Natural Rights of Man": what about the rights of those who did not fit these categories, such as women, people of color, disabled, children, or gays? From a postmodern perspective, "man" is a social construction, an invention by society. The fact is that human experience is much too diverse and exuberant to be contained by a category. So the task is to "deconstruct" exclusive concepts, to open up a space for Others, in the arts, literature, painting, music, etc. Postmodernism means the tearing down of rigid concepts about art and a free-for-all experimentation.

right. See **political spectrum.**

sovereignty. Sovereignty refers both to the powers exercised by an autonomous **state** in relation to other countries and to the supreme powers exercised by a state over its own members. In the context of international law, a sovereign state is independent and free from all external control; enjoys full legal equality with other states; governs its own territory; selects its own political, economic, and social systems; and has the power to enter into agreements with other nations, to exchange ambassadors, and to decide on war or peace. A protectorate, because it has ceded some of its powers to another state, is not sovereign. Although a sovereign state theoretically enjoys absolute freedom, its freedom is in fact often abridged by the need to coexist with other countries, as well as by treaties, international laws, and the strength of its military. Sovereign power, which is the power to make and enforce the law and to control the nation's finances and military establishment, may be vested in one person (a monarchy, for example), in a small group of people (an oligarchy), or in all the people, either directly or through representatives (a democracy). It may be limited by natural or divine law, constitutions, or customs. See also **state.**

state. The state is frequently defined as the highest or most comprehensive political association having a recognized claim to primacy—first allegiance or ultimate authority. According to another common definition, statehood is the stable possession of preponderant power by a single authority within a delimited territory. There are two impediments, however, to any simple definition of the state. The first is that the term has been used quite loosely, to designate any sort of political rule at any period in history ("the Byzantine state," "the Papal states"), and at the same time quite restrictively, to designate the kind of political structure mainly characteristic of post-Renaissance Western societies. The second impediment is that notions about what the state is vary systematically with the various political philosophies: a Lockean liberal who advocates a minimalist state that merely enforces natural law and protects natural rights will never be able to agree with a Hegelian, who sees the state as the concrete actualization of rational freedom on earth, or with a marxian, who sees the state as a mere committee for the management of the interests of the social class owning the means of economic production. Defining the state is not easy unless one is prepared to declare dogmatically that a particular theory of statehood is correct, to the exclusion of all others. The same difficulty afflicts any effort to say what the state's purpose is. A Benthamite utilitarian will urge that the end of the state is the greatest happiness of the greatest number, and that the pursuit of this end gives the state legitimate authority. A Kantian will suggest that the state exists to provide a legal context within which good will and respect for persons is more nearly possible.

Nor is the tracing of the origin of the state free of this same difficulty: some have traced the foundation of the state to a desire for security and peace (Thomas Hobbes); some have insisted on natural sociability as creating states, believing that the stateless human is either a beast or a god (Aristotle); some have put forward economic motives, such as a desire for the division of labor and an economy of scale, which can be obtained only by centralizing power and authoritatively allocating work (Edmund Burke); still others have stressed human depravity in a fallen world creating the need for the state (Saint Augustine). In trying, then, to say what the state is, what its purposes are, and where its origin is, the problem always exists that the state itself is not simply a fact but a conceptual artifact. The most reasonable and candid way to treat the state, therefore, is to offer a history of theories about it.

taxonomy. A particular way to categorize, classify, organize things.

PERMISSIONS

PART I: HISTORICAL ORIGINS/THEORETICAL AND FEMINIST(S) CONTEXTS

1. Maria Linda Apodaca, *Latin American Perspectives* 4, no. 2, pp. 70–89, copyright © 1977 by Maria Linda Apodaca. Reprinted by permission of Sage Publications, Inc.

2. From *Latina Politics, Latino Politics: Gender, Culture, and Political Participation in Boston* by Carol Hardy-Fanta. Reprinted by permission of Temple University Press. © 1993 by Temple University. All rights reserved.

4. Rodolfo "Corky" Gonzales, *I Am Joaquín: An Epic Poem* (1967). Used with the permission of the author.

6. From Jesús de la Teja, editor, *The Making of a Tejano, a Revolution Remembered: The Memoirs and Selected Correspondence of Juan N. Seguín* (Austin, TX: State House Press, 1991). Used with permission.

8. From *On Becoming Cuban: Identity, Nationality, and Culture* by Louis A. Pérez. Copyright ©1999 by the University of North Carolina Press. Used by permission of the publisher.

10. From *Puerto Rico: The Trials of the Oldest Colony in the World* by José Trías Monge. Copyright © 1997 by the Yale University Press. Used with permission.

Poem: From Gustavo Pérez-Firmat, *Life on the Hyphen: The Cuban-American Way* (Austin: University of Texas Press, 1999), p. 181. Used with permission.

PART II: LIFE WITHIN THE EMPIRE: (DE)CONSTRUCTING POLITICAL POSITIONS AND IDENTITIES

11. Yamila Azize-Vargas, "The Emergence of Feminism in Puerto Rico, 1870–1930." *Unequal Sisters,* Vicky L. Ruiz and Ellen Carol DuBois, editors. New York: Routledge, 1994, pp. 260–67.

12. From *Puerto Rico: Independence Is a Necessity* edited by Rafael Cancel Miranda. Copyright © 1998 by Pathfinder Press. Reprinted by permission.

13. From *In the Land of Mirrors: Cuban Exile Politics in the United States* by María de los Angeles Torres. Copyright © 1999 by The University of Michigan Press. Used with permission.

14. Marta Cotera, "Our Feminist Heritage," *The Chicana Feminist,* Austin, TX: Information System Development, 1977.

15. José E. Limón, "El Primer Congreso Mexicanista de 1911: A Precursor to Contemporary Chicanismo," *Aztlán* 5, nos. 1/2, pp. 85–106. Used with permission.

16. Francisco E. Balderrama and Raymond Rodríguez, "Epilogue/Fin," *Decade of Betrayal: Mexican Repatriation in the 1930s* (Albuquerque: University of New Mexico Press, 1995), pp. 214–23. Used with permission.

17. César E. Chávez's name and writings are used with permission from the César E. Chávez Foundation. For licensing or further information, contact the César E. Chávez Foundation at 213–362–0267 or via e-mail at info@cecfmail.org.

18. Cherríe Moraga, *The Last Generation* (Cambridge, MA: South End Press, 1993), pp. 145–74. Used with permission.

19. Jorge Duany, *Latin American Perspectives* 25, no. 3, pp. 147–72, copyright © 1998 by Jorge Duany. Reprinted by permission of Sage Publications, Inc.

20. Patricia Guadalupe, "No Regrets," *El Andar* 11, no. 1 (Spring 2000), pp. 40–43. Used with permission.

21. María Cristina García, *Havana USA: Cuban Exiles and Cuban Americans in South Florida, 1959–1994* (Berkeley: University of California Press, 1996), pp. 108–19, 137–46, 162–68, 208–12, 236–39, 249–51, and 257. Copyright © 1996 The Regents of the University of California. Used with permission.

PART III: ON THE NATIONAL QUESTION

22. David Sánchez, "Brown Beret National Policies," *La Causa,* Los Angeles, California, 1972, pp. 4–6. Used with permission.

23. Fred A. Cervantes, "Chicanos as a Postcolonial Minority: Some Questions Concerning the Adequacy of the Paradigm of Internal Colonialism," *Perspectives in Chicano Studies,* Vol. 1, R. Flores Macias, editor, National Association for Chicana and Chicano Studies, 1977, pp. 123–35.

24. "Young Lords Party 13-Point Program and Platform," from *Young Lords Party,* Michael Abramson, editor (New York: McGraw-Hill, 1971), pp. 150–51. Copyright © The McGraw-Hill Companies, Inc. Used with permission.

25. Ramón Grosfoguel, "The Divorce of Nationalist Discourse from the Puerto Rican People," from *Puerto Rican Jam: Rethinking Colonialism and Nationalism,* edited by Frances Negron-Muntaner and Ramón Grosfoguel (University of Minnesota Press, 1997), pp. 57–76. Used with permission.

Poem: Chloé S. Georas, "Native of Nowhere," from *Puerto Rican Jam: Rethinking*

Colonialism and Nationalism, edited by Frances Negrón-Muntaner and Ramón Grosfoguel (University of Minnesota Press, 1997). Used with permission.

PART IV: BEYOND THE
NATIONAL/COLONIAL DICHOTOMY

26. From "Transnational Political and Cultural Identities: Crossing Theoretical Borders," by María de los Angeles Torres as it appears in *Borderless Borders: U.S. Latinos, Latin Americans and the Paradox of Interdependence* edited by Frank Bonilla et al. Reprinted by permission of Temple University Press. © by Temple University. All rights reserved.

27. Victor Valle and Rodolfo D. Torres, "Class and Culture Wars in the New Latino Politics," from *Latino Metropolis* (University of Minnesota Press, 2000), pp. 167–95, 218–20. Used with permission.

28. From *Decolonial Imaginary: Writing Chicanas into History* by Emma Pérez (Bloomington: University of Indiana Press, 1999). Used with permission.

29. Guillermo Gómez-Peña, "A Postdemocratic Era," in *Dangerous Border Crossers: The Artist Talks Back* (London: Routledge, 2000), pp. 269–71. Used with permission.

Note: Every effort has been made to contact the original copyright holders of the articles reprinted in this book. Anyone who has reason to claim an outstanding or unresolved permissions issue is urged to immediately contact the publisher.

INDEX

ABOUT THE AUTHORS

Francisco H. Vázquez is professor of the history of ideas in the Hutchins School of Liberal Studies and director of the Hutchins Center for Interdisciplinary Learning at Sonoma State University, California. Among his publications are "Philosophy in Mexico: The Opium of the Intellectuals or a Prophetic Insight" (*Canadian Journal of Political and Social Theory* 4, no. 3, 1980) and "Chicanology: A Postmodern Analysis of Meshicano Discourse" (*Perspectives in Mexican American Studies* 3, 1992).

Rodolfo D. Torres is associate professor of education, political science, and urban and regional planning, and is a member of the Focused Research Program in Labor Studies at the University of California, Irvine. Among his books are *Latino Metropolis* (2000), *Latino Social Movements* (1999), and *Race, Identity, and Citizenship* (1999). He is currently associate editor of *New Political Science* and on editorial boards for *Urban Affairs Review* and *Ethnicities*.

To the memory of
Lucy Hernández Reynozo (February 5,
1925–December 15, 1973),
la autora de mis dias.
While your body succumbed much too
soon to the harshness of life,
your love and kindness live on
as an example and inspiration to us all.
—FHV

To the memory of
Dr. Jeff Marcos Garcilazo (July 4,
1956–May 4, 2001),
who taught me new ways to theorize
the Chicana and Chicano
working class.
I miss you, Jeff.
—RDT